R. Gupta's®

POPULAR MASTER GUIDE

DSSSB–TEACHERS

PGT

COMMERCE

Recruitment Exam

by

RPH Editorial Board

2027
EDITION

RAMESH PUBLISHING HOUSE, NEW DELHI

Published by
O.P. Gupta *for* Ramesh Publishing House

Admin. Office
12-H, New Daryaganj Road, Opp. Officers' Mess,
New Delhi-110002 ☏ 23275224, 23245124

E-mail: info@rameshpublishinghouse.com
For Online Shopping: www.rameshpublishinghouse.com

Showroom
- Balaji Market, Nai Sarak, Delhi-110006 ☏ 23282525 📱 9354373464
- 4457, Nai Sarak, Delhi-110006

Book Code: R-1303

ISBN: 978-93-5012-002-6

Price: ₹ 360

Printed at: Deepak Offset, Delhi

CONTENTS

Scheme of Examination

Section-I

S.No.	Subject	Questions	Marks
1.	Mental Ability and Reasoning Ability	20	20
2.	General Awareness	20	20
3.	English Language & Comprehension	20	20
4.	Hindi Language & Comprehension	20	20
5.	Numerical Aptitude & Data Interpretation	20	20
	Total	**100**	**100**

Section-II

S.No.	Subject	Questions	Marks
1.	MCQs pertaining to Post-Graduation qualification and teaching methodology required for the post.	**200**	**200**

Previous Years' Paper

Delhi Subordinate Services Selection Board (DSSSB)

PGT (Commerce) Recruitment Exam, 2025

(Exam held on 29-07-2025)

Subject Knowledge – Commerce & Teaching Methodology

1. Which form of organisation offers the greatest potential for raising capital through public stock offerings?
1. Limited Liability Company (LLC)
2. Corporation
3. Sole proprietorship
4. Partnership

2. Which among the following is a voluntary association of persons who join together with the primary motive of welfare of its members?
1. Joint Stock Company
2. Limited Liability Partnership
3. Cooperative Organisation
4. Angel Investing Association

3. Which of the following is NOT an example of a franchise?
1. Bata outlets
2. Domino's
3. Haldiram's
4. PVR Cinema

4. Which of the following is considered an economic activity?
1. A mother cooking for her family
2. A teacher teaching her child at home
3. A person listening to music for relaxation
4. A farmer growing crops for sale

5. The banking service that provides financial advice and services tailored specifically for high net worth individuals is called:
1. commercial banking
2. private banking
3. retail banking
4. corporate banking

6. Cattle-breeding farms, poultry farms or fish hatchery come under the class of:
1. processing industries
2. tertiary industries
3. extractive industries
4. genetic industries

7. In the event of the absence of a partnership deed, the profit and/or loss is to be shared among partners:
1. proportionately as per time devoted
2. in an equal ratio
3. as per their capital contribution ratio
4. as per the sacrificing ratio

8. What does 'VoIP' stand for in the context of business communication?
1. Virtual Online Interaction Platform
2. Voice Over Internet Protocol
3. Video Over Internet Protocol
4. Virtual Office Information Process

9. The statutory corporations are set up under the:
1. Government Corporate Act
2. Special Act of the Parliament
3. Companies Act, 2013
4. Indian Companies Act, 1956

10. Who among the following has the ultimate control over the business based on a Joint Hindu Family (HUF)?

1. The eldest member of the HUF
2. The Karta of the HUF
3. The senior most female member of the HUF
4. The elder son in the HUF

11. Which of the following is a type of liability insurance that covers claims that exceed homeowners' or auto insurance limits?

1. Collision insurance
2. Comprehensive insurance
3. Excess liability insurance
4. Umbrella insurance

12. Firms that aid the company in promoting, selling and distributing its goods to final buyers are:

1. Marketing Intermediaries
2. Publics
3. Wholesalers
4. Retailers

13. In which form of business is the owner personally liable for all debts?

1. Sole Proprietorship
2. Corporation
3. Limited Liability Partnership (LLP)
4. Cooperative Society

14. Select the odd one out with respect to the characteristics of business.

1. Risk and uncertainty
2. No profit motive, but service motive
3. Continuous process
4. Economic activity

15. Which of the following is NOT a benefit of e-banking services?

1. Unlimited network to the bank
2. 24 hours, 365 days a year services
3. Security of personal information
4. Digital payments

16. _____ concentrates on the structure of the organisation for the achievement of organisational goals and certain principles of management.

1. Neo classical theory
2. Contingency approach
3. Bureaucracy
4. Classical theory

17. Commercial banks are governed by the Indian Banking Regulation Act of:

1. 1949
2. 1948
3. 1935
4. 1956

18. Which of the following are considered as various forms of business organisations?

(*i*) Sole proprietorship
(*ii*) Joint Hindu family business
(*iii*) Partnership
(*iv*) Cooperative societies

1. All (*i*), (*ii*), (*iii*) and (*iv*)
2. Only (*ii*) and (*iii*)
3. Only (*i*) and (*ii*)
4. Only (*i*), (*ii*) and (*iii*)

19. Which of the following is NOT a primary industry?

1. Extracting
2. Genetic
3. Agriculture
4. Assembling

20. The partnership form of business is governed by the _____.

1. Indian Partnership Act, 1930
2. Indian Partnership Act, 1932
3. Partnership Act, 1932
4. Partnership Act, 1881

21. Money raised from within the firm, from operations or through the sale of ownership in the firm is known as:

1. Debt Financing
2. Short Term Financing
3. Medium Term Financing
4. Equity Financing

22. Which document is essential for the operation of a partnership firm, and outlines the duties, powers and obligations of the partners?

1. Memorandum of Association
2. Partnership Deed
3. Articles of Association
4. Shareholders' Agreement

23. Which of the following best describes the 'principle of scalar chain' in management?

1. The process of arranging jobs in a hierarchy
2. The flow of command or line of authority from the top management to the lowest ranks
3. The process of matching job roles with individual skills
4. The method of delegating tasks based on complexity

24. Which approach in the evolution of management thought emphasises the importance of understanding individual behaviours and group dynamics within an organisation?

1. Scientific Management
2. Classical Theory
3. Behavioural Science Approach
4. Bureaucratic Approach

25. Which of the following statement(s) is/are true?

(*i*) Sole trader or partnership forms are desirable when direct control of business is preferred.

(*ii*) Nature of the business does not have any influence on the choice of organisation form.

(*iii*) If the area of operation is very wide, partnership form is ideal.

1. Only (*i*) and (*iii*)
2. Only (*i*) and (*ii*)
3. Only (*i*)
4. (*i*), (*ii*) and (*iii*)

26. An industry that converts raw materials into usable products, like furniture or clothing, belongs to which classification?

1. Secondary 2. Primary
3. Quaternary 4. Tertiary

27. Planning is essential at _____ level(s) of management.

(1) Lower (2) Middle
(3) Higher

1. 1 & 2 only 2. 2 only
3. 1, 2 and 3 4. 3 only

28. _____ includes determining what tasks are to be done, who is to do them, how the tasks are to be grouped, who reports to whom, and who will make decisions.

1. Leading 2. Organising
3. Planning 4. Controlling

29. Under the Companies Act, 2013, for every company other than a One Person Company, not more than _____ shall elapse between the date of one annual general meeting and that of the next.

1. Fifteen months 2. Six months
3. Twelve months 4. Eighteen months

30. In a Joint Hindu Family Business, who will take the position after the death of the Karta?

1. The Eldest Female Member
2. Any of the eldest male or female member of the family
3. The Eldest Male Member
4. Any Male Member

31. In a sole proprietorship, the owner has:

1. limited liability for business debts
2. unlimited personal liability
3. liability restricted to invested capital
4. no liability for employee actions

32. A _____ is a broad explanation of why a firm exists and where it is trying to march ahead.

1. Goal 2. Objective
3. Mission 4. Vision

33. In the context of globalisation, what does the term 'race to the bottom' refer to?

1. A competition among nations to have the lowest tax rates
2. A trend where countries reduce their technological advancement to save costs
3. A competition among nations to have the highest GDP growth
4. A process company, state, or nation attempts to undercut the competition's prices by sacrificing quality standards

34. An effective team exercise building goes beyond simply bringing individuals together. It involves:

1. micromanaging individual team member's activities
2. creating a sense of shared purpose, clear roles, effective communication and trust within the team
3. encouraging competition and conflict within the team for better results
4. focusing on individual performance evaluations only

35. Separation of Ownership from the Management is the biggest advantage of:

1. Joint Stock Company
2. Cooperative Organisation
3. Sole Proprietorship
4. Limited Liability Partnership

36. XYZ is a listed company, having engaged into the services of Finance and Auditing, where a single individual promoter holds 70% of the ownership stakes. Which among the following would describe its type?

1. Government Company
2. Public Limited Company
3. Private Limited Company
4. Chartered Company

37. What is/are the main economic objectives of privatisation in the New Industrial Policy of 1991?

(1) To reduce the role of public sector
(2) To increase disinvestment in the PSUs
(3) To achieve rapid industrial development

1. 1 & 3 only 2. 2 & 3 only
3. 1, 2 & 3 4. 1 & 2 only

38. Which of the following statements about liability in a Joint Hindu Family business is correct?

1. Liability of Karta is unlimited, but coparceners have limited liability.
2. Liability of all coparceners is unlimited, and the Karta has no liability.
3. Liability of all members is unlimited.
4. Liability of Karta is limited to his share.

39. Which of the following is NOT an implied characteristic of management according to classical theorists?

1. It involves a continuous process of planning, execution and control.
2. It applies only to profit-making organisations.
3. It is a universal process applicable to all types of organisations.
4. It is a goal-oriented process.

40. The principle that each member of a co-operative has one vote, regardless of the amount of capital contributed, is known as:

1. capital control
2. majoritarian rule
3. equal equity
4. democratic control

41. Which of the following best distinguishes a joint stock company from a partnership firm?

1. Business organisation
2. Profit-sharing ratio
3. Maximum number of members
4. Registration process

42. Which of the following is NOT a channel of distribution under internal trade?

1. Producer - Exporter - Importer
2. Producer - Agent - Retailer - Consumer
3. Producer - Consumer
4. Producer - Retailer - Consumer

43. Which of the following sources of finance DOES NOT carry any financial cost (like interest or dividend)?

1. Bank loans
2. Preference shares
3. Debentures
4. Retained earnings

44. Which of the following is NOT a feature of liberalisation?

(*i*) Freedom in fixing price of goods and services
(*ii*) Simplifying the procedure for imports and exports
(*iii*) Increase in tax rates
(*iv*) Restriction on foreign capital

1. (*iii*) and (*iv*) only
2. (*i*), (*iii*) and (*iv*) only
3. (*iii*) only
4. (*i*) and (*ii*) only

45. If the proprietor of a business invests ₹ 50,000 in his business, it is deemed that the proprietor has given that much amount to the business as a loan that will be shown as a liability for the business. Which of the following Accounting Concepts supports this?

1. Accounting Period Concept
2. Entity Concept
3. Going Concern Concept
4. Dual Aspect Concept

46. _____ orientation favours the staffing of foreign operations on a regional basis.

1. Ethnocentric
2. Polycentric
3. Geocentric
4. Regiocentric

47. Which dimension of Corporate Social Responsibility (CSR) focuses on promoting human welfare and goodwill, and being a good corporate citizen contributing to community and quality of life?

1. Ethical
2. Legal
3. Philanthropic
4. Economic

48. On the basis of the nature of activity, industry can be classified into which of the following types?

(*i*) Extractive industries
(*ii*) Genetic industries
(*iii*) Manufacturing industries
(*iv*) Construction industries

1. Only (*i*) and (*ii*)
2. Only (*ii*) and (*iii*)
3. (*i*), (*ii*), (*iii*) and (*iv*)
4. Only (*i*), (*ii*) and (*iii*)

49. Match Column I with Column II with respect to the degree of skills required in different levels of organisational hierarchy.

Column I	Column II
1. Top Level Managers	A. Technical Skills
2. Middle Level Managers	B. Conceptual and Design Skills
3. Lower Level Supervisors	C. Human Skills

1. 1-A, 2-C, 3-B
2. 1-B, 2-C, 3-A
3. 1-B, 2-A, 3-C
4. 1-A, 2-B, 3-C

50. Which of the following is NOT true about Departmental Undertakings?

1. The employees of the enterprise are Government servants.
2. The funding of these enterprises come directly from the Government Treasury.
3. They are accountable to the concerned ministry.
4. The bureaucrat's over-cautious and conservative approval allow them to take risky ventures.

51. Which among the following statements is true with respect to Basel III Norms?

1. Banks must maintain a minimum Common Equity Tier 1 (CET1) capital ratio of 10% of risk-weighted assets (RWAs).
2. Banks must maintain a minimum total capital ratio of 12% of risk-weighted assets (RWAs).
3. Banks must maintain a minimum Tier 1 capital ratio of 7% of risk-weighted assets (RWAs).
4. Banks must hold enough high-quality liquid assets (HQLA) to cover net cash outflows over a 15-day stress period.

52. The Royal Caribbean cruise-liner has the requirement of a big cruise ship, having 10 swimming pools, 3 big theatres, 5,000 plus rooms and suites alongside two dining halls on each deck. They approached Black Rock Shipping Company and ultimately, the order was placed. For a big, customised order like this, the appropriate costing method to be adopted by Black Rock must be:

1. job costing
2. standard costing
3. marginal costing
4. batch costing

53. In the context of company liquidation, what is the correct ranking of payment priority among the following instruments?

1. Debentures > Preference shares > Equity shares
2. Equity shares > Debentures > Preference shares
3. Equity shares > Preference shares > Debentures
4. Preference shares > Debentures > Equity shares

54. Under the Companies Act 2013, a company CANNOT buy back its shares from:

1. its free reserves
2. bank balance
3. the proceeds of the issue of any shares or other specified securities
4. securities premium account

55. Which of the following American Depository Receipts is considered to be the most prestigious, and often enables a foreign firm to issue public offerings of ADRs in the US stock markets while establishing a substantial trading preference in the US market in raising capital?

1. Level III ADRs 2. Global ADRs
3. Level II ADRs 4. Level I ADRs

56. Which of the following correctly shows the stages in the formation of a joint stock company?

1. Promotion → Raising of Capital → Incorporation → Commencement of Business
2. Incorporation → Promotion → Raising of Capital → Commencement of Business
3. Raising of Capital → Commencement of Business → Incorporation → Promotion
4. Promotion → Incorporation → Raising of Capital → Commencement of Business

57. Ramesh received ₹ 2,00,000 as rent. Which of the following journal entries correctly records this transaction?

1. Bank A/c Dr.
   To Rent A/c
2. Rent A/c Dr.
   To Bank A/c
3. Bank A/c Dr.
   To Ramesh A/c
4. Ramesh A/c Dr.
   To Bank A/c

58. The free flow of which of the following is NOT typically associated with globalisation?

1. Goods and services
2. Capital
3. Labour and technology
4. Currency devaluation

59. In which of the following industries is job costing applicable?

(*i*) Printing press
(*ii*) Automobile garages
(*iii*) Shipbuilding

1. Only (*i*)
2. Only (*ii*) and (*iii*)
3. (*i*), (*ii*) and (*iii*)
4. Only (*i*) and (*iii*)

60. What is the name of those warehouses built for those industries that have to pay excise duty on the production of goods?

1. Cargo Warehouses
2. Bonded Warehouses
3. Shipping Warehouses
4. Excise Warehouses

61. Who has given the concept of time and motion study?

1. Frederick Winslow Taylor
2. Henry Feyol
3. Peegou
4. Peter F. Druker

62. Which of the following statements accurately describes the concept of management?

1. Management solely involves making decisions for lower-level employees.
2. Management is primarily concerned with overseeing financial transactions within an organisation.
3. Management is a function only performed by top executives.
4. Management is the process of planning, organising, leading, and controlling an organisation's resources to achieve its goals.

63. Human Resource Management is a process, which consists of four main activities, namely, _____, as well as maintenance of human resources.

1. acquisition, development, real
2. acquisition, development, motivation
3. primary, secondary, residual
4. real, nominal, personal

64. Which of the following lays down the course of action selected to guide and determine present and future decisions?

1. Methods
2. Plans
3. Policy
4. Procedures

65. Which of the following securities are equity-linked debt securities that are to be converted into equity or depository receipts after a specific period?

1. Convertible bonds
2. Eurobonds
3. Foreign currency convertible bonds
4. Masala bonds

66. Management is a/an _____.

1. Science
2. Art
3. Profession

1. 1, 2 and 3 2. 1 & 2 only
3. 1 & 3 only 4. 2 & 3 only

67. Which of the following statements best explains the nature of Management?

1. It is only scientific application
2. It is not pervasive
3. It is both art and science
4. It is only an art

68. Which of the following is NOT a method of privatisation?

1. Contracting
2. Management Buy-out
3. Divestiture
4. Franchising

69. Social trends, like growing health consciousness, can create opportunities for businesses by:

1. creating avenues for innovation and diversification
2. focusing solely on traditional marketing strategies
3. having no impact on product development strategies
4. reducing the need for customer service

70. Public deposits are often used by the companies to:

1. fund research and development activities
2. meet short-term working capital needs
3. pay dividends to shareholders
4. finance long-term capital expenditures (e.g., building a new factory)

71. There are mainly two types of business environment, _____.

1. fixed and flexible
2. internal and external
3. real and subsidiary
4. primary and secondary

72. Which among the following approaches of Management Theories draws together the pertinent knowledge of management by relating it to the managerial job?

1. Systems Approach
2. Bureaucratic Approach
3. Contingency Approach
4. Operational Approach

73. _____ is acknowledged as the father of Scientific Management.

1. Henry L Gantt
2. Frank Gilbreth
3. Henri Fayol
4. FW Taylor

74. How does the dividend distribution typically differ between equity shares and preference shares?

1. Equity shareholders have priority in dividend payments over preference shareholders.
2. Equity shareholders are paid dividends only after preference shareholders receive their dividends.
3. Equity shareholders are guaranteed a fixed dividend, while preference shareholders receive variable dividends.
4. Preference shareholders can vote on dividend distribution, whereas equity shareholders cannot.

75. Which of the following is NOT a micro environmental factor?

1. Customers
2. Economic condition
3. Suppliers
4. Employees

76. _____ was popularised as an "Approach to Planning" by Peter Drucker in 1954 in his famous book "The Practice of Management".

1. MBO
2. MBWA
3. Kaizen
4. 360 Degree Feedback

77. Which of the following statements is INCORRECT regarding a disadvantage of preference shares?

1. If the company earns returns less than the cost of preference share capital, it may result in an increase in earnings per share (EPS) for the equity shareholders.
2. For tax calculation, dividend on preference shares is not a deductible expense.
3. The preference shareholders do not have voting rights.
4. The cumulative preference shares become a permanent burden so far as the payment of dividend is concerned.

78. _____ allow a manager to visualise the entire organisation and work with ideas and the relationships between abstract concepts.

1. Conceptual Skills
2. Technical Skills
3. Secular Skills
4. People Skills

79. Which of the following tools is most commonly used in TQM for identifying the root cause of problems?

1. Bar Chart
2. Fishbone Diagram (Ishikawa)
3. Scatter Diagram
4. Gantt Chart

80. A global strategy in which a firm (the licensor) allows a foreign company (the licensee) to produce its product in exchange for a fee (a royalty) is known as:

1. franchising
2. licensing
3. exporting
4. contract manufacturing

81. Which of the following is excluded as a decision support tool for Total Quality Management?

1. Benchmarking
2. Affinity charting
3. Bin card system
4. Balanced scorecard

82. Which type of accounting is concerned with the provision of information to external parties such as investors, creditors, and regulators?

1. Management accounting
2. Cost accounting
3. Tax accounting
4. Financial accounting

83. Which of the following is a limitation of cost reduction techniques?

1. Increased customer satisfaction
2. Potential decrease in product quality
3. Increased short-term profits
4. Enhanced employee morale

84. What is the primary goal of Business Process Reengineering (BPR)?

A. To reduce the cost of production
B. To improve customer satisfaction
C. To expand the company globally
D. To increase the number of products manufactured

1. B, C and D 2. A and B
3. B and C 4. A, B and C

85. Which of the following are the objectives of personal financial planning?

1. Tax planning
2. Risk planning
3. Investment planning

1. All 1, 2 and 3 2. 1 and 2 only
3. 2 and 3 only 4. 1 and 3 only

86. Which of the following is NOT a method of entry into a foreign market for a domestic firm?

1. Exporting
2. Joint Venturing
3. Licensing/Franchising
4. Importing

87. The classification of items in ABC analysis is done on the basis of:

1. quantity of materials consumed
2. frequency or priority of consumption of materials
3. investment in materials only
4. value and importance

88. What does marketing control primarily focus on?

1. Training new HR staff
2. Buying raw materials
3. Measuring marketing performance and correcting deviations
4. Auditing accounts

89. Calculate the P/V ratio from the given information.

Sales in Period-1 ₹ 2,00,000
Profit in Period-1 ₹ 20,000
Sales in Period-2 ₹ 3,00,000
Profit in Period-2 ₹ 40,000

1. 13.33% 2. 10%
3. 25% 4. 20%

90. What is NOT included in the scope of commerce?

1. Trade 2. Export
3. Manufacturing 4. Aids to trade

91. Which of the following capital budgeting methods adjusts for the time value of money by discounting cash flows?

1. Payback Period
2. Profitability Index (PI)
3. Accounting Rate of Return (ARR)
4. Net Present Value (NPV)

92. Select the correct option regarding the Modern Portfolio Theory (MPT).

1. It is an investment approach that focuses on diversification and the relationship between risk and return when constructing investment portfolios.
2. Focus on maximising return regardless of risk or minimising risk without considering return.
3. Risk can be entirely eliminated through diversification.
4. The expected return of a portfolio is unrelated to the risk profile of the assets it contains.

93. Goods about which customers do not know much or do not normally think of buying and which require the greatest amount of promotions are called:

1. unsought goods
2. shopping goods
3. regular goods
4. convenience goods

94. Which of the following bodies takes care of the investors' protection for the investments exclusively made in National Pension Schemes?

1. PFRDA
2. RBI
3. SEBI
4. IRDA

95. Which of the following is NOT a right explicitly recognised under the Consumer Protection Act, 1986?

1. Right to Seek Redressal
2. Right to Information
3. Right to Safety
4. Right to Property

96. Financing Decisions are mainly related with deciding:

1. the quantum of finance to be raised from various long-term sources
2. the quantum of finance to be raised from various short-term sources
3. the quantum of finance to be raised from various short-term as well as long-term sources
4. the optimum mix of debt and equity

1. 1 & 4 only   2. 1, 3 & 4 only
3. 1 & 2 only   4. 1, 2, 3 & 4

97. A technique used by a team to generate ideas on a particular subject is known as:

1. Calibration
2. Benchmarking
3. Brainstorming
4. Conformity

98. What role does a facilitator play in a Quality Circle?

1. Guide discussions, encourage participation and help in implementation of solutions.
2. Make all the decisions and assign tasks.
3. Take detailed minutes of every meeting.
4. Act as a representative of management and enforce company policies.

99. In terms of debentures, _____ DO NOT carry any security.

1. Convertible Debentures
2. Registered Debentures
3. Unsecured Debentures
4. Mortgage Debentures

100. Green Marketing incorporates a broad range of activities, EXCEPT:

1. product modification
2. changes in production process
3. changes in advertising strategies
4. changes in pricing process

101. The identification of specific short-range objectives by lower-level managers is known as:

1. Tactical Planning
2. Operational Planning
3. Strategic Planning
4. Contingency Planning

102. Gordon's Model of Dividend Policy suggests that dividends are relevant because:

1. retained earnings do not affect stock value
2. future dividends are discounted at a lower rate
3. dividends have a higher tax shield than retained earnings
4. investors prefer current dividends over future capital gains

103. Which technology is commonly used in automating routine accounting tasks?

1. Machine learning
2. Blockchain
3. Virtual reality
4. Robotic process automation

104. In relation to Risk v/s Return concept in Financial Planning, which of the following statements are correct?

(*i*) Every individual has their own risk-taking capacity.

(*ii*) Conservative risk means an individual takes minimal risks ensuring funds are secure.

(*iii*) Aggressive risk means an individual is willing to take high risks and prefers investing in equity, commodities markets, and even be speculating for returns.

1. Only (*i*) and (*ii*)
2. Only (*i*) and (*iii*)
3. All (*i*), (*ii*) and (*iii*)
4. Only (*ii*) and (*iii*)

105. In accounting DBMS, the query language used to retrieve, update or delete data is generally:

1. XML
2. C++
3. SQL
4. HTML

106. Which of the following statement(s) is/are correct?

Statement 1: Financial planning is essentially the preparation of the financial blueprint of an organisation's future operations.

Statement 2: The objective of financial planning is to ensure that enough funds are available at the right time.

1. Only statement 2 is correct.
2. Both statements 1 and 2 are correct.
3. Only statement 1 is correct.
4. Both statements 1 and 2 are incorrect.

107. Responsibility centres whose managers are normally accountable for only those costs that are under their control are called _____, which are also known as cost centres.

1. Revenue Centres
2. Profit Centres
3. Investment Centres
4. Expense Centres

108. The SCORES platform by SEBI primarily aims to:

1. predict stock market performance using AI
2. rate the risk level of mutual fund schemes
3. score the compliance behaviour of listed companies
4. resolve investor grievances electronically

109. A short-term unsecured promissory note, issued by corporations mostly on a discount basis, is called:

1. commercial paper
2. treasury bill
3. zero coupon bond
4. certificate of deposit

110. Match Column I with Column II to get meaningful associations:

Column-I	Column-II
1. Goals	A. General Statements or understanding that guide or channel thinking in decision making
2. Policies	B. Specific required actions or non-actions allowing no discretion
3. Procedures	C. The ends towards which activity is aimed
4. Rules	D. Plans that establish a required method of handling future activities

1. 1-C, 2-A, 3-D, 4-B
2. 1-A, 2-C, 3-D, 4-B
3. 1-C, 2-B, 3-A, 4-D
4. 1-B, 2-A, 3-D, 4-C

111. In a matrix organisational structure, the employees:

1. report to only one supervisor
2. work in isolated teams with little cross-departmental interaction
3. are organised strictly by function
4. report both to a functional manager and a project manager

112. Which of the following is regarded as the managerial function of Human Resources Management?

1. Planning
2. Compensation to Personnel
3. Maintaining Good Industrial Relation
4. Development of Personnel

113. In the context of strategic planning and analysis, which of the following is NOT a component of the BCG Matrix?

1. Question Marks
2. Dogs
3. Cash Cows
4. Bulls

114. Which regulatory body oversees the acceptance of public deposits by non-banking financial companies (NBFCs) in India?

1. Ministry of Finance
2. Reserve Bank of India (RBI)
3. Securities and Exchange Board of India (SEBI)
4. Insurance Regulatory and Development Authority (IRDA)

115. Which Clause of Listing Obligations and Disclosure Regulations (LODR) of the SEBI Act, 1992, deals with the concept of corporate governance?

1. 50 2. 48
3. 51 4. 49

116. A stable Dividend Policy where a fixed percentage of net earnings is paid in the form of dividends is termed as:

1. constant pay-out ratio
2. regular dividend
3. stable rupee dividend
4. constant dividend per share

117. Which of the following are components of the Macro Environment?

(*i*) Economic Environment
(*ii*) Political and Legal Environment
(*iii*) Competitive Environment
(*iv*) Technological Environment

1. (*ii*) and (*iv*) only
2. (*i*), (*ii*), (*iii*) and (*iv*)
3. (*iii*) and (*iv*) only
4. (*i*), (*ii*) and (*iv*) only

118. Which of the following statements are true?

(*i*) Stock exchange provides liquidity to investment.
(*ii*) Fluctuations in the value of securities reflect the economic and business conditions in the country.
(*iii*) Stock exchange does not lead to excessive speculation.

1. (*i*) & (*iii*) only 2. (*i*), (*ii*) & (*iii*)
3. (*i*) & (*ii*) only 4. (*ii*) & (*iii*) only

119. Globalisation can pose challenges for businesses, such as:

1. elimination of competition from domestic companies
2. guaranteed success in international markets
3. a decrease in the need for marketing and advertising
4. navigating cultural differences and complex regulations in foreign markets

120. Which of the following instruments offers features similar to mutual funds, such as diversification and low cost, but also has the added advantage of being freely traded on a stock exchange?

1. Exchange Traded Funds
2. Sovereign Bonds
3. Corporate Bonds
4. Bank NIFTY Indices

121. When a consignor incurs expenses on sending goods to a consignee, what is the journal entry in the books of the consignee?

1. Consignment A/c Dr
   To Cash/Bank A/c
2. Consignment A/c Dr
   To Consignee's Personal A/c
3. Consignee's Personal A/c Dr
   To Consignment A/c
4. No Entry

122. Under which accounting principle must a business assume that it will continue to operate indefinitely, unless there is evidence to the contrary?

1. Accrual Principle
2. Full Disclosure Principle
3. Going Concern Principle
4. Historical Cost Principle

123. The end of the license-permit-quota raj means:

1. Privatisation 2. Liberalisation
3. Globalisation

1. 2 only 2. 1 only
3. 1, 2 and 3 4. 3 only

124. In relation to Corporate Restructuring, _____ is a merger that takes place upon the combination of two companies which are operating in the same industry but at different stages of the production or distribution system.

1. Co-generic merger
2. Conglomerate merger
3. Vertical merger
4. Horizontal merger

125. Which of the following is an outcome expected from the successful implementation of Quality Circles?

1. Improved communication within teams
2. Reduced employee workload
3. Elimination of all production errors
4. Mandatory participation in all decisions

126. The Lean System of production developed by Toyota in Japan primarily used in Total Preventive Maintenance (TPM), where cards of visible records are used to move and control the flow of production in a factory, is popularly known as:

1. Quality Circles
2. Kaizan
3. Total Quality Management
4. Kanban

127. _____ refers to the learning opportunities designed to help employees grow.

1. Training 2. On-the-job training
3. Development 4. Experience

128. _____ was a major contributor to Administrative Management Approach.

1. Charles Babbage
2. FW Taylor
3. Henri Fayol
4. Henry L Gnatt

129. Match Column I with Column II in connection with Transport Management System for meaningful associations.

Column-I	Column-II
(*i*) Routing	A. Product Dimension, Damage Risk Assessment Capacity
(*ii*) Load Planning	B. Optimisation of Routine, Cost Analysis and Capacity
(*iii*) Load Tendering	C. In-transit control, GPS monitoring
(*iv*) Status Tracking	D. Selection of carrier in that route, Transit Capabilities

1. (*i*)-D, (*ii*)-B, (*iii*)-A, (*iv*)-C
2. (*i*)-B, (*ii*)-A, (*iii*)-D, (*iv*)-C
3. (*i*)-A, (*ii*)-B, (*iii*)-D, (*iv*)-C
4. (*i*)-D, (*ii*)-A, (*iii*)-B, (*iv*)-C

130. Which of the following are included in redressal machinery for Consumer Grievances?

(*i*) National Commission
(*ii*) State Commission
(*iii*) District Forum

1. Only (*i*) and (*ii*)
2. Only (*i*) and (*iii*)
3. (*i*), (*ii*) and (*iii*)
4. Only (*ii*) and (*iii*)

131. A company is launching a new line of fitness trackers. They want to make the product readily available to potential customers. Which distribution strategy would be most appropriate?

1. Limited distribution through fitness centres with personal trainers
2. Direct sales through the company website only
3. Selective distribution through specialty sporting goods stores
4. Intensive distribution through various retail channels (such as electronics stores and big-box stores)

132. _____ is intended to broaden the knowledge of managers or potential managers in different enterprise functions.

1. Job rotation
2. Job enrichment
3. Job valuation
4. Job enlargement

133. The digital age has transformed consumer behaviour. How can consumer awareness initiatives adapt to this changing landscape?

1. By focusing on traditional media channels like newspapers and television
2. By developing marketing campaigns that target specific demographics
3. By creating lengthy and detailed reports on consumer rights
4. By utilising social media platforms for educational content and peer-to-peer information sharing

134. Which Section of the Consumer Protection Act, 1986, deals with 'unfair trade practices'?

1. Section 2(1)(t)
2. Section 2(1)(r)
3. Section 2(1)(u)
4. Section 2(1)(s)

135. The correct sequence of the process of Environment Analysis is _____.

1. Forecasting, Scanning, Monitoring, Assessment
2. Assessment, Scanning, Monitoring, Forecasting
3. Scanning, Monitoring, Forecasting, Assessment
4. Monitoring, Scanning, Forecasting, Assessment

136. In the context of corporate restructuring, a 'poison pill' is a strategy used by the target company to:

1. prevent a hostile takeover
2. facilitate a merger
3. increase the company's debt
4. attract potential buyers

137. When forfeited shares are reissued at a price higher than the forfeited amount, the excess is transferred to:

1. Capital Reserve
2. Securities Premium
3. Share Capital
4. General Reserve

138. Under the Consumer Protection Act, 1986, which of the following forums has jurisdiction to entertain complaints, where the amount involved exceeds ₹ 5 lakhs but DOES NOT exceed ₹ 20 lakhs?

1. District Forum
2. State Commission
3. Supreme Court
4. National Commission

139. Which of the following is NOT a feature of debentures?

1. Debenture holders have ownership rights.
2. They can be secured or unsecured.
3. They can be either redeemable or irredeemable.
4. They bear a fixed interest rate.

140. Which of the following statements are correct?

(*i*) The year 1987 brought the ISO 9000 standards into reality and visible strategies emerged.

(*ii*) CII organised training programmes in ISO 9000 quality systems for international standards and certification in the year 1989.

(*iii*) From the year 1991, Indian companies started to get the ISO 9000 certifications.

1. Only (*ii*) and (*iii*)
2. Only (*i*) and (*iii*)
3. Only (*i*) and (*ii*)
4. (*i*), (*ii*) and (*iii*)

141. _____ is otherwise known as Revenue Recognition Concept.

1. Matching Concept
2. Realisation Concept
3. Cost Concept
4. Money Measurement Concept

142. Which of the following is a copy of a firm's account with a bank?

1. Bank Reconciliation Statement
2. Cash Book
3. Pass Book
4. Cash Flow Statement

143. Expenditure made on a foreign tour to purchase a machinery and the technical know-how for long-term use can be categorised as:

1. Hybrid Expenditure
2. Capital Expenditure
3. Revenue Expenditure
4. Deferred Revenue Expenditure

144. Which of the following techniques are used to measure the impact of inflation on financial statements?

1. Calculative Purchasing Power Method and Current Cost Accounting Method
2. Current Purchasing Power Method and Current Cost Accounting Method
3. Cost Purchasing Power Method and Current Cost Accounting Method
4. Composite Purchasing Power Method and Current Cost Accounting Method

145. The cost price of the asset less scrap value of the asset is known as the:

1. Book Value
2. Market Value
3. Salvage Value
4. Depreciable Value

146. What does the concept of materiality mean in the context of accounting standards?

1. Accounting methods should be changed frequently to reflect market trends.
2. Only significant and relevant information that impacts decision-making needs to be disclosed.
3. Financial statements should be brief and easy to understand for everyone.
4. All financial information must be disclosed, regardless of significance.

147. Which accounting concept requires that financial statements be prepared at regular intervals?

1. Periodicity Concept
2. Realization Concept
3. Consistency Concept
4. Accrual Concept

148. Application Amount payable on the securities applied is marked as lien on amount payable as Application Money on Securities applied. After the company has allotted securities, bank debits the applicant's bank account by the amount payable on allotted securities and removes the lien on the balance amount. Such a phenomenon as recognised by SEBI is popularly known as:

1. Application Through Demat Blocking (ATDB)
2. Allotment Order through Account Block (AOAB)
3. Applications Supported by Blocked Amount (ASBA)
4. Share Application by Lien Amount (SALA)

149. Which of the following are the usual causes of difference(s) between the balances as shown by a cash book and a pass book?

(*i*) Cheques issued but not presented for payment

(*ii*) Cheques deposited with the bank but not yet collected and credited by bank

(*iii*) Bank charges not entered in the cash book

1. Only (*i*) and (*iii*)
2. (*i*), (*ii*) and (*iii*)
3. Only (*i*) and (*ii*)
4. Only (*ii*) and (*iii*)

150. Which of the following is NOT a part of the three main branches of accounting?

1. Human resource accounting
2. Management accounting
3. Financial accounting
4. Cost accounting

151. According to the matching concept of accounting, expenses should be recognised:

1. when the invoice is received
2. at the end of the accounting period
3. in the same period in which revenue is recognised
4. when the cash is paid

152. Which accounting principle mandates that the financial statements should include all information that could affect the decision-making of users?

1. Consistency principle
2. Materiality principle
3. Full disclosure principle
4. Conservatism principle

153. _____ have been defined as "the body of doctrines commonly associated with the theory and procedure of accounting, serving as an explanation of current practices and as a guide for the selection of conventions or procedures where alternatives exist".

1. Accounting jargons
2. Accounting principles
3. Accounting postulates
4. Accounting standards

154. Mr. Shyam is the owner of the company, and he withdrew goods and eventually used them for personal purposes. The cost of the goods being ₹ 500 and the selling price being ₹ 600, which of the following journal entries will be appropriate for such transaction?

1.

Particulars	Dr.	Cr.
Drawings A/C Dr.	500	
To Purchases A/C		500

2.

Particulars	Dr.	Cr.
Drawings A/C Dr.	600	
To Goods A/C		600

3.

Particulars	Dr.	Cr.
Shayam's A/C Dr.	500	
To Purchases A/C		500

4.

Particulars	Dr.	Cr.
Shayam's A/C Dr.	600	
To Sales A/C		600

155. Under the current purchasing power (CPP) approach in inflation accounting, which adjustment is made to historical costs?

1. Restating all assets and liabilities at current market values
2. Adjusting depreciation expense for inflation effects
3. Applying a general price index to all transactions
4. Discounting future cash flows to present values

156. Which of the following statements are INCORRECT in relation to rules of debit and credit?

(*i*) Personal Accounts: 'Debit the receiver and credit the giver'

(*ii*) Nominal Accounts: 'Debit what comes in and credit what goes out'

(*iii*) Real Accounts: 'Debit all expenses and losses and credit all incomes and gains'

1. All (*i*), (*ii*) and (*iii*)
2. Only (*i*) and (*ii*)
3. Only (*ii*) and (*iii*)
4. Only (*i*) and (*iii*)

157. Which of the following CANNOT be considered as debt capital?

1. Capital Raised from Issuing Bonds
2. Capital Raised from Long Term Loans
3. Capital Raised through Equity Shares
4. Debentures

158. Which of the following is NOT regarded as a qualitative characteristic of financial statements?

1. Liquidity
2. Comparability
3. Understand ability
4. Relevance

159. The process of recording business transactions in a book of original entry is known as:

1. Balance 2. Casting
3. Journalising 4. Posting

160. Indian Accounting Standard (IND AS) 16 deals with:

1. Recognition of Liability
2. Funds Flow and Cash Flow
3. Branch and Departmental Accounting
4. Property, Plant and Equipment

161. Which of the following ratios tests an organisation's ability to meet short term obligations?

1. Operating Ratio
2. Assets Turnover Ratio
3. Current Ratio
4. Leverage Ratio

162. Job costing method is adopted in:

1. automobile making
2. paper making
3. furniture making
4. oil extraction

163. Which method starts with net income and adjusts for changes in working capital and non-cash items to calculate cash flow from operating activities?

1. Direct Method 2. Indirect Method
3. Equity Method 4. Cost Method

164. The expression '(Net Income – Preferred Dividends)/Weighted Average Common Shares Outstanding' will essentially give us:

1. Market Capitalisation (MC)
2. Price to Earnings per Share (PE)
3. Price to Book Value (PB)
4. Earnings per Share (EPS)

165. _____ is a list of all accounts with their balances to provide a check on the equality of the debits and credits.

1. Cash Flow Statement
2. Balance Sheet
3. Trial Balance
4. Funds Flow Statement

166. Which of the following financial statements is the one which gives the financial position of a firm on a given day and not for an entire period?

1. Cash Flow Statements
2. Profit & Loss Account
3. Receipts and Payments Account
4. Balance Sheet

167. Which of the following is NOT a source of cash?

1. Cash from operations
2. Issue of debentures
3. Sale of fixed assets
4. Purchase of fixed assets

168. In relation to Financial Statement Analysis, which of the following statements are correct?

(*i*) The trend analysis of ratios indicates whether the financial position of a firm is improving or deteriorating over the years.

(*ii*) Ratios not only reflect the financial position of a firm but also serve as a tool for remedial actions.

(*iii*) Ratios are useful to assess and measure the profitability of the firm in respect of sales and investments.

1. Only (*i*) and (*ii*)
2. Only (*i*) and (*iii*)
3. (*i*), (*ii*) and (*iii*)
4. Only (*ii*) and (*iii*)

169. Which ratio measures a company's ability to meet its short-term obligations with its most liquid assets?
1. Return on equity (ROE)
2. Debt ratio
3. Quick ratio
4. Current ratio

170. Donations received for a specific purpose (e.g., building fund) are treated as:
1. Capital receipt
2. Surplus in Income and Expenditure Account
3. Deferred revenue
4. Revenue income

171. If the market price of an equity share is ₹ 20 and the earnings per share is ₹ 5, the price earnings ratio will be:
1. 5
2. 4
3. 0.25
4. 10

172. What is the primary purpose of a financial statement analysis?
1. To prepare financial statements for external reporting
2. To record transactions in the accounting system
3. To calculate taxes payable based on financial data
4. To interpret and evaluate the financial performance of a company

173. The process of bringing a business to an end and distributing its assets to claimants is called:
1. liquidation
2. depreciation
3. amortisation
4. consolidation

174. Horizontal analysis in Financial Statement Analysis involves:
1. analysing cash flow statements
2. analysing ratios to determine financial health
3. comparing financial statements of different companies
4. comparing financial statements of companies over different periods of time

175. In case of fund flow statement, the term 'funds' means:
1. cash and marketable securities
2. working capital
3. cash and bank balances
4. cash only

176. Which of the following activities result in changes in the size and composition of the owner's capital and borrowings of the firm?
1. Operating activities
2. Investing activities
3. Financing activities
4. Operating and investing activities

177. The FIFO method of pricing issues is suitable:
1. during the period of constant prices
2. during the period of falling prices
3. during the period of rising prices
4. during the period when prices move erratically

178. In what order (from the given list) does the liquidator of a company distribute the payment from the amount received from the assets not specifically pledged and the amounts contributed by the contributories?

(*i*) Expenses of winding up including the liquidators remuneration
(*ii*) Unsecured creditors
(*iii*) Creditors secured by the floating charge on the assets of the company
(*iv*) Preferential creditors

1. (*i*), (*iii*), (*iv*) and (*ii*)
2. (*i*), (*ii*), (*iv*) and (*iii*)
3. (*iii*), (*iv*), (*i*) and (*ii*)
4. (*iv*), (*iii*), (*ii*) and (*i*)

179. Under the weighted average method in process costing, cost per equivalent units is calculated by:

1. dividing the total units completed for current period by the units in closing work in process
2. dividing the total units completed by the units of opening work in process and units completed for current period
3. dividing the total costs incurred by the units in closing work in process
4. dividing the total costs incurred by the units of opening work in process and units completed for current period

180. Common-size analysis is also known as _____ analysis.

1. horizontal 2. vertical
3. dynamic 4. trend

181. The project method was developed by _____.

1. B.F. Skinner
2. Ivan Pavlov
3. Friedrich Wilhelm August Frobel
4. William Heard Kilpatrick

182. Which of the following is the process of assessing a students's performance qualitatively and expressing it in terms of letter grades and preferred in the assessment of co-scholastic learning outcomes?

1. Absolute grading
2. Indirect grading
3. Relative grading
4. Direct grading

183. In the Rights of Persons with Disabilities (RPWD) Act, 2016, how many specified types of disabilities are officially recognised by the Government of India?

1. 14 2. 25
3. 7 4. 21

184. The Herbartian model emphasises on the development of the _____ abilities of the learner.

1. mental 2. physical
3. corporeal 4. somatic

185. People listen to distinguish sounds and to develop sensitivity to nonverbal communication. What is this type of listening called?

1. Efferent listening
2. Discriminative listening
3. Aesthetic listening
4. Critical listening

186. The United Nations declared _____ as the International Women's Year to concentrate attention on the advancement of women all over the world.

1. 1979 2. 1974
3. 1978 4. 1975

187. The main objective of the National Repository of Open Educational Resources (NROER) is to make available _____.

1. printed textbooks to schools
2. teaching certification
3. digital learning resources
4. online examinations

188. What is the fundamental cognitive skill that involves the retention and recall of information?

1. Language 2. Affection
3. Memory 4. Attention

189. What is the quantitative description of phenomena or attributes or variables called?

1. Evaluation
2. Achievement test
3. Test
4. Measurement

190. It is physically not possible to teach everything in school; therefore, many topics and subject areas are excluded intentionally. This type of curriculum is called _____.

1. specified curriculum
2. hidden curriculum
3. overt curriculum
4. null curriculum

191. Which of the following learning activities best represents the psychomotor domain?

1. Performing a lab experiment
2. Solving a math problem
3. Writing an essay
4. Participating in a classroom debate

192. _____ can be effectively used in the classroom to provide real-world scenarios to help students learn.

1. Drama 2. Art
3. Dance 4. Role plays

193. An approach to teaching in which the entire process is guided by the learners' needs, interests, abilities and developmental level is known as _____.

1. content-driven approach
2. pupil-centred approach
3. teacher-centred approach
4. subject-centred approach

194. In which type of learning, the learner attempts to investigate questions, scenarios, often assisted by the teacher?

1. Cooperative Learning
2. Expository Learning
3. Collaborative Learning
4. Inquiry based Learning

195. _____ is the process of teaching individuals how to behave according to the social expectations associated with their gender, which are known as gender roles.

1. Gender identity
2. Gender stereotype
3. Gender socialisation
4. Gender schema

196. Diverse and _____ foster creativity and improve performance in workplaces.

1. mainstreaming environments
2. integrative environments
3. special environments
4. inclusive environments

197. What is the key educational implication of acknowledging individual differences among learners?

1. Teaching should be tailored to address the diverse needs of learners.
2. All students should follow the same learning path.
3. Priority should be given only to high achieving students.
4. There is only one effective way to learn

198. In the Herbartian model, the role of the 'apperceptive mass' in the learning process is to _____.

1. block new information from being processed
2. store emotional responses to learning
3. encourage rote memorisation of content
4. help organise and integrate new knowledge with past experiences

199. The term 'discipline' originates from two _____ words 'discipulus', which means pupil, and 'disciplina', which means teaching (noun).

1. French 2. Greek
3. German 4. Latin

200. Piaget has explained cognitive development through _____ important stages of development that occur in a sequence.

1. four 2. three
3. six 4. five

ANSWERS

1	2	3	4	5	6	7	8	9	10
2	3	4	4	2	4	2	2	2	2
11	**12**	**13**	**14**	**15**	**16**	**17**	**18**	**19**	**20**
4	1	1	2	3	4	1	1	4	2

21	22	23	24	25	26	27	28	29	30
4	2	2	3	3	1	3	2	1	3
31	**32**	**33**	**34**	**35**	**36**	**37**	**38**	**39**	**40**
2	3	4	2	1	2	3	1	2	4
41	**42**	**43**	**44**	**45**	**46**	**47**	**48**	**49**	**50**
4	1	4	1	2	4	3	3	2	4
51	**52**	**53**	**54**	**55**	**56**	**57**	**58**	**59**	**60**
3	1	1	2	1	4	1	4	3	2
61	**62**	**63**	**64**	**65**	**66**	**67**	**68**	**69**	**70**
1	4	2	3	1	1	3	4	1	2
71	**72**	**73**	**74**	**75**	**76**	**77**	**78**	**79**	**80**
2	4	4	2	2	1	1	1	2	2
81	**82**	**83**	**84**	**85**	**86**	**87**	**88**	**89**	**90**
3	4	2	2	1	4	4	3	4	3
91	**92**	**93**	**94**	**95**	**96**	**97**	**98**	**99**	**100**
4	1	1	1	4	4	3	1	3	4
101	**102**	**103**	**104**	**105**	**106**	**107**	**108**	**109**	**110**
2	4	4	3	3	2	4	4	1	1
111	**112**	**113**	**114**	**115**	**116**	**117**	**118**	**119**	**120**
4	1	4	2	4	1	4	3	4	1
121	**122**	**123**	**124**	**125**	**126**	**127**	**128**	**129**	**130**
4	3	1	3	1	4	3	3	2	3
131	**132**	**133**	**134**	**135**	**136**	**137**	**138**	**139**	**140**
4	1	4	2	3	1	1	1	1	4
141	**142**	**143**	**144**	**145**	**146**	**147**	**148**	**149**	**150**
2	3	2	2	4	2	1	3	2	1
151	**152**	**153**	**154**	**155**	**156**	**157**	**158**	**159**	**160**
3	3	2	1	3	3	3	1	3	4
161	**162**	**163**	**164**	**165**	**166**	**167**	**168**	**169**	**170**
3	3	2	4	3	4	4	3	3	1
171	**172**	**173**	**174**	**175**	**176**	**177**	**178**	**179**	**180**
2	4	1	4	2	3	3	1	4	2
181	**182**	**183**	**184**	**185**	**186**	**187**	**188**	**189**	**190**
4	4	4	1	2	4	3	3	4	4
191	**192**	**193**	**194**	**195**	**196**	**197**	**198**	**199**	**200**
1	4	2	4	3	4	1	4	4	1

EXPLANATORY ANSWERS

1. A Corporation offers the greatest potential for raising capital through public stock offerings because it has the legal authority to issue shares of stock to the public through stock exchanges. This allows it to attract investment from a large number of investors, both individuals and institutions. In contrast, LLCs, partnerships, and sole proprietorships typically have restrictions on ownership and cannot easily access public capital markets.

2. A Cooperative Organisation is a voluntary association of individuals who come together with the main aim of promoting the welfare of their members rather than earning profits. Each member contributes capital and participates in management decisions on a democratic basis, typically following the principle of "one member, one vote." Examples include credit cooperatives, housing cooperatives, and agricultural cooperatives.

3. PVR Cinema is not an example of a franchise. It is a company-owned chain of multiplexes operating under its own brand and management. In contrast, Bata outlets, Domino's, and Haldiram's operate through the franchise model, where independent owners run outlets under the brand's established system and guidelines.

4. An economic activity refers to any activity undertaken with the intention of earning income or profit. Among the options, a farmer growing crops for sale qualifies as an economic activity because it involves production for the market and aims to generate income. The other activities listed (cooking for family, teaching one's child, listening to music) are personal or non-economic.

5. Private banking is the specialized banking service designed for high-net-worth individuals (HNWIs). It offers personalized financial advice, wealth management, investment planning, estate management, and other tailored services to meet the specific needs of affluent clients.

6. Cattle-breeding farms, poultry farms, and fish hatcheries fall under the class of genetic industries. These industries are involved in the breeding and multiplication of plants and animals with the objective of improving their quality and yield. Unlike extractive industries, which draw resources from nature, genetic industries focu on reproducing and enhancing living organism through scientific and selective breeding methods

7. In the absence of a partnership deed, the Indian Partnership Act, 1932 specifies that profits and losses are to be shared equally among all partners, regardless of their capital contribution or the time they devote to the business. This default rule applies unless there is a written agreement (partnership deed) stating otherwise.

8. VoIP stands for Voice Over Internet Protocol. It refers to the technology that allows voice communication and multimedia sessions to be transmitted over the Internet instead of traditional telephone lines. Examples include applications like Skype, Zoom, and WhatsApp calls, which use VoIP for communication.

9. Statutory corporations are public enterprises established under a Special Act of the Parliament or State Legislature. These Acts define their powers, functions, and structure. Examples include the Life Insurance Corporation of India (LIC) and the State Bank of India (SBI). They are autonomous bodies with a distinct legal identity separate from the government.

10. In a Joint Hindu Family Business (HUF), the Karta holds the ultimate control and authority over business operations. The Karta is typically the senior-most male member of the family and manages all business affairs, makes decisions, and represents the HUF legally. Other members, known as coparceners, have ownership rights but limited managerial control.

11. Umbrella insurance is a type of liability insurance that provides coverage beyond the limits of a homeowner's, auto, or boat insurance policy. It offers additional protection against major claims and lawsuits, helping safeguard the insured's assets when the underlying insurance coverage is exhausted. For instance, if an auto accident claim exceeds the auto policy's limit, the umbrella policy covers the excess amount.

12. Marketing intermediaries are firms or individuals that assist companies in promoting, selling, and distributing goods to final buyers. They act as a link between the producer and the consumer,

helping in efficient movement of goods and services. Examples include wholesalers, retailers, agents, and distributors who facilitate the marketing process.

13. In a Sole Proprietorship, the owner is personally liable for all debts and obligations of the business. There is no legal distinction between the owner and the business, meaning personal assets can be used to pay business debts. While this form offers full control and profits to the owner, it also carries unlimited personal risk.

14. The characteristic "No profit motive, but service motive" does not belong to business. Businesses are driven by the profit motive and involve economic activities carried out continuously under conditions of risk and uncertainty. A service motive characterizes non-profit or social organizations rather than business enterprises.

15. Security of personal information is not a guaranteed benefit of e-banking services. While banks employ advanced security measures, risks such as phishing, hacking, and identity theft still exist. The other options — unlimited network access, round-the-clock services, and digital payments — are recognized advantages of e-banking.

16. The Classical theory of management focuses on the structure of the organisation and emphasizes achieving efficiency and organisational goals through well-defined roles, hierarchy, and division of labour. It also stresses principles such as unity of command, specialization, and a clear chain of authority, aiming for maximum productivity and order within the organisation.

17. Commercial banks in India are governed by the Indian Banking Regulation Act of 1949. This Act provides the legal framework for the regulation, supervision, and control of commercial banks in India, covering aspects like licensing, management, and business operations to ensure financial stability and public confidence.

18. The various recognised forms of business organisations include Sole Proprietorship, Joint Hindu Family Business, Partnership, and Cooperative Societies. These forms differ in ownership structure, liability, management control, and legal status, offering options suited to different business needs and scales.

19. Assembling is not a primary industry. Primary industries are involved in the extraction or production of natural resources, such as agriculture, mining, fishing, and forestry. Assembling, on the other hand, belongs to the manufacturing or secondary sector, where finished goods are produced by combining various components.

20. The partnership form of business in India is governed by the Indian Partnership Act, 1932. This Act outlines the rights, duties, liabilities, and relationships among partners, as well as rules concerning the formation, registration, and dissolution of partnerships.

21. Equity Financing refers to money raised from within the firm through the sale of ownership interests, such as shares of stock, or from profits retained from operations. Unlike debt financing, it does not involve borrowing or repayment with interest. Instead, investors or shareholders gain ownership rights and a share in the company's profits.

22. A Partnership Deed is the essential document for the operation of a partnership firm. It defines the duties, powers, and obligations of each partner, outlines the profit-sharing ratio, capital contribution, and rules regarding admission or retirement of partners. While not legally mandatory, it helps prevent disputes and ensures smooth business functioning.

23. The Principle of Scalar Chain in management refers to the flow of command or line of authority from the top management to the lowest ranks in an organisation. It establishes a clear communication channel, ensuring that instructions, information, and accountability flow in an orderly and hierarchical manner. This concept was introduced by Henri Fayol as one of his 14 principles of management.

24. The Behavioural Science Approach emphasizes understanding individual behaviour and group dynamics within an organisation. It focuses on human relations, motivation, leadership, communication, and teamwork as key factors influencing productivity and morale. This approach emerged as a response to the limitations of classical and scientific management theories that ignored human needs and emotions.

25. **Statement (*i*)** is true because sole proprietorship or partnership forms are suitable when direct control of business is desired.

Statement (*ii*) is false, as the nature of the business (e.g., scale, capital needs, risk) strongly influences the choice of organisational form.

Statement (*iii*) is also false, as a partnership is not ideal for a wide area of operation; large-scale businesses usually prefer companies due to better capital and management resources.

26. Industries that convert raw materials into usable products such as furniture, clothing, or machinery belong to the Secondary industry. These industries take the outputs of primary industries (like wood, cotton, or minerals) and process or manufacture them into finished or semi-finished goods ready for use or further production. Examples include textile, automobile, and furniture industries.

27. Planning is essential at all levels of management — lower, middle, and higher. At the higher level, it involves strategic planning and goal setting; at the middle level, it includes departmental and tactical planning; and at the lower level, it focuses on operational or day-to-day activities. Effective planning at every level ensures alignment with organisational objectives.

28. Organising refers to the process of determining what tasks are to be done, who will perform them, how they will be grouped, who reports to whom, and who will make decisions. It involves creating a structure for efficient coordination and allocation of resources to achieve the organisation's objectives.

29. Under the Companies Act, 2013, the maximum period that can elapse between two Annual General Meetings (AGMs) is fifteen months. This ensures regular accountability to shareholders and periodic review of company performance and financial statements.

30. In a Joint Hindu Family Business, after the death of the Karta, the position is automatically taken over by the eldest male member of the family. The Karta holds the highest authority in the family business, managing and representing it on behalf of all coparceners.

31. In a Sole Proprietorship, the owner has unlimited personal liability. This means that there is no legal distinction between the owner and the business, and the owner is personally responsible for all business debts and obligations. If the business cannot meet its liabilities, the owner's personal assets may be used to settle them.

32. A Mission is a broad statement that explains why a firm exists and what its core purpose is. It defines the business's reason for being, its primary goals, and its approach toward stakeholders. It acts as a guiding framework for decision-making and strategy development.

33. In the context of globalisation, the term 'race to the bottom' refers to a process in which a company, state, or nation attempts to undercut competitors' prices by sacrificing quality standards, environmental regulations, or labor protections. It often occurs when countries compete to attract foreign investment by offering cheaper production costs and weaker regulations.

34. Effective team building involves creating a sense of shared purpose, defining clear roles, establishing effective communication, and fostering trust among team members. This leads to better collaboration, higher motivation, and improved productivity. Team building goes beyond assembling people—it focuses on developing cohesion and alignment toward common goals.

35. Separation of Ownership from Management is the biggest advantage of a Joint Stock Company. In this form, shareholders (owners) provide capital and elect a board of directors, while professional managers handle daily operations. This separation allows for specialization, efficient decision-making, and professional management of large-scale enterprises.

36. Since XYZ is a listed company, it means its shares are traded publicly on a stock exchange. Even though one promoter holds 70% of ownership, it remains a Public Limited Company because it is listed and offers shares to the public. The key feature of such companies is that they can raise capital from the public and are governed by the Companies Act, 2013.

37. The main economic objectives of privatisation under the New Industrial Policy of 1991 were to reduce the role of the public sector, increase disinvestment in PSUs, and achieve rapid industrial development through greater efficiency, competitiveness, and private participation. All three statements align with these objectives.

38. In a Joint Hindu Family Business, the Karta's liability is unlimited, meaning his personal assets can be used to pay off business debts, while the liability of coparceners is limited to their share in the joint family property. This reflects the hierarchical control and responsibility within the HUF structure.

39. The statement "It applies only to profit-making organisations" is not an implied characteristic of management. Classical theorists viewed management as a universal process applicable to both profit and non-profit organisations, involving planning, organising, directing, and controlling to achieve goals efficiently.

40. The principle that each member of a co-operative has one vote, regardless of capital contribution, is known as democratic control. This ensures equality among members, reflecting the cooperative spirit of mutual help and joint decision-making rather than financial dominance.

41. The key distinction between a Joint Stock Company and a Partnership Firm lies in their registration process. Registration is compulsory for a joint stock company under the Companies Act, whereas it is optional for a partnership firm under the Indian Partnership Act, 1932. This registration grants the company a separate legal identity, perpetual succession, and limited liability — advantages a partnership does not automatically possess.

42. The channel Producer – Exporter – Importer is not part of internal trade, as it involves cross-border transactions, making it a form of external or international trade. Internal trade occurs only within a country's boundaries, involving producers, wholesalers, retailers, and consumers.

43. Retained earnings do not carry any financial cost like interest or dividends because they are profits reinvested back into the business rather than distributed to shareholders or borrowed from external sources. Although there is an opportunity cost (since shareholders could have received dividends), there is no explicit financial outflow.

44. Features such as freedom in pricing, and simplified import/export procedures are part of liberalisation. However, increasing tax rates and restricting foreign capital are opposite to the principles of liberalisation, which aim to reduce government control and attract foreign investment.

45. The Entity Concept in accounting treats the business and the owner as two separate entities. Hence, when a proprietor invests ₹ 50,000, it is considered as capital given to the business, which becomes a liability from the business's perspective. This separation helps in maintaining clarity and objectivity in financial records.

46. The Regiocentric orientation favours the staffing of foreign operations on a regional basis. In this approach, the company groups countries into regions and recruits or transfers employees within those regions. It balances global coordination with regional responsiveness, unlike ethnocentric (home-country focus) or polycentric (host-country focus) orientations.

47. The Philanthropic dimension of Corporate Social Responsibility (CSR) emphasizes promoting human welfare, goodwill, and contributing to the community and quality of life. It involves voluntary actions such as donations, education support, healthcare initiatives, and community development, going beyond what is legally or ethically required.

48. On the basis of the nature of activity, industries are classified into Extractive, Genetic, Manufacturing, and Construction industries. Extractive industries obtain raw materials from nature; genetic industries breed plants and animals; manufacturing industries transform materials into goods; and construction industries create infrastructure like buildings and roads.

49. The correct matching of managerial levels with required skills is as follows:

- Top Level Managers → Conceptual and Design Skills (B) – for strategic planning and overall direction.
- Middle Level Managers → Human Skills (C) – for coordination and communication between top and lower levels.
- Lower Level Supervisors → Technical Skills (A) – for direct supervision of operational work.

Hence, the correct order is 1-B, 2-C, 3-A.

50. The statement "The bureaucrat's over-cautious and conservative approval allow them to take risky ventures" is NOT true about Departmental Undertakings. In fact, such bureaucratic control usually prevents them from taking risky ventures or innovative steps. These undertakings operate as government departments, with employees being government servants, funded through the treasury, and accountable to a ministry.

51. Under the Basel III Norms, banks are required to maintain a minimum Tier 1 capital ratio of 7% of risk-weighted assets (RWAs). This includes a Common Equity Tier 1 (CET1) ratio of at least 4.5%, plus a 2.5% capital conservation buffer. These norms aim to strengthen bank capital requirements and promote stability in the global financial system.

52. For large, customised orders, such as a specially designed cruise ship with unique features, the appropriate costing method is Job Costing. Under this method, costs are recorded and monitored separately for each job or project since each job is distinct and tailor-made to the client's specifications.

53. In the event of company liquidation, the order of payment priority is:

Debenture holders (secured creditors) are paid first, followed by Preference shareholders, and finally Equity shareholders. Debentures represent loans, hence have repayment priority; preference shares have fixed dividends and preferential rights over equity shares.

54. Under Section 68(1) of the Companies Act, 2013, a company can buy back its shares using only certain specific sources:

- Free reserves
- Securities premium account
- Proceeds from the issue of any shares or other specified securities (but not of the same kind being bought back)

However, a company cannot use its regular bank balance as a direct source for buyback, since it must come from the specific reserves or proceeds mentioned above.

55. Level III ADRs are the most prestigious type of American Depository Receipts. They allow a foreign company to issue public offerings and establish significant trading presence in U.S. stock markets such as NASDAQ or NYSE. This level requires full compliance with U.S. GAAP and SEC reporting standards, enhancing visibility and access to capital.

56. The correct sequence of stages in the formation of a Joint Stock Company is:

Promotion → Incorporation → Raising of Capital → Commencement of Business.

- Promotion: Identifying a business idea and taking necessary steps to form the company.
- Incorporation: Getting the company registered and obtaining a Certificate of Incorporation.
- Raising of Capital: Issuing shares to raise necessary funds.
- Commencement of Business: Public companies can start operations only after obtaining the Certificate of Commencement of Business.

57. When Ramesh receives ₹ 2,00,000 as rent, the business is earning income, and cash/bank balance increases. Hence, the correct journal entry is:

Bank A/c Dr. ₹ 2,00,000

To Rent A/c ₹ 2,00,000

This entry records the increase in bank assets (debit) and income earned (credit).

58. Currency devaluation is not typically associated with globalisation. Globalisation involves the free flow of goods, services, capital, labour, and technology across borders. Currency devaluation, on the other hand, is a governmental monetary policy tool used to influence trade balances and exports, not a direct feature of globalisation.

59. Job costing is applicable in industries where work is done according to specific customer orders, and each job differs from the other. Industries such as printing presses, automobile garages, and shipbuilding all involve customised orders and unique jobs, making job costing suitable for all three.

60. Bonded Warehouses are those used by industries that have to pay excise duty on the production of goods. Goods are stored here without immediate payment of duty, which is only paid when the goods are removed for sale or export. These warehouses help defer tax payments and manage cash flow efficiently.

61. The concept of Time and Motion Study was introduced by Frederick Winslow Taylor, the father of Scientific Management. He analyzed tasks by breaking them into smaller components (motion study) and timing each element (time study) to determine the most efficient way of performing a job, aiming to increase productivity and reduce waste.

62. Management is best described as the process of planning, organising, leading, and controlling an organisation's resources to achieve its goals. It is a universal function that involves coordinating people and other resources efficiently and effectively at all levels of an organisation.

63. The process of Human Resource Management (HRM) consists of four key activities: acquisition, development, motivation, and maintenance of human resources. Acquisition involves hiring the right people; development focuses on training; motivation deals with employee engagement; and maintenance ensures retention and satisfaction.

64. A Policy lays down the course of action selected to guide and determine present and future decisions. It provides a broad framework or guideline for decision-making, ensuring consistency in operations and helping managers handle recurring issues systematically.

65. Convertible bonds are equity-linked debt instruments that can be converted into equity shares or depository receipts after a specific period. They start as debt instruments (earning fixed interest) but give the holder the option to convert them into equity, thus combining features of both debt and equity.

A specific variant used internationally is the Foreign Currency Convertible Bond (FCCB), which functions similarly but is denominated in a foreign currency.

66. Management is considered a science, an art, and a profession.

- As a science, it uses systematic knowledge, principles, and cause-effect relationships.
- As an art, it involves the creative application of knowledge, experience, and skills to achieve desired results.
- As a profession, it follows a code of conduct and requires specialized knowledge, though it is not fully professionalized like law or medicine.

67. The nature of Management is that it is both an art and a science. It is a science because it relies on principles, techniques, and systematic knowledge; it is an art because effective application requires personal skills, creativity, and experience. Thus, management blends theoretical knowledge with practical execution.

68. Franchising is not a method of privatisation. Privatisation involves transferring ownership or management of state-owned enterprises to the private sector, typically through methods like contracting, management buy-outs, and divestiture. Franchising, however, is a business model for private enterprises to expand through licensing arrangements.

69. Social trends such as growing health consciousness create opportunities for innovation and diversification. Businesses can develop new products like organic foods, fitness apps, or wellness services to meet changing consumer preferences. Adapting to such trends helps companies remain competitive and relevant.

70. Public deposits are funds raised directly from the public for a fixed period at a prescribed interest rate. Companies typically use these deposits to meet short-term working capital needs, such as financing day-to-day operations, managing inventory, or covering immediate expenses, rather than for long-term capital investments.

71. There are mainly two types of business environment — Internal and External.

The internal environment includes factors within the organisation such as employees, management, and culture, while the external environment consists of factors outside the organisation like competitors, customers, technology, and government policies. Both influence business operations and decision-making.

72. The Operational Approach to management draws together relevant knowledge from various management theories and relates it to the managerial job. It integrates the contributions of different schools—scientific, human relations, and systems—to develop a comprehensive understanding of management functions and practices.

73. Frederick Winslow Taylor (F.W. Taylor) is acknowledged as the Father of Scientific Management. He introduced scientific principles to improve industrial efficiency, such as time and motion studies, standardization, and performance-based incentives, which revolutionized management practices worldwide.

74. Equity shareholders are paid dividends only after preference shareholders have received their fixed dividends. Preference shareholders have a prior claim on profits and assets during liquidation, whereas dividends for equity shareholders are variable and depend on the company's performance and profit availability.

75. Economic conditions are not a micro environmental factor; they belong to the macro environment, which affects all businesses in an economy. Micro environmental factors include customers, suppliers, competitors, intermediaries, and employees, which directly influence a specific company's operations.

76. The concept of MBO (Management by Objectives) was popularised by Peter F. Drucker in 1954 in his book "The Practice of Management."

MBO is an approach to planning where managers and employees collaboratively set, monitor, and achieve specific, measurable goals within a defined timeframe. It aligns individual objectives with organisational goals, improving motivation and performance.

77. The incorrect statement regarding a disadvantage of preference shares is:

"If the company earns returns less than the cost of preference share capital, it may result in an increase in earnings per share (EPS) for the equity shareholders."

This statement is false because lower returns actually decrease EPS for equity shareholders, as preference dividends must be paid before equity holders receive anything. The other statements correctly describe limitations of preference shares.

78. Conceptual skills enable a manager to visualise the entire organisation, understand how different functions interrelate, and work with abstract ideas and strategies. These skills are crucial for top-level managers involved in long-term planning and overall decision-making.

79. The Fishbone Diagram (Ishikawa Diagram) is the tool most commonly used in Total Quality Management (TQM) to identify the root cause of problems. It helps in visually mapping potential causes of an issue under categories such as manpower, methods, materials, machinery, and environment, enabling structured problem-solving.

80. A Licensing strategy allows a foreign company (licensee) to produce and sell the licensor's product in exchange for a royalty or fee. This enables global expansion without heavy investment in foreign operations. Examples include technology licensing and brand name usage in foreign markets.

81. The Bin Card System is excluded as a decision support tool for Total Quality Management (TQM).

TQM focuses on continuous improvement through tools like Benchmarking, Affinity Charting, and the Balanced Scorecard, which help in quality analysis, performance tracking, and goal alignment. The Bin Card System, however, is a storekeeping tool used for recording inventory movements, not for quality management.

82. Financial Accounting is concerned with providing information to external parties such as investors, creditors, regulators, and tax authorities. It involves preparing financial statements — the balance sheet, income statement, and cash flow statement — to communicate a company's financial position and performance objectively.

83. A major limitation of cost reduction techniques is the potential decrease in product quality. When excessive emphasis is placed on reducing costs, it can lead to inferior materials, reduced quality control, or compromised service standards, which may harm brand reputation and customer satisfaction in the long run.

84. The primary goal of Business Process Reengineering (BPR) is to achieve dramatic improvements in performance such as reducing production costs and improving customer satisfaction by redesigning core business processes. It is not primarily focused on global expansion or increasing product count but on efficiency and value creation.

85. The objectives of personal financial planning include Tax Planning, Risk Planning, and Investment Planning. Together, these ensure financial stability, wealth growth, and protection against uncertainties. A sound financial plan helps individuals manage income, control expenses, and meet long-term goals effectively.

86. Importing is not a method of entry into a foreign market for a domestic firm.

Exporting, joint venturing, and licensing/franchising are methods by which a firm enters foreign markets to sell its products or services. Importing, on the other hand, involves buying goods from foreign countries into the domestic market, which is the reverse of foreign market entry.

87. In ABC Analysis, items are classified based on their value and importance.

- 'A' items are high-value but low-quantity items requiring strict control,
- 'B' items are moderate in both value and control, and
- 'C' items are low-value, high-quantity items with minimal control.

This method helps optimise inventory management and focus on critical items.

88. Marketing control primarily focuses on measuring marketing performance and correcting deviations to ensure that objectives are achieved efficiently. It involves evaluating sales performance, market share, and profitability, and taking corrective actions when results deviate from the marketing plan.

89. We can calculate the P/V ratio (Profit/Volume ratio) using the change in profit and change in sales:

$$\text{P/V Ratio} = \frac{\text{Change in Profit}}{\text{Change in Sales}} \times 100$$

$$\text{Change in Profit} = 40{,}000 - 20{,}000 = 20{,}000$$

$$\text{Change in Sales} = 3{,}00{,}000 - 2{,}00{,}000 = 1{,}00{,}000$$

$$\text{P/V Ratio} = \frac{20{,}000}{1{,}00{,}000} \times 100 = 20\%.$$

90. Manufacturing is not included in the scope of commerce.

Commerce involves all activities related to the exchange and distribution of goods, such as trade (internal and external) and aids to trade (transport, banking, insurance, warehousing, communication, etc.). Manufacturing, however, falls under industry, not commerce.

91. The Net Present Value (NPV) method adjusts for the time value of money by discounting future cash flows to their present value. It compares the present value of cash inflows with the initial investment, and a positive NPV indicates that the project is financially viable and profitable.

92. The Modern Portfolio Theory (MPT) is an investment approach that focuses on diversification and the relationship between risk and return when constructing portfolios. Developed by Harry Markowitz, it suggests that investors can achieve an optimal portfolio by balancing expected return with acceptable risk through diversification.

93. Unsought goods are products that customers do not think of buying regularly or are unaware of, such as life insurance, funeral services, or fire extinguishers. These goods require intensive promotion and personal selling efforts to create awareness and interest among consumers.

94. The Pension Fund Regulatory and Development Authority (PFRDA) is the body responsible for investor protection and regulation of the National Pension System (NPS) in India. It oversees pension fund operations, ensures transparency, and safeguards the interests of subscribers.

95. The Right to Property is not a right explicitly recognised under the Consumer Protection Act, 1986. The Act ensures consumer rights such as Right to Safety, Right to Information, Right to Choose, and Right to Seek Redressal, among others, but property rights fall under constitutional or civil law, not consumer law.

96. Financing decisions encompass all aspects of how a company acquires funds. This includes deciding:

- The quantum of finance to be raised from long-term sources,
- The quantum of finance to be raised from short-term sources,
- The total funds needed from both short-term and long-term sources, and
- The optimum mix of debt and equity to maintain an ideal capital structure.

These decisions ensure that the company maintains financial stability, minimizes cost of capital, and maximizes shareholder wealth.

97. The technique used by a team to generate a large number of creative ideas on a particular subject without immediate criticism or evaluation is called Brainstorming. It encourages open participation and helps in problem-solving, innovation, and decision-making processes.

98. In a Quality Circle, the facilitator plays the role of a guide and motivator. They help steer discussions, encourage participation among members, and support the implementation of solutions proposed by the circle. The facilitator does not make decisions but ensures smooth teamwork and communication.

99. Unsecured debentures do not carry any security or charge on the company's assets. They are also called naked debentures, as investors rely solely on the company's creditworthiness for repayment. In contrast, secured or mortgage debentures are backed by specific assets.

100. Green marketing involves strategies aimed at promoting environmentally friendly products through product modification, production process changes, and advertising adjustments. However, it does not involve changes in pricing process — pricing depends on cost, demand, and competition, not necessarily environmental objectives.

101. Operational Planning involves the identification of specific short-range objectives by lower-level managers. It focuses on day-to-day activities, resource allocation, and achieving immediate targets that contribute to broader tactical and strategic goals. Operational plans typically cover short periods such as weeks or months.

102. According to Gordon's Model of Dividend Policy, dividends are relevant because investors prefer current dividends over uncertain future capital gains. This is based on the "bird-in-hand" theory, which suggests that immediate returns are less risky and more valued by investors compared to potential future profits.

103. Robotic Process Automation (RPA) is commonly used in automating routine accounting tasks such as data entry, reconciliation, invoice processing, and report generation. It enhances efficiency, accuracy, and speed by performing repetitive rule-based operations without human intervention.

104. All three statements correctly describe the Risk vs. Return concept in Financial Planning:

(*i*) Risk tolerance varies by individual.

(*ii*) Conservative risk implies minimal risk-taking with focus on security.

(*iii*) Aggressive risk indicates willingness to take higher risks for higher returns through investments in equities or commodities.

105. In accounting database management systems (DBMS), SQL (Structured Query Language) is used to retrieve, update, or delete data. It is the standard programming language for managing and manipulating relational databases effectively and securely.

106. Both statements correctly describe the concept and objective of financial planning:

Statement 1: Financial planning indeed involves preparing a financial blueprint for an organisation's future operations, outlining resource allocation and fund requirements.

Statement 2: The main objective of financial planning is to ensure that adequate funds are available at the right time to meet business needs and avoid liquidity crises.

107. Expense Centres (also known as Cost Centres) are responsibility centres where managers are accountable only for the costs they can control. They do not directly generate revenue or profit, and their efficiency is measured by how well they control costs within the budgeted limits.

108. The SCORES (SEBI Complaints Redress System) platform by SEBI is designed to resolve investor grievances electronically. It allows investors to lodge complaints against listed companies or intermediaries online and track their resolution status, ensuring transparency and accountability in grievance redressal.

109. A Commercial Paper (CP) is a short-term unsecured promissory note issued by creditworthy corporations to meet their short-term financing needs. It is typically issued at a discount to face value and redeemed at par on maturity, with maturities ranging from 7 to 364 days.

110. The correct matching is:

1. **Goals → C:** The ends towards which activity is aimed.
2. **Policies → A:** General statements or understandings that guide decision-making.
3. **Procedures → D:** Plans that establish required methods of handling future activities.
4. **Rules → B:** Specific required actions or non-actions allowing no discretion.

111. In a Matrix Organisational Structure, employees report to both a functional manager and a project manager. This dual authority system combines functional and project-based structures, facilitating better communication, flexibility, and resource sharing across departments, though it can sometimes create role conflicts.

112. Among the given options, Planning is regarded as a managerial function of Human Resource Management (HRM). Managerial functions in HRM include Planning, Organising, Directing, and Controlling, while operative functions include recruitment, compensation, training, and maintaining industrial relations.

113. In the BCG Matrix (Boston Consulting Group Matrix), the four components are Stars, Cash Cows, Question Marks, and Dogs — each representing a business unit's market share and growth potential. The term "Bulls" is not a component of the BCG Matrix.

114. The Reserve Bank of India (RBI) is the regulatory body that oversees the acceptance of public deposits by Non-Banking Financial Companies (NBFCs) in India. The RBI sets norms regarding deposit-taking, liquidity, capital adequacy, and governance to safeguard depositor interests.

115. Clause 49 of the Listing Obligations and Disclosure Requirements (LODR) under the SEBI Act, 1992 deals with the concept of Corporate

Governance. It sets out principles and mandatory requirements related to board composition, audit committees, disclosures, and shareholder rights to ensure transparency and accountability in listed companies.

116. A stable dividend policy where a fixed percentage of net earnings is distributed as dividends is known as a constant pay-out ratio. Under this approach, the dividend amount varies with profit levels, maintaining a consistent relationship between earnings and dividends.

117. The macro environment includes external forces that broadly affect all businesses in an economy. These are the Economic Environment, Political and Legal Environment, Technological Environment, Socio-cultural Environment, and Natural Environment. The Competitive Environment belongs to the micro environment.

118. (*i*) True — Stock exchanges provide liquidity by allowing investors to easily buy and sell securities.

(*ii*) True — Security value fluctuations reflect economic and business conditions.

(*iii*) False — Stock exchanges can sometimes lead to excessive speculation.

Hence, only (*i*) and (*ii*) are correct.

119. Globalisation poses challenges such as navigating cultural differences, understanding foreign legal systems, and complying with complex international regulations. Businesses must adapt to diverse consumer preferences and competitive pressures across countries.

120. Exchange Traded Funds (ETFs) are investment instruments that combine the diversification and low cost benefits of mutual funds with the liquidity of stocks, as they can be freely traded on stock exchanges throughout the day. ETFs track indices, commodities, or sectors.

121. When the consignor incurs expenses on sending goods to the consignee, these are not recorded in the consignee's books, as the consignee does not bear or pay for them. Such expenses are entered only in the consignor's books. Therefore, no entry is passed in the consignee's records.

122. The Going Concern Principle assumes that a business will continue its operations indefinitely and will not be liquidated or significantly reduced in the near future. This principle allows assets to be valued based on their ongoing use rather than liquidation value.

123. The end of the license-permit-quota raj refers to Liberalisation, which began with India's New Industrial Policy of 1991. It removed restrictions on business operations, simplified procedures, and reduced government control, allowing private and foreign investment to flourish.

124. A Vertical Merger occurs when two companies in the same industry but at different stages of production or distribution combine — for example, a manufacturer merging with a supplier or distributor. The aim is to enhance efficiency, reduce costs, and improve supply chain control.

125. A successful Quality Circle leads to improved communication within teams, as employees collaborate to identify, analyse, and solve work-related problems. This fosters teamwork, motivation, and mutual respect, though it does not necessarily reduce workload or eliminate all errors.

126. The Lean System of Production developed by Toyota uses a card-based visual signal system called Kanban. Kanban is used in Total Productive Maintenance (TPM) and Lean Manufacturing to control workflow, manage inventory, and ensure smooth movement of materials through production stages.

127. Development refers to learning opportunities designed to help employees grow in their overall capabilities, not just their current job performance. It focuses on preparing employees for future roles, improving leadership, decision-making, and adaptability.

128. Henri Fayol was a major contributor to the Administrative Management Approach. He developed 14 principles of management and identified five primary functions — planning, organising, commanding, coordinating, and controlling — forming the foundation of modern management theory.

129. In a Transport Management System (TMS):

(*i*) Routing → B: Optimisation of routine, cost analysis, and capacity.

(*ii*) Load Planning → A: Product dimension, damage risk assessment, and capacity.

(*iii*) Load Tendering → D: Selection of carrier in that route, transit capabilities.

(*iv*) Status Tracking → C: In-transit control, GPS monitoring.

130. The Consumer Grievance Redressal Machinery under the Consumer Protection Act includes three tiers:

- District Forum (District Commission),
- State Commission, and
- National Commission.

These bodies handle consumer complaints based on the value of the claim and ensure speedy resolution of disputes.

131. For a new line of fitness trackers, the best approach is intensive distribution, which ensures the product is widely available across multiple retail channels such as electronics stores, supermarkets, and online platforms. This strategy maximizes visibility and accessibility for consumers in a competitive market.

132. Job rotation is intended to broaden the knowledge and skills of managers or potential managers by moving them through different jobs and functions within the organisation. This exposure enhances their understanding of operations and prepares them for higher responsibilities.

133. In the digital age, consumer awareness initiatives can adapt effectively by utilising social media platforms to share educational content, raise awareness about consumer rights, and encourage peer-to-peer information sharing. This ensures a wider, faster, and more engaging reach to diverse audiences.

134. Section 2(1)(r) of the Consumer Protection Act, 1986 defines and deals with 'unfair trade practices', which include misleading advertisements, false representation of products, and deceptive promotions intended to exploit consumers.

135. The correct sequence in the process of Environmental Analysis is:

Scanning → Monitoring → Forecasting → Assessment.

This sequence ensures systematic identification of trends, observation of developments, prediction of their future impact, and evaluation of their relevance to the organisation.

136. In corporate restructuring, a 'poison pill' is a defensive strategy used by a target company to prevent a hostile takeover. It makes the company less attractive to potential acquirers—often by allowing existing shareholders to buy additional shares at a discount, thereby diluting the ownership of the hostile bidder.

137. When forfeited shares are reissued at a price higher than the forfeited amount, the excess amount received is treated as a capital profit and is transferred to the Capital Reserve Account. This reserve cannot be used for distributing dividends but may be used for issuing bonus shares.

138. Under the Consumer Protection Act, 1986, the District Forum had jurisdiction to entertain complaints where the amount involved exceeded ₹ 5 lakhs but did not exceed ₹ 20 lakhs. (Note: This threshold was later revised in the 2019 Act.)

139. Debenture holders do not have ownership rights in the company; they are creditors who earn a fixed rate of interest. Ownership rights, such as voting or profit-sharing, belong only to shareholders.

140. All the statements are correct:

(*i*) ISO 9000 standards were introduced in 1987, marking a global shift toward quality management.

(*ii*) The Confederation of Indian Industry (CII) organised ISO 9000 training in 1989.

(*iii*) From 1991, Indian companies began obtaining ISO 9000 certifications.

141. The Realisation Concept is otherwise known as the Revenue Recognition Concept. It states that revenue should be recognised when it is earned — that is, when goods are delivered or services are rendered — regardless of when cash is received.

142. A Pass Book is a copy of a firm's account with the bank, maintained by the bank and issued to the customer. It records all banking transactions such as deposits, withdrawals, and charges, and serves as a reference for reconciling the firm's Cash Book.

143. Expenditure incurred on a foreign tour to purchase machinery and technical know-how for long-term use is a Capital Expenditure. It provides long-term benefits to the business and is treated as an asset rather than an immediate expense.

144. The techniques used to measure the impact of inflation on financial statements are the Current Purchasing Power Method and the Current Cost Accounting Method. These adjust financial figures to reflect the current value of money and assets under inflationary conditions.

145. The cost price of an asset less its scrap (residual) value is known as the Depreciable Value. It represents the total amount of cost that will be allocated as depreciation over the useful life of the asset.

146. The concept of materiality in accounting means that only significant and relevant information which could influence the decision-making of users of financial statements needs to be disclosed. Trivial details that do not affect understanding or decisions can be omitted.

147. The Periodicity Concept (also known as the Accounting Period Concept) requires that financial statements be prepared at regular intervals, such as quarterly or annually, so that performance and position can be evaluated periodically.

148. The process where the application money for securities is blocked in the applicant's bank account until allotment, and the amount is debited only for the allotted securities, is known as Applications Supported by Blocked Amount (ASBA). It ensures transparency and prevents misuse of investor funds.

149. The usual causes of differences between the Cash Book and Pass Book balances include:

(*i*) Cheques issued but not presented for payment,

(*ii*) Cheques deposited but not yet collected, and

(*iii*) Bank charges not recorded in the Cash Book.

All three lead to temporary timing differences between the two balances.

150. The three main branches of accounting are Financial Accounting, Cost Accounting, and Management Accounting. Human Resource Accounting is an emerging, specialised area and not one of the main traditional branches.

151. According to the Matching Concept of Accounting, expenses should be recognised in the same period in which the related revenues are recognised. This ensures that income and expenses are properly matched to show an accurate profit for the period.

152. The Full Disclosure Principle requires that all information that could influence the decision-making of users (such as investors and creditors) must be disclosed in the financial statements. This enhances transparency and accountability.

153. The statement refers to Accounting Principles, which are the body of doctrines that explain current accounting practices and guide the selection of conventions or methods where alternatives exist.

154. When the owner withdraws goods for personal use, it is treated as drawings, and the cost price (not selling price) is used for recording the transaction.

Journal Entry:

Drawings A/c Dr. ₹ 500

To Purchases A/c ₹ 500

155. Under the Current Purchasing Power (CPP) Approach in inflation accounting, all historical costs are adjusted by applying a general price index to reflect changes in the purchasing power of money over time.

156. The rules of debit and credit are:

- Personal Accounts: Debit the receiver, Credit the giver
- Real Accounts: Debit what comes in, Credit what goes out
- Nominal Accounts: Debit all expenses and losses, Credit all incomes and gains

In the question:

- (*ii*) and (*iii*) are incorrectly matched.

157. Debt capital refers to borrowed funds that a company must repay over time, often with interest. It includes debentures, bonds, and long-term loans.

On the other hand, equity share capital represents ownership — shareholders are owners, not lenders — and hence, it cannot be treated as debt capital.

158. The qualitative characteristics of financial statements, as defined by accounting frameworks, include:

- **Relevance:** Information must influence users' decisions.
- **Understandability:** Should be easily interpretable by users.
- **Comparability:** Enables users to compare performance across periods or entities.

Liquidity, however, is a financial metric, not a qualitative characteristic.

159. The process of recording business transactions in a book of original entry (Journal) in chronological order is called Journalising.

It is the first step in the accounting cycle, where each transaction is analyzed and recorded using debit and credit rules.

160. Indian Accounting Standard (IND AS) 16 relates to Property, Plant, and Equipment (PPE).

It prescribes guidelines for:

- Recognition (when to record assets),
- Measurement (initial and subsequent valuation),
- Depreciation, and
- Derecognition (when assets are disposed or no longer generate benefits).

161. The Current Ratio evaluates a company's ability to meet its short-term obligations using its current assets (like cash, receivables, and inventory).

It is calculated as:

Current Ratio = Current Assets/Current Liabilities

A ratio above 1 indicates sound liquidity.

162. Job costing is used when products are manufactured to specific customer orders or are distinct in nature.

Industries like furniture making, printing presses, and shipbuilding use this system since each job differs in cost and specification.

163. The Indirect Method of preparing a Cash Flow Statement starts with net income and adjusts for non-cash items (like depreciation) and changes in working capital to compute cash flow from operating activities.

164. The formula

(Net Income – Preferred Dividends)/Weighted Average Common Shares Outstanding

represents Earnings per Share (EPS) — a key profitability indicator showing how much profit is attributable to each equity share.

165. A Trial Balance is a statement that lists all ledger accounts with their debit and credit balances at a particular date to ensure total debits equal total credits.

It serves as an accuracy check before preparing financial statements.

166. The Balance Sheet provides a snapshot of the financial position of a firm on a specific date, showing assets, liabilities, and owner's equity.

In contrast, statements like the Profit & Loss Account or Cash Flow Statement reflect performance over a period of time.

167. Sources of cash are activities that bring funds into the business, such as cash from operations, issue of debentures, or sale of assets.

However, purchasing fixed assets results in cash outflow, not inflow — hence it is not a source of cash.

168. All three statements are correct:

(*i*) Trend analysis helps assess whether a firm's financial health is improving or deteriorating.

(*ii*) Ratios highlight problem areas and guide remedial actions.

(*iii*) Profitability ratios measure returns on sales and investments.

Thus, ratio analysis is both diagnostic and evaluative in nature.

169. The Quick Ratio (also known as the Acid-Test Ratio) measures a company's ability to meet short-term obligations using its most liquid assets, excluding inventory and prepaid expenses.

$$\text{Quick Ratio} = \frac{\text{Current Assets} - \text{Inventory}}{\text{Current Liabilities}}$$

170. Donations received for a specific purpose, like a building fund or library fund, are treated as capital receipts since they are non-recurring and used for a designated purpose, not general operations.

171.
$$\text{P/E Ratio} = \frac{\text{Market Price per Share}}{\text{Earnings per Share}}$$
$$= \frac{20}{5} = 4.$$

172. The primary purpose of financial statement analysis is to interpret and evaluate the financial performance and position of a company.

It helps stakeholders such as investors, creditors, and management to understand how efficiently the business is operating, its profitability, solvency, and liquidity position.

This analysis supports better decision-making by highlighting trends and financial strengths or weaknesses.

173. Liquidation refers to the formal process of bringing a business to an end, settling all its liabilities, selling off assets, and distributing the remaining proceeds among creditors and shareholders.

It is usually carried out when a company becomes insolvent or when its owners decide to close it down.

174. Horizontal Analysis (also known as Trend Analysis) involves comparing financial data such as revenue, expenses, or profits across multiple accounting periods.

This helps to identify trends — whether the company's performance is improving, deteriorating, or remaining stable over time.

For example, comparing sales and net income over five years gives a clear view of growth patterns.

175. In a Fund Flow Statement, the term 'funds' does not mean only cash — it refers to working capital, which is the difference between current assets and current liabilities.

The fund flow statement shows how working capital has changed during a given period and helps in understanding the movement of financial resources within the business.

176. Financing activities are those that change the size and composition of the owner's capital and borrowings of a firm.

These include issuing shares or debentures, obtaining loans, repaying borrowings, and paying dividends.

They show how a business finances its operations and growth through debt or equity.

177. The FIFO (First In, First Out) method assumes that materials purchased first are issued first.

It is most suitable during periods of rising prices, as it results in lower cost of goods sold (since older, cheaper stock is issued first) and higher closing stock values.

178. In company liquidation, the order of payment from unpledged assets and contributories' contributions is as follows:

1. Expenses of winding up, including liquidator's remuneration
2. Creditors secured by a floating charge
3. Preferential creditors (like wages, taxes, etc.)
4. Unsecured creditors

Hence, the correct order is (*i*), (*iii*), (*iv*), and (*ii*).

179. Under the Weighted Average Method in process costing, the cost per equivalent unit is calculated by dividing the total costs (opening WIP + current period costs) by the total equivalent units of production (which includes units completed and equivalent units in closing WIP).

180. Common-size analysis expresses each item in financial statements as a percentage of a base item (e.g., sales in income statement or total assets in balance sheet).

It is also called Vertical Analysis, as figures are compared within the same period.

181. The Project Method was developed by William Heard Kilpatrick, an American educator and a follower of John Dewey.

He introduced this method as a student-centered approach where learning happens through purposeful, real-life projects that integrate various subjects and skills.

It encourages creativity, critical thinking, and practical application of knowledge.

182. Direct grading is the process of qualitatively assessing a student's performance and expressing it in the form of letter grades (like A, B, C, etc.) rather than marks.

It is most commonly used to evaluate co-scholastic areas such as behavior, participation, and attitudes where numerical marking isn't suitable.

183. The Rights of Persons with Disabilities (RPWD) Act, 2016 expanded the list of officially recognized disabilities from 7 (under the 1995 Act) to 21.

These include conditions like autism spectrum disorder, muscular dystrophy, acid attack victims, and others, ensuring broader inclusion and legal protection.

184. The Herbartian model of teaching, developed by Johann Friedrich Herbart, focuses on the development of the learner's mental abilities through systematic steps — preparation, presentation, association, generalization, and application.

It emphasizes structured learning and logical thinking.

185. Discriminative listening is when listeners pay attention to differences in sounds, tone, and nonverbal cues to understand emotions and intentions behind speech.

It's the foundation for effective communication and helps interpret meaning beyond words.

186. The United Nations declared 1975 as the International Women's Year to focus global attention on women's rights, equality, and development.

This declaration led to the first World Conference on Women held in Mexico City the same year and initiated the UN Decade for Women (1976–1985).

187. The National Repository of Open Educational Resources (NROER) was launched by the Ministry of Education, Government of India, to make digital learning resources freely available.

It includes e-content such as videos, images, documents, interactive modules, and textbooks to support teachers and students in digital learning.

188. Memory is the fundamental cognitive skill that allows a person to retain, store, and recall information when needed.

It forms the basis for learning, comprehension, and problem-solving, as all higher mental processes depend on effective memory functioning.

189. Measurement refers to the quantitative description of attributes or variables such as knowledge, ability, or attitude.

It involves assigning numbers or scores to represent the extent or degree of a characteristic, forming the basis for evaluation in education and psychology.

190. The Null Curriculum refers to the content that is intentionally omitted or excluded from what is taught in schools.

These are topics educators or policymakers decide not to include, often due to limited time, perceived irrelevance, or cultural sensitivity.

191. The psychomotor domain of learning involves physical movement, coordination, and the use of motor skills.

Performing a lab experiment requires precise hand–eye coordination and the practical application of physical skills — making it the best example of this domain.

192. Role plays are effective classroom techniques that simulate real-life situations to help students develop problem-solving, communication, and interpersonal skills.

They encourage experiential learning and allow students to apply theoretical knowledge in a realistic context.

193. A pupil-centred approach focuses on the learner's needs, interests, and developmental stage, rather than rigidly following the syllabus or teacher's preferences.

It promotes active participation, creativity, independence in learning.

194. In Inquiry-Based Learning, students expl questions, problems, or scenarios to constr knowledge through investigation and reasoni

The teacher acts as a facilitator, guiding inquiry process rather than delivering di answers.

195. Gender socialisation is the process through wh individuals learn societal expectations, roles, a behaviors associated with their gender.

It occurs through family, education, media, ar culture, shaping perceptions of masculinity an femininity.

196. Inclusive environments are those that value diversity and ensure equal participation for everyone, regardless of differences such as gender, ability, or background.

Such environments promote collaboration, creativity, and innovation, ultimately improving workplace performance and morale.

197. Recognising individual differences means understanding that students have varied learning styles, abilities, and interests.

Hence, teaching should be differentiated and tailored to meet the unique needs of every learner, ensuring equitable learning opportunities.

198. In the Herbartian model, the apperceptive mass refers to the learner's existing knowledge and experiences that help in organising and connecting new information.

It plays a key role in meaningful learning by integrating new ideas with prior understanding.

199. The term 'discipline' originates from Latin — discipulus means "pupil" and disciplina means "teaching" or "instruction."

Together, they highlight the concept of learning through guidance and training.

200. Jean Piaget explained cognitive development through four sequential stages—

1. Sensorimotor (0–2 years)
2. Preoperational (2–7 years)
3. Concrete Operational (7–11 years)
4. Formal Operational (12+ years)

Each stage represents a distinct way of thinking and understanding the world.

Previous Paper (Solved)

Delhi Subordinate Services Selection Board

DSSSB–PGT (Commerce) Recruitment Exam, 2021*

1. Which one of the following statements is true?
   A. India's share in world exports of agricultural commodities is very high.
   B. India is the fifth largest producer of fruits and vegetables in the world.
   C. Indian meat is exported only in frozen form.
   D. USA is the leading market for India's agricultural products.

2. Which of the following statements is false about sole proprietorship form of business?
   A. A proprietor's knowledge and skills in various fields like production, finance, marketing, etc. leads to better functioning.
   B. The sole trader is the monarch of business.
   C. The proprietor's personal property can be utilized when the business is in loss.
   D. A proprietor is not bound to publish his accounts to the public.

3. Match the items of List-II with the items of List-I relating to Methods of Raising Finance and select the code of correct matching.

List-I	***List-II***
(*a*) Short-term Capital	(*i*) Issue of equity shares
(*b*) Medium-term Capital	(*ii*) Clean advance from banks
(*c*) Long-term Capital	(*iii*) Public deposits
	(*iv*) Factoring
	(*v*) Discounting of bills
	(*vi*) Issue of preference shares

	(*a*)	(*b*)	(*c*)
A.	(*i*), (*iv*), (*v*)	(*ii*), (*iii*)	(*iv*)
B.	(*iv*), (*v*)	(*ii*), (*iii*)	(*i*), (*iv*)
C.	(*iii*), (*iv*), (*v*)	(*ii*), (*iii*)	(*i*), (*iv*)
D.	(*iii*), (*v*)	(*ii*)	(*i*), (*iv*)

4. What is the unique role of IDBI that is different from other development banks?
   A. It grants loans and advances to companies repayable between 8 to 10 years.
   B. Providing financial assistance directly to industrial units, as well as to refinance loans granted by other financial institutions.
   C. It subscribes directly to the issue of shares and debentures made by industrial concerns.
   D. It undertakes underwriting of the public issue of shares and debentures made by companies.

5. Who stated "business is not mere money chasing but it also should aim at serving the community"?
   A. Henry Ford B. Elton Mayo
   C. Henri Fayol D. Lyndall Urwick

6. Which one of the following is not of a benefit of trade liberalisation?
   A. For producers and suppliers, markets are enlarged and sales opportunities are increased
   B. Consumers enjoy lower prices and greater choice in products
   C. Workers gain new employment opportunities
   D. Income disparity and productivity differences

7. The principle of "Esprit de corps" was listed by:
   A. Frederick Taylor B. Ralph Davis
   C. Lyndall Urwick D. Henry Fayol

* Online exam held on 28/06/2021.

8. The composition of the total capital consisting partly of long-term funds with fixed charge and partly of ownership funds is known as:
A. Working Capital B. Revolving Capital
C. Capital Gearing D. Capital Structure

9. "______ consists of buying and selling commodities, or securities, or other property, in the hope of a profit from anticipated changes of value".
A. Arbitrage B. Speculation
C. Initial Margin D. Margin Trading

10. Which of the following is/are not considered as an economic activity?
(*i*) a doctor working in a government hospital
(*ii*) a teacher working in a school
(*iii*) a farmer working in the field for his own consumption
(*iv*) domestic work by housewife
A. Only (*ii*) B. Only (*i*) and (*iii*)
C. Only (*iv*) D. Only (*iii*)

11. What does the term Underwriting mean?
A. undertaking to subscribe to shares or debentures if public subscription is not adequate.
B. assuring public subscription to the issue of shares.
C. promise to buy debentures.
D. promise to buy shares.

12. The Indian Partnership Act, 1932 defined partnership as:
A. "A partnership is a form of business organization in which two or more persons up to a maximum of twenty join together to undertake some form of business activity".
B. "A partnership is an arrangement where parties, known as business partners, agree to cooperate to advance their mutual interests".
C. "The relation between persons who have agreed to share the profits of business carried on by all or any of them acting for all".
D. "As an association of two or more persons to carry on as co-owners a business for profit".

13. It is the manager's ability to coordinate all organisational activities and varied interests involved in it. It involves viewing the organisation in its totality and understanding the interdependence of its individual parts. Name the managerial skill?
A. Technical skill B. Human skill
C. Functional skill D. Conceptual skill

14. Under which of the following corporations does "The Reserve Bank of India" come?
A. Chartered Company
B. Statutory Company
C. Government Company
D. Registered Company

15. If a particular partner of a firm represents that another person is also a partner of the firm, and if such a person does not disclaim the partnership relationship even after coming to know about it, such person is called:
A. Partners by holding out
B. Dormant partner
C. Partner in profits
D. Partner by estoppels

16. When the goods are imported from one country and the same are exported to another country, such trade is called:
A. External trade B. International trade
C. Export trade D. Entrepot trade

17. This is a document which is issued by the master of the ship or the ship owner or an agent, stating that the goods mentioned in it have been taken on board the ship for transportation as per terms and conditions specified in it. It also serves as a contract of affreightment and as a document of title to the goods. This document is termed as:
A. Mate's Receipt
B. Bill of Lading
C. Dock's Receipt
D. Custom Export Pass

18. Which of the following statements is untrue about World Trade Organization (WTO)?
A. Its headquarters is located in Lusanne, Switzerland.
B. It came into existence in 1995

C. The only international organisation which deals with the global rules of trade between nations.
D. WTO is the successor to the General Agreement on Tariffs and Trade (GATT)

19. Which of the following factors does not influence the choice of organization at the time of starting a business unit?
A. Increase in tax liability
B. Governmental controls and regulations
C. Extent of risk and liability
D. The area of operation of the business

20. Which one of the following statements is true?
A. Long-term finance is associated with long-term return on the investment.
B. Long-term finance is generally required for a period of 20 years or more.
C. Long-term finance can be withdrawn at a short notice.
D. Long-term finance is not required in all types of business activities-manufacturing, trading as well as transport business, etc.

21. The central task of a manager is to get work done with the cooperation of people for the attainment of organisational objectives. Thus it is the duty of every manager to study the behaviour of people working under him and adopt the necessary techniques to inspire people to cooperate and contribute their best efforts towards organisational goals.

This process is known as:
A. Motivation B. Leadership
C. Communication D. Supervision

22. Which of the following Five Year Plan's basis was formed by the strategy popularly known as the 'Nehru-Mahalanobis Strategy'?
A. First plan B. Second plan
C. Third plan D. Fifth plan

23. Choose the false statement.
A. Comparison of two sets of data can only be done by relative measures of dispersion.
B. Variability itself may be some times used in decision-making.
C. The only purpose of measuring dispersion is to assess the reliability of an average.
D. A good measure of dispersion should preferably use all the items of the data.

24. According to the Section 2(1)(d) of the Consumer Protection Act, 1986, the term "consumer" is defined as:
(*a*) A person who buys any goods for a consideration.
(*b*) A person who hires or avails of any services for a consideration.

Choose the correct option.
A. Neither (*a*) nor (*b*)
B. Only (*b*)
C. Only (*a*)
D. Both (*a*) and (*b*)

25. What is a "BANK RATE"?
A. The rate of interest charged by the RBI on loans to Agricultural banks
B. The rate of interest charged by the RBI on loans to Government of India
C. The rate of interest charged by the RBI on loans to Commercial banks
D. The rate of interest charged by the RBI on loans to State banks

26. A document issued by Reserve Bank of India on behalf of the Central Government for meeting its temporary deficits and financing the expenditure, is known as:
A. Commercial bill
B. Short-term liability bill
C. Treasury bill
D. Money bill

27. What is the objective of The MRTP Act, 1969?
(*a*) No monopolies
(*b*) To ensure that the operation of the economic system does not result in the concentration of economic power to the common detriment.
(*c*) To prohibit restrictive and unfair trade practices, which are prejudicial to public interest.
A. Only (*a*) B. All (*a*), (*b*), (*c*)
C. Only (*b*) D. Only (*c*)

28. What is a "POLICY"?

A. General statements or understandings which guide or channel thinking and action in decision-making.

B. A unified and critical plan of action to achieve an objective or set of objectives. It is a plan prepared for meeting the challenge posed by the environmental forces. It addresses the 'how' aspects of achieving an objective.

C. A set of steps determined in advance and standardised for initiating, carrying through and completing a time-bound activity.

D. A planned target of performance or the desired end result of an activity which one attempts to realise.

29. A ______ in relation to any goods means a person who sells or distributes any goods for sale.

A. Seller B. Buyer
C. Manufacturer D. Trader

30. Which of the following terms refers to "the number of individuals a manager can effectively supervise."?

A. Leadership
B. Span of Control
C. Unity of Command
D. Chain of Command

31. According to whom "Statistics are numerical statements of facts in any department of enquiry placed in relation to each other"?

A. Bowley B. Yule and Kendall
C. Thomas Malthus D. Webster

32. Which of these is not a salient feature of the Consumer Protection Act, 1986?

A. It is indeed a very unique and highly progressive piece of social welfare legislation and is acclaimed as the magna carta of Indian consumers.

B. It applies to all goods and services unless otherwise expressly notified by the Central Government.

C. The hallmark of the ACT is that it has not set a time-frame for the disposal of cases.

D. It allows filing of 'class action' complaints on behalf of groups of consumers having common interests.

33. A graph of frequency distribution depicting cumulative frequencies is:

A. Mixed Graph B. Whiskers Graph
C. Historiagram D. Ogive

34. In order to protect consumers from unscrupulous and unethical practices by business people, the Indian Government, from time to time, has enacted different laws. Which one of the following Acts does not come under that list?

A. The Indian Standards Institution Certification Act, 1952
B. The Standards of Purchasing and Measures Act, 1956
C. Sales of Goods Act, 1930
D. The Drugs and Cosmetics Act, 1940

35. ______ which was originally used to measure the distribution of wealth and income; is now also used to study the distribution of profits, wages and turnover, etc. It is a graphic method of studying dispersion. It is a double cumulative percentage graph used in determining the extent of inequalities of items.

A. Bell Curve B. Frequency Curve
C. Lorenz Curve D. Reverse Curve

36. Which of these persons can file a complaint under the Consumer Protection Act, 1986?

(*a*) Any voluntary consumer association, registered under the Companies Act, 1956 or under any other law for the time being in force
(*b*) A consumer
(*c*) The central government
(*d*) One or more consumers, where there are numerous consumers having the same interest.
(*e*) Any state government

A. Only (*a*), (*b*), (*c*)
B. (*a*), (*b*), (*c*), (*d*), (*e*)
C. Only (*a*)
D. Only (*a*), (*b*), (*d*)

37. Which of the following is not a principal goal of planning laid down by Planning Commission of India in 1950?

A. To establish a socialist pattern of society based on equality and social justice and absence of exploitation.

B. To increase production to the maximum possible extent so as to achieve higher levels of national and per capita income.

C. To achieve full employment.

D. To nationalise banking and insurance.

38. Which of these is a method of collecting primary data?

1. Personal Interviewing
2. Schedule
3. Through Local Reports and Correspondents

A. Only 2 B. Only 1
C. All 1, 2, 3 D. Only 3

39. Choose the correct statement.

A. Foreign direct investment is an investment where the foreign party retains control over the investment.

B. GDRs is a convertible bond.

C. FCCBs cannot be converted into GDRs.

D. Portfolio investment is an investment where the foreign party does not seek control over the investment.

40. Choose the false statement about coordination.

A. Coordination provides unity of action in the organisation.

B. The need for coordination increases with an increase in the interdependence between organisational units.

C. Coordination between various positions at the same level in the organization is called vertical coordination.

D. Coordination helps in resolving the conflict of personal goals and organisational goals.

41. A person who reports unethical practices by their employer to outsiders is known as:

A. perceiver

B. reporter

C. whistle blower

D. informer

42. ______ is defined as the change in total cost as a result of change in the level of output, investment etc.

A. Marginal opportunity cost

B. Marginal cost

C. Incremental cost

D. Opportunity cost

43. Match the organisational objective with the marketing concepts given below; and choose the correct code:

Organisational Objectives	***Marketing Concepts***
(*a*) Effective distribution	(*i*) Product concept
(*b*) Large scale selling and Promotional effort	(*ii*) Societal concept
(*c*) Produce what consumer need	(*iii*) Selling concept
(*d*) Product improvement	(*iv*) Production concept
(*e*) Improve society's well being	(*v*) Marketing concept

	(*a*)	(*b*)	(*c*)	(*d*)	(*e*)
A.	(*iv*)	(*i*)	(*v*)	(*iii*)	(*ii*)
B.	(*iv*)	(*iii*)	(*v*)	(*ii*)	(*i*)
C.	(*v*)	(*iii*)	(*iv*)	(*i*)	(*ii*)
D.	(*iv*)	(*iii*)	(*v*)	(*i*)	(*ii*)

44. Define "Strategy".

A. A series of functions or steps performed to accomplish a specific task or undertaking.

B. It is a comprehensive plan laying down the principle steps for accomplishing a specific objective and sets an approximate time limit for each stage.

C. It is hierarchy of intentions ranging from a board vision through mission and purpose down to specific objectives.

D. A unified, comprehensive and integrated plan that relates the calculated advantage of the firm to the challenges of the environment.

45. Read the Assertion and Reasoning and select the correct option.

Assertion (A) : The Reserve Bank of India is the apex organisation in the Indian money market.

Reasoning (R) : In April, 1988, it set up the Discount and Finance House of India (DFHI) to perform the function of stablising the money market in India.

A. (A) is correct, but (R) is incorrect.
B. Both (A) and (R) are incorrect.
C. (A) and (R) both are correct, but (R) is not the right explanation of (A).
D. (A) and (R) both are correct and (R) is the right explanation of (A).

46. "Organisational Behaviour is a field of study that investigates the impact that individuals, groups and structures have on behaviour within organisations for the purpose of applying such knowledge towards improving an organisation's effectiveness."

Who has said this?
A. Fred Luthans
B. Keith Davis
C. Joe Kelly
D. Stephen P. Robbins

47. What is known as the process of dividing the total market for a product or service into several smaller groups, such that the members of each group are similar with respect to the factors that influence demand?
A. Market segmentation
B. Market break down
C. Market separation
D. Market partition

48. A strategy, which is directed at producing goods and services considered unique in its industry and directed at consumers who are relatively price-insensitive, is known as:
A. Differentiation B. Focus
C. Cost Leadership D. Low-cost strategy

49. Read the situation given below and classify it.

A customer walks into a general merchant's shop and while buying 'Dove' soap discovers that he can get a stainless steel spoon free if she buys 'santoor' soap. Therefore, she bought 'santoor' soap.

A. It is neither advertisement nor publicity.
B. It is a Publicity.
C. It is both, advertisement as well as publicity.
D. It is an Advertisement

50. In which of the following streams was Classical theory of organisation developed?
1. Bureaucracy
2. Administrative Theory
3. Scientific Management

A. Only 1 B. Only 2
C. Only 3 D. All 1, 2, 3

51. In PESTEL framework, what does 'L' stand for?
A. Liberalisation B. Logistics
C. Legal D. Linguistic

52. Which of these is/are the method of making Capital Issue:
(*a*) Offer for sale (*b*) Private placement
(*c*) Rights issue (*d*) Bid and Offer
A. Only (*a*), (*c*), (*d*) B. Only (*a*), (*b*), (*d*)
C. Only (*a*), (*b*), (*c*) D. Only (*a*), (*d*)

53. Read the Assertion and Reason and select the correct option.

Assertion (A) : The channel of distribution is a network of institutions that perform a variety of interrelated and coordinated functions in the movement of goods from producers to consumers.

Reason (R) : Most producers do not sell goods directly to the consumers. They make use of a variety of intermediaries known as middlemen. These middlemen who take title to goods or assist in transferring the title to goods as they move from the producer to the consumer.

A. (A) and (R) both are correct; and (R) is the right explanation of (A).
B. (A) is correct; but (R) is incorrect.

C. Both (A) and (R) are incorrect.
D. (A) and (R) both are correct; but (R) is not the right explanation of (A).

54. Inside trading refers to trading in the scripts of a company by persons having access to ______ price sensitive information to make private gains or reduce losses.
A. published B. unpublished
C. analysed D. synthesized

55. Which of the following is not one of the four central questions that the study of economics is supposed to answer?
A. Who produces what?
B. When are goods produced?
C. How are goods produced?
D. Who consumes what?

56. What are Speciality Goods?
A. Products bought by individuals or households for their personal non business use.
B. A class of consumer goods that people buy frequently with the least possible time and effort.
C. A class of consumer goods with perceived unique characteristics such that consumers are willing to spend special effort to buy them.
D. A class of consumer goods that are purchased only after the buyer has spent some time and effort comparing price, quality, style, colour, etc. of alternative products in competing stores.

57. Choose the statement which is incorrect.
A. Companies which want to create a "prestige image" for their products normally price them high.
B. Price stabilization policy seeks to prevent price wars.
C. Sales maximisation will automatically lead to profit maximisation.
D. Pricing is governed by not only the internal factors of a company but also external environmental factors.

58. If good growing conditions increase the supply of coconut and hot weather increases the demand for coconut water, the quantity of coconuts bought:
A. does not change but the price rises
B. increases and the price might rise, fall or not change
C. increases and the price rises
D. does not change but the price falls

59. What is the source of formation of attitude?
1. Social Learning
2. Instrumental Conditioning
3. Direct Experience
A. Only 2 and 3 B. Only 1 and 2
C. Only 1 and 3 D. Only 1

60. Which of the following statements about price elasticity of demand is correct?
(*a*) Price elasticity of demand is a measure of how much the quantity demanded of a good responds to a change in the price of that good.
(*b*) Price elasticity of demand is computed as the percentage change in quantity demanded divided by the percentage change in price.
(*c*) Price elasticity of demand in the long run would be different from that of the short run.
A. All (*a*), (*b*), (*c*) B. Only (*b*)
C. Only (*a*) D. Only (*c*)

61. Which of these is an example of models of e-commerce?
A. A watermelon farmer opens a farm stand
B. Watermelons bought by a restaurant owner from a farmer
C. A watermelon farmer advertises his watermelon online
D. A watermelon farmer sells his watermelon to another farmer

62. Loading is usually involved in all such items which are recorded at the invoice price in the Consignment Account. Which of these is not one of those items?
A. Opening Stock
B. Goods Sent on Consignment
C. Goods Returned by the Consignee
D. Expenses incurred by the consignor

63. What are benefits of e-commerce to society at large?

(*i*) E-Commerce enables more individuals to work at home and to do less travelling for shopping resulting in less traffic on the roads and lower air pollution.

(*ii*) E-commerce enables public to shop or do other transactions 24 hrs a day, all year round from almost any location.

(*iii*) Ability for creation of highly specialized business.

(*iv*) E-Commerce enables people in rural areas to enjoy products and services that are not available to them.

(*v*) E-commerce provides people with more choices they can select from many vendors and from many products.

Choose the correct option.

A. Only (*i*) and (*ii*)
B. All (*i*), (*ii*), (*iii*), (*iv*), (*v*)
C. Only (*i*) and (*iv*)
D. Only (*ii*) and (*iii*)

64. In practice, a compound journal entry is not recorded when:

(*a*) one account is to be debited and two or more accounts are to be credited

(*b*) two or more accounts are to be debited and one account is to be credited

(*c*) two or more accounts are to be debited and two or more accounts are to be credited

(*d*) only one account is debited and another account is credited.

Choose the correct option.

A. Only (*a*) B. Only (*d*)
C. Only (*b*) D. Only (*a*) and (*b*)

65. Which of the following ratios does come under Activity/Operating ratios?

A. Quick ratio
B. Current ratio
C. Inventory turnover ratio
D. Proprietary ratio

66. Which of the following statements is false in relation to consignment?

A. The consignee does not become the debtor of the consignor on receipt of goods.
B. Despatch of goods on consignment amounts to sale of goods by the consignor.
C. The legal ownership and title of goods is not transferred to the consignee.
D. The relationship between the consignor and the consignee is that of a principal and an agent.

67. Which of the following is not a method of costing?

A. Job Costing B. Operating Costing
C. Contract Costing D. Standard Costing

68. It is a popular technique for generating new ideas. A group of persons sit together and generate as many business ideas as possible. One idea leads to another.

What is this technique/process called as?

A. Brain Writing B. Starbursting
C. Brain storming D. Stepladder

69. This is a basic concept of accounting. According to this concept every business transaction has a two-fold effect. In commercial context it is a famous dictum that "every receiver is also a giver and every giver is also a receiver".

Name the concept.

A. Business Entity Concept
B. Money Measurement Concept
C. Dual Aspect Concept
D. Objective Evidence Concept

70. A bill drawn on June 16 for a period of 30 days and unfortunately July 19 is a public holiday. Then what will be the maturity date of the bill?

A. 20th July B. 19th July
C. 17th July D. 18th July

71. Which of these is a kind of company categorised on the basis of liability of shareholders or members?

A. Government Company
B. Public Company
C. Unlimited Company
D. Private Company

72. Which of the following expenditures is considered as deferred revenue expenditure?
A. ₹ 4,000 spent on dismantling, transportation and reinstalling plant and machinery to a new site
B. ₹ 60,000 spent on construction of railway siding
C. ₹ 2,000 spent on repairs of machinery
D. ₹ 20,000 spent on some major alterations to a theatre which made it more comfortable and attractive

73. Which of these books is not related to 'Non Trading concerns'?
A. Minutes Books B. Stock Register
C. Members Register D. Donation Books

74. E-cash is not based on which of the following systems?
A. Electronic Data Exchange
B. Digital Name
C. Cryptocurrency
D. Digital Signatures

75. Memorandum Joint Venture Account is prepared to find out:
(*a*) Amount due from the co-venturers
(*b*) Profit or loss on the joint venture
A. Only (*a*)
B. Only (*b*)
C. Neither (*a*) nor (*b*)
D. Both (*a*) and (*b*)

76. Which of the following is not an individual component of systematic risk?
A. Interest rate risk
B. Inflation risk
C. Purchasing power risk
D. Market risk

77. ______ is also referred to as e-website. It allows the customers to purchase goods from various sellers using Internet. Its aim is to provide a global, reliable, 24 × 7 web based effective sales management system.
A. e-store B. e-mall
C. e-visibility D. e-shop

78. Noida Toll Bridge is an example of ______ type of project financing.
A. Build, own & operate type (BOO)
B. Build, own, operate & transfer type (BOOT)
C. Build, operate & Transfer type (BOT)
D. Bridge financing

79. A company forfeited 400 equity shares of ₹ 10 each issued at a discount of 10 per cent for non-payment of two calls of ₹ 2 each. What will be the amount forfeited by the company?
A. ₹ 1,600 B. ₹ 2,400
C. ₹ 2,000 D. ₹ 4,800

80. Which is not a direct or indirect cost?
A. Overhead cost
B. Oncosts
C. Down cost
D. Supplementary costs

81. Which media is very effective for advertisement, but is the most expensive medium?
A. television B. hoarding
C. radio D. exhibition

82. Match the items of List-II with the items of List-I and indicate the code of correct matching. The items relate to the Balance Sheet of a Company.

List-I	*List-II*
(*a*) Miscellaneous Expenditure	(*i*) Unclaimed Dividend
(*b*) Current Liabilities	(*ii*) Forfeited Shares Account
(*c*) Subscribed Capital	(*iii*) Work-in-Progress
(*d*) Current Assets	(*iv*) Discount on Issue of Shares

	(*a*)	(*b*)	(*c*)	(*d*)
A.	(*iv*)	(*i*)	(*ii*)	(*iii*)
B.	(*ii*)	(*i*)	(*iii*)	(*iv*)
C.	(*iii*)	(*iv*)	(*i*)	(*ii*)
D.	(*i*)	(*ii*)	(*iii*)	(*iv*)

83. The Foreign Exchange Management Act (FEMA) was passed by Lok Sabha on?
A. 11th December, 1973
B. 9th December, 1973
C. 2nd December, 1999
D. 9th December, 1999

84. Which of the following is prepared for distribution of profits among the partners?
A. Profit and Loss Appropriation account
B. Profit and Loss account
C. Partner's Current account
D. Profit and Loss Adjustment account

85. The State Bank of India Act was passed in 1959 and in course of time, 8 major State associated banks were amalgamated with the main bank as its subsidiaries. Which one of the following is not one of those banks?
A. The Hyderabad State Bank
B. Bank of Punjab
C. Bank of Saurashtra
D. Bank of Rajasthan

86. What is the chief characteristic of foreign aid?
A. Countries would need foreign exchange which they can acquire only by having surpluses in their balance of payments.
B. It is made accessible on concessional terms inferring that the pace of interest is lower and the development time frame is longer.
C. Loans and grants are provided for development purposes.
D. Rarely involves any foreign exchange problems when it is provided.

87. X sets up a new business on October 1, 1987 and does not close his books on March 31, 1988. What will be the period of previous year for the assessment year 1989-90?
A. 24 months B. 12 months
C. 18 months D. 9 months

88. Read the following statements and select the correct option.
(*a*) A company's financial performance is dependant on the shares issued by the company.
(*b*) A company's financial performance is dependant on the investment in assets.
(*c*) A company's financial performance is dependant on the liquidity or cash flow statement.
(*d*) A company's financial performance is based on the profits earned during the period.
A. Only (*c*) is correct
B. (*a*), (*b*) and (*c*) are correct
C. (*c*) and (*d*) are correct
D. (*a*) and (*b*) are correct

89. Which of the following statements is true?
A. Market gridding is a method of survey of expert's opinion.
B. Market gridding means establishing and running a web marketing facility
C. Market gridding means managing brands and developing brand equity
D. Market gridding is an analytical technique which facilitates dividing a market into segments.

90. Which one of the following is a disadvantage of a tailor made software?
A. It can be developed according to the customer's requirement
B. The high cost of installation and maintenance
C. Can link with another information system
D. It is difficult to learn and require high tech training

91. When marketing practices are condemned for lessening rivalry, the analysis falls under which general space of social marketing issues?
A. Marketing's impact on other businesses.
B. Marketing's impact on society as a whole.
C. Marketing's impact on the individual.
D. Marketing's impact on the company.

92. Who appoints NABARD chairman?
A. Appointment Committee of NABARD
B. President of India
C. Reserve Bank of India
D. Appointments Committee of the Union Cabinet

93. Which income from the following is partially exempted?
A. Interest on certain government securities
B. Shares from unregistered firm
C. Payment of lease rent
D. Agricultural income

94. The gold standard was briefly reinstated from which to which year as the Gold Exchange Standard?

A. 1914-39 B. 1925-31
C. 1927-32 D. 1920-30

95. Who said "Recruitment is a business, and it is a big business"?

A. Dales S. Beach B. Edwin B. Flippo
C. Dale Yoder D. Lord

96. Which of the following statements is true?

A. Agricultural income is totally exempted from tax
B. Tax incidence is the lowest in the case of non-resident
C. Gratuity or Pension is partially exempted income
D. Incidence of tax is relatively highe of resident when compared with 'non-resident'.

97. For calculating pre-incorporation profits in the case of a public limited company the relevant date is:

A. The date of Certificate to Commence Business
B. The date of Certificate of Incorporation
C. The date of take over
D. The date of issuing shares

98. Which of the following is not an objective of IMF today?

A. Discouraging adoption of exchange controls
B. Developing a multilateral system of payments.
C. Maintaining Exchange rate stability
D. Assisting member countries to restore equilibrium in balance of payments

99. Which of the following proformas of Balance Sheet of a company does require that figures of the previous year should be shown in separate column along with the figures of the current year with respect to each of the items of liabilities and assets?

(*a*) Horizontal form
(*b*) Vertical form

A. Neither (*a*) nor (*b*)
B. Only (*a*)
C. Both (*a*) and (*b*)
D. Only (*b*)

100. What is on the X and Y axis of the graph of a product life cycle?

A. X-sale, Y-Time
B. X-Growth, Y-Time
C. X-time, Y-demand
D. X-demand, Y-sales

101. Where is the headquarters of Bank of International Settlement situated?

A. France B. Switzerland
C. Germany D. Belgium

102. Which of the following statement(s) is/are true about monetary policy of RBI?

(*a*) Monetary policy is one of RBI's controlled expansion.
(*b*) RBI possesses extensive powers of credit control, only quantitative in nature.
(*c*) The monetary policy of the RBI has been rather weak.
(*d*) The monetary policy of RBI has been very effective.

A. (*a*) and (*d*) are correct
B. Only (*b*) is true
C. (*a*) and (*c*) are true
D. Only (*a*) is True

103. In which year did the income tax act come into force?

A. 1922 B. 1962
C. 1958 D. 1961

104. A method used in a comparative analysis of financial statement is:

A. Comparative Analysis
B. Graphical Analysis
C. Returning Analysis
D. Common Size Analysis

105. What is the slope of the positive supply curve like?

A. It slopes up and to the left
B. It slopes up and to the right
C. It slopes down and to the right
D. It slopes down and to the left

106. Which of the following is an example of cash flows from investing activities?
A. Issue of shares
B. Purchase of raw material in cash
C. Repayment of long term loan
D. Sale of investment by non financial enterprise

107. While recruiting, a test is conducted to find out whether a candidate is interested in the job for which he is a candidate and to find out which area of the job range the candidate is interested in. Which test is being talked about?
A. Cognitive ability test
B. Personality test
C. Situational test
D. Aptitude test

108. The word 'downsizing' was coined by:
A. Morgan Roach
B. Stephen Stanley
C. Morgan Roach and Stephen Stanley
D. Stefan Roach and Morgan Stanley

109. Which of the following statements is false?
A. Efficient customer service is an objective of physical distribution system.
B. Physical distribution system creates time and place utilities in products.
C. In total cost approach of physical distribution system, the cost of each element is considered in isolation.
D. Total cost approach envisages the use of total cost while choosing the alternative courses of action in respect of physical distribution.

110. Bank of Venice was established in:
A. 1154 B. 1157
C. 1517 D. 1514

111. Which of the following does not hold short-term claims as working balance against the major reserve centres?
A. RBI B. Central Bank
C. Commercial Banks D. Business Firms

112. Annual report is given by an organization to its:
A. shareholders B. directors
C. auditors D. management

113. The intrinsic value of a bond or any fixed income security is equal to:
A. The economic value of a bond
B. The realisable value of a bond
C. The previous year's value of cash flows
D. The present value of expected cash flows

114. What is an index of operational efficiency?
A. Financial Leverage
B. Operating Leverage
C. Return on Investment Leverage
D. Combined Leverage

115. Which of the following is not an advantage of departmental stores?
A. These stores can afford to have effective advertising through press, radio and television
B. These stores are able to offer various products at more reasonable prices than most other retailers.
C. Their central location attracts a large number of customers leading to a large turnover.
D. Bulk-buying from these stores enables them to obtain heavy discounts from manufacturers

116. Which market becomes necessary at the saturation stage?
A. Concentrated
B. Undifferentiated
C. Product differentiation
D. Differentiated

117. This type of interview helps the interviewer in appraising certain skills of the candidates like initiative and inter-personal skills. Which interview is being talked about?
A. Group discussion interview
B. Phone interview
C. Panel interview
D. Depth interview

118. alt + F3 is the shortcut key for:
A. changing period in tally
B. calculator

C. payment voucher
D. company creation

119. Goods sent on consignment is debited to:
A. Consignee's account
B. Goods sent on Consignment account
C. Profit and Loss account
D. Consigment account

120. Payroll software is an example of which software?
A. Application software
B. System software
C. Programming software
D. Utility software

121. Equal remuneration act was enacted which prohibits discrimination in matters relating to remuneration on the basis of religion, region or gender. In which year was this act enacted?
A. 1948 B. 1981
C. 1976 D. 1965

122. Insurance works on the Principle of:
A. Sharing of losses
B. Law of contract
C. Large numbers
D. Probabilities

123. Which of the following statements is/are true?
(*a*) When the required rate of return is equal to nominal rate, the value of bond is equal to its par value.
(*b*) If the required rate of return is greater than the nominal rate, the value of a bond is more than its par value.
(*c*) When the required rate of return is less than nominal rate, the value of bond is less than its par value.
A. Only (*b*) is correct
B. Only (*a*) is correct
C. (*a*) and (*c*) are correct
D. Only (*a*) and (*b*) are correct

124. Read the Assertion and Reason given and select the correct option.
Assertion (A) : Capital is treated as liability
Reason (R) : Capital is treated as a liability due to money measurement concept.
A. Both Assertion (A) and Reason (R) are true and Reason (R) is the correct explanation of Assertion (A)
B. Assertion (A) is true, but Reason (R) is false.
C. Assertion (A) is false, but Reason (R) is true.
D. Both Assertion (A) and Reason (R) are true and Reason (R) is not the correct explanation of Assertion (A).

125. The banker takes care of funds of the customer as a:
A. security guard B. attorney
C. executor D. correspondent

126. This type of contract involves a mutual agreement that comes into being after an unexpected occurrence, accident, or a natural calamity. In this type of contract both the parties have an element of risk. Identify the type of contract.
A. Aleatory contract
B. Bilateral contract
C. Express contract
D. Adhesion contract

127. Rekha and Arjun entered into a contract whereby Rekha agreed to sell Arjun ₹ 1,000 worth of heroin, an illegal substance.

Which type of a contract is this?
A. Unlawful contract
B. Void contract
C. Unconstitutional contract
D. Voidable contract

128. In India, the first step towards building up a structure of development finance institutions was taken up with which establishment?
A. Industrial Credit and Investment Corporation of India
B. Industrial Finance Corporation of India
C. State Financial Corporations
D. State Industrial Development Corporations

129. What is the the first factor influencing a buyer's decision?
A. Occupation B. Age
C. Family D. Education

130. Which of the following statements is/are false?

(*a*) The cash reserve ratio affects the credit creation.

(*b*) Business conditions of the banks like inflation, depression, etc. affect the credit creation process.

(*c*) Credit Policy of the Central Bank affects the cash reserve ratio.

(*d*) All the banks have the same nature and extent of programmes of credit sanction and disbursement.

A. (*a*) and (*b*) are false
B. Only (*c*) is false
C. Only (*d*) is false
D. Only (*a*) is false

131. A, B and C share profit and loss in the ratio 3 : 2 : 1, what will be the new profit sharing ratio of A and C, if B retiers from the business?

A. 3 : 1 B. 2 : 1
C. 1 : 3 D. 3 : 2

132. What is a program or policy of a company that aims to eliminate discrimination by providing equal opportunities and thereby improving his/her profession?

A. Performance appraisal
B. Affirmative action
C. Decentralisation
D. Inclusive growth

133. This technique of performance appraisal was first developed in USA and UK in 1943 and is focused on observation of behaviours across a series of select exercises or work samples. Which technique is being referred to?

A. Assessment Centers
B. Psychological Appraisals
C. Paired comparison method
D. Ranking Methods

134. Fictitious assets are included in:

A. Fixed liabilities
B. Current liabilities
C. Capital
D. Long term liabilities

135. Which of the following terms is dissimilar to the other four in the context of insurable interest in life insurance?

A. Debtor B. Employer
C. Employee D. Creditor

136. On which of the deposits, interest is not paid?

A. Recurring deposit
B. Current account deposit
C. Fixed deposit
D. Saving bank deposit

137. Read the given Assertion and Reason and select the correct option.

Assertion (A) : Central tendency is the tendency of most raters to give average ratings to all or the center of the scale.

Reason (R) : A very high rating or a very low rating could invite questions, criticisms or explanations.

A. Both Assertion (A) and Reason (R) are true and Reason (R) is not the correct explanation of Assertion (A).
B. Assertion (A) is true, but Reason (R) is false.
C. Both Assertion (A) and Reason (R) are true and Reason (R) is the correct explanation of Assertion (A)
D. Assertion (A) is false, but Reason (R) is true.

138. What is the maturity term for most of the treasury bills when issued?

A. 91 days B. 90 days
C. 81 days D. 60 days

139. Which is the most ancient bank in the world?

A. Bank of ancient France
B. Bank of ancient Rome
C. Bank of Greece
D. Bank of Venice

140. Which statement from the following is false?

A. A private company doesn't issue the prospectus
B. The rate of dividend is fixed on equity shares
C. The lump sum amount can received on shares
D. During the calls in advance the bank account is debited and calls in advance account is credited

141. What percentage of tax is taxable on long-term capital gain arising from transfer of securities, bonds, units, debenture?

A. 12 per cent B. 20 per cent
C. 5 per cent D. 10 per cent

142. The Hawthorne studies were aimed at finding out the factors that really influenced the productivity and work performance of labourers. Under which of the following management approaches this study was conducted by Elton Mayo and his associates?

A. Human Relations Approach
B. Contingency Approach
C. Modern Systems Approach
D. Behavioural Approach

143. Which of the following is Adam Smith's definition of the concept of price?

A. Pricing is a very important aspect in the marketing as it directly affect the sales and profits of the company.
B. Price is the exchange value of a product expressed in terms of rupees or any other monetary unit.
C. The price of everything, what everything really costs, is the toil and trouble of acquiring it.
D. Price is an important element of marketing. After developing a product, the next thing a company has to decide is the price.

144. What is mentioned under Sec-44AE of the Income Tax Act, 1961?

A. Special Provisions for Computing Profits and Gains of business of plying, hiring or leasing goods carriages
B. Expenses deductible from commission earned by insurance agents etc.
C. Meaning of capital gains
D. Special Provisions for Computing Profits and Gains of small business of civil construction, etc

145. Identify which of the following statements is/are true?

(*a*) There can be a stranger to a contract and consideration.
(*b*) There can be a stranger to a contract.
(*c*) There can be a stranger to consideration.
(*d*) There cannot be a stranger to any contract.

A. (*a*) is true B. (*d*) is true
C. (*c*) is true D. (*b*) is true

146. Who first gave the concept of MBO to the world in 1954?

A. Dale Yoder B. Dales S beech
C. Edwin B. Flippo D. Peter F. Drucker

147. Reconstituion of partnership is:

A. Change in profit sharing ratio of partners
B. To raise goodwill account by its value
C. Additional capital introduced by partner
D. Allowing interest on capital

148. Read the Assertion and Reaso and select the correct option.

Assertion (A) : Bank rate is also called as credit rate.

Reason (R) : Banks need funds to expand credit facilities to their clients, specially during busy season.

A. Both Assertion (A) and Reason (R) are true and Reason (R) is the correct explanation of Assertion (A)
B. Both Assertion (A) and Reason (R) are true and Reason (R) is not the correct explanation of Assertion (A).
C. Assertion (A) is false, but Reason (R) is true.
D. Assertion (A) is true, but Reason (R) is false.

149. Which of the following is not a benefit of Human Source Information System (HRIS)?

A. Higher accuracy of information
B. Reduction in duplication
C. Quality of response depending on the accuracy of the input
D. Higher speed of retrieval of information

150. Industrial Finance Corporation of India (lFCl) is managed by a Board of Directors, which consists of partly elected and partly nominated directors. The Central Government appoints the whole-time Chairman of the Board in

consultation with the Industrial Development Bank of India (IDBI). How many directors are appointed by the Reserve Bank of India?
A. Two directors
B. Three directors
C. One director
D. Reserve Bank of India does not appoint directors

151. Which bank first evolved the function of clearance, settlements and transfer of mutual claims?
A. World Bank
B. Bank of Venice
C. Bank of England
D. Bank of Ancient Rome

152. Which of the following statements is false?
A. The needs of borrowers differ in terms of amounts, the length or period for which borrowings are needed, and the currency in which borrowings are raised.
B. International finance focuses on areas such as foreign direct investment and currency exchange rates.
C. Borrowers are the issuers of debt instruments in the form of Promissory Notes, Bonds and Commercial Paper.
D. When the dollar rises in value relative to a foreign currency, the current assets and current liabilities of a U.S. foreign subsidiary increase in dollar value

153. Reader's Digest magazine offers diaries to its regular subscribers for introducing new subscribers. Which method of conditional premium of consumer promotion is this an example of?
A. Refill Packs
B. Coupon Premium Plan
C. Consumer Contests
D. User to User scheme

154. Which of the following is a significant justification for insurers to sell life insurance strategies through agents?
A. Many people require personalised guidance for selecting the right policy
B. Agents have to meet their marketing targets
C. Individuals can choose which strategy is best for them
D. The advantages of life insurance policy are basic and clear to all

155. The intrinsic value of a bond or any fixed income security is ______ the present value of the expected cash flows.
A. less than B. equal to
C. more than D. not related to

156. The premium on issue of debentures is showed in Balance Sheet under:
A. secured loan
B. current liabilities
C. share capital
D. reserve and surplus

157. Which trade promotion leads to quick profits for wholesalers and retailers?
A. Cooperative advertising
B. Gift to dealers
C. Merchandise deals
D. Price deals

158. Preeti is a person who is usually of unsound mind, but occasionally of sound mind. Can she make a contract?
A. No, she cannot make a contract
B. Cannot be determined
C. She can make a contract when she is sound mind
D. She can always make a contract

159. Exemptions for newly established industrial undertaking in free trade zones is mentioned in which section?
A. Section 10 (B) B. Section 10 (AA)
C. Section 10 (BA) D. Section 10 (A)

160. Which of the following does not fall under the accepted classification of Standard Industrial Classification (SIC) Code?
A. Transportation
B. Agriculture
C. Mining
D. Communication

161. Which statement from the following is false?
A. Company can issue debentures for consideration other than cash
B. Coupon rate debenture has fixed rate of interest
C. Mortgaged debentures are called secured debentures
D. Bearer debentures can be transferred to any person

162. Securities and Exchange Board of India has laid down which of the following?
A. Minimum subscription of a company must be 60 per cent of shares issued for subscription before it allots the shares.
B. Maximum subscription of a company must be 90 per cent of shares issued for subscription before it allots the shares.
C. Minimum subscription of a company must be 90 per cent of shares issued for subscription before it allots the shares.
D. Maximum subscription of a company must be 60 per cent of shares issued for subscription before it allots the shares.

163. Which of the following statements is false?
A. Working capital is an excess of current asset over current liabilities
B. Debt equity ratio measures the short term financial position
C. The activity issue and turn over ratio are same
D. The ideal ratio between current assets and current liabilities is 2 : 1

164. Who announces the foreign trade policy in india?
A. Reserve Bank of India
B. Ministry of Finance
C. Ministry of Commerce
D. FEDAI

165. Under which section of the contract act is 'Agent' defined?
A. Section 152 B. Section 192
C. Section 182 D. Section 172

166. In India currency notes are issued by
A. RBI
B. Axis Bank
C. Central Bank of India
D. Government of India

167. Who stipulates the rate of interest in Savings Bank Account?
A. Government of India
B. Indian Bank Association
C. Concerned Bank
D. RBI

168. The person who conceives the business idea, brings the organisation into existence and carry on the business activity and top of it bears risk is called.
A. Professional B. Entrepreneur
C. Manager D. Employer

169. Which of the following is not the feature of sole tradership?
A. No personal property can be claimed to pay out the debts of the firm.
B. One man ownership.
C. All profit of the business are enjoyed by the owner.
D. No separate entity of business with its owner.

170. Which one of the following activities does not come under auxiliaries to trade?
A. Preservation of goods to make them available as and when needed by consumers.
B. Movement of those goods that are not consumed at the same place where they are produced to the place where they are demanded.
C. Conversion and transformation of raw-materials and semi-finished goods into finished goods.
D. Banks providing a variety of credit to the public.

171. The voluntary association of persons who are not financially stable come together to overcome the disability arising due to inadequate financial resources are called.
A. Corporate
B. Joint hindu family
C. Partnership
D. Co-operative societies

172. The importance of Central Bank's function as the lender of the last resort was stressed by Walter Bagehot in which year?
A. 1872 B. 1873
C. 1871 D. 1870

173. As per companies act 2013 to form a partnership firm, there should be atleast two persons and maximum ______.
A. 100 B. 50
C. 40 D. unlimited

174. An individual who acquires required qualification or skill or training for the particular employment is called
A. Employee B. Professional
C. Entrepreneur D. Employer

175. Which statement is correct?
A. Business includes the exchange of goods and services carried with the intention of domestic fulfillment.
B. Business includes the exchange of goods and services carried with the intention of return in term of money as well as goods.
C. Business includes the exchange of goods and services carried with the intention of charity.
D. Business includes the exchange of goods and services carried with the intention of return in term of money.

176. The errors on one side of the ledger account are compensated by errors of the same amounts on the other side or on the same side. Which error is being talked about?
A. Compensating errors
B. Error of principle
C. Compensatory errors
D. Errors of commission

177. What are the web sites that aggregate information across the entire organization or for groups within the organization such as project teams called?
A. Content/Document Management systems
B. Groupware
C. Workflow systems
D. Enterprise Portals

178. Select the following activities as economic activities by choosing the correct alternatives.
1. Selling groceries.
2. Teaching in an institution.
3. Gift a house of the family.
4. Donation of goods in an old age home.
A. 1 and 2 only B. 1 and 4 only
C. 2 and 4 only D. 1 and 3 only

179. The following are the examples of which type of industry. Nursery, fish culture, poultry farms etc.
A. Genetic Industries
B. Manufacturing Industries
C. Construction Industries
D. Extractive Industries

180. As of 2019 which country leads the world in manufacturing of electronic goods.
A. China B. India
C. Russia D. U.S.A.

181. Which is not one of the various dimensions of commerce education?
A. Privatization B. Globalization
C. Industrialization D. Liberalization

182. A class room procedure should not be emphasized on:
A. Skill of questioning
B. Informal environment of classroom
C. Clear aims and objectives of the lesson
D. Property selected and organized institutional material

183. The effective means of teaching commerce in this modern age is:
A. Audio visual aids
B. Using only one standard book
C. By different books
D. Preparing notes in the copies

184. It is the term which includes testing and measurement and also qualitative description of the pupil behaviour, what is it called?
A. Testing. B. Judgement
C. Evaluation D. Measurement

185. Which of the following low cost teaching aids is/are used in commerce?
A. Commerce Club B. Commerce Lab
C. Graphic Aids D. Commerce Library

186. A good commerce teacher is who:
A. Supplies the keeping material to the students according to the interest.
B. Has rigid behaviour to students.
C. Guides the students to the right direction.
D. Keep himself updated with current affairs

187. In display whose photos and study material are not displayed in commerce lab?
A. Business icons and their ideas
B. Film celebrities
C. Government publications
D. Trade periodicals

188. Which is not the part of Commerce Education?
A. Applying economic principle in business.
B. Develop skills to face the business situations.
C. Study about the current and future market situations.
D. Learn about the political skills.

189. A commerce teacher should have:
A. A master's degree in Commerce.
B. A master's degree in Political Science.
C. A bachelor's degree in Economics.
D. A bachelor's degree in Science.

190. A commerce professional can hold the job as ______.
A. Mechanical advisor B. Financial advisor
C. Legal advisor D. Political advisor

191. What is commerce club?
A. It is the club where the students gather and study with the books, chalk, duster & blackboard.
B. It is the club to throw the party.
C. It is the place where students unite and tend to be open in their issues and learn under the guidance of adult teacher.
D. It is the place where students get together for fun under the guidance of a teacher.

192. Commerce Education deals with the study of:
A. Domestic Science B. Trade
C. History D. Science

193. ______ is where students practice their theoretical knowledge gained in the classroom by different activities.
A. Commerce lab B. Assembly hall
C. Commerce library D. Classroom

194. What does the term 'commerce' mean?
A. None of these
B. It is concerned with exchange of goods and services in return of money.
C. It is merely concerned with distribution of goods and services.
D. It is restricted to the exchange of goods only in return of money.

195. Who says this 'Teaching is a progressive occupation and teacher must ever be a student'?
A. Binning
B. None of these
C. Business school of Delhi
D. Dr. Radhakrishanan

196. Which of the following is not the product of learning?
A. Physical structure
B. Maturation
C. Skill
D. Knowledge

197. Which method of teaching for a commerce teacher is useful for teaching practical subjects like public relation, communication etc?
A. None of these
B. Demonstration method
C. Lecture method
D. Project method

198. ______ is a piece of work involving careful study of a subject over a period of time, done by students under the guidance of teacher.
A. Lecture
B. Demonstration
C. Lecture–cum demonstration
D. Profit Method

199. Who is the father of Management?
A. Pigou B. Robinson
C. F.W. Taylor D. Henery Fayol

200. To evaluate the commerce student's quality, which of the following techniques is used?
A. Rating scales B. Checklists
C. None of these D. Project Report

ANSWERS

1	2	3	4	5	6	7	8	9	10
D	A	C	B	A	D	D	D	B	C
11	**12**	**13**	**14**	**15**	**16**	**17**	**18**	**19**	**20**
A	C	D	B	A	D	B	A	A	A
21	**22**	**23**	**24**	**25**	**26**	**27**	**28**	**29**	**30**
A	B	C	D	C	C	B	A	D	B
31	**32**	**33**	**34**	**35**	**36**	**37**	**38**	**39**	**40**
A	C	D	B	C	B	D	C	D	C
41	**42**	**43**	**44**	**45**	**46**	**47**	**48**	**49**	**50**
C	C	D	D	D	D	A	A	A	D
51	**52**	**53**	**54**	**55**	**56**	**57**	**58**	**59**	**60**
C	C	A	B	B	C	C	B	C	A
61	**62**	**63**	**64**	**65**	**66**	**67**	**68**	**69**	**70**
C	D	C	B	C	B	D	C	C	D
71	**72**	**73**	**74**	**75**	**76**	**77**	**78**	**79**	**80**
C	A	D	B	B	B	D	B	B	C
81	**82**	**83**	**84**	**85**	**86**	**87**	**88**	**89**	**90**
A	A	C	A	B	B	C	C	D	D
91	**92**	**93**	**94**	**95**	**96**	**97**	**98**	**99**	**100**
A	D	B	B	C	A	B	C	C	A
101	**102**	**103**	**104**	**105**	**106**	**107**	**108**	**109**	**110**
B	C	B	D	B	B	C	D	C	B
111	**112**	**113**	**114**	**115**	**116**	**117**	**118**	**119**	**120**
A	A	D	C	B	D	A	D	D	A
121	**122**	**123**	**124**	**125**	**126**	**127**	**128**	**129**	**130**
C	B	B	B	A	A	C	B	B	C
131	**132**	**133**	**134**	**135**	**136**	**137**	**138**	**139**	**140**
A	B	A	B	A	B	C	A	D	B
141	**142**	**143**	**144**	**145**	**146**	**147**	**148**	**149**	**150**
D	A	C	A	C	D	A	C	C	C
151	**152**	**153**	**154**	**155**	**156**	**157**	**158**	**159**	**160**
C	D	D	A	B	D	D	C	D	B
161	**162**	**163**	**164**	**165**	**166**	**167**	**168**	**169**	**170**
B	C	B	C	C	A	D	B	A	C
171	**172**	**173**	**174**	**175**	**176**	**177**	**178**	**179**	**180**
D	B	B	B	D	C	D	A	A	A
181	**182**	**183**	**184**	**185**	**186**	**187**	**188**	**189**	**190**
C	B	A	C	C	B	B	D	A	B
191	**192**	**193**	**194**	**195**	**196**	**197**	**198**	**199**	**200**
C	B	A	B	A	B	D	D	D	A

Previous Paper (Solved)

DSSSB—PGT (COMMERCE) Recruitment Exam, 2018*

1. ______ is NOT an elementary component in the BCG Matrix.
A. Elephant B. Star
C. Dog D. Cash Cow

2. A strategic option that entails reduction or termination of any existing product or service line, along with the level of objectives set below the past achievements, can be termed as:
A. Turn-Around strategy
B. Retrenchment strategy
C. Diversification strategy
D. Growth strategy

3. ____________ is a tool for evaluating how satisfactorily a corporate entity has discharged its social responsibilities.
A. Corporate Audit
B. Social Audit
C. Corporate Social Responsibility
D. Management Audit

4. Considering an example in the textile industry, if a dyeing unit takes over a spinning and a weaving unit, such an integrtion is called as:
A. Horizontal integration
B. Diagonal integration
C. Conglomerate integration
D. Vertical integration

5. Which of the following costing methods usually compares the actual data with estimated data to arrive at a conclusion?
A. Batch costing method
B. Activity-based costing method
C. Job costing method
D. Standard costing method

6. Capital Budgeting decisions are primarily taken for:
A. Absolute short term purposes
B. Short term purposes
C. Medium term purposes
D. Long term purposes

7. Who among the following is considered as the 'Father of Accounting'?
A. Henry Dunant
B. Robert Stephenson
C. Luca Pacioli
D. Elton Mayo

8. Which one of the following is NOT a component as per Porter's Model in Strategic Management?
A. Place Leadership Strategy
B. Differentiation Strategy
C. Cost Leadership Strategy
D. Focused/Positioning Strategy

9. Which among the following methods is essentially an integrated ratio analysis?
A. BCG Matrix Analysis
B. Trial Balance Analysis
C. DuPont Analysis
D. Cash Flow Analysis

10. If we draw a matrix of SWOT analysis, in which quadrant will the entry of other market players be placed?
A. Weakness B. Opportunity
C. Strength D. Threat

11. Select the option which correctly arranges the following events in ascending order according to their occurrences.

Events:
1. Management by Objective
2. Scientific Management

* Online exam held on 04/07/2018.

3. Hawthorne Studies
4. Industrial Unrest

A. 2, 4, 3, 1 B. 4, 2, 3, 1
C. 3, 2, 1, 4 D. 1, 3, 4, 2

12. A Balanced Score Card is:
A. A tool to balance current and capital liability.
B. A method to evaluate financial performance of a firm.
C. Essentially a balance sheet of financial matters.
D. A tool for assessing strengths and weaknesses in a balanced way.

13. Which of the following is usually NOT a characteristic of a successful strategic alliance?
A. Confrontation
B. Balancing contributions
C. Goal compatibility
D. Synergy

14. Which among the following is NOT a factor the determines capital structure of a company?
A. Debtor turnover ratio
B. Financial leverage
C. Legal framework
D. Cash Flow abilities

15. The United Nations established the United Nations Commission on International Trade Law (UNCITRAL) in the year:
A. 1966 B. 1945
C. 1960 D. 1950

16. ABC Ltd. buys 77% of available shares (ownership) of XYZ Corp. Which of the following can be said about XYZ Corp?
A. It is no longer a company
B. It is a holding company
C. It is an independent company
D. It is a subsidiary company

17. The ability of two or more units generating greater value by working together than they will be working individually is typically called as:
A. Management by Exception
B. Management by Objectives
C. Strategy
D. Synergy

18. Find the odd one out with regard to Performance Evaluation Technique.
A. Management by Objective
B. Confidential Reporting
C. Behavioural Anchored Rating Scale
D. 360 Degree Evaluation

19. The purchase price of a lock is ₹ 100 per unit, while the carrying cost comes to 5% and consumption of raw material is 24000 units p.a. Ordering cost is ₹ 10 per order. What will be the EOQ (Economic Order Quantity)?
A. 310 B. 300
C. 250 D. 210

20. Who among the following propounded 14 basic principles of management?
A. Henry Fayol B. David Ricardo
C. F.W. Taylor D. Alfred Marshall

21. Which among the following is a reason for Under Capitalisation?
A. High efficiency
B. Unduly high price paid for assets
C. Liberal dividend policy
D. When fair return is not realised on capital employed

22. In the short run, in order to survive the cut-throat competition, which among the following can be adopted as a last resort for survival?
A. Marginal Cost < Sales
B. Total Cost = Sales
C. Marginal Cost > Sales
D. Total Cost < Sales

23. Which among the following may be an effect of Under Capitalisation?
A. Dividends may be paid even if no profits are made
B. Market value of shares may go up
C. Market value of share may drastically fall
D. Company may manipulate accounts to show profits in the event of loss

24. Which of the following errors CANNOT be detected through Trial Balance?
A. Posting wrong amount
B. Treating an expense as an asset
C. Posting an amount on the wrong side
D. Wrong Totalling

25. Which among the following is primarily NOT a finance function?
A. Diversification decisions
B. Financing decisions
C. Dividend decisions
D. Investment decisions

26. Which of the following Depreciation Accounting policies is usually suitable for mining companies under normal circumstances?
A. Annuity Method
B. Insurance Policy Method
C. Depletion Method
D. Written Down Value Method

27. Which one among the following is NOT a subsidiary book in Accounting?
A. Cash Book B. Sales Book
C. Journal Book D. Sales Return Book

28. During an inflationary period, _____ method of material issue would help to ensure that the cost of production determined is approximately the current prevailing price level.
A. FIFO
B. Specific Price Method
C. Base Stock Method
D. LIFO

29. What is the point of 'No Profit No Loss' termed as?
A. Contribution B. Break Even
C. Margin of Safety D. Angle of Incidence

30. The excess of Current Asset over Current Liability in typical financial terms is called as:
A. Cash Flow Analysis
B. Net Working Capital
C. Gross Working Capital
D. Current Ratio

31. Which of the following companies has acquired Indian e-retail giant Flipkart?
A. Procter & Gamble B. Starbucks
C. Walmart D. Marks & Spencer

32. When the real valuation of assets is less than the amount of capital invested, such a situation is called as:
A. Capital rationing B. Capital gearing
C. Under capitalisation D. Over capitalisation

33. Which of the following transactions may NOT be categorised as "error of principle" as far as Accounting is concerned?
A. Treating an income as liability
B. Treating a liability as income
C. Treating an asset as expense
D. Omitting the entire amount to record after transaction

34. The process of mapping the current demand for manpower and making sure of the availability of the right kind of manpower at the right time, and bridging the gap of current and future manpower requirements is typically the function of:
A. Human Resource Development
B. Human Resource Training
C. Human Resource Management
D. Human Resource Planning

35. A Secret Reserve can be created through:
A. Undervaluation of assets and liabilities
B. Undervaluation of current assets and undervaluation of current liabilities
C. Over valuation of assets and liabilities
D. Over valuation of assets and under valuation of liabilities

36. As per _______ accounting concept, a business is treated as separate from its owner's personal affairs.
A. Business Entity
B. Dual Aspect
C. Historical Cost
D. Perpetual Succession

37. Find the odd one out with regard to application of costing principles?
A. Margin of Safety
B. Break Even Analysis
C. Cost Volume Profit Analysis
D. Variance Analysis for Materials

38. Which among the following is the regulatory body for insurance business in India?
A. AMFI B. SEBI
C. RBI D. IRDA

39. Suppose that a company only pays dividends when it cannot profitably reinvest its earnings.

What can such a dividend decision be categorised as?
A. Strict Dividend Decision
B. Liberal Dividend Decision
C. Active Dividend Decision
D. Residual Passive Dividend Decision

40. What is the style of leadership called whereby the leader assumes all the power and loves to dictate the followers as all the decisions are centralised?
A. Autocratic Leadership
B. Paternalistic Leadership
C. Free-Reign Leadership
D. Democratic Leadership

41. What does the term 'Esprit De Corps', one of Henry Fayol's 14 management principles, mean?
A. Proper Leadership
B. Adequate Knowledge
C. Individual Performance
D. Team Spirit

42. Who developed the Management Grid as a tool of Performance Evaluation?
A. Harold Koontz and Cyril O'Donnell
B. Robert Blake and Jane Mouton
C. Alfred Marshall
D. Peter F. Drucker

43. Which of the following costing techniques is suitable for manufacturing biscuits of similar description for a biscuit company throughout the year?
A. Standard Costing B. Contract Costing
C. Batch Costing D. Process Costing

44. Which among the following is NOT an emerging challenge for an HR manager in the contemporary context?
A. Globalisation
B. Management of various cultural issues of employees
C. Payroll management
D. Matching various employee expectations with a career path

45. Which of Henry Fayol's 14 principles of management depicts the phrase "One head, One Plan"?
A. Unity of Direction B. Unity of Command
C. Order D. Equity

46. The term 'SEZ' stands for:
A. Social Ecological Zone
B. Social Economic Zone
C. Social Environmental Zone
D. Special Economic Zone

47. Who is considered as the 'Father of Scientific Management'?
A. David Ricardo B. F.W. Taylor
C. Alfred Marshall D. Henry Fayol

48. Which of the following does NOT form a primary part of the general functional areas of Human Resource Management?
A. Measuring performance and developing employees' potential
B. Determining and staffing for employment needs
C. Anticipating and coping with organisational change
D. Taking care of quality while procuring raw materials

49. Prof. Elton Mayo can rightly be categorised as a:
A. Legendary Leader
B. Religious Guru
C. Physical Scientist
D. Behavioral Scientist

50. Which of the following is NOT a tool for analysing financial statements?
A. Trend Analysis
B. Profit and Loss Account Statement.
C. Funds Flow Analysis
D. Ratio Analysis

51. Mr. Ambani wants a fully customised private jet which must have a big dining lounge in it unlike other aircrafts. He offers the contract to Luft Dreamliners Pvt. Ltd. for manufacturing. Which costing principle shall the company use to manufacture the said aircraft for Mr. Ambani?
A. Job Costing B. Batch Costing
C. Standard Costing D. Process Costing

52. In a _____ Statement, each account is expressed as a percentage of the value of sales.
A. Fund Flow B. Liquidator's
C. Common Size D. Cash Flow

53. Suppose there are two partners A and B. A brings ₹ 2,00,000 while B brings in ₹ 1,00,000 capital for the firm. A is actively involved in the business, while B is not at all contributing to it. The profit and Loss account reveals a profit of ₹ 30,000 for the year. How will the profit be distributed among A and B, respectively in the absence of a Partnership deed?
A. ₹ 30,000 and ₹ 0
B. ₹ 10,000 and ₹ 20,000
C. ₹ 15,000 and ₹ 15,000
D. ₹ 20,000 and ₹ 10,000

54. The term 'LPG' in a business environment stands for:
A. Liquefied Petroleum Gas
B. Liberalisation, Privatisation and Globalisation
C. Loss Per Gram
D. Localisation, Promotion and Geo-extrication

55. What is the person who, without being a real partner, so behaves as to lead others to believe him to be a partner called?
A. Partner by Estoppel
B. Dormant Partner
C. Sub Partner
D. Sleeping Partner

56. The study of organisation behavior conducted in the 1920s by Western Electric Company located at Chicago is popularly known as:
A. Michigan Studies
B. Hawthorne Studies
C. California Studies
D. Detroit Studies

57. Putting a right man in the right job according to his qualification and ability is called as:
A. Recruiting B. Controlling
C. Staffing D. Selecting

58. Which of Henry Fayol's 14 principles of management depicts the phrase "A place for everything and everything in its place"?
A. Order
B. Unity of Command
C. Equity
D. Unity of Direction

59. Which of the following strategies allows a firm to excel over competitors by offering products or services at the least cost?
A. Promotional Leadership
B. Cost Leadership
C. Market Leadership
D. Place Leadership

60. Rajan and Sajan started a business on 1st January 2017 with capital of ₹ 30,000 and ₹ 20,000, respectively. According to the Partnership deed, Sajan is entitled to a salary of ₹ 500 per month while interest to be allowed on capital is @6% for both the partners. The remaining profit must be distributed in the ratio of 5 : 3. After 31st December, 2017, the firm earned a gross profit of ₹ 25,000. During the year, Rajan and Sajan withdraw ₹ 8,000 and ₹ 10,000, respectively. Calculated the closing balance of Rajan and Sajan respectively assuming profits were credited in their respective capital accounts.
A. ₹ 33,800, ₹ 23,200
B. ₹ 32,500, ₹ 21,500
C. ₹ 31,800, ₹ 22,200
D. ₹ 31,600, ₹ 22,400

61. When the completion stage of a contract is more than half, the profit to be credited to Profit and Loss account will be equal to:
A. 100% of Notional Profit × (Cash Received/Work Certified)
B. 2/3 × Notional Profit × (Cash Received/Work Certified)
C. 1/3 × Notional Profit × (Cash Received/Work Certified)
D. 1/2 × Notional Profit × (Cash Received/Work Certified)

62. The focal point of the Uruguay Round of GATT on agreement of TRIPS was:
A. Intellectual Property
B. Cross-Border Trading of Goods
C. Liberalisation
D. Tariffs on Trade

63. Which of the following Acts has replaced the Monopolistic, Restrictive & Unfair Trade Practices (MRTP) Act?
A. Essential Commodities Act
B. Consumer Protection Act
C. Competition Act
D. Food Safety and Standards Act

64. The VIIIth Round of GATT (Uruguay Round) finally resulted in the conversion of GATT into _______ .

A. World Bank
B. International Monetary Fund
C. World Trade Organization
D. International Court of Justice

65. _____, in reference to international trade, is the export by a country or company of a product at a price that is lower in the foreign market than the price charged in the domestic market.

A. Foreign Trade B. EXIM
C. Dumping D. TRIPS

66. "Debit all Expenses and Losses, Credit all Gains or Income" is a rule that is applicable for:

A. Natural Personal Accounts
B. Representative Personal Accounts
C. Nominal Accounts
D. Intangible Real Accounts

67. The General Agreement on Tariffs and Trade (GATT) as signed by 23 major countries including India came into force in the year:

A. 1935-1936 B. 1947-1948
C. 1990-1991 D. 1955-1956

68. The 'Management by Objective' concept was developed by:

A. Henry Ford B. Harry Potter
C. Frederick W. Taylor D. Peter F. Drucker

69. The Consumer Protection Act was enacted in the year:

A. 1975 B. 1979
C. 1982 D. 1986

70. Generally, a/an _________ in a contract provides that the contract price would be suitably enhanced on the happening of a specified contingency.

A. Escalation Clause
B. Contract Clause
C. Key-Man Clause
D. Ownership Clause

71. Which of the following is treated as per the principles of Nominal Account?

A. Bad Debts Recovery Account
B. Drawings Account
C. Commission Received in Advance
D. Bills Payable Account

72. In Line and Staff structure of an organisation, the authority lies with:

A. More in Line and Less with Staff Personnel
B. Line Personnel
C. Staff Personnel
D. Equally with Line and Staff Personnel

73. Which of the following costing principles is based on comparison of actual and estimated cost?

A. Contract Costing
B. Activity Based Costing
C. Standard Costing
D. Job Costing

74. As per the Consumer Protection Act, who among the following is NOT regarded as a Consumer?

A. Anyone who hires or avails any services
B. Anyone who obtains goods for resale
C. Anyone who uses/is benefitted from services without making any payment
D. Anyone who buys any goods or services

75. The aggregate of total Indirect Costs are termed as:

A. Cost of Production B. Overhead Cost
C. Prime Cost D. Works Cost

76. Payment to a contractor is made on the basis of _______.

A. Percentage of Notional Profit
B. Notional Profit
C. Certified Work
D. Contract Price

77. The following are the expenditures for a contract of ₹ 6,00,000 commenced in January 2017.

- Materials : ₹ 1,20,000
- Wages : ₹ 1,64,400
- Plant : ₹ 20,000
- Business Charges : ₹ 8,600
- Work Certified : 80%
- Cash Received (31.12.17) : ₹ 2,40,000
- Depreciation of Plant : 10%

Calculate the notional profit as per the contract costing principles.

A. ₹ 10,000 B. ₹ 25,000
C. ₹ 20,000 D. ₹ 15,000

78. According to Section 44 of the Competition Law, the penalty for making false statements or omission to furnish material information by any party is:
A. Minimum penalty of ₹ 50 lakh and Maximum penalty upto ₹ 1 crore
B. Minimum penalty of ₹ 25 lakh and Maximum penalty upto ₹ 1 crore
C. Minimum penalty of ₹ 5 lakh and Maximum penalty upto ₹ 50 lakh
D. Minimum penalty of ₹ 10 lakh and Maximum penalty upto ₹ 50 lakh

79. _________ was propounded by Prof. William Ouchi.
A. Theory X B. Theory Y
C. ERG Theory D. Theory Z

80. Management by Exception, a style of business management, typically talks about which of the following?
A. Targets should be achieved within a defined time limit.
B. Management should be involved in day-to-day working without allowing any exceptions.
C. Management should not involve themselves in routine things and must rather concentrate on strategies.
D. Exceptional cases must not be included in management and be treated as special cases.

81. International Finance Corporation, an affiliate of the World Bank, was established in the year:
A. 1960 B. 1956
C. 1972 D. 1985

82. Which of the following statements is correct?
A. Merger does not form a part of Amalgamation
B. Under no circumstances, Amalgamation leads to liquidation of an existing company
C. Amalgamation includes Absorption
D. Internal Reconstruction is an integral part of Amalgamation

83. What is the full form of 'UNCTAD', a body of the United Nations?
A. United Nations Conference on Trade and Development
B. United Nations Committee on Trips and Development
C. United Nations Consortium on Transport and Dodges
D. United Nations Conference on Tariffs and Development

84. Accounting for taxes on income is dealt with in:
A. Accounting Standard 22
B. Accounting Standard 13
C. Accounting Standard 20
D. Accounting Standard 9

85. Which of the following is NOT an assumption of Economic Ordering Quantity (EOQ)?
A. Anticipated usage of material in units is not known.
B. The quantity of material ordered is received immediately *i.e.* the lead time is zero.
C. Ordering cost per order and carrying cost per unit are known and they are fixed.
D. Cost per unit of the material is constant and is known as well.

86. UNCTAD was established by the United Nations in the year:
A. 1958 B. 1964
C. 1950 D. 1968

87. Which of the following statements regarding National Commission is NOT true as per the Consumer Protection Act?
A. The Commission consists of 8 members, out of which minimum 2 members are women.
B. The Commission hears the appeals made against the decisions of the State Commission.
C. The Commission hears the appeals or complaints where the value/compensation exceeds ₹ 1 crore.
D. The Chairman of the Commission must be a sitting or retired judge of the Supreme Court.

88. Where the headquarters of the World Trade Organisation (WTO) is located?
A. Washington D.C., USA
B. Paris, France

C. New York, USA
D. Geneva, Switzerland

89. While preparing a Cash Flow Statement, cash receipts from royalties, fees, commission etc. come under:
A. Production activities
B. Operating activities
C. Financing activities
D. Investing activities

90. _____ is an area in which business and trade laws are different from the rest of the country and are located within a country's national borders. However, they are treated just like foreign territory for the purpose of trade and commerce.
A. SEZ
B. SHG
C. Trade Zone
D. Industrial Corridor

91. Find the odd one out with regard to tariff and non-tariff barriers in foreign trade?
A. Consular Formalities
B. Licensing
C. Voluntary Export Restraints
D. Import Duties

92. Abnormal effectiveness or wastage valuation is done on the basis of:
A. Cost per unit of goods
B. Amount received from sale of normal wastage
C. Valuation of closing stock in each process
D. Cost of raw material purchased

93. Who propounded the 'Two-Factor Theory' of Motivation?
A. Abraham Maslow
B. Clayton Alderfer
C. Henry Mintzberg
D. Frederick Herzberg

94. According to Halsey Premium Plan, time wage is guaranteed with a bonus of _______ wages for time saved.
A. 33.33%
B. 50.00%
C. 66.66%
D. 90.00%

95. _________ involves the examination and redesign of a set of related work activities that are performed by employees to achieve business goals and workflows in an organisation.
A. Strategic Management
B. Total Quality Management
C. Business Process Re-engineering
D. Knowledge Management

96. The goal of matching the knowledge, skills and abilities (KSAs) that are central to perform a job, as determined by job analyis, with the prospective employee's knowledge, skills and abilities is called (technically in Management language) as:
A. Person-Job Fit
B. KSA Fit
C. Competency Mapping
D. Potential Appraisal

97. Which list does India belong in the UNCTAD Membership?
A. List C
B. List D
C. List A
D. List B

98. Grapevine must be categorised under:
A. Style of Leadership
B. Communication
C. Organisational Structure
D. Human Resource Development

99. _______ is a work group of employees who meet regularly to discuss their problems, investigate causes, recommend solutions and take corrective actions. This is generally a small group of employees belonging to the same work area.
A. Line Organisation
B. Quality Circle
C. Committee Organisation
D. Staff Organisation

100. Which one of the following may help in building an 'Innovation Enabled Organisation'?
A. Strong formal orientation with adequate bureaucracy
B. Strictly adhering to targets at any cost
C. Following the principles of Management by Objectives (MBO)
D. Following effective cross-functional teams

101. Which of the following is a contract in which a bonding company agrees to reimburse a firm up to a started amount for financial losses caused exclusively by dishonest acts of managers or other employees?

A. Zero Coupon Bond
B. Indemnity Bond
C. Fidelity Bond
D. Corporate Bond

102. ________ is the interest earned on a given deposit or principal that has become a part of the principal at the end of a specified period.
A. Simple Interest
B. Time Value of Money
C. Capital
D. Compound Interest

103. Which among the following aims at promoting corporate fairness, transparency and accountability?
A. Corporate Governance
B. Corporate Netting
C. Lifting of Corporate Veil
D. Corporate Social Responsibility

104. United Nations Conference on Trade and Development (UNCTAD) is the principal organ of:
A. UN International Court of Justice
B. UN General Assembly
C. UN Social Council
D. UN Security Council

105. The formula is $\frac{1}{3}$ Notional Profit $\frac{\text{Cash Received}}{\text{Work Certified}}$ is used in contract costing when:
A. the completion of contract is more than 75% but less than 90%
B. the completion of contract is more than 25% but less than 50%.
C. the completion of contract is more than 50% but less than 75%
D. the completion of contract is less than 25%.

106. BOGEY standard in Cost Accounting is also known as:
A. Basic Waste Control standard
B. Attainable standard
C. Ideal standard
D. Abnormal loss standard

107. Consider the following journal entry:
Royalties A/c Dr.
Shortworking A/c Dr.
To Landlord's A/c

Find the correct situation of the usage of the above entry.
A. When royalty payable is more than the minimum rent
B. When there is a normal payment of lease royalty
C. When there is a profit in lease
D. When royalty payable is less than the minimum rent

108. _____ is a quality which should NOT ethically be followed by a critical thinker while in the process of critical thinking.
A. Open mindedness
B. Reservation in arriving at a conclusion
C. Contextual
D. Non-Experimental and judgmental

109. The annuity with an indefinite life which makes continuous annual payment is termed as:
A. Regular Annuity
B. Perpetuity
C. Depreciating Annuity
D. Continuous Annuity

110. ______ is defined as consistency or agreement of individual goals with company goals.
A. Goal Fixation B. Goal Congruence
C. Goal Ambiguity D. Goal Restructuring

111. ______ is concerned with the design and delivery of financial products and advice to individuals, businesses and governments.
A. Financial Management
B. Financial Leverage
C. Finance
D. Financial Services

112. In management, when managers place their personal goals ahead of corporate goals, such a problem is called as:
A. Agency Problem
B. Mission Problem
C. Goal Congruence
D. Corporate Restructuring

113. In which of the following accounting processes is Deficiency Account exclusively opened?
A. Branch and Department Accounting
B. Insolvency Accounting
C. Accounting of Banking Companies
D. Royalty Accounting

114. Decrease in the working capital is connected with:
A. Non-trading expenses
B. Application of fund
C. Sources of fund
D. Non-trading income

115. The process of determining the present value of a future amount is typically called in finance language as:
A. Cannibalising B. Valuation
C. Discounting D. Compounding

116. ______ is an approach to Ethics that focus on the rightness or wrongness of actions themselves, as opposed to the rightness or wrongness of the consequences of those actions.
A. Pragmatic Ethics
B. Consequentialism Ethics
C. Deontological Ethics
D. Virtue Ethics

117. While treating funds, _______ recognises revenue at the point of sale and expenses when they are incurred.
A. Realisation Method
B. Revenue Generation Method
C. Accrual Method
D. Recognition Method

118. ______ is equal to after tax operating profits of a firm less the cost of funds used to finance investments.
A. Fixed Cost
B. Gross Sales
C. Marginal Cost
D. Economic Value Added

119. "The moral principle that governs a person's behaviour or how an activity is conducted" best describes the term:
A. Commerce B. Trade
C. Business D. Ethics

120. "A Rupee earned today is more valuable than earning the same rupee tomorrow." Which of the following term in the language of Financial Management explains this theory?
A. Time Value of Money
B. Valuation Concept
C. Investment Concept
D. Compounding of Money

121. India Ltd. is a fully government owned company whereas Sharma Ltd. is a company that is fully managed by a private management. Subsequently, India Ltd. took over Sharma Ltd. in a hostile takeover by buying 72% shares of Sharma Ltd. Select the option which best describes the status of Sharma Ltd. after the takeover.
A. Chartered Company
B. Government Subsidiary Company
C. Holding Company
D. Private Limited Company

122. A platform of an organised and regulated financial market where securitites (bonds, shares, etc.) are bought and sold at prices governed by the forces of demand and supply and often regulated by a professional body is called as:
A. Money Market
B. Indigenous Lending
C. Financial Intermediary
D. Stock Exchange

123. Which one of the following is generally NOT a characteristic of a Traditional Accounting System?
A. It is historical in nature
B. It matches current revenues with historical costs
C. It considers inflation
D. Profit and Loss account does not consider increase in net asset value

124. Reliance Industries Ltd., which is listed on the BSE and NSE, is an example of a:
A. Government Company
B. Public Ltd. Company
C. Private Company
D. Public Sector Undertaking

125. Which of the following is NOT a feature of Book-keeping?
A. A person responsible for book-keeping is called a Book-keeper
B. It is the recording phase of an accounting system
C. Book-keeping does not require any special skills
D. It compiles clerical activities not analytical in nature

126. ______ describes the relationship between the required return or cost of Equity Capital and the non-diversifiable risks of a firm measured by Beta Coefficient.
A. Stock Market Operations
B. Systematic Risk Analysis
C. Capital Assets Pricing Model
D. Cost-Volume-Profit Analysis

127. As per Profitability Index, a project will qualify for acceptance, if:
A. PI < 1 B. PI < 0
C. PI > 0 D. PI > 1

128. ____ is the business practice of hiring a party outside a company to perform services and create goods, usually done as a cost-cutting measure, that traditionally were being performed in-house by the company's own employees and staff.
A. Outperforming
B. External Searching
C. Outsourcing
D. Over Timing

129. "The use of borrowed fund in anticipation of higher return to the shareholders."—This is a concept called as:
A. Stakeholder Optimising
B. Reverse Trading
C. Trading on Equity
D. Debenture Trading

130. Which one of the following is NOT a transaction as per Accounting Principles?
A. Mr. X started a business with capital (brought in cash) of ₹ 40,000
B. Mr. X paid salaries worth ₹ 5,000 to staff
C. Mr. X purchased machinery worth ₹ 20,000 in cash
D. Mr. X placed an order with D'Souza & Co. for goods worth ₹ 10,000

131. The NIFTY comprises stocks of Indian companies belonging to ____ sectors in India.
A. 8 B. 15
C. 12 D. 5

132. The Over-the-Counter Exchange of India (OTCEI) has its headquarters in the city:
A. Mumbai B. Hyderabad
C. Delhi D. Kolkata

133. Which of the following is NOT a primary purpose for holding cash?
A. Transaction Motive
B. Precautionary Motive
C. Storage Motive
D. Speculative Motive

134. Which of the following is primarily NOT responsible for change in the Working Capital?
A. Change in the level of sale
B. Change in the members of the Board of Directors
C. Change in the operating expenses
D. Changes in the technology

135. Which of the following methods takes into consideration the time value of money?
A. Accounting Rate of Return Method
B. Pay Back Method
C. Accounting Rate of Return
D. Discounted Cash Flow Techniques

136. The ability of a firm to use fixed financial charges to magnify the effects of changes in EBIT on the earnings per share is otherwise termed as:
A. Combined Leverage
B. Operating Leverage
C. Long Term Leverage
D. Financial Leverage

137. Which of the following is NOT correct with regard to a company registered in India as per Companies Act, 2013?
A. Every company must have Perpetual Succession
B. Every company can sue and can be sued
C. Every company must possess Articles of Association
D. Every company should have a common seal

138. Find the odd one out with regard to branches of Accounting.
A. Corporate Accounting
B. Management Accounting
C. Financial Accounting
D. Cost Accounting

139. The argument that current dividends are less risky as compared to future/distant dividends and that the shareholders prefer dividends over retained earnings is known as:

A. Interim Dividend Argument
B. Bird in Hand Argument
C. Apple in the Basket Argument
D. Fish in the Net Argument

140. The different Rankings of the same projects as given by the NPV and IRR methods may take place. One of the following is NOT associated with it. Find out the same.
A. Unequal Expected Lives
B. Management Disparity
C. Size-Disparity Problem
D. Time-Disparity Problem

141. Software that allows collective and collaborative working as a team from different geographical location on a real-time basis is otherwise called as:
A. Cross platform mobile app
B. VOIP
C. Groupware
D. Peer-to-Peer software

142. Calls in arrear is shown in statement of affairs under:
A. List B B. List C
C. List A D. List D

143. The choice of investment proposals under financial constraints in terms of a given size of capital expenditures budget is known as:
A. Capital Sponsoring
B. Capital Gearing
C. Capital Rationing
D. Capital Diluting

144. The appearance of a contingent liability in the footnote of a company's balance sheet is a result of _____ accounting principle.
A. Conservatism B. Disclosure
C. Consistency D. Materiality

145. Which of the following is NOT an element for setting up of objectives?
A. Starting point or the present position
B. Terminal point or the expected result
C. Initiation of Proper Control Mechanism
D. Specified time duration by which the objectives are to be achieved

146. The value of assets are usually shown in the balance sheet on the basis of:
A. Unexpired Cost Value
B. Replacement Cost Value
C. Market Value
D. Revaluated Cost Value

147. For promoting a beauty salon, which of the following marketing models would give the best results?
A. Cloud Marketing
B. Seasonal Marketing
C. Personal Selling
D. Mass Selling

148. Which of the following will be the journal entry when notary charges are paid by a third party in connection with Bill of Exchange?
A. Third Party A/c Dr.
To Acceptor's A/c
B. Bank A/c Dr
To Acceptor's A/c
C. Acceptor's A/c Dr.
To Bank A/c
D. Drawer's A/c Dr.
To Bank A/c

149. The subject matter of Accounting Standard 20 is:
A. Accounting for Amalgamation
B. Earnings per Share
C. Consolidated Balance Sheet of Holding Company
D. Employee Stock Option Plan

150. Which of the following is NOT a part of the 4Ps of Marketing?
A. Place B. Price
C. Projection D. Product

151. Which of the following options best explains a Bank Reconciliation Statement?
A. It is a part of Cash Book
B. It is a separate statement
C. It is a sub-division of a journal entry
D. It is a ledger account

152. This entity is created by a special law. Defining its objectives, powers and privileges while prescribing the form of management and its relationship with government departments are the feature of:

A. Government Companies
B. Departmental Undertakings
C. Multi-National Companies
D. Public Corporations

153. ______ is a type of marketing research method whereby information is collected from published and other written sources to analyse and interpret the outcome.
A. Observation Method
B. Desk Research
C. Field Investigation
D. Experimental Method

154. Which of the following is the primary difference between the old and new concept of marketing?
A. Product Focus
B. Production
C. Consumer Satisfaction
D. Distribution and Sales

155. Which of the following is NOT a part of the scope of Marketing?
A. Distribution channel
B. After sales service issues
C. Pricing methods and policies
D. Recruiting people for marketing

156. Which of the following theories has NO direct bearing on Capital Structure?
A. Net Income Approach
B. Net Operating Income Approach
C. Arbitrary Pricing Approach
D. Modigliani-Miller Approach

157. Which of the following is primarily NOT a key activity performed by a Finance Manager?
A. Making Retrenchment Strategies
B. Making Investment Decisions
C. Performing Financial Planning
D. Doing Financial Analysis

158. ______ is NOT a credit rating agency.
A. CARE B. CRAII
C. ICRA D. FITCH

159. Which of the following authors belongs to the Modern Era of Marketing?
A. Tousley and Clark
B. E.J. McCarthy
C. Edward and David
D. Pyle

160. Which of the following software assists in accounting?
A. MS Access B. Audacity
C. Corel Draw D. Tally

161. Acquiring a machinery for long-term use by selling a part of building will result in ______ in a fund flow statement.
A. proportionate increase in the application of funds
B. increase in the source of funds
C. no flow of funds
D. increase in the application of funds

162. ________ is the process of creating, sharing using and managing the existing learning and information of an organisation while facilitating a multidisciplinary approach of achieving organisational objectives by making the best use of the learning coupled with thought processes.
A. Personnel Management
B. Strategic Management
C. Knowledge Management
D. Logistics Management

163. ISO, as a process of business standardisation, stands for:
A. Integrated Organization for Standardization
B. Indian Organization for Standardization
C. International Organization for Standardization
D. Inter-Globe Organization for Standardization

164. _______ comprises a range of accounting models designed to correct problems arising from historical cost accounting in comparison to rise in the prices subsequently.
A. Branch and Departmental Accounting
B. Inventory Accounting
C. Inflation Accounting
D. Human Resource Accounting

165. Who among the following is closely associated with Marketing Management?
A. Alfred Marshall B. Alfred Nobel
C. Philip Kotler D. Mohammad Younis

166. The Process of reaching out to the maximum number of possible candidates having potential to perform a job and encouraging them to apply for the same job is called:

A. Motivation B. Placement
C. Recruitment D. Selection

167. Which of the following reports is NOT a part of Management Information System?
A. Cash Flow Statements
B. Books of Original Entry
C. Master Budget Statements
D. Funds Flow Statement

168. Following information has been given:
Annual Usage : 8000 units
Cost per Unit : ₹ 30
Buying Cost : ₹ 15 per order
Calculate the Economic Order Quantity.
A. 420 B. 450
C. 380 D. 400

169. The distinction between capital and revenue transactions are necessary for preparation of:
A. Cash Flow Statement
B. Fund Flow Statement
C. Final Account
D. Receipt and Payment Account

170. Which of the following is NOT an element of a Cash Flow Statement?
A. Operating Activity
B. Procuring Activity
C. Financing Activity
D. Investing Activity

171. Which of the following items should NOT be entered in Receipts and Payment Account of a club formulated for social gatherings?
A. Loss on sale of old furniture
B. Various payments made towards expenses incurred
C. Sale of old newspapers
D. Subscription received in advance

172. Which of the following is NOT a contemporary impact of business service through techno-logical advancement?
A. Mobile apps for banking and other services
B. Advertisements in print media
C. Emergence of paperless transactions
D. e-Retailing and doorstep delivery

173. Find the odd one out with regard to Export-Import business.
A. Letter of Credit B. SEZs
C. Micro Finance D. EXIM Bank

174. Which of the following is the highest level need as per Professor Abraham Maslow's hierarchy of needs?
A. Social Need
B. Physiological Need
C. Safety Need
D. Self-Actualisation Need

175. Impatient, achievement-oriented people are classified as:
A. Introvert Personality
B. Extrovert Personality
C. Type A Personality
D. Type B Personality

176. Which among the following is NOT a Database Management Software?
A. Oracle B. Audacity Pro
C. IBM DB2 D. My SQL

177. As a byproduct of Quality Circle, _____ means improvement over an improvement, simply saying continuous improvement.
A. Kaizen
B. Funso
C. Hinshitshu
D. Total Quality Management

178. Which of the following CANNOT be regarded as a business service?
A. Transportation and logistics
B. Insurance services
C. Donation given
D. Personal banking

179. The basic difference between Traditional Accounting and Human Resource Accounting is:
A. Identifying and reporting investments made in employees
B. Method of valuation of stock in trade
C. Basic principles of accounting
D. Method of revenue recognition

180. Which of the following is the primary differentiating factor between ADR and GDR, as a part of depository receipt?
A. Validity of the Instruments
B. Type of Financial Product
C. Area of Operation
D. Negotiability

181. Special educators help teachers in:
A. Talking to students B. Remediation
C. Instructing D. Reporting

182. In machine language, the presence of an electric pulse followed by the absence of another electric pulse is represented as:
A. (01) B. (1)
C. (10) D. (0)

183. Leela at 11 months looked for help from her mother to pick up a doll from the top of a table but at the age of two she pulled a chair and climbed on it to reach the dell. What development had taken place?

Complete the sentence choosing the correct option.
A. Physical development
B. Emotional development
C. Cognitive and physical development
D. Language development

184. Education of girls is seen as "Education for social cohesion rather than Social progress". in which of the following documents?
A. NPE 1986 B. NPERC 1990
C. NCFSE 2000 D. NCF 1975

185. The class scheduled to go on an educational tour to a fort. What could be the best alternate plan the teacher can have for Ashish who uses crutches to walk?
A. Give him a holiday
B. Ask him to stay back in class and complete an assignment
C. Buddy system for mutual support
D. A movie show

186. Ramesh secured 15th rank. Which type of test was this evaluation based on?
A. Norm referenced
B. Standardized
C. Criterion referencing
D. Diagnostic

187. Concept formation is a result of:
A. Teaching B. Drilling
C. Perceptions D. Memorising

188. Inclusive Education policy is an initiative to support the larger objective of _____. Choose the right option.
A. Girl child education
B. Special needs education
C. Minority education
D. Education for all

189. The objective of poems in languages is to learn:
A. Action
B. Aesthetics and varied expression
C. Singing
D. Rhythm

190. A social science lesson takes responsibility of the following values?
A. Appreciation of land, culture and heritage
B. Knowledge about location of resources
C. Understanding population trends
D. Awareness about technology

191. Which of the following is the epistemological basis for scientific knowledge, according to pragmatists?
A. Problem solving B. Experiments
C. Opinions D. Interpretations

192. Technology aided learning can substitute a teacher effectively when we use:
A. Interactive e-lessons
B. Programmed learning
C. PowerPoint presentations
D. Audio-visual aids

193. What does the acronym HTML stand for?
A. Hyper Text Multiple Language
B. Hyper Transfer Marking Language
C. Hypertext Marking Logic
D. Hypertext Markup Language

194. Which element do debate and extempore speech help to develop?
A. Reading fluency
B. Writing skill
C. Emotional intelligence
D. Being articulate in speech

195. Constructivist development model by Vygotsky signifies:
A. Learning by doing
B. Reading
C. Working individually
D. Discussing with peers

196. Which of the following is a key mathematical skill?
A. Illustrating B. Observing
C. Drawing D. Computing

197. Science teachers can enhance their proficiency through reading by:
A. Discussion with colleagues
B. Updating with latest scientific developments
C. Substantiating lessons with latest scientific developments
D. Giving home assignments

198. Taking feedback from children after the lessons is:
A. A Classroom Assessment Technique
B. Lesson planning
C. Reporting
D. Assessment

199. Which quality of a test reflects its desired outcome?
A. Reliability B. Validity
C. Functionality D. Feasibility

200. Story telling comes from the art of:
A. Explaining B. Narrating
C. Memory D. Acting

ANSWERS

1	2	3	4	5	6	7	8	9	10
A	B	B	D	D	D	C	A	C	D
11	12	13	14	15	16	17	18	19	20
B	D	A	A	A	D	D	B	A	A
21	22	23	24	25	26	27	28	29	30
A	A	B	B	A	C	C	D	B	B
31	32	33	34	35	36	37	38	39	40
C	D	D	D	D	A	D	D	D	A
41	42	43	44	45	46	47	48	49	50
D	B	C	C	A	D	B	D	D	B
51	52	53	54	55	56	57	58	59	60
A	C	C	B	A	B	C	A	B	A
61	62	63	64	65	66	67	68	69	70
B	A	C	C	C	C	B	D	D	A
71	72	73	74	75	76	77	78	79	80
A	B	C	B	B	C	D	A	D	C
81	82	83	84	85	86	87	88	89	90
B	A	A	A	A	B	A	D	B	A
91	92	93	94	95	96	97	98	99	100
C	A	D	B	C	A	C	B	B	D
101	102	103	104	105	106	107	108	109	110
C	D	A	B	B	C	D	D	B	B
111	112	113	114	115	116	117	118	119	120
D	A	B	B	C	C	C	D	D	A
121	122	123	124	125	126	127	128	129	130
B	D	C	B	C	C	D	C	C	D
131	132	133	134	135	136	137	138	139	140
C	A	C	B	D	D	C	D	B	B
141	142	143	144	145	146	147	148	149	150
C	C	C	B	C	A	C	C	B	C
151	152	153	154	155	156	157	158	159	160
B	D	B	C	D	C	A	B	B	D
161	162	163	164	165	166	167	168	169	170
C	C	C	C	C	C	B	D	C	B
171	172	173	174	175	176	177	178	179	180
A	B	C	D	C	B	A	C	A	C
181	182	183	184	185	186	187	188	189	190
B	C	C	C	C	A	C	D	B	A
191	192	193	194	195	196	197	198	199	200
B	A	D	D	D	D	C	A	B	B

Previous Paper (Solved)

DSSSB—COMMERCE TEACHER (PGT) Recruitment Exam, 2015

1. Fixed cost remain at the same level irrespective of change in:
A. Volume B. Cost
C. Quality D. Fashion

2. Decision-making is a future oriented activity. If involves forecasting and planning. The function of decision-making is to choose alternatives for the:
A. Future B. Present
C. Profit D. Loss

3. Which concept of marketing is based on 'Customer Satisfaction' key point?
A. Old concept of marketing
B. Modern concept of marketing
C. Entity concept of business
D. All of the above

4. Which of the following is not an economic factor?
A. Gross National Product
B. Per Capita Income
C. Trends in the price of goods and services
D. All of the above

5. "The Environment of business consists of all those external things to which it is exposed and by which it may be influenced, directly or indirectly" said by:
A. Copen
B. Wleer and Torch
C. Reinecke and Shcoell
D. None of the above

6. Which of the following is not component of environment?
A. Economical factors
B. Geographical factors
C. Political factors
D. None of the above

7. Which of the following control the working of share market in India?
A. MRTP Act B. FERA
C. BIFR D. SEBI

8. Which tax is collected by Panchayat?
A. Tax on local fairs
B. Sales Tax
C. Custom Duty
D. Land Revenue

9. The Consumer Protection Act came into force on:
A. 1 July, 1987
B. 1 July, 1986
C. 1 June, 1986
D. 1 June 1987

10. Goods means:
A. All movable property
B. All immovable property
C. Auctionable claims
D. Decree

11. Which one of the following services is not covered under Consumer Protection Act?
A. The Services of a Teacher
B. The Services of a Banker
C. The Services of a Doctor
D. The Services of a Lawyer

12. Corporate tax is:
A. Indirect tax B. Gift tax
C. Direct tax D. Service tax

13. Who are the drivers of Globalisation?
A. International trade
B. Financial flows
C. Communications
D. All of the above

14. Which of the following is component of social cultural environment?
A. Education B. Agriculture
C. Population D. A and B

15. Socialism came into force for social development but it has one limitation which is:
A. Maximum use of national resources
B. Full employment
C. Production planning
D. Bureaucratic tendency

16. Capital economic system consists of:
A. Right to own private property
B. Profit motive
C. Existence of competition
D. All of the above

17. Memorandum of Association of a company consists:
A. Name clause
B. Place clause
C. Objective clause
D. All of these

18. Product proliferation represent introducing different brands in same:
A. Product line
B. Product quality
C. Product price
D. Product design

19. Mission is a statement which define the role that an organisation plays:
A. Society B. Market
C. Shop D. Capital

20. Indian Mercantile Law is based on:
A. American Law
B. European Law
C. English Mercantile Law
D. Japani Law

21. An implied agreement is created by:
A. Orally B. Registration
C. Conduct D. Automatically

22. A void agreement is an agreement which is:
A. Enforceable at law
B. Not enforceable at law
C. Enforceable at the option of one of the parties
D. Restricted by government

23. Residential status of an assessee can be:
A. Different for different assessment years
B. Different for current years
C. Different for previous years
D. None of the above

24. Tax incident is highest in the case of:
A. Resident and ordinarily resident
B. Non-resident
C. Resident but not ordinarily resident
D. None of the above

25. Preference shareholders are:
A. Creditors of the company
B. Trustee of the company
C. Employee of the company
D. Owners of the company

26. Doctrine of subrogation is related to:
A. General Insurance Act, 1971
B. Indian Contract Act, 1872
C. The Sale of Goods Act, 1930
D. Indian Companies Act, 1956

27. Performing assets means:
A. Money at call and short notice
B. Cash Balance with RBI
C. Bank Balance with RBI
D. Loans and advance who generate income

28. General Reserve created from:
A. Capital profit
B. Revenue profit
C. Only profit
D. By sale of assets

29. Premium received on the issue of shares is shown in:
A. Debit side of profit and loss Account

B. Credit side of Profit and loss Account
C. Assets side of the Balance Sheet
D. Liabilities side of the Balance Sheet

30. In case the shares are forfeited capital account in debited by:
A. Nominal value of shares
B. Paid up amount of shares
C. Called up amount of shares
D. Uncalled up amount of shares

31. If earnings price ratio is 0.5 and earning per share is ₹ 8, the market price of the share will be:
A. ₹ 40 B. ₹ 100
C. ₹ 160 D. ₹ 0.40

32. Accounting standard – 14 is related with:
A. Amalgamation
B. Valuation of stock
C. Depreciation accounting
D. Valuation of assets

33. The basic purpose of funds flow statement is to indicate the following:
A. Financial position
B. Increase or decrease in assets
C. Increase or decrease in liabilities
D. Increase or decrease in working capital

34. Which of the following is not normally paid from the working capital?
A. Payment of wages
B. Payment to creditors
C. Redemption of debentures
D. Purchase of raw materials

35. Which one of the following is liverage ratio?
A. Debt equity ratio
B. Current ratio
C. Operating ratio
D. Inventory ratio

36. Cash from operation is equal to:
A. Net profit + increase in current assets
B. Net profit + decrease in current liabilities
C. Net profit + non cash expenditure + decrease in current assets
D. Net profit after tax

37. Material cost variance is due to:
A. Change in price of material
B. Change in quantity used
C. Change in material mix
D. All of the above

38. Sales for the year ₹ 40,000, purchase ₹ 30,000, expenses, ₹ 5,000 creditors at the start ₹ 10,000, creditors at the end ₹ 15,000 cash from operation with:
A. ₹ 20,000 B. ₹ 5,000
C. ₹ 10,000 D. ₹ 15,000

39. Which one of the following items shall be taken as of a capital nature?
A. ₹ 2,000 spent on dismantling plant and machinery to the convenient site
B. ₹ 1,000 paid for removal of plant to a new site
C. ₹ 5,000 paid for erection of new machine
D. A sum of ₹ 5,000 was expenses on reinstalling plant and machinery

40. Depreciation of fixed assets is an example of:
A. Revenue expenditure
B. Capital expenditure
C. Deferred revenue expenditure
D. All of the above

41. Which of the following expenses will be allocated on time basis?
A. Salary B. Wages
C. Interest D. All of the above

42. Pre-incorporation profit is credited to:
A. Profit and Loss A/c
B. P and L Appropriation A/c
C. General Reserve A/c
D. Capital Reserve A/c

43. Financial stability refers to the capacity of an undertaking to meet its financial obligation, both .... and ....
A. Short-term and long-term
B. Current and fixed assets
C. Bills receivables and bills payables
D. Financial position and solvency position

44. Which of the following is non-trading charges?
A. Preliminary expenses written off

B. Discount on issue written off
C. Provision for taxation
D. All of the above

45. Which one of the following formula will be used for computing the price elasticity of demand?

A. $\frac{\text{\% change in quantity demand}}{\text{\% change in price}}$

B. $\frac{\text{Change in quantity demand}}{\text{National Income}}$

C. $\frac{\text{\% change in quantity demand}}{100}$

D. $\frac{\text{\% change in price}}{\text{\% change in supply}}$

46. A firm that is the sole seller of a product without close substitutes called:
A. Monopoly B. Oligopoly
C. Competition D. Bureaucracy

47. Which is not part of market structure?
A. Oligopoly
B. Monopolistic competition
C. Perfect competition
D. None of the above

48. Profit = Total revenue – ....
Choose the suitable answer for:
A. Total cost B. Total price
C. Total sale D. None of these

49. Which cost known as periodical cost?
A. Fixed cost
B. Variable cost
C. Revenue cost
D. Marginal cost

50. The change in total revenue from an additional unit sold called as:
A. Marginal revenue
B. Average revenue
C. Revenue
D. Profit

51. Demand curve is a graph of the relationship between the price of a goods and the:
A. Quantity demanded
B. Supply
C. Quantity supplied
D. Demand

52. The marginal revenue equation can be derived from the:
A. Demand equation
B. Supply equation
C. Cost equation
D. Price equation

53. Price elasticity is defined as the percentage change in .... that results from a 1 per cent change in price.
A. Supply demanded
B. Quantity demanded
C. Quantity
D. Supply

54. Pricing decisions are affected by the .... in which the firm operates.
A. Political environment
B. Economic environment
C. Business
D. Demand

55. If one input is variable and all of the inputs are fixed the firm's product function exhibits the:
A. Law of variable proportions
B. Law of capital proportions
C. Law of supply
D. Law of demand

56. Which is/are methods of measuring national income?
A. Product method
B. Income method
C. Expenditure method
D. All of the above

57. Price discrimination occurs when variation in prices for a product in different markets does not occur variation in:
A. Costs B. Price
C. Demand D. All of these

58. Market equilibrium of a commodity determined by:
A. Balancing of demand and supply position

B. Aggregate demand
C. Aggregate supply
D. Govt. intervention

59. A market structure characterised by having only one buyer of a product or service known as:
A. Monopsony
B. Monopoly
C. Digopoly
D. None of the above

60. In which case the law of demand does not apply?
A. Expectations regarding further prices
B. Status goods
C. Giffen goods
D. All of the above

61. Which is not sources of oligopoly?
A. Huge capital investment
B. Economic of scale
C. Patent of rights
D. None of the above

62. Contribution is a combination of:
A. Fixed cost + profit
B. Fixed cost + loss
C. Fixed cost + variable cost
D. Fixed cost + sales

63. Tabulation of data is a:
A. Need of statistics
B. Function of statistics
C. Objects of statistics
D. (A) and (B) both

64. Which one of the following is not included under the characteristics of useful hypothesis?
A. Related with available technique
B. Empiricism
C. Related with existing theorics
D. Sampling

65. Which of the following is the source of errors?
A. Errors of origin
B. Errors of inadequacy
C. Errors of manipulation
D. Errors of interpretation

66. If we have a population of size 4000 units and we want to select a sample of 500 units, then ratio is:
A. 9.2 B. 9
C. 9.3 D. 9.4

67. A coin is tossed 4 times. What is probability of getting exactly 2 head:
A. $\frac{2}{8}$ B. $\frac{1}{8}$
C. $\frac{3}{8}$ D. $\frac{4}{8}$

68. Hypothesis is:
A. A statement about the population
B. A tool of calculation
C. A tool of auditing
D. A tool of production

69. Which of the following is/are the tool of measure of the variation of the items?
A. Mean B. Dispersion
C. Mode D. Hypothesis

70. Principle of parity of authority and responsibility is related to:
A. Decentralisation
B. Delegation
C. Divisionalisation
D. Autonomy

71. Which is not the management function?
A. Co-operation B. Planning
C. Organising D. Control

72. "Although delays are costly the cost of eliminating all delay may be even more costly". This thesis is based on the:
A. Queuing theory
B. Game theory
C. Probability theory
D. Linear programming

73. Horizontal co-ordination is related to:
A. Co-operation
B. Interested parties
C. Different level of management
D. Equal level of management

74. The principle of 'Unity of Comman' implies:
A. Unity of through and action
B. Unity among subordinates
C. Instructions from staff authority
D. Instruction from line authority

75. Job rotation means:
A. Rearrangement of job contents
B. Rotation of jobs between various sections
C. Changing people in the job
D. None of the above

76. Matrix organization is:
A. A monolithic functional organisation
B. A consulative nature
C. One where a project is assignd to a project manager
D. One where project manager and rest of others are of specific skills expertise

77. The process of evaluating employees' performance is known as:
A. Job analysis B. Job rotation
C. Induction D. Merit rating

78. Grapevine communication is a type of:
A. Formal communication
B. Informal communication
C. Horizontal communication
D. SWOT communication

79. The scalar principle of organisation implies:
A. A subordinate should have only one superior
B. Line of authority must be clearly defined
C. All authority must vest in one single person
D. Manager should directly supervise only a limited number of subordinates

80. Unity of command is practised in:
A. Functional organisation
B. Staff organisation
C. Project organisation
D. Line organisation

81. SWOT is related to:
A. Organisation B. Stalling
C. Planning D. Control

82. The technique of 'Carrot and Stick' is used for:
A. Reducing absenteeism
B. Rewarding
C. Controlling
D. Motivating

83. Who developed the theory Z of management?
A. Douglas McGregor
B. William G. Ouchi
C. Cheter Barnard
D. Rensis Likert

84. Span of control refers to:
A. A number of units under company
B. Supply area of a company
C. Numbers of subordinates under a manager
D. Controlling techniques

85. Which one of the following is forms of organisation?
A. Line organisation
B. Staff organisation
C. Functional organisation
D. Committee organisation

86. When a cement mill, a steel mill and a chemical company combine, in this case of:
A. Diagonal combination
B. Vertical combination
C. Horizontal combination
D. Circular combination

87. Communication between the management and the employee is known as:
A. Inter scalar
B. Extra organisational
C. Intra scalar
D. Crosswise

88. Indian railway is an example of:
A. A departmental undertaking
B. A public corporation
C. A government company
D. None of the above

89. Which of the following statements is correct?
A. Authority cannot be delegated
B. Responsibility cannot be delegated

C. Authority and responsibility cannot go together
D. None of the above

90. Eiton Mayo is main contributor to:
A. Classical approach
B. Bureaucracy
C. Modern theory of management
D. Human relations approach

91. Management is today considered as a process of:
A. Getting work done through others
B. Working with others
C. Working with and through others
D. None of the above

92. Which of the following statements correct?
A. Authority and responsibility always flow upwards
B. Authority and responsibility always flow downwards
C. Authority flows downwards and responsibility flows upwards
D. Authority flows upwards and responsibility flows downward

93. MBO is a technique to:
A. Split the organisational goods into goals of individuals
B. Delegate the authority
C. Define the span of control
D. Laydown the objective of the organisation

94. The term 'strategy' is mainly relation to:
A. Planning
B. Motivating employees
C. Decentralisation
D. Co-ordination

95. Which one of the following is not principle of business organisation?
A. Principle of objectives
B. Principle of efficiency
C. Principle of division of labour
D. Principle of profit

96. The concept of 'Bounded Rationality' in decision-making has been given by:
A. Line authority
B. Staff authority
C. Informal authority
D. All of the above

97. "Leadership qualities are inborn" this notion forms part of which of the following?
A. The followership theory of leadership
B. The behavioural theory of leadership
C. The path goal theory of leadership
D. The great men theory of leadership

98. That form of business organisation for which Specific Act has not been passed is:
A. Partnership
B. Company
C. Co-operative society
D. Sole proprietorship

99. Workers oppose rationalization because:
A. Of dominance of capital
B. Of lockout
C. Of retrenchment
D. They will have to work more

100. The process in which actual result are compared with desired result is called:
A. Co-ordination B. Direction
C. Control D. Planning

101. "One man control is the best in the world" is a statement of:
A. Haney
B. Kimball and Kimball
C. William R. Baset
D. F.W. Taylor

102. Which one of the following is the principle of business ethics?
A. Principle of universality
B. Principle of humanity
C. Principle of autonomy
D. Principle of dissatisfaction

103. Which one of the following form may be used for calculating the equity ratio?
A. $\frac{\text{Net worth}}{\text{Total debt}}$ B. $\frac{\text{Total debt}}{\text{Net worth}}$
C. $\frac{\text{Assets}}{\text{Liabilities}}$ D. $\frac{\text{Current Assets}}{\text{Current Stock}}$

104. Stock dividend .... the number of equity share.

A. Increase B. Decrease
C. Neutral D. Even

105. If initial investment is ₹ 2,00,000 and the annual cash flow is ₹ 50,000, then the pay back reciprocal will be:

A. 0.25% B. 0.30%
C. 0.34% D. 0.50%

106. Which formula may be used for certainty equivalent coefficient in cash risk analysis in capital budgeting?

A. $\frac{100}{\text{Risk}} \times \text{Investment}$

B. $\frac{\text{Riskless cash flow}}{\text{Risky cash flow}}$

C. $\frac{\text{Risk}}{\text{Investment}} \times 100$

D. $\frac{\text{Risky cash flow}}{100} \times \text{Investment}$

107. .... meets the short term financial requirements of a business enterprise.

A. Share Capital
B. Debenture
C. Working Capital
D. Assets

108. The principle of trading on equity provides a basis for using fixed interest bearing capital as a source of .... finance.

A. Permanent B. Adhoc
C. Temporary D. None of these

109. The rate of dividend on equity share is not:

A. Fixed B. Floating
C. Equal D. Suitable

110. The cost of depreciation fund calculated according to:

A. Opportunity Cost Theory
B. Maximum Cost Theory
C. M.M. Theory
D. Swat'z model

111. Stock dividend is known as:

A. Fund B. Profit
C. Inventory D. Bonus share

112. Which Bank is known as a Central Bank of India?

A. Reserve Bank of India
B. State Bank of India
C. Punjab National Bank
D. All of the above

113. Liquidity means the ability of the Bank to convert its non-cash assets into cash easily and without:

A. Loss B. Profit
C. Interest D. Risk

114. Which of the following transactions would cause a change in 'Owners' equity?

A. Repayment of a Bank loan
B. Payment of dividends and unprofitable operations
C. Sale of land on credit
D. Purchase of assets and incurrence of liabilities

115. Which of these are outside the domain of macro economics?

A. Consumer behaviour
B. National Income
C. Economic growth
D. Balance of payment and trade

116. Macro economics is the study of:

A. Inflation B. Unemployment
C. Growth D. All of above

117. Personal taxes in India best illustrates a:

A. Proportional tax system
B. Progressive tax system
C. Indirect tax system
D. Value added tax system

118. Break even point refers to the situation when:

A. Total revenue is equal to total cost
B. Total revenue is more than total cost
C. Total revenue is less than total cost
D. Total revenue is equal to total variable cost

119. A monopoly firm makes more profit because:
A. It has ability to choose among price and output combination
B. It can discriminate price
C. It leave the consumer win no consumer surplus
D. It acts as a market leader

120. Which of the following statement is true?
A. Monopolists are price taken
B. Monopoly firm earn abnormal profits
C. A monopoly firm faces straight demand line
D. Supply curve of a monopoly is positive stoped

121. Which of these are not include tertiary sector?
A. Banking B. Insurance
C. Agriculture D. Transport

122. In .... in fact "No leadership at all".
A. Democratic B. Autocratic
C. Free rein D. Bureaucratic

123. Which of the following is an environmental force that shapes personality?
A. Gender B. Height
C. Experience D. Brain size

124. The final step of the strategic management process is:
A. Doing an internal analysis
B. Formulating strategies
C. Implementing strategies
D. Evaluating results

125. According to Abraham Maslow, the most elevated type of need is:
A. Self-actualization
B. Physiological
C. Esteem
D. Safety

126. What three words define motivation?
A. Persistence, Fairness, Ambition
B. Ambition, Direction, Intensity
C. Desire, Persistence, Fairness
D. Intensity, Direction, Persistence

127. The salary of factory cleark is treated as:
A. Direct labour cost
B. Indirect labour cost
C. Conversion cost
D. Prime cost

128. Loss by fire is an example of:
A. Normal loss
B. Abnormal loss
C. Incremental loss
D. Cannot be determined

129. In case of rise in price levels, the most suitable method for valuing material issued is:
A. LIFO
B. FIFO
C. Simple average
D. Weighted average

130. The main purpose of cost accounting is to:
A. Maximize profits
B. Help in inventory valuation
C. Aid in the fixation of selling price
D. Provide information to management for decision-making

131. A store ledger card is similar to the:
A. Stock ledger
B. Bin card
C. Material card
D. Purchase requisition card

132. A standard rate is paid to the employee when he completed his job:
A. In time less than the standard
B. In standard time
C. In time more than standard
D. Both in standard time and more than the standard time

133. .... is the date on which a bill falls due for payment.
A. Settlement date B. Maturity date
C. Payment date D. Due date

134. Joint venture is a partnership:
A. With no firm name
B. For indefinite period
C. Formed for 5 years
D. All the three

135. Owing of the business are called:
A. Liabilities B. Capital
C. Net worth D. Assets

136. Cash sales will be recorded in:
A. Sales Day Book
B. Cash Book
C. Purchase Book
D. Return inward Book

137. The Receipts and Payments Account of a non-profit organization is a:
A. Nominal Account
B. Real Account
C. Income Statement Account
D. Financial Account

138. Cost of goods sold excludes:
A. Opening stock
B. Closing stock
C. Wages and Salary
D. Salesmen Commission

139. A customer returning the goods purchased on credit, may inform the seller by sending:
A. Debit Note B. Credit Note
C. Court Notice D. Return Invoice

140. Which of these is an appropriation of profit?
A. Provision for payment of bonus
B. Provision for depreciation
C. Provision for dividend
D. Provision for doubtful debts

141. Which of the following is not depreciated?
A. Building
B. Land
C. Plant and Machinery
D. Office equipment

142. Interest on own capital is a:
A. Cash cost B. Notional cost
C. Sunk cost D. Part of prime cost

143. Merit rating helps the following except:
A. Determining right worker for the right job/work
B. Delinking rewards with merits
C. Simplifying wage structure
D. Improving labour relations and reducing labour turnover

144. Non-monetary Incentives may include the following except:
A. Health and safety
B. Housing facilities
C. Education and Training
D. Dearness allowance

145. The basic research cost should be treated as:
A. Product cost
B. Production cost
C. Production overhead
D. Period cost

146. Two coins are tossed five times, find the probability of getting an even number of heads.
A. 0.5 B. 1
C. 0.4 D. 0.25

147. In a map 2 cm denotes a distance of 3 km, then the scale in the map is:
A. 1 : 1,50,000 B. 1 : 15,000
C. 1 : 1,500 D. 2 : 3

148. Public notice is required to be given in the case:
A. Admission of minor
B. Death of a partner
C. Retirement by sleeping partner
D. Exercising option to continue or not, on attainment of majority by the minor

149. Property of the firm does not include:
A. Trademark owned by the firm
B. Property acquired by or for the firm
C. Goodwill of the business
D. Property belonging to the partners

150. Where the unpaid seller has obtained a decree for the price of the goods the right of lien?
A. can be exercised
B. is lost
C. is at the option of the court
D. is at the option of the seller

151. A contract stands discharged:
A. By performance of the contract
B. By breach of the contract
C. By agreement and novation
D. All of these

152. Demand is a function of:
A. Price B. Firm
C. Product D. Cost

153. Elasticity of demand measures the:
A. Sensitivity of sales to changes in a particular casual factor
B. Sensitivity of production to changes in a particular cost
C. Value of price and cost
D. Volume of product

154. An indifference curve is always:
A. A vertical straight line
B. Convex to the origin
C. Concave to the origin
D. A horizontal straight line

155. The total utility is maximum when:
A. M.U. is zero
B. M.U. is equal to A.U.
C. M.U. is the highest
D. A.U. is the highest

156. Consumer's surplus is highest in the case of:
A. Necessities
B. Luxuries
C. Comforts
D. Conventional necessities

157. In Vroom's Expectancy Theory, Valence means:
A. Strength of an individual's preference for a particular outcome
B. Salary
C. Supervision
D. Knowledge of planning

158. Capital budgeting involves the:
A. Planning of purchase
B. Planning of sales
C. Planning of expenditure for assets
D. All of the above

159. Which is not the form of dividend?
A. Optional dividend
B. Interim dividend
C. Composite dividend
D. Zero dividend

160. Price ratio method is:
A. Earning yield method
B. Growth method
C. Asset method
D. Dividend yield method

161. Marketing segmentation should be followed by the targeting and product positioning activities for effective planning and implementation of the:
A. Marketing plans
B. Business control
C. Marketing process
D. None of these

162. Marketing mix involves:
A. Product mix
B. Promotional mix
C. Service mix
D. All of the above

163. Which is not the 'P' of marketing?
A. Product B. Promotion
C. Price D. Policy

164. Internet marketing does not deal:
A. Advertising
B. Interactive marketing
C. E-mail marketing
D. Display advertising

165. PERT and CPM are:
A. Network techniques
B. Assignment techniques
C. Project evaluation techniques
D. All of the above

166. Linear programming identifies:
A. The optimum quantities of the variables
B. The maximum profit or minimum cost that can be expected
C. Both (A) and (B)
D. None of the above

167. Elements of TQM includes:
A. Continuous improvement
B. Supplier quality
C. Supplier partnership
D. All of above

168. Strategic management is the set of decisions and actions in formulation and implementation of strategies designed to achieve the objectives of:
A. A organisation B. A planning
C. A customer D. A management

169. Which is intellectual quality?
A. Enthusiasm
B. Exerting
C. A high degree of intelligence
D. Integrity

170. Good ethics is good:
A. Customers and suppliers
B. Value
C. Business
D. Human

171. Right shares enjoy preferential right with regard to:
A. Repayment of capital
B. Payment of retained earnings
C. Payment of dividend
D. None of the above

172. Profits are maximised at a point where:
A. MR = MC B. MR > MC
C. MR < MC D. AC > MC

173. Which of the following is not a capital asset under capital gains head of Income?
A. Stock in Trade
B. Goodwill of business
C. Agricultural land in urban
D. Jewellery

174. Market sub-divided on the basis of behavioural characteristics is called:
A. Segmentation
B. Aggregation
C. Precision
D. None of the above

175. Business ethics relates to:
A. Society's decisions
B. Customer's decisions
C. An individual's or work group's decisions
D. Government decisions

176. Opportunity cost is the best example of:
A. Sunk cost B. Standard cost
C. Relevant cost D. Irrelevant cost

177. Wage, Rent and Materials are examples of:
A. Implicit cost
B. Explicit cost
C. Direct cost
D. Manufacturing cost

178. Which of the following cost is used in the calculation of cost per unit?
A. Total production cost
B. Cost of goods sold
C. Cost of goods manufactured
D. Cost of goods available for sales

179. Sales commissions are classified as:
A. Prime costs
B. Period costs
C. Product costs
D. Indirect labour

180. If the direct labour is ₹ 42,000 and FOH is 40% of conversion cost, what will be the amount of FOH?
A. ₹ 63,000 B. ₹ 30,000
C. ₹ 28,000 D. ₹ 16,800

181. Economics cannot be considered as perfect science because:
A. Human Behaviour is unpredicated
B. It is difficult to make correct prediction of economic variables
C. Economist do not have common opinion about a particular economic event
D. All of the above

182. In the long run price is governed by:
A. Cost of production
B. Demand supply forces
C. Marginal utility
D. None of these

183. A Monopoly's demand curve is:
A. Same as its average revenue curve
B. Same as its supply curve
C. Same as its cost curve
D. Same as that of the factor inputs

184. Total profit of a firm in a pefect competitive market is:
A. Total revenue less total cost
B. Marginal revenue less marginal cost
C. Total revenue less marginal cost
D. Total revenue less variable cost

185. GDP is defined as:
A. Current value of all the capital goods produced in the country
B. Sum of goods and services exported during the year
C. All the capital goods and consumable goods produced and sold during the year
D. The market value of all goods and services produced in the domestic economy during the year

186. Which is the apex bank for agricultural credit in India?
A. RBI B. SIDBI
C. NABARD D. IDBI

187. Manipulation in CRR enables the RBI to:
A. Influence the lending ability of the Commercial Banks
B. Check unemployment growth
C, Check proverty
D. Increase GDP

188. Supply of money refers to:
A. Total money held by the public
B. Total money held by RBI
C. Total money with all the Commercial Banks and RBI
D. Total money in Government account

189. Optional money is a:
A. Legal tender money
B. Non-legal tender money
C. Limited legal tender money
D. Full bodied money

190. If RBI wants to decrease the money supply in order to check inflation it will:
A. Sell bonds
B. Increase CRR
C. Hike bank rate
D. All of the above

191. CRR means:
A. Cash Reserve Ratio
B. Current Rate of Return
C. Cumulative Rate of Return
D. Current Rate of Rupee

192. Deflation is a state when:
A. Collapse of sensex
B. Fall in GDP
C. Consistent increase in prices
D. Prices are falling

193. Expectancy theory is an example of a:
A. Process theory
B. Goal-setting theory
C. Needs theory
D. Cognitive Evaluation theory

194. The functional approach to leadership emphasises that:
A. The various functions of leadership cannot be shared among members of a group
B. Leadership resides in a particular person and not in the functions
C. Both of the above
D. Neither of the above

195. A .... is the combining of two or more companies into one organization.
A. Merger
B. Acquisition
C. Diversification
D. Reconstruction

196. Which of the following is not an element of the management process?
A. Pricing B. Planning
C. Staffing D. Leading

197. Centralization refers to:
A. The geographic dispersion of an organization
B. The decision-making process
C. The development and maintenance of power in the organization
D. The degree to which decision making is concentrated at a single point in the organization

198. During the downturn portion of a business cycle, the economy is characterized by:
A. Falling output and rising unemployment
B. Rising profits and falling wages
C. Falling unemployment and falling output
D. Rising unemployment and rising investment

199. The recently emerged type of managerial job is:
A. Top manager
B. Middle manager
C. First line manager
D. Team leader

200. A .... organizational structure is the simplest form and has clear lines of authority and ease of decision making.
A. Horizontal B. Line
C. Vertical D. Staff

ANSWERS

1	**2**	**3**	**4**	**5**	**6**	**7**	**8**	**9**	**10**
A	A	B	D	C	D	D	A	A	A
11	**12**	**13**	**14**	**15**	**16**	**17**	**18**	**19**	**20**
A	C	D	A	D	D	D	A	A	C
21	**22**	**23**	**24**	**25**	**26**	**27**	**28**	**29**	**30**
C	B	A	A	D	A	D	B	D	C
31	**32**	**33**	**34**	**35**	**36**	**37**	**38**	**39**	**40**
C	A	D	C	A	C	D	C	C	A
41	**42**	**43**	**44**	**45**	**46**	**47**	**48**	**49**	**50**
D	D	A	D	A	A	D	A	A	A
51	**52**	**53**	**54**	**55**	**56**	**57**	**58**	**59**	**60**
A	A	B	B	A	D	A	A	A	D
61	**62**	**63**	**64**	**65**	**66**	**67**	**68**	**69**	**70**
D	A	D	D	D	A	C	A	B	B
71	**72**	**73**	**74**	**75**	**76**	**77**	**78**	**79**	**80**
A	A	A	D	C	C	D	B	B	D
81	**82**	**83**	**84**	**85**	**86**	**87**	**88**	**89**	**90**
C	D	B	C	B	D	C	A	B	D
91	**92**	**93**	**94**	**95**	**96**	**97**	**98**	**99**	**100**
B	C	A	A	D	A	D	D	C	C
101	**102**	**103**	**104**	**105**	**106**	**107**	**108**	**109**	**110**
C	D	A	A	A	B	C	A	A	A
111	**112**	**113**	**114**	**115**	**116**	**117**	**118**	**119**	**120**
D	A	A	B	A	D	B	A	A	A
121	**122**	**123**	**124**	**125**	**126**	**127**	**128**	**129**	**130**
C	C	C	D	A	D	B	A	A	D
131	**132**	**133**	**134**	**135**	**136**	**137**	**138**	**139**	**140**
B	B	B	A	A	B	B	D	A	C

141	142	143	144	145	146	147	148	149	150
B	B	B	D	C	A	C	D	D	A
151	**152**	**153**	**154**	**155**	**156**	**157**	**158**	**159**	**160**
D	A	A	B	A	A	A	C	D	A
161	**162**	**163**	**164**	**165**	**166**	**167**	**168**	**169**	**170**
A	D	D	A	C	C	D	A	D	C
171	**172**	**173**	**174**	**175**	**176**	**177**	**178**	**179**	**180**
B	B	A	A	C	C	B	C	B	C
181	**182**	**183**	**184**	**185**	**186**	**187**	**188**	**189**	**190**
D	A	A	A	D	C	A	A	B	D
191	**192**	**193**	**194**	**195**	**196**	**197**	**198**	**199**	**200**
A	D	A	D	A	A	D	A	D	B

COMMERCE

PART-I
BUSINESS STUDIES AND MANAGEMENT

1. INTRODUCTION TO BUSINESS

MEANING, NATURE AND OBJECTIVES OF BUSINESS

Human beings have unlimited wants and desires and they are busy in one activity or the other to satisfy these wants and desires. All human activities may be broadly classified into two categories — economic and non-economic.

Economic Activities : All those human activities which are undertaken with the object of earning one's living are called economic activities. Economic activities of man thus deal with the business of earning a living. In order to earn one's living, every one follows an occupation in accordance with one's talents and capabilities. Economic activities may be broadly devided into four categories :

(a) Business .... e.g., Vegetable Vendor, Shopkeeper, Industrialist, etc.
(b) Profession ... e.g., Doctor, Lawyer, Chartered Accountant, etc.
(c) Employment ..... Clerk, Officer, Manager, etc.
(d) Vocation .... Painter, Nurse, Musician, etc.

Non-economic activities : These are those activities which are not undertaken with the purpose of earning one's living. These activities are performed just for the sake of them and may be inspired by sentiments, love, sympathy, patriotism, humanity etc. The driving force here is the feelings of the person who is performing such activities. Examples are morning walk, social work, visiting temple, housewife's cooking for the family etc.

An activity may be a non-economic activity for one person and the same activity may be an economic activity for another person. For example, cooking by a housewife is a non-economic activity whereas cooking by a cook in a hotel is an economic activity.

Meaning of Business

As stated earlier, business is an economic activity. The literal meaning of the term 'business' is 'busyness' or the state of being busy. But in economic sense, business may be defined 'the regular production or purchase and sale of goods undertaken with the object of earning profits through the satisfaction of human wants. In order that an activity should be called business, it should have the following characteristics :

1. **Sale or transfer of title :** It is a basic characteristic of business to transfer or sell goods or services for value. Producing goods for self consuption is not included in business. For example, cooking by housewife is not business but cooking by a cook in restaurant is business because the latter is for sale.
2. **Dealings in goods/services :** Business means dealings in goods or services. Goods may be consumers goods (like tooth-paste, shoes, cloth, furniture etc.) or producer or capital goods (like machinery, tools, factory building etc.). A business may also be engaged in providing services like transport, electricity, banking insurance etc.
3. **Regularity of dealings :** In order an activity may be called business, dealings in goods and services should be on a regular basis and should

be of recurring nature. When a person sells his old black and white T.V. set, his this activity does not constitute business because it is not a recurring nature. But Videocon Company is a business concern because it sells TV set on a regular basis.

4. **Profit motive :** Business is an activity which is undertaken with the object of making profit. Profit is the biggest stimulus for maintaining the continuity of business. In other words, a business cannot service for long unless it makes profit.

TYPES OF BUSINESS ACTIVITIES

Business activities may be broadly divided into two categories :

(a) Industry and

(b) Commerce

Industry and commerce are further sub-divided as shown in fig.

INDUSTRY

The term industry is used to refer to those of the business activities which are concerned with the production of goods. Industry is created from utility. It aims to ensuring supply of goods in that form which suits the objects, needs and convenience of the person for whom these are meant.

Goods produced by an industry may be as "Producer goods" or "Consumer goods". Producer goods are those which are used in the production of other goods. For example, coal or steel is used in the production of other goods like machinery, blades, motor car, etc.

Consumer goods are those which are used by the consumers without further processing, e.g. soaps, drugs, radio sets, cloth, etc.

CLASSIFICATION OF INDUSTRY

An industry may be either primary or secondary.

(i) **Primary Industry :** It is that in which nature plays a more important role than man.

(ii) **Secondary Industry :** It is that where a man plays a more important role than nature.

Primary industry is further classified into two categories: Extractive Industry and Genetic Industry.

(a) **Extractive Industry :** It is that primary industry whereby various forms of resources are drawn out, extracted or grew from soil, air or water. Examples – hunting, fishing, mining, fruit gathering, lumbering, etc.

(b) **Genetic Industry :** It is that primary industry which is engaged in reproducing and multiplying certain species of plants and animals. Examples – animal husbandry, fish culture, cultivation of forests, etc.

Secondary Industry is also of two types : Manufacturing Industry and Construction Industry.

(i) **Manufacturing Industry :** It is that which is concerned with converting raw materials into finished goods. Examples – steel, cement, engineering, textiles, paper, chemicals, etc.

(ii) **Construction Industry :** It is concerned with constructional activities aiming at building of houses, dams, roads, bridges etc. The main characteristic feature of construction industry is that their products are made at fixed sites and not within the factory premises. These products cannot be carried to the market for the purpose of sale.

COMMERCE

Commerce is concerned with sale, purchase and distribution of goods. It consists of the trades and all such activities which facilitate trades. In the words of James Stephenson, "Commerce covers not only the function of buying and selling of goods and handling goods but also the many services which must be provided to finance, insurance, store and transport goods in the course of these exchanges." Its main function is to take the goods from their place of production to the people who actually want to make use of them. In this sense commerce performs the function of a link between producer and consumer. The main branches of commerce are as follows :

TRADE

Trade is the sale and purchase of goods. Thus, the producer who sells raw material to the manufacturer, the wholesaler who buys the finished goods from the manufacturer and sells them to the retailer and the retailer who sells them to his customers are all engaged in trade.

Trade relieves the botheration of the producer related to availability of customers and disposal of goods. An other hand, it saves the time and trouble of customers regarding selection of goods.

TYPE OF TRADE

(i) **Home Trade :** Also called internal trade, it consists the sale and exchange of goods within the bounds of a country. Home trade is conducted on either of the following bases :

(a) **Wholesale Trade :** It involves purchase of large quantities of goods from manufacturers and selling them to retailers who sell direct to the consumers. It is a link between producers and retailers.

(b) **Retail Trade :** It is a link between the wholesalers and the consumers. Retail trade consists the supply of requirements made by the consumers in small quantities.

(ii) **Foreign Trade :** Also known as international trade, it consists of trade between two countries. Such trade is mostly conducted on wholesale basis. Foreign trade is divided into three categories :

(a) **Import Trade :** When goods are brought into a country for use in the domestic market.

(b) **Export Trade :** When goods of a country are sold in foreign market.

(c) **Entreport Trade :** Also known as re-export trade, it consists of import of goods in order to re-export to other countries.

AUXILIARIES TO TRADE

As stated earlier, commerce includes trade and also several services which facilitate trade. These auxiliaries to trade include banking, insurance, transport, warehousing, advertising etc. These are briefly described below :

(i) **Banking :** It is an important commercial function. Without the services offered by bank it would become greatly difficult to carry on production and distribution functions. Banks provided finance or credit in the forms of loans, overdrafts and cash credits. Banks offer the facilities of discounting bills and also act as agents on behalf of customers in such matters as raising capital for companies, collection and payment of cheques etc.

(ii) **Insurance :** All types of businesses are exposed to the risk of losing property, goods and money by fire, burglary and theft. Goods may also be damaged and destroyed and money stolen while in transit. Such losses would cause individuals and companies financial loss. Insurance considerably softens the effect of such risks to the concerned persons. Insurance companies annually collect from vast numbers of people small payments called premiums. Out of the built up funds, they can compensate insured persons for any losses they suffer and also make a profit for themselves.

(iii) **Transport :** Transport assists trade in moving goods from one place to another. A good transport system in which goods can be carried by ships, aircrafts, railways, motor lorries and delivery vans etc. increases the numbers of customers which can be supplied, widens the markets for goods and encourages production. As a result of fast means of transport, geographical barriers between the producer and consumer have vanished and practically all areas of the world have been closely linked up.

(iv) **Warehousing :** As goods are produced in anticipation of demand, it becomes necessary to make suitable arrangements of their storage so that these can be made available as and when these are needed by customers. The function of storage and preservation is performed by warehouses.

(v) **Advertising, Packing etc. :** These facilitate in the marketing of goods. For example, advertising brings goods and services to the knowledge of prospective customers. Packing facilitates the delivery of goods to the customers.

Industry, commerce and trade are very closely related to each other and cannot be separated from each other.

OBJECTIVES OF BUSINESS

There is a lot of misunderstanding about the purpose of business. It is a common belief that money making is the purpose of business. Of course, a business must make profits if it is to continue to exist. But it would be wrong to think that the sole purpose of business is to make profit. In the words of Urwick "Earning of profit cannot be the objectives of a business any more than eating is objective of living" Henry Ford was also of the same opinion as he said "mere money chasing is not business." He firmly believed that to succeed in business service of the community should be one's primary motive. A truly great business can be built up only if the objective of service to community is constantly kept in mind. If this is done, profits will automatically come.

Thus besides making profits, a business has social objectives. In fact the twin objective— economic objectives (profit) and social objectives (service) are quite intimately related. In order to earn profit, a business should aim at meeting the needs of the community by ensuring a continuous supply of goods and services to people.

Profit is an important indicator of the success of business. If profits are earned, it may be taken as an indication that community appreciates the services renderd by the business. It cannot be denied that a business must earn a reasonable profit necessary to justify its existence and to cover its own future risks. Profits provide not only a test of its efficiency but also a check against its failure. Profits bring the prestige and power to business. It is the return on capital and a reward for the risk of entrepreneurship. Profit is the driving force behind private enterprise.

To sum up, economic objectives of a business comprise of satisfactory profit, creation of customers and provision for future growth. Social objectives include supply of goods at reasonable price, fair deal to customers, fair returns to investors, fair dealing with the suppliers of materials and avoiding anti-social practices.

The objectives of a business are demonstrated in fig. below :

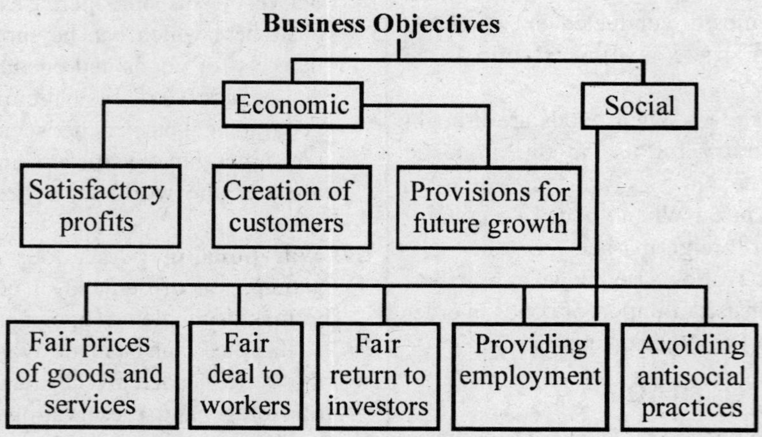

2. FORM OF BUSINESS ORGANIZATION

A business enterprise may be classified under mainly three heads based on the ownership:

(1) Public enterprise
(2) Private enterprise
(3) Joint enterprise

In case of public enterprises, the ownership is with the government whereas in case of private enterprises, individuals own the enterprise.

FORMS OF PRIVATE ENTERPRISES

Among the private enterprises, the following classification can be made :

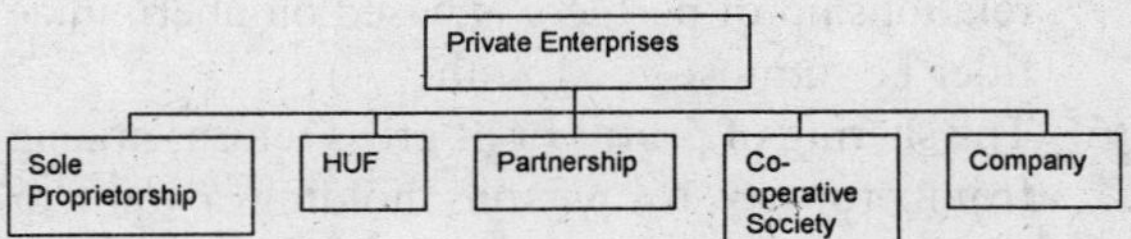

We shall understand each form of organization in detail.

SOLE PROPRIETORSHIP

A sole proprietorship is a form of enterprise which is owned, managed and controlled by an individual entrepreneur. The sole-proprietor arranges the finance, manages the business affairs and takes the profits or bears the losses. The main features of such enterprises are as below :

1. The liability of the proprietor is unlimited. It means that if the business does not have enough property to pay off its debts, the personal property of the owner can be used to pay off the debts of business.
2. The proprietor arranges for the capital himself, conducts the business himself and shares the profits and losses also himself.
3. All the decisions are taken by the proprietor himself.
4. Owner has personal contact with all the employees as well as the customers.
5. It is easy to bring any change in the management and the activities to be undertaken.
6. Full secrecy of business activities can be maintained as they are known to the proprietor only.

Advantages

Sole proprietorship form of organization offers following advantages:

(a) It is easy to form a sole proprietorship as no registration is required.
(b) As the owner himself has to bear the profit or losses, he works very hard and efficiently.
(c) Decision making is very fast as the owner need not take permission from anyone.
(d) The business activities are flexible. The owner can make any change in the product or business activity as per his wishes.
(e) It is beneficial to the country as large number of people can earn money and provide growth to the economy.
(f) Sole proprietorship firm is the biggest employment generating form of business organization.
(g) There are very less government regulations in the day to-day functioning of such organization.
(h) Such organization can be closed at any time without any government interference.

Disadvantages

But, such form of organization is also subject to certain limitations or disadvantages:

(a) The availability of capital is very limited which reduces the scope of expansion and growth of business.

(b) The sole proprietor has limited managerial skills and need not possess expertise in all areas like production, finance, marketing etc.

(c) Such organizations lack continuity as it is dependant on one person only. Death of proprietor may lead to closure of business.

(d) Sole proprietorship form is not suitable for large scale operations.

(e) Banks and other financial institutions generally avoid to lend money to sole proprietorship firms. Therefore, the cost of borrowing money is very high for such firms.

Suitability

This form of organization is suitable in following cases:

(1) Where business is small and small capital is required

(2) The activities of business are such that one person can manage them.

(3) Risk involved in the business is not very high.

(4) Where customers need personal attention.

PARTNERSHIP FIRM

Partnership is an intermediary stage organization between sole proprietorship and company. It combines the benefits of both the organizations while avoiding the limitations of them. According to Section 4 of Indian Partnership Act, 1932, "Partnership is the relation between two or more persons who have agreed to share the profits of a business carried on by all or any of them acting for all."

The Partnership Act specifies that minimum 2 persons are required to form partnership but does not specify the maximum number of partners. Section 11 of the Companies Act, 1956 states that any association having a membership of more than 10 persons incase of banking business or 20 persons in case of non-banking business is illegal association if it is not registered as a corporate body. So, this sets a limit on number of partners. The following are the main features of partnership organizations :

(1) Since the relation of partnership arises out of contract, the person willing to become partner must be competent to contract. According to the Indian Contract Act, a Minor, Person of unsound mind and Persons disqualified by law for this purpose are not capable to enter into a contract.

(2) The partnership agreement may be in writing or oral.

(3) There is 'Mutual Agency' relationship between partners. This means that each partner is an agent as well as principal. He can bind all other partners by his acts done in ordinary course of business (as an agent) and he is also bound by the acts done by other partners (as a principal).

(4) Partners have unlimited liability i.e. if the assets of the firm are not sufficient to discharge the debts of the firm, the creditors can recover their debts from personal property of the partners.

(5) A partner cannot transfer his share in partnership to any other person without the consent of all other partners because the relationship of partners is based on uberimmae fidei i.e. utmost good faith.

(6) The sharing of profits or of gross returns arising from property by persons holding a joint or common interest in that property does not of itself make such persons partners.

(7) Where no provision is made by contract between the partners for the duration of their partnership, or for the determination of their partnership, the partnership is "partnership at will".

REGISTRATION OF PARTNERSHIP FIRM

The agreement of the partners in writing is called 'Partnership Deed'. It contains the details regarding the partners, business and the rules as to the conduct of the partnership business.

Registration of firm means getting the firm registered with the Registrar of Firms of the place where the business is located. If the firm wants to get registered it must have partnership deed in writing. Under the Act, the registration of firm is not compulsory. But, the Act creates certain limitations on the firms which are not registered. The effects of non-registration are as below:

(i) A partner cannot file a suit against the firm or any partner to enforce any right arising from contract.

(ii) The firm cannot file a suit against a third party to enforce any right arising from contract.

(iii) Unregistered firm or partner cannot claim a set off (if value exceeds Rs. 100) in proceeding instituted against the firm by the third party to enforce a right arising from a contract.

But, the following rights of a partner are not affected even if the firm is not registered:

1. The right of a partner to sue for the dissolution of the firm
2. The right of the firm to sue any partner
3. The right of a partner to sue for the accounts of a dissolved firm or for claiming share of the assets of a dissolved firm
4. Rights arising otherwise than out of a contract
5. Rights of a firm having no place of business in India
6. Right to claim set off, if the amount of set off is less than Rs. 100

TYPES OF PARTNERS

There are various types of partners which are briefly explained hereunder :

1. Active/Ostensible Partner. He is the partner who takes active interest in the day to day conduct of the business. He, like other partners, is liable for the acts of other partners and can bind other partners by his acts. He must give a public notice of his retirement within 6 months from the date of retirement to stop himself becoming liable for the acts of the firm.

2. Sleeping/Dormant Partner. He does not take active interest in the business of the firm. He need not give public notice of his retirement. He merely shares profit/loss of the firm.

3. Nominal Partner. He merely lends his name to the firm without having any real interest in the firm. He neither contributes to the capital nor shares the profit or loss of the firm or take part in the business of the firm. But, he is liable for all the acts of the firm, like other partners. He must give public notice of his retirement.

4. Partner in Profits only. He shares only profits of the firm and not losses. But, he is liable to third parties for the liabilities of the firm, like other partners. He also must give public notice of his retirement.

5. Sub-Partner. He is a third person with whom a partner agrees to share his profits derived from the firm. He has no rights against the firm nor any liability for the acts of the firm. Legally, he is not considered as a partner. He has a personal agreement with a partner and not with the firm.

6. Partner by Estoppel or Holding Out. A person is held liable as a partner by estoppel if the following conditions are satisfied :

1. He must have represented himself to be a partner by word spoken or written or by his conduct or he must have knowingly permitted himself to be represented as a partner, and
2. The other person acting on the faith of such representation must have given credit to the firm.

Such a partner is liable only for the credit given to the firm by a third party based on such a representation. Such a partner does not share the profits or losses of the firm. This kind of partnership is based on the principle that a person should be estopped(stopped) from denying what he has said.

7. Minor as a Partner. According to Section 11 of Indian Contract Act, 1972, a minor is not capable of entering into a contract and hence an agreement by or with a minor is void-ab-initio (Mohiri Bibi v. Dharmodas Ghosh case). Since partnership is formed by an agreement, a minor cannot become a partner. But he can be entered into partnership as a beneficiary. According to Section 30 of Partnership Act, "With the consent of all the partners for the time being, a minor may be admitted to the benefits of partnership." But at the same time, there cannot be a partnership consisting of all the minors or of one major and all other minors.

As a beneficiary, a minor is entitled to the profits of the partnership business. But he is not personally liable for the debts of the firm. Only his share in the partnership and not his personal property can be used to discharge the liabilities of the firm. On becoming major, the minor has to decide within 6 months whether he wants to become a regular partner in the firm or not by giving a public notice. On electing to become partner, he personally becomes liable to the debts of the firm from the date of his admission as a minor and not from the date of becoming a regular partner.

IMPLIED AUTHORITY OF A PARTNER

According to the Partnership Act, the act of a partner which is done to carry on, in the usual way, business of the firm is binding upon the firm. This authority of a partner to bind the firm is called his "implied authority". So, a partner has implied authority to do all the acts necessary to carry on business of the firm in normal way. The firm is bound by such acts of the partner even if some of the acts have been prohibited by the firm in the partnership agreement. But in absence of any custom to the contrary, implied authority of a partner does not include following acts:

(a) Submit a dispute relating to the business of the firm to arbitration.

(b) Open a banking account on behalf of the firm in his own name.

(c) Compromise or relinquish any claim or portion of a claim by the firm.

(d) Withdraw a suit or proceeding filed on behalf of the firm.

(e) Admit any liability in a suit or proceeding against the firm.

(f) Acquire immovable property on behalf of the firm.

(g) Transfer immovable property belonging to the firm, or

(h) Enter into partnership on behalf of the firm.

RETIREMENT OF A PARTNER

Section 32 of the Act deals with the provisions relating to the retirement of a partner which are as below :

(1) A partner may retire from the firm :
   (i) in accordance with an express agreement; or
   (ii) with consent of all other partners; or
   (iii) where the partnership is at will, by giving a notice in writing to all the other partners of his intention to retire.

(2) A retiring partner may carry on business competing with that of the firm and may advertise such business. But he has no right to
   (a) use the name of the firm,
   (b) represent himself as carrying on the business of the firm, or
   (c) solicit the custom of the old customers of the firm except when he obtains these rights by an agreement with the other partners of the firm.

(3) A retiring partner will not be liable for liabilities incurred by the firm after his retirement. However, he must give a public notice to that effect. Such a notice is not necessary in case of sleeping partner or a deceased or insolvent partner.

RIGHTS OF AN OUTGOING PARTNER

Section 37 provides that where any partner of a firm has died or otherwise ceased to be a partner, and the surviving or continuing partners carry on the business with the property of the firm without finally settling the accounts of the outgoing partner, such partner or his legal representative, in the absence of any contract to the contrary can claim at his option:

(a) Such share of the profits after his leaving the firm as may be attributable to the use of his share of property of the firm, or

(b) Interest @6% p.a. on the amount of his share in the property of the firm.

DISSOLUTION OF PARTNERSHIP AND FIRM

First of all, we should make it clear that dissolution of partnership is different from dissolution of partnership firm. Any change in the relations of the partners is called dissolution of partnership. Thus in all cases of admission or retirement of a partner, death of a partner, change in the profit sharing ratio etc. the partnership gets dissolved and the new partnership comes into existence.

The dissolution of partnership between all the partners of the firm is called the dissolution of partnership firm. In this case, the business of the firm is closed down and the affairs are settled. The assets are realized and the liabilities are paid off. So, the dissolution of partnership may or may not result into dissolution of firm but dissolution of firm definitely means dissolution of partnership also.

MODES OF DISSOLUTION OF FIRM

A partnership firm may be dissolved with or without the intervention of the Court.

DISSOLUTION WITHOUT INTERVENTION OF COURT

In the following cases, the firm may be dissolved without the intervention of the Court :

1. By mutual consent of all the partners i.e. by agreement
2. Compulsory dissolution of the firm when all the partners or all but one are declared insolvent or the business of the firm becomes unlawful on happening of any event.
3. In the absence of any contract to the contrary, firm may be dissolved on happening of certain contingencies, as mentioned below :
   (a) On expiry of fixed period for which the partnership was constituted
   (b) On completion of adventure or undertaking for the carrying out of which the firm was constituted
   (c) On the death of a partner
   (d) On the adjudication of a partner as insolvent
4. When the partnership is at will, the firm may be dissolved by any partner giving a notice in writing to all the other partners of his intention to dissolve the firm.

DISSOLUTION BY COURT

In the following cases, the Court may, on the suit by a partner, order the dissolution of the firm:

(a) When a partner has become of unsound mind
(b) When a partner, other than the one suing, has become permanently incapable of performing his duties as partner
(c) When a partner, other than the one suing, is guilty of misconduct which may prejudicially affect the carrying on of the business
(d) When a partner, other than suing partner, willfully or persistently commits breach of agreement regarding the conduct of the business
(e) When a partner, other than suing partner, has transferred the whole of his interest in the firm to a third person without the consent of other partners
(f) When the business of the firm cannot be carried on except at a loss
(g) Any other just and equitable ground, as the court considers

Note : The explanation regarding Partnership Deed, Rights and Duties of partners have already been mentioned in the accounts section.

HUF (HINDU UNDIVIDED FAMILY)

HUF is a unique form of business organization prevailing only in India. It represents a business organization which is owned by the members of a joint Hindu family. It is governed by Hindu Law. According to Hindu Law, " HUF is a family which consists of all persons lineally descended from a common ancestor and include their wives and unmarried daughters." In such a business, the senior most member is called 'Karta' who manages the business and the other members are called 'Coparceners'. The main features of such an organization are as below :

1. A male member becomes a member merely by his birth. No contract is required. The membership is restricted to three successive generations. No female member of the family is a member of such business.
2. The business is managed by Karta and other members assist him in the business.
3. The liability of Karta is unlimited whereas the liability of other members is limited to the extent of their share in the property of the family business.
4. The coparceners do not have right to inspect and copy the account books, and ask for the account of past dealings.
5. It continues to operate even after the death of a coparcener or Karta. It comes to an end when the members so decide by mutual agreement.
6. Only Karta has implied authority to bind the HUF business by acts done in the ordinary course of the business of the firm.

Advantages

HUF form of business organization offers all the advantages of sole proprietorship. Besides that, it has following additional advantages:

1. Since the business is managed by all the male members of the family, the collective advice of them leads to effective decisions.
2. Each member of the business can look after one or more activity of business.
3. It has advantage of perpetual succession as even after the death of Karta, the senior most member becomes Karta and the firm continues.
4. There is no limit on maximum number of members as in the case of partnership firm.

So, HUF form of organization is suitable in cases where one person cannot run the business, it requires assistance from others also, but at the same time the owner does not want to involve any outsider in the business to share the profits.

JOINT STOCK COMPANY

Popularly called as 'Company', this form of organization came into existence from the limitation on maximum number of partners a firm can have (10 in case of banking business and 20 in all other cases). So, when the business requires large capital which cannot be contributed by a few persons and participation of large number of people is required, the company form of organization is adopted.

The detailed explanation regarding the definition and characteristics of the company, types of companies, registration of company etc. has been given in the section on Company Law.

CO-OPERATIVE ORGANIZATION

Meaning

It is a voluntary association of persons who come together to promote their common economic interests through the principle of self help. According to Section 4 of Co-operative Societies Act, 1912, co-operative society is a society which has objective of promotion of economic interests of its members in accordance with cooperative principles.

A minimum of 10 persons are required to form a co-operative society. It is required to be registered with the Registrars of cooperative societies of the concerned state in which the society's registered office is situated. There is no maximum limit for membership. The following are the key features of a cooperative organization :

1. It is a voluntary organization of persons who wants to promote their common interest.
2. Each member has one vote irrespective of number of shares held by him.
3. The management vests in the committee elected by the members annually.
4. Like company, a registered cooperative society enjoys a separate legal entity distinct from its members.
5. The primary objective of the society is to provide services to its members and not to earn profits.
6. Profits are distributed in the form of dividend and bonus. Bonus is the surplus profit left after distributing dividend, which is distributed in the proportion of the volume of business transacted by each member.
7. The liability of the members is limited to the extent of the capital contributed by them.

Types of Co-operative Societies

Various types of co-operative societies can be classified into following categories based on the objective for which they are established:

(a) Consumers' Co-operatives
(b) Producers' Cooperatives
(c) Marketing Co-operative societies
(d) Credit Co-operative societies
(e) Housing Co-operatives
(f) Co-operative banks

Advantages

(1) Registration of co-operative society is very simple and not costly.
(2) The management of the society is based on democratic principles.
(3) It provides a platform to a group of persons to promote their cause as a whole.
(4) It also enjoys perpetual succession as even upon death of few members the remaining members continue the organization.
(5) Income Tax Act grants certain exemptions to co-operative societies in taxing their income.
(6) Liability of the members may be limited or unlimited.

3. BUSINESS OWNERSHIP

FORMS OF PUBLIC ENTERPRISES

Public enterprises are those which are owned and managed by the Central/State government. The following are the main forms of public enterprises:

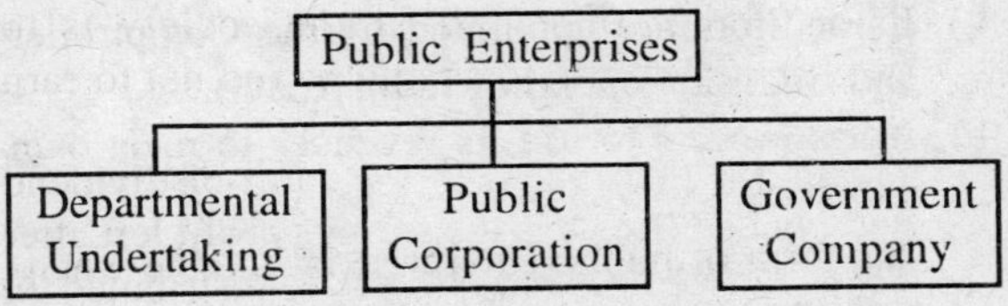

DEPARTMENTAL UNDERTAKING

Departmental undertaking is a public enterprise which is organized, controlled and financed by the government in the same way as any other government department. The main difference between a government department and undertaking is that departmental undertaking does some work like construction, manufacturing etc. similar to one performed by private enterprises. For example, Railways, Public Works Department, Ordinance factories, Postal department etc. The main features of such undertakings are as below :

1. It is created by the concerned government (Central or State) and attached to a particular ministry who controls and manages it.
2. It is not a registered organization and hence does not have separate legal entity.
3. It is wholly financed by the government budget.
4. It has no authority to use its revenues to meet the expenditures. Revenues are deposited into government treasuries.
5. It has no power to borrow funds.
6. The employees of the undertaking are government servants.
7. The concerned Minister is accountable to the legislature for functioning of undertakings under his control.

This form of organization is suitable where -

(a) Government desires to have full control over the services to be provided
(b) Secrecy is required to be maintained for strategic importance like atomic energy and defence industries
(c) The project is in initial stage of planning and require continuous funds and constant monitoring

PUBLIC CORPORATION

Public corporation is an autonomous organization established by a special Act of the Central or State Legislature. The Act defines the functions, powers, management and other aspects regarding the functioning of the corporation. They are also known as Statutory Corporation as they are created by a Statute. They act like other private companies but are governed by the enabling Act and not Companies Act, 1956. Examples are LIC, Indian Airlines, Reserve Bank of India, IDBI, Unit Trust of India etc. It has following features :

1. Like other companies, it has separate legal entity.
2. It is managed by the Board of Directors which is appointed according to the provisions of the Special Act.
3. It is wholly financed by the government.
4. It has power to borrow funds from the government as well as public.
5. It has authority to use its revenues to meet the expenditures.
6. It prepares its own budget and the employees are not government servants.
7. It is formed primarily with the objective of public service and not profit earning.

This form of organization is suitable when -

(i) The project requires a huge amount of initial capital

(ii) Autonomy is required to be given to so that decisions are taken in time without bureaucratic delays.

(iii) Public interest must be kept in mind while taking decisions

(iv) Enterprise is required to be run on business lines

GOVERNMENT COMPANY

According to Section 617 of Companies Act, government company is a company in which at least 51% of the paid up share capital is held by

(i) Central Government, or

(ii) Any State govt. or governments, or

(iii) Partly by Central govt. and partly by one or more State governments

Government company includes a company which is subsidiary of a government company. Examples are State Trading Corporation, Steel Authority of India Ltd., ONGC etc. They are similar to other private company except the fact that majority of shares are owned by the government. Such companies has below mentioned characteristics:

(a) It is registered and governed by the provisions of Companies Act. But, government may, by notification, exempt such companies from certain provisions of Companies Act.

(b) Like other companies, it has separate legal entity.

(c) It is managed by Board of Directors consisting of directors appointed by the shareholders as well as nominated by the government.

(d) It can raise funds from the public as well as the government.

(e) Its employees are not government servants.

(f) They are run on commercial principles and enjoy higher degree of autonomy from government as compared to other forms of public enterprise.

(g) Its auditors are appointed by the Comptroller and Auditor General of India (CAG).

(h) It has powers to use its revenues to meet own expenses.

This form of public enterprise is suitable when-

1. Private participation in capital is required but they are not ready to take full risk
2. Enterprise is to run on the business principles

Multinational Companies

A multinational company is one which operates in several countries. It is defined as "a corporation, which operates, in addition to the country in which it is incorporated, in one or more other countries". Apparently, such companies are very larger in size. Some of multinational companies operating in India are - Coca Cola, Pepsi, Uniliver Ltd. IBM. ABB, Philips etc.

4. BUSINESS SERVICES

COMMERCE

Commerce is a composite term which includes many activities. Many a times, it is used interchangeably with industry, business etc. Let us first try to understand what commerce is and where it stands.

People do different kinds of economic activities. These activities can be classified under three categories:

1. Profession
2. Employment
3. Business

Among these, business activities refer to the activities which are connected with the production or purchase and sale of goods or services with the object of earning profit. It relates to the creation of three utilities :

(a) Form utility through processing or production
(b) Time utility through storage
(c) Place utility through transportation

Business activities can be classified into two broad divisions :

(i) Industry
(ii) Commerce

MEANING OF COMMERCE

Commerce includes all those activities which

(a) Establish a link between the producers and consumers of goods, and
(b) Maintain a smooth and uninterrupted flow of goods from producers to consumers.

To perform, the aforesaid activities, the various hindrances of persons, place, time, risk, finance and information are to be removed. The following activities remove such hindrances and hence are part of commerce:

(i) Trade
(ii) Transportation
(iii) Storage and Warehousing
(iv) Insurance
(v) Banking
(vi) Advertising

The whole range of commerce activities can be broadly classified as under :

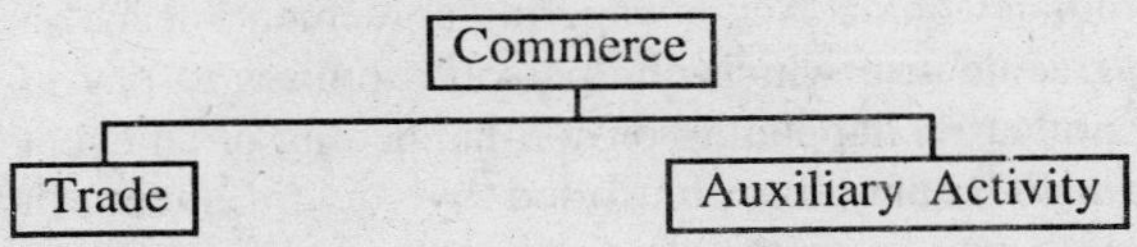

Trade

Trade refers to the sale, transfer or exchange of goods and services for a certain price. Trade removes the hindrance of person in commerce by establishing a link between producers and consumers. Goods acquire place utility through trade since the traders make the goods available to consumers in different markets.

Auxiliary Activities

Auxiliary activities are aid to trading activity and remove various hindrances which arise in the production and distribution of goods. They, as mentioned above, are transportation, warehousing, insurance, banking and advertising.

INSURANCE

MEANING. Insurance is a contract in which the insurer (insurance company) undertakes to indemnify the insured on the happening of a certain event in consideration of a specified amount. The document which covers the terms and conditions of insurance is known as Insurance Policy. The basic principle underlying insurance is pooling of risks.

Insurance spreads the loss over a large number of people who insure themselves against some risk. For example, a person takes fire insurance of Rs. 1,00,000 for a premium of Rs. 110. the probability of fire occurring is 1 house per thousand houses. Now, if the house of a person is destroyed by fire, he need not worry as the insurance company will pay him 1,00,000. Had the insurance not been there, it would have been great loss to him. Through insurance, this loss has been borne by the rest of 999 people whose houses are not destroyed but has paid insurance premium.

Insurance And Wagering

Many people consider that the contract of insurance is similar to a wagering agreement. According to Indian Contact Act, a wagering agreement means an agreement in which one person promises to pay to another on happening or non-happening of an event which cannot be controlled by any of them. In other words, wagering agreement is like gambling or speculation. Here, it is important to understand that an insurance contract is not like a wagering agreement. The following are the distinction between the two:

(a) In case of general insurance the contract is to indemnify the loss suffered by the insured. So, suffering a loss by insured is the primary condition of payment of insurance. In case of wagering agreement, neither party suffers any loss and hence no question of indemnity.

(b) The purpose of insurance is to provide the security to the insured. In wagering agreement, the purpose of the parties involved is to earn by way of speculation.

(c) One primary difference is that in insurance, the insured has insurable interest in the object of insurance, but in wagering agreement none of the parties have any interest in the subject matter.

(d) Insurance contract is legal and can be enforced under law, but wagering agreement has been declared to be void by the Indian Contract Act being opposed to public policy.

(e) One of the principles of insurance is observing utmost good faith by parties which is absent in case of wagering agreement

(f) In insurance the loss of one person is distributed over a number of persons and hence all get the benefit. In wagering the loss of one party is the profit of another: one person gains and the other loses.

Principles of Insurance

In addition to the essential elements of contract, the following principles are also applicable to insurance contracts as fundamental conditions :

1. Principle of Utmost Good Faith. Insurance contract is a contract of *uberrimae fidei* i.e. a contract of utmost good faith. This means that each of the parties to the contract is bound to disclose all material facts which may affect the decision of the other party to enter into such contract or the premium to be charged. There must be neither concealment nor the mis-statement of material facts. If this principle is violated by any party, the insurance contract is considered to be invalid.

2. Principle of Indemnity. A contract of insurance is a contract of indemnity (except contract of life insurance). The insurer compensates the insured for the actual loss suffered by him. The insured is not permitted to make a profit out of the contract.

3. Principle of Insurable Interest. According to this principle, the insured must have insurable interest in the subject matter of the insurance. Insurance interest is a pecuniary interest in the preservation of the subject matter. A person is said to have insurable interest only when he will derive monetary benefit from the preservation of subject matter or he will suffer monetary loss on the happening of the event insured. So, the insured need not be the actual owner of the property. For example, a creditor has insurable interest in the life of the debtor.

The point of time when the insured must have insurable interest in the subject matter differs from contract to contract. In life insurance, the insurable interest must exist at the time of making the contract only. In fire insurance, the interest must exist both at the time of making the contract and at the time of actual loss whereas, in marine insurance, the insurable interest should exist only at the time of actual loss.

4. Principle of Causa Proxima. According to this principle, an insured can recover only that loss which is proximately caused by the risk insured against. When there is more than one causes of loss, the principle of proximate cause of loss is followed and the nearest cause of loss is considered.

5. Principle of subrogation. The term 'Subrogation' means substitution. Under this principle, once the claim of the insured has finally settled, the insurer steps into the shoes of the insured and becomes entitled to exercise all the rights of the insured regarding the subject matter of the insurance. Accordingly, if the insured had any right to recover his losses from anyone who is responsible for the loss, the insurance company can recover that money.

6. Principle of Mitigation of Loss. According to this principle, an insured must take all reasonable steps which a man of ordinary prudence will take under those circumstances to reduce the loss. For example, if the insured does not take enough steps to stop the fire in his godown, the insurance company can reduce the claim to that extent.

7. Principle of Contribution. When the goods are insured with more than one insurance company, it is called double insurance. In such cases, the principle of contribution applies. According to this principle, if one property is insured with two insurance companies then in the event of loss, the amount of loss shall be borne by all the companies in proportion to the amount of insurance given by each company. For example, A has taken insurance of Rs. 1,00,000 with X Co. and Rs. 2,00,000 with Y. Co. Now A suffers a loss of Rs. 90,000. in this case, the loss shall be borne by both the companies. X Co. will pay Rs. 30,000 and Y Co. will pay Rs. 60,000. If one of them pays full amount i.e. 90,000 then he is entitled to recover the share of other insurance companies from them.

RE-INSURANCE

This phenomenon has arisen with the creation of large projects involving thousands of crores of rupees. In such projects, loss due to fire, flood or other natural calamities may turn out to be hundreds of crores of rupees. If an insurance company does not want to take such a high risk, he re-insures some part of risk with another insurance company in consideration of sharing the premium. For example, A takes insurance of Rs. 20,000 crore with X Co with annual premium of Rs. 150 crores. X Co. does not want to carry such a higher risk. So, it reinsures Rs. 8,000 crores with Y Co. paying it premium of Rs. 60 crores. Now, there is loss of Rs. 600 crores in particular year. This loss shall be paid by X Co. to A. Then X Co. shall recover Rs. 240 crores from Y Co. as insurance. Contract of re-insurance is similar to a contract of insurance of loss. It is subject to all the conditions of original policy.

TYPES OF INSURANCE

Insurance can be taken for any loss to a person or business. It can be divided into two broad categories:

(a) Life Insurance
(b) General Insurance

Under general insurance, various types of risks for which insurance is taken are as under:

(1) Fire Insurance (For risk of loss due to fire)
(2) Marine Insurance (For risk of loss to ship or cargo)
(3) Health insurance
(4) Fidelity insurance
(5) Other types of Insurance (For risk of loss due to theft, accidents etc.)

LIFE INSURANCE

In a contract of life insurance, the insurer undertakes to pay a fixed amount on the death of the insured or on the expiry of the term whichever is earlier. It is called protection cum investment contract. The policy holder gets the protection of indemnity in case of death and if he does not die within the period of the policy he gets an amount which is more than the premium he had paid and thus gets return on his investment.

Kinds Of Life Insurance Policies

Various kinds of life insurance policies are offered by the insurance companies considering the varying requirements of people for money at different stages of life. The important types of policies are explained hereunder:

(a) Endowment Policy : Nowadays, this is the most popular type of policy. Under such a policy, the insured pays annual premium for a number of years ranging form 10-25 years and he is paid back a lumpsum amount at the end of specified period, or upon death, whichever is earlier. This kind of policy is suitable for those who need a big amount after certain years for expenses like marriage of children, education etc. Examples of such polices are Jeevan Anand, Jeevan Shri etc.

(b) Money Back Policy : This kind of insurance is suitable to those who do not have large sum to invest but want to insure their lives with a view to earn returns on their investment. In this kind of policy, the insured pays premium regularly. The insurance company pays back to the insured certain amount of profit at regular intervals. The insurance amount becomes payable at the end of the maturity or the death of insured, whichever is earlier.

(c) With Profit Policy : The holder is entitled to receive the bonus at the declared rates on the sum assured. The bonus declared by the insurance company gets accumulated year after year but is paid at the time of maturity of the policy.

(d) Whole Life policy : In this kind of insurance, the insured pays a small premium throughout his life and the insurance amount is payable on his death only.

(e) Limited Payment Life Policy : Under this, the insured pays the insurance premium for a specified number of years, but the amount of insurance is payable only on his death.

(f) Joint Life Policy : This kind of policy gives insurance to two or more persons. The insurance is payable at the end of the specified period or upon the death of any of them, whichever is earlier.

(g) Accident Policy : In case of with accident policies, the holder is entitled to double or triple the sum assured on death due to accident.

Surrender Value of Life Policy. Surrender value of a policy is the amount payable by the insurance company to the policyholder if the policyholder decides to discontinue his policy before the date of its maturity. Insurance company decides the surrender value for each year for every kind of policies. In case of surrender of policy, the policyholder surrenders his rights under the policy to the insurance company.

FIRE INSURANCE

In fire insurance contract, the insurer undertakes to compensate the insured for the actual loss suffered by him due to the damage or destruction of property by fire subject to the maximum limit of the sum insured. It is to be noted that fire insurance policies are always subject to **Average Clause**. This clause is applicable in case of under insurance i.e. where the sum insured of the policy is less than the value fo the subject matter of insurance. In such cases, the actual claim is proportionately reduced by applying the following formula:

$$\text{Actual Claim} = \text{Actual Loss} \times \frac{\text{Sum Insured}}{\text{Sum Insurable}}$$

The same property can be inured with different insurers. In this case, all the insurers are jointly liable to bear the loss. But in no case, the total amount payable to the insured can exceed the amount of actual loss. Apart from the loss of goods, a person can also take Loss of Profit Policy which protects the insured against the loss of profit due to dislocation of business because of fire.

Types of Fire Policies

The following types of fire polices are in practice:

(a) Valued Policy : In this kind of policies, the amount payable in the event of destruction is fixed irrespective of the actual amount of loss.

(b) Specific Policy ; In such policies, the insured gets his property insured for a certain sum. The liability of the insurer is limited to the sum insured or actual amount of loss, whichever is lower.

(c) Average Policy : It is a policy which contains 'Average Clause'. As already explained in such policies, if the goods are insured for an amount less than their actual value, the amount of insurance to be paid gets reduced from the actual loss.

(d) Replacement Policy : Under this policy, the insurer does not pay cash to the insured, instead he replaces the property of the insured.

(e) Consequential Loss Policy : Under this system, the insured is also paid for loss of profit due to stoppage of production/business due to fire.

(f) Comprehensive Policy : This policy covers losses against risks like fire, theft, burglary, strikes, riots etc.

MARINE INSURANCE

In a contract of marine insurance, the insurer undertakes to compensate the insured in return for the premium for the actual loss suffered by him due to perils of the sea. It may be in respect of ship, cargo, freight or any other subject connected with a marine voyage. In this type of insurance the insurer is called 'Underwriter'.

Types of Marine Policies

The following kinds of marine policies are in use:

(1) Time Policy : In this type of policy, the property is insured for a specified period of time, generally not exceeding one year.

(2) Voyage Policy : This kind of policy is taken for a particular voyage only, from one place to another.

(3) Valued Policy : This type of policy is taken for a specified amount of the property to be insured.

(4) Floating Policy : This is a kind of open policy. The insurance is taken for a particular amount without any details. The details of the ship under insurance are given afterwards by a declaration. This type of policy is useful for cargo owners who own a number of vessels. Whenever, a vessel is loaded for journey the cargo company gives a declaration to the insurance company of the particulars of that vessel.

TERMS USED IN INSURANCE BUSINESS

Barratry. Barratry is a fraudulent act committed by a master or crew of a vessel which damages the vessel or its cargo, including desertion, illegal scuttling, and theft of the ship or cargo

Actuaries. A professional usually involved in the life insurance industry, who applies mathematical theories of probabilities and statistical techniques in risk calculation. Actuaries are becoming increasingly involved in general insurance in relation to loss reserving and premium calculations.

Demurrage. Demurrage is the loss of use a vessel owner incurs if his vessel is restricted to port as a result of damage to the vessel or delays in loading or unloading.

Ex-Gratia Settlement. A claim settlement made by an insurer even when the loss is not covered by the policy. Usually made for commercial reasons where the claims experience has otherwise been good.

Inland Container Depot. Inland Container Depot is a dry port wherein facility to clear goods of imports received in containers by sea is facilitated. It also facilitates keeping the imported goods and their subsequent clearance for export or home use. ICD is also used by exporter to keep the goods before finally sending them to the port. Most of the formalities to be done for import is doe at the ICD for the convenience of the importer. It is managed and controlled by the Customs authorities.

Stowage. The lacing of cargo in a vessel in such a manner as to provide the utmost safety and efficiency for the ship and the goods it carries.

Bonded Warehouse. A warehouse storage area or manufacturing facility in which imported goods may be stored or processed without payment of customs duties.

5. TRADE

RETAIL DISTRIBUTION

"Retail outlets are shops from whom the consumer ultimately buys."

Retailer perhaps is the last link of the chain of distribution who sell goods to the ultimate consumer and has no other alternative.

Retailing is a must and cannot be eliminated. In a bid to remove wholesaler, however, certain big produces have started direct selling to consumer by opening chain stores or some other forms of large scale retaining. But in the sense, they function as a retailer because they sell goods direct to the consumer.

Retailer serves the manufacturer by passing on to them the exact feelings, desires, need and preferences of the ultimate customers and on the reverse, he introduces the product to the consumers. In this way, they serve the consumer by presenting the new product before them.

Today, large scale retailing has got momentum and in India especially multiples shops have become a popular form of large scale retailing. But still retailing at small scale cannot be said to be out-moded. Their service to various sections are innumerable and invaluable.

RETAIL TRADE

According to the report of the definition committee America, "Retailing includes all activities incidental to selling to the ultimate consumer," In the words of William J. Stanton, "A retailer or a retail store is a business enterprise which sells primarily to the ultimate consumer for non-business use." Lundiff and Still define it as "retailing consist of those activities involved in selling directly to ultimate consumers."

Many dictionaries define retailing as the sale of goods in small quantities to the ultimate consumer." The word retailer has a French origin meaning "to cut again". It is exactly and literary so and is meaningful. Retail trade is one that cuts off smaller portion from large lumps of goods from the bulk of product processed by the wholesaler. Small lots are cut and distributed through retailers. The retailer is the last link in the chain of distribution between the manufacture and the ultimate consumer. Without retailer to make the goods of industry conveniently available to millions of consumer there could be no mass production. Even the industrial revolution would not have taken place in the absence of retailers. The retail shop is one of the oldest and most widely used business establishments in any country of the world.

Retailer and retailing : A retailer or a retail store is a business enterprises which sell primarily to ultimate consumer. The retailer is also known as a dealer. The word distributor is sometimes used wrongly to denote a retailer. The distributor is a whole selling middle-man and not at all a retailer.

Retailing on the other hand, includes all activities directly related to the sale of goods or service to the ultimate consumer, irrespective of who sells.

The distinction of retailing is normally made on the basis to whom the product is sold. For example, if a manufacturer sells direct to the consumer that also is retailing even a wholesales is said to be engaged in retailing when he sells directly to an ultimate consumer although his main business, may still be whole-selling. Therefore, it is most of the buyer in the transaction is a ultimate consumer, the seller in the same quantities is engaged in retailing." In other words, anyone selling to the ultimate consumer is performing the functions of a retailer, regardless of what he call himself.

Retailer have been portrayed as the buying agents for their consumer. It has been marked that the marketing an marchandisity arm of many manufactures. Retailing is subjected to context changes which increases both the risk and opportunities of the participants. It is influenced by many forces such as population and the mobility of consumer, increased personal income, changes in information of income, consumer credit and competitive change etc. Technological innovation is yet another cause that affect retailing. Finally, there is influence of Government policies which prevails over social, economic and scientific influences.

Retailing functions : Retailing constitutes the final link in the distributive chain. Therefore, it is responsible for the performances of serval important marketing functions. Some of these functions are :

1. Assembling of goods from various wholesalers.
2. The physical movement and storage of goods for the supply to the final consumer to meet their needs and requirements.
3. Providing of information concerning the nature and use of goods to the wholesaler and product. It also informs about the market trends to them.
4. The standardisation, grading and final processing of goods which have been left in grading or unstandardised by wholesaler.
5. The provision of ready availability of goods of various qualities and of various manufacture.
6. The provision of risk concerning the price and nature extend of demand of goods as long as they remain unsolved.
7. The financing of inventory and extension of credit to consumer for a short period.

Services Rendered by the Retailers

Retailer offers valuable service to:

(i) Wholesaler/producer and

(ii) Consumer

I. Service to Wholesaler and Producers

Retailers serve the wholesaler and producer in the following ways :

1. Advertisement of new products : If the retailers are in the direct touch with consumer and they know the consumer wants and need, they are in a position to influence decision of the consumer to buy a new product. Consumers consult the retailer to know the characteristics and utilities of the new product. They serve as the best media of advertisement for the producer and wholesaler. They also make local publicity of the product.

2. Arrangement to sell the goods : Retailers and only retailer sell the product to innumerable small consumers and thus receive the wholesaler from selling the good to ultimate consumer in small quantities.

3. Information about consumer's habit tastes and needs : As the retailers are in close touch with consumer and have full knowledge of their habits, tastes, need and preference, they also know the change in their tests, habits etc. They provide all such information to wholesalers/producers.

II. Services to Consumer

Retailers are served by the consumers in innumerable way as follows :

1. Selection : The retailer keeps stock of different varieties of goods of an average consumer cannot afford to stock goods that he requires for every day use. In other words, by holding stock of these goods the retailer relieves the consumer performing their stock for himself.

2. Variety of goods : The retailers keep a good assortment of various varieties of a product manufactured by different firms. In this way he provides a variety of choice to his customer.

3. Demand creations: Most of the demand creation method are undertaken by retailer for the manufacture and wholesaler. They arrange for the display of goods, supply necessary information to the customer and provide various similar services.

4. Distribution : The retailer is an expert in the distribution of consumer goods. Out of their experiences, training and ultimate knowledge of the goods, they are in a position to keep the customer in the proper selection of goods. The retailers success in their business ultimately rest on the effective rendering of these services.

5. Credit facilities : The retailer often extends credit facilities to the consumer. These alone account for the large scale.

6. Personal service : The retailer provides many personal services to the customer such as home delivery, after-sales service, liberal exchange of goods etc.

7. Sale on approval : As the retailers are very close to the consumers they sell the goods on approval basis. Under this type of sellings, the consumer is given the facilities that if goods are not of their choice or are not approved by the family members they can return the same within a specific time. Besides the above service rendered by the retailers, they make the good available in all seasons according to the needs, tastes and preference of the customers. They give advice to customers in selecting the goods, provide facility of return goods, increases the knowledge of customers about new varieties of goods and also render other periodical services.

Essential elements for a successful retail trade in order to get success in retailing : The retailer must consider the following facts.

1. Selection of proper goods : It should be able to select proper good which can meet the requirement of his customer selection he should exercise his foresight, use his past experience and keep in view the changing fashions.

2. Perfectly knowledge about goods : A retailer should have through knowledge about the goods he deals in only then he will be able to satisfy his customer and answer their questions.

3. Sales policy : He should adopt the policy of buying in bulk and increases his sales by satisfying himself with a lower margin of profit instead of charging higher prices and limiting his sales. By this policy he can also face local competition from other retailers in the market.

4. Adequate capital : Adequate capital is a vital factor for the success of any business. A retailer should command adequate capital at his disposal because he has to follow some credit facilities also to his customer.

5. Selection of suitable business location : It is very necessary that a suitable business location should be selected. The place should be easily accessible to the customer. What should be a suitable location will depend on the nature of goods to deals in.

6. Necessary business education : He should be well versed with the art of a salesmanship underlined his habits and temperament of his customers.

7. Attractive display and advertisement : He should arrange things in an attractive style as to attract more customers. Goods should be prominently displayed.

8. To provide credit facility : In modern times providing credit facilities has also become necessary. For this, the retailers should know the financial position of his customer and their habit also.

Besides, he should also provide free advice.

Facility of return of goods if possible home delivery facing of durable item.

Different Forms of Retail Trade Organisation

It is retailing that has changed very drastically during the last two decades. Some institutions have disappeared whereas never ones have been added. This process of deletion and addition still continues in newer firms. They range from hawkers and dealers who have no permanent place to well organised settled shop like departmental stores, super bazars etc. Some of the importance kinds of retailing business units on the basic of their places of business are categorised as :

1. Itinerant Retailers
2. Fixed shop Retailers

1. Itinerant Retailers : These traders have no fixed business places and move from place to place as the season changes. They sell low-priced item generally in very small lots. They generally invest a very small capital and does not stick to a particular line of business. Some of them are :

(a) Hawkers and pedlars : Sale by hawkers and pedlars is of very old origin. With the help of a beast of burden or a hand-cart they carry the goods from place to place and sell them at very doors of the customer. While the same function is done even by pedlars, the point of difference is that they carry their goods on their persons. Both of these retailers do not have any fixed place of business. Hence they keep on moving from locality to localilty on the basis of prospects of the business.

They generally handle cheap goods with low unit value like pens, kerchiefs, knifes, comb, cheap cosmetics, toys etc. There cannot be any guarantee about the quality of goods as they are of inferior variety. So, while buying goods from hawkers and pedlars one must be careful about their quality. Generally these retailers sell goods at very tempting prices which are considerably lower than the market value. They are seen outside the temple or bathing ghats.

(b) Market traders : Market traders are those retailers who open their shops at different places on fixed days known as marketed day like some bazar. Such days are fixed on weekly, fortnightly and monthly basis. Such traders may carry on their business in one locality or at different places on different days. The retailers also hold their shop on important festivals and have roaring business on those days.

(c) Cheaps Jacks : A cheap jack has independent shop in a business locality. Though he keeps a shop, it is not of permanent nature and he may shift his shop the moment he finds that another locality is more profitable.

(d) Street traders : This type of retailers carry on their business in the busy streets or foot-paths of busy town roads.

2. Fixed shop Retailers : These retailers generally retain permanent place of business. Fixed shop retailing may further be classified on the basic of their size of operation as small scale and large scale.

A. Small Scale Retailing

(a) The street stall-holders : The street stall-holders have their stalls in a street where they may find heavy traffic. They exercise much care in selecting the location as the site once selected is more or less permanent. Though the stall-holders handle goods on a very small-scale, they deal in different types of articles like pen, towels, underwear, socks etc.

(b) Second hand goods dealers : They deal in second hand goods or articles like books, clothes etc. They purchase and sell such goods particularly to those customers who cannot afford to buy new goods at higher price. These dealers mainly get their suppliers from public section.

(c) Speciality shops : Goods of a particular variety are sold in such shops. The dealer specialises and deals only in one line of good shops exclusively meant for books, leather goods toys, medicines, readymade etc.

(d) General shops : These shops sell all the item of product required for every day use. The size of such shops is generally decided on the basis of productions they have to serve. These shops claims permanent local customers.

(e) Independent shops : These are small non-integrated retail establishment having a lesser degree of specialisation in their management. The owner himself manages the business. He maintains intimate personal contact with customers. He gets supplies from the whole-salers. These independent stores may be classified into : (i) general stores (ii) single line stores and speciality stores.

(f) Automatic vending machines : Vending machines have assumed importance in recent years. A variety of products are sold through coin operated machine which automatically vend merchandise without the load of any sales assistant. The use and importance of such types of retailing is yet to prove its viability in India.

(g) Discount houses : These are post-war development. The discount houses grew out of the practise of manufactures giving large discount to retailers on certain types of goods. A discount house is a retailing business unit which features consumer durable items like jewellery, household appliances. These house operate on a relatively low make up and a minimum customer service.

(h) Syndicate stores : A syndicate store is in fact an extension of the chain and mail order house but relatively on a small scale. One of the chief characteristic of syndicate stores is that while they offer a variety of merchandise to customer they seldom well-known brands. Most of the merchandise they sell would be of their own. Why they buy unbranded merchandise. Later on, these are under their own brands.

B. Large Scale Retailing

In modern times, several types of large scale retail organisations have sprang up in a bid to eliminate the wholesaler middleman and to get the economies of larger scale operations. Some of the large scale retail organisations are (a) Departmental stores (b) Chain stores or multiple shops (c) M.O.B (d) Hire purchase and instalment (e) Consumer cooperative stores (f) Super bazar and (g) Hyper markets. For the full description of these retail organisation refer to next question on next page.

THE CLASSICAL THEORY OF INTERNATIONAL TRADE-I

INTERNATIONAL BUSINESS

The fundamental task of international trade theories is to explain why nations trade together. The theories also show which goods will be exported and imported and what conditions are necessary for exchange of goods to take place between the countries.

Theories of international trade can be a broadly grouped into two :

(a) Classical theory popularly known as Theory of Comparative Cost and,

(b) Modern Theory.

Classical Theory : Theory of comparative cost

The seeds of the classical theory of international trade were sown by Adam Smith. But today, it is linked with the name of David Ricardo, who gave it classical formulation in his principles of political economy. Prof. Taussing and John Stuart made important additions to it. The theory was further developed and generalised by Alfred Marshall who employed the so called reciprocal demand and supply curves for solving certain problems in international trade.

The basic contention of the theory is that which country will produce those goods for the production of which it is specially the suited on account of its climate, of the qualities of its soil, of its other natural resources of the innate and acquired the capacities of its people and import those goods which it is suited to produce or which it cannot produce at all. It is for these reasons that the classical theory of international trade is also known as the theory of comparative cost since according to the theory what each country will export and what it will import is determined by the comparative difference in labour costs.

This unit deals with the classical theories of trade propounded by Adam Smith and David Ricardo, as also with Prof. Taussing's re-statement of the Recardo's theory in terms of money.

Adam Smith : The law of absolute cost advantage

Smith was the first economist to present in a systematic way the argument that the wealth of a nation would expand most rapidly if the Government would abandoned controls over domestic and foreign economic activities and follow a policy of free trade. In such a situation, according to Adam Smith, each nation would import goods from the cheapest overseas source and would, in turn, export those products in which it has a cost advantage. As, will be seen, considerable efficiency gains arise when each nation specialises in the goods it can produce most cheaply within a system of international division of labour.

ILLUSTRATION

The following hypothetical example illustrates the absolute cost difference.

Smith : Absolute cost advantage (in man-hours per unit of output)

	Rice	Steel
U.S.A	50	40
India	20	80

In the above example, there are only two countries – India and U.S.A. The two commodities are rice and steel. From the cost table, one can see to produce a unit of rice, United States requires 50 man-hours of labour. In India the cost of the same is only 20 man-hours. Rice, thus costs more to produce in the United States than it does in India. However, one unit of steel can be produced in U.S.A. for 40 man-hours but costs 80 man-hours in India. India thus, has an absolute advantage over U.S.A. in the production of rice but U.S.A. enjoys an absolute advantage in the output of steel. As both India and U.S.A. have an absolute advantage in the production of the one commodity, trade between the two countries will benefit both.

India having absolute cost advantage over U.S.A. in the production of rice will concentrate upon the production of rice, producing more of them than it requires for its own needs and exchange the surplus with the United States against steel, in the production of which (steel) India has absolute cost disadvantage. U.S.A., on the other hand, will concentrate upon the production of steel, in which it has absolute cost advantage over India and exchange the same against rice from India in the production of which it is less suited.

What is prudence in the conduct of every private family can scarce be folly in that of a great kingdom. If a foreign country can supply as with a commodity cheaper than we ourselves than make it, better buy it of them with some part of the produce of our own industry, employed a way in which we have some advantage. The increased amount of goods resulting from specialisation constitute the real gain of trade.

David Ricardo : Comparative advantage

Dissatisfied with certain looseness Adam Smith's analysis, David Ricardo developed the principle of comparative advantage of comparative cost as the basis of international trade. Adam Smith has implied that a natural or technical advantage should exist to give each country at least one low cost product it could sell internationally and share in the gains of trade. But what would happen when a country does not have a cost advantage in the production of even one product?

Assumptions of the theory : The classical trade theory of Ricardo rests on seven cornerstone assumptions which are as a follows :

1. There are two countries and two commodities. Ricardo simplified his argument by regarding the number of nations to two and the number of products to two.
2. The labour is the only factor used for producing these goods, i.e., the cost of production consists of labour cost only.
3. Production is subject to constant returns to scale, i.e, cost of production per unit of output does not vary with the level of output.
4. There are no transport costs. In other words, cost of production consists of only production cost.
5. There is perfect competition in all products and factor markets.
6. Free trade does not affect the relative income position of a nation's citizens. The gains of trade must be distributed in such a way as to leave the distribution of income undisturbed.
7. Trade is carried on only by barter.

Given the above set of assumptions the Ricardo explains that the countries engaged in international trade derive specific benefit if they specialise in producing one commodity.

ILLUSTRATION

Ricardo takes into account a situation of the two countries, one has absolute cost advantage and another country has absolute cost disadvantage in producing both the goods. Suppose the following cost conditions for producing cloth and wine prevailed in England and Portugal :

Ricardo : Comparative cost advantage (In man-hours per unit of output)

	Cloth	Wine
Portugal	90	80
England	100	120

In Portugal, a unit of cloth costs 90 man-hours and a unit of wine costs 80; in England a unit of cloth costs 100 man-hours and a unit of wine costs 120. Smith's absolute cost advantage argument cannot explain how trade would take place under these conditions. The cost of producing both the goods is lower in Portugal than in England. Portugal has absolute cost advantage in the production of both the goods–cloth and wine.

To examine how trade can take place in this situation to the benefit of cloth and wine, let us turn to the above arithmetical example.

Suppose there was no trade between the two countries. In the absence of trade, the domestic exchange ratio that can be established in Portugal is 1 unit of wine against 0.88 units of cloth (80/90) and in England 1 unit of wine against 0.88 units of cloth (120/100). Ricardo argues that Portugal will have sufficient inducement to engage in trade if 1 unit of wine commands a little more 0.88 units of cloth. For England, there will be inducement to enter into trade if a little less than 1.2 units of cloth is given for 1 unit of wine. In order to derive this benefit, both the countries should specialise in the production of one commodity. The principle of specialisation is "Comparative Cost Difference."

The localisation of production as between different countries follows the principle of comparative cost. Each country will tend to specialise in the production of the commodities in which its labour costs are comparatively the lowest. After specialisation, total production of wine in Portugal is 2.125 units and total production of cloth in England is 2.2 units. The total production of both the commodities, after specialisation is increased.

However, the individual benefits depend upon the establishment of an actual international exchange ratio. Ricardo assumes that the exchange ratio can be established as 1 unit of wine against 1 unit of cloth. In this case, for every 100 labour-hours which England sends to Portugal embodied in the form of commodity cloth, she receives 1 unit of wine, which in the absence of international trade, would have costed her 120 labour-hours produce for herself. Portugal, on the other hand, obtains 1 unit of cloth at the cost of 80 labour-hours, which would have otherwise costed her 90 labour-hours in the absence of trade. Thus, Ricardo includes that the basis of international trade is the comparative cost advantage and the result of international trade is the specialisation in production with the minimum cost.

Conclusion

It is clear, that the doctrine of 'comparative cost' marks a real advance in Adam Smith's statement of the basis of international trade. Comparative cost doctrine is more general, as it explains situations not covered by Smith's theory and includes the latter as a special case, one where a country's comparative advantage is also an absolute advantage.

Although Ricardo's principle gives a more convincing and adequate proof of the benefits of trade, it left the actual ratios of international exchange and international prices undermined. He failed to further and establish the precise terms of the profitable exchange. He focused exclusively upon the supply or cost side of international trade and paid no attention to the demand side.

Prof. Taussing : Comparative cost expressed in money

One of the shortcomings of Ricardo's theory of comparative cost is that the money and prices are not a part of the comparative cost model. In the above example, Portugal and England simply barter units of cloth and wine. In the modern economy, which practices division of labour, goods are not exchanged directly against other goods but bought with money. The flow of international trade is determined directly by absolute difference in money prices and not by comparative difference in labour costs as assumed by Ricardo. Prof. Taussing, therefore has restated the theory in terms of money prices and has shown that the essentials of the model remains unchanged with the introduction of money. Comparative differences in the money cost, instead of Ricardo's comparative labour cost difference, the basis of the trade.

ILLUSTRATION

The arithmetical example given by Prof. Taussing is as under :

In the United States :

10 days of labour produce 20 units of wheat.

10 days of labour produce 20 units of linen.

In Germany :

10 days of labour produce 10 units of wheat.

10 days of labour produce 15 unit of linen.

From the above it is clear that the United States has an absolute advantage in both of branches of production but a comparative advantage in wheat. Germany has an absolute advantage in both wheat and linen but her comparative disadvantage is less in the case of linen. Hence the United States will specialise in the wheat and Germany in linen.

Stated in money terms, the position is as follows :

Country	Daily wage $	Total wage $	Production of 10 days of labour	Money cost
U.S.A.	1.5	15	20 units of wheat	0.75
U.S.A.	1.5	15	20 units of linen	0.75
Germany	1.0	10	10 units of wheat	1.00
Germany	1.0	10	10 units of linen	0.66

The price of wheat in the United States is lower than in Germany, so that the wheat will be exported from U.S.A. to Germany. The price of linen is lower in Germany than in U.S.A., so that linen will be exported from Germany. Even though the money wage rate has been arbitrarily chosen, it can be shown that ratio of money wages between the two countries must always lie between an upper and a lower limit, and it is only the choice of a ratio within these limits which is arbitrary. Let us suppose that the daily wage in U.S.A. cannot exceed $ 2.00, it cannot be more than double German wage because the cost advantage of the U.S.A. in wheat is 20 to 10. Suppose the American wages were to rise to $2.00. The position would then be as under :

As can be seen, with the rise in U.S. wage rate to $2.00 the U.S. price per unit of both wheat and linen would be $1.00. U.S.A. will no longer export as the money cost of production of the unit of wheat is the same in both the countries, yet linen would continue to be imported as it is cheaper to import than to produce domestically.

Country	Daily wage $	Total wage $	Production of 10 days of labour	Money cost = price per unit
U.S.A.	2.00	20	20 units of wheat	1.00
U.S.A.	2.00	20	20 units of linen	1.00
Germany	1.00	10	10 units of wheat	1.00
Germany	1.00	10	10 units of linen	0.66

Her balance of payment would turn adverse, resulting in the gold outflow from U.S.A. as she has to make payments for linen in term of gold. On the other hand, there is no corresponding payments in gold for U.S.A. as she exports nothing. The result would be net outflow of gold from U.S.A. With the outflow of gold, money, supply prices and wages would have to fall in U.S.A. (under gold standard, the supply of money bears a fixed relation to supply of gold).

Similarly, it can be shown that the daily wage in the United States cannot be lower than $ 1.33 which is fixed by the cost advantage of the U.S. in linen, *viz.*, 20 to 15. If the American wage rate were to follow below $1.33 the German wage being by hypothesis $1.00 the situation would be as shown in the table below :

Country	Daily wage $	Total wage $	Production of 10 days of labour	Money cost = price per unit
U.S.A.	1.33	13.3	20 units of wheat	0.66
U.S.A.	1.33	13.3	20 units of linen	0.66
Germany	1.00	10	10 units of wheat	1.00
Germany	1.00	10	15 units of linen	0.66

With the U.S. wage rate falling to $1.33, it would no longer be profitable for Germany to export linen as the money cost of producing linen is then the same in both the countries. Yet, she would import wheat, the result being, the Germany's balance of payments would become adverse. There will be gold outflow from Germany into U.S.A. and the supply of money, prices and wages would again rise in U.S.A. and fall in Germany.

Conclusion

Though Taussing has been successful in attempting to re-state the theory of comparative cost in terms of money cost and in showing that the principle of comparative cost is steel adhered to, it suffers from the same weakness as that of Ricardo's, namely, its failure to show the exact equilibrium the international exchange ratio. Just as the Ricardian theory only sets the upper, lower limits between which the actual international exchange ratio must lie at any time. The credit goes to J.S. Mill for the making this important addition to the theory of comparative cost. Mill's theory is discussed in the following chapter.

Classical Trade Theory : A Critique

Perhaps the most celebrated doctrine of the classical economics is the theory of comparative cost of David Ricardo.

Despite the elegance and simplicity Ricardo's model in the demonstrating the welfare proposition that trade is beneficial to who engaged in it, his theory of comparative advantage has come in for serious criticisms on the various counts. We may list some of these criticisms as follows :

(a) The Assumption of Labour Cost : The most serious attack on Ricardo is that he tied his theory of trade to labour cost alone. In essence, he relied on the labour theory of value which stated that the value of goods were determined by their labour content. However, goods are not produced by labour alone but by a combination of all factors of production. Hence critics assert that it is not labour cost but money cost alone that can serve as the basis of comparison.

(b) The Assumption of Constant Cost : As the mentioned exposition of the doctrine of the comparative costs has assumed that the values of commodities produced within a country are proporuional to their labour time cost. In other words, the doctrine of comparative cost depends upon the real cost concept. The serious difficulty that arises from this dependence is that the theory can analyse the situation of trade only under the condition of constant cost of production. Under constant cost, a country does not both import and produce for itself any commodity. There is complete specialisation which leads to larg-scale production. Prof. Jacob Viner has claimed either that the doctrine of comparative cost must be rejected because of its the dependence on real cost of value or else that it must be re-stated in terms of modern value theory without reference to real cost.

To the extent that the internal markets are not perfectly competitive and labour and capital are not completely mobile, the full benefit of free trade will not be realised. In addition, we must be concerned about those workers who may trap in poverty and unemployment by the decline of their industry in the face of foreign competition.

(c) Non-Consideration of Demand Factor : Ricardo's theory of comparative advantage was only a theory on the supply side of the international trade, it took no account of demand. This important addition was made by J.S. Mill and further elaborated by Alfred Marshall.

(d) Absence of Transport Costs : Ricardo took no account in his theory of the effects of a transport costs on prices. In the real world, transport costs play an important part in determining the prices of internationally traded commodities. Therefore, account should be taken of their effect when the considering theory of trade.

(e) Absence of Technological Changes : Another limitation of the Ricardian model is his assumption that there is no technological change or economic development and therefore world economy is static.

In Ricardo's abstract world, no inventor event discovers a new product or even discovers a more effective way of producing the wine and cloth. There is no economic development and the economy is static. According to Ricardo, a nation cannot experience a change in its comparative advantage and thereby shift the basis of trade. England will continue produce cloth and Portugal wine until the end of time.

Double Model System : Ricardo dealt with only a two country-two commodity model. The theory is therefore restrictive in its operation. In actual practice, international trade is done among various countries with many commodities. Therefore, Haberler has generalised the theory of comparative cost by applying it to more than two goods, which is discussed in the Appendix 'A'.

THE CLASSICAL THEORY OF INTERNATIONAL TRADE-II

Mill's Theory of Reciprocal Demand

J.S. Mill proceeds to examine question of international values or the ratios at which the commodities would be exchanged for each other. As seen in the previous unit, one of weaknesses of Ricardo's theory of comparative cost was its failure to explain the exact terms on which the commodities would be traded between the countries. In the words of J.S. Mill the "inclination and circumstances of the consumers on both sides would determine where between the two international cost ratios, the terms of trade will be."

ILLUSTRATION

Instead of taking the output of each commodity in two countries with the given labour cost difference, Mill assumes given almost of labour in each country with different labours of output. Thus, his formulation runs in terms of comparative effectiveness of labour as contrasted with Ricardo's comparative labour cost.

Ricardo's illustration, in terms of Mill's formulation would be like this :

Input of labour (days)	Country	Wine (casks)	Output of cloth (metres)
300	Portugal	100	75
300	England	50	60

For the same input of labour, Portugal and England can quite produce different outputs of wine and cloth. Portugal has an absolute advantage in the production of both commodities but it has a clear the comparative advantage in wine. England has least comparative disadvantage in cloth. It is the comparative advantage that indicates the lines of profitable specialisation if trade develops.

Expressed in general terms, the principle of comparative effectiveness can be stated as follows : If a_1 and b_1 are the levels of output for the given amount of labour in production of commodities 'A' and 'B' respectively in country I and a_2 and b_2 the corresponding labour output ratios for country II, then country I will export commodity 'A' and import commodity 'B' if :

$$\frac{a_1}{b_1} > \frac{a_2}{b_2}$$

Reciprocal Demand

Turning to the question of what factors determine the terms of trade within the range of

Wine	Cloth
100	75+
	120–

price ratio as given above, Mill's answer is that it is the reciprocal demand that will determine the actual exchange ratio. Reciprocal demand means the relative strength of demand of the two countries for each other's products in terms of the own product.

Turning to our example, let suppose that trade between Portugal and England is opened on terms of 100 casks of wine for 95 metres of cloth. If, at this internal price, England's demands for wine is in multiples of 100 casks of wine say, 1,000 and Portugal's demand is also a similar multiple of 95 metres of cloth, say 950 there would be equilibrium of reciprocal demand with each country export just paying for its imports.

Suppose at the same price of 100W/95C England desired to consume only $8 \times 100 = 800$ casks of wine, it is clear that at the exchange ratio of 100W/95C, 8000 casks of wine would not be sufficient to pay for Portugal's imports of 950 metres of cloth.

Portugal could obtain at 100W/95C only 8 × 95 or 760 metres of cloths to obtain 190 additional metres of cloth to Portugal's buyers need. Suppose Portugal offers slightly more than 100, say 108 casks of wine for 95 metres of cloth or 100 casks of wine for 87.5 metres of cloths. At this more favourable price to England, England would have to accept more wine, say 9 × 100 casks or 900 in all. But with cloth now higher in price for Portugal, its buyers would take less, perhaps 9 × 87.5 or 787.50 metres of cloth. Equilibrium would now be established since at the new price of 100W/87.5 C, Portugal's wines exports of 900 casks just pay for England's cloth exports of 787.50 metres. At this point, the sacrifice made by a country, in the terms of exports is equal to the gain of that country, in term of imports.

Conclusion

To Conclude :

1. The possible range of better terms is given by the respective domestic terms of trade as set by comparative efficiency in such country.
2. Within this range, the actual terms depend on each country's demand for the other country's produce and
3. Only those terms of trade will stable at which the exports offered by each country just suffice to pay for the imports it desires.

Marshall's Theory of Offer Curves

J.S. Mills theory of reciprocal demand fails to explain the exact equilibrium position of international exchange ratio. Marshall has explained this position with the help of offer-curves. The offer-curve is a typical demand curve, which denotes the amount of a commodity the country is willing to offer for a given amount of some other commodity. In other words, the offer-curve denotes the demand of one commodity in terms of the supply of another commodity.

Derivation of offer curve : For deriving the offer curve, Marshall has applied the same principle which he applies in deriving the demand curve in the internal economy. The demand curve in the internal economy indicates that more is demanded at a lower price because marginal utility of the commodity diminishes as more of the same commodity is available and therefore the consumer is ready to consume more of it only at the lower price. In case of offer-curves, the country is ready to offer more of a commodity in which it has the specialised until more of the other commodity is not available. Once the supply of the other commodity is increased, the offer of a commodity from a trading country increases less than proportionately.

Price (Rs)	Quantity of oil (barrels)	Expenditure (Rs)
70	9	0
60	100	600
50	200	1000
40	300	1200
30	400	1200
20	500	1000
10	600	600

Before we derive an offer-curve let as first recapitulate a standard demand curve diagram. The horizontal axis-OX is labelled quantity and the vertical axis-OY is called the price axis. The demand curve DD slopes downwards from left to right indicating inverse relationship between price and quantity demanded.

This figure shows Indian demands for oil in barrels at varying rupee prices.

From the above demand curve for oil one can derive an expenditure curve OE for oil as shown in this figure. In this figure horizontal axis OX shows the quantity of oil and vertical axis OY shows the total expenditure.

The quantity of oil demanded by India will now be related to its money value expressed in Indian rupees but to the quantity of cotton India must exchange in export.

At point L on the offer curve OC, India demands 100 barrels of oil and in turn is willing to offer 200 bales of cotton. The terms at L is 2 bales to 1 barrel i.e., 2 : 1. At point M, India is willing to offer 300 bales of cotton in exchange of 200 barrels, *i.e.,* 1.5 : 1. At point N India is willing to offer 400 bales

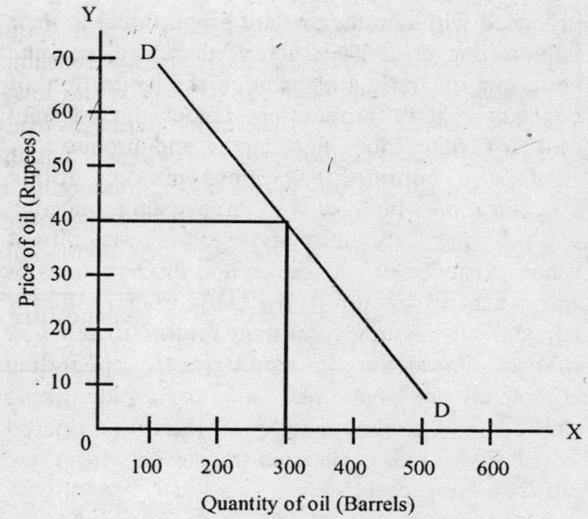

Fig. India's demand curve for oil

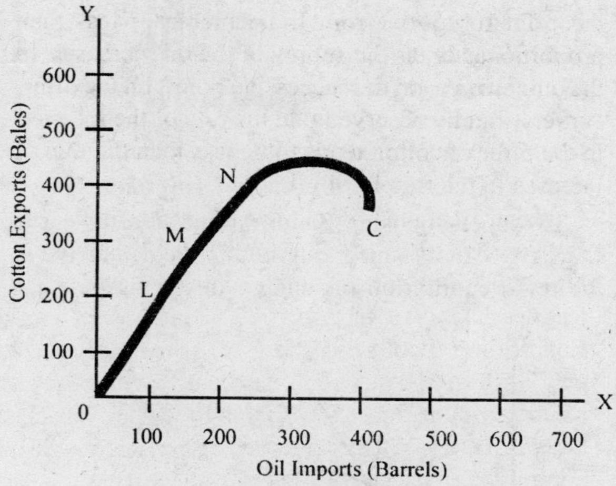

Fig. India's cotton-oil offer-curve

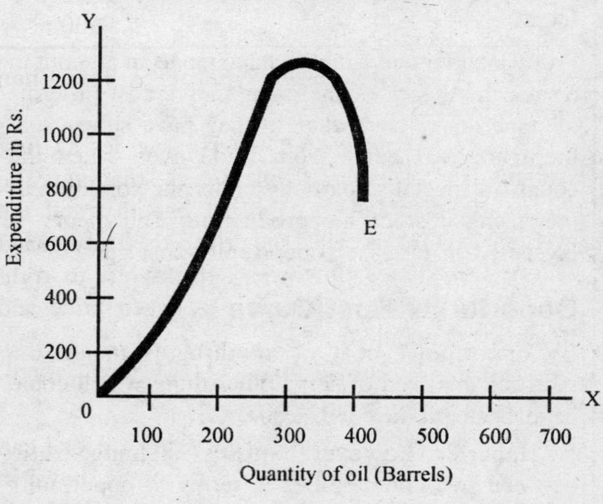

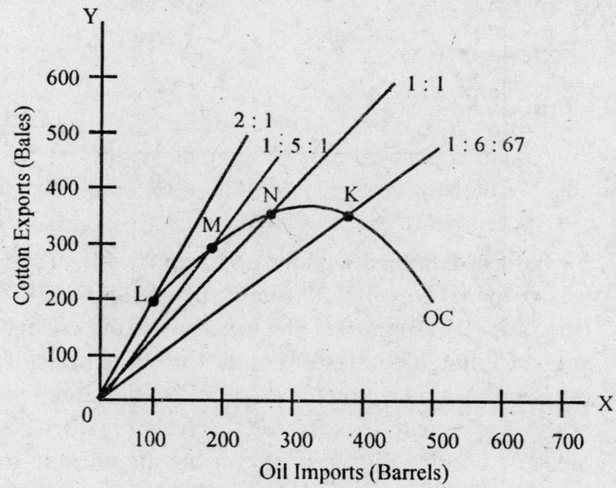

of cotton only if 400 barrels of oil is offered by her trading partners. Here terms of trade is 1:1.

The shift in the terms of trade, from 2 bales of cotton to 1 barrel of oil to 1 bale of cotton to 1 barrel of oil, is because at point L India experiences a relative scarcity of cotton and hence, the marginal utility of cotton for India increases. On the other hand, the marginal utility of oil decreases, as more of it is acquired.

Terms of trade lines may now be add to show the connection between cotton ; oil exchange ratio and offer curve of India OC. This is shown in this Fig :

Each line from the origin indicates particular terms of trade, the ratio along any given terms of trade line is constant.

At M the price of a barrel of oil is 1.5 bales of cotton and India increases her cotton exports from 200 to 300 bales of the cotton for which she receives 200 barrels of oil in return. At N the price is 1 bale of cotton per barrel, exports and imports equal 400. At K exports are lower in quantity than imports, viz, 360 and 600 respectively.

Thus it can be seen that the slope of the offer curve is increasing from a left to right indicating that the offer to cotton from India increases less than proportionately, as the supply of the oil increases. In the other words, on the successive points on the offer-curve, it can be observed that the rate of the increase in the offer of cotton tends to be less than the rate of increase in the supply of oil.

By super-imposing Saudi Arabia's offer curve OCSA ON India's offer-curve OC_1 we can arrive at the trade equilibrium as shown in the figure.

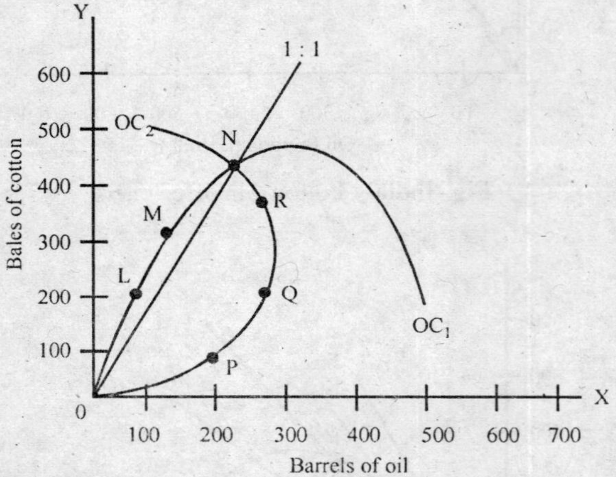

India is delighted with the opportunity. Infact she was prepared to offer 200 bales of cotton for 100 barrels of oil or supposing that India proposing trading at L, offering 200 bales of cotton for 100 barrels of oil, Saudi Arabia would happily yield to the situation as she was prepared to offer 200 barrels of oil for 100 bales of cotton. Similarly it can be shown that at points M and Q one country's demands are more than satisfied by the supply response of the other. At point R on Saudi Arabia's offer-curve and N of India's offer curve, however the demand and the supply elements are in full equilibrium in both the countries. Beyond R both become the reluctant to export more of their own product because of the unfavourable terms sought by the other.

RESTATEMENT OF THE THEORY OF COMPARATIVE COST IN TERM OF OPPORTUNITY COST

The Ricardian doctrine of comparative cost is based on the labour theory of value of commodities produced within a country are proportional to their labour time cost. The theory, therefore, can the situation of trade only under the condition of constant cost of production. Under the constant cost, a country does not import and produce for itself any commodity. There is a complete specialisation which leads to large-scale production and it is very difficult to envisage the possibility of a non-existence of economies and diseconomics of large-scale production. However, theory conveniently assumes constant returns to scale so that it can allow the countries to specialise completely and obtain real gains from trade. In the process the theory has completely neglected possibility of real gains from trade even when there are increasing costs.

International Trade Under Increasing Cost

Prof. Haberler and Liontief have made an attempt to restate the theory of the comparative cost in terms of opportunity cost wherein they have shown that there are real gains from trade even when the countries specialise partially under the condition of increasing cost of the production. The theory is presented in terms of opportunity cost curves.

Opportunity Cost Curve

By opportunity cost of anything is meant the sacrifice involved of some other thing which could have been produced instead.

Haberler, however exposes exchange ratio between two commodities in terms of opportunity costs which may expressed in the form of production or transformation curve. Haberler derives a country's opportunity cost curve (or transformation curve) under the following assumption.

(a) There is perfect competition in all factors and commodity markets.
(b) Price of every commodity equals the marginal cost of production of that commodity.
(c) The economy is at full employment equilibrium.
(d) Supply of factors is fixed.
(e) Given the technology good from given resources are produced most efficiently.

Given the production possibilities of two commodities of a given resource under the condition of increasing cost, opportunity cost curve will be concave towards the origin as shown in this figure :

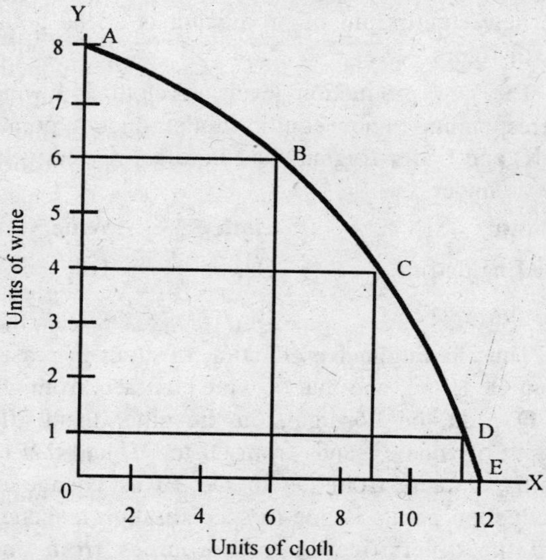

Fig. Opportunity cost curve under Increasing cost

In this figure units of cloth are measured on the horizontal axis OX and units of wine on the vertical axis OY. The curve AE is the opportunity cost curve and shows that with the given resource in this condition a country, say England, can produce either maximum of OA(8) units of wine alone or OE(12) units of cloth alone, or various alternative combinations of units of cloth and wine such as 6 units of cloth, 9 units of cloth and 4 units of wine. The curve AE denotes how much of one commodity is to be scarificed for getting a unit more of other commodity. The concavity of opportunity cost curve in this figure shows that the law of the increasing cost is operating in the production of both the commodities. This implies that as the production of wine is substituted for that of cloth the opportunity cost of wine in terms of cloth will go on increasing.

Pre-trade Situation : England

Given the internal demand condition in England, the domestic price ratio is shown by the price line MM in this figure. The equilibrium domestic production of the two commodities in the absence of internal trade will take place at K the point of tangency between the given domestic price line MM and transformation curve AE and the highest indifference curve MM as shown in this figure.

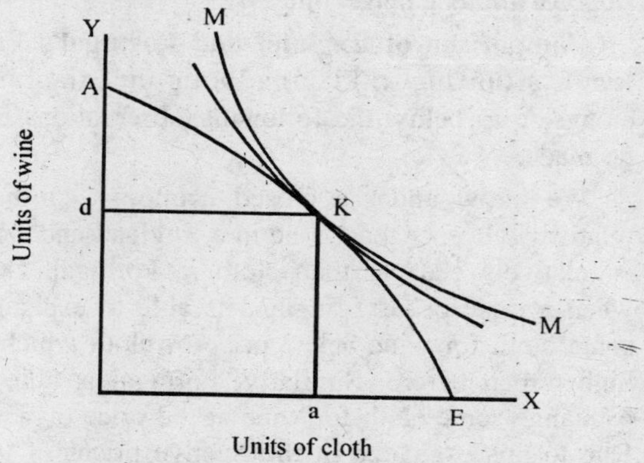

Fig. Pre-trade equilibrium of England

The curve MM is the consumption indifference curve for England. An indifference curve is defined in the theory of value, as the curve representing an indefinite point of alternative combination of two goods yielding the same amount of satisfaction to the consumer. The consumption indifference curve for a country is a collection commodity combinations between which the consumer together are different.

Pre-trade Situation : Portugal

For Portugal given the existing stock of its resources and internal demand conditions for wine and cloth the production and consumption of both the commodities, in the absence of trade would be as shown in this figure :

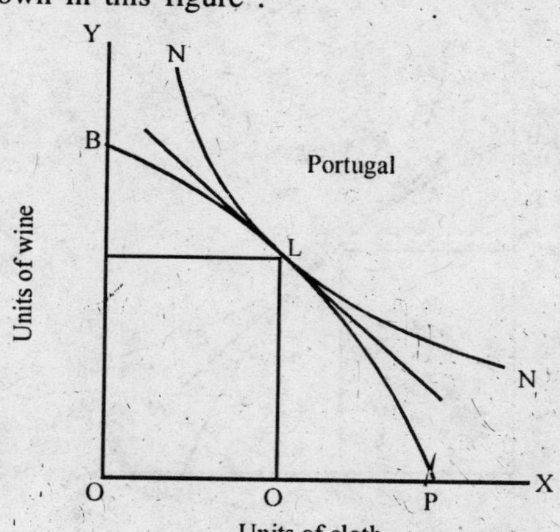

In the case of Portugal equilibrium at Point L, with the units of wine and OE units of cloth being consumed and produced at the relative price by the slope of the exchange line NN.

Comparison of England and Portugal's Pre-trade situation : Placing both the diagrams alongside as below the following observations can be made.

We know under a closed economy, cloth is relatively cheaper than wine in a England and wine is relatively cheaper than cloth in Portugal. Now when a trade occurs, England is able to exchange some cloth for wine at the price of cloth which is higher than before. Similarly, Portugal is able to exchange some cloth for wine at the price of wine. Due to this exchange in the relative prices of two goods, wine and cloth producers in Portugal tend to specialise in wine making and those in England in cloth.

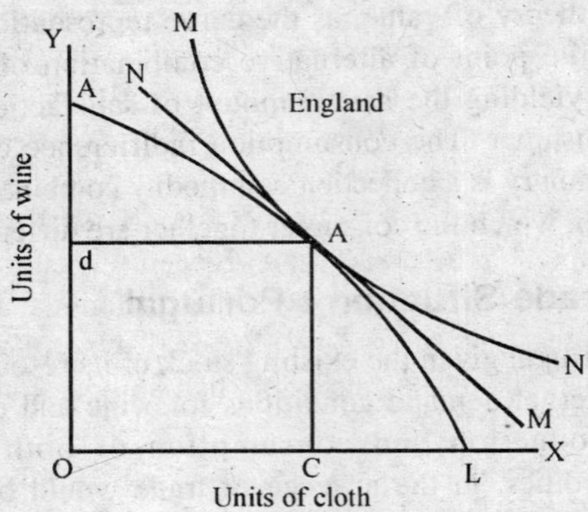

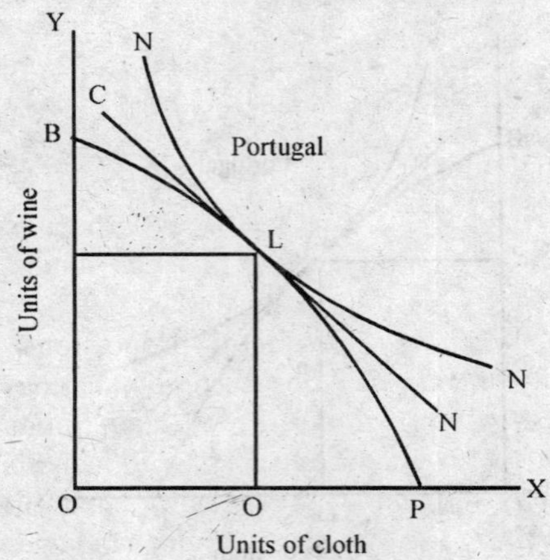

Post-trade Production : England and Portugal

After trade, new equilibrium of the production in England's case takes place at K in figure. In Portugal the new equilibrium of production is at the point L_1, in figure.

The new production levels of cloth and wine corresponding to new equilibrium production points of K^1 and L^1 for England and Portugal respectively are as under :

Country	Cloth	Wine
For England	Oc_1	Od_1
For Portugal	Oe_1	Of_1

Thus in England production of cloth increases from Oc to Oc_1 and that of wine contracts from Od to Od_1. In the Portugal, on the other hand, the output of wine expands from Of to Of_1 and that of cloth contracts from Oe to Oe_1. This change in production points is due to specialisation tendency and the diversification of resources from one industry to another. Under specialisation, each country produces more of the good due to increased efficiency. Similarly, in the case of Portugal, ff_1 expansion of wine is more than the contraction of cloth by ee_1.

Post-trade Consumption : England and Portugal

On account of the increased efficiency in the exportables of England and Portugal due to trade, both countries are able to consume more and more and move on to a higher indifference curve and before. In the case of England, the new consumption is denoted by L^2 in figure.

The new levels of consumption of cloth and wine represented by the new consumption equilibrium points K^2 and L^2 for England and Portugal respectively are as follows :

Country	Cloth	Wine
England	Oc_2 units	Od_2 units
Portugal	Oe_2 units	Of_2 units

England consumes dd_2 more of wine against cc_2 decline in the consumption of cloth ($dd_2 > cc_2$). Likewise after trade Portugal consumes ee_2 more of cloth against ff_1 decline in the consumption of wine ($ee_2 > ff_2$). Thus both the countries gain in consumption and enjoy and increased welfare which is depicted in the diagrams by a movement on to the higher in difference curve after opening of trade between both the countries.

MODERN THEORY OF INTERNATIONAL TRADE

Introduction

An alternative approach to explaining the pattern of international trade was developed by Eli Heckscher and Bertil Ohlin.

This approach breaks away from the Ricardian model and works in terms of an analytical form of work which is in striking contract to the classical theory. As we have seen, the Ricardian model assumes one factor thereby makes the factor supply irrelevant in determining the trade pattern. On the other hand, Heckscher-Ohlin model explains trade advantages in terms of the three factors of neo-classical production theory, labour and capital and makes international difference in factor endowments the crucial and sale factor determining comparative advantages.

Secondly, whereas the former attributes to international differences in production functions the explanation of comparative advantage, the latter explicitly postulates the international identity of production function. The Heckscher-Ohlin theory is also different from the Ricardin analysis in defining cost at the total money prices of factor inputs, rather than the outmoded labour theory of value.

By laying great stress on the notion that mutually interdependant product and factor markets and price guided trade the Heckscher-Ohlin theory extended the discussion for beyond the barter model of Ricardo.

Heckscher-Ohlin Theory

It should be remembered at the cost that the Heckscher-Ohlin theory does not invalidate, the classical theory of comparative cost is rather powerfully supplements in since it also accepts comparative advantage as the basic of international trade. According to the classical theory the basis of trade lay in the fact that the production function for a given commodity varied from one country to another, and the extent of this variation differed for various goods. But classical theory made little attempt to explain the causes of such comparative cost difference. Heckscher and Ohlin's alternative formulation of comparative cost doctrine attempted to explain why comparative cost difference exist internationally. Heckscher and Ohlin's theory thus enquires more fundamentally into the climate basis of trade.

Basis of Trade

Heckscher and Ohlin see the immediate basis of international trade not in the difference in the comparative costs of producing a commodity between the countries (which is the case with Ricardo and others) but in the difference in the final price of a commodity between countries. Then they attribute this difference in the final price of a commodity as between countries to the difference in the comparative cost of production of that commodity. Thereafter they proceed to examine the root causes which produces this difference in the comparative costs. What follows in their explanations to the causes of such comparative cost difference.

It was Heckscher who originated the idea that though comparative cost difference is the basis of international trade. The root causes in the conditions which produce this difference. The difference is comparative costs advantage occurs because of (i) the difference in relative scarcity of factor of production in the two countries and (ii) the input of different factor proportions required in the production function of different commodities. This thought was further elaborated by Prof. Ohlin. called his theory the factor proportions factor intensity theory. He observed that nations have different internal mixtures of land, labour and capital. Some countries such as United States in their early years had a great deal of land relative to labour and capital. China and India had huge labour resources, less land and very little capital. Since the factor of production are unevenly distributed among nations, factor proportion or factor inducement is said to be different.

Further, different amounts of land, labour and capital are required to produce different goods. Agricultural products such as wheat usually require much land, textiles much labour and machine tools and other industrial products much capital. In shorts different products have different factor intensities.

Thus it was the difference in factor intensities in the production function of goods alongwith actual difference in relative factor endowments of the countries (*i.e.,* one country might possess a lot of land relative to other factor) which explained the international difference in comparative costs of productions. A country can produce a commodity more cheaply by matching its abundant factor with the factor intensity of the commodity because when a nation has relatively more a particular factor, the costs of that factor to a producer will be comparatively lower. The lower the price of the major input the greater is the price advantage the producer will have in the trade.

In nut-shell, this is the basic idea lying behind the Heckscher Ohlin theory of commodity trade which can be stated thus, a country will specialise in the production and exports of goods whose production requires a relatively large amounts (relative to other factor of production) of the factor with which the country is relatively will endowed (relative to other factors).

It is a known facts that nations are very differently endowed with facilities for the productions of various goods as they are differently supplied with the productive factor. In country A the supply of the factor capital may be abundant but labour may be scarce. In the B the reverse may be the case. In country A the costs of producing capital intensive goods may be cheaper due to the abundant availability of capital at the resulant lower interest rate. On the other hand, the costs of producing labour intensive goods may be costlier because of the relative scarcity of labour and the resulting higher wage rate.

In country B, on the other hand, because of her abundant availability of labour, wage rate and hence the costs of production labour-intensive goods may be lower. Capital-intensive goods may be costiler due to higher interest rate resulting from the scarce availability of capital. Naturally, country A will possess a comparative costs advantage in the production of goods which employ more of the factor that the relatively abundant and so cheap *viz.*, capital-intensive goods. Country B will possess a comparative costs advantage in the productions of goods which employ more of the factor that the relatively abundant there namely labour-intensive goods country D will specialise in the production and exports of goods which employ more of its relatively abundant and less of its relatively scant factor (such as machines) and will import those goods (such as rice) which call for factor in the reverse proportion. The reverse will hold good for country B.

This means that when a country specialises in the production and exports of the commodities which for their production require more of the factor which are abundantly and hence cheaply available to her, she indirectly exports her abundant and cheap factor embodied in the forms of goods. On the other hand, when she imports commodities which for their production require more of the factor which are only scantily available to her and hence costly, she in turn, imports scarce factors embodied in the form of goods. Thus, indirectly factors in abundant supply are exported and factors in scarce supply and imported by a country.

ILLUSTRATION

In support of his factor-proportion theory of international trade Ohlin gives an illustration of trade between Australia and England. Australia has abundant supply of agricultural land but a scanty population. Land is cheap and wages are high in comparison with England. She therefore specialises in the production of wheat and wool and trades the same against the manufacturers of England, which require large quantities of labour and capital like coal and iron which are scantly available in Australia. Things are contrary with England. When

Australia exports wheat, wool, etc., she is indirectly exporting factors in abundant supply there, namely land and when she imports manufacturers she indirectly impacts factors in scant supply, *viz.*, the capital and labour. Similarly, when the England exports manufacturers, she the indirectly exports capital and the labour and imports land via wheat, and wool.

We shall now proceed to examine the theory of Heckscher and Ohlin.

Assumption of Theory : The basic model is constructed from a number of the explicit and implicit assumptions using "double" model system.

1. Perfect competition exists in both the product and factor markets in the each country.
2. Factor mobility within a country is complete *i.e.*, perfect mobility of factors of production within a country but a factor mobility between the countries is non-existent.
3. Factors are identical qualitatively in both the countries.
4. Factors supply in each country are fixed and fully employed.
5. Trade is free and costlier *i.e.*, no barriers to trade of any sort and no costs of transport.
6. The physical amounts of each productive factor possessed by countries are different.
7. Techniques of production identical to goods are the same in both the countries. The same amount of factor inputs applied to the production of a given commodity will yield exactly the same output in both the countries.
8. Constant returns to scale applies to the production function for the goods.

Ohlin argues that once we know from assumption 6 above what the relative factor endowments are for each country. We can infer from this what the relative factor price structures will be for each country. A country endowed with relatively more labour and less capital will have a factor price structure such that the capital will be more expensive relative to the labour.

In considering the Heckscher-Ohlin model one must constantly think in terms of relative quantities. We cannot say simply because one country say, X has greater physical amount of one factor more than another country Y that the country X is relatively well endowed of each country. Thus only if the ratio $\frac{\text{Labour}}{\text{Capital}}$ in country X is greater than the $\frac{\text{Labour}}{\text{Capital}}$ ratio is country Y, we can say that country X is relatively well endowed with labour.

Thus,

(L/K) X may be 10 units/5 units = 2

(L/K) Y may be 8 units/2 units = 4

where L stands for labour, K for the capital, X and Y for two countries.

In this example, though country Y, possesses a smaller absolute amount of a labour than country X is nevertheless relatively well endowed with labour.

Let us now consider how Ohlin derives from his assumption the basis of their theory of international trade.

According to Ohlin, the factor price structure will be the same in both the countries, only if the relative factor endowments are indentical, *i.e.*, only if (L/K) in country X = (L/K) in country Y. Otherwise factor price structure will differ between countries and so each country will its factors in a differing proportions, the labour abundant country using labour-intensive production methods, their capital abundant country using capital-intensive production methods.

Thus in this figure, at any given factor price ratio, commodity A will always be relatively labour-intensive in production relative to commodity B and B will always be capital-intensive relative to A. For, a unit of commodity A requires O_1 of factor labour whereas a unit of commodity of B requires only OL, of the factor labour which is less than OL on the other hand, a unit of commodity good B requires only OL, O+ the factorlabour which is less than OL. On the other hand, a unit Of commodity good B requires Oc, units of factor capital. The more than Oc units of factor capital the required for production of one the unit of commodity A. It should however be remembered that a commodity can only be judged to be capital or (labour-intensive relative to the production requirements of another commodity at the same factor price ratio.)

Now, according to the law of the comparative advantage trade will occur only if commodity prices differ internationally that is the price of A relative to the price of B in country Y. Given the perfect competition assumption in both factor and product markets, this is the same thing saying the cost of producing A relative to the cost of producing B in country Y.

Suppose in our two countries two goods, two factors model country X is relatively more endowed with capital and that for all factor price ratio commodity B is a relatively capital-intensive in production. According to Ohlin, since country X is capital abundant the price of capital relative to the price of labour will be low. It follows, therefore that the country X will be able to produce commodity A relatively cheaply. Therefore, the price ratio between goods A and B will differ between the two countries and would take place, each country, exporting the goods in whose production a relatively large amount of its relatively abundant factor is required.

Appendix B contains a geometric the treatment of the Heckscher-Ohlin model.

Superiority of Heckscher-Ohlin theory over the classical theory of comparative cost.

1. General Equilibrium Analysis : In the determination of the pattern of trade the Ricardian theory of comparative cost focused exclusively on the supply side by stating that it is the difference in the original cost of production of commodity that leads to specialisation and hence international trade. Their Ricardian theory, therefore is one-sided as it ignored the demand factors in the determination of the pattern of international trade and specialisation. Heckscher-Ohlin theory overcomes this weak new of the Ricardian theory. According to Heckscher-Ohlin though the ultimate cause of trade is the difference in the costs of producing identical, goods among countries, the immediate basis of the international trade is the difference in the final price of a commodity as between countries. By combining the demand and supply elements. Heckscher-Ohlin have brought about an integration between the theory of value, *i.e.*, the theory of pricing and the theory of international trade.

Thus the modern theory of international trade is an improvement over the Ricardian theory in that it is based on the general equilibrium analysis where the demand and supply aspects are brought to the fore in the determination of the basis of international trade. It is for this reason that the modern theory of international trade is also known as the General Equilibrium Theory.

2. Enquiry into the Ultimate Cause of Trade : Secondly the theory inquires more the fundamental into the ultimate cause of trade. The classical comparative theory was not able to provide the satisfactory answer to the question of why after all, is there a difference in comparative cost of producing the commodities between countries. The Heckscher-Ohlin model provides the complete answer to this question.

3. No Need for a Separate Theory of the International Trade : Thirdly Heckscher and Ohlin theory of international trade also does away with the need for the separate theory of international trade.

As we have seen, Ricardo's analysis was conducted in terms of two countries-two commodities situation only at one factor input-labour time. This input was more efficient in one country than another with the result that wages to be higher in the more efficient country.

However, the disparity in the wage level between the two countries would not be igroned out by the movements of labour from the less highly paid to the more highly paid country. Since, Ricardo argues that factors of production, though not completely immobile were exceedingly immobile between countries as compared with movement within a country and that between countries is the basis of Ricardo's differentiation between international and inter-regional trade.

According to Ohlin, therefore international trade is only a special case of inter-regional trade. There are no fundamental difference but only a quantitative difference between inter-regional and international trade. Different regions within the same country have different factor endowments just as there are differences in the factor endowments between countries. Hence each region is best equipped to produce the goods that require a large proportion of the factors relatively abundant and it is least fit to produce goods which require a large proportion of factors available to it in small quantities or not at all. Thus, the ability of different regions to produce different goods differ because of difference in factor endowment. This argument was extended to provide the explanation for the difference in comparative costs of producing commodity between different countries by Heckscher.

The ultimate basis of both inter-regional and international trade is their difference in the comparative cost of producing identical commodities.

Criticism of Heckscher-Ohlin Theory

As we have seen before, Heckscher and Ohlin model is based on number of the highly simplified and realistic assumption and it is precisely this assumption which have been attacked by the critics. Criticism levelled against the theory are as follow:

1. Factor identity : The theory assumes that factors are identical qualitatively in both the countries and that these factors are capable of being measured in order to calculate factor-endowment ratios.

In the real world of course, it is obvious that : (a) Factors are not identical in quality between countries and (b) more than one type of each factor exists. The problems of measurements and comparison would arise in real world.

2. Correlation between Factor Availability and Factor Price : Ohlin argued that relative factor price would reflect the exactly relative factor endowments. This means a country possessing relatively abundant capital will have a factor price structure such that capital will be cheap compared to labour. He asserts that once the relative physical quantities of each productive factor endowments in both the countries are known, the relative factor price structure for each country can be clearly inferred.

Also countries with identical factor endowments ratio could engage in the trade, so long as relative production costs and therefore relative commodity prices differed. This would happen if a demand conditions for factor supplies differed between countries. Thus unless we assume that relative factor prices will reflect relative factor endowment the conclusion of Heckscher-Ohlin theorem as the sole explanation of a trade will not follow.

3. Identical Production Techniques : Ohlin assumed that production technique for a given commodity is the same in all countries. This is not a very realistic assumption as there are always the spectrum of techniques available for producing each commodity, some of which may be capital-intensive techniques producing the given commodity and an economic relatively well endowed with capital and hence having cheap capital can go in for capital-intensive technique for producing identical commodity. When this happens, comparative cost difference will cease to exist and so trade will not take place.

INTERNATIONAL MONETARY FUND (IMF)

Even before the second world war come to an end, monetary experts in U.S.A. and U.K. started thinking over the monetary problems likely to be faced after the war. Two different plans were chalked out, one by Mr. Keynes an American author and the other by Mr. White a British author and were named after them as Keynes plan and White plan. The two sets of proposal were subjected to intensive discussion and served as the basis for the Brettenwood conference. The conference decided to set up two organisations :

(i) International Monetary Fund (IMF)

(ii) International Bank of Reconstruction and Development popularly known as a IBRD.

Objectives of the IMF

According to the Article I of IMF, its main objectives are :

1. To promote international co-operation.
2. To facilitate the expansion and the balance growth of international trade and contribute

thereby to the production and maintenance of high levels of the employment and real incomes.

3. To help re-establish a multilateral system of trade and payments and to eliminate foreign exchange restrictions.
4. To provide means for international adjustment international reserves.

Functions of IMF

The functions of the IMF can be discussed under the following three heads :

1. Regulatory Functions : In its regulatory aspect the IMF administers a code of a good behaviour in international payments.

2. Financial Functions : As a financial institution the IMF offers medium term loans to the national monetary authorities to enable them to make up their balance of payment deficits. The IMF resources come from the member countries based on an established quota as fixed by the IMF in terms of the SDR. IMF may borrow from industrial member countries under certain conditions as set for in the General arrangements to Berrone.

3. Consultative Functions : As a consultant the IMF provides a forum for international co-operation and is a source of counsel and technical assistance to its members.

As explained IMF funds come from the member countries based on the quota fixed by the fund. In Novemeber 1983, the aggregate fund quotas are 61.06 billion SDR approximately and now expected to increase as a result of Eighth General Review of Quotas to SDR 90.035 billion.

Quotas are used to determine :

1. The voting powers of members.
2. Their contribution to fund resources.
3. Their share in the allocation of SDR's. India's quota in the fund is SDR 1,717.5 million but is expected to increase to SDR 2207.7 million.

Main features of the International Monetary System

There was a big departure from the existing international monetary system in 1973 hence we can study the monetary system under two heads.

A. Monetary System up to 1973

The main features of international monetary system, which existed up to 1973 were as follows :

1. Par Value System : The exchange value of member's currency was fixed by the IMF in terms of gold, *i.e.*, price of gold was officially fixed at 85 per ounce or in other words, the values of different currencies were fixed in terms of dollar. Dollar was used as an intervention currency and was as good as gold.

2. Change in Par Value : In order to maintain short term equilibrium in the balance of payment situation, if the IMF did not serve the purpose. For this purpose there were no need to take as permission for devaluation for currency as was necessary if the proposed change was more than 10 per cent. It could be allowed provided IMF was to satisfy that:

(i) there was a fundamental disequilibrium,

(ii) the devaluation would be the right remedy in the circumstance for solving the fundamental disequilibrium.

3. Restriction on exchange control : There was restriction on exchange control except

(i) when a member's currency was under massive attack, and

(ii) when fund declared certain currency was scarce.

B. Monetary System since 1973

There was a big change in the monetary system in 1973. Since then the system is :

1. Pegging of currency : A member can now peg its currency to : (i) either a single major currency, (ii) as based of currencies, (iii) allow it to float independently; and (iv) adjust it to a set of indicators.

Thus there is a complete departure from the par value system. It is however subject to surveillance by the fund.

2. Reduction in the role of gold : Now the role of gold is not so bold. There is no statutory price for gold. Infact one-third of the gold reserve with IMF was disposed off to create a Trust fund to provide the additional support to 59 eligible member countries in balancing there balance of payments at concesssional terms. SDR is not the unit of account for funds transactions.

Charges for the use of Funds Resources

A service charge of 0.5 per cent is payable on purchase other than purchase from reserve branch. In addition their fund levies charges on balances of member currencies resulting from purchases. The charge is determined annually at beginning of each financial year. The maximum reduction of 3 per cent cost is allowed on the borrowing of 69 countries and 1.5 per cent on 14 countries. The use of funds resources enables member countries to get necessary foreign exchange resources in times of the difficult and domestic use of export production.

International Liquidity and Special Drawing Rights (SDR)

Before the IMF was established, countries had to make payments to other countries either in gold or in internationally accepted currencies such as the pound sterling and the dollar. Every country, therefore accumulated and kept reserves of gold. The reserves also brought good return by way of interest. These currencies therefore came to be known as "International reserve currencies." They do not serve at present as good monetary reserve as they did before.

The S.D.R plan proposed that the fund would write into its books new reserve of about $ 3.5 billion per year for the next three years. Each member should be given proportionate share in the reserve pool. This share will depend upon a country's existing subscription to the fund. The SDRs thus represent entirely a new form of paper money, unconditionally and automatically and is therefore called "paper gold."

A deficit member country can make use of these ights during a balance of payments crisis. These are intended to supplement gold and carry on the absolute gold value guarantee. Each unit of the SDR's is expressed as being equivalent to the present value of the US dollar, *viz*, 0.888671 grams fine.

The composition of currencies in the basket, underwent a change in July, 1978 and in a move to further enchance the attractiveness of the SDR's the IMF has switched to the simplified basket of five currencies. The five currencies now included are the US Dollar, Deuteche Mark, Japanese Yen, French Franc and Pound Sterling. The SDR is the unit of account for all purpose of the fund.

The creation of additional liquidity through the SDR scheme helps the member countries to supplement their reserve resources. The interest of SDRs to be paid for the use of SDRs by participants and payable to the holders of SDRs on the holding in excess on cumulative of SDR is currently stated 100 per cent by the average market rate on the chosen 5 countries whose currencies comprise the SDR valuation basket. Interest is payable quarterly.

WORLD BANK OR IBRD

The International Bank for Reconstruction and Development was set up as a result of the decision taken in Brettonwoods conference, New Hompshire. The conference was held in July 19 and attended by 44 nations. It decided to set up two organizations, the IMF and the IBRD to solve the monetary and financial problems of the less developed countries likely to be faced in Post World War II.

Activities : In order to achieve these purposes the charter authorises of the World Bank to engage in the following financing activities.

(a) It may lend funds directly, either from its capital funds it borrows in the private investments market.

(b) It may guarantee loans advanced by other or it may participate in such loans.

(c) Loans may be advanced to member countries directly or to private business on agricultural enterprises in the territories of members.

Some basic provision of Bank Loan

Some characteristics of Bank loans are :-

(i) They are meant for high priority productive purposes mainly to develop the infrastructure for the development such as generation and distribution of electric power, rail, roads, ports and inland water-ways, airlines and airports etc.

(ii) They must be used to meet only the foreign exchange component of the projects.

(iii) They are not tied.

There are two subsidiaries of World Bank :

International Development Association (IDA) : Considering the need for the structuring the economy of less developed countries, the World Bank set up the IDA in 1960. It is an aiding centre for several developing countries, who look up to it for financial assistance.

Credits

The main criteria for the allocation of IDA credit is the per capita income of the recipient country. Countries which have an annual per capita Gross National Product (GNP) of less than $681 are the eligible for IDA credits. Other parametres taken into consideration are country's credit worhiness, its economic performance, the density of its population and the existence of variable projects in the borrowing nations.

The purposes for which the IDA has an advanced credits are agriculture, rural development, education, energy, industrial development, population and nutrition, transportation and tourism, telecommunication etc.

IDA and India

India has been the largest beneficiary from IDA. Since its inception India's share is 40 per cent of IDA funds. It touched a new height of nearly $5581 (current) during the fifth plan. However India has not been able to utilise this aid fully both because of infrastructural difficulties at home and the adverse conditions imposed by donor countries such aid.

IDA credits have helped various sectors of our economy such as agriculture, rural development, construction, irrigation, power ports, industrial imports, fertiliser production, shipping etc.

Some of the important projects financed by IDA in India are the Sone irrigation project, Bihar, Punjab, Bombay water supply and sewage project, Rajasthan canal command area development project, etc. IDA has also been providing funds to the Industrial Development Bank of India (IDBI) as also Agricultural Refinance and Development Corporation (ARDC) for their developmental activities pertaining to industry and rural areas.

International Finance Corporation (IFC)

It is also an affiliate of World Bank and was set up in 1956. It extends credits to private business enterprises. It provides equity and loan capital for private and management, encourages the development of local capital market and stimulates the international form of private capital, it supports joint ventures and other conditions with the techniques available in the industrial nations.

The corporation has 124 members as on 30th June 1983. Its paid up capital as on date was 544 million and dollars its retained earning were 204 million dollars. IFC had made commitments total 5520 million dollars to 711 private enterprises.

The project for which the corporation advanced assistance, must satisfy the following conditions :

1. It should have the prospects of the earning profits.
2. It should boost the economy of the host country.
3. Local investors should be able to participate in the project in beginning of the project or later.
4. The management should be capable and experienced.
5. The sponsor of the project has the substantial holding in the enterprise.

INTERNATIONAL BUSINESS

International Business includes transactions between two different countries. It engages business either private or government across the national boundaries. These transactions include the transfer of goods, services, technology, managerial knowledge and capital to other countries. International business has gained greater visibility and importance because of the growth of large multinational corporations.

Characteristics of International Business

The characteristics of business in Domestic and in International level are quite different from one another. The characteristics of I.B. and practices followed can be summarised under following environments :

(a) Educational Environment : Educational environment plays a vital role in I.B., since I.B.

involves relationship of a firm with many countries it follows a multiple language system.

It may be either in spoken, written or official form but it comes across a multiple language system. The education system of different countries varies from each other in their quality, level and extent and there sometimes pose constraints in I.B.

(b) Sociological-Cultural Environment : In International Business the values and attitudes of people towards achievement, risk taking, scientific method and work are heterogenous. In case of multinational organization in terms of authority, status, roles, institutions, mobility and social systems are different as opposed to domestic business in which there are similar.

(c) Political Legal Environment : As in the domestic business which is country centered in international business the political orientation in terms of power and ideologies are transnational. The legal environment which includes laws, codes and regulations are different. National sovereignties are many and Govt. policies and regulations are different.

(d) Economic Environment : In I.B. the economic development is found at different stages. Since I.B. is performed in different countries across the national boundaries the economic system is different. It may be either capitalist mixed or Marxist. In I.B. the contact between the parent firm and the host country is affected by several facters some are unifying, others can cause conflicts.

Unifying effects : Unifying influences occur when the parent company provides and shares technical and managerial know-how, the assisting the host company in the development of human and material resources. Moreover, the parent corporation and the firm in the host country may it profitable to be integrated into a global organization structure. Whatever, the interaction, policies must provide for equity and results in benefits for both the parent firm and host company. Only, then one can expect a long lasting relationship.

Potentials for Conflict

Many factors can cause conflicts between the parent firm and the host country. Nationalistic self-interest may over-shadow the benefits obtained through co-operation. Similarly, sociological, cultural differences can lead to breakdowns in communications and subsequent misunderstanding. Some international corporations have been charged with making excessive profits, hiring the best local people away from local firms, and operating country to social customs.

The international corporations must develop social and diplomatic skills in its managers in order to prevent such conflicts and to resolve those that unavoidably occur.

Forms of International Business

As said earlier, I.B. is the interaction between two countries. This transaction of a firm with the host country can take many forms. One is the exporters of goods and services. Another is a licensing agreement for producing goods in another country. The parent company may also engage in management contracts that provide for operating foreign companies. Still another form of interaction is the joint venture with a firm in the host country. Finally, multinationals may set up wholly owned subsidiaries or branches with production facilities in the host country. Once a firm has decided to go international it has many alternatives for getting the entry into foreign market. The choice depends very much on the resources of firm and the market potentials for its products in the importing country. The various forms of international business is as follow :

1. Exporting : A firm may choose to enter the international market for the first time by exporting its surplus production through any of the following form

(a) By approaching the consumers directly in overseas market.

(b) By selling the production to an import house and buying agent in India.

(c) By selling the product to an exporting house in India for export purpose.

These forms are the most common and simplest for entering the overseas market for the first time. This is so because the risk attached to such venture is minimum.

2. Licensing : The another form of international business is to grant a license to a foreign firm to manufacture the product by using the firms name, patent, trademark and technology under the terms of agreement. The company granting the license gets an agreed percentage on gross sales as its remuneration such a right to use patent, trademarks and technology to produce the goods may be granted with or without any financial involvement. Generally such an agreement works in the following situations :

(a) When the importing country puts curbs on imports.
(b) When a country is sensitive to foreign ownership.
(c) When it is necessary for a firm to protect its patent and trademark against cancellation for non-use and
(d) Where there is a danger of its patent and trademark being initiated.

This strategy which gained prominence in the seventies because a sufficiently large number of countries became sensitive to foreign ownership.

This form is generally suitable for small and medium sized firms. The main advantage of this strategy is that it does not require a large capital investment.

3. Joint Ventures : Another made of entering a foreign market is through joint ventures i.e. joining the management and sharing the profit of the firm in the importing country. This venture may be for manufacturing or marketing the product. This strategy, like licensing got prominence in seventies because most of the developing countries viewed with suspician direct foreign investment.

Advantages

(a) Lack of adequate capital or human resources inhabiting a company plan of internationalising its operation.
(b) A company's desire to take advantage of the local firms distribution system.
(c) Prospects of a company in the foreign market if it utilises the skills of a partner in the importing country.

Under this system, the firm enters into collaboration with a local company in the importing company to share the management and profits of such venture. This method reduces the political and economic risks substantially associated with the internationalization. However, an important limitation of this method is that it might lead to loss of absolute control and perhaps also loss of freedom of action in production marketing operations.

4. Manufacturing in a foreign country : When a firm finds that it is not possible or profitable to export the goods to a foreign country due to :

(a) high cost of exporting or
(b) tariff and non-tariff barriers on its goods in the importing country or
(c) the lower cost of materials and labour in a foreign country and hence lower cost of production.

It may decide to manufacture and market the goods locally in the host country and thus it may keep itself away from the host country's barriers on the import of goods and other restrictions on imports.

But the decision to manufacture and market the goods locally is very risky because the success depends very much in the fair assessment of the market potentials in the foreign country concerned. In other words, this strategy works well when the market for a specific type of goods in a particular country is substantial and is likely expand further.

5. Management Contracts : This method of serving a foreign country is rarely adopted by the firm itself. Rather, it is the result of the external political pressures from the host country Government. This arrangement generally comes into being when the firm's investments in a foreign country are appropriated by the host country Govt. and when no suitable and adequate managerial capability exists in the host country.

6. Consultancy services : Under this arrangement, the countries which are lagging behind in technical field offer facilities to firms from other countries to serve the host country and invite them to participate in their developmental programmes through their expertise service in different specialised field. Firms having such expertise may enter into contracts with the host country's Govt. or firms for the export of such project exports. The project exports, may include turn key project, engineering services contracts, civil construction contracts etc.

Thus, a firm may choose any of the above methods to serve its foreign markets. The different methods may be adopted by different firms taking the potentials of foreign markets into consideration, or a firm may adopt different methods for the different foreign markets.

BALANCE OF PAYMENT

As I.B. engages transactions either private or Govt., between two or more countries it maintains a systematic record of all its economic transactions with the outside world in a given year. This is called Balance of Payment. It is a statistical data which include characters and dimensions of the country's economic relationship, with the rest of the world.

In the words of Baroderston "The Balance of Payment is merely a way of listing receipts and payments in international transaction for a country."

According to Kindle Berger "The Balance of Payment of a country is a systematic record of all economic transaction between the residents of reporting country and residents of foreign countries during a given period of time."

Thus, we can say that the balance of payment is comprehensive summary of the international transactions among the host country and parent country in a fixed period of time.

The Accounts of Balance of Payment are of following two types :

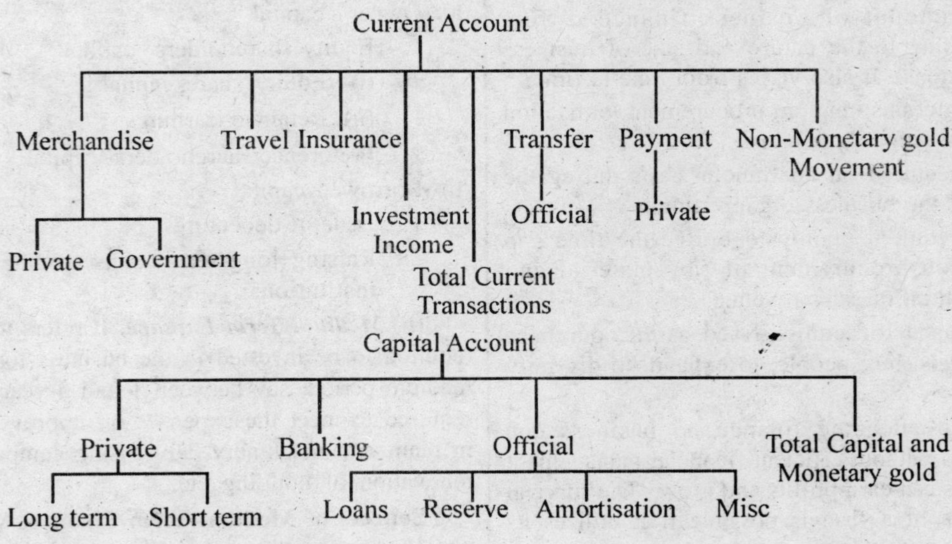

6. BUSINESS FINANCE

MEANING

Finance (money used for the activity) is required by every type of organization whether profit seeking or non-profit seeking. Business finance refers to money and credit employed in business. It involves procurement and utilization of funds for business purposes. The following are the characteristics of business finance :

(a) It includes all types of funds used in business whether provided by the owner or borrowed from outside.

(b) The amount of business finance differs according to the nature and size of business operations. It also varies from time to time.

(c) It involves estimation, procurement, utilization and investment of funds.

(d) It is required on continuous basis during the life of the business organization.

(e) It is required mainly to bridge the time gap between procurement of raw material and realization of sales revenue.

(f) It is used to acquire fixed assets, purchase materials, hire people, to expand, to diversify etc.

Without adequate finance no business can survive and without efficient financial management no business can earn profits and grow. The survival and growth of a firm is possible if it utilizes its funds in an effective manner.

TYPES OF BUSINESS FINANCE

The types of finance required by business organizations may be broadly divided into three categories:

(a) Long term finance
(b) Medium term finance
(c) Short term finance

(a) *Long Term Finance.* It refers to the funds required to be invested in the business for a long period, say for more than 5 years. It is required to acquire assets like land, building, plant and machinery etc. and to finance permanent working capital (that part of working capital which is permanently required to hold a minimum level of current assets irrespective of the level of operations).

Sources of Long Term Finance. The sources of long term finance may be divided into certain categories as below :

(a) Owner's capital
  1. Equity shareholders' capital
     (i) Equity share capital
     (ii) Retained earnings
  2. Preference shareholders' capital

(b) Borrowed capital
  1. Issue of debentures
  2. Raising long term loans from Financial institutions

(b) *Medium Term Finance.* It refers to funds required to be invested in the business for medium period, say between 1 and 5 years. It is required to meet the expenses on improvement in plant and machinery, advertising campaign, renovation of building etc.

Sources of Medium Term Finance. Medium term finance can be raised from the following sources:

(a) Loan from commercial banks
(b) Public deposits
(c) Retained earnings
(d) Redeemable debentures
(e) Loan from financial institutions

(c) *Short Term Finance.* It is required to meet the day-to-day operating expenses and for holding stock of raw material, work in progress, consumables, finished goods, debtors etc. This finance is generally taken for a period up to 1 year. This finance is required as per the length of operating cycle of business i.e. conversion of inventory into sales and sales into cash.

Sources of Short Term Finance. Following are the sources from which short term finance can be raised:

(a) Trade credit from supplier
(b) Advance from customers
(c) Discounting bill of exchange
(d) Bank overdraft
(e) Cash credit
(f) Factoring
(g) Public deposits

WORKING CAPITAL

Working capital is that part of capital which is required to keep the business going and meet the day to day expenses of the business. It keeps on changing with the size of operations of business. There are two concepts of working capital viz. Gross working capital and Net working capital. Gross working capital refers to firm's investment in current assets whereas Net working capital refers to the difference between current assets and current liabilities. In general, if nothing is specifically mentioned, working capital means net working capital only.

Factors Determining Requirement of Working Capital. The working capital requirement of an enterprise depends on following factors:

(a) The Nature of Business i.e. manufacturing or construction firms require higher working capital whereas financial services firm require low working capital

(b) Size of Business : bigger the business, higher is the requirement of working capital

(c) Manufacturing Cycle : longer the cycle, higher is the working capital required

(d) Business Cycle : more working capital required in boom period and less in depression

(e) Production Policy : If products are manufactured in demand season then during that period higher working capital is required.

(f) Availability of Credit from suppliers

(g) Level of Inflation : higher the inflation, higher working capital required

(h) Profit Margin : higher the margin, lower the working capital required

Working Capital Cycle. Working capital cycle refers to conversion of cash into various current assets in a sequence and finally ending with cash. The working capital cycle is explained as below:

Cash – Raw material and operating expenses – Finished goods – Credit sale – Debtors – Cash

The above process explains that the working capital begins with cash balance with the owner. With that cash the owner purchases raw material and pays for operating expense which results into finished goods. These goods are either sold for cash or credit. Credit sale leads to creation of debtors. When debtors pay it is finally again converted into cash and the cycles starts again.

RAISING SECURITIES FOR FINANCE

As we saw in the sources of long term and medium term finance, the business organization may raise securities to raise the required finance. The organization has following options of securities to raise finance:

(a) Equity share capital
(b) Preference share capital
(c) Debentures
(d) Public Deposit

The composition of debt and equity in the long term finance of a firm is called **'Capital Structure'** of the firm. Utilization of these capital into various projects of the firm is called **'Capital Budgeting'**.

Raising Equity Share Capital

Meaning. Equity share is an ordinary share which does not carry the preferential rights attached to the preference share. The holder of such share is called equity shareholder. The following are the features of equity shares:

1. They enjoy voting rights in the company and hence elect the manag ment of the company.

2. The rate of dividend on equity share is neither fixed nor guaranteed. It depends on the availability of profit after meeting all liabilities and paying dividend to preference shareholders.
3. It is generally not redeemable during the life of the company unless shares are bought back.

Advantages of Raising Equity Capital

The following are the advantages of raising capital through issue of equity shares:

1. It is permanent capital and the company need not bother about its redemption
2. There is no obligation to pay dividend every year as it depends on availability of profits
3. Equity shares are issued without any charge on assets
4. It raises the capacity of the company to raise further debt
5. There is no risk of financial insolvency by issuing equity share capital

Disadvantage of Raising Equity Capital

The disadvantages of issuing equity shares are as below :

(a) The cost of issuing equity shares is very high because of higher expenses on advertising, brokerage, consultancy etc. while issuing new shares.

(b) Equity shareholders expect higher rate of return (as they take higher risk) and hence if the project is not attractive, it is difficult to raise equity capital.

(c) Company has to pay tax on distribution of dividend and also dividend is not a deductible expense under Income tax Act.

(d) The promoter has the risk of losing control of the company if someone acquires large number of shares from market.

(e) Raising high amount of equity capital does not permit the company to take advantage of 'Trading on Equity'.

(f) As equity capital is not redeemed, many a times it leads to over capitalization by companies.

Here, it should be remembered that generally companies do not pay interest on capital. But sometimes it may pay interest on capital during the construction of the project prior to the commencement of its business. Once the company commences its business commercially, it cannot pay interest on capital. Interest paid during the construction period is considered as part of the fixed cost.

Raising Preference Share Capital

Meaning. A preference share is one which carries a right to receive dividend at a stipulated rate before any dividend is paid on equity shares and a right to receive repayment of capital on winding up of company before the capital of equity shareholders is returned.

Types of Preference Shares

Based on various rights attached with the preference shares, in addition to above two rights, they can be categorized in the following ways:

(1) Cumulative and Non-Cumulative. In case of cumulative preference shares, if the company cannot pay the dividend in a year, it gets accumulated and has to be paid in the next year. The unpaid dividend does not accumulate in case of non-cumulative preference shares. Unless otherwise stated, preference shares are deemed to be cumulative.

(2) Participating and Non-Participating. Participating preference shares get a right to participate in the profits of the company (other than the usual dividend) left after paying dividend to the equity shareholders. Non-participating preference shareholders only gets dividend.

(3) Convertible and Non-convertible. Convertible preference shares are issued with a condition that after expiry of certain period, they may be converted into equity shares and not redeemed. Non-convertible preference shares are redeemed after expiry of fixed period.

Advantages

The merits of issuing preference shares are listed as below:

(a) Preference dividend is payable at a fixed rate only.

(b) In case of non-cumulative preference shares, the dividend is to be paid only if the profits are available.
(c) They are issued without any charge on the assets.
(d) There is no risk of losing the management control of company as preference shares does not carry voting rights.
(e) The cost of issuing preference shares is lower than issuing equity shares.
(f) The company can take advantage of trading on equity by issuing preference shares.

Disadvantages

(1) The cost of preference share is higher than cost of debt capital.
(2) Dividend paid to preference shareholders is not deductible expense under Income Tax Act.
(3) Since irredeemable preference shares cannot be issued now, the company has to make arrangement for redemption of shares.
(4) It does not attract many investors as the rate of return is fixed with high risk of capital.

Issue of Debentures

Meaning. A debenture is a written instrument acknowledging a debt by the issuer and containing provisions as regards the repayment of principal and interest at a fixed rate. It represents debt capital of the company which has to be redeemed after a fixed period.

Advantages

1. The cost of issuing debentures is lower than that of equity shares.
2. The interest paid on debentures is a deductible expense and hence the effective interest rate is very low.
3. There is no risk of losing management control, as debentures do not carry voting rights.
4. The company has an advantage of trading on equity by issuing debentures.
5. It attracts lot of investors who want safe, though low, return on their investment.

Disadvantages

(i) There is higher risk of financial insolvency as the interest has to be paid even if the company has incurred losses.
(ii) Debentures are issued against the security of some asset. So, the company must have enough assets before issue of debentures.
(iii) Small companies find it difficult to raise finance by issue of debentures.
(iv) The company has to make arrangement for the redemption of debentures at the end of stipulated period.

Public Deposits

Public deposits are like any other deposits with bank. Companies invite shareholders, employees and general public to deposit their savings with the company in the form of deposits for a fixed rate of return. It is raised by companies to raise medium term or short term finance. The provisions of Companies Act regarding issue of public deposits have been covered under company law section.

Advantages

1. Public deposits are not covered by any mortgage. They are like unsecured debentures.
2. The floatation cost of raising finance though public deposit is less than that of equity capital.
3. It gives flexibility to company, as it can raise them at any time and redeem when not needed.
4. It does not involve much legal and regulatory compliance as in case of issue of shares.
5. It helps the company to take advantage of trading on equity.
6. The interest paid on deposits is a deductible expenditure.

Disadvantage

(a) As the public deposits are unsecured, not many investors are willing to put their savings.
(b) The interest rate on public deposits is very high compared to debentures.
(c) There is a limit on the period for which deposits can be raised. (Max. 36 months)
(d) Only companies having higher reputation in the capital market can raise fixed deposits.

TRADING ON EQUITY

Use of funds bearing fixed interest payments like debentures, bank loans, preference shares etc. to derive benefit of higher rate of return on equity capital is known as 'Trading on Equity'. It is also called 'Financial Leverage'. This benefit is available only when the rate of return on capital employed is more than the rate of fixed interest payment, otherwise it may affect the equity shareholders adversely. The use of trading on equity will be clear with the following example :

Total funds required - Rs. 10,00,000

Plan A - 10,000 equity shares of Rs. 100 each

Plan B - 5,000 equity shares of Rs. 100 each and debentures of Rs. 5,00,000 with 15% interest

Tax rate - 40%

Earning Before Interest and Taxes

Situation (a) Rs. 2,00,000 ; Situation (b) Rs. 50,000

The following is the statement showing the effect of use of Trading on Equity

Particulars	EBIT Rs. 2,00,000		EBIT Rs. 50,000	
	Plan A	Plan B	Plan A	Plan B
Earnings Before Interest and Taxes	2,00,000	2,00,000	50,000	50,000
Less : Interest on debentures	—	75,000	—	75,000
Earning before Taxes	2,00,000	1,25,000	50,000	(-) 25,000
Taxes @ 40%	80,000	50,000	20,000	—
Earnings after Taxes	1,20,000	75,000	30,000	(-) 25,000
No. of Equity shares	20,000	5,000	10,000	5,000
Earning per share	Rs. 1.2	Rs. 1.5	Rs. .3	Rs. (-) 0.5
Return on Equity capital	12%	15%	3%	(-)5%

From the above example two inferences can be drawn:

(a) If return on capital employed is more than rate of interest payable, Trading on equity leads to higher return to the equity shareholders.

(b) If rate of return is lower than rate of interest, trading on equity leads to lower return to the equity shareholders.

CAPITALIZATION

It refers to the composition of long term finance of the business. All types of long term funds, whether owned or borrowed are part of capitalization. It is generally used in relation with companies. The company has to first determine the amount of capitalization required in the business. There are two methods to calculate requirement of capitalization:

(a) Cost method

(b) Earning method

Cost Method : Under this method, the company first calculate the requirement of fixed assets in the business like land, building, machinery, patents, vehicles etc. As most of fixed assets are financed by long term funds, the capitalization required will be equal to the requirement of fixed assets.

Earnings Method : Every industry has certain parameters regarding requirement of capitalization for a particular level of earning. So, a company can also determine its capitalization level based on estimated earnings. For example, if the company expects to earn Rs. 5,00,000 per annum and the normal capitalization rate is 8%, the company would require 4,00,000 *100 / 8 i.e. Rs. 50,00,000 as long term capital.

Over Capitalization

A company is said to be over capitalized when the actual capitalization is more than the normal capitalization required considering the earning capacity of the company. For example, in the above example, for earning of Rs. 4,00,000 capitalization required is Rs. 50,00,000. Now, if the company has raised long term funds to the tune of Rs. 60,00,000, company is said to be over capitalized by

Rs. 10,00,000. it may result due to one or more of the following reasons:

1. When the company raises more of capital than required because the capital market is bullish and it is easy to raise equity capital
2. The promoters of the company had wrongly estimated the future earnings of the company
3. The normal capitalization rate assumed by the promoters is less than actual industry average.
4. Company is paying high interest resulting into lower profits
5. Company could not materialize some of the major contracts it was expecting to get
6. Due to change in government policy, the industry has suffered heavily.
7. Excessive amount is paid for goodwill and other fixed assets
8. Higher rates of taxation resulting into lower profits
9. Due to sudden increase in cost of raw material, profitability has come down

Watered capital. Capital of a company is said to be watered, if the some part of capital is not represented by the fixed assets. It happens when a company pays heavy price for the goodwill which does not result into much gain for the company. It also happens in the promotional stage of company as it has to incur heavy expenditure during promotion.

Under Capitalization

As against over capitalization, under capitalization is a situation when the actual capitalization of the company is less than warranted by its earnings. Here, it should be seen whether the company has large secret reserves. Because if there are secret reserves on paper, company may seem to be under capitalized whereas in fact it is not. Following are some of the reasons of under capitalization:

(a) Under estimation of future earnings
(b) Over estimating the rate of capitalization by the promoters
(c) Getting some big unexpected contracts resulting into higher profits
(d) Drop in the tax rates by government
(e) Operating the company and production at very high efficiency levels.

7. SOCIAL RESPONSIBILITY OF BUSINESS

By social responsibility, we mean the intelligent and objective concern for the welfare of society that restrains individual and corporate behaviour from ultimately destructive activities, no matter how immediately profitable, and leads in the direction of positive contributions to human betterment, variously as the latter may be defined.

Why Social Responsibility of Business?

Why should business be concerned about social responsibilities, is a question that has attracted the attention of many thinkers, both from academics as well as from practitioners. There have been arguments and counter arguments in favour of and against social responsibility of business and its role as an objective of business, it is worthwhile to present briefly the arguments against and for it that have surfaced over time. It should be pointed out, however, that each argument for and against social responsibility assumes a certain understanding of the concept that may vary.

Arguments against Social Responsibility

The core of arguments against business's assumption of any responsibilities other than to produce goods and service efficiently and to make as much money as possible is that, business is an economic institution and economic values should be the sole determinant of its performance. The manager of a business is an employee of owners of business and is responsible only to owners. In this context, arguments against social responsibility of business run on the following lines:

1. Contrary to Basic Functions of Business: **Milton Friedman**, a widely respected economist, holds the classical view that the only responsibility of business is to earn profit. He says: "There is one and only one responsibility of business – to use its resources and engage in activities designed to increase its profit so long as it stays within the rules of the game, which is to say, engages in open and free competition, without deception or fraud. Few trends could so thoroughly undermine the very traditions of our free society as the acceptance by corporate officials of a social responsibility other than to make as much money for their stockholders as possible. This is fundamentally subversive doctrine."

The basic contention of Friedman is that social responsibility is contrary to basic business functions. The basic argument is that if price of a product in the market does not truly reflect the relative costs of producing it, but includes costs for social action, the allocative mechanism of the market place is distorted. Either the customer pays a price greater than that necessary to call the goods into market or the firm's product-mix provides less consumer satisfaction. Moreover, the doctrine of social responsibility means acceptance of the socialist view that political mechanisms rather than market mechanisms are the appropriate ways to allocate scarce resources of alternative uses.

Another basis of suggesting social responsi-bility against the basic business function is that as manager moves further away from the simple rule of profit maximization that guides his actions into the social and political realm, he has no guides to help him know what social responsibility he should take in the public interest. Furthermore, the business should try to determine what is public interest because the economic system is not a playground on which businessmen may exercise their peculiar preferences. Closely associated with this argument is the view that businessmen have no special skills to deal with social matters. **Henderson** observes that "spectacle of otherwise sophisticated people going on bended, knees to companies and pleading with them to have the kind of conscience and moral responsibilities only rarely found in individuals is nothing less than laughable."

2. Domination of Business Values : Business should not be socially responsible otherwise business values will dominate the social values. Therefore **Levitt**, the famous psychologist, holds the view that : "The danger is that all these things (social aspects of business functioning) will turn the corporation into twentieth-century equivalent of the medieval Church. The corporation would eventually invest itself with all-embracing duties, obligations, and finally powers – ministering the whole man and molding him and society in the image of the corporation's narrow ambitions and its essentially unsocial needs."

His fear is true because in the past the results were not so good when the values of a society were dominated by one major institution, whether it was the church, the military, business, or something else.

3. Inefficiency in the System : There is no substitute for the power of self-interest to get people to act. Any replacement of altruism for self-interest will, therefore, be fatal to the efficiency of the system. The rigour of the market mechanism will place in jeopardy the competitive position of that system which adds to its costs by assuming social responsibilities. Therefore, managers should manage only in the interests of the shareholders, and shareholders should be put in a position to decide how their property will be used. In this context, **Heyne** asserts that : "Taken seriously, the doctrine of social responsibility fosters megalomania in its adherents. It places upon the businessman's conscience intolerable burdens that tempt him continually to arrogance and pharisaism."

Arguments for Social Responsibility

Though there is no one core idea in the argument that business has no social responsibility, there are several ideas about social responsibility of the business. Over the period of time, the things have changed too much giving new thoughts and replacing the classical view of business's objectives. These arguments run in the following directions :

1. Business : A Part of the Society : Business organizations are creatures of society and must respond to social demands. A business operates within a set of cultural norms and restraints. These are certainly not only economic but also legal, political, social, and technical. They are powerful and business should know instinctively that as they change, they must be incorporated in the decision – making process. There is another point in this. Since business is a subsystem of society, its functioning should contribute to the welfare of the system as a whole and not only to the subsystem alone. Therefore, organizational decisions should be made in a way which not only provide welfare to the organization but also to other subsystems of the society so that total welfare of the system is maximum. When a particular subsystem becomes more powerful and efficient, other subsystems look for the support from it. This is true for business also. For example, **Steiner** comments that : "The managers of the biggest companies know that as a business gets larger, the public takes more interest in it because it has a greater impact on the community. The antennae of these managers are tuned to public opinion and they react to it. They seek to maintain a proper image of their company in the public mind. This leads to the assumption of greater social responsibilities."

2. Avoidance of Government Regulations : When business is unable to fulfil its social roles, it invites more government intervention in the business system. Therefore, in order to avoid government regulation of business, it is preferable to go for social responsibility programmes. In any case, government regulation is costlier than the cost of social responsibility programmes. Government regulation cuts flexibility and freedom of doing business, concentrates power in government which may be against the basic features of free and democratic country. For example, **G. L. Mehta** has observed that : "Business cannot remain a small basis of influence in a vast desert of poverty. Increasingly those who are deprived of opportunity for lack neither of skill nor of willingness to work, will look upon the existing social order with hostility."

Such hostility may break the present social system and hence may jeopardize the economic objective of the business.

3. Long-run Self-interest of Business : Discharge of social responsibility ensures long-run self-interest of business. It is possible that at the initial stage, the cost of discharging social responsibility may be high but in the long run, the business can do better by creating better public image among the various interest groups. In fact, many managers have realized that taking welfare measures for workers have paid rich dividends to the business in the form of improved productivity. In this regard, one committee has observed as follows :

"It is in the enlightened self-interest of corporations to promote the public welfare in a positive way. Indeed, the corporate interest broadly defined by management can support involvement in helping to solve virtually any social problem, because people who have good environment, education, and opportunity make better employees, customers, and neighbours for business than those who are poor, ignorant, and oppressed."

4. Traditional Values : In any country, economic growth is not possible without the active cooperation of people. People cannot be enthused to participate for development unless they have a reasonable assurance that they will share the fruits of growth. Thus, the urge for social justice is widespread and universally accepted. The need for our society is to convert this urge into a programme of action which would be in tune with our culture and way of life. Our way of life can be well described by the following verse (translated from Sanskrit) which teachers and the taught used to chant everyday before starting their studies in the Ashram. The verse reads as : "May we prosper together and enjoy our prosperity in common. Let our exploits be joint adventures. May our studies be full of light. May we not quarrel each other. Let there be peace, peace, peace."

Similarly, the first verse of Ishavashya Upanishad describes that : "All that exists in this universe is the abode of the Almighty. Therefore, enjoy the good things in life by sharing them with others. Do not covet the possession of others."

These traditional thoughts hold good today to guide the economic activities of the country. From this point of view, business can do better if it is concerned with social aspects of life in the country.

Conclusions

The argument of those who argue that business organizations have nothing to do with social responsibility and expect the maximization of shareholders' wealth are weak on two points.

First : They overstate the trend and ultimate magnitude of business's voluntary assumption of social responsibility.

Second : They want business organizations to do somethings they cannot do, that is to ignore disregard to its social concern. Many forces will come in its way to destroy it. Therefore, even if business is involved in making profit, it is done through the creation of utility to the social needs. Better these social needs are served, better will be the prospect of its survival and progress. Even in Western countries, where economic activities are comparatively free from controls, it has been accepted that profit is not the sole criterion for measuring the success of a business organization. For example, **Day** has observed that : "As a statement of purpose, maximizing of profit is not only unsatisfying; it is not even accurate. A more realistic statement has to be more complicated. The corporation is a creation of society whose purpose is the production and distribution of needed goods and services, for profit of society and itself. Each element of that statement is needed if the whole is to be accurate: you cannot drop one element without doing violence to the fact."

The proponents of social responsibility say that society is not submitting one set of expectations for another. Rather it is broadening the standards by means of which corporate performance is to be judged. The old concept of profit maximization has vanished and even economists have accepted it. They have substituted profit maximization with satisfactory profit. Today, business decision-making is a mixture of altruism, self-interest, and good citizenship. Managers do take actions which are in the social interest even though there is a cost involved and the connection with long-range profit is quite remote. Therefore, the issue is not whether the business has social responsibility; it has. The issue is how to identify this responsibility and act upon that.

ETHICS AND MANAGEMENT SYSTEM

Ethics can be defined as the systematic attempt to make sense of individual, group, organizational, professional, social, market, and global moral experience in such a way as to determine the desirable, prioritized ends that are worth pursuing, the right rules and obligations that ought to govern human conduct, the virtuous intentions and character traits that deserve development in life, and to act accordingly. Put more simply, ethics is the study of individual and collective moral awareness, judgement, character, and conduct.

Sometimes the term morality is used interchangeably with ethics in every day conversion, but at other times it can be conceptually distinguished from ethics. The morality of a society is related to its mores – the customs accepted by a society or group as being right and wrong-as well as to those laws of a society that add legal prohibitions and sanctions to many activities considered to be immoral. Morality, therefore, can be defined as the customary, sociolegal practices and activities that are considered importantly right and wrong; the rules that govern those activities; and the values that are embedded, fostered, or pursued by those conventional, sociolegal activities and practices.

In some instances, management morality and management ethics are diametrically opposed to each other. For example, in the South before the Civil War, the fugitive slave, if recaptured, was often maimed by his or her managers/owners frequently by chopping off one foot. Although this act of maiming was condoned by customary morality and sociolegal practices, at the time, some ethically sensitive, progressive managers objected to it. They argued that this cruel and vindictive act may have been morally acceptable but was ethically repulsive. Whereas management morality may allow one to succeed temporarily by conforming to current social norms or organizational mazes, management ethics calls for a sensitive, reflective, and systematic endorsement of those norms only after they have withstood critical challenge. A classic business example of a transition from stakeholder morality to stakeholder ethics is represented in the Ford V. Dodge lawsuit from the turn of the century. Henry Ford wanted to share profits from his automobile company with his employees to improve the quality of their lives, but the Supreme Court sided with the position of Dodge that the fiduciary moral relationship with investors precluded the ethical sharing and gain sharing with designated stakeholders has been ethically justified in terms of prioritized ends and obligations that overcame the conventional morality of earlier forms of capitalism. Many times, moral managers and ethical managers engage in the same behaviour patterns, but the latter must critically challenge accepted norms before endorsing them.

The study of ethics can occur on at least three levels of analysis: **Macro/Global**, **Molar/organizational**, and **Micro/individual**. Macro/global ethics focus on world economic contexts-conflicts between market and command economies. Molar/organizational ethics addresses ethical issues encountered within and between institutions-company codes of business conduct or ethical issues in mergers and acquisitions. Finally, Micro/individual ethics focuses on personal group conduct — lying, cheating, or stealing at work by employees.

In addition, moral values are part of a person's philosophy of life. A philosophy of life consists of ongoing, critical reflection about logically fundamental beliefs regarding what is real, true, and of value and acting in accord with those reasoned commitments. Moral values, along with economic, aesthetic, political, and other values, indicate what people regard as important in life and worth acting on. Reflection on beliefs about what is real, called *metaphysics*, and reflection on beliefs about what is true, called *epistemology*, can result in either religious or secular conclusions, and both can provide conceptual foundations for moral values. For example, a person who believes that a real God created the world and humanity, that these truths are known by faith in divine revelation disclosed through sacred writings, and that his or her highest ethical value is spiritual salvation after death has adopted a religious foundation for ethics. Another person who believes that nature is the only reality that always existed, that humans created gods out of fear, that these truths are known through science and reason, and that the highest moral value is ethical integrity in this life has adopted a secular foundation for ethics. Both persons can act ethically, but from different metaphysical and epistemological foundations.

In addition to reducing tangible and intangible costs, management ethics adds value to individual, group, and organizational performance. Management ethics can be defined as the descriptive and normative study of moral awareness, judgement, character, and conduct as they relate to all levels of managerial practice. Individual business judgement and performance can be enhanced through management ethics in the following ways:

- Stimulation of the moral imagination
- Moral identification and ordering
- Moral evaluation
- Tolerating moral disagreement and ambiguity
- Integrating managerial competence and moral competence
- Eliciting a sense of moral responsibility

Although it is tempting for managers to suppose that economic and legal factors determine rational business decisions, empathy for the web of moral relationships and obligations imaginatively enlarges the awareness of the business impact of integrity.

For a manager, exhibiting ethical integrity involves achieving good consequences or ends by adhering to standards of right conduct (duty-oriented theories emphasized in deontological ethics), while habitually being motivated by proper intentions and developing virtuous character traits (character-oriented theories emphasized in virtue ethics), in an ethically supportive, holistic context (system-oriented theories emphasized in system development ethics). Although all four theories of ethics (teleological, deontological, virtues, and system development) can be isolated, the main point is that all four theories are necessary to understand moral phenomena fully, to make balanced ethical judgements, and to act with managerial integrity. Just as handling behaviour complexity is required of master managers, handling moral complexity is required of ethical managers.

More important, management theory and practice implicitly endorse some ethical values over others. For example, *rational goal,* "bottom line" managers who use results as the exclusive per-formance standard logically endorse and tacitly choose to accord outcome-oriented ethical values preeminence over other ethical values. Rational goal managers, who have strong role competencies in directing and producing, implicitly subscribe to outcome-oriented ethical values in their daily practice. *Internal process* managers, who exhibit strong role competencies in monitoring and coordinating, implicitly subscribe to duty-oriented ethical values in their daily practice. These "by the book" managers who use compliance with internal policies as the exclusive performance standard are tacitly endorsing and logically choosing to accord duty-oriented ethical values priority over other ethical values. *Human relations* managers, who have strong role competencies in facilitating and mentoring, implicitly subscribe to a virtues-oriented ethical value in daily practice. These "true grit" managers who focus on "the right stuff in persons" and use virtuous character as the exclusive performance standard are tacitly endorsing and logically choosing to accord character-oriented ethical values preeminence over other ethical values. Finally, *open systems managers,* who excel in innovating and brokering for resources, implicitly subscribe to systems-oriented ethical values in daily practice. These "change agent" managers who use continuous system improvement as the exclusive performance standard, are tacitly endorsing and logically choosing to accord systems oriented ethical values priority over other ethical values.

8. MANAGEMENT

DEFINITION

In the management literature, we find a large number of definitions of management given by different authors. However, the different view-points may be classified into the following categories, namely:

1. Management as an art of getting thing done.
2. Management as a function
3. Management as a process
4. Management as a body of individuals.

These viewpoints are explained below.

MANAGEMENT AS AN ART OF GETTING THINGS DONE

Some people define management as "*an art of getting things done through others.*" This definition represents the traditional view of management under which workers are treated as a factor of production only. This definition is incomplete in the present context. Its deficiencies are as follows :

1. This definition is vague as it does not give the functions which a manager has to perform to get results from others.
2. It gives the impression of the manipulative character of the practice of management.
3. The employess are merely treated as means for getting results. In other words, their position is like a *cog in the wheel.* This definition ignores the needs of the workers and does not offer them human treatment.

MANAGEMENT AS A FUNCTION

Management is the key function in any organisation. According to Dalton E. McFarland, "Management is the fundamental integrating and operating mechanism underlying organised effort." William Spriegel viewed management "as that function of an enterprise which concerns itself with the direction and control of various activities to attain the business objectives." It is the function of working with people and coordinating their efforts so as to accomplish the objectives of the organisation.

An enterprise concerns itself with the direction and control of various activities to attain the business objectives. "It is the function of working with people and coordinating their efforts so as to accomplish the objectives of the organisation."

MANAGEMENT AS A PROCESS

Henri Fayol viewed management as a process consisting of five functions which every manager performs. According to Fayol, "*To manage is to forecast and plan, to organise, to command, to coordinate, and to control.*" Management is a process by which managers create, direct and operate purposive organisation through systematic, coordinated and cooperative human efforts.

According to George R. Terry, "*Management is a distinct process consisting of planning, organising, actuating, and controlling performed to determine and accomplish stated objectives by the use of human beings and other resources.*" Management is a process since it comprises a series of functions which lead to the achievement of organisational objectives. The functions of

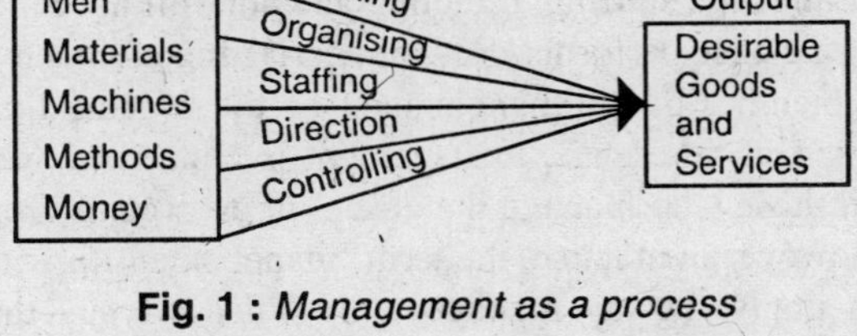

Fig. 1 : *Management as a process*

management are : planning, organising, staffing, directing and controlling as shown in Fig. 1. These functions are inter-dependent and inter-related. There is no specific sequence of their performance. More or less, they are performed simultaneously by the managers.

The functions of management, considered as a whole, make up the management process. As shown in Fig. 2 *Management process involves planning, organising, staffing, directing and controlling.* These are the basic functions which every manager performs for the achievement of certain goals. The manager draws plans to translate these goals into reality. But planning is of no use unless the manager organises, directs, and controls the activities of the people working under him to execute the plans. In this way the managerial functions are interdependent and interrelated.

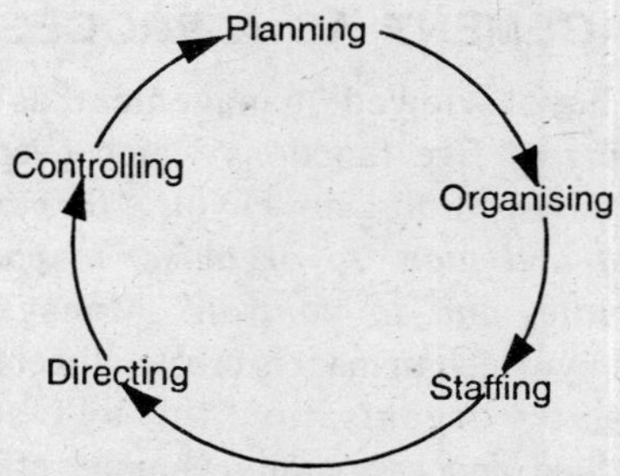

Fig. 2 : *Elements of Management Process*

MANAGEMENT AS A GROUP

The term 'management' is frequently used to denote a group of managerial personnel. Management is the body or group of people which performs managerial functions for the accomplishment of certain goals. These people are individually known as '*managers*'. In other words, a manager is a person who performs the managerial functions of planning, organising, staffing, directing and controlling. Since a manager performs the managerial functions he is a member of the management of the organisation. Used in this sense, management is concerned with all those who manage the affairs of an organisation. However in practice, the term 'management' is used to imply the top management. When we say that Management of Alpha Company is very efficient, we are referring to its Chairman and Managing Director, Board of Directors and Divisional Heads.

NATURE OR CHARACTERISTICS OF MANAGEMENT

We now embark upon certain features or characteristics of management which illustrate the nature of management. Such features are as follows:

1. Management is an Integrative Process: The essence of management is integration of human and other resources in a manner that it leads to effective performance. All these resources are made available to those who manage. Managers apply know-ledge, experience, and principles for getting the results.

2. Management is a Multi-disciplinary Discipline: Here we are taking management in the sense of a discipline. Since the available resources are heterogeneous, i.e., living and non-living, the performance depends upon the proper knowledge and skill of various disciplines. Management has grown as a body of discipline taking the help of so many social sciences like Anthropology, Sociology, Psychology, etc. Much of the management literature is the result of the association of these diciplines. In fact, one of the approaches, known as behavioural approach to management, got currency after the impact of these sciences.

3. Management is Universal: The principles and techniques of management have universal application. They are not rigid. They can be applied with certain modifications in different situations. Thus, the principles and techniques of management are flexible in nature.

4. Management is Activity Based: Although the class of people engaged in managing is referred to as management, yet it is essentially the task of managing by such class of people which is called management. As such management refers to distinct class of activities about which knowledge can be obtained and skill in its application acquired.

5. Management is Accomplished by, with and through the efforts of others: While defining management it has already been said that some management scientists defined management as the art of getting things done through people. Thus, management in a sense amounts to the ability and skill of a person in getting work accomplished through people at work.

6. Management is Intangible: Management has been called an unseen force. Its presence is evidenced by the result of its efforts – orderliness, informed employees, buoyant spirit, and adequate work output. Thus feeling of mangement is result-oriented. One may not see with the naked eye the functioning of management but its result are apparently known. People often remark of the effectiveness or ineffectiveness of mangement on the basis of the end results, although they are incapable of observing it during operation.

7. Management is Purposeful: Management is concerned with the achievement of certain objectives. Commonly, managerial success is measured by the extent to which the objectives are achieved. Management exists because it is an effective means of getting needed work accomplished.

MANAGER

A manager is a person who plans, organize, directs and controls the allocation of human, material, financial and information resources in pursuit of the organization's goals.

Since every group requires some sort of management, the management practices started with human civilization when people began living together in groups. But, this discipline got the attention of researchers only in 20th century. Various thinkers and researchers analysed management with their perspective and explained the subject with the hlep of studies and experiences. But, the real development of management thoughts began with the development of scientific management given by Taylor.

TAYLOR'S SCIENTIFIC MANAGEMENT

F.W. Taylor and others like Gilbreth and Gantt investigated the effective use of human beings in industrial organizations, particularly at shop floor levels (Production level). Taylor has defined management as the art of "knowing exactly what you want men to do and then see in that they do it in the best and cheapest way." He is called the father of Scientific Management. During his job, Taylor made many experiments about how to increase the efficiency of people. On the basis of his experiments, he published many papers and books and all his contributions were compiled in his book "Scientific Management". His contributions can be described in two parts: main features of Scientific Management and principles of scientific management.

Main Features of Scientific Management

Based upon his experiments, Taylor identified how human beings could be made more efficient by standardizing the work and better method of doing work. This has resulted into following features of scientific management :

1. Separation of Planning and Doing. Taylor, emphasised the separation of planning aspect from actual doing of the work. Earlier, the worker himself was doing the planning of his work and the instruments required for it and supervisor was only supposed to see how the worker is performing. This was creating lot of problems and so, Taylor, said that planning should be left with the supervisor and worker should emphasise only operational work.

2. Functional Foremanship. For separation of planning and doing, Taylor evolved the concept of functional foremanship based on specialization of functions. In this system, 8 persons were involved to direct activities of workers. Out of this, four persons were concerned with planning and four were concerned with doing aspect of the work. The following chart shows the work set up :

3. Job Analysis. Job analysis is to find out the one best way of doing the thing. The best way of doing a job is one which requires the least movements, consequently less time and cost. This can be determined by doing **Time-Motion-Fatigue Study**. Time study involves the determination of time a movement takes to complete. The movement which takes minimum time is the best. Motion study involves the study of movements in parts which are involved in doing a job and thereby eliminating the wasteful movements and performing only

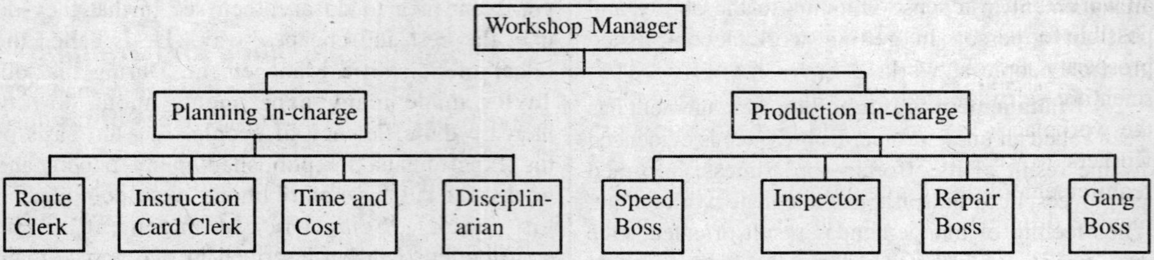

necessary movements. Fatigue study shows the amount and frequency of rest required in completing the work. After certain period of time, workers feel fatigue and cannot work with full capacity. Therefore, they require rest in between. Based on this study, Taylor standardised each part of a process and ensured that the wastage of time is minimum and output is higher.

4. Standardisation. Taylor emphasized that standardization should be maintained in respect of instruments and tools, period of work, amount of work, working conditions, cost of production etc. These things should be fixed in advance on the basis of job analysis and various elements of costs that go in performing a work.

5. Scientific Selection and Training of Workers. Taylor has suggested that workers should be selected on scientific basis taking into account their education, work experience, aptitude, physical strength etc. A worker should be given work for which he is physically and technically most suitable. Apart from selection, proper emphasis should be given on training of workers which makes them more efficient and effective.

6. Financial Incentives. Financial incentives can motivate workers to put in their maximum efforts. Taylor himself applied the concept of differential piece rate system which was highly motivating. In this scheme, there is considerable difference in wages between those who complete the work and those who do not complete in time.

7. Economy. While applying scientific management, adequate consideration should be given to economy and profits. For this purpose, techniques of cost estimates and control should be adopted. The economy and profit can be achieved by making resources more productive as well as by eliminating the wastages.

8. Mental Revolution. Scientific management depends upon the mutual cooperation between management and workers. For this, there should be mental change in both the parties. Taylor feels that this is the most important feature of scientific management because in its absence, no principle of scientific management can be applied.

Principles of Scientific Management

Taylor has given following basic principles of scientific management.

(a) Replacing Rule of Thumb with Science. Taylor has emphasised that organized knowledge should be applied which will replace rule of thumb. While the use of scientific method denotes precision in determining any aspect of work, rule of thumb emphasises estimation. This approach can be adopted in all aspects of managing.

(b) Harmony in Group Action. Taylor suggested that attempt should be made to obtain harmony in group action rather than discord. Group harmony suggests that there should be mutual give and take situation and proper understanding so that group as a whole contributes to the maximum.

(c) Co-operation. Scientific management is based upon mutual confidence, cooperation and goodwill. Cooperation between the management and the workers can be developed through mutual understanding and a change in thinking.

(d) Maximum Output. Scientific management involves continuous increase in production and productivity instead of restricted production either by management or by worker. Therefore, he advised the management and the workers to turn their attention towards increasing the size of the surplus until the size of the surplus becomes so large that it is necessary to quarrel over how it shall be divided.

(e) Development of Workers. According to him, all workers should be developed to the fullest extent possible for their own and for the company's highest prosperity. Development of workers requires their scientific selection and providing them training at the workplace. Training should be provided to the workers to keep them fully fit according to the requirement of new methods of workings which may be different than the non-scientific methods.

Evaluation of Scientific Management Theory

The principles of scientific management were more concerned with problems at the operating levels and did not emphasise management of an organization from the manager's point of view. This was probably due to the reasons that during that period industrial revolution was in full swing and most of economic activities were concentrated on manufacturing activity. Therefore, it was more relevant from the engineering point of view rather than that of management.

HENRY FAYOL'S ADMINISTRATIVE MANAGEMENT

Henry Fayol is considered as the father of Modern Management Theory. His contributions are generally termed as 'Operational Management' of 'Administrative Management'. Fayol looked at the problems of managing an organization from top management point of view. He has used the term 'administration' instead of 'management'. He also emphasised that principles of management are flexible and not absolute and are usable regardless of changing and special conditions.

According to Fayol, the activities of an industrial organization could be divided into six groups :

1. Technical
2. Commercial
3. Financial
4. Security
5. Accounting
6. Managerial

He said that these activities exist in business of every size. But, he devoted most of his analysis on the managerial activity only. He divided his approach of studying management into three parts:

A. Managerial Qualities and Training
B. General Principles of Management
C. Elements of Management

(A) Managerial Qualities and Training

He identified the qualities required in a manager. According to him, there are six types of qualities that a manager requires. They are :

(a) Physical (health, vigour and address)
(b) Mental (ability to understand and learn, judgement and adaptability)
(c) Moral(energy, firmness, loyalty, initiative and dignity)
(d) Educational (general acquaintance with matters)
(e) Technical (peculiar to the function being performed)
(f) Experience (arising from work)

Fayol has observed that the most important ability for a worker is technical. As one goes up the scalar chain, the relative importance of managerial ability increases, with insight becoming the most important ability for top level executives. He recognized a widespread need for principles of management and management teaching. He held that managerial ability should be acquired first in school and later in the workshop.

(B) General Principles of Management

Fayol has given 14 principles of management. He said that management principles are not exhaustive but suggestive and they are not rigid but flexible. It is a matter of knowing how to use them which is a difficult art requiring intelligence, experience and proportion. The principles are as below :

(1) Division of Work. Fayol advocated division of work to take advantage of specialization. This was because each change in the work brings in it training and adaptation which reduces output. This division of work, though upto certain limits only, should be applied throughout the organization.

(2) Authority and Responsibility. The authority and responsibility are related, with the latter the corollary of the former and arising from it. So, in order to discharge the responsibility properly, there should be parity of authority and responsibility.

(3) Discipline. All the personnel serving in the organization should be disciplined. Discipline may be self imposed or command discipline. While self imposed discipline comes from within the individual, command discipline stems from a recognized authority and utilizes deterrents to secure compliance with a desired action, which is expressed by established customs, rules and regulations.

(4) Unity of Command. Unity of command means that a person should get orders and instructions from only one superior. Otherwise, it creates conflict and confusion. This is contrary to Taylor's Functional Foremanship where a worker has two superiors, one is operational and one does the planning.

(5) Unity of Direction. It means that each group of activities with the same objective must have one head and one plan. It is concerned with functioning of the organization in respect of its grouping of activities or planning. Unity of direction provides better coordination among various activities to be undertaken by an organization.

(6) Subordination of Individual to General Interest. It refers to that individual interest must be subordinate to general interest of the organisation in case of conflict between the two. However, factors like ambition, laziness, weakness, etc. tend to reduce the importance of general interest. Therefore, superiors should set an example in fairness.

(7) Remuneration of Personnel. Remuneration of employees should be fair and provide maximum possible satisfaction to employees and employers. Fayol did not favour profit sharing programme for workers but advocated it for managers. He was also in favour of non-financial benefits though these were possible only in the case of large scale organizations.

(8) Centralization or Decentralization. According to Fayol, centralization and decentralization are the question of proportion. In small firms, centralization brings faster decisions and better execution of work, but in large firms a series of intermediaries are required and hence decentralisation is more effective.

(9) Scalar Chain. There should be a scalar chain of authority and of communication ranging from highest to the lowest. It suggests that each communication going up or coming down must flow through each position in the line of authority. It can be short circuited only in special circumstances. For this purpose, Fayol suggested **'Gang Plank'** in which the two persons at par can communicate to each other without going through the whole of scalar chain provided that it is authorized by their superior and the superior is informed of the communication.

(10) Order. This principle relates to the arrangement of people and things. It implies that there should be a place for everything and everything should be in its place. Similarly, there should be right man in the right place.

(11) Equity. Equity is the combination of justice and kindness. Equity in treatment and behaviour is liked by everyone and it brings loyalty in the organization.

(12) Stability of Tenure. No employee should be removed within short time. There should be reasonable security of jobs. Stability of tenure is essential to get an employee accustomed to new work and succeeding in doing it well.

(13) Initiative. Within the limits of authority and discipline, managers should encourage their employees for taking initiative.

(14) Esprit de Corps. This means 'unity is strength'. The manager should encourage esprit de corps among the employees for establishing team work.

(C) Elements of Management

Fayol said that management should be viewed as a process consisting of 5 elements. He regarded these elements as functions of management. They are

1. Planning
2. Organizing
3. Commanding
4. Coordination
5. Controlling

He has regarded planning as the most important managerial function. Creation of organization structure and commanding function is necessary to execute plans. Coordination is necessary to make sure that every one is working together, and control looks whether everything is proceeding according to the plan.

9. BUSINESS ENVIRONMENT

The term business environment cannotes external forces, factors and institutions that affect a business enterprise. It means the external conditions or forces within which a business firm operates. It includes all factors which are external to and beyond the control of individual business enterprises and their managements. *Thus, business environment may be defined as all those conditions and forces external to a business unit under which it operates.* These forces include customers, creditors, competitors, suppliers, government, sociocultural organisations, political parties,international organisations, etc. Some of these forces may have direct influence over the business firm while others may operate indirectly.

Kinds of Business Environment

For the purpose of proper understanding, business environment may be classified into : (*i*) Economic environment, (*ii*) Politico-Legal environment, (*iii*) Socio-cultural environment, (*iv*) Educationai environment, (*v*) Historical environment, and (*vi*) Physical environment. All enviroments other than economic environment may also be labelled as *non-economic environment.*

1. Economic Environment. The broad national economic environment is set by the nature of economic system embodying the nature of property right, ownership of means of production, production relations, role of planning, functioning of price mechanism, etc. Judged from these angles, the economic system of a country may be characterised as capitalist (free enterprise), socialist, communist, or mixed. The functioning of the business is greatly influenced by the economic environment of the country which is directed by the national government through fiscal policies, industrial regulations, economic controls, import-export policies, etc. For instance, if the Government announces a cut in the exise duty on refrigerators. the sales of business firms manufacturing refrigerators will go up. Similarly, if the Government allows liberal finance to export-oriented units on concessional rates, such units will get a boost.

The economic environment of a firm also includes all markets in which it buys and sells, raises funds, gets labour, etc. The business is invariably influenced by the conditions of various markets. For instance, if there is uncertainty in the capital market, it will not be advisable to issue shares and debentures to the public because of risk of under-subscription.

2. Politico-Legal Environment. It provides the legal framework within which the business is to function. The viability of business depends upon the ability with which it can meet the challenges arising out of the politico-legal environment. The politico-legal enviornment of a country is influenced by political organisations, political stablitity, Government's intervention in business, constitutional provisions affecting business, foreign policy, etc. All these factors have a bearing on business. For instance, bottling and sale of Coca Cola was discontinued in India in the late seventies because of the government policy of restricting the growth of multinational companies in the country. In 1989, the Government allowed another multi-national company, Pepsi Cola, to enter the Indian market to give boost to the food processing industry. In August 1993, the Supreme Court passed an order for the closure of iron foundaries around the famous Taj Mahal because of air pollution caused by them leading to an adverse impact on the beauty of Taj Mahal.

Stability of the Government is also an important factor from the point of view of growth of business. Businessmen prefer to start new units in those states where there is political stability and where rule of law prevails.

3. Socio-Cultural Environment. The socio-cultural environment of a nation determines the value system of the society which in turn affects the functioning of business. Sociological factors such as caste structure, mobility of labour, customs and conventions, cultural heritage, view towards scientific methods, respect for seniority, etc. might have a far reaching impact on business. For instance, the nature of goods and services in demand depends upon people's attitudes, customs, socio-cultural values, etc. In India, the attitudes of people have changed with respect to food and clothing as a result of industrialisation, employment of women in factories and offices and increased level of education. This has resulted in the growth of food processing and garment manufacturing units.

Socio-cultural environment determines the code of conduct the business should follow. If a business follows unethical practices, various social groups and Government will intervene to discipline it. For instance, if an industrial unit is not paying fair wages to workers, trade unions and Government will intervene. If it is indulging in adulteration, hoarding or black marketing, there are consumer forums and several government agencies to take action against it.

4. Technological Environment. In any country, the state of technolgy plays an important role in determining the type and quality of goods and services to be produced and the type of plant and equipment to be used. In the modern world, the pace of technological changes is very fast. Technological environment influences business oganisations in terms of investment in technology, consistent application of technology and the effects of technology on markets. Therefore, every big organisation has to be actively engaged in technological forecasting. Advancements in automation and information technology will create challenging situations for the organisations in the future.

5. Educational Environment. The type and level of education influence the quality of human resources available to the business. Educational environment factors which are relevant in relation to business are : attitude towards education, type of education, design of courses to meet the requirements of industry, literacy level, professional education, facilities for research and development, role of specialised institutions, etc.

6. Historical Environment. The historical heritage of the country also influences the current environment of business. The business environment in a number of newly independent nations has been largely determined by the colonial status which those countries enjoyed earlier. The French Revolution had much to do with the emergence of capitalist spirit of business and investment, World War I and the Soviet Revolution provided a perspetive to relaise the ambition of a State-owned and controlled business system. The declaration of Emergency in India in 1975 forced some business ethics and practices in India. Such examples can be multiplied. History is not be treated as "dead past" ; historical events and ideologies may exercise a strong impact on the current state of business.

7. Physical Environment. The physical and geographical factors can play a predominant role in constituting the non-economic environment and thereby affecting the business. The application of modern technology in industry leads to rapid economic growth at a huge social cost—deterioration of the physical environment around us, *i.e., air pollution, noise pollution, water pollution*, so on and so forth. The nature of such costs is being assessed by biologists, ecologists, sociologists and conserva-tionists. In the light of this, much talk is there about the social responsibilities of business. Business now has to calculate social net profitability (social benefit minus social cost) of its ventures. In this calculation, business must consider the physical environmental factors such as the quantity and quality of existing forest wealth, possibility of artificial rain, the exploitation of sea products like fish, the health hazards out of pollution, etc.

BUSINESS ENTREPRENEURSHIP

Plant Location

The location of an industrial unit is an important problem which its promoters have to deal with. It is the responsibility of the promoters to search out that location at which the unit will have easy access to raw materials, labour, power, market and certain services like banking, transportation, communication, insurance and warehousing. As far as possible, the location must be optimum so that the costs of production and distribution are the lowest. If the location of a plant is not suitable, it may cause many problems. For instance, transportation cost may be higher and the right type of labour may not be available. It may also restrict the growth of the firm.

The problem of location is faced not only by new concerns but also by the running concers which have growth plans. The growing concerns have to take decisions about the location of their new plants and sometimes, they are also faced with the problem of shifting the entire operations to a new place because of limitations of existing location and accommodation. Therefore, the new concerns should also take into consideration the growth factor and the possibility of changes in the environmental conditions while selecing the location.

FACTORS AFFECTING LOCATION

One of the important problems in launching an industrial enterprise is the choice of suitable location which will help in minimisation of production costs and maximisation of profit. In order to select an optimum location, the promoters must carefully study the impact of the following factors :

1. Availability of Raw Materials: The availability of the required quality and quantity of raw materials at a reasonable cost is an important factor for determining the location of an industrial unit. In many industries, the cost of raw material forms more than 50% of the total cost of their products. The impact of raw materials on location depends upon their nature and the source of their deposits. Weber classified raw materials into upiquities and localised materials. Generally, ubiquities like water, clay and sand which are found at all places have very little influence on location. That means the place of production would be fixed independently. But in some cases, materials of ubiquitous nature may so vary in quantity and quality that they are in fact regarded as fixed. For example, paper manufacturing plants require a regular supply of a large quantity of pure water and they are, therefore, located near the banks of the rivers.

Localised raw materials may be further subdivided into *pure mterials* such as raw cotton and wool, and *gross materials* such as sugarcane, iron ore and coal. The latter type of raw materials lose their weight in the process of production. If a large quantity of weights losing material is to be used during production, it is better to locate the plant near the source of material because there will be greater savings of transportation costs. For instance, iron and steel industry which uses coal and iron ore as raw materials has localised near the coal and iron ore mines.

2. Labour Supply: Every plant requires an adequate supply of labour with appropriate skills. Weber deducted that an industrial unit will deviate from the point of minimum transportation cost to the cheaper labour centre if the additional cost of transportation at the new centre is more than compensated by the savings in labour cost. But this hypothesis has lost its significance in the recent years becase of many reasons. Labour is easily moblie and there is a level of minimum wages fixed by law below which an industrial concern cannot go. Moreover, cartain industries are capital intensive and they require less labour. Therefore, it can be said that supply of labour, particularly in a country where there is large scale unemployment, is not as important as it used to be half a century ago.

3. Proximity to the Market: Industrial units using non-weight losing raw materials tend to locate near the markets because of so many advantages. A manufacturer can improve his customer relations and render rapid services to his customers. Industries producing perishable commodities and those producing for a local market are also drawn towards the market, because it would reduce the cost of transport in distributing the finished products. The industrial units end to disperse only if they fing new markets for their products.

4. Transport and Communication Facilities: Transport services are required for assembling materials and distribution of products. While selecting the location, it should be seen that transportation facilities are easily available at reasonable rates. The junction points of waterways, roadways and railways have the tendency to become industrial centres because of this reason only. If an industrial unit is directly linked with the means of transportation, its transportation costs are lower. Besides transportation, communication services also play an important role in the location of industrial units. Every business firm requires information as regards raw materials, finished goods and market price which can be made available only when there are communication facilities. Since transport and communication facilities are not adequately available in rural areas, entrepreneurs are reluctant to start their operations in those areas.

5. Power and Fuel: An adequate supply of power and fuel is an important factor for the uninterrupted operations of any enterprise. In the initial days of industrial revolution, industrial units were located near coal deposists because coal was the major source of power and fuel and is of weight losing nature and quite bulky. But with the introduction of other sources of power like electricity, gas, oil, etc, the power factor has become more mobile. This has helped in dispersal of industries. The industrial units which mainly depend on electric power tend to shift from a place if they do not get its regular supply. But iron and steel industry, where coal is still the major source of fuel, is located near the coal mines.

6. Climatic Considerations: Natural and climatic considerations like level of ground, topography (hilly and rocky surface) of a region, and drainage facilities influence the location of industries in certain cases. For example, cotton textile mills require a humid climate. The humid climate of Bombay offered great scope for the development of cotton textile industry. But the development of artificial humidification and air-conditioning has reduced the importance of climate to some extent. Entrepreneurs do not prefer to locate their units in hilly and rocky areas because of higher transport cost. Similarly, regions which are subject to frequent floods, earth-quakes, etc. do not attract industrial units.

7. Supply of Capital: Finance is the life-blood of any industrial venture. Availability of adequate funds at low rates of interests in an important factor influencing industrial location. But in these days, capital has become a highly mobile factor of production. Despite this fact, availability of funds at cheaper rates of interest is an important consideration. For instance, there are State Financial Corporations in various states which offer loans at a very low rate of interest if the entrepreneurs start their projects in the notified backward areas. Similarly, technocrat entrepreneurs who do not have sufficient capital to implement their projects will naturally be attracted towards those areas where they can get sufficient supply of finance.

8. External Economies: Sometimes, industrial units are located in those centres where other industrial units are already located. It is because of the fact that transportation, warehousing, banking, communication and other services are easily available. Secondly, the raw materials may be easily available at cheaper rates. For instance, by-product of one unit my be the raw material for another. Distilleries are located near the sugar factories because molasses which is a by-product of sugar industry is a raw material for the distilleries.

9. Strategic Considerations: Strategic considerations like law and order, political stability and safety also influence location. Naturally, entrepreneurs will like to locate their units in those areas which are safe and where there are least disturbances on account of law and order problems.

10. Government Policy: In planned economies, the role of government policy with respect to location of industries is crucial. In India, the Central Government follows the policy of balanced regional development of the country which is necessary from the point of view of social problems like slum, disparity of income and wealth and optium use of resources. In order to implement this policy, the

Government encourages the industrialists to invest their money in backward areas by giving various tax incentive in the form of remission of excise duty and sales tax. Government also offers certain non-tax incentives like loan at cheaper rates, factory sheds etc. to attract the entrepreneurs. The Government has also put restrictions on granting of licences to certain industries to be set up in metropolitan cities with a population of more than 10 lakhs and urban areas with more than 5 lakhs population as per 1981 census.

11. Miscellaneous Factors: Miscellaneous factors like historical incidents and attitude of the community also influence location of industries. In Mughal days, cottage industries thrived near the courts of rulers due to the patronage of state. Industrial relations atmosphere in the region also affects the location. Facilities like housing, medical, recreation, banking and credit also attract the location of certain industrial units.

CHOICE OF AN ORGANISATION (BUSINESS)

Choice of a suitable form of ownership organisation is an important problem while launching a new business enterprise. It is the form of ownership organisation which determines the power and responsibility of the entrepreneur. Once a form of orgnisation of chosen, it is very difficult and costly to switch over to another form of organisation. Hence, the form of ownership should be chosen after considerable thought and deliberation.

Essential Features of an Ideal Form of Organisation

In certain lines of business like insurance and banking, business can be undertaken only by the incorporated organisations. But in other cases, a large number of factors have to be considered while choosing a particular form of organisation. The important characteristics of an ideal form of organisation are discussed below.

1. Ease of Formation : The comparative ease or difficulty with which a business can be brought into existence makes one form preferable to another. The question of finding suitable business partners/ associates, promotion expenses and legal formalities are some of the components which make the formation easy or difficult depending upon the fact whether they are required to be gone through or not.

2. Ease of Raising Capital : Another important feature of a good form of organisation is its capacity to raise adequate funds. Generally speaking, an investor while investing his money looks to the safety of his investment, reasonable return on investment, transferability of investment and limited liability. Safety of investment, transferability of investment and limited liability are all present if the investors decide to invest their money in the form of company shares or debentures.

3. Limit of Liability : The form of organisation which can reduce the risk should be preferred to others. Except sole proprietorship and partnership, in all other forms of business organisations, the liability of the owner (s) is limited to the extent of investment in shares. In case of sole proprietorship and partnership, the liability of the owner (s) in unlimited in the sense that his personal estate (personal property and belongings) can be used to pay off the debts and losses sustained in the business. But unlimited liability has one great merit in that it provides the spur for initiative, drive and involvement in business.

4. Effectiveness of Management : Management constitutes one of the most crucial factors in business success. It is the effectiveness of management which can bring business prosperity and success and its ineffectiveness may push the business on the door of bankruptcy. The effectiveness of management depends upon three factors; (*i*) Motivation, (*ii*) Skill, and (*iii*) Flexibility. Motivation for effective management is high where ownership and management go hand in hand because of the direct relation of the rewards to the efforts put in. So far as the skill and flexibility are concerned, in case the owner is unable to contribute them, he brings in these by introducing outside talents either as partner(*s*) or as hired manager.

5. Ownership Control : If an entrepreneur wants to have a direct control over his business, the preferable form would be sole proprietorship. If a partnership is created he has to share control with other partners. In a private company the promoters may be able to retain effective control over the business of the company. But in case of a public company, the owners will have indirect control over the management of the company.

6. Flexibiility of Operation : An ideal form of business organisation is one which allows for maximum flexibility of operations. In other words. It should provide enough scope to the entrepreneur to adjust and adapt to changes. Any rigidity in regard to taking in of new members or raising of additional capital will not serve the interests of business.

7. Maintenance of Secrecy : Ordinarily a form of organisation which enables retention of business secrets is preferred to the one wherein business secrets are difficult to preserve. From this point of view, the sole proprietorship is the most ideal form of organisation. In case the partners have been chosen carefully, partnership form comes next to proprietory form of organisation in this respect. On the contrary, the company form is under legal obligation to put forward a number of important details by way of disclosure to the shareholders and the general public.

8. Stability or Continuity : The long life of business concern is desired both by the owners and the employees because the owner is able to reap the fruits of his investment over a long period of time and the employees find a source of continuous employment if the business continues for long. From the point of view of stability, company form is the ideal form of organisation because it remains unaffected by the continuance or discontinuance of its members, whereas sole proprietorship and partnership get affected immediately if the partner or the sole proprietor ceases to exist.

9. Freedom from Government Regulations : A form of organisation which does not attract too many Government regulations in its day-to-day working is preferred to a form in which there are frequent Government regulations. Some of the Government regulations apply on the basis of the size of the business enterprise rather than on the basis of the form of its ownership. But still a company form of organisation is subjected to more regulations by the Government than any other form. Sole proprietorship and partnership to that extent are in a preferable position.

10. Impact of Taxation : Everybody wants to minimise the burden of income tax. While selecting the form of organisation, impact of taxation should be given due consideration. Tax liability is not the same in all forms of ownership. Sole traders and partnership firms are liable to pay income-tax on a slab rate system. The rate of tax increases if their income exceeds a particular slab. But in case of companies, a flat rate of income tax is to be paid. The impact of tax burden should be considered in the light of the prevailing rates of tax.

INITIAL CHOICE OF ORGANISATION

The choice of the form of organisation at the time of launching a new enterprise depends upon the nature of business activity. Volume and area of operations, degree of control desired, initial capital requirement, extent of liability, continuity of business, Government regulation and tax burden. It is important to point out that these factors are inter-related and inter-dependent. The relationship between the various factors must be clearly identified. The impact of various factors on the choice of the suitable form or orgnisation is discussed below :

1. Nature of business activity: Initially, the entrepreneur has to decide about the kind of business activity he is going to undertake, namely, trading activity, manufacturing activity, service activity, etc., and then decide in favour of a particular form of organisation. A trading activity proposed to be undertaken on a small scale can be done thorugh sole proprietorship. The same will be the case if he wants to render service as an hair dresser, a tailor, or a jeweller. But if he wants to undertake a manufacturing business then he will have to think of either partnership or company form of organisation.

2. Expected volume of business: If the good to be produced and sold are going to be on a large scale, then a company form of organisa-tion would be suitable. But if the volume of business proposed to be handled is small then a sole proprietor-ship or partnership form of organisation will do.

3. Area of operation: In case a widespread area is proposed to be covered through the business operation, a company form is better suited than any other form. But if the area of operation is confined to a particular locality, sole proprietory or partnership form of organisation will be adequate.

4. Degree of control desired: If a businessman aims at having a direct control over his business operations, the preferable form would be sole proprietorship. But if he is not interested in direct control and is instead interested in the large size of operation, it would be preferable to go in for a company form or co-operative form of organisation.

5. Initial finance required: If the finance required to start the business is quite huge, then there is no choice except to start it in the form of a company organisation. But if the initial finance proposed to be invested is small then a sole proprietary form or a partnership form of organisation would be more suitable.

6. Liability: If the entrepreneur is not deterred by unlimited liability if the business runs into losses, then he would not mind starting the business as a sole proprietary one. But in case of his hesitation to shoulder the entire risk single handedly or bear the unlimited liability, he would like to go in for either partnership or company form of organisation.

7. Continuity of business: If the entrepreneur wishes the business to continue indefinitely, he would decide to start it in the form of company or co-operative organisation. But if he is not interested in its long life, he may start as a sole proprietary or as a partnership business.

8. Government regulations: If the entrepreneur wishes to avoid too much Government controls and regulations of business, he would prefer sole proprietorship or partnership. Business undertaken through company and co-operative forms of organisations are subjected to a lot of Government controls and regulations through the Companies Act and the Co-operative Societies Act.

9. Tax burden: There is a single (or flat) rate of tax on corporate profits which is quite high. The rate of tax remains the same irrespective of the volume of corporate profits. But sole traders and partnership firms are subjected to a progressive rate of income tax, *i.e.,* the rate of tax goes on increasing with the increase in the volume of profits. That means the income tax payable will be lower in cases of lower slabs of income of sole traders and partnership firms. Therefore, if low profits are expected from the business, it should be organinsed on a sole proprietorship or partnership basis. But if large profits are expected from the business, it should be organised as a joint stock company because this form of organisation has an edge over the other forms as regards amount of capital, limited, liability and continuity of business.

GROWTH STRATEGY

Strategy is an essential ingredient of management of all enterprises. The term 'strategy' has been adapted from war and has been applied to a wide range of administrative thinking. According to Chandler, "*Strategy is the determination of the basic long-term goals and objectives of an enterprise and the adoption of courses of action and the allocation of resources necessary to carry out these objectives.*" Strategy is a firm's planned course of action to fight competition and to increase its market share. It is implemented by the direction of operations for fulfilment of the strategic plans. Thus, strategy is the action element of business operations.

Significance of Growth Strategy

Every business should have a strategy or an overall plan of action to meet the challenges of environment in future. Moreover, a strategy must be accompanied by the use of proper tactics or it will fail. An effective strategy would enhance the likelihood of business survival. It would be able to meet aspirations of employees for opportunities of advancement in the company.

Creation of effective business strategy requires a basic knowledge of economic theory, management principles, and administrative practices. A knowledge of the tools of analysis like accounting, statistics and finance is also necessary. The strategic planner should understand the significance of business strategy in clear terms. Strategy is important as it makes possible the implementation of policy and long-range plans for achieving organisational goals. It is also important in defining the kind of business in which the organisation engages itself and its reliance on ethical business practices.

TYPES OF GROWTH STRATEGIES

There are three types of growth strategies which may be followed by the business firms. These include:

1. Intensive growth strategy.
2. Diversification strategy.
3. Integrative growth strategy.

The strategies represent strategic decision of the management regarding the growth of the firm. They provide answer to question like what rate of growth, hw fast and slow? The first two strategies represent internal growth of business.

Intensive Growth Strategy

It is a strategy of '*aggregation*' or expansion under which growth is achieved by expanding the scale of operations. This strategy involves expansion of firm's product range and market. Three alternative strategies in this regard are as follows :

(a) Market Penetration: This strategy aims to seek increased sales of the present products in the present markets through more aggressive promotion and distribution. The firm tries to penetrate deeper into the market to increase its market share. More money is spent on advertising and sale promotion to increase sale volume.

(b) Market Development: This strategy aims to increase sales volume by selling the present products into new markets. For example, Pepsi Cola had achieved growth by capturing foreign markets. The existing product is pushed into new markets by changing its packaging, or brand name, etc.

(c) Product Development: Under this strategy, a business seeks to grow by developing improved products for the present markets. The current product may be replaced or the new products may be introduced in addition to the existing products. The introduction of "Colgate-gel" by Colgate-Palmolive (India) Ltd. is and example in this regard.

To sum up, the intensive growth strategy involves the internal growth of the concern within its existing corporate structure. It is also known as growth through aggregation. The management of a firm may decide to grow through expansion of scale of operations in order to attain optimum size The firm will achieve many economies in purchasing, production, financing, marketing and management.

Advantages

The advantages of intensive growth strategy are as under :

(*i*) The growth is gradual and it is easier to handle growth. The working of the organisation is smooth.

(*ii*) Intensive growth is possible through internal financing. Profit of the firm may be reinvested for improving and expanding product range.

(*iii*) The existing resources of the firm are fully utilised.

(*iv*) The managers are involved since the inception of growth strategy. There is no problem of managing new products or markets as the managers are fully prepared to handle new operations.

(*v*) Economies of large scale operations are achieved.

Limitations

The limitations of intensive growth strategy are as under :

(*i*) It takes a long time to achieve the target rate of growth and it is a very slow growth strategy.

(*ii*) The business firm may not be able to exploit present opportunities in the market if it is to grow gradually

(*iii*) The scope for expansion of product and market may be limited.

DIVERSIFICATION STRATEGY

Under this growth strategy, the company seeks increased sales by developing new products for new markets. The diversification does not add variety in any one product but introduces entirely different types of products. Products added may be complementary *i.e.,* they fit in the product mix. Such expansion will permit greater utilisation of special talents and know-how, of common overheads, of the marketing organisation, of the research programme and staff, of the brand name or of other facilities. For example, a manufacturer may diversify his activities by manufacturing, VCPs and VCRs alongwith TV sets. Such an expansion is known as *Concentric diversification* as it is related to existing products and facilities.

It may also happen that the new product is in no way related to the existing product line. Such type of growth is called *conglomerate diversification.* For example, a cement manufacturer may enter into the production of sugar.

The distinction between intensive growth strategy and diversification strategy must be carefully noted. In the case of intensive growth, the firm increases the production and sale of its existing products. But in case of diversification, there is addition of new products and new markets. A firm may choose the strategy of diversification under the following situations :

(*a*) When the firm cannot meet its growth target by the strategy of intensive growth only.

(*b*) When diversification promises a greater profitability than expansion.

(*c*) When the firm has huge funds at its disposal which can be utilised for expansion of products and market.

A firm may also choose both the intensive growth strategy and diversification strategy simultaneously if it has adequate capital to finance growth and human resources to handle growth. Ansoff has designed the following matrix (Table 1) to decide the choice between intensive growth strategy and diversification strategy.

Market/Product	*Present*	*New*
Present	Market Penetration	Product Development
New	Market Development	Diversification

Table 1. *Product-Market Matrix and Growth Strategy.*

Advantages

The advantages of diversification strategy are as under :

(*i*) Diversification offers greater scope for growth and probability as compared to intensive growth strategy.

(*ii*) Because of diversification, the business risks are scattered. New products are added, Loss in one product is made good by profit in other products.

(*iii*) The existing facilities such as machines overheads, marketing organisation, etc. are fully utilised.

(*iv*) The firm producing a large number of products can absorb the shocks of business cycles. For instance, if there is a depression in the sale of a product, the firm will survive if it is doing good business in other products.

(*v*) The growth is systematic and does not affect the normal functioning of the firm.

Limitations

The limitations of diversification are as given below:

(*i*) Adequate funds are required for diversification. The internal savings of the business may not be sufficient to finance growth.

(*ii*) Diversification may involve new technology and new markets. The existing staff may experience problems in adapting to this growth pattern.

(*iii*) The tasks and responsibilities of top executives increase because of need to handle new product, technology and markets.

INTERGRATIVE GROWTH STRATEGY (GROWTH BY COMBINATION)

It is a strategy of *growth by combination.* Two or more firms may decide to combine or merge to form a bigger enterprise. When one firm takes over another firm, it is called merged or absorption. But if a new firm is created by combining (or merging) two existing firms, it is called amalgamation.

The alternatives of integrative growth strategy are as discussed below :

(a) Backward Integration: A company engaged in production of a product may integrate, backward upto the sources of raw materials. This would ensure continuous supply of raw materials for the production processes of the company. The acquisition of a textile mill by a ready-made garments manufacturer is a case of backward integration.

(b) Forward Integration: A company may decide to grow through forward integration with the distribution channels of its products. It may acquire certain distribution channels to have a greater control over the distribution of its products. The manufacturer of readymade garments may take over certain retail shops to ensure ready market for his products.

(c) Horizontal Integration: It takes place by merging of units engaged in manufacturing similar products or rendering similar services. That means competing firms are brought together under single ownership and management. For instance, if two or more sugar mills are combined under the same ownership, it will be a case of horizontal integration. The benefits of this type of integration are economies of large scale operations and evasion of unnecessary competition.

(d) Conglomerative Growth: A company is said to follow the conglomerative growth strategy if it acquires another firm which is engaged in altogether different line of business and is using different trade channels. In other words, it seeks its future growth through entering lines of business unrelated to its present market channels or technology. For instance a textile company may take over units engaged in chemicals, fertilisers, suger, electrical equipments, etc.

Advantages

The merits of integrative growth strategy are as under :

(*i*) It ensures acquisition of running manufacturing units. The problems of promotion are not to be faced.

(*ii*) Business growth is quick because running units are acquired.

(*iii*) The business takes over sources of raw materials. Some sort of self-sufficiency is achieved as far as raw materials are concerned.

(*iv*) Acquisition of established market channels facilitate the marketability of the products.

Limitations

The limitations of integrative growth strategy are as under :

(*i*) Integrative growth strategy can be implemented only if huge capital is available with the business firm.

(*ii*) Competent and professional executives are needed to handle the affairs of new units. The existing staff of the acquired units may not be able to adjust with the new management.

(*iii*) There is a need of overall revision of the organisation structure to meet new challenges. If it is not done, there will be problems of coordination in the working of acquired units.

10. MANAGEMENT FUNCTION

Management is an essential activity in every sphere of organised activity. The efficient management of human and material resources is essential for the achievement of objectives of any group. management pervades virtually every aspect of organised life. It is a process of taking certain decisions and putting them into action. Both these activities, *i.e.,* deciding and doing, are very important in every field of life. The significance of management will be more clear by going through the following points :

1. Determination of Objectives: The objectives of any organisation are determined by the management. They are put into writing and communicated to all others in the organisation. No organisation can succeed in its operations unless its objectives are identified and well defined.

2. Achievement of Objectives: Management is an important force for the accomplishment of the objective of any group. The perfect coordination and integration of human and non-human resources is brought about by the management or the individuals known as 'managers'. Managers reconcile the objectives of the enterprise and those of the individuals comprising it. They direct and coordinate the activities of the individuals comprising it. They direct and coordinate the activities of the individuals in the use of material resources for the achievement of pre-determined goals.

3. Brain of Enterprise: Management is the brain of any enterprise. All the policy decisions are taken by it. Management keeps itself in touch with the current environment and supplies foresight to the enterprise. It helps in predicting what is going to happen in future which will influence the working of the enterprise. It also takes steps to ensure that the enterprise is able to meet the demands of changing environment.

4. Efficient use of Resources: The role of expert and professional managers has increased these days because of the separation of ownership from management and growth of capital intensive techniques of production. Only the expert managers can meet the new challenges. They can increase the productivity by proper utilisation of the exiting resources. An efficient management can lead a business towards growth and prosperity. It provides leadership to the business and hepls in achieving its objectives. In short, managing is no more restricted to the mere exercise of authority, but it also involves scientific thinking, deciding and thoughtful organisa-tion, direction and control to ensure better results.

5. Economic Development: Efficient management is equally important at the national level. According to Peter Drucker, "Management is the crucial factor in economic and social development." The development of a country is virtually dependent upon the quality of management of its resources. No amount of capital investment and import of technical now-how and equipment will succeed in further economic development of a country if such wealth producing resources are not managed properly. Thus, it can be concluded that efficient management is a key to the growth of economy of any country.

FUNCTIONS OF MANAGEMENT

Many management writers have discussed the functions of management. But there is no unanimity among them about the nomenclature of the functions of mangement. Henri Fayol classified management functions as forecasting and planning, organising, commanding, coordination, and controlling, But Ralph Davis classified managerial functions into three categories, *viz.*, planning, organising and control. He was of the view that command and coordination facilitate control and, therefore, should be considered as part of it. However, some authors argue that coordination is not a separate function as it is the essence of management.

Luther Gulick coined the word 'PODSCORB' to describe the functions of management. This word is made up of the initials of the following functions, namely (*i*) *planning,* (*ii*) *organising,* (*iii*) *directing,* (*iv*) *staffing,* (*v*) *coordinating,* (*vi*) *reporting,* (*vii*) *budgeting.* Thus, there is no universally accepted classification of managerial functions. Though there is disagreement over the grouping and classification, there is general agreement that certain management functions exist.

In classifying the functions of management, one must distinguish clearly important operations such as marketing, manufacturing, accounting, engineering and purchasing. These differ from one enterprise to another but the functions of managers are common to all. We can broadly classify the functions of manage-ment under the following five broad categories: (1) Planning; (2) Organising; (3) Staffing; (4) Directing; (5) Controlling.

1. Planning: Planning is the determination of a course of action to achieve in advance the desired results. It is selecting and relating of facts and making and using of assumptions regarding the future in the visualisation and information of proposed activities believed to be necessary to achieve the desired results. *It involves deciding in advance what to do, when to do it, where to do it, how to do it and who is to do it and how the results are to be evaluated.* Thus, planning is the systematic thinking about the ways and the means for the accomplishment of pre-determined objectives. The goals or objectives have to be clarified first before taking any other decision. Goals provide the basis for looking into the future and for evaluating the performance with the pre-determined standards.

Systematic planning is necessary for any business activity, otherwise it will be done in a haphazard manner. It will ensure proper utilisation of human and non-human resources to achieve the desired goals. Planning has to be done at all levels of management. Since planning involves taking important decisions, top management devotes more time on planning as compared to lower levels of management.

The process of planning involves the following steps :

(*i*) determination of goals or objectives of the enterprise,
(*ii*) forecasting,
(*iii*) search of alternative courses of action,
(*iv*) evaluation of various alternative and formulation of a plan,
(*v*) formulation of policies and procedures,
(*vi*) preparation of schedules, programmes and budgets.

2. Organising: Organising involves the determination and providing of various resources required to achieve the organisational objectives. In order to put its plan into action, management has to employ people and allocate them the work each has to do. Management has also to provide them the work each has to do. Management has also to provide them with material resources like money, materials, machines and equipment to do their jobs well. According to Fayol, "*To organise a business is to provide it with everything useful to its functioning – raw materials, tools, capital and personnel.*" Thus organising is an important managerial activity by which mangement brings together the manpower and material resources for the achievement of certain objectives.

Organisation as a function of management involves *identificaion and grouping the activities to be performed and dividing them among the individuals and creating authority and responsibility relationship among them.* The process of organisation involves the following steps :

(*i*) Determination of objectives and identification of main activities
(*ii*) Division of activities and creation of jobs
(*iii*) Fitting individuals into jobs
(*iv*) Developing relationship in terms of authorities and responsibilities

3. Staffing: The staffing function has assumed great importance these days because of repid advancement of technology, increasing size of organisations and complex behaviour of human beings. According to Harold Koontz and Cyril O'Donnell, "*Staffing involves manning the organisational structure through proper and effective selection, appraisal, and development of personnel to fill the roles designed into the structure.*"

The staffing function involves recruitment, selection, training, development and appraisal of personnel. Every manager is continuously engaged in performing the staffing function. He is actively associated with the recruitment, selection, training and appraisal of his subordinates. The Board of Directors of a company undertakes staffing function by selecting, helping develop and appraising a chief executive who in turn performs these functions in relation to the heads of various divisions or departments of the enterprise. The departmental heads also select, train and appraise their assistants and so on. Finally, the first line managers or supervisors perform the staffing function when they participate in selecting, training and appraising their subordinates. Thus it can be said that staffing is also a pervasive function of management like other functions of mangement.

4. Direction: *Direction is that part of the management process which actuates the organisational members to work efficiently and effectively for the attainment of organisational objectives.* It constitutes the life spark of the enterprise which, like electric power, sets it into motion. Planning, organising and staffing are merely preparations for doing the work and the work actually starts when the managers start performing the direction function. Direction is the *inter-personal aspect of management* which deals directly with influencing, guiding, supervising and motivating the subordinates for the accomplishment of pre-determined objectives.

According to Joseph Massie, "Directing concerns the total manner in which a manager influences the actions of subordinates. It is the final action of a manager in getting others to act after all preparations have been completed." It consists of three sub-functions :

(*a*) Communication : It is the process of passing information and understanding from one person to another. A manager has always to tell the subordinates what to do, how to do it and when to do it. he has to create an understanding in their minds in regard to these things in his department.

(*b*) Leadership : Leadership may be defined as the process by which a manager guides and influences the work of his subordinates. It is the quality of the behaviour of a manager whereby he guides his subordinates or their activities in the desired direction. A manager, as an effective leader, should consult his subordinates and among the subordinates.

(*c*) Motivation : Motivaiton means inspiring the subordinates with a zeal to do work for the accomplishment of organisational objectives. A manager should make appropriate use of motivation to actuate the subordinates to work harmoniously towards the achievement of organisational goals. Different people are motivated by different types of rewards. To some financial incentives like job security, job enlargement, freedom to work, recognition, achievement, etc.

5. Controlling: Controlling is seeing that actual performance is guided towards expected performance. It is related to all other management functions. All other management functions cannot be completed effectively without performance of the control function. According to Haimann, "*Control is the process of checking to determine whether or not proper progress is being made towards the objectives and goals and acting, if necessary, to correct any deviation.*"

Koontz and O'Donnell have defined controlling "*as the measurement and correction of the performance of activities of subordinates in order to make sure that enterprise, objectives and the plans devised to attain them are being accomplished.*" Thus, controlling involves the following elements :

1. Setting standards of performance
2. Measurement of actual performance
3. Comparing of actual performance with the standards
4. Taking corrective measures if the performance does not meet the standards of performance

11. FINANCIAL MANAGEMENT

NATURE

The term 'nature' as applied to financial management refers to its relationship with the closely-related fields of economic and accounting, its functions, scope and objectives. Financial management, as an academic discipline, has undergone fundamental changes in its scope and coverage. In the early years of its evolution it was treated synonymously with the raising of funds. In the current literature pertaining to financial management, a broader scope so as to include, in addition to procurement of funds, efficient use of resources is universally recognised. Similarly, the academic thinking as regards the objective of financial management is also characteristics by a change over the years. Financial management, as an integral part of overall management, is not a totally independent area. It draws heavily on related disciplines and fields of study, such as economics, accounting, marketing, production and quantitative methods. Although these disciplines are inter-related, there are key differences among them.

Finance and Economics

The relevance of economics to financial management can be described in the light of the two broad areas of economics: macroeconomics and microeconomics.

Macroeconomics is concerned with the overall institution environment in which the firm operates. It looks at the economy as a whole. Macro-economics is concerned with the institutional structure of the banking system, money and capital markets, financial intermediaries, monetary, credit and fiscal policies and economic policies dealing with, and controlling level of, activity within an economy. Since business firms operate in the macroeconomics environment, it is important for financial managers to understand the broad economic environment. Specifically, they should (1) recognise and understand how monetary policy affects the cost and the availability of funds; (2) be versed in fiscal policy and its effects on the economy; (3) be aware of the various financial institutions/financing outlets; and (4) understand the consequences of various levels of economic activity and changes in economic policy for their decision environment and so on.

Microeconomics deals with the economic decisions of individuals and organisations. It concerns itself with the determination of optimal operating strategies. In other words, the theories of microeconomics provide for effective operations of business firms. They are concerned with defining actions that will permit the firms to achieve success. The concepts and theories of microeconomics relevant to financial management are, for instance, those involving (1) supply and demand relationships and profit maximisation strategies, (2) issues related to the mix of productive factors, 'optimal' sales level and product pricing strategies, (3) measurement of utility preferences, risk and the determination of value, and (4) the rationale of depreciating assets. In addition, the primary principle that applies in financial management is marginal analysis, it suggests that financial decision should be made on the basis of comparison of marginal revenue and marginal cost. Such decisions will lead to an increase in profits of the firm. It is therefore, important that financial managers must be familiar with basic microeconomics.

Thus, a knowledge of economics is necessary for a financial manager to understand both the financial environment and the decision theories which under-lie contemporary financial management. He should be familiar with these two areas of economics. Macroeconomics provides the financial manager with an insight into policies by which economic activity is controlled. Operating within that institutional framework, the financial manager draws on microeconomic theories of the operations of firm and profit maximisation.

Finance and Accounting

The relationship between finance and accounting, conceptually speaking, has two dimensions :

1. They are closely related to the extent that accounting is an important input in financial decision making; and
2. There are key differences in viewpoints between them.

Accounting function is a necessary input into the finance function. That is, accounting is a sub function of finance. Accounting generates information/data relating to operations/activities of the firm. The end-product of accounting constitutes financial statements such as the balance sheet, the income statement (profit and loss account) and the statement of changes in financial position (sources and uses of funds statement). The information contained in these statements and reports assists financial managers in assessing the past performance and future directions of the firm and in meeting certain legal obligations, such as payment of taxes and so on. Thus, accounting and finance are functionally closely related.

But there are key differences between finance and accounting. The first difference relates to the treatment of funds while the second relates to decision making.

Finance and Other Related Disciplines

Apart from economics and accounting, finance also draws for its key day-to-day decisions on supportive disciplines such as marketing, production and quantitative methods. For instance, financial managers should consider the impact of new product development and promotion plans made in the marketing area since their plans will require capital outlays and have an impact on the projected cash flows. Similarly, changes in the production process may necessitate capital expenditures which the financial managers must evaluate and finance. And, finally, the tools of analysis developed in the quantitative methods area are helpful in analysing complex financial management problems.

The marketing, production and quantitative methods are, thus, only indirectly related to day-to-day decision making by financial managers and are supportive in nature while economics and accounting are the primary disciplines on which the financial manager draws substantially.

The relationship between financial manage-ment and supportive disciplines is depicted in the following Fig. 1.

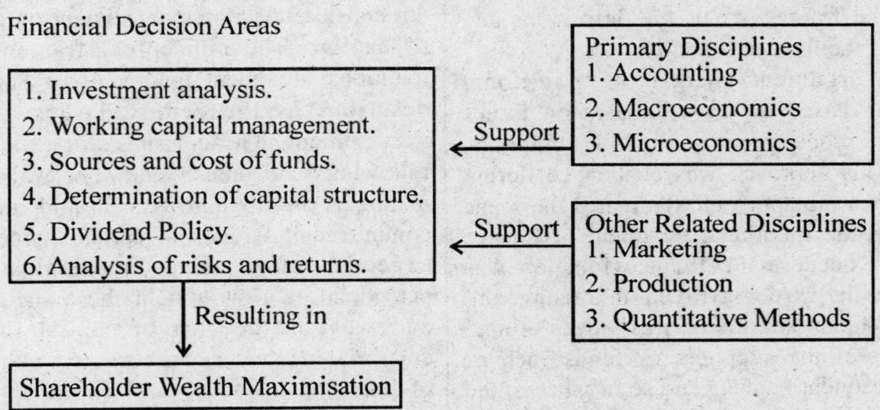

Fig. 1. *Impact of other Disciplines on Financial Management*

SCOPE OF FINANCIAL MANAGEMENT

The approach to the scope and functions of financial management is divided, for purpose of exposition, into two broad categories :

(*a*) The Traditional Approach, and

(*b*) The Modern Approach

(*a*) Traditional Approach: The traditional approach to the scope of financial management refers to its subject matter, in academic literature in the initial stages of its evolution, as a separate branch of academic study. The term 'corporation finance' was used to describe what is now known in the academic world as 'Financial management'. As the name suggests, the concern of corporation finance was with the financing of corporate enterprises. In other words, the scope of the finance function was treated by the traditional approach in the narrow sense of procurement of funds by corporate enterprise to meet their financing needs. The term 'procurement' was used in a broad sense.

The traditional approach to the scope of the finance function evolved during the 1920s and 1930s and dominated academic thinking during the forties and through the early fifties. The weakness of the traditional approach falls into two broad categories:

(*i*) those relating to the treatment of various topics and the emphasis attached to them; and

(*ii*) those relating to the basic conceptual and analytical framework of the definitions and scope of the finance function.

The first argument against the traditional approach was based on its emphasis on issues relating to the procurement of funds by corporate enterprises. This approach was challenged during the period when the approach dominated the scene itself. Further, the traditional treatment of finance was criticised because the finance function was equated with the issue involved in raising and administering funds, the theme was woven around the viewpoint of the suppliers of funds such as investors, investment bankers and so on, that is, the outsiders. It implies that no consideration was given to the viewpoint of those who had to take internal financial decisions. The traditional treatment was, in other words, the outsider-looking-in approach. The limitation was that internal decision making (i.e., insider-looking-out) was completely ignored.

The second ground of criticism of the traditional treatment was that the focus was on financing problems of corporate enterprises. To that extent the scope of financial management was confined only to a segment of the industrial enterprises, as non-corporate organisations lay outside its scope.

Another basis on which the traditional approach was challenged, was that the treatment was built too closely around episodic events, such as promotion, incorporation, merger, consolidation, reorganisation and so on. Financial management was confined to a description of these infrequent happenings in the life of an enterprise. As a logical corollary, the day-to-day financial problems of a normal company did not receive much attention.

Finally, the traditional treatment was found to have a lacuna to the extent that the focus was on long term financing. Its natural implications was that the issues involved in working capital were not in the purview of the finance function.

The limitations of the traditional approach were not entirely based on treatment or emphasis of different aspects. In other words, its weaknesses were more fundamental. The conceptual and analytical shortcomings of this approach arose from the fact that it confined financial management to issues involved in procurement of external funds, it did not consider the important dimension of allocation of capital. The conceptual framework of the traditional treatment ignored what Solomon aptly describes as the central issues of financial management. These issues are reflected in the following fundamental questions which a finance manager should address. Should an enterprise commit capital funds to certain purpose? Do the expected returns meet financial standards of performance? How should these standards be set and what is the cost of capital funds to the enterprise? How does the cost vary with the mixture of financing methods used? In the absence of the coverage of these crucial aspects, the traditional approach implied a very narrow scope for financial management. The modern approach provides a solution to these shortcomings.

(*b*) Modern Approach: The modern approach views the term financial management in a broad sense and provides a conceptual and analytical framework for financial decision making. According to it, the finance function covers both acquisition of funds as well as their allocations. Thus, apart from the issues involved in acquiring external funds, the main concern of financial management is the efficient and wise allocation of funds to various uses. It is an integral part of overall management.

The new approach is an analytical way of viewing the financial problems of a firm. The main contents of this approach are: What is the total volume of funds an enterprise should commit? What specific assets should the enterprise acquire? How should the funds required be financed? Alternatively, the principal contents of the modern approach to financial management can be said to be :

(*i*) How large should an enterprise be, and how fast should it grow?
(*ii*) In what form should it hold assets? and
(*iii*) What should be the composition of its liabilities?

The three questions posed above cover between them the major financial problems of a firm. In other words, financial management, according to the new approach, is concerned with the solution of three major problems relating to the financial operations of a firm, corresponding to the three questions of investment, financing and dividend decisions. Thus, financial management, in the modern sense of the term, can be broken into three major decisions as functions of finance:

(*i*) The investment decision,
(*ii*) The financing decision, and
(*iii*) The dividend policy decision.

(*i*) The Investment Decision: The investment decision relates to the selection of assets in which funds will be invested by a firm. The assets which can be acquired fall into two broad groups :

(*i*) long-term assets which yield a return over a period of time in future,
(*ii*) short-term or current assets, defined as those assets which in the normal course of business are convertible into cash without dimunition in value, usually within a year.

The first of these involving the first category of assets is popularly known in financial literature as **capital budgeting**. The aspect of financial decision making with reference to current assets or short-term assets is popularly termed as working capital management.

Capital Budgeting: Capital budgeting is probably the most crucial financial decision for a firm. It relates to the selection of an asset or investment proposal or course of action whose benefits are likely to be available in future over the life time of the project. The long-term assets can be either new or old/existing ones. The first aspect of the capital budgeting decision relates to the choice of the new asset out of the alternatives available or the reallocation of capital when an existing asset fails to justify the funds committed. Whether an asset will be accepted or not will depend upon the relative benefits and return associated with it. The measurement of the worth of the investment proposals is, therefore, a major element in the capital budgeting exercises. This implies a discussion of the methods of appraising investment proposals.

The second element of the capital budgeting decision is the analysis of risk and uncertainty. Since the benefits from the investment proposals extend into the future, their accrual is uncertain. They have to be estimated under various assumptions of the physical volume of sale and the level of prices. An element of risk in the sense of uncertainty of future benefits is, thus, involved in the exercise. The returns from capital budgeting decisions should, therefore, be evaluated in relation to the risk associated with it.

Finally, the evaluation of the worth of a long-term project implies a certain norm or standard against which the benefits are to be judged. The requisite norm is known by different names such as cut-off rate, hurdle rate, required rate, minimum rate of return and so on. This standard is broadly expressed in terms of the cost of capital. The concept and measurement of the cost of capital is, thus, another major aspect of capital budgeting decision.

In brief, the main elements of capital budgeting decisions are:

(*i*) The long-term assets and their composition,
(*ii*) The business risk complexion of the firm, and
(*iii*) Concept and measurement of the cost of capital.

Working Capital Management: Working capital management is concerned with the management of current assets. It is an important and integral part of financial management as short-term survival is a pre-requisite for long-term success. One aspect of working capital management is the trade-off between profitability and risk (liquidity). There is a conflict between profitability and liquidity. If a firm does not have adequate working capital, that is, it does not invest sufficient funds in current assets, it may become illiquid and consequently may not have the ability to meet its current obligations and, thus, invite the risk of bankruptcy. If the current assets are too large, profitability is adversely affected. The key strategies and considerations in ensuring a trade-off between profitability and liquidity is one major dimension of working capital management. In addition, the individual current assets should be efficiently managed so that neither inadequate nor unnecessary funds are locked up. Thus, the management of working capital has two basic ingredients:

1. an overview of working capital management as a whole, and
2. efficient management of the individual current assets such as cash, receivables and inventory.

(*ii*) Financing Decision: The second major decision involved in financial management is the financing decision. The investment decision is broadly concerned with the asset-mix or the composition of the assets of a firm. The concern of the financing decision is with the financing-mix or capital structure or leverage. The term capital structure refers to the proportion of debt (fixed-interest sources of financing) and equity capital (variable-dividend securities source of funds). The financing decision of a firm relates to the choice of the proportion of these sources to finance the investment requirements. There are two aspects of the financing decision. First, the theory of capital structure which shows the theoretical relationship between the employment of debt and the return to the shareholders. The use of debt implies a higher return to the shareholders as also the financial risk. A proper balance between debt and equity to ensure a trade-off between risk and return to the shareholders is necessary. A capital structure with a reasonable proportion of debt and equity capital is called the optimum capital structure. Thus, one dimension of the financing decision whether there is an optimum capital structure? And in what proportion should funds be raised to maximise the return to the shareholders? The second aspect of the financing decision is the determination of an appropriate capital structure, given the facts of a particular case. Thus, the financing decision covers two inter-related aspects : (1) Capital structure theory, and (2) Capital structure decision.

(*iii*) Dividend Policy Decision: The third major decision of financial management is the decision relating to the dividend policy. The dividend should be analysed in relation to the financing decision of a firm. Two alternatives are available in dealing with the profits of a firm : they can be distributed to the shareholders in the form of dividends or they can be retained in the business itself. The decision as to which course should be followed depends largely on a significant element in the dividend decision, the dividend pay out ratio, that is, what proportion of net profits should be paid out to the shareholders. The final decision will depend upon the preference of the shareholders and investment opportunities available within the firm. The second major aspect of the dividend decision is the factors determining dividend policy of a firm in practice.

To conclude, the traditional approach had a very narrow perception and was devoid of an integrated conceptual and analytical framework. It had rightly been discarded in current academic literature. The modern approach has broadened the scope of financial management which involves the solution of three major decisions, namely, investment, financing and dividend. These are inter-related and should be jointly taken so that financial decision-making is optimal. The conceptual framework for optimum financial decisions is the objective of financial management. In other words, to ensure an optimum decision in respect of these three areas, they should be related to the objectives of financial management.

Objectives of Financial Management

To make wise decisions a clear understanding of the objectives which are sought to be achieved is necessary. There are two widely discussed approaches :

(*i*) Profit Maximisation Approach, and
(*ii*) Wealth Maximisation Approach.

VALUATION CONCEPTS AND VALUATION OF SECURITIES

Time Value of Money: Recognition of the time value of money in financial decision-making is extremely important. A financial decision taken today has implications for a number of years, that is, it spreads into the future. For example, firms have to acquire fixed assets for which they have to pay a certain sum of money to the vendors. The benefits arising out of the acquisition of such assets will be spread over a number of years in the future, till the working life of the assets. On the other hand, funds have to be procured from different sources such as raising of capital through new issues, bank borrowings, term loans from financial institutions, sale of debentures and so on. These involve a cash inflow at the time of raising funds as well as an obligation to pay interest/dividend and return the principal in future. It is on the basis of a comparison of the cash outflows (outlays) and the benefits (cash inflows) that financial decisions are made. For a meaningful comparison the two variables must be strictly comparable. One basic requirement of comparability is the incorporation of the time element in the calculations. In other words, in order to have a logical and meaningful comparison between cash flows that accrue in different time periods, it is necessary to convert the sum of money to a common point of time.

Rationale: Conceptually, 'Time value of money' means that the value of a unit of money is different in different time periods. The value of a sum of money received today is more than its value received after sometime. Conversely, the sum of money received in future is less valuable than it is today. In other words, the present worth of a rupee received after sometime will be less than a rupee received today. Since a rupee received today has more value, rational investors would prefer current receipt to future receipts. The time value of money can also be referred to as time preference for money.

The main reason for time preference for money is to be found in the reinvestment opportunities for funds which are received early. The funds so invested will earn a rate of return; this would not be possible if the funds are received at a later time. The time preference for money is, therefore, expressed generally in terms of a rate of return or more popularly as a discount rate. The expected rate of return as also the time value of money will vary from individual to individual depending, inter alia, on his perception. We illustrate the time value of money using a simple example :

Suppose, Mr. X is given the choice of receiving Rs. 1,000 either now or one year later. His choice would obviously be for the first alternative as he can deposit the amount in his saving bank account and earn a nominal rate of interest, say, five per cent. At the end of the year, the amount will accumulate to Rs. 1,050. In other words, the choice before Mr. X is between Rs. 1,050 and Rs. 1,000 at the end of the year. As a rational person, Mr. X should be expected to prefer the larger amount (i.e. Rs. 1,050 here). Here we say that the time value of money, that is, the rate of interest is five percent. It may, thus be seen that future cash flows are less valuable because of the investment opportunities of the present cash flows.

Techniques: There are two techniques for evaluating future incomes in terms of the present. These techniques are given below :

1. Compounding Technique, and
2. Discounting Technique.

1. Compounding Technique: Interest is compounded when the amount earned on an initial deposit (the initial principal) becomes part of the principal at the end of the first compounding period.

The term principal refers to the amount of money on which interest is received.

Example 1 : If Mr. X invests in a saving bank account Rs. 1,000 at 5% interest compounded annually, at the end of the first year, he will have Rs. 1,050 in his account. This amount constitutes the principal for earning interest for the next year. At the end of the next year, there would be Rs. 1,102.50 in the account. This would represent the principal for the third year. The amount of interest earned would be Rs. 55.125. The total amount appearing in his account would be Rs. 1,157.625. Following Table 1 shows this compounding procedure:

Table 1. Annual Compounding

Year	1	2	3
Beginning amount	Rs. 1,000	Rs. 1,050	Rs. 1,102.50
Interest Rate	0.05	0.05	0.05
Amount of interest	50	52.50	55.125
Beginning principal	1,000	1,050	1,102.50
Ending principal	1,050	1,102.50	1,157.625

This compounding procedure will continue for an indefinite number of years. The compounding of interest can be calculated by the following equation:

$$A = P(1 + i)^n \quad ...(1)$$

in which

A = amount at the end of the period
P = principal at the beginning of the period
i = rate of interest
n = number of years

The amount of money in the account at the end of various years is calculated by using equation (1).

Amount at the end of year

1 = Rs. 1,000 (1 + .05) = Rs. 1,050

2 = Rs. 1,050 (1 + .05) = Rs. 1,102.50

3 = Rs. 1,102.50 (1 + .05) = Rs. 1,157.625

The amount at the end of year 2 can be ascertained by substituting Rs. 1,000 (1 + .05) for Rs. 1,050, that is, Rs. 1,000 (1 + .05) (1 + .05) = Rs. 1,102.50.

Similarly, the amount at the end of year 3 can be determined in the following way : Rs. 1,000 (1 + .05) (1 + .05) (1 + .05) = Rs. 1,157.625.

Thus, after substituting the actual figures for the investment of Rs. 1,000 in the formula $A = P(1 + i)^n$, we arrive at the same result as shown in the Table 1. This is the fundamental equation of compound interest.

Two important observations can be made from the Table 1. The first is that as the interest rate increases for any given year, the compound interest factor also increases. Thus, the higher the interest rate, the greater is the future sum. The second point is that for a given interest rate the future sum of a rupee increases with the passage of time. Thus, the longer the period of time, the higher is the compound interest factor. However, it should be borne in mind that for an interest rate of zero per cent, the compound interest factor always equals 1 and, therefore, the future amount always equals the initial principal.

Semi-annual and Other Compounding Periods: Very often the interest rates are compounded more than once in a year. Savings institutions, particularly, compound interests semi-annually, quarterly and even monthly.

Semi-annual Compounding : Means that there are two compounding periods within the year. Interest is actually paid after every six months at a rate of one-half of the annual rate of interest.

Example 2: Assume Mr. X places his savings of Rs. 1,000 in a two-year time deposit scheme of a bank which yields 6% interest compounded semi-annually. He will be paid 3% interest compounded over four periods—each of six months' duration. Following Table 2 presents the calculations of the amount Mr. X will have from the time deposit after two years.

Table 2 shows that his savings will amount to Rs. 1,060.90 and Rs. 1,125.51 respectively at the end of the first year and second year.

Quarterly Compound : Means that there are four compounding periods within the year. Instead of paying the interest once a year, it is paid in four equal instalments after every three months. Using the Example 2, there will be eight compounding periods and the rate of interest for each compounding period will be 1.5 per cent, that is (1/4 of 6%).

Table 2. Semi-annual Compounding

Year	6 months	1 year	18 months	2 years
Beginning amount	Rs. 1,000.00	Rs. 1,030.00	Rs. 1,060.90	Rs. 1,092.73
Interest rate	0.03	0.03	0.03	0.03
Amount of interest	30.00	30.90	31.83	32.78
Beginning principal	1,000.00	1,030.00	1,060.90	1,092.73
Ending principal	1,030.00	1,060.90	1,092.73	1,125.51

Table 3 presents the relevant calculations regarding the amount he will have at the end of two years, when interest is compounded quarterly. At the end of the first year, his saving will accumulate to Rs. 1,061.363 and at the end of the second year he will have Rs. 1,126.49.

Table 3. Quarterly Compounding

Period (months)	Beginning Amount (Rs.)	Interest Factor	Amount of Interest (Rs.)	Beginning Principal (Rs.)	Ending Principal (Rs.)
3	1,000.000	0.015	15.000	1,000.000	1,015.000
6	1,015.000	0.015	15.225	1,015.000	1,030.225
9	1,030.225	0.015	15.453	1,030.225	1,045.678
12	1,045.678	0.015	15.685	1,045.678	1,061.363
15	1,061.363	0.015	15.920	1,061.363	1,077.283
18	1,077.283	0.015	16.159	1,077.283	1,093.442
21	1,093.442	0.015	16.401	1,093.442	1,109.843
24	1,109.843	0.015	16.647	1,109.843	1,126.490

The Table 4 presents a comparative picture of Mr. X's savings at the end of two years when they are compounded annually, half-yearly and quarterly. The table warrants the generalisation that the more frequently the interest is compounded, the greater is the amount of money accumulated. This is primarily because interest is earned more frequently.

The effect of compounding more than once a year can also be expressed in the form of a formula:

Table 4. Comparison of Annual, Semi-annual and Quarterly Compounding

End of year	Compounding Period		
	Annual	Half-Yearly	Quarterly
1	1,060.00	1,060.90	1,061.36
2	1,123.60	1,125.51	1,126.49

$$P\left\{1+\frac{i}{m}\right\}^{mn} = A$$

in which m is the number of times per year compounding is made. For semi-annual compounding, m would be 2, while for quarterly compounding it would equal 4 and if interest is compounded monthly, weekly and daily, would equal 12, 52 and 365 respectively.

2. Present Value or Discounting Technique: The concept of the present value is the exact opposite of that of compound value. In this approach money received at some future date and will be worthless because the corresponding interest is lost during the period. In other words, the present value of a rupee that will be received in the future will be less than the value of a rupee in hand today. Thus, in contrast to the compounding approach where we convert present sums into future sums, in present value approach future sums are converted into present sums. Given a positive rate of interest, the present value of future rupees will always be lower. It is for this reason, therefore, that the procedure of finding present values is commonly called **discounting**. It is concerned with determining the present value of a future amount, assuming that the decision maker has an opportunity to earn a certain return on his money. This return is designated in financial literature as the discount rate, the cost of capital or an opportunity cost.

Example 3: Mr. X has been given an opportunity to receive Rs. 1,060 one year from now. He knows that he can earn 6% interest on his investments. The question is : What amount will he be prepared to invest for this opportunity?

To answer this question, we must determine how many rupees must be invested at 6% today to have Rs. 1,060 one year afterwards.

Let us assume that P is this unknown amount, we have P(1 + 0.06) = Rs. 1,060

$$\Rightarrow P = \frac{\text{Rs. } 1{,}060}{1.06} = \text{Rs. } 1{,}000.$$

Thus, Rs. 1,000 would be the required investment to have Rs. 1,060 after the expiry of one year. In other words, the present value of Rs. 1,060 received one year from now, given the rate of interest of 6%, is Rs. 1,000. Mr. X should be indifferent to whether he receives Rs. 1,000 today or Rs. 1,060 one year from today. If he can either receive more than Rs. 1,060 by paying Rs. 1,000 or Rs. 1,060 by paying less than Rs. 1,000, he would do so.

Mathematical Formulation

Finding present value is simply the reverse of compounding, the formula for compounding of the sum can be readily transferred into a present value formula. According, to the compounding formula, $A = P(1 + i)^n$. Therefore, the present value equation becomes :

$$P = \frac{A}{(1+i)^n} = A\left\{\frac{1}{(1+i)^n}\right\}$$

in which P is the present value for the future sum to be received or spent; A is the sum to be received or spent in future; i is interest rate, and n is the number of years. Thus, the present value of money is the reciprocal of the compounding value.

Present Value of a Series of Cash Flows

In capital budgeting decisions, the present value of a series of receipts received by a firm at different time periods. In order to determine the present value of such a mixed stream of cash inflows, all that is required is to determine the present value of each future payment and then to aggregate them to find the total present value of the stream of cash flows. Symbolically :

$$P = \frac{C_1}{(1+i)} + \frac{C_2}{(1+i)^2} + \frac{C_3}{(1+i)^3} + \ldots + \frac{C_n}{(1+i)^n}$$

$$= \sum_{t=1}^{n} \frac{C_t}{(1+i)^t}$$

in which P = the sum of the individual present values of separate cash flows; C_1, C_2, C_3, ... C_n, refers to cash flows in time periods 1, 2, 3, ... n.

This is the general form of the present value formula. To put the formula in a more practical perspective, we will have

$$P = C_1(IF_1) + C_2(IF_2) + C_3(IF_3) + \ldots + C_n(IF_n)$$

$$= \sum_{t=1}^{n} C_t(IF_t)$$

in which IF_1, IF_2, IF_3, ... IF_n represents relevant present value factors in different time periods, 1, 2, 3, ... n.

If the time value of money is 10%, we can easily find the present value of the following series of yearly payments. Consider the following examples:

Example 4:

Year	Cash flows (Rs.)
1	500
2	1,000
3	1,500
4	2,000
5	2,500

In order to solve this problem, the present value of each individual cash flow discounted at 10% for the appropriate number of years is to determined. The sum of all these individual values is then calculated to get the present value of the total stream. The present value factors required for the purpose are obtained from 'Present Value Table'. The results are given below :

Present Value of a Mixed Stream of Cash Flows

Year End (1)	Cash Flows (2)	Present Value Factor (3)	Present Value (2) × (3) (4)
1	Rs. 500	0.909	Rs. 454.50
2	1,000	0.826	826.00
3	1,500	0.751	1,126.50
4	2,000	0.683	1,366.00
5	2,500	0.621	1,552.00
			5,325.50

Annuity: An annuity as a series of equal cash flows of an amount each time. Due to this nature of an annuity, short cut is possible.

Example 5: Mr. X wishes to determine the present value of the annuity consisting of cash inflows of Rs. 1,000 per year for 5 years. The rate of interest he can earn from his investment is 10%.

Solution: Long Method for Finding Present Value of an Annuity of Rs. 1,000 for five years.

Year End (1)	Cash Flows (2)	Present Value Factor (3)	Present Value (2) × (3) (4)
1	Rs. 1,000	0.909	Rs. 909.00
2	1,000	0.826	826.00
3	1,000	0.751	751.00
4	1,000	0.683	683.00
5	1,000	0.621	621.00
			3,790.00

This procedure yields a present value of Rs. 3,790. Calculations can be cut short as the present value factor for each year is to multiplied by the annual amount of Rs. 1,000. This method of calculating the present value of the annuity can also be expressed as an equation :

$$P = \text{Rs. } 1{,}000\,(0.909) + \text{Rs. } 1{,}000\,(0.826) + \text{Rs. } 1{,}000\,(0.751) + \text{Rs. } 1{,}000\,(0.683) + \text{Rs. } 1{,}000\,(0.621) = \text{Rs. } 3{,}790.$$

Thus, the present value of an annuity can be found by multiplying the annuity amount by the sum of the present value factors for each year of the life of the annuity table.

Present Value of an Infinite Life Annuity

An annuity that goes on for ever is called a perpetuity. The present value of a perpetuity of Rs. C amount is given by the formula :

$$\frac{C}{i}$$

This is because as the length of time for which the annuity is received increases, the annuity discount factor also increases but if the length goes on extending, this increase in the annuity factor slows down. In fact, as annuity life becomes infinitely long ($n \rightarrow \phi$), the annuity discount factor approaches an upper limit. Such a limit is 1/i. In other words, the appropriate factor is found by merely dividing 1 by the discount rate. The validity of this method can be seen by looking at fact.

Practical Applications of Compounding and Present Value Techniques

Compounding and discounting techniques have a number of important applications, relevant to the task of the financial manager and investor.

1. A financial manager is often interested in determining the size of annual payments to accumulate a future sum to repay an existing liability at some future date or to provide funds for replacement of an existing machine/asset after its useful life.
2. When the amount of loan taken from financial institutions or commercial banks is to be repaid in a specified number of equal annual instalments, the financial manager will be interested in determining the amount of the annual instalments.

3. An investor may often be interested in finding the rate of growth in dividend paid by a company over a period of time. It is because growth in dividends has a significant bearing on the price of the shares. In such a situation compound interest tables are used.
4. To determine the current values of debentures, the present values tables can be of immense use. The cash flow from a debenture consists of two parts : first, interest inflows at periodic intervals, say, semi-annually or annually and, second, the repayment of the principal on maturity. Since the interest payments on a debenture are made periodically throughout its life, it is easy to calculate the present value of this annuity type interest inflow by Consulting Table and the present value of the face value of the debentures can be ascertained by discounting it at the market rate of interest by Consulting Table. The sum of the two values so obtained will be current worth of a debenture. If the interest is paid after six months, the factors are obtained for one half of the discount rate and the number of years is doubled.

VALUATION OF LONG-TERM SECURITIES

The value of a long-term security is the present value of cash flow stream promised to, and expected by, the investor, discounted at a required rate of return (RoR) duly adjusted for the risk involved.

Valuation of Debentures/Bonds

Debenture/Bond is a security acknowledging long-term debt, issued by a corporate firm/government organisation to investors, with the undertaking of paying interest, period after period till the security matures. There are three major features of such securities :

1. They have face value (say of Rs. 100 or Rs. 1,000);
2. They have stated maturity period, and
3. They carry coupon rate/annual rate of interest, stated on the face value of security (say 15% debentures, 14% bonds).

The main concern in valuing a bond is discounting/capitalising the cash-flow stream that the investor would receive over the life of the instrument. The terms of a bond involve a legally binding payment pattern. The cash flow pattern consists of the interest payments for a specified time span of the security, coupled with a final payment, when the security matures. The discount rate (K_d) is the RoR (rate of return), depending on the risk structure of the security.

Perpetual Debentures/Bonds

Such bonds never mature as far as repayment of principal is concerned. The issuer of such securities pays a fixed rate of interest in perpetuity.

The present value of perpetual Bond, V, is the capitalised value of an infinite stream of interest payment, I. Symbolically :

$$V = \sum_{t=1}^{\infty} \frac{I}{(1+K_d)^t} \quad \text{or} \quad \frac{I}{K_d}$$

Suppose, an investor buys debenture that pays Rs. 120 interest per year foreover and his RoR on this type of debenture is 15%, V = Rs. 120/0.15 = Rs. 800. In case the market price is less than Rs. 800, it will be worth buying.

Debentures/Bonds with Definite Maturity

These may be classified into the following types :

1. Interest Paying Debentures/Bonds : Also called non-zero coupon debentures, pay maturity/terminal value on their maturity (MV) in addition to the periodic interest payment to investors. Symbolically :

$$V = \sum_{t=1}^{n} \frac{I}{(1+K_d)^t} + \frac{MV}{(1+K_d)^n}$$

$$= I\left(PVIFA_{Kd,n}\right) + MV\left(PVIF_{Kd,n}\right)$$

$PVIFA_{Kd,n}$ = Present value interest factor of annuity for n numbers of years (in which interest is to be received) corresponding to the investor's RoR.

$PVIF_{Kd,n}$ = Simple present value of maturity sum received in the nth year, discounted at the investor's RoR.

Suppose an interest of Rs. 120 is payable for 10 years, RoR is 15%, and at maturity, Rs. 1,000 is payable, the value of bond would be : Rs. 120 (5.019) + Rs. 1,000 (0.247) = Rs. 849.28.

Semi-annual Compounding of Interest

In case, interest is paid twice a year (on half-yearly basis)

$$V = \sum_{t=1}^{2n} \frac{I/2}{(1+K_d/2)^t} + \frac{MV}{(1+K_d/2)^{2n}}$$

$$= \frac{I}{2}\left(PVIFA_{Kd/2,n}\right) + \left(MV\left(PVIF_{Kd/2,2n}\right)\right)$$

2. Zero Coupon Bonds : Do not make periodic interest payments. The return to the investor consists of the difference between the redemption/face value of the security on maturity data and the 'below face value' at which he purchases. Since no interest is to be received, its value is equivalent to discounted value of MV only. Symbolically,

$$V = \frac{MV}{(1+K_d)^n}$$

$$= MV\left(PVIF_{Kd,n}\right)$$

Suppose a firm issues a zero coupon bond having a 15 year maturity and face value of Rs. 1,000. If the investor's required rate of return is 15%, V = Rs. 1,000 ($PVIF_{0.15,15}$) = Rs. 1,000 (0.123) = Rs. 123. In other words, an investor buying zero coupon bond for Rs. 123 today can get Rs. 1,000 after 15 years and his investment of Rs. 123 will earn for him a 15% compound annual rate of return. Since there is a significant difference between the issue price and maturity value of such bonds, they are appropriately referred to as deep discount bonds.

Valuation of Preference Shares

Preference shares, like debentures, are usually subject to a fixed rate of return/dividend. In case of no stated maturity, their valuation is similar to that of perpetual bonds. Symbolically :

$$V = \sum_{i=1}^{\infty} \frac{D_p}{(1+K_p)^t} \text{ or } \frac{D_p}{K_p}$$

The valuation of redeemable preference shares is given

$$V = \sum_{t=1}^{n} \frac{D_p}{(1+K_p)^t} + \frac{MV}{(1+K_p)^n},$$

$$= D_p\left(PVIFA_{Kp,n}\right) + MV\left(PVIF_{Kp,n}\right)$$

Valuation of Equity Shares

The value of equity shares is the discounted value of all expected future dividends (D_t) to be paid by the company to its equity shareholders. The discounted value represents the investor's required rate of return on such investment. Symbolically,

$$V = \sum_{t=1}^{\infty} \frac{D_t}{(1+K_e)^t}$$

Dividend Discount Models

They are designed to compute the value of equity shares under specific assumptions, that is, the expected growth pattern of future dividends and the appropriate discount rate (K_e).

Constant Growth

In case dividends are expected to grow at a uniform compound rate (say g) perpetually, V is given

$$V = \sum_{t=1}^{\infty} \frac{D_0(1+g)^t}{(1+K_e)^t} \text{ or } = \frac{D_1}{K_e - g}$$

The constant growth dividend discount model is also known as the Gordon Growth Model.

No Growth

When a stable/constant dividend is expected to be maintained for a long period of time (i.e., dividends are subject to no growth)

$$V = D_1^{lK_e}$$

Varied Growth Rates

In a situation in which equity dividends exhibit above normal growth for a number of years in as much as g may even be greater than K_e, and then eventually taper off to normal/sustainable growth. For instance, if dividend per share is expected to grow at 15% compound rate for 5 years and thereafter at 6%. Following equation will indicate the value of equity share, assuming 14% as K_e.

$$V = \sum_{t=1}^{5} \frac{D_0(1.15)^t}{(1.14)^t} + \sum_{t=6}^{\infty} \frac{D_5(1.06)^{t-5}}{(1.14)^t}$$

It may be noted that the growth in dividends in the second phase uses the expected dividends in period 5 as its base. It is for this reason that the growth term exponent is t – 5; it implies that the exponent in year 6 means 1, in year 7 means 2 and so on. The second phase in equation is similar to constant growth model following a period of abnormal growth. Accordingly :

$$V = \sum_{t=1}^{5} \frac{D_0(1.15)^t}{(1.14)^t} + \left[\frac{1}{(1.14)5}\right]\left[\frac{D_6}{0.14 - 0.06}\right]$$

Assuming current dividend (D_0) as Rs. 10 per share, value of equity share would be Rs. 189.62 as shown in the Table 5.

Present Value of Constant Growth Component (Second Phase)

Expected dividend in year 6 = Rs. 20.11 (1.06)
= Rs. 21.32

Expected market price of share at the end of year 5

$$= \frac{\text{Rs. } 21.32}{0.14 - 0.06} = \text{Rs. } 266.50$$

Present value of Rs. 266.50 = Rs. 266.50 × 0.519 = Rs. 138.31

Present Value of equity share = Rs. 51.31 + Rs. 138.31

= Rs. 189.62

RISK AND RETURN

The two key determinants of security prices/value are risk and return. The financial managers must understand how to measure and price financial risk.

Risk and Return of a Single Asset

Definition of Return and Risk:

Return : The (rate of) return on an asset/ investment for a given period, say a year, is the annual income received plus any change in market price, usually expressed as a per cent of the opening market price. Symbolically, the one-period actual (expected) return, R

$$= \frac{D_t + (P_t - P_{t-1})}{P_{t-1}}$$

where,

D_t = annual income/cash dividend at the end of time period, t.

P_t = security price at time period, t (using/ ending security price)

Table 5. Present Value of Dividend, Phase 1 (Years 1-5)

End of Year	Dividend	PVIF (0.14)	Total PV
1	Rs. 10 $(1.15)^1$ = Rs. 11.50	0.877	Rs. 10.09
2	10 $(1.15)^2$ = 13.22	0.769	10.17
3	10 $(1.15)^3$ = 15.21	0.675	10.27
4	10 $(1.15)^4$ = 17.49	0.592	10.35
5	10 $(1.15)^5$ = 20.11	0.519	10.43
	$\sum_{t=1}^{5} \frac{D_0(1.15)^t}{(1.14)^t}$		51.31

P_{t-1} = security price at time period, t – 1 (opening/beginning security price)

If the price of a share on April 1 (current year) is Rs. 25, the annual dividend received at the end of the year is Re. 1 and the year end price on March 31 is Rs. 30, the rate of return

$$= \frac{[\text{Re. } 1 + (\text{Rs. } 30 - \text{Rs. } 25)]}{\text{Rs. } 25} = 0.24 = 24\%.$$

The rate of return of 24% has two components :

(*i*) **Current yield :** i.e. annual income ÷ beginning price

$$= \frac{\text{Re. } 1}{\text{Rs. } 25} = 0.04 \text{ or } 4\%, \text{ and}$$

(*ii*) **Capital gain/loss :** (ending price – beginning price) ÷ beginning price

$$= \frac{(\text{Rs. } 30 - \text{Rs. } 25)}{\text{Rs. } 25} = 0.20 = 20\%.$$

Risk: The variability of the actual return from the expected returns associated with a given asset/ investment is defined as risk. The greater the variability, the riskier the security (shares) is said to be. The more certain the return from an asset (T-bill), the less the variability and, therefore, the less the risk.

Measurement of Return

The return associated with a single asset is assessed from both a **behavioural** and a **quantitative/ statistical point** of view. The behavioural view of point of return can be obtained by using :

(*i*) Sensitivity Analysis, and

(*ii*) Probability (Distribution).

The **statistical measures** of return of an asset are :

1. Standard Deviation, and
2. Coefficient of Variation.

CAPITAL STRUCTURE

The term designing capital structure, capital structure decision, factors determining capital structure and capital structure planning are used interchangeably here.

Theoretically a combination of debt and equity does affect the cost of capital as also the total value of the firm. There is, in other words, an optimum capital structure. The capital structure is said to be optimum when the marginal real cost (explicit as well as implicit) of each available source of financing is identical. With an optimum debt and equity mix, the cost of capital is minimum and the market price per share is maximum. The use of debt in capital structure or financial leverage has both benefits as well as costs. While the principal attraction of debt is the tax benefit, its cost is financial distress and reduced commercial profitability. The term financial distress includes a broad spectrum of problems ranging from relatively minor liquidity shortages to bankruptcy. The problem of financial distress will magnify with an increase in financial leverage. Beyond a certain point, the expected cost of financial distress will outweigh the tax benefit.

The key factors governing the capital structure decisions are :

1. Profitability Aspect
2. Liquidity Aspect
3. Control
4. Leverage ratios in industry
5. Nature of industry
6. Constitution with investment bankers/lenders
7. Commercial strategy
8. Timing of Issue
9. Company characteristics, and
10. Tax Planning

1. Profitability Aspect

Earnings Before Interest and Tax (EBIT)—Earning Per Share (EPS) Analysis (EBIT-EPS Analysis): Keeping in view the primary objective of financial management of maximising the market value of the firm, the EBIT-EPS analysis should be considered logically as the first step in the direction of designing a firm's capital structure. The EBIT-EPS analysis shows the impact of various financing alternatives on EPS at various levels of EBIT. This analysis is, useful for two reasons :

(*i*) the EPS is a measure of a firm's performance given the P/E ratio, the larger the EPS, the larger would be the value of a firm's shares; and

(*ii*) given the importance of EPS and the function of the EBIT-EPS analysis to show the value of EPS under various financial alternatives at different levels of EBIT, the EBIT-EPS analysis information can be extremely useful to the finance manager in arriving at an appropriate financing decision.

If the probability of EBIT falling below the indifference point is high, the equity-alternative should be preferred. In general, the higher the level of EBIT and the lower the probability of downward fluctuation, the greater is the amount of debt that can be employed. While taking a decision in this respect, it should be remembered that P/E ratio is less for a levered financial plan due to increased financial risk. Therefore, increase in EPS should be greater so that its advantage is not completely offset or more than offset by using debt in the capital structure. Moreover, if the debt alternative entails a provision for creating a sinking fund, the finance manager should keep in mind that earnings available for payment of dividends and reinvestment to further expand facilities would be reduced by the amount of the sinking fund payment. The indifference point would then be computed as follows :

$$\text{UEPS – Debt Plan} \quad\quad \text{UEPS – Equity Plan}$$
$$\frac{(\text{EBIT} - 1)(1 - t) - \text{SF}}{N_1} = \frac{(\text{EBIT})(1 - t)}{N_2}$$

where,

UEPS = uncommitted earnings per share

SF = sinking fund payment per annum

I = interest payments

Coverage Ratio: Apart from the EBIT-EPS analysis, the ability of a firm to use debt, from the profitability point of view, can also be judged in terms of a coverage ratio, namely :

$$\frac{\text{EBIT}}{\text{I}}$$

or $$\frac{\text{EBIT}}{\text{I} + \left[\frac{\text{SF}}{1 - t}\right]}$$

The ratio measures the size of the interest payments relative to the EBIT. The reciprocal of this ratio (I/EBIT) measures the proportion of EBIT devoted to interest payments. The higher the coverage ratio, the greater is the certainty that the firm would be in a position to meet its obligations of interest payment.

The coverage ratio can be calculated, like the EPS for various levels of EBIT. This would provide a better picture of the firm's most likely EBIT to meet out specific-commitments. It will throw light on the adequacy of EBIT to meet the firm's annual burden of payments connected with interest on loan, preference dividend, contribution to sinking fund (if any) and other repayment of principal.

2. Liquidity Aspect

Cash Flow Analysis: EBIT-EPS analysis and coverage ratios are very useful in making explicit the impact of leverage on EPS and on the firm's ability to meet its commitments at various levels of EBIT. But the EBIT/interest ratio is less than a perfect measure to analyse the firm's ability to service fixed charges because the firm's ability to do so depends on the total payments required, that is, interest and principal, in relation to the cash flow available to meet them. Therefore, the analysis of the cash flow ability of the firm to service fixed charges is an important exercise to be carried out in capital structure planning in addition to profitability analysis. The exercise is of overwhelming significance in the context of the risk of bankruptcy. If the firm borrows more than its debt capacity and, therefore, fails to meet its obligations in future, the lenders may seize the assets of the company to satisfy their claims. Thus, the basic existence of the company would be endangered.

It may be possible that the company's EBIT is adequate to cover its specific commitments, arising out of debt obligations; but, the firm may not have sufficient cash to pay as its income is blocked within the firm in the form of higher in ventory, receivable and/or sometimes purchases of fixed assets, particularly, when the company is a growing one. In the absence of cash flow analysis a company, which is otherwise profitability sound, would in case of default, run into great difficulties. Thus, cash flow analysis is an essential ingredient of any sound capital structure decision.

Cash flow analysis yields a number of distinct advantages in the crucial task of setting debt policy: (*i*) it focuses on the solvency of the firm during adverse circumstances in contrast to EBIT-EPS analysis which is concerned with the effects to leverage under normal circumstances; (*ii*) it takes into consideration the balance sheet change and other cash flows that do not appear in the profit and loss account; (*iii*) it gives an insight into the inventory of financial resources available in the event of recession; and (*iv*) finally, it views the problem in a dynamic context over time whereas EBIT/EPS and coverage analysis normally consider only a single year. From all these points, it can be concluded that the cash flow analysis evaluates the risk of financial distress and should be recognised as a good supporting supplement to the EBIT/EPS analysis in framing the firm's capital structure.

In assessing the liquidity position of a firm in its cash flow analysis, various measures can be employed. One such measure is the ratio of fixed charges to net cash inflows. This ratio measures the coverage of fixed financial charges (interest plus repayment of principal, if any) to net cash inflows. In other words, it indicates the number of times the fixed financial requirements are covered by the net cash inflows. The greater the coverage ratio, the greater is the amount of debt that a firm can use.

Another measure to analyse the cash flow ability of a firm to service fixed charges in determining an appropriate capital structure is to prepare a cash budget to determine whether the expected cash flows are sufficient to cover the fixed obligations. The purpose of preparing the cash budget is to find out possible deviations in actual cash flows from those that are expected. Therefore, cash budgets should be prepared for a range of possible cash inflows with a probability attached to each of them. This information can be used to evaluate the ability of the firm to meet its fixed obligations. Since the probability of various cash flow pattern is known, the firm can work out the amount of fixed charges as well as the debt that the firm can employ and still remain within an insolvency limit tolerable to the management.

Suppose, the firm is of the view that 5% is the maximum probability of not having cash to meet charges that can be tolerated. Further, suppose that the actual probability of being out of cash on the basis of the cash budget prepared under adverse circumstances is also 5%. In such a situation, according to Van Horne, debt can be employed up to a point where the cash balance is just sufficient to cover the fixed charges. That is to say, debt can be increased up to the point at which the additional cash drain would cause the probability of cash insolvency to equal the risk tolerance specified management. It is, of course, not necessary that the debt would be increased to that point. This method of analysis suggested by Van Horne provides a means for assessing the effect of increase in debt on the risk of cash insolvency. On the basis of the information available from this analysis the firm would determine the most appropriate level of debt.

A similar type of analysis has been suggested by Gordon Donaldson. It is argued that firm will normally be able to meet its fixed obligations in terms of interest as well as repayment of principal. It is only during adverse circumstances that firms will not be able to maintain their ability to meet contractual obligations and would be exposed to the risk of bankruptcy or the extreme form of risk of financial distress. Donaldson terms these as recession conditions. To examine the impact of alternative debt policies on the risk of bankruptcy, therefore, what is required is a careful analysis of how a firm's cash flows would be affected by recession conditions.

3. Control

Another consideration in planning, the types of funds to use is the attitude of the management towards control. Lenders have no direct voice in the management of a company. They may, of course, place certain restrictions in the loan agreement on the management's activities. So long as there is no default in the payment of interest or the repayment of the principal, there is a littlè that they can do legally against the company. For all practical purposes, they have very little say in the policy-decisions of the company or in the selection of the board of directors. Likewise, preference shareholders do not have the right to vote for the appointment of the board of directors. However, if the financial affairs of the company have deteriorated to such an extent that dividends on preference shares have not been paid for a certain number of years, they are given the right to attend the meetings and participate in the voting. In most of the cases, they, like the creditors, do not have any say in the selection of the management. The power to choose the management in most cases rests with the equity holders. Accordingly, if the main object of the management is to maintain control, they will like to have a greater weightage for debt and preference shares in additional capital requirements, since by obtaining funds through them the management sacrifices little or no control. However, it should be remembered that if the company borrows more than what it can service or repay, the creditors may seize the assets of the company to satisfy their claims. In that situation, the management would lose all control. It might be better to sacrifice a measure of control by some additional equity financing rather than run the risk of losing all control to creditors by employing too much debt. The same holds true for preference shares. In such a situation, equity would be a better source of financing. However, if the firm has the ability, as determined by profitability and solvency considerations and the management wants to maintain control in its own hands, the issue of senior securities will be recommended as the issue of additional equity shares would involve the risk of losing control. This will be all the more true if the company is closely held. The management of widely-held companies runs little risk of losing continuation of control. The shares of such companies are widely distributed. Most of the shareholders are interested simply in the return and have neither the time nor the inclination to participate in management. If they are not satisfied, they will switch over to other companies.

4. Leverage Ratios for Other Firms in the Industry

Yet another approach to the capital structure decisions is to make a comparison with the debt-equity ratios of companies belonging to the same industry, having a similar business risk. The rationale of the use of industry standards is that debt-equity ratios appropriate for other firms in a similar line of business should be appropriate for the company as well. Industry standards provide a useful benchmark. If the firm is out of line, it is conspicuous in the market place. This does not necessarily imply that the firm's capital structure planning is inappropriate. It may well be possible that other firms may not be using appropriate debt-equity ratios. They may be more conservative or more aggressive risk-takers than desired. However, comparison is helpful as it acts as a red signal to the management that there may be something wrong with the debt-equity mix of the company. In other words, what it suggests is that if a firm is out of line, it should know the reasons why and be satisfied that there are good reasons for it.

5. Nature of Industry

The nature of industry is one of the most important elements in determining the degree of financial leverage a firm can carry safely without any risk of bankruptcy. If an industry's sales are subject to wide fluctuations, over a business cycle, the firm should have low degree of financial leverage. Such firms will already have a high operating leverage. In case both are high, the total risk of the firm as determined by the combined leverage (the product of operating leverage and financial leverage) would become unduly high. The firms with high debt ratios belonging to industries such as refrigeration, televisions, machine tools and capital equipment manufacturing, run the risk of not being able to meet the required payments in lean years which would cause financial distress. Clearly, such firms should have a more conservative capital structure and rely less on debt. On the other hand, industries dealing with non-durable consumer goods (food) or with inexpensive items (paper clips, match boxes) or with items in habitual use (cigarettes) or all those products which have an inelastic demand are not likely to be subject to wide fluctuations in sales. Such industries can afford to have higher debt proportions in capital structure as in lean years they do not run the risk of being unable to meet their commitments.

Judging industry by its competitive nature, it may be inferred that those industries which have keen competition among themselves should have a relatively greater proportion of equity than debt. For example, in the garment industry much of the competition is based on style. The styles being unpredictable and transitory the profits also fluctuate accordingly. Therefore, such firms should emphasise equity over debt because of the excessive risk is not being able to meet payments on borrowed funds. At the other extreme, there are public utility undertakings involved in the production of electricity, gas, water, transportation services or telephone services, which are relatively free from intra-industry competition. Their sales are more stable and predictable. Therefore, such companies can afford to use more debt.

The stage of the life-cycle of the industry has also a crucial bearing in assigning relative weightage to various sources of raising finance. If the industry is in its infancy, the probability of the rate of mortality would be high. Therefore, more emphasis needs to be placed on equity capital. The firm would do well to avoid seeking funds from senior securities which require fixed payments. At such a stage, risk outweighs the attractions of financial leverage. When the industry has reached maturity and is passing through the period of rapid growth, the firm should pay special attention to manoeuverability to assure that as it grows it obtains funds when needed and under acceptable terms. If the outlook is for a long term decline in business, the firm should build such a plan which allows for easy contraction in the sources of the funds used. For this purpose, the firm can have 'call' provision in the case of senior securities.

6. Consultation with Investment Bankers and Lenders

Another useful approach in deciding the proportion of various securities in a firm's structure is to seek the opinion of investment analysts, institutional investors, investment bankers and lenders. These analysts, having been in business for a considerable period of time, acquire expertise and have access to information regarding securities of a large number of companies and know how the market evaluates them. They are, therefore, in a better position to assess a particular financial plan.

Similarly, the opinions of prospective lenders and investors are likely to be very useful to the firm; it is they who will ultimately provide funds to the firm. Therefore, the type of securities which they will prefer to buy is very significant information for the financial manager and helps him in taking a decision regarding the form of securities to be issued. It is imperative that if a financial decision is to contribute to the valuation of the firm, the finance manager must think in a way similar to that of the investors.

7. Maintaining Manoeuverability for Commercial Strategy

Manoeuverability refers to a firm's ability to adjust its sources of funds in either direction— increase or decrease in response to changes in the need for funds. That is, the finance manager must keep himself in a situation where he can change positions. Therefore, while designing the capital structure, he should not lose sight of the future impact on the present financial plan. For instance, the firm may adopt an aggressive debt policy as it looks good at one point but if in future the firm is in need of additional funds, it may be forced to issue equity shares on unfavourable terms as the firm has a too heavy debt and is, therefore, unable to obtain funds in this form. Due to increased financial risk, the cost of equity would be higher. Clearly, the opportunity cost of an unwise debt-policy could turn out to be very high. Therefore, in order to preserve operating flexibility, a firm is well advised to have unused debt capacity for future needs, that is, it should operate below the maximum safe debt level. The preservation of unused debt capacity can be an important consideration for the company whose funds requirements are sudden and unpredictable. It gives the company financial manoeuverability by virtue of leaving the options open.

There should be room for flexibility not only in obtaining funds but also in refunding them. To provide the desired flexibility, the firm might incorporate a call provision as one of the covenants of the agreement with the suppliers of funds. The call provision implies that the firm with an adequate notice can repay their principal sum.

Flexibility, however, can be obtained only at a cost. When a finance manager achieves flexibility, it means that the party at the other end of the transaction is foregoing something and for doing this would like to be compensated. Callable preference shares and options for advance payment of long term debt are devices for maintaining flexibility. But, they will require higher yield to be paid than non-callable preference shares and long term debts for a definite number of years. Therefore, the finance manager faces the task of risk/return trade-off. He is to assure himself that he is not buying flexibility at a higher cost than is warranted by gains achieved through flexibility.

8. Timing of Issue

Closely related to flexibility in deciding the types of funds to be used, is the question of timing. Frequently very substantial savings may be obtained by proper timing of security issues. Thus, the timing of the public offerings is also an important consideration in capital structure decisions of a firm. Public offering should be made at a time when the state of the economy as well as the capital market is ideal to provide the funds. The monetary and fiscal policies that are pursued by the government are also important in this regard. The government follows a cheap money policy to boost the economy during a recession and a dear money policy during inflationary period. The type of policy pursued by the government reflects itself in prices as well as yields on senior securities and equity. High debenture yields are associated with relative scarcity of debt money and low P/E ratios on shares are an indication of the relative scarcity of equity funds. Frequently, therefore, the company has to decide whether to finance initially with an equity issue and later with a debt issue, or vice-versa. Consequently, it is forced to evaluate the alternative methods of financing in the light of general market conditions and expectations for the company itself. If the management feels that borrowed funds will become costly or scarce, the firm may like to use the benefit of financial leverage immediately. An expected decline in interest rates may encourage the firms to postpone borrowings, and remain in a flexible position which helps to take advantage of lower interest rates in the future.

At times, funds will be needed and must be obtained if they are relatively costly. This aspect is related to the internal rate of return (IRR). If the project materialises just when demand for the product involved is strong, the early return to flow of funds is higher; the IRR is higher and perhaps a somewhat higher cost of capital can be profitably tolerated. The differential increase in the rate of return, at this time, is more than the differential in the cost of money. It is foolhardly for a finance manager to chase the lowest cost of money only to find that he has procured the funds at bargain rates when the time for their usefulness has passed.

However, it should be borne in mind, that timing is not the only consideration. The timing analysis may suggest, for instance, use of debt. But the company cannot go in for debt if its existing capital structure is already top-heavy with debt. Agreements with the existing lenders of the funds may impose certain other restrictions. Thus, timing in obtaining funds is exercised within limits imposed by the timing of needs for funds, the extent of flexibility, and existing explicit agreements, sometimes an implicit understanding, with lenders and owners.

9. Characteristics of the Company

The characteristics of a company in terms of size and credit standing, among others, also play a vital role in determining the share of senior securities and equity in its capital structure.

The management's freedom of choice is extremely limited in the case of small and very large companies. Companies that are very small must rely, to a considerable degree, upon the owner's funds for their financing; they find it very difficult to obtain long term debts. In the minds of investors, generally, small firms are considered to be more risky than large firms. Therefore, such firms do not have ready access to different types of funds from various sources. They are generally in a weak bargaining position in obtaining funds. Since their sources of raising funds are limited, they can assign larger weights to the factor of flexibility. In contrast, very large companies are compelled to make use of different sources of raising funds as no single source can cater to their total requirements of funds.

Firms enjoying a high credit standing among investors/lenders in the capital market are in a better position to get funds from the source of their choice. If the credit standing is poor, the firm's choice of obtaining funds is rather limited.

10. Tax Planning

Finally, tax planning is likely to have a significant bearing on capital structure decisions. Under the Income Tax Act, 1961, while interest on borrowed funds is allowed as a deduction under Section 36(1)(iii), dividend on shares is not deductible from the operating profits of a company. With effect from June 1, 1997, distributed profits are subject to an extra 10% tax under Section 115, O/P/Q. Secondly, cost of raising finance through borrowings is deductible in the year of incurrence. If, however, it is incurred during pre-commencement of business period, it has to be capitalised. The cost of issue of shares is allowed as a deduction in 10 years Section 35D. As a result, corporate taxation is an important determinant of the choice between different sources of financing. For a widely held company with expansion involving Rs. 100 lakh, the implication on taxes on the rate of return on equity capital with reference to the alternative capital structures are depicted in the Table 6 : (1) Alternative I, Rs. 100 lakh equity capital; (2) Alternative II, equity capital, Rs. 40 lakh + debentures, Rs. 40 lakh + institutional loans, Rs. 20 lakh, and (3) Alternative III, equity capital Rs. 20 lakh + debentures, Rs. 30 lakh + loans from financial institution, Rs. 50 lakh. The before -tax expected rate of return = 25%. The rate of dividend is 20%.

Table 6. Effect of Taxes on Capital Structure Decision (Rs. 000)

	Alternative I	Alternative II	Alternative III
Return (Rs. 100 lakh × 0.25)	Rs.2,500	Rs.2,500	Rs.2,500
Less interest on debentures (0.14)	–	560	420
Less interest on loan (0.18)	–	360	900
Taxable profit	2,500	1,580	1,180
Tax (0.35)	875	553	413
Return on equity capital	1,625	1,027	767
Rate of return on equity	16.25	25.68	38.35
Capital (before dividend tax)			

The alternative III is obviously the best.

12. FINANCIAL MARKET

The financial market of any country can be broadly divided into two types of markets :

(1) Money market

(2) Capital market.

MONEY MARKET

Money market is a market for securities that account paid back in the short term usually less than one year. Since equity capital is not paid back within a year, debt market generally comprises of only debt securities. It is regulated by the guidelines issued by RBI from time to time. This market is further divided into various sub markets which are as below:

(a) Call Money market

(b) Treasury Bills market

(c) Short term bank loans

(d) Unorganized market of moneylenders

Here, call money market refers to the market for short term borrowings between banks. According to RBI guidelines, all banks are supposed to maintain certain level of liquidity and report o the RBI on fortnight basis. A bank which is falling short in its liquidity position borrows from the bank having excess liquidity for one or few days. The rate of interest is called 'Call rates' and is considered as the benchmark in the determination of overall interest rate in the economy. Treasury bills market refers to the market of trading in government securities through which the central government raises money in the market. They are also known as 'Gilt edged securities' because there is virtually no risk of default on these securities.

CAPITAL MARKET

Capital market is a market for long-term debt and equity shares. In this market, the capital funds comprising of both equity and debt are issued and traded. Capital market is regulated by the guidelines issued by SEBI (Securities and Exchange Board of India). Capital market can be further divided into two parts :

1. Primary market
2. Secondary market

1. Primary Market (IPO Market). Primary market means a market where the securities of a company are offered to the public for the first time for subscription. People apply for the securities of the company which in turn allots the securities to the applicants. It is also called Initial Public Offering (IPO).

2. Secondary Market (Stock Exchange). Secondary market refers to a market where securities are traded after being initially offered to the public in the primary market. The trade in securities takes place through a well regulated market called stock exchange.

STOCK EXCHANGE

The term 'Stock Exchange' consists of two words 'Stock' and 'Exchange'. Stock means a part or fraction of capital of any company. Exchange means a market for purchasing and selling. Thus, stock exchange can be described as a market where securities are bought and sold. It is also called 'secondary market' for securities because only the securities already issued can be bought and sold on a stock exchange. The word 'Securities' include ;

1. Shares, scrips, stocks, bonds, debentures or other marketable securities of alike nature in or of any incorporated company or other body corporate;
2. Government securities;

3. Such other instruments as may be declared by the Central govt. to be securities; and
4. Rights or interest in securities.

FUNCTIONS OF STOCK EXCHANGE

The stock exchange performs various functions which are beneficial to the investors, the companies as well as the whole economy. The major functions of stock exchange can be explained as below :

1. It provides a ready market where the existing securities can be easily bought and sold thereby enhances the liquidity of the security.
2. It provides the quotation of prices for various securities which is helpful in knowing the worth of the company as well as useful in calculation of taxes like Income Tax and Wealth Tax.
3. Stock exchange protects the investors against malpractices of companies by enforcing strict disclosure and other rules.
4. It helps the companies raise funds for investment for their projects thereby helping capital formation. People invest in the shares because of the assurance that they can sell them and recover the investment at any time in future through stock exchange.
5. Stock exchanges also influence the management and working of the companies by enforcing certain rules and regulations.

LISTING OF SECURITIES

Listing of securities refers to the inclusion of securities in the official trade list of securities which are permitted to be traded on a stock exchange. Only the listed securities are allowed to be traded at the stock exchange. Every company intending to offer shares or debentures to the public by issue of a prospectus is required to make an application before the issue, to one or more of the recognized stock exchanges for permission for its shares or debentures to be dealt with at the exchange. Thus listing is compulsory if the shares are issued by public offer. If the shares are issued without issuing a prospectus i.e. through private placement the listing of security is not compulsory.

INTERMEDIARIES IN THE CAPITAL MARKET

There are various intermediaries in the capital market which help the companies raise capital in the market. They are explained as below :

(1) Lead Manager (Pre and Post Issue). In the pre-issue process, the Lead Manager (LM) takes up the due diligence of company's operations/ management/ business plans etc. Other activities of the LM include drafting and design of Offer documents, Prospectus, statutory advertisements and memorandum containing salient features of the Prospectus. The Lead managers shall ensure compliance with stipulated requirements and completion of prescribed formalities with the Stock Exchanges, RoC and SEBI including finalization of Prospectus and RoC filing, Appointment of other intermediaries viz., Registrar(s), Printers, Advertising Agency and Bankers to the Offer is also included in the pre-issue processes. The LM also draws up the various marketing strategies for the issue.

The post issue activities including management of escrow accounts, coordinate non-institutional allocation, intimation of allocation and dispatch of refunds to bidders etc are performed by the LM. The post Offer activities for the Issue will involve essential follow-up steps, which include the finalization of trading and dealing of instruments and dispatch of certificates and demat or delivery of shares, with various agencies connected with the work such as the Registrar(s) to the Issue and Bankers to the Issue and the bank handling refund business. The lead manager shall be responsible for ensuring that these agencies fulfill their functions and enable it to discharge this responsibility through suitable agreements with the Company.

(2) Registrar. The Registrar finalizes the list of eligible allottees after deleting the invalid applications and ensures that the corporate action for crediting of shares to the demat accounts of the applicants is done and the dispatch of refund orders to those applicable are sent. The Lead manager coordinates with the Registrar to ensure follow up so that the flow of applications from collecting bank branches, processing of the applications and other matters till the basis of allotment is finalized, dispatch security certificates and refund orders completed and securities listed.

(3) Bankers to the issue (Lead Merchant Banker). Bankers to the issue, as the name suggests, carries out all the activities of ensuring that the funds are collected and transferred to the Escrow accounts. The Lead Merchant Banker shall ensure that Bankers to the Issue are appointed in all the mandatory collection centers as specified in DIP Guidelines. The LM also ensures follow-up with bankers to the issue to get quick estimates of collection and advising the issuer about closure of the issue, based on the correct figures.

BOOK BUILDING

"Book Building" means a process undertaken by which a demand for the securities proposed to be issued by a body corporate is elicited and built up and the price for the securities is assessed on the basis of the bids obtained for the quantum of securities offered for subscription by the issuer. This method provides an opportunity to the market to discover price for securities.

Book building is a process of price discovery. Hence, the Red Herring prospectus does not contain a price. Instead, the red herring prospectus contains either the floor price of the securities offered through it or a price band along with the range within which the bids can move. The applicants bid for the shares quoting the price and the quantity that they would like to bid at. Only the retail investors have the option of bidding at 'cut-off' price i.e. the price which is finally decided as the price of the security after the process of book building is over. After the bidding process is complete, the 'cut-off' price is arrived at on the lines of Dutch auction method. The basis of Allotment is then finalized and letters of allotment/refund is undertaken. The final prospectus with all the details including the final issue price and the issue size is filed with ROC, thus completing the issue process.

Reservation for Retail Individual Investor

1. A minimum 50% of the net offer of securities to the public shall initially be made available for allotment to retail individual investors, as the case may be.
2. The balance net offer of securities to the public shall be made available for allotment to:
   (i) individual applicants other than retail individual investors, and;
   (ii) other investors including corporate bodies/ institutions irrespective of the number of shares, debentures, etc. applied for.
3. The unsubscribed portion of the net offer to any one of the categories specified in (a) or (b) shall be made available for allotment to applicants in the other category, if so required.

Retail individual investor means an investor who applies or bids for securities of or for a value of not more than Rs.1,00,000.

Minimum Application Value. The minimum application value shall be within the range of Rs. 5,000 to Rs, 7,000. The issuer company, in consultation with the merchant banker, shall stipulate the minimum application size (in terms of number of shares) falling within the aforesaid range of minimum application value and make upfront disclosures in this regard, in the offer document.

SEBI GUIDELINES ON PUBLIC ISSUE

The following are certain guidelines of SEBI in relation to public issue / book building :

1. The spread between the floor and the cap of the price band shall not be more than 20%. In other words, it means that the cap should not be more than 120% of the floor price.
2. Subscription list for public issues shall be kept open for at least 3 working days and not more than 10 working days. In case of Book built issues, the minimum and maximum period for which bidding will be open is 3 – 7 working days
3. In case of initial public offer by an unlisted company,
   (a) If the issue price is Rs. 500/- or more, the issuer company shall have a discretion to fix the face value below Rs. 10/- per share subject to the condition that the face value shall in no case be less than Rs. 1 per share;

(b) If issue price is less than Rs. 500 per share, the face value shall be Rs.10/- per share;

4. If the subscription money is proposed to be received in calls, the calls shall be structured in such a manner that the entire subscription money is called within 12 months from the date of allotment.
5. If the issue size is above Rs.500 crores, it shall not be necessary to call the entire subscription money within 12 months.
6. All the public issues of size in excess of Rs.10 crores, are to made compulsorily in the demat mode.

SEBI GUIDELINES ON TAKEOVER

The SEBI (Substantial Acquisition of Shares and Takeovers) Regulations, 1997 has defined substantial quantity of shares or voting rights distinctly for two different purposes:

(a) Threshold of Disclosure to be Made by Acquirer(s). The following rules require an acquirer to disclose his shareholding in the target company at different stages of his acquisition of shares to maintain transparency.

1. 5% and more shares or voting rights: A person who, along with persons acting in concert, if any, acquires shares or voting rights (which when taken together with his existing holding) would entitle him to more than 5% or 10% or 14% shares or voting rights of target company, is required to disclose at every stage the aggregate of his shareholding to the target company and the Stock Exchanges within 2 days of acquisition or receipt of intimation of allotment of shares.
2. Any person who holds more than 15% but less than 55% shares or voting rights of target company, and who purchases or sells shares aggregating to 2% or more shall within 2 days disclose such purchase/ sale along with the aggregate of his shareholding to the target company and the Stock Exchanges.
3. Any person who holds more than 15% shares or voting rights of target company and a promoter and person having control over the target company, shall within 21 days from the financial year ending March 31 as well as the record date fixed for the purpose of dividend declaration, disclose every year his aggregate shareholding to the target company.

(b) Trigger Point for Making an Open offer by an Acquirer. These rules require the acquirer to make an open offer to the public for purchase of shares at different stages so ensure that the public at large also gets the benefits of higher valuation of the company's shares.

(a) 15% shares or voting rights: An acquirer who intends to acquire shares which alongwith his existing shareholding would entitle him to exercise 15% or more voting rights, can acquire such additional shares only after making a public announcement (PA) to acquire atleast additional 20% of the voting capital of target company from the shareholders through an open offer.

(b) Consolidation of holding: An acquirer who holds 55% or more but less than 75% shares or voting rights of a target company, can acquire further shares or voting rights only after making a public announcement to acquire atleast additional 20% shares of target company from the shareholders through an open offer.

A public announcement is an announcement made in the newspapers by the acquirer primarily disclosing his intention to acquire shares of the target company from existing shareholders by means of an open offer. The acquirer has to make an offer for a minimum of 20% (less only in specified cases).

INSIDER TRADING

Insider trading is one of the menaces of stock market culture which still have not been eliminated by the regulatory authorities. According to the insider trading regulations framed by SEBI, "Insider" means any person who, is or was connected with the company or is deemed to have been connected with the company, and who is reasonably expected to have access to unpublished price sensitive information in respect of securities of a company, or who has received or has had access to such unpublished price sensitive information. In brief, insider is a person who knows what is happening in a company.

Price sensitive information means any information which relates directly or indirectly to a company and which if published is likely to materially affect the price of securities of company;

Explanation: - The following shall be deemed to be price sensitive information

(1) Periodical financial results of the company;
(2) Intended declaration of dividends (both interim and final);
(3) Issue of securities or buy-back of securities;
(4) Any major expansion plans or execution of new projects;
(5) Amalgamation, mergers or takeovers;
(6) Disposal of the whole or substantial part of the undertaking;
(7) Any significant changes in policies, plans or operations of the company.

Under the insider trading regulation, SEBI has banned an insider and his relative from trading into the shares of the company for which he is an insider. Moreover, he cannot even suggest or advice any person to deal into shares of such company.

DEMATERIALISATION

Dematerialisation is the process by which physical certificates of an investor are converted to an equivalent number of securities in electronic form and credited in to the investor's account with his/her DP (Depository Participant). It is similar to holding money as cash in hand or in electronic form with the banks.

DEPOSITORY SERVICES

Meaning. A depository is an organization which holds securities of investor in electronic form at the request of the investor through a registered Depository Participant. It also provides services related to transactions in securities. It can be compared with a bank, which holds the funds for depositors. A Bank – Depository Analogy is given in following table:

BANK	DEPOSITORY
• Holds funds in an account	• Hold securities in an account
• Transfers funds between accounts on the instruction of the account holder i.e. A cheque	• Transfers securities between accounts on the instruction of the account holder through delivery instruction slip.
• Facilitates transfers without having to handle money	• Facilitates transfers of ownership without having to handle securities.
• Facilitates safekeeping of money	• Facilitates safekeeping of shares.

At present two Depositories viz. National Securities Depository Limited and Central Depository Services (I) Limited are registered with SEBI.

Depository Participant

A Depository Participant (DP) is an agent of the depository through which it interfaces with the investor. A DP can offer depository services only after it gets proper registration from SEBI. A Depository can be compared with a bank, like wise a DP may be compared with a branch of a Bank. An investor can open his account with any of the depository participants. So, the relationship of the depository, depository participant and investor can be shown as below :

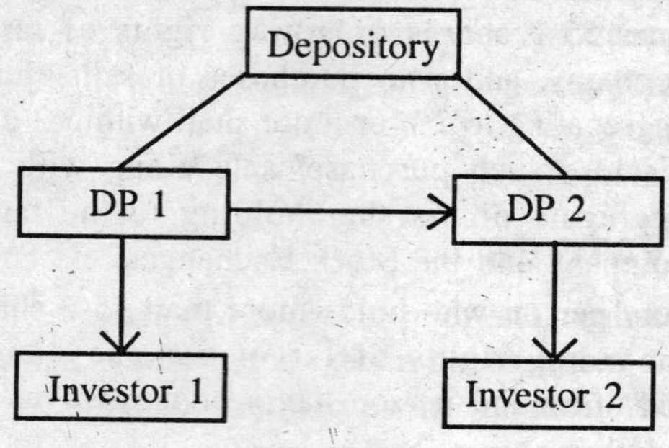

To understand how the depository system works, the above diagram is useful. According to it, two DP are the agents of a depository. (They can be agent of different depositories also) Investor 1 has account with DP 1 and the investor 2 has account with DP 2. Now, if the investor 1 sells shares of some company to investor 2, investor 1 will issue a Delivery Instruction Slip similar to a cheque) to investor 2 which in turn will be deposited with DP 2. DP 2 will send this slip to DP 1 who will transfer those shares to DP 2 to be credited to the account of investor 2. This is very similar to any bank transaction.

Benefits of Depository

Benefits of having securities in depository form are enumerated as below :

1. A safe, convenient way to hold securities;
2. Immediate transfer of securities;
3. No stamp duty on transfer of securities;
4. Elimination of risks associated with physical certificates such as bad delivery, fake securities, Delays, thefts etc.;
5. Reduction in paperwork involved in transfer of securities;
6. Reduction in transaction cost;
7. No odd lot problem, even one share can be sold;
8. Nomination facility;
9. Change in address recorded with DP gets registered with all companies in which investor holds securities electronically eliminating the need to correspond with each of them separately;
10. Transmission of securities is done by DP eliminating correspondence with companies;
11. Automatic credit into demat account of shares, arising out-of bonus or split or consolidation or merger etc.

DERIVATIVES

Meaning. The term "Derivative" indicates that it has no independent value, i.e. its value is entirely "derived" from the value of the underlying asset. The underlying asset can be securities, commodities, bullion, currency, livestock or anything else. In brief, derivatives has no physical presence, it is merely a contract. With Securities Laws (Second Amendment) Act, 1999, Derivatives has been included in the definition of Securities. The term Derivative has been defined in Securities Contracts (Regulations) Act, as:

A Derivative includes: -

(i) A security derived from a debt instrument, share, loan, whether secured or unsecured, risk instrument or contract for differences or any other form of security;

(ii) A contract which derives its value from the prices, or index of prices, of underlying securities;

Types of Derivatives

Derivative products or contracts are of many types. They can be classified into following categories:

(1) Forward contract

(2) Futures

(3) Options

(4) Swap

From the viewpoint of capital market, only futures and options derivatives are important. Therefore, we shall discuss about them only.

Future Contract. Futures Contract means a legally binding agreement to buy or sell the underlying security on a future date. Future contracts are the organized/standardized contracts in terms of quantity, quality (in case of commodities), delivery time and place for settlement on any date in future. The contract expires on a pre-specified date which is called the expiry date of the contract. On expiry, futures can be settled by delivery of the underlying asset or cash. Cash settlement entails paying/receiving the difference between the price at which the contract was entered and the price of the underlying asset at the time of expiry of the contract.

Options Contract. Options Contract is a type of Derivatives Contract which gives the buyer/holder of the contract the right (but not the obligation) to buy/sell the underlying asset at a predetermined price within or at end of a specified period. The buyer / holder of the option purchases the right from the seller/writer for a consideration which is called the Premium. The seller/writer of an option is obligated to settle the option as per the terms of the contract when the buyer/holder exercises his right. The underlying asset could include securities, an index of prices of securities etc.

Under Securities Contracts (Regulations) Act, 1956 options on securities has been defined as a contract for the purchase or sale of a right to buy or sell, or a right to buy and sell, securities in future, and includes a teji, a mandi, a teji mandi, a galli, a put, a call or a put and call in securities;

An Option to buy is called Call option and option to sell is called Put option. Further, if an option that is exercisable on or before the expiry date is called American option and one that is exercisable only on expiry date, is called European option. The price at which the option is to be exercised is called Strike price or Exercise price.

As in the case of futures contracts, option contracts can be also be settled by delivery of the underlying asset or cash. However, unlike futures cash settlement in option contract entails paying/receiving the difference between the strike price/exercise price and the price of the underlying asset either at the time of expiry of the contract or at the time of exercise / assignment of the option contract.

Index Futures and Index Options. Futures contract based on an index i.e. the underlying asset is the index, are known as Index Futures Contracts. For example, futures contract on NIFTY Index and BSE-30 Index. These contracts derive their value from the value of the underlying index.

Similarly, the options contracts, which are based on some index, are known as Index options contract. However, unlike Index Futures, the buyer of Index Option Contracts has only the right but not the obligation to buy / sell the underlying index on expiry. Index Option Contracts are generally European Style options i.e. they can be exercised only on the expiry date.

By its very nature, index cannot be delivered on maturity of the Index futures or Index option contracts therefore, these contracts are essentially cash settled on Expiry.

REGULATION OF DERIVATIVES TRADING

Dr. L.C Gupta Committee constituted by SEBI had laid down the regulatory framework for derivative trading in India. SEBI has also framed suggestive bye-law for Derivative Exchanges which lay's down the provisions for trading and settlement of derivative contracts. Derivative products have been introduced in a phased manner starting with Index Futures Contracts in June 2000. Index Options and Stock Options were introduced in June 2001 and July 2001 followed by Stock Futures in November 2001. SEBI has also specified that the value of a derivative contract should not be less than Rs. 2 Lakh at the time of introducing the contract in the market.

MUTUAL FUNDS

Meaning. Mutual fund is a mechanism for pooling the resources by issuing units to the investors and investing funds in securities in accordance with objectives as disclosed in offer document. Investments in securities are spread across a wide cross-section of industries and sectors and thus the risk is reduced. Diversification reduces the risk because all stocks may not move in the same direction in the same proportion at the same time. Mutual fund issues units to the investors in accordance with quantum of money invested by them. Investors of mutual funds are known as unit holders. A mutual fund is required to be registered with Securities and Exchange Board of India (SEBI) which regulates securities markets before it can collect funds from the public.

A mutual fund is set up in the form of a trust, and it has three entities to manage the whole working of a mutual fund :

(1) Trustee company

(2) Asset management company (AMC), and

(3) Custodian.

The trustee company is established by one or more than one sponsor who is like promoter of a company. The trustee company of the mutual fund hold its property for the benefit of the unit holders. Asset Management Company (AMC) approved by

SEBI manages the funds by making investments in various types of securities. Custodian, who is registered with SEBI, holds the securities of various schemes of the fund in its custody. The trustee company is vested with the general power of superintendence and direction over AMC. They monitor the performance and compliance of SEBI Regulations by the mutual fund.

Net Asset Value. Mutual funds invest the money collected from the investors in securities markets. In simple words, Net Asset Value is the market value of the securities held by the scheme. Since market value of securities changes every day, NAV of a scheme also varies on day-to-day basis. The NAV per unit is the market value of securities of a scheme divided by the total number of units of the scheme on any particular date. For example, if the market value of securities of a mutual fund scheme is Rs 200 lakhs and the mutual fund has issued 10 lakhs units of Rs. 10 each to the investors, then the NAV per unit of the fund is Rs.20. NAV is required to be disclosed by the mutual funds on a regular basis - daily or weekly - depending on the type of scheme.

Types of Mutual Funds. Mutual funds can be divided into various categories based on two criteria:

(a) Schemes according to Maturity Period

(b) Schemes according to Investment objective

(a) Schemes According to Maturity Period

A mutual fund scheme can be classified into open-ended scheme or close-ended scheme depending on its maturity period.

1. **Open-ended Fund:** An open-ended fund or scheme is one that is available for subscription and repurchase on a continuous basis. These schemes do not have a fixed maturity period. Investors can conveniently buy and sell units to the issuing company itself at Net Asset Value (NAV) related prices which are declared on a daily basis. The key feature of open-end schemes is liquidity.

2. **Close-ended Fund:** A close-ended fund or scheme has a stipulated maturity period e.g. 5-7 years. The fund is open for subscription only during a specified period at the time of launch of the scheme. Investors can invest in the scheme at the time of the initial public issue and thereafter they can buy or sell the units of the scheme on the stock exchanges where the units are listed. So, the main difference in open ended and closed ended scheme is that in case of former, the units can be sold to the issuing company itself whereas in case of later, the units are sold in the open market through stock exchange.

(b) Schemes According to Investment Objective

A scheme can also be classified considering its investment objective. Such schemes may be open-ended or close-ended schemes as described earlier. Such schemes may be classified mainly as follows:

1. **Growth Equity Oriented Scheme :** The aim of growth funds is to provide capital appreciation over the medium to long- term. Such schemes normally invest a major part of their corpus in equities. Such funds have comparatively high risks. These schemes provide different options to the investors like dividend option, capital appreciation, etc. and the investors may choose an option depending on their preferences. The investors must indicate the option in the application form. Growth schemes are good for investors having a long-term outlook seeking appreciation over a period of time.

2. **Income/Debt Oriented Scheme :** The aim of income funds is to provide regular and steady income to investors. Such schemes generally invest in fixed income securities such as bonds, corporate debentures, Government securities and money market instruments. Such funds are less risky compared to equity schemes. However, opportunities of capital appreciation are also limited in such funds. The NAVs of such funds are affected because of change in interest rates in the country. If the interest rates fall, NAVs of such funds are likely to increase in the short run and vice versa. These funds are useful for those investors who prefer less risk and regular income.

3. **Balanced Fund :** The aim of balanced funds is to provide both growth and regular income as such schemes invest both in equities and fixed income securities in the proportion indicated in their offer documents. These are appropriate for investors looking for moderate growth.

4. **Money Market or Liquid Fund:** These funds are also income funds and their aim is to provide easy liquidity, preservation of capital and moderate income. These schemes invest exclusively in safer short-term instruments such as treasury bills, certificates of deposit, commercial paper and inter-bank call money, government securities, etc. Returns on these schemes fluctuate much less compared to other funds. These funds are appropriate for corporate and individual investors as a means to park their surplus funds for short periods. They are popularly called "Money Market Mutual Funds of MMMF".

5. **Gilt Fund :** These funds invest exclusively in government securities. Government securities have no default risk. NAVs of these schemes also fluctuate due to change in interest rates and other economic factors as is the case with income or debt oriented schemes.

6. **Index Funds :** Index Funds replicate the portfolio of a particular index such as the BSE Sensitive index, S&P NSE 50 index (Nifty), etc. These schemes invest in the securities in the same weightage comprising of an index. NAVs of such schemes would rise or fall in accordance with the rise or fall in the index, though not exactly by the same percentage due to some factors known as "tracking error" in technical terms.

There are also exchange traded index funds (ETF) launched by the mutual funds which are traded on the stock exchanges.

Recent announcements of SEBI : SEBI has recently made following announcements on 30th December 2005.

(i) Investors will be given a unique identifiction number (UIN) to transact deals in the stock market.

(ii) It has decided to make biometric identification like electronic finger printing compulsory for all trade value over Rs. 5,00,000.

(iii) SEBI will soon introduce optional grading of IPOs by SEBI registered credit rating agencies.

(iv) SEBI has allowed mutual funds to launch gold exchange traded funds (GETF) in India

(v) In order to rationalise regulations for FPOs and rights issues, SEBI has decided to do away with the repetitive disclosures.

TERMS USED IN CAPITAL MARKET

Spot Delivery Contract. It refers to a contract for the purchase or sale of securities which is settled on the same day on which the transaction takes place or latest by the following day.

Initial Public Offering (IPO) . When an unlisted company makes either a fresh issue of securities or an offer for sale of its existing securities or both for the first time to the public, it is called and IPO. This paves way for listing and trading of the issuer's securities on a stock exchange.

Closely Held Company. This term is used for a company whose most of the shares are held by a few persons and there is a small quantity of shares held by general public which is available in the market.

Red Herring Prospectus. It is a prospectus which does not have details of either price or number of shares being offered or the amount of issue. This means that in case price is not disclosed, the number of shares and the upper and lower price bands are disclosed. On the other hand, an issuer can state the issue size and the number of shares are determined later.

Green-shoe Option. A Green Shoe option means an option of allocating shares in excess of the shares included in the public issue and operating a post-listing price stabilizing mechanism. This is an arrangement wherein the issue would be over allotted to the extent of a maximum of 15% of the issue size. For example, if a company makes an issue of Rs. 100 crores with a green shoe option and the applications have been received for Rs. 150 crores, the company can exercise the option and allot shares upto Rs. 115 crores. From an investor's perspective, an issue with green shoe option provides more probability of getting shares and also that post listing price may show relatively more stability as compared to market.

Cut-off Price. In Book building issue, the issuer is required to indicate either the price band or a floor price in the red herring prospectus. The actual discovered issue price can be any price in the price band or any price above the floor price. This issue price is called "Cut off price". This is decided by the issuer and LM after considering all the bids. SEBI (DIP) guidelines permit only retail individual investors to have an option of applying at cut off price.

Persons Acting in Concert. PACs are individual(s) /company(ies)/ any other legal entity(ies) who are acting together for a common objective or for a purpose of substantial acquisition of shares or voting rights or gaining control over the target company pursuant to an agreement or understanding whether formal or informal. Acting in concert would imply co-operation, co-ordination for acquisition of voting rights or control. This co-operation/ co-ordinated approach may either be direct or indirect.

Qualified Institutional Buyer (QIBs). Qualified Institutional Buyers are those institutional investors who are generally perceived to possess expertise and the financial muscle to evaluate and invest in the capital markets.

In terms of clause 2.2.2B (v) of DIP Guidelines, a 'Qualified Institutional Buyer' shall mean:

(a) Public financial institution as defined in section 4A of the Companies Act, 1956;

(b) Scheduled commercial banks;

(c) Mutual funds;

(d) Foreign institutional investor registered with SEBI;

(e) Multilateral and bilateral development financial institutions;

(f) Venture capital funds registered with SEBI.

(g) Foreign Venture capital investors registered with SEBI.

(h) State Industrial Development Corporations.

(i) Insurance Companies registered with the Insurance Regulatory and Development Authority (IRDA).

(j) Provident Funds with minimum corpus of Rs. 25 crores

(k) Pension Funds with minimum corpus of Rs. 25 crores

These entities are not required to be registered with SEBI as QIBs. Any entities falling under the categories specified above are considered as QIBs for the purpose of participating in primary issuance process.

Forward Delivery Contract. It refers to a contract for the purchase or sale of securities, which is due for settlement on the following settlement day but which can be postponed to the next settlement day if so desired. Such postponement is known as 'Badla'.

Ex and Cum Dividend. Ex means 'without'. When the securities are quoted ex-dividend, the buyer is not entitled to receive the first dividend to be declared after the sale of such shares. Cum means 'including'. The cum-dividend price includes the amount of dividend which the company may declare. The shares are quoted cum-dividend before the book closure or record date and ex-dividend after that date.

ISIN. ISIN (International Securities Identification Number) is a unique identification number for a security.

Zero Coupon Bond. Bond issued at a discount and repaid at a face value. No periodic interest is paid. The difference between the issue price and redemption price represents the return to the holder. The buyer of these bonds receives only one payment i.e. at the maturity of the bond.

Commercial Paper. A short term promise to repay a fixed amount that is placed on the market either directly or through a specialized intermediary. It is usually issued by companies with a high credit standing in form of a promissory note redeemable at par to the holder on maturity and therefore doesn't require any guarantee. Commercial paper is a money market instrument issued for the tenure of 90 days.

Pay-in Day and Pay-out Day. Pay in day is the day when the brokers shall make payment or delivery of securities to the exchange. Pay out day is the day when the exchange makes payment or delivery of securities to the broker. Since settlement cycle has been reduced from T+3 rolling settlement to T+2 w.e.f. April 01, 2003, the exchanges have to ensure that the pay out of funds and securities to the clients is done by the broker within 24 hours of the payout.

Rolling Settlement. Settlement refers to the settlement of all the purchases and sales taken place at the stock exchange. In the earlier system, if a person has bought some shares, he would get upto 5 days to sell those shares without having the liability to take the delivery of shares. He will only receive or pay the difference in the price at which share are bought and sold. Under rolling settlement system, all the trades outstanding at the end of the day have to be settled. So, if a person buys some shares and does not sell them on the same day, he will have to take the delivery of shares and pay the full price. This has reduced the scope of speculation. At present we are following the system of T+2 under rolling settlement from April 1, 2003. It means that the securities and cash are transacted 2 days after the day on which the trade has taken place.

Corporatisation of Stock Exchanges. Corporatisation is the process of converting the organizational structure of the stock exchange from a non-corporate structure to a corporate structure. Traditionally, some of the stock exchanges in India were established as "Association of persons", e.g. BSE, ASE and MPSE. Corporatisation of such exchanges is the process of converting them into incorporated Companies

Demutualisation of Stock Exchanges. Demutualisation refers to the transition process of an exchange from a "mutually-owned" association to a company "owned by shareholders". In other words, transforming the legal structure of an exchange from a mutual form to a business corporation form is referred to as demutualisation. The above, in effect means that after demutualisation, the ownership, the management and the trading rights at the exchange are segregated from one another.

Corporate Governance. As Kumar Managalam Committee Report on Corporate Governance enumerates, the fundamental objective of corporate governance is the "enhancement of shareholder value, keeping in view the interests of other stakeholder". This definition harmonizes the need for a company to strike a balance at all times between the need to enhance shareholders' wealth whilst not in any way being detrimental to the interests of the other stakeholders in the company.

Wash Sales. It refers to the fictitious transaction of selling and buying of particular securities at higher prices to push up prices of those securities so that broker and speculator is able to reap profits by selling his holdings to the public.

Cornering. It means a situation in the stock market in which almost the entire supply of a particular security is held by an individual or group.

Rigging. Rigging refers to a situation in the stock market in which those who hold large blocks of securities buy and sell their holdings to have a control over the market quotations and thereby pushing the market prices up and then start selling the shares gradually once the prices have risen substantially.

Blank Transfer. When the name of the buyer is not mentioned in the transfer form and seller merely signs it, it is known as blank transfer.

Lame Duck. When a bear speculator finds it difficult to meet his commitments immediately, he is said to be struggling like a lame duck. This happens when he has been cornered because he cannot buy the shares for delivery at any price, as no shares are available in the market.

Stag. A stag is a speculator who applies for shares of new issue for being sold at a premium. He is bullish in nature as he always hopes for a rise in the prices.

Contango. Contango is a badla charge paid by a bear to a bull for a badla.

Remisers. They are agents of full flagged members of a stock exchange. They cannot carry on business in their own name. They are paid commission out of brokerage collected by them. They are also called sub-brokers.

Global Depository Receipts (GDR). It is a negotiable financial instrument issued by a bank to represent a foreign company's publicly traded securities. When any foreign company wants to raise capital in the country, it issues shares to a depository bank which in turn issues depository receipts to the people of the country which are traded on the stock exchange. when such depository receipts are issued by a bank in USA, it is called American Depository Receipts (ADR). In case of banks of other countries, it is known as Global Depository receipts (GDR). Recently government has allowed foreign companies to raise capital in India by way of issue of Indian depository receipts. Depository receipts make it easier to buy shares in foreign companies.

NASDAQ. National Association of Securities Dealers Automated Quotation (NASDAQ) is a stock exchange based in New York which pioneered in facilitating the trading of small and newly floated companies specially in the information technology sector. Today, it is one of the most popular stock exchange.

Securities Transaction Tax. This tax was introduced in budget 2004-05 and was made applicable from October 1, 2004. It is a tax on transactions done in the financial securities through a recognized stock exchange which includes shares, debentures, government securities, etc. This tax is charged on the transaction value @ 0.15% on the delivery based transactions, 0.015% for trades that do not involve delivery of shares and 0.010% for futures and options.

13. HUMAN RESOURCE MANAGEMENT

CONCEPT OF HUMAN RESOURCE MANAGEMENT

The term 'human resources' may be defined as the total knowledge, skills, creative abilities, talents and aptitudes of an organization's workforce, as well as the values, attitudes, approaches and beliefs of the individuals involved in the affairs, of the organization. It is the sum total or aggregate of inherent abilities, acquired knowledge and skills represented by the talents and aptitudes of the persons employed in an organization.

Several terms have been used by various management thinkers to represent human resources. These includes 'personnel', 'people at work', 'manpower', 'staff' and 'employees'. Whatever may be the term used, the human resources of an organization include all individuals engaged in various organizational activities at different levels. According to **Leon C. Megginson**, "From the national point of view, human resources may be defined the knowledge, skills, creative abilities, talents and aptitudes obtained in the population; whereas from the viewpoint of the individual enterprise, they represent the total of the inherent abilities acquired knowledge and skills as exemplified in the talents and aptitudes of its employees". **Jucius Michael** calls these resources, 'human factor', which refer to "a whole consisting of inter-related, inter-dependent and interacting physiological, psychological, sociological and ethical components." Thus, human resources are multi-dimensional in nature. People working in the organization have different needs at different times. These needs may physiological, social and psychological.

According to the Institute of Personnel Management (U.K.), "Personnel management is an integral but distinctive part of management, concerned with people at work and their relationships within the enterprise. It seeks to bring together into an effective organization the men and women who staff the enterprise, enabling each to make his/her best contribution to its success, both as a member of a working group and as an individual. It seeks to provide relationships within the enterprise that are conducive both to effective work and human satisfaction".

Scott, Clothier and Spriegel have defined personnel management as that branch of management which is responsible on a staff basis for concentrating on those aspects of operations which are primarily concerned with the relationship of management to employees and employees to employees and with the development of the individual and the group. The objective is to attain maximum individual development, desirable working relationship between employees and employers, and employees and employees, and effective moulding of human resources as contrasted with physical resources.

PERSPECTIVES OF HUMAN RESOURCE MANAGEMENT

The growth of human resource management in U.S.A. and U.K. was evolutionary in nature. It took place because of the voluntary efforts of the employers. But in countries like India human resource management grew because of compulsions made by the Government. In 1931, the Royal Commission on Labour recommended the abolition of jobber system and the appointment of labour officers in the industries to look after recruitment and welfare of employees. In 1948, the Factories Act made it obligatory for certain industrial enterprises to appoint welfare officers.

The scope of human resource management has expanded considerably throughout the world. Over the last forty years or so, new techniques and styles of managing the human resources have been developed as a result of the researches and experiences in the field. The task of the human manager is not confined only to the recruitment of workers, but also to looking after their welfare and handling their grievances.

Under the influence of technological development, organizational complexities are growing. The impact on the work, working methods, work rules, tools, equipment, etc. is inevitable. Jobs have become more complex and need specialized skills and professionals. As a result of this, emphasis is being given to the training and development aspects. In order to meet the growing needs of such human, management institutes, universities and other bodies have started training and executive development programmes.

Human management is no longer restricted only to the wage earners in the factories. It has become equally important in offices, sales organizations, hospitals, research and development institutions and in the ranks of management itself. Human management is not needed by private industry alone. No-profit institutions, government departments and armed services also need human management for better employer-employee relations.

Some companies have labour relations directors whose primary job is to advise and assist top management, superintendents and departmental heads in their dealings with union representatives. This official may or may not report to the personnel manager, although this function should be subordinate to personnel management in the broad sense. In a unionized company where there is no labour relations, director or the personnel manager usually has these responsibilities.

The other terms used frequently in discussion of personnel problems and techniques are "labour relations" and "industrial relations". Something, these are used interchangeably with "personnel management or administration", but it is useful to distinguish between them. The term "labour relations" refers primarily to the relations between management and unionized labour. The subject-matter of labour relations includes the negotiation of contracts with unions and day-to-day relations with union leaders and business agents in the handling of differences arising under the contract, arbitration and government regulations of the terms and conditions of employment.

The use of the term 'industrial relations' as synonymous with 'human resource/personnel management' has been very common in United States of America.

In India, the field of personnel management has three branches, viz (i) personnel administration, (ii) industrial relations and (iii) labour welfare. Personnel administration deals with the administrative aspects of personnel functions such as recruitment, selection, placement, promotion, transfer, wages and incentives, etc. Industrial relations deals broadly with employer-employee relationship, negotiations and collective bargaining, settlement of grievance and disputes, joint consultation. Labour welfare programmes seek to improve the working and living conditions of the employees by the provision of facilities such as crèche, canteen, housing, recreation, education etc.

In the Indian context, these three areas have developed some kind of identity of their own and have been recognized as integral parts of the broad field of personnel management. However, these three are not watertight compartments. This kind of division has facilitated convenient grouping of personnel functions. It also worth noting that these three groups of personnel functions have been generally dealt with by officers with three different sets of designations. The first have been usually dealt with by officers designated as personnel officers, while the second and third are handled generally by those with designations of labour officer and welfare officer respectively.

HUMAN RESOURCE PLANNING

Manpower, personnel or human resources may be regarded as the quantitative and qualitative measurement of work-force required in an organization and planning in relation to manpower may be regarded as establishing objectives to develop human resources in line with broad objectives of organization. Human resource planning is the process of developing and determining objectives, policies and programmes that will develop, utilize and distribute manpower so as to achieve the goals of the organization. In the words of **Coleman**, "Manpower planning is the process of determining manpower requirements and the means for meeting those requirements in order to carry out the integrated plan of the organization".

According to **Geisler**, "Manpower planning is the process including forecasting, developing and controlling by which a firm ensures that it has the right number of people and the right kind of people at the right places, at the right time doing work for which they are economically most useful." Thus, manpower planning consists of projecting future manpower requirements and developing manpower plans for the implementation of the projections. Manpower planning cannot be rigid or static; it is amenable to modifications, review and adjustments in accordance with the needs of the organizations or the changing circumstances.

NATURE OF HUMAN RESOURCE PLANNING

The following points emerge from the study of definition of manpower planning:

(i) Manpower planning aims at ascertaining the manpower needs of the organization both in number and kind.

(ii) It presents an inventory of exiting manpower of the organization. An analysis of the inventory of manpower helps in ascertaining the status of the available with the organization.

(iii) It helps in determining the shortfall (or surplus) of manpower by comparing the total manpower needs with the present supply of manpower. It also helps in projecting future manpower needs.

(iv) It is concerned with the initiation of various organization programmes depending upon the demand and supply of human resources. If the future needs exceed presently available talent, this gap becomes the basis for a programme of employment and training. And, if the presently available talent exceeds the future needs, this difference may become the basis for a programme of retirements, discharge, etc.

(v) Effective manpower planning must encompass the acquisition, utilization, improvement, and preservation of the organization's human resources.

OBJECTIVES OF HUMAN RESOURCE PLANNING

The major objectives of manpower planning in an organization are:

(i) ensure optimum use of human resources currently employed;

(ii) avoid balances in the distribution and allocation of human resources;

(iii) assess or forecast future skill requirements of the organization's overall objectives;

(iv) provide control measure to ensure availability of necessary resources when required;

(v) control the cost aspect of human resources;

(vi) formulate transfer and promotion policies.

SCOPE OR ELEMENTS OF HUMAN RESOURCES PLANNING

The basic activities involved in human resource planning are as under:

(i) Listing of current manpower or human resources.

(ii) Assessing the extent to which the current manpower is utilized to the advantage of the organization.

(iii) Phasing out the surplus manpower, if any.

(iv) Analyzing the requirements of manpower in future in the light of expansion plans retirement of personnel, etc.

(v) Making manpower forecasts.

(vi) Designing training programmes for different categories of manpower.

BENEFITS OF MANPOWER PLANNING

Manpower planning is an important tool of Human Resource Management as it helps in the following ways:

1. Manpower planning results in reduced labour costs as it helps the management to anticipate shortages and/or surpluses of manpower and correct these imbalances before they become unmanageable and expensive.
2. It is a better basis for planning employee development that is designated to make optimum use of workers' skills within the organization.
3. It enables identification of the gaps of the existing manpower so that corrective training could be imparted. Thus, the training programme becomes more effective.
4. It leads to improvement in the overall business planning process.
5. It helps in formulating managerial succession plan as a part of the replacement planning process which is necessitated when job-change plans for managers are formulated. Besides, this exercise would provide enough lead time for identifying and developing managers to move up the corporate ladder.
6. It leads to a greater awareness of the importance of sound manpower management throughout the organizations.
7. It serves as a tool to evaluate the effect of alternative manpower actions and policies.

PROCESS OF HUMAN RESOURCES PLANNING

The process of manpower planning involves the following steps:

1. Determination of objectives of manpower planning
2. Current manpower inventory
3. Demand forecasting
4. Job requirements
5. Employment plan
6. Training and development programme

Manpower planning is a continuous process as shown in the Fig. 1. The manager responsible for manpower planning has to be concerned with all the steps at all type. He may have to revise employment plan and training and development programme from time to time depending upon the changes in circumstances such as sudden changes in volume in production, unexpected high rate of labor turnover, obsolescence of existing skills and so on. A brief explanation of the steps in the manpower planning process is given below:

1. Determination of Objectives of Manpower Planning : The persons concerned with manpower planning must be clear about the goals of manpower planning. According to Sikula, "The ultimate purpose of manpower planning is to relate future human resources to future enterprise needs so as to maximize the future return on investment in human resources."

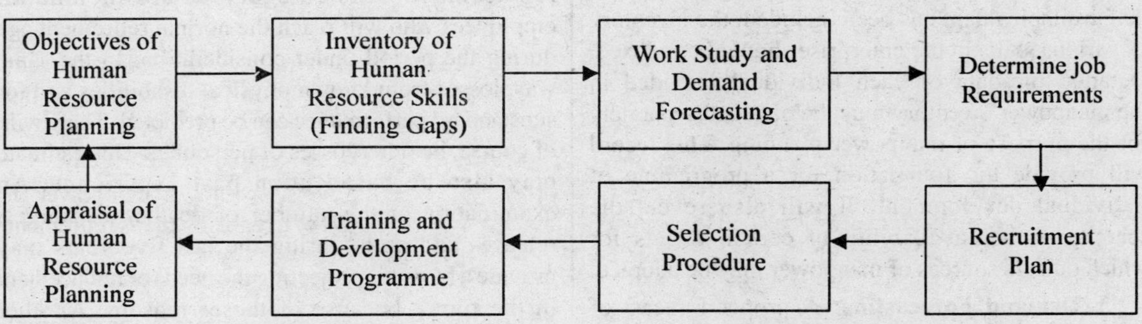

Fig. 1. *Human Resources Planning Process*

Manpower planning is an integral part of the corporate planning. It must be integrated with the overall organizational plans. Manpower planning should be done carefully as it has got long-term repercussions. Once the wrong forecast of future requirement of human resources and wrong analyses of the available manpower inventory are made, it may not be possible to rectify the errors in the short-run. Therefore, manpower planning should be more concerned with filling future vacancies with right type of people rather than with matching existing personnel with existing jobs.

Current Manpower Inventory: Analysis of current manpower supply may be undertaken by department, by function, by occupation, or by level of skill or qualifications. Appropriate adjustments in these would need to be made in the light of any foreseeable changes in weekly hours of work, holidays, leave entitlements, etc. It may be noted that assessment of demand for the operative personnel presents less problems of uncertainty and current manpower supply can be adjusted accordingly. But projections of manpower requirements for supervisory and managerial levels present a complex problem because the required talents are not available at a short notice. This explains the need to ascertain the present manpower inventory in the enterprise. This will also help in drawing recruitment and development plans to meet the needs of certain skills in the future.

Systematic steps must be taken in order to ensure that a reservoir of talent is available when vacancies occur. The search for talented employees in the organization must be continuous. To be sure that available talent has been included; the inventory of various skills in the enterprise should be indexed. Detailed bio-data of each individual included in the manpower inventory must be obtained separately for the purpose of manpower planning. This record will provide the foundation for a programme of individual development. It will also reveal the scarcity or non-availability of certain talents for which outside sources of manpower may be adopted.

3. Demand Forecasting: A proper forecast of manpower required in the future (say, after one year, two years, three years and so on) must be attempted. The factors relevant for manpower forecasting are as follows:

(*i*) **Employment Trends:** The manpower planning committee at the corporate level should make an examination of number of the employees on the payroll during the past five years to know the trend within each group. With the help of this, it would be possible to determine whether a particular group has been stable or unstable and whether it has been expanding or contracting.

(*ii*) **Replacement Needs:** The need for replacement arises due to death, retirement, resignation and termination of employees. The examination of replacement needs may relate to specific manpower groups : supervisory, skilled, clerical, unskilled, etc. For some groups like managerial or supervisory, it is very difficult to predict the needs. One of the major difficulties involved in predicting the need for managerial skill is that the management development cycle takes a long time. So the needs for managerial manpower should be anticipated sufficiently in advance.

Forecasts of manpower may be based to a great extent on the analysis of historical data. It is presumed that the factors causing past occurrences will also play a similar role in the future. But these data must be adjusted in the light of other known information about the future. Certain losses of key personnel can be predicted with a substantial degree of accuracy. These include losses from retirement, physical disabilities and cases of sub-standard performance. But retirement is the most common type of anticipated separation which gives rise to the need for replacement. This category would include all employees who will reach the normal retirement age during the period under consideration. In the same way, losses from known physical disabilities and for substandard performance can be predicted. There will, of course, be other losses of personnel. This estimate may also be based upon past experience. An examination of the number of deaths, discharges, releases and quits during the last five years may provide a basis for projecting the need for replacement in the future because of theses reasons. Another important factor influencing the replacement needs is transfer of some employees to other departments of the organization or promotion of some employees to higher jobs. This number can be estimated on the basis of a review of the persons promoted or transferred during the previous years and the records of performance of various employees during the past years.

***(iii)* Productivity:** An important area to which the manpower planning is related is the improvement in productivity. Gains in productivity add to the growth potential of the organization and can make possible healthy wage increase. Gains in productivity will also influence the requirements of manpower.

Planning for productivity gains has several aspects. The first and the important one relates to affecting gains by improvements in existing manpower utilization. Current levels of utilization and indications about the needed improvement can be obtained by the application of various analytical techniques of industrial engineering or work study such as activity charts, flow charts, multiple activity charts, and activity sampling studies and so on. Methods improvement techniques help reduce work content. Conceptually, similar approaches aimed at upgrading management performance help secure productivity gains at the managerial level.

The second aspect relates to installation of more productive tools, equipments or processes. Any anticipated change due to the introduction of automation will affect manpower needs in the plants as well as in the divisional offices. The manpower planning experts should attempt to learn about such changes with sufficient time to appraise their possible impact on the number and kinds of employees required in the future.

The last aspect relates to the matching of skills with the requirements of the jobs. Job analysis techniques facilitate a clear specification of the skills and experience requirements of jobs. The immediate products of this analysis are job description and job specification.

***(iv)* Growth and Expansion:** Another aspect relevant for manpower planning is personnel requirements for growth and expansion of the organization. The expansion plans of various plants and divisions should be carefully reviewed to assess their probable effects on the number of employees required in each group. The accuracy with which such manpower requirements can be forecast will depend, among other things, on the degree of accuracy which can be achieved in relation to the expansion programme. Where the expansion programme is less specific and the time perspective is larger, uncertainties will also be greater.

A going concern is a living and growing organism. It is not contended with the exiting level of production or profits. It also wants to grow and increase its share in the total activities of industry. One of the basic aspirations of most business managers is to perpetuate the enterprise in which they are engaged. In this world of competition, perpetuation would mean that every organization has its plans ahead of its activities and aims at a better growth rate and at diversification of its activities and at a better image of itself. All these aims and aspirations result in expansion and growth creating numerous positions for work-force at various levels. These aims and aspirations can be fulfilled if there are a sufficient number of capable persons to handle various positions in the organization.

A good organization always tries to adapt itself to change in the methods and techniques of production. Developments in scientific world like the emergence of space science, nuclear science, electronics, etc. has considerably opened up new avenues of business investment avenues expansion and has also introduced great complexities in the management of companies. These changes have completely thrown out of gear the capacity and ability of existing employees to meet the new situations unless they are adequately educated and trained. Manpower planners should take all these factors into account while studying the impact of various business expansion plans on manpower requirements.

***(v)* Absenteeism:** It means a situation when a person fails to come for work when he is scheduled to work. The rate of absenteeism can be calculated by the following formula:

$$\text{Absenteeism} = \frac{\text{Man-days lost}}{\text{Man-days worked + Man-days lost}}$$

There are certain employees who are more prone to absenteeism in any organization. 10 to 20 per cent of such employees may account for 70 to 80 per cent of absences. It should be noted that excessive absenteeism (more than the irreducible minimum, say 3% to 5%) involves a considerable cost to the firm even when the absent employees receive no pay. Work schedules are upset leading to overtime work which in turn leads to increase cost of production. The management should go into the causes of absenteeism and attempt to reduce the absenteeism as far as possible. The manpower planning experts will have to consider the known rate of absenteeism in their-decision regarding estimation of manpower requirements.

(*vi*) **Work Study:** Work study technique can be used when it is possible to apply work measurement to know how long operations should take and the amount of labour required. This is also known as **'Workload analysis'**. On the basis of the work-load of each plant during the forthcoming years, workforce analysis is done considering the rates of absenteeism and labour turnover.

4. Job Requirements: Job analysis is the qualitative aspect of manpower requirement since it determines the demands of a job in terms of responsibilities and duties and then translates these demands in terms of skills, qualities and other human attributes. It helps in determining the number and kinds of jobs and qualifications needed to fill these jobs because with the help of job analysis it is known that what is the quantum of work which an average person can do a job in a day. It facilitates the division of work into different jobs. Thus, it is an essential element of effective manpower planning. At managerial levels, accurate job descriptions help in preparation of inventories of executive talent.

5. Employment plans: This phase deals with planning how the organization can obtain the required number of right type of personnel as reflected by the personnel forecasts. In other words, there is a need to prepare programmes of recruitment, selection, training, transfer and promotion so that personnel needs of various departments of the organization are met.

6. Training and Development Programme: The preparation of skill inventory helps in identifying the training and development needs of the organization. Training is necessary not only for new employees, but also for old employees. Executive development programmes have to be devised for the development of managerial personnel. No enterprise has a choice of whether to provide training or not, the only choice is that of method or technique. All types of jobs usually require some sort of training for their efficient performance even when the persons appointed have some job experience, they must be given some training to renew their knowledge and skills and to tell them what they are expected to do. The talents of the employees are not fully productive without a systematic programme of training and development.

7. Appraisal of Manpower Planning: After the employment and training programmes have been implemented, an appraisal must be made of the effectiveness of manpower planning. Deficiencies in the programme should be pointed out and the catalogue of manpower inventory should be updated periodically. Corrective actions should also be taken wherever it is necessary to remove the deficiencies in manpower planning. An appraisal of the existing manpower plans will also serve as a guide in the future manpower planning. Human resource planning is closely linked to the goals of human resource management and those of the organization. Shortage or surplus of human resources in any department or at any level should be minimized. Human Resource Planning programme will be effective if it can anticipate the deficiencies of various skills will in time so that steps are initiated for recruitment of required human resources. Similarly, if some types of personnel are surplus, they should be adjusted after giving them appropriate training. If it is not possible, they may be phased out through voluntary retirement scheme.

TECHNIQUES OF HUMAN RESOURCE PLANNING

The quantitative aspects of human resource planning involve demand forecasting and supply forecasting as discussed further.

DEMAND FORECASTING

It is the process of estimating the requirement of different kinds of personnel in future. The basis of manpower forecasts should be the annual budget and long-term corporate plan, translated into activity levels for each function and department. In a manufacturing company, the sales budget would be translated into a manufacturing plan giving the number and types of products to be made in each period. From this information, the number of man-hours by skill categories to make the quota for each period would be computed. In an insurance company, forecasts of new business would be translated into the number of proposals that would have to be processed by the underwriting department. In a mail order company, forecasts would be made of the number of orders that might have to be processed, assembled and dispatched.

There are three basic demand forecasting methods:

1. Managerial judgement;
2. Work study techniques;
3. Statistical techniques.

SUPPLY FORECASTING

Supply forecasting is concerned with the estimate of supply of manpower given the analysis of current resources and.future availability. Here the personnel planner must consider both the external supply (employees available for higher position in the organization's geographic work force) and the internal supply (organization's current employees). External supply of personnel is important for two reasons. First, the normal separation of employees through voluntary turnover, retirements, illness death and discharge may require that the organization look to employment agencies, colleges and universities and other sources to replenish lost personnel. Second organizational growth and diversification require the use of external sources to obtain additional numbers and types of employees.

The internal supply of personnel is influenced by the following factors:

(*a*) existing manpower resources;
(*b*) potential losses to existing resources through labour wastage;
(*c*) potential changes to exiting resources through internal promotions;
(*d*) effect of changing conditions of work and absenteeism;
(*e*) sources of supply from the firm.

SELECTING HUMAN RESOURCES

RECRUITMENT

Meaning of Recruitment: The process of identification of different sources of personnel is known as recruitment. According to Edwin B. Flippo, "*Recruitment is the process of searching the candidates for employment and stimulating them to apply for jobs in the organization*". It is a linking activity that brings together those offering jobs and those seeking jobs.

Date S. Beach observed, "*Recruitment is the development and maintenance of adequate manpower resources. It involves the creation of a pool of available labour upon whom the organization can draw when it needs additional employees.*" Recruitment refers to the attempt of getting interested applicants and providing a pool of prospective employees so that the management can select the right person for the right job from this pool. Recruitment precedes the selection process, i.e., selection of right candidates for various positions in the organization.

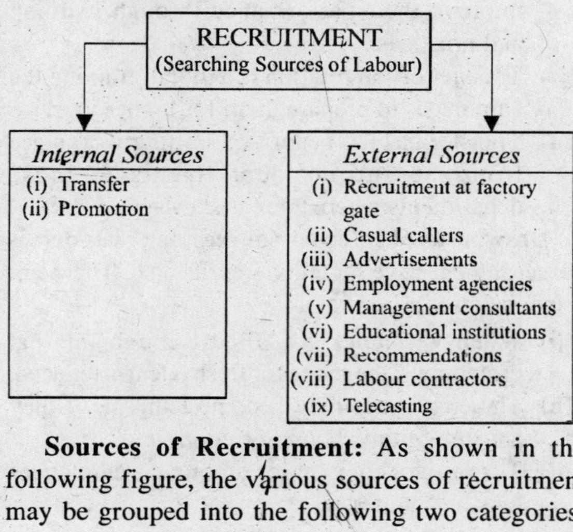

Sources of Recruitment: As shown in the following figure, the various sources of recruitment may be grouped into the following two categories:

1. Internal Sources (recruitment form within the enterprise); and
2. External Sources (recruitment from outside).

Internal Sources

There are two important internal sources of recruitment, namely, *transfer* and *promotion* which are given below in details

(*i*) Transfer: It involves the shifting of an employee from one job to another, one department to another or from one shift to another. Transfer is a good source of filling vacancies.

(*ii*) Promotion: It leads to *shifting an employee to a higher position, carrying higher responsibilities, facilities, status and pay.*

Advantages of Internal Sources: Filling vacancies in higher jobs from within the organization or through internal transfers has the following merits:

(*i*) Employees are motivated to improve their performance
(*ii*) Morale of the employees is increased
(*iii*) Industrial peace prevails in the enterprise because of promotion avenues
(*iv*) Filling of jobs internally is cheaper as compared to getting candidates from external sources
(*v*) A promotion at a higher level may lead to a chain of promotions at lower levels in the organization. This motivates the employees to improve their performance through learning and practices.
(*vi*) Transfer or job rotation is a tool of training the employees to prepare them for higher jobs.
(*vii*) Transfer has the benefit of shifting workplace from the surplus departments to those departments where there is shortage of staff.

Drawbacks of Internal Sources: Internal sources of recruitment have certain demerits also. These are listed below:

(*i*) When vacancies are filled through internal promotions, the scope for fresh talent is reduced.
(*ii*) The employees may become lethargic if they are sure of time bound promotions.
(*iii*) The spirit of competition among the employees may be hampered.
(*iv*) Frequent transfers of employees may reduce the overall productivity of the organization.

External Sources

Every enterprise has to tap external sources for various positions. Running enterprises have to recruit employees from outside for filling the positions whose specifications cannot be met by the present employees, and for meeting the additional requirements of manpower. The following external sources of recruitment are commonly used by the big enterprises:

(*i*) Direct Recruitment: An important source of recruitment is direct recruitment by placing a notice on the notice board of the enterprise specifying the details of the jobs available. It is also known as *recruitment at factory gate*. The practice of direct recruitment is generally followed for filling casual vacancies requiring unskilled workers. Such workers are known as *casual or badli workers* and they are paid remuneration on daily-wage basis.

This method of recruitment is very cheap as it does not involve any cost of advertising vacancies. It is suitable for filling casual vacancies when there is greater rush of work or when a number of permanent workers are absent.

(*ii*) Casual Callers or Unsolicited Applications: The organizations which are regarded as good employers draw a steady stream of unsolicited applications in their offices. This serves as a valuable source of manpower. If adequate attention is paid to maintain pending application folders for various jobs, the personnel department may find the unsolicited applications useful in filling the vacancies whenever they arise. The merit of this source of recruitment is that it avoids the costs of recruiting workforce from other sources.

(*iii*) Media Advertisement: Advertisement in newspapers or trade and professional journals is generally used when qualified and experienced personnel are not available from other sources. Most of the senior positions in industry as well as commerce are filled by this method. The advantage of advertising is that more information about the organization, job descriptions and job specifications can be given in advertisement to allow self-screening by the prospective candidates. Advertisement gives the management a wider range of candidates form which to choose. Its disadvantage is that it may bring in a food of response, and many times, from quite unsuitable candidates.

(iv) **Employment Agencies:** Employment exchanges run by the Government are regarded as a good source or recruitment for unskilled, semi-skilled and skilled operative jobs. In some cases, compulsory notification of vacancies to the employment exchange is required by law. Thus, the employment exchanges bring the job givers in contact with the job seekers. However, in the technical and professional area, private agencies and professional bodies appear to be doing most of the work. Employment exchanges and selected private agencies provide national-wide services in attempting to match personnel demand and supply.

(v) **Management Consultants:** Management consultancy firms help the organizations to recruit technical, professional and managerial personnel. They specialize in middle level and top level executive placements. They maintain data bank of persons with different qualifications and skills and even advertise the jobs on behalf of their to recruit right type of personnel. These days, professional bodies of accountants, engineers, etc. also help their members to get suitable placements in industrial organizations.

(vi) **Educational Institutions or Campus Recruitment:** Jobs in commerce and industry have become increasing technical and complex to the point where school and college degrees are widely required. Consequently, big organizations maintain a close liaison with the universities, vocational institutes and management institutes for recruitment to various jobs. Recruitment form educational institutions are a well-established practice of thousands of business and other organizations. It is also known as *campus recruitment.*

(vii) **Recommendations:** Applicants introduced by friends and relatives may prove to be a good source of recruitment. In fact, many employers prefer to take such persons because something about their background is known. When a present employee or a business friend recommends some one for a job, a type of preliminary screening is done and the person is placed on a job. Some organizations have agreements with the trade unions to give preference to blood relations of existing or retired employees if their qualifications and experience are sited to fill the vacant jobs.

(viii) **Labour Contractors:** Labour contractors are an important source of recruitment in some industries in India. Workers are recruited through labour contractors who are themselves employees of the organization. The disadvantage of this system is that if the contractor leaves the organization, all the workers employed through him will also leave. That is why, this source of labour is not preferred by many businesses organizations.

(ix) **Telecasting:** The practice of telecasting of vacant posts over T.V. is gaining importance these days. Special programmes like 'Job Watch', 'Youth Pulse', etc. over the T.V. have become quite popular in recruitment for various types of jobs.

Merits of External Sources

The merit of external sources is as under:

(i) **Qualified Personnel:** By using external sources of recruitment, the management can get qualified and trained people.

(ii) **Wider Choice:** When vacancies are advertised widely, a large number of applicants apply. The management has a wider choice to select people for employment.

(iii) **Fresh Talent:** External sources facilitate infusion of fresh blood with new ideas into the enterprise. This will improve working of the enterprise.

(iv) **Competitive Spirit:** If a company can tap external sources, the existing staff will have to compete with the outsiders. They will work hard to show better performance.

Demerits of External Sources

The demerits of filling vacancies from external sources are as follows:

(i) **Dissatisfaction among Existing Staff:** External recruitment may lead to dissatisfaction and frustrations among existing employees. They may

feel that their chances of promotion are reduced.

(*ii*) **Lengthy Process:** Recruitment from outside takes a long time. The business has to notify the vacancies and wait for applications to initiate the selection process.

(*iii*) **Costly Process:** It is very costly to recruit staff from external sources. A lot of money has to be spent on advertisement and processing of applications.

(*iv*) **Uncertain Response:** The candidates from outside may not be suitable for the enterprise. There is no guarantee that the enterprise will be able to attract right kinds of people from external sources.

RECRUITMENT PROCEDURE

Responsibility for Recruitment: In a small organization, recruitment is usually done rather informally by the owner or manager. But in a larger organization, the human resource department is usually responsible for developing sources of applicants. Within the human resource department, there is likely to be an employment office to do the recruiting and even initial selection of candidates for a job. Big organizations employing large number of professional and managerial employees may have a separate department engaged entirely in recruiting.

At the same time, individual managers and employees may be referring promising applicants to the personnel department. Similarly, the human managers as may be the case when campus recruitment is assistance from the managers or as may be the case when campus recruitment is proposed at the alma mater of one of the managers. Still other firms prefer to put together recruiting teams consisting of human resource specialists and other executives. For example, one or more engineers may accompany the team of campus recruiters for recruitment of engineering personnel at technical institutes.

Regardless of who does the recruiting, it is important for one department to coordinate the recruitment function in order to develop adequate sources, avoid duplication, and ensure that human resource needs for the whole organization are met.

Factors affecting Recruitment: There are many factors that limit or affect the recruitment policy of an organization. The important factors are listed below:

(*i*) Size of the organization and the kinds of human resources required.

(*ii*) Effect of past recruitment efforts.

(*iii*) Nature of labour market of the region.

(*iv*) Extent and strength of unionization in the region.

(*v*) Working conditions, wages and other benefits offered by other concerns.

(*vi*) Social and political environment

(*vii*) Legal obligations created by various statutes.

Requisition for Recruitment: Recruitment is an on-going process whereby the firm attempts to develop a pool of qualified applicants for future human resource needs even though specific vacancies do not currently exist. This practice is also necessary to maintain contacts with sources of recruitment.

In most cases, recruitment starts when a manager initiates an employee requisition for a specific vacancy. The requisition should contain the basic information describing the position to be filled, the duties to be performed, and the experience and qualifications required of the candidate for the job.

SELECTION

Selection involves a series of steps by which the candidates are screened for choosing the most suitable persons for vacant posts. The process of selection leads to employment of persons who possess the ability and qualifications to perform the jobs which have fallen vacant in an organization. It divides the candidates for employment into two categories, namely, 'those who will be offered employment and those who will not be'. This process should be called '*rejection*' since more candidates may be turned away than employed. That is why, selection is frequently described as a negative process in contrast with the positive nature of recruitment.

Purpose of Selection

The basic purpose of the selection process is to *choose right type of candidates to man various positions* in the organization. In order to achieve this purpose, a well-organized selection procedure involves many steps and at each step, unsuitable candidates are rejected. In other words, the aim of selection process is to reject the unsuitable candidates. But recruitment, on the other hand, is a positive process. Its aim is to attract applicants for vacant jobs in the organization. Various sources of recruitment are used for this purpose.

Thus, recruitment is a positive process because it aims at attracting applicants for various jobs. But selection is a negative process because it aims at rejecting applicants who are unsuitable and offering jobs to those who are found fully suitable.

Distinctive Features of Selection

(*i*) Selection means employment of workers or establishing a *Contractual relationship* between the employer and the worker.

(*ii*) Selection is a *negative process* because it involves rejection of unsuitable candidates.

(*iii*) Selection aims at *eliminating unsuitable candidates* and ensuring most competent people for the vacant job.

(*iv*) Selection is a *complex process* under which each candidate is required to cross a number of hurdles before getting the offer for a job.

Significance of Selection

Selection is a critical process these days because it requires a heavy investment of money to get right types of people. Induction and training costs are also high. If the right types of persons are not chosen, it will lead to huge loss of the employer in terms of time, effort and money. Therefore, it is essential to devise a suitable selection procedure. Each step in the selection procedure should help in getting more and more information about the applicants to facilitate decision-making in the area of selection.

Absenteeism and employee turnover are the important problems which are being faced by most of the organizations. The intensity of these problems can be reduced if in the future all selections are made carefully so that there are 'round pegs in the round holes'. Whenever unsuitable employees are appointed, the efficiency of the organization will go down. Such employees will shirk work and absent themselves from the work more often. They may also be compelled to leave their jobs. If this happens, all the expenses incurred on the selection and training of such employees will go waste.

Scientific selection and placement of personnel will go a long way towards building up a stable work-force. It will keep the rates of absenteeism and labour turnover low and will increase the morale of the employees. If the employees are suitable according to the requirements of the jobs, they will show higher efficiency and productivity. This will also enable the organization to achieve its objectives effectively.

The benefits of selecting right kinds of people for various jobs are as follows:

(*i*) Proper selection and placement of personnel go a long way towards building up a suitable workforce. It will keep the rates of absenteeism and labour turnover low.

(*ii*) Competent employees will show higher efficiency and enable the organization to achieve its objective effectively.

(*iii*) The rate of industrial accidents will be considerably low if suitable employees are placed on various jobs.

(*iv*) When people get jobs of their taste and choice, they get higher job satisfaction. This will build up a contended workforce for the organization.

(*v*) The morale of the employees who are satisfied with their jobs is often high.

Scientific Selection

Fitting the worker to the job is the first and the most important step in promoting individual efficiency in industry. Scientific selection of employees is an important function of the Personnel Department. The object of scientific selection is to place on each job a worker who can maintain a given output with minimum expenditure of energy and who will be best fitted to the job.

The factors to be considered for selecting the right person for the right job are as under:

1. Physical Characteristics: Sound body, limbs, height, weight, sight, etc.

2. Personal Characteristics: Age, sex, marital status, number of children, family background, etc.

3. Proficiency or Skill and Ability: Qualifications and previous experience.

4. Competency: Potentiality of an individual for learning and becoming proficient in a job. Competency points out capacity to acquire knowledge and skill for success on the job.

5. Temperament and character: Emotional, moral and social qualities, honesty, loyalty, etc. A high degree of intellectual competency can never serve as a substitute for such qualities as honesty and trust worthiness. It is important to know about individual's character, his habits of work, his way of reacting in this or that situation, his driving forces in determining his fitness for the job.

6. Interest: Without interest, work is colourless and worthwhile to the individual and abilities are developed as well as accomplishments are realized. If a person has skill, and competency, but he has no interest in the job, he will be unhappy in his work.

Role of Personnel Department in Selection

Personal department plays an important role in the selection process. However, it should be kept in mind that decision to add persons on the payroll in a particular department of the organization is not made by the personnel department. The requisition for the employees must originate from the department where it is necessary to hire some persons to particular jobs in the near future. For this purpose, the use of a standard requisition form by the departmental head is preferable as it will make clear the number of vacancies, types of jobs, pay scale and any special characteristics or skills required. After receiving the requisition, the personnel department will see the catalogue of job description and job specifications to obtain a picture of the job and will tap some source or sources of recruitment according to the circumstances of the case.

Selection process will start when some applications are received from the candidates. The personnel department will classify and file the applications and will screen out the applicants which are found unsuitable. After this, it may call the other applicants for initial interview or employment tests.

Selection Procedure

The procedure of selection will vary from organization to organization and even from department to department within the same organization according to the kinds of the jobs to be filled. The number of steps in the procedure and the sequence of steps also vary. For instance, some organizational do not hold preliminary interview, test or screening, whereas in other organizational such as commercial banks, preliminary tests are given to eliminate a large numbers of applicants. Similarly, in some cases, medical examination is given before final selection and in others, medical check up follows final selection. Thus, every organization will design a selection procedure that suits its requirements. However, the main steps could be incorporated in the selections procedures are as under:

1. Preliminary interview
2. Receiving applications
3. Screening of applications
4. Employment test
5. Employment Interview
6. Physical examination
7. Checking references
8. Final selection

As shown in the Fig. 2, every candidate for a job has to clear a number of hurdles before getting selected for the job. If he is not found suitable at any stage, he is not considered for the further stages. Thus, he will be rejected. For instance, if a candidate's particulars in the application are not found suitable, he will not be called for the interview.

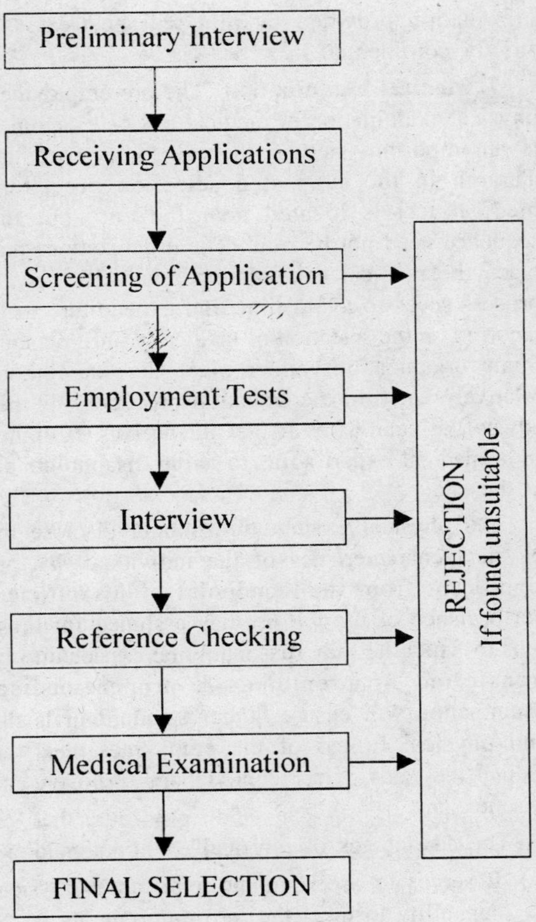

Fig. 2

The successive stages in the selection process are discussed below:

1.. Preliminary Interview: In the most of the organizations, the selection programme begins with preliminary interview or screening. The preliminary interview is generally brief and does the job of eliminating the totally unsuitable candidates. The preliminary interview offers advantages not only to the organization, but also to the applicants. If an applicant is eliminated at this stage, the organization will be saved from the expenses of processing him through the remaining steps of the selection procedure and the unsuitable candidate.

2. Receiving Applications: Whenever there is a vacancy, it is advertised or enquires are made from the suitable sources, and applications are received from the candidates. Standard application forms may be drawn up for different jobs supplied to the candidates on request. The application form is useful for several reasons. It gives a preliminary idea about the candidate to the interviewer and helps him in formulating questions to have more information about the candidate. The written information about age, qualifications, experience, etc. may prove to be of greater value to the interviewers. It makes the processing of applications very easy since there is uniformity of filling the date in the application form.

3. Screening of Applications: After the applications are received, they are screened by a screening committee and a list is prepared of the candidates to be interviewed. Applicants may be called for interview on some specific criteria like sex, desired age group, experience and qualifications. The number of candidates to be called for interview is normally five to seven times the number of posts to be filled up. The screened applications are then reviewed by the Personnel Manager and interview letters are dispatched by registered post or under certificate of post.

4. Employment Tests: Individual differ in almost all aspects one can think of. They differ with respect to physical characteristics, capacity, level of mental ability, their likes and dislikes and also with respect to personality traits. The pattern of physical, mental and personal variables gives rise to thousand and one combinations and the particular pattern makes the individual suitable for several classes of activities, jobs or fields of work. Matching of individual's physical, mental and temperamental pattern with the requirements of job or filed of training is a difficult task. But where this matching takes place, the result is happiness for the individual and prosperity for the organization and the society. But instances of round pegs in square holes and vice versa are not rare. So before deciding upon the job or jobs suitable for a particular individual, one should know the level of his ability and the knowledge, the pattern of his interest and aptitudes in detail. This will require the use of employment tests which are listed below:

(*a*) Intelligence tests
(*b*) Aptitude tests
(*c*) Trade of proficiency tests
(*d*) Interest tests
(*e*) Personality tests

Employment tests are widely used for judging the applicant's suitability for the job. They bring out the qualities and weaknesses of individuals which could be analyzed before offering jobs to them. The tests must be designed properly.

5. Employment Interview: Employment tests provide a lot of valuable information about the candidate, yet they don't provide the complete information required of the applicant. Interview may be used to secure more information about the candidate. The main purposes of an employment interview are:

(a) To find out the suitability of the candidate
(b) To seek more information about the candidate, and
(c) To give him an accurate picture of the job with details of terms and conditions and some idea of organization's policies.

For the selection of right types of people, employment interview is very important. The communication skill of the candidate can be judged in the interview. His way of thinking can also be known. Interview is very important where the candidate has to go through employment tests. The information contained in the application can be checked during the interview.

6. Checking References: A referee is potentially an important source of information about a candidate's ability and personality if he holds a responsible position in some organization or has been the boss or employer of the candidate. Prior to final selection, the prospective employer normally makes an investigation on the reference supplied by the applicant and undertakes more or less thorough search into the candidate's past employment, education, personal reputation, financial condition, police record, etc. However, it is often difficult to persuade a referee to give his opinion frankly. The organization may persuade him to do so by giving an assurance that all information provided by him will be treated as strictly confidential.

7. Medical Examination: The pre-employment physical examination or medical test of a candidate is an important step in the selection procedure. Though in the suggested selection procedure, medical test is located near the end, but this sequence need not be rigid. The organizations may place the medical examination relatively early in process so as to avoid time and expenditure to be incurred on the selection of medically unfit persons. Some organizations either place the examination relatively early in the selection procedure or they advise the candidates to get themselves examined by a medical expert so as to avoid disappointment at the end.

The physical examination should disclose the physical characteristics of the individual that are significant from the standpoint of his efficient performance of the job he may assigned for those jobs to which he may reasonably be expected to be transferred or promoted. A proper medical examination will ensure higher standard of health and physical fitness of the employees and will reduce the rates of accident, labour turnover, and absenteeism.

The advantages of physical examination are:

(*a*) It serves to ascertain the applicant's physical capability to meet the job requirements;
(*b*) It serves to protect the organization against the unwarranted claims under workers' compensation laws or against law suits for damages; and
(*c*) It helps to prevent communicable diseases entering the organization.

8. Final Selection and Appointment Letter: After a candidate has cleared all the hurdles in the selection procedure, he is formally appointed by issuing him an appointment letter or by concluding with him a service agreement. Generally, the candidates are not appointed on permanent basis because it is considered better to try them for a few months on the job itself. This is because no procedure of selection is complete in itself to find out the whole picture of the personality and qualities of a candidate. It is only by observing a person at work that one can find out how he does his work and behaves with fellow employees and supervisors. If during the probation period, an employee is found unsuitable, the management may transfer him to some other job to which he may be expected to do justice. But if the organization cannot offer him a job which he can do well, the management may either sack him or give him time and training to improve him.

INDUCTION (ORIENTATION OR PRELIMINARY TRAINING)

Induction is the welcoming process to make the new employee feel at home and generate in him feeling of belongingness to the organization. It is concerned with the problem of introducing or orienting a new employ to his work-group, supervisor and the organization. It is the beginning of the fusion process which helps integration between the organization goal and the personal goals of the new employee. After selecting compatible personnel, the organization must communicate to the new employees its philosophy, policies and customs and practices. Planned induction welcomes the new employee, creates a good attitude, reduces labour turnover and the employee feels at home right from the beginning.

When a new employee reports for work, he must be helped to get acquainted and adjusted with the work environment and the fellow employees. It is better to give him a friendly welcome when he joins the organization, get him introduced to the organization and help him to get a general idea about the rules and regulations, working conditions, etc. of the organization. Induction may also be viewed as the *socializing process* by which the organization seeks to make an individual its agent for the achievement of its objectives and the individual seeks to make an agency of the organization for the achievement of his personal goals.

Purpose: An induction or introduction programme should try to achieve the following objectives:

(*i*) To build up the new employee's confidence in the organization and in himself so that he may become an efficient employee.

(*ii*) To promote a feeling of belonging and loyalty to the organization among new-comers.

(*iii*) To ensure that the new employee may not form false impression regarding the new place of work because first impression is the last impression.

(*iv*) To give the new entrant the information he needs such as location of locker room, cafeteria and other facilities, time to break off, leave rules, etc.

(v) To foster a close relationship between the new workers and the old workers and supervisors.

Contents

The induction programme is generally informal in case of small firms. It may be formal of the duration of two to four weeks in case of big organizations. Orientation training course should not be too lengthy. It need not necessarily be given on the day when the new employee joins. But if a formal course is to be attended after two or three weeks on the job, the initial introduction and the immediately needed information may be given by the supervisor to the new employee. The range of information that may be covered under orientation training is as follows:

(*i*) Company's history and philosophy
(*ii*) Products of the company
(*iii*) Company's organization structure
(*iv*) Location of departments and employee services
(*v*) Personnel policies and practices
(*vi*) Employees' activities
(*vii*) Rules and regulations
(*viii*) Grievance procedure
(*ix*) Safety measures
(*x*) Standing orders

Socialization: Familiarization with Organization Culture

Socialization is a process of indoctrinating the new employees into the organization culture. The organization takes steps to get them adapt to its existing culture. It socializes the new employees and moulds them to accept its standards and norms.

Socialization is a process of adaptation by which employees are able to understand the basic values, norms and customs for becoming the accepted members of organization and assuming organizational roles. People who do not learn to adjust with the culture of organization are labelled as 'rebels' or 'nonconformists' and may even be turned out of the organization. Socialization performs two functions:

(*i*) It creates uniform behaviour in members, increases understanding, reduces conflicts, etc. and

(*ii*) It reduces role ambiguity of employees as they will come to know what is expected of them

As shown in the Fig. 3, Maanen and Schein have conceptualized three stages in the process of socialization: pre-arrival, encounter and metamorphosis or transformation. These are briefly discussed below:

1. Prearrival Stage: It denotes the period of learning in the socialization process that occurs before a new worker joins the organization. The new worker has a set of values, beliefs, attitudes and expectations. Such factors must be taken care of at the selection stage. Those types of people should be selected who might be able to fit into the organization's culture. The candidates must be made aware of the organization's values and expectations during the selection process so that the chances of wrong selection are reduced to the minimum.

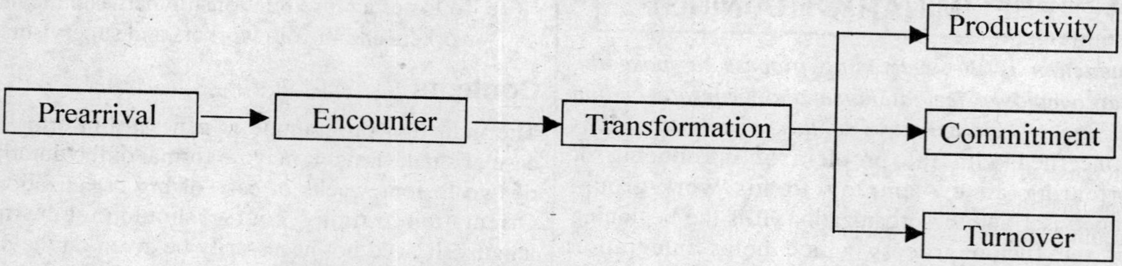

Fig. 3. *Stages in Socialization Process*

2. Encounter Stage: The new employee enters this stage when he joins the organization. He comes to know what the organization is really like and may find divergence between his expectations and those of the organization. If this is so, the new employee must undergo socialization that will detach him from his previous notions and assumptions about the organization and make him learn another set the organization deems desirable. The induction process is helpful in many of the cases. But if the employee is not able to change his expectations and adapt to the requirements of the organization, he might have to leave the organization.

3. Metamorphosis or Transformation Stage: Under this stage, the real transformation in the new employee takes place. He adjusts to this work-group's values and norms and becomes comfortable with the organization and his job. His internalization of organization's culture wins him acceptability among his colleagues and creates confidence in him. This makes him a contended employees and he likes the place of work and enjoys the company of his colleagues. As a result, he will feel committed to the organizational and his productivity will increase. His search for job elsewhere will also come to the end. If, in any case, the employee is not able to adapt himself to the organization culture, the result will be productivity, lack of commitment and even leaving the organization.

TRAINING

Need and Rationale of Training

Training is important not only from the point of view of the organization, but also for the employees. Training is valuable to the employees because it will give them greater job security and an opportunity for advancement. A skill acquired through training is an asset for the organization and the employee. It can be taken away only by the complete elimination of the need for that skill because of technological changes.

The need for training arises because of the following reasons:

(i) **Changing Technology:** Technology is changing at a fast pace. The workers must learn new techniques to make use of advanced technology. Thus, training should be treated as a continuous process to update the employees in new methods and procedures.

(ii) **Quality Conscious Customers:** The customers have become quality conscious and their requirements keep on changing. To satisfy the customers, quality of products must be continuously improved through training of workers.

(iii) **Greater Productivity:** It is essential to increase productivity and reduce cost of production for meeting competition in the market. Effective training can increase productivity of the workers.

(iv) **Stable Workforce:** Training creates a feeling of confidence in the minds of the workers. It gives them a security at the work place. As a result, labour turnover and absenteeism rates are reduced.

(v) **Increased Safety:** Trained workers handle the machines safely. They also know the use of various safety devices in the factory. Thus, they are less prone to industrial accidents.

(vi) **Better Management:** Training can be used as an effective tool of planning and control. It develops skills among workers for the future and also prepares them for promotion. It helps in reducing the costs of supervision, wastages and industrial accidents. It also increase productivity and quality.

Definition of Training

Training is an organized activity for increasing the knowledge and skills of people for a definite purpose. It involves systematic procedures for transferring technical know-how to the employees so as to increase their knowledge and skills for doing specific jobs with proficiency. In other words, the trainees acquire technical knowledge, skills and problem solving ability by undergoing the training programme.

According to **Edwin B. Flippo**, "Training is the act of increasing the knowledge and skills of an employee for doing a particular job." Its purpose is to achieve a change in the behaviour of those trained and to enable them to do their jobs better. Training is a continuous process.

Objectives of Training

The objectives of training are as follows:

1. To increase the knowledge of workers in doing specific jobs
2. To impart new skills among the workers systematically so that they learn quickly
3. To bring about change in the attitudes of the workers towards fellow workers, supervisor and the organization
4. To improve the overall performance of the organization
5. To make the workers handle materials, machines and equipment efficiently and thus to check wastage of time and resources.
6. To reduce the number of accidents by providing safety training to workers
7. To prepare workers for higher jobs by developing advanced skills in them

Benefits of Training to Employees

Training helps the employees or workers in the following ways:

(i) **Confidence:** Training creates a feeling of confidence in the minds of workers. It gives a feeling of safety and security to them at the work-place.

(ii) **New Skills:** Training develops skills which serve as a valuable personal asset of a worker. It remains permanently with the worker himself.

(iii) **Promotion:** Training provides opportunity for quick promotion and self-development.

(iv) **Higher Earnings:** Training helps in earning higher remuneration and other monetary benefits to the workers as their productivity is increased.

***(v)* Adaptability:** Training develops adaptability among workers. They don't worry when work procedures and methods are changed.

***(vi)* Increased Safety:** Trained workers handle the machines safely. They also know the use of various safety devices in the factory. Thus, they are less prone to accidents.

Types of Training

On the basis of purpose, several types of training programmes are offered to the employees. It should be noted that these programmes are not mutually exclusive. They invariable overlap and employ many common techniques. The important types of training programmes are as follows:

1. Induction or orientation training
2. Job training
3. Apprenticeship training
4. Internship training
5. Refresher training or retraining
6. Training for promotion

1. Induction or Orientation Training: Induction is concerned with *introduction or orientation a new employee to the organization and its procedures, rules and regulations.* When a new employee reports for work, he must be helped to get acquainted with the work environment and fellow employees. It is better to give him a friendly welcome when he joins the organization, get him introduced to the organization and help him to get a general idea about the rules and regulations, working conditions, etc. of the organization.

2. Job Training: Job training relates to specific job which the worker has to handle. It gives information about machines, process of production, instructions to be followed, and methods to be used and so on. It develops skills and confidence among the workers and enables them to perform the job efficiently.

3. Apprenticeship Training: Apprenticeship training programme tends more towards education than merely on the vocational training. Under this, both knowledge and skills in doing a job or a series of related jobs are involved. The governments of various countries have passed laws which make it obligatory on certain classes of employers to provide apprenticeship training to the young people. The usual apprenticeship programmes combine on the job training and experience with class-room instructions in particular subjects.

The trainees receive wages while learning and they acquire valuable skills which command a high wage in the labour market. In India, here are so many 'earn when you learn' schemes both in the private as well as public sector undertakings. This is also advantageous to the trainees. Some employers look upon apprentices as a source of cheap labour. Apprenticeship training is desirable in industries which require a constant flow of new employees expected to become all round craftsmen. It is very much prevalent in printing trades, building and construction, and crafts like mechanics, electricians, welders, etc.

4. Internship Training: Under this method, the educational or vocational institute enters into arrangement with an industrial enterprise for providing practical knowledge to its students. Internship training is usually meant for such vocations where advanced theoretical knowledge is to be backed by practical experience on the job. For instance, engineering students are sent to big industrial enterprise for gaining practical work experience and medical students are sent to big hospitals to get practical knowledge. The period of such training varies from six months to two years. The trainees do not belong to the business enterprises, they come from the vocational or professional institutions. It is quite usual that enterprise giving them training absorb them by offering suitable jobs.

5. Refresher Training or Retraining: As the name implies, the refresher training is meant for the old employees of the enterprise. The basic purpose of refresher training is to acquaint the existing workforce with the latest methods of performing there jobs and improve their efficiency further. In the words of Dale Yoder, "Retraining programmes are designed to avoid personnel obsolescence." The skills with the existing employees become obsolete because of technological changes and because of the tendency of human beings to forget. Thus refresher training is essential because of the following factors:

(*a*) The workers require training to bring them up-to-date with the knowledge and skills and to relearn what they have forgotten.

(*b*) Rapid technological changes make even the qualified workers obsolete in course of time because new technology is associated with new work-methods and job requirements. The workers need to learn new work methods to use new techniques in doing their jobs.

(c) Refresher training becomes necessary because many new jobs which are created due to changes in the demand for goods and services are to be handled by the existing employees.

6. Training for Promotion: The talented employees may be given adequate training to make them eligible for promotion to higher jobs in the organization. Promotion of an employee means a significant change in his responsibilities and duties. Therefore, it is essential that he is provided sufficient training to learn new skills to perform his new duties efficiently. The purpose of training for promotion is to develop the existing employees to make them fit for undertaking higher job responsibilities. This serves as a motivating force to the employees.

Methods of Training

As shown in the following Exhibit, a wide range of training methods and techniques have been developed over the years by various organizations and training experts. Different training methods are suitable for different categories of personnel in the organization: Managerial and Non-managerial, technical, administrative, skilled, unskilled, senior, junior and so on. Each organization has to choose those methods and techniques of training which are relevant for its training needs.

EXHIBIT: Methods of Training

I. **Vestibule Training** (adapted to the environment at the place of work)

II. **On-the-job training** (at the place of work)
   - (*i*) Coaching
   - (*ii*) Understudy
   - (*iii*) Position Rotation

III. **Off-the-job Training** (away form the place of work)
   - (*i*) Special Lecture-cum-Discussion
   - (*ii*) Conference
   - (*iii*) Case Study
   - (*iv*) Sensitivity Training
   - (*v*) Special Projects
   - (*vi*) Committee Assignments

The various methods of training may be classified into the following categories:

I. Vestibule training
II. On-the-job training
III. Off-the-job training

I. Vestibule Training: The term 'vestibule training' is used to designate training in a class-room for semi-skilled jobs. It is more suitable where a large number of employees must be trained at the same time for the same kind of work. Where this method is used, there should be well qualified instructors in charge of training programme. Here the emphasis tends to be on learning rather than production. It is frequently used to train clerks, machine operators, typists, etc.

Vestibule training is adapted to the same general type of training problem that is faced by on-the-job training. A vestibule school is run as a special endeavor of the personnel department. An attempt is made to duplicate, as nearly as possible, the actual material, equipment and conditions found in the real work-lace. Now the question arises why to have a vestibule school. The vestibule school may be started when the training work exceeds the capacity of the line supervisor. Thus, in vestibule training, the workers are trained on specific jobs in a school run by the organization. An attempt is made to create working conditions which are similar to the actual workshop conditions. The learning conditions are also carefully controlled.

Vestibule training is particularly suitable where it is not admissible to put the burden of training on line supervisors and where a special coaching is required. The staff of the vestibule school consists of expert and specialist instructors. The trainees avoid confusion and pressure of the work situation and are thus able to concentrate on training. Their activities do not interfere with the regular processes of production. Moreover, trainees get an opportunity to become accustomed to work routine and recover from their initial nervousness before going on to actual jobs.

Vestibule training has certain demerits also. The artificial training atmosphere may create the adjustment problem for the trainees when they return to the place of job. Vestibule training is relatively expensive because there is duplication of materials, equipment and conditions found in a real work-place.

II. On-the-job Training: On-the-job training is considered to be the most effective method of training the operative personnel. Under this method, *the worker is given training at the work place by his immediate supervisor.* In other words, the worker learns in the actual work environment. It is based on the principle of '*learning by doing*'.

On-the-job training is suitable for imparting skills that can be learnt in a relatively short period of time. It has the chief advantage of strongly motivation the trainee to learn. It is not located in an artificial situation. It permits the trainee to learn on the equipment and in the work-environment. On-the-job training methods are relatively cheaper and less time consuming. Another important factor about On-the-job training is that supervisors play an important part in training the subordinates.

There are four methods of On-the-job training describing below:

(*i*) Coaching: Under this method, the supervisor imparts job knowledge and skills to his subordinate. The emphasis in coaching or instructing the subordinate is on learning by doing. This method is very effective if the superior has sufficient time to provide coaching to his subordinates.

(*ii*) Understudy: The superior gives training to a subordinate as his understudy or assistant. The subordinate learns through experience and observation. It prepares the subordinate to assume the responsibilities of the superior's job in case the superior leaves the organization.

The subordinate chosen for under-study is designated as the heir-apparent and his future depends upon what happens to his boss. The purpose of under study is to prepare someone to fill the vacancy caused by death, retirements, promotion, or transfer of the superior.

(*iii*) Position Rotation: The purpose of position rotation is to broaden the background of the trainee in various positions. The trainee is periodically rotated from job to job instead of sticking to one job so that he acquires a general background of different jobs. However, rotation of an employee from one job to another should not be done frequently. He should be allowed to stay on a job for a sufficient period so that he may acquire the full knowledge of the job.

Job rotation is used by many organizations to develop *all-round-workers*. The employees learn new skills and gain experience in handling different kinds of jobs. They also come to know the inter-relationship between different jobs. Job rotation is also used to place workers on the right jobs and prepare them to handle other jobs in case of need.

III. Off-the-job Training: It *requires the worker to undergo training for a specific period away from the work-place*. Off-the-job methods are concerned with both knowledge and skills in doing certain jobs. The workers are free of tension of work when they are learning.

There are several Off-the-job methods of training and development as described below:

(*i*) Special Lecture cum Discussion: Training through special lectures is also known as '*class-room training*'. It is more associated with imparting knowledge than with skills. The special lectures may be delivered by some executives of the organization or specialists from vocational and professional institutes. Many firms also follow the practice of inviting expert for special lectures for the staff on matters like health, safety, productivity, quantity, etc.

***(ii)* Conference Training:** A conference is a group meeting conducted according to an organized plan in which the members seek to develop knowledge and understanding by oral participation. It is an effective training device for persons in the positions of both conference member and conference leader. As a member, a person can learn from others by comparing his opinion with those of others. He learns to respect the viewpoints of others and also realizes that there is more than one workable approach to any problem.

***(iii)* Case Study:** The case method is a *means of simulating experience in the classroom.* Under this method, the trainees are given a problem or case which is more or less related to the concepts and principles already taught. They analyse the problem and suggest solutions which are discussed in the class. The instructor helps them reach a common solution the problem. This method gives the trainee an opportunity to apply his knowledge to the solution of realistic problems.

Designing a Training Programme

The training programme is an integral part of human resource management. As shown in the Fig. 4, it consists of the following inter-related steps:

(*i*) Identification of training needs
(*ii*) Setting training objectives
(*iii*) Organization of training
(*iv*) Evaluation of training

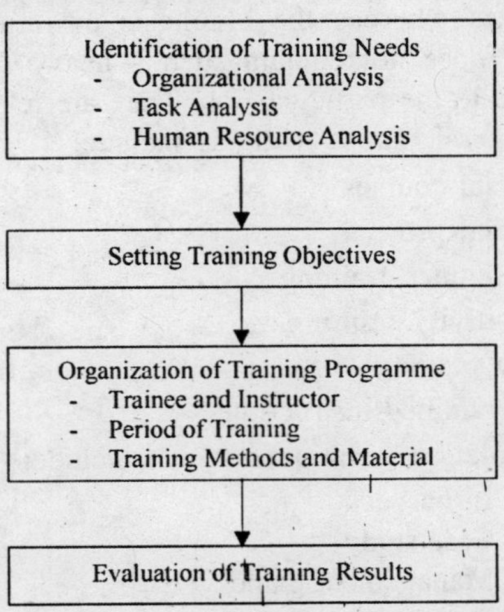

Fig. 4. *Design of a Training Programme*

Essentials of Good Training

Training is an important tool of management capable of making significant contribution to the goals of the organization. Training tends to improve the performance of employees by narrowing the gap between expectations and achievements. Because of its significant role, it is essential to have an effective training programme in the enterprise. An effective training programme should possess the following characteristics:

(*a*) Training programme should be chalked out after identifying the training needs or goals. It should have relevance to the job requirements.

(*b*) An effective training programme should be flexible. It should make due allowance for the differences among the individuals as regards ability, aptitude, learning capacity, emotional make-up, etc.

(*c*) A good training programme should prepare the trainees mentally before they are imparted any job knowledge or skill.

(*d*) An effective training programme should be conducted by well qualified and experience trainers.

(*e*) An effective training programme should emphasis both theory and practice. It should help in acquiring knowledge and its application.

(*f*) An effective training programme should have the top management's support. The top management can greatly influence the quality of training in the organization by the policies it adopts and the extent to which it supports the training programme.

DEVELOPMENT

Executive or management development consists of all activities by which executives learn to improve their behaviour and performance. It is designed to improve the effectiveness of managers in their present jobs and to prepare them for higher jobs in future. Executive development denotes planned efforts to improve current and future performance of the organization.

Management or executive development includes *"all those activities and programmes which have substantial influence on changing the capacity of the individual to perform his present assignment better and in so doing are likely to increase his potential for future management assignment"*.

Nature of Development

(*i*) Educational Process: Development is more ask in of education than it is to specific training in skills.

(*ii*) Behavioural Change: Executive or management development is a planned process of learning and growth designed to bring behavioural change among the executives. It implies that there will be a change in knowledge and behaviour of the individuals undergoing development programme. The individual will be able to perform his present assignment better and will increase his potential for future assignment.

(*iii*) Self Development: Managers develop themselves by participating in training courses organized by the organization. They also make use of actual job experience in learning new behaviours.

(*iv*) Continuous Process: Executive development is an ongoing or never ending exercise rather than an 'oneshot' affair.

Objectives of Development

The objectives of management of executive development programme of any business concern are:

(*i*) To increase the overall knowledge and conceptual and decision-making skills of executives;

(*ii*) To improve the performance of managers in their present positions;

(*iii*) To ensure an adequate reserve of capable well-trained managers for future needs;

(*iv*) To influence the behaviour of workers through the executives;

(*v*) To introduce change in the organization by developing executives into change agents or facilitators;

(*vi*) To provide opportunities to the mangers for their career advancement; and

(*vii*) To prevent obsolescence of executives by providing them opportunities for updating their knowledge and skills.

Methods of Development

A large variety of methods of management development have come into prominence these days. These methods can be classified into two broad categories, namely:

(*i*) On-the-job Methods

(*ii*) Off-the-job methods

(*i*) On-the-job Methods: The main feature of on-the-job methods is to increase the ability of the executives to work while performing their duties. They aim at exposing the trainees to the real work situation. Generally, support is provided by immediate superior in the conduct of these development programmes. On-the-job methods include:

(*a*) On-the-job coaching

(*b*) Understudy

(*c*) Job rotation

(*d*) Multiple Management

(*e*) Committee assignments

(*ii*) Off-the-job Methods: The focus in off-the-job methods of development is to improve general behavioural and decision-making skills of the executives whereas the emphasis of on-the-job methods does not contain such a heavy dose of reference to the particular job. They are rela-tively more general. Those methods include:

(*a*) Special courses

(*b*) Special projects

(*c*) Conference training

(*d*) Sensitivity training

(*e*) Role playing

(*f*) Programmed instruction

(*g*) Simulation techniques which include:

(*i*) In-basket

(*ii*) Case study

(*iii*) Management games

(*h*) Transactional analysis

Classification of Development Methods According to Purpose

Management development programmes help in acquiring and developing managerial skills and knowledge. Different types of techniques are used to acquire and develop various types of managerial skills and knowledge as shown in the following Exhibit:

Exhibit: Methods of Executive Development

Purpose	Method/Technique
1. Job Knowledge	(*a*) On-the-Job experience
	(*b*) Coaching
	(*c*) Understudy
2. Organizational Knowledge	(*a*) Job Rotation
	(*b*) Multiple Management
3. General Knowledge	(*a*) Special Courses
	(*b*) Specific Readings
4. Decision-making Skills	(*a*) In-basket
	(*b*) Business Game
	(*c*) Case Study
5. Inter-personal Skills	(*a*) Role Play
	(*b*) Sensitivity Training
6. Specific Individual Needs	(*a*) Special Projects
	(*b*) Committee Assignment
	(*c*) Specific Readings

Organization of Executive Development Programme

The important steps in the organization of a management development programme are as follows:

1. Analysis of development needs
2. Inventory of management talents
3. Appraisal of present talents
4. Planning of individual development programme
5. Establishment of development programme

1. Analysis of Development Needs: Before deciding to launch a management development programme, a close and critical examination of the present and future development needs of the organization has to be made. It should be clear as to how many and what type of managers are required to meet the present and future requirements. A comparison of the existing talents with those required to meet the projected needs will help the top management to determine the need of executive development.

2. Inventory of Management Talents: This is prepared to have complete information about each executive in each position. For each member of executive team, a card is prepared listing such data as name, age, length of service, education, work experience, health record, psychological test results and performance appraisal data, etc. The selection of the individuals for a management development programme is made on the basis of the kind of background they possess.

3. Appraisal of Talents: A qualitative assessment of the existing executives is made to determine the type of executive talent available within the organization. The performance of every executive is compared with the standard excepted of him. His personal traits are also analysed to estimate his potential development. Such information will disclose the strengths as well as weakness or deficiencies of managers in certain functions relating to the future needs of the organization.

4. Establishment of Development Programme: It is the duty of Human Resource department to provide the developmental opportunities. For this, it will identify the existing level of skills, knowledge etc. of various executives and compare them with their respective job requirements. Thus, it will identify developmental needs and establish specific development programmes like special courses, management games, sensitivity training, conference training, etc.

5. Planning Development Programmes for Individuals: The performance appraisal of each executive will identify strengths and weaknesses of each executive. Based on this information, special programmes for development of executives may be chalked out. These might include special projects, committee assignment, or specific readings.

6. Evaluation of Executive Development: Executive development is a lengthy and costly process. It is necessary to determine the results of money and time spent on executive development. A systematic evaluation of executive development will reveal the relevance of the development for the organization. Survey of trainee's behaviour, opinion surveys, interviews with the trainees, etc. could be used to judge the effectiveness of executive development. Indicators such as changes in productivity, quality and costs can also be used to measure effectiveness of executive development programme.

Essential Principles of Executives Development

Irrespective of the type of training and development techniques, a sound training programme must be based on the following basic principles:

1. Training and development programme must be based on the principles of individual differences. It must be borne in mind that individuals differ in ability and speed to learn, interests and other personal characteristics.
2. The need for and the depth and nature of training to be provided should be worked out from the job analysis and organizational analysis.
3. For effective motivation of learners or trainees, suitable incentives must be provided.
4. Both the trainer as well as the trainees must take active part in the training activities, so that all concerned evince genuine interest in the training.
5. The trainer selected for imparting training should undergo special training for the purpose. A well qualified trainer is one who not only has mastery of the technical details of the particular job, but knows how to train, i.e., to teach.
6. All development is self-development. Learner's participation is essential for development and spoon feeding seldom brings long-lasting growth.
7. Feedback of performance should be made available to the learner so that he can take steps to improve himself. There is always a scope for improvement due to gap between actual performance and capacity of the individual.

EXIT POLICY

Exit Policy is a part of the Liberalization policy adopted by the Government. Exit Policy was in air in 1991 itself which aimed at closing down the sick and inefficient industries and making hand shakes with excess employees so as to reduce the financial burden on the economy. In March 1992, Government approved this exit policy.

World Bank and IMF are insisting to implement this exit policy for reform in the economy. Goswami Committee constituted for investigating the problem of industrial sickness, also suggested to adopt this Exit policy.

PERFORMANCE APPRAISAL AND EVALUATION

Concept

Performance appraisal goes by various names such as performance evaluation, progress rating, merit rating, merit evaluation, etc.

Performance appraisal means systematic evaluation of the personality and performance of each employee by his supervisor or some other person trained in the techniques of merit rating. It employs various rating techniques for comparing individual employees in a work group, in terms of personal qualities or deficiencies and the requirements of their respective jobs. To quote Dale Yoder, "*Performance appraisal includes all formal procedures used to evaluate personalities and contributions and potentials of group members in a working organizational. It is a continuous process to secure information necessary for making correct and objective decisions on employees.*" The comparison of performance with job requirements helps in finding out the merit of individual employees in a work group. Rating may be done by supervisor or an independent appraiser.

Performance appraisal is a formal programme in an organization which is concerned with not only the contributions of the members who form part of the organization, but aims at spotting the potential also. The satisfactory performance is only a part of the system as a whole and the management needs more information than mere performance ratings of the subordinates. There are no two opinions about the necessity of performance appraisal which can meet these requirements of the management to achieve the organizational goals.

Purposes of Performance Appraisal

The objectives of performance appraisal fall in two categories:

1. Administrative; and
2. Self-improvement

1. *Administrative Objectives*

(*i*) Promotions: This is perhaps the most important administrative use of performance appraisal. It is to the common interests of both the management and employees to promote employees into positions where they can most effectively utilize their abilities. It is mismanagement to promote employees into positions where they cannot perform effectively at the time in question. A properly developed and administered performance appraisal system can aid in determining whether individuals should be considered for promotions. The system must rate the rate for the present job and his potentialities for the higher job. A person performing his job well does not necessarily mean that he is fit for promotion.

(*ii*) Transfers: In an organization, it may be necessary to consider various types of personnel actions such as transfers, layoffs, demotions, and discharges. In some cases, such actions are called for because of unsatisfactory performance while in other cases it may be called for due to economic conditions over which the organization has no control because of changes in production process. Such actions can be justified if they are based on performance appraisal.

(*iii*) Wage and salary Administration: In some cases, the wage increases are based on the performance appraisal reports. In some cases, appraisals and seniority are used in combination.

(*iv*) Training and Development: An appropriate system of performance appraisal can be helpful in identifying the areas of skills or knowledge in which certain employees are not upto par, thus pointing out general training deficiencies which presumably should be corrected by additional training, discussions, or counseling. Performance appraisal can also help in spotting the talented employees so as to train and develop them to create an inventory of executive skills. It can also provide the areas where the employee/executives could be further trained and positioned to meet retirement and expansion situations.

(*v*) Personnel Research: Performance appraisal helps in research in the field of personnel management. Various theories in human relationships are the outcome of efforts to find out the cause and effect relationship between the personnel and their performance.

2. *Self Improvement*

The performance appraisals bring out the deficiencies and shortcomings of the employees. A discussion between the boss and the subordinate conducted in a spirit of co-operation and mutual understanding gives the chance to employee to have an insight on his performance in the general set up of the organization. The way these discussions are conducted gives chance to the employees to take suitable steps to improve their performance or the employee like 'How am I doing?' and 'Where do I stand?'

Performance appraisal helps human resources development in another way also. A promotion minded individual can ask for the target programmes of a position he seeks and use the information given by performance appraisal to prepare him for the job and enhance his candidacy.

Performance appraisal also helps to spot out a person's ability to see an organization problem, devise ways of attacking it, translate his ideas into action, incorporate new information as it arises and carry his plans through the results. It highlights a sort of total managerial action in contrast to things we customarily factor out as conceptual entities – things such as the planning function, leadership ability, or financial knowledge. The manager's selection will often be improved by this emphasis on the whole managerial job. It should be noted that best predictor of future success as a manager is past success in managerial duties. The appraisal programme asks the rater to look at the record of managerial success, not the manager's personality.

Benefits of Performance Appraisal

The important reasons or benefits which justify the existence of a system of performance appraisal in an enterprise are as under:

(*i*) A good system of performance appraisal helps the supervisor to evaluate the performance of his employees systematically and periodically. It also helps him to assign that work to individuals for which they are best suited.

(*ii*) Performance rating helps in guiding and correction of employees. The supervisor may use the results of rating for the purpose of constructively guiding employees in the efficient performance of work.

(*iii*) The ability of the staff is recognized and can be adequately rewarded by giving them special increments.

(*iv*) Performance appraisal can be used as a basis of sound personnel policy in relation to transfers and promotions. If the performance of an employee is better than others, he can be recommended for promotion, but if a person is not doing well on a job, he may be transferred to some other job.

(*v*) Ratings can be used to evaluate the effectiveness of training programmes. Weaknesses of employees are revealed by merit rating and the training programmes can be modified accordingly.

(*vi*) Performance appraisal provides an incentive to the employees to better their performance in a bid to improve their rating over others.

(*vii*) Systematic appraisals will prevent grievances and develop confidence amongst the employees if they are convinced of the impartial basis of evaluation. The records of merit rating are available in permanent form to protect the management against subsequent charges of discrimination which might be leveled by the trade union leaders.

Limitations of Performance Appraisal

Performance appraisal may not yield the desired results because of the following deficiencies:

(*i*) If the factors included in the assessment are irrelevant, the result of merit rating will not be accurate.

(*ii*) Different qualities to be rated may not be given proper weightage in certain cases.

(*iii*) Some of the factors are highly subjective like initiative and personality of the employees; so the actual rating may not be on scientific lines.

(*iv*) Supervisors often do not have critical ability in assessing the staff. Sometimes, they are guided by their personal emotions and likes. So the ratings are likely to be biased.

Methods of Performance Appraisal

There are various methods of merit rating which may be classified into:

(I) Traditional Methods, and

(II) Modern Methods

(I) Traditional Methods

Traditional methods are very old techniques of performance appraisal. They are based on trait-oriented appraisal. Evaluation of employee is done on the basis of standards of personal traits or qualities such as attitudes, judgement, versatility, initiative, dependability, leadership, loyalty, punctuality, knowledge of job, etc. There are seven traditional methods of appraisal as shown below:

1. Unstructured appraisal
2. Employee ranking
3. Forced distribution
4. Graphic-rating scales
5. Check-lists
6. Critical incidents
7. Field review

1. Unstructured Appraisal: Under this, the appraiser is required to write down his impression about the person being appraised in an unstructured way. However, in some organizations, comments are required to be grouped under specific headings such as quality of job performance, reasons for specific job behaviors, personality traits, and development needs. This system is highly subjective and has got its merit in its simplicity and is still in use especially in the small firms.

2. Employee Ranking Method: Ranking is a simple process of placing employees in a rank according to their job performance. It permits comparison of all employees in any single rating group regardless of the type of work. All workers are judged on the same

3. Forced Distribution Method: Some appraisers suffer from a constant error, i.e., they either rate all workers as excellent, average or poor. They fail to evaluate the poor, average or excellent employees clearly. The forced distribution system is devised to force the appraiser to fit the employees being appraised into predetermined ranges of scale. It has an advantage over the paired comparison system in that two or more employees can be given equal ratings. This system is based on the presumption that employees can be divided into five points scale of outstanding, above average, average, below average and poor. In this system the appraiser is asked to distribute the employees into these categories in such a way that about 10% of the men are in group 'outstanding', 20% 'above average', 40% 'average', 20% 'below average', and 10% 'poor'.

4. Graphic Rating Scales: Under this method, scales are established for a number of specific factors and qualities. Five degrees are established for each factor and general definitions appear at points along the scale. Generally, the rater is supplied with a printed form, one for each person to be rated. The selection of factors to be measured on the graphic rating scale is an important point under this system. These are of two types: (i) characteristics, such as initiative and dependability, and (ii) contributions, such as quantity and quality of work since certain areas of job performance cannot be objectively measured, it is likely that graphic scale will continue to use a mixture of both characteristics and contribution.

5. Check List: It also consists of two techniques:

(*a*) Weighted Check List, and

(*b*) Forced Choice

(*a*) Weighted Check List: Under this method, various statements are prepared in such a manner that they describe various types and levels of behaviours for a particular job. Each statement is attached with a scale value. At the time of rating the employees, the supervisor just collects and checks all the statements. After the weights or values are attached to the individual traits, the rating upto this level is gathered on the rating sheet. Then the weights are averaged and employee is evaluated. The weighted check-list should be prepared by the persons thoroughly acquainted with job and perfect at preparing and weighing statements. When this process is over, rating is placed on separate cards. Then these cards are sorted by raters who actually observed the accomplishment of the work. They rank the employees from poor to excellent. Weights are then assigned to the statements in accordance with the way they are ranked by the raters.

(*b*) Forced Choice: This method is used particularly with the objective of avoiding scope for personal prejudices. Under this method, the rater is forced to choose between descriptive statements of seemingly equal worth describing the person in question. Statements are choosen of both the sides (favourable as well as unfavourable). For example, the following two pairs of statement may be given to the rater and they may be asked to select one statement from each pair that is represented by supervisor.

(*a*) Gives clear instructions to his subordinate

(*b*) Can be depended upon to complete any job assigned

(*c*) Makes promises that he knows he cannot keep

(*d*) Shows favouritism to some employee

6. *Critical Incident Method:* A critical incident means a significant act by an employee exceeding or failing any of the requirements of his job. It represents an exceptional behaviour of an employee at work, as for instance, Resisted the implementation of change; became upset over work; refused to help a fellow worker; suggested an improvement in the work method; tried to get a fellow worker to accept the management decision; welcome new ideas.

This method requires every supervisor to record all such significant incidents in each employee's behavior which indicate effective or successful action and those which indicate ineffective or poor behaviour. These are recorded in a specially designed notebook which contains categories or characteristics under which various behaviours can be recorded. Examples of such types of job requirements for workers are judgement, learning ability, productivity, and dependability, accuracy of work, responsibility and initiative. Daily recording of these items seems to be essential because the supervisor may forget the incidents with his subordinates.

Under the critical incident method, the supervisor is supposed to refrain from passing overall judgements and concentrate upon discussing facts as he sees them. Theoretically, this should provide a sound and an objective basis for appraisal of performance of an employee. Strictly speaking, the critical incident method is not a rating method as it requires the supervisor to pay close attention to what an employee is doing.

7. Field Review Method: Under this method, the supervisors are interviewed by an expert from the personnel department. The expert questions the supervisor to obtain all the pertinent information on each employee and takes notes in his note book. Thus, there is no rating – form with factors or degrees, but overall ratings are obtained. The workers are usually classified into three categories as outstanding, satisfactory and unsatisfactory.

The interviewer questions the supervisor about the requirements of each job in his unit and about the performance of each man in his job. He probes to find out not only how a man is doing but also why he does that way and what can be done to improve or develop him. The supervisor is required to give his opinion about the progress of his subordinates, the level of the performance of each subordinate, his weaknesses, good points, outstanding ability, promotability, and the possible plans of action in cases requiring further consideration. The questions are asked and answered verbally.

The success of filed review method depends upon the competence of the interviewer. If he knows his job, he can contribute significantly to accurate appraisals. Field review method releaves the supervisors of the tedious writing work of filling in appraisal forms. It also ensures a greater likelihood that the supervisors will give adequate attention to the appraisals because the personnel department largely controls the process. Superficial judgement can be eliminated if the appraiser probes deeply.

Criticism of Traditional Methods

The general criticism of traditional performance appraisal systems is that they are too subjective in nature because all of them are based on personal judgement of the rater. The personal judgement is always subjected to personal bias or prejudice as well as pressure from certain other areas. The appraiser may not be able to judge the competence of the employee because of lack of training.

Because of the jundgemental role of the superiors under the traditional systems, performance ratings are frequently subject to a number of errors and weakness which are discussed below:

1. Halo Error: This type of error occurs when the rater allows one aspect of a man's character or performance to influence his entire evaluation. It is the tendency of many raters to let the rating they assign to one characteristic excessively influence their ratings on all subsequent characteristics. Many supervisors tend to give an employee approximately the same rating on all factors. The error can be recognized quite easily on factor scales. The rating scale technique of performance appraisal is particularly susceptible to the halo supervisor judge all of his subordinates on a single factor or trait before going to the next. In this manner, he can consider all of the men relative to a standard or to each other on each trait.

2. Central Tendency: This error occurs when the rater is in doubt about the subordinates or has inadequate information about them or is giving less attention and effort to the rating process. Because of these reasons, generally the raters are reluctant to rate people at the outer ends of the scale. The rater knows that he has to appraise his subordinates at periodic intervals. But if he is unfamiliar with some of the subordinates or does not have sufficient time to devote to the rating process, he may play it safe by neither condemning nor praising. So he may rate them 'average'. It is possible for this type of rating i.e., all average to be a true rating, but its probability is less than its frequency.

3. Leniency or Strictness: Some supervisors have a tendency to be easy raters and others have a tendency to be harsh in their ratings. Lenient or easy rater assign consistently high values or scores to their subordinates and strict or harsh raters give consistently low ratings. Both the trend can arise from varying standards of performance among supervisors and form different interpretations of what they observe in employee performance.

4. Recent Behaviour Bias: Some raters evaluate persons on the basis of their performance in recent few weeks; average constant behaviour is not checked. Some employees being aware of this tendency show better results when they feel that they are being observed and the report of their performance is to be compiled soon.

5. Miscellaneous Biases: In many cases, the rater may give higher ratings because he thinks that it would look bad for him if employees in the other departments received higher pay increases than his group. Supervisors will tend to rate their subordinates near the middle of the spectrum (average) if their bosses put pressure on them to correct the worker's average rates or to get rid of the subordinates. Some supervisors show bias against members of the opposite sex or of another caste, religion or nationality. They also give higher ratings to senior employees because they are not ready to admit that they have not improved under their leadership. Many a times, a rater is influenced by organizational positions and may give higher ratings to those holding the higher positions.

Many people have attacked the reliability and validity of traditional systems on different grounds, but the fundamental criticism has been founded upon the judgement role of the supervisor and the antagonistic response of the subordinates. In a study of appraisal systems in General Electric Co. USA, the investigators found that traditional approach to performance appraisal resulted in the following responses:

(A) Criticism arises from the very nature of the system
(B) Criticism has negative effect upon achievement of goals
(C) Criticism increases antagonism and defensiveness which lead to interior performance
(D) Praise the little effect, one way or the other

(II) Modern Methods

There are two important methods of performance appraisal which are used by the modern concerns. The first is Management by Objectives which represents result-oriented appraisal. The second is Behaviourally-Anchored Rating Scale which is based on rating the behaviour of the subordinates.

Management by Objectives

It was Peter Drucker who proposed goal setting approach to performance appraisal which he called 'Management by Objective and Self Control'. This approach was further strengthened by Douglas McGregor. McGregor was concerned with the fact that most traditional appraisal systems involved ratings of traits and personal qualities that he felt were highly unreliable. Besides, the use of such trait ratings produced two main difficulties:

1. The manager was uncomfortable about using them and resisted making appraisals, and
2. It had a damaging effect on the motivation and development of the subordinate

Goal setting approach or "*management by objectives (MBO)*" is the same as behavioural approach to subordinate appraisal, actually called "*work planning and review*" in case of General Electric Co., USA. Under this approach, an employee is not appraised by his recognizable traits, but by his performance with respect to the agreed goals or objectives. Thus, the essential feature of this approach is mutual establishment of job goals. The application of goal setting approach to performance appraisal involves the following steps:

1. The subordinate discuses his job description with his superior and they agree on the contents of his job and the key results areas.
2. The subordinate prepares a list of reasonable objectives for the coming period of six to twelve months.
3. He sits with his superior to discuss these targets and plans, and a final set is worked out.
4. Check-points are established for the evaluation of progress, and the ways of measuring progress are selected.
5. The superior and the subordinate meet at the end of the period to discuss the results of the subordinate's efforts to meet the targets mutually established.

The goal setting approach is based on clear and time bound objectives from the corporate level to the operative level. This approach can be applied with great success if the performance appraisal programme consists of the following elements:

- Good job descriptions are available to help setting of goals for different positions.
- Superiors have trust in the subordinates to establish reasonable goals; and
- There is emphasis on problem solving rather than criticism of the performance of the subordinates.

The goal setting approach has done away with the judgement role of the superiors in the appraisal of their subordinates. It has led to greater satisfaction, greater agreement, greater comfort, and less tension and hostility between the workers and the management. This approach is considerably superior to the traditional approach of performance appraisal. It emphasizes training and development of individuals. It is problem solving approach rather than tell and sell approach. This approach has also got a built-in device of self-appraisal by the subordinates because they know their goals and the standards by which their performance will be measured.

Behaviourally Anchored Rating Scales

Behaviourally anchored rating scales (BARS) are designed to identify the critical areas of performance for a job, and to describe the more effective and less effective job behaviour for getting results. Performance is evaluated by asking the rater to record specific observable job behaviours of an employee and then to compare these observations with a "behaviorally anchored rating scale". As a result, the supervisor is in a position to compare the employee's actual behavioral with the behaviour that has been previously determined to be more or less effective.

Proponents of BARS claim many advantages of this approach. They argue that such a system differentiates among behavior, performance, and results, and consequently is able to provide a basis for setting development goals for the employee. Because it is job-specific and identifies observable and measurable behavior, it is a more reliable and valid method for performance appraisal.

Requirements of a Sound Performance Appraisal Programme

A sound system of performance appraisal must fulfill the following essentials:

1. The appraisal plan should be simple to operate and easy to understand.
2. The performance appraisal system would be performance based, uniform and non-variable, fair, just and equitable. It should be ensured that the appraisers are honest, rational and objective in their approach, judgement and behavioural orientation.
3. The employees should be made aware of the performance in terms of goals, targets, behaviour, etc. expected of them. A personal equation between the appraiser and the employee has to be developed to achieve mutual understanding of the criteria of evaluation.
4. The appraisal plan should be devised in consultation with the subordinates. This will increase their commitment to the plan and their understanding of expected performance.
5. The appraisal plan should take into account the appraisal practices prevailing in other units in the industry as well as the latest thinking on

performance appraisal. It should fit in the structure and operations of the organization.

6. The top management must create a climate of reliable appraisal throughout the organization. Goal-orientation, open communications, mutual trust information relationships, etc. are the basic elements of such a climate.
7. The appraisal plan should be designed to achieve specific objectives. The objectives of the appraisal programme may be to evaluate current performance on the job and to determine the potential for higher jobs. In some cases, performance appraisal is linked with specific objectives like pay raise, training, promotion, transfer, etc. The number of factors to be considered and the data to be collected should be tailor-made to achieve the objective of the appraisal.
8. The appraisers should be selected and trained properly so that they have no personal bias and possess the necessary capabilities for objective evaluation of employees. In order to ensure objectivity in appraisal, an individual may be rated by more persons independently.
9. There should be provision of appeals against appraisals to ensure confidence of the employees and their associations or unions. The results of appraisal must be discussed with the rates so that they may get an opportunity to express their feelings on their progress reports.

POTENTIAL ASSESSMENT

In most Indian organizations, people earn promotions on the basis of their past performance. The past performance is considered a good indicator of future job success. This could be true, if the jobs to be played by the promotee are similar. However, in actual practice, the roles that a role holder played in the past may not be the same that he is expected to play if he assumes a different job after his transfer or promotion to a new position. Past performance, therefore, may not be a good indicator of the suitability of an indicator for a higher role.

To overcome this inadequacy, organizations must think of a new system called potential appraisal. The objective of potential appraisal is to identify the potential of a given employee to occupy higher positions in the organization hierarchy and undertake higher responsibilities.

Potential Assessment is required to:

- Inform employees about their future prospects;
- Help the organization chalk out of a suitable succession plan;
- Update training efforts from time to time;
- Advise employees about what they must do to improve their career prospects.

Steps to be followed while introducing a Good Potential Assessment System

The following are some of the steps required to be followed while introducing a potential assessment system:

- **Role Description:** Organizational roles and functions must be defined clearly. To this end, job descriptions must be prepared for each job.
- **Qualities needed to perform the roles:** Bases on job descriptions, the roles to be played by people must be prepared (i.e., technical, managerial jobs and behavioural dimensions).
- **Rating mechanism:** Besides listing the functions and qualities, the potential assessment system must list mechanisms of judging the qualities of employees such as:

1. Rating by others: The potential of a candidate could be rated by the immediate supervisor who is acquainted with the candidate's work in the past, especially his technical capabilities.

2. Test: Managerial and behavioural dimensions can be measured through a battery of psychological tests.

3. Games: Simulation games and exercise (assessment centre, business games, in-basket, role play etc.) could be used to uncover the potential of a candidate.

4. Records: Performance records and ratings of a candidate on his previous jobs could be examined carefully on various dimensions such as initiative, creativity, risk taking ability, etc., which might play a key role in discharging his duties in a new job.

- **Organizing the system:** After covering the above preliminaries, he must set up a system that will allow the introduction of the scheme smoothly giving answers to some puzzling questions:
  - (i) How much weightage to merit in place of seniority in promotions?
  - (ii) How much weightage to each of the performance dimensions – technical, managerial, behavioural qualities?
  - (iii) What are the mechanisms of assessing the individual on different indicators of his potential and with what reliability?
- **Feedback:** The system must provide an opportunity for every employee to know the results of his assessment. "He should be helped to understand the qualities actually required for performing the role for which he thinks he has the potential, the mechanisms used by the organizations to appraise his potential and the results of such an appraisal".

JOB EVALUATION

Job evaluation is an orderly and systematic technique which aims at determining the worth of jobs. It is a formal system of determining the base compensation of jobs.

The International Labour Organization (ILO) has defined job evaluation thus: "*Job evaluation may be defined simply as an attempt to determine and compare the demands which the normal performance of particular jobs makes on normal workers without taking into account of the individual abilities or performance of the workers concerned.*" The British Institute of Management offered this definition: "*Job evaluation is the process of analysis and assessment of jobs to ascertain reliably their relative worth using the assessment as a basis for a balance structure*".

The basic object of job evaluation is to ascertain the relative worth of each job through an objective evaluation so that relative remuneration may be fixed for different jobs.

Objectives of Job Evaluation

The major objectives of job evaluation are to help management to achieve (1) equitability of wage structure within the firm, i.e., internal consistency, and (2) consistency of firm's overall wage structure with that of the industry in which the firm operates. Apart from these two major or primary objectives, job evaluation serves many other objectives also, those are given here below:

1. Establishment of sound wage foundation for incentive and bonus programmes
2. Maintenance of consistent wage policy
3. Enable management to gauge and control its payroll costs more accurately
4. Provide a framework for periodic review of wages and salaries
5. Classify functions, authority and responsibility which in turn aids in work simplification and elimination of duplicate operations.
6. Reduce grievances and labour turnover and, thereby, increase employee morale and improve management-employee relationships
7. Serve as a basis for negotiation with the union

Significance of Job Evaluation

Job evaluation leads to the following benefits:

(*i*) Job evaluation is a valuable technique in the hands of management by which a more rational and consistent (internal and external) wage and salary structure can be evolved. Internal consistency is concerned with the maintenance of relative wages within the firm and external consistency refers to a desired relativity of a firm's structure to that of the industry or region.

(*ii*) Job evaluation helps in bringing or maintaining harmonious relations between labour and management since it tends to eliminate wage inequalities within the organization and the industry.

(*iii*) Because of increasing mechanization and automation in industry, it has become unrealistic to pay workers primarily on the basis of their output. In many cases, it is the machine that determines the rate of production, so job evaluation will be of much use in fixing the wages.

(*iv*) Job evaluation standardizes the process of determining the wage differentials for various jobs. It means uniform standards will be applied to all jobs in the organization to know their relative worth.

(*v*) Job differences should not be based on skill differences only. Job evaluation takes into account various other factors like risks and working conditions also to determine the worth of jobs. Jobs are no longer differentiated mainly by the degree of skills required as differences in other job characteristics such as responsibility, effort required and nature of work have assumed greater importance for such jobs. There is thus no justification for paying wages according to skill requirements only. Job evaluation takes all relevant factors into account to determine wages.

(*vi*) Job evaluation provides a rate for the job and not for the man. Because of division of labour and specialization any large enterprise may have hundreds or thousands of different jobs to be performed by a substantial number of workers. Many workers work together on the same, similar or technically interdependent jobs. An attempt should be made to precisely define the jobs and fix wages accordingly. This is possible only by job evaluation.

(*vii*) Job evaluation helps in keeping down the costs of recruitment and selection of workers. It also assists in retaining the workers or, in other words, keeping down the rate of labour turnover because worker's wages are determined systematically by the process of job evaluation. Job evaluation involves job analysis which is of great use while recruiting new employees. Selection can be made objective by matching the qualifications of the candidate with the job specifications.

Limitations of Job Evaluation

The limitations of job evaluation are as under:

(*i*) There is no standard list of factors to be considered for job evaluation. Moreover, all job factors can't be measured accurately. Thus, job evaluation lacks scientific precision.

(*ii*) The wages fixed for a job on the basis of job evaluation might not retain workers who can make much money else-where because of law of demand and supply.

(*iii*) There is a strong feeling among the workers that individual merit should be rewarded as some kind of merit rating scheme has to be superimposed upon evaluated wage rates.

(*iv*) It presumes that jobs of equal worth will be equally attractive to the employees, but it is not true in real life. If a job offers no prospects of a rise, while another job rated equal to it has bright prospects, the later will attract more people.

(*v*) It tends to be inflexible in so far as it does not place right deal of emphasis on the wage rates prevalent in the industry as a whole.

(*vi*) Trade unions often regard job evaluation with suspicion because some of the methods are not scientific and are difficult to understand. They fear that the job evaluation will do away with collective bargaining for settlement of wages.

Job Evaluation Programme

The process of job evaluation involves the following steps:

1. A thorough examination of the jobs.
2. The preparation of job descriptions and usually an analysis of job requirements needed for its successful performance.
3. The comparison of one job with others.
4. The arrangement of jobs in their correct sequence in terms of value to the firm.
5. The relation of the sequence to a money scale.

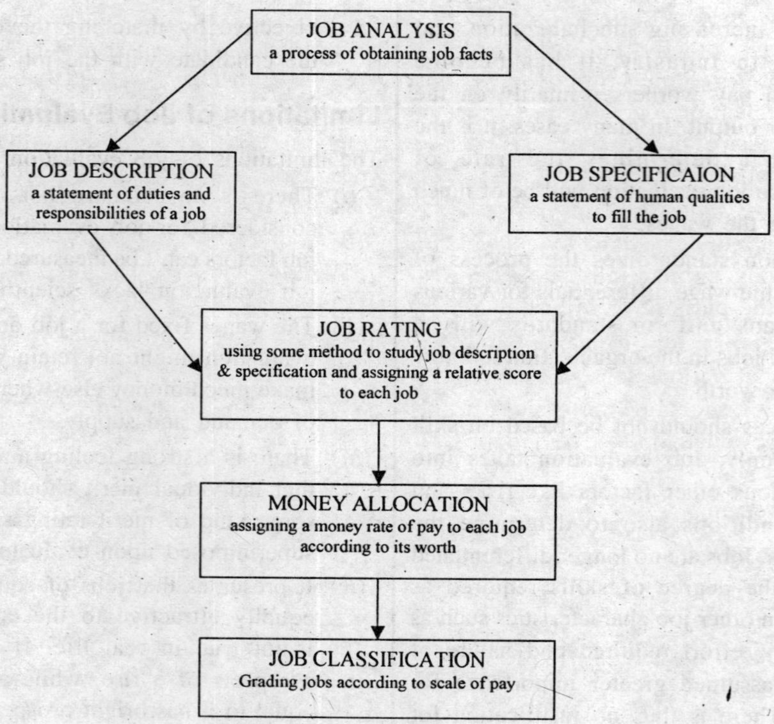

Fig. 5. *The process of Job Evaluation*

An effective job evaluation system (see Fig. 5) should fulfill the following conditions:

(*a*) It should be carried out with a high degree of integrity and fair mindedness.

(*b*) It calls for mutual trust between management and unions.

(*c*) The evaluator or committee of evaluators should have a wide knowledge of all the jobs dealt with.

(*d*) The workers should be informed of what is intended and be reassured early in the discussions that no rate of pay would be cut as a result of job evaluation, and

(*e*) The details of the scheme should not clash with provisions of a collective agreement.

Principles of Job Evaluation

In establishing the systematic approach to measuring job worth, there are certain *principles* which must be followed. Those are given here below:

1. Consideration of Job
2. Clarity of Job Information
3. Pooling of Knowledge
4. Grouping of Jobs

1. Consideration of Job: The job evaluators must rate the job and not the employee. In deciding how much money a particular job is worth, there is always a temptation to be influenced in one's judgement by the qualifications and caliber of the individual who is presently performing the job. But he may be either over or under-qualified. So the job evaluators should not commit the error of rating the individuals.

2. Clarity of Job Information: Job analysis must be done before job evaluation is initiated. Clear and accurate job descriptions and specifications must be available to provide data concerning the factors to be measured.

3. Pooling of Knowledge: As far as possible, the pooled or combined judgements of several persons should be employed in evaluating jobs. Job evaluation is a systematic, orderly, and logical way of setting the rates of wages within a firm. However, it is not exact measurement, it is grading or rating. The decisions of a number of qualified persons will reduce the likelihood of serious errors.

4. Grouping of Jobs: A decision must be made concerning what jobs are to be covered by a single evaluation system. Only similar jobs should be grouped together for the purpose of evaluation.

Selection of Job Factors: Job evaluation should involve the evaluation of various jobs in terms of certain factors. The important factors to be considered under job evaluation may be grouped under the following heads:

(*a*) *Skill :* mental and manual,
(*b*) *Experience*
(*c*) *Effort and initiative*
(*d*) *Responsibility to be undertaken*
(*e*) *Working environments, and*
(*f*) *Supervision needed*

Methods of Job Evaluation

The more difficult the job, the more is its worth. The more scarce the labour supply and higher the demand, the more a job is worth. The more skill, education and responsibility required in a job, the more is its worth. These generalizations usually hold true for most jobs and serve as indicators of what the level of pay should be, but they are so general that they are of little use in translating specific jobs into rates of monetary compensation. Therefore, several systems of job evaluation have been developed which take into account the above mentioned factors either directly or indirectly.

There are four types of job evaluation methods. These can be divided into two categories:

1. **Non-quantitative methods**
   (*i*) Ranking or job comparison
   (*ii*) Grading or job classification
2. **Quantitative methods**
   (*iii*) Point rating
   (*iv*) Factor comparison

The first category covers the simple methods which apparently make no use of detailed job factors. But they remain in the minds of the evaluators and thus affect the results. The job is treated as a whole, and job descriptions are often utilized. But the methods under the second category use detailed analysis. Job factors are selected and measured and job specifications are definitely given consideration.

(*i*) Ranking Method: The job ranking method is the simplest of all the methods. A committee of several executives is constituted which evaluates the job descriptions and ranks them in order of importance beginning with the most important job to the least important job in the organization. No specific factors are used for consideration. The purpose of ranking is to determine whether a job involves the same level of duties, responsibilities and requirements as others in the series or a higher or lower level than they do. By comparing the jobs, the rank order of importance of each can be determined. In this method, jobs are not split up into their component parts. Instead comparison is made on the basis of whole jobs. Three techniques are generally used for ranking purposes, namely:

(a) Utilizing job descriptions
(b) Making paired comparisons, and
(c) Ranking also a number line

(*ii*) Job Grading or Classification Method: This method is considered to be an improvement over ranking method in that a predetermined scale of values is provided. This method involves (1) establishing of job classes or grades, (2) definition of each grade and (3) classification of individual jobs according to how well their characteristics match those of the different grade definitions.

The job evaluation committee goes through each job description and carefully weighs it in the light of certain factors like skill, experience, etc. In this way, it assigns each job to a particular grade or class. For each grade or class, there is a different rate of wage. In fact, this method arrives at a series of classes or grades, which is precisely the point at which both the point and factor-comparison system also arrive. It is also a relatively simpler and inexpensive system to operate.

The main disadvantages of the job grading method are that broad generalizations must be used in defining grades. Another difficulty is that grading approach usually requires multiple systems for different types of jobs, e.g., description of office jobs differs widely from those of production jobs. Moreover, the installation of this method is not appropriate for big organizations.

***(iii)* Point Method:** This is the most widely used method of job evaluation. It alongwith factor comparison system, involves a more detailed, quantitative and analytical approach to the measurement of job worth. Under this method, a quantitative evaluation of different jobs in terms of various factors is made. Maximum point values are assigned to each of the job factors required to be considered. Then each job is awarded points for each of the factors. The wage level appropriate for each job is fixed on the basis of total points scored by it.

It contrasts to the ranking and grading methods, which measure jobs as whole jobs, the point system is a more analytical approach and deals with job factors. A job factor is a specific requirement levied upon the job-holder which he must contribute, assume or endure. The major factors are: skill, effort responsibility and working conditions. These factors or points are later converted into money value. The procedure for the design of 'Point Method' is discussed below:

1. List the type of jobs to be evaluated
2. Determine the factors to be used in this method like skill efforts, initiative, etc. and define them properly
3. Determine the number of degrees to be allocated to each factor and prepare a suitable definition of each
4. Assign points to each degree of each factor
5. Select a certain number of key jobs, say 10-15, and evaluate each in terms of scale so constructed
6. Design the wage structure

***(iv)* Factor Comparison Method:** Thoman E. Hitten was the first to originate factor comparison method of job evaluation. This method determines the relative rank of the jobs to be evaluated in relation to monetary scale. It is often used for evaluating white collar, professional and managerial positions, although it is equally suitable for grading other jobs as well. It is essentially a combination of the ranking and point systems. Like rank order method, it rates jobs by comparing one job with another and, like the point system, it is more analytical in the sense of subdividing jobs into compensable factors. Final ratings are expressed in terms of number.

In this method, five factors are generally evaluated for each job. These are comparatively fewer than the point system but are nevertheless sufficient, because each factor is defined broadly. The number of factors may be more than five also. The five factors with are customarily used are:

- Mental requirements
- Skills
- Physical requirements
- Responsibilities
- Working conditions

The evaluation of job under this method consists of following steps:

1. Select the factors and define them clearly.
2. Select the key job which would serve as standard against which all other jobs are compared. A key job is one whose content has become stabilized over a period of time and whose wage rate is considered to be presently correct by the management and the union.
3. Allocate wage for each key job to different factors.
4. Develop a job comparison scale and insert key jobs in them. When all of the key jobs have been evaluated and wages allocated in this manner, a job comparison scale can be constructed.
5. Evaluate the job in question factor by factor in relation to key jobs on job comparison scale. Then each job is to be evaluated and compared to other jobs in terms of each factor.
6. Design, adjust and operate the wage structure.

14. MARKETING

NARROW DEFINITION

Marketing may be narrowly defined as an economic process by which goods and services are exchanged and the values determined in terms of money prices. The American Marketing Association has defined marketing as "*the performance of business activities that direct the flow of goods and services through producers to consumers or users.*" That means marketing includes all those activities carried on to transfer the goods from the manufactures or producers to the consumers. It involves the exchange of goods and services for money. This way of defining marketing represents '*product orientation.*' It concentrates on selling whatever has been produced or manufactured by a business concern without caring for the requirements or demands of the customers. This definition suited the earlier days of seller's market when there was shortage of goods.

Product oriented definition of marketing is inappropriate in the present day business environment where there are a large number of substitutes and keen competition in the market. It presumes that the process of marketing begins after goods have been produced and ends with their sale. But in the present day business, marketing begins long before the goods are produced. The demands of the customers must be forecast before the product development and production take pace. Marketing decisions must also be made regarding the market, pricing and promotion of the product. Marketing does not end with the final sale. The customer must be satisfied if a business enterprise expects his repeat orders. Because of these reasons, the concept of marketing has undergone a change. Progressive firms of the world follow '*consumer orientation*' in marketing because they recognise that consumers are often responsible for changes in business policies. Consumers are the force which give direction to the business activities. Consumers' satisfaction should be the main aim of the business activities.

BROAD DEFINITION

According to Cundiff and Still, "*Marketing is the business process by which products are matched with the market and through which transfers of ownership are effected.*" Matching products with the market means determining the requirements of potential customers and supplying the products which meet their requirements. If a business organisation produces the products after assessing the requirements of prospective customers, it is more likely to be successful to achieve its objectives. The consumer-oriented marketing has given rise to a new philosophy in business known as '*marketing concept*'. The marketing concept emphasises the determination of the requirements of potential customers and supplying products to satisfy their requirements. Modern marketing has, thus, become an integrated process of identification, assessment and satisfaction of human wants. "Marketing is the process of discovering and translating consumer wants into products and services and then in turn making it possible for more and more people to enjoy more and more of these products and services."

MARKETING CONCEPT

Modern authors view marketing more than a physical process of distributing goods and services. They feel that marketing represents a distinct philosophy of business or a course of business thinking that has emerged over the recent years. The businessmen following this philosophy recognise and accept '*customer-oriented*' way of doing the business. They perceive *the creation of customer and satisfaction of his wants as the justification of business.* Determination of needs of customers takes precedence over production. In other words, product is not created according to the availability of the materials, machines and technical know-how with the firm, but is created according to the needs of the customers.

Under marketing concept the emphasis is on selling satisfaction and not merely on selling a product. 'The marketing concept is a consumer orientation backed by integrated marketing aimed at generating customer satisfaction as the key to satisfying organisational goals.' The objective of marketing is not the maximisation of profitable sales volume, but profits through the satisfaction of customers. All the marketing activities are integrated to achieve organisational goals through the satisfaction of customers.

Marketing concept is based on three fundamental beliefs. *First,* all company planning, policies and operations should be oriented towards the customer. *Second,* profitable sales volume should be the goal of a firm. *Third,* all marketing activities in a firm should be organisationally integrated and co-ordinated. Under the marketing concept, customer is the fulcrum around which the business moves. The objective of a firm is not the maximisation of profitable sales volume but profits through the satisfaction of the customers. And all the marketing activities in a firm are integrated and directed towards this objective. The managers practising this philosophy think in terms of what benefits the market or what needs are they satisfying.

The business firms pursuing the marketing concept achieve the following benefits :

1. Marketing concept has philosophical and strategic implications as it allow the business firm to direct its activities towards the broader and long range objectives like sustained interaction with the customers, and stability and growth of the firm.

2. Marketing concept leads to follow an integrated and co-ordinated apporach to marketing. By concentrating on consumers' wants, management can evaluate contribution made by the different parts of the firm in a better way.

3. Concern about market or customers' needs rather than product reduces the chances of a business firm becoming a sick unit. It is obvious that the firm will produce those products which will satisfy the wants of the customers and they will be easily accepted by the customers.

DISTINCTION BETWEEN MARKETING AND SELLING

The marketing concept is a course of business thinking, while marketing is a process or a course of business action. Naturally, marketing is influenced by the course of business thinking (*i.e.,* customer-oricntation). Marketing concept focuses on customers for earning profits through customers' satisfaction and follows integrated marketing. But formerly marketing focussed on products to earn profits through sales volume and followed sales promotion techniques for this purpose. Thus, marketing concept makes a sharp distinction between marketing and sellling.

Marketing is a total system of interacting business activities designed to plan, promote and distribute want satisfying goods and services to present and potential customers. It is concerned with all the functions of the enterprise which are performed to satisfy the wants of the customers. Used in this sense, marketing is a very wide term and includes selling. Selling may be defined as the performance of those activities which lead to obtaining orders from customers and direct the flow of goods and services from the seller to the buyer. Thus, it involves activities connected with the transfer of goods, already produced, to the customer.

Selling is a sub-activity of marketing and is basically administrative in nature confined to physical transfer of ownership and possession of goods and services from the seller to the buyer. Selling concentrates merely on increasing the volume of sales whereas marketing concerned with satisfaction of wants, needs and preferences of the customers.

Marketing has philosophical and strategic implications as it is directed towards the broader and iong-range objectives. But selling is a mere tactical and routine activity with a short-run perspective of increasing sales. It comes after the production of goods and services whereas marketing comes at the begining of the production cycle.

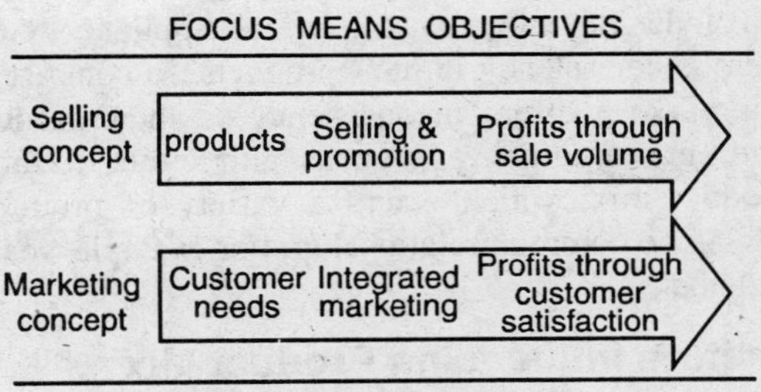

Fig. 1. *Selling vs. marketing.*

Difference between Marketing and Selling

Marketing	*Selling*
1. Marketing focuses on customer's needs of want-satisfying goods.	1. Selling focuses on seller's needs of converting his goods into cash.
2. Emphasis is given on product planning and development to match products with the market.	2. Emphasis is placed on sale of goods already produced.
3. Customer is treated as a king. He is given supreme importance.	3. Seller/product enjoys supreme importance.
4. Marketing aims at profits through customer satisfac-ion.	4. Selling aims at profit through sales volume.
5. The principle of caveat vendor (let the seller beware) is followed.	5. The principle of caveat emptor (let the buyer beware) is followed.
6. Integrated approach to marketing is practised.	6. Fragmented approach to selling is practised.

FUNCTIONS OF MARKETING

In most of the business enterprises, marketing department is set up under supervision of the Marketing Manager. The major purpose of this department is to generate revenue for the business by selling want satisfying goods and services to the customers. In order to achieve this purpose, the Marketing Manager performs the following functions:

(*i*) Marketing reasearch.
(*ii*) Product planning and development.
(*iii*) Buying and assembling.
(*iv*) Selling.
(*v*) Standardisation, garding and branding.
(*vi*) Packaging.
(*vii*) Storage.
(*viii*) Transportation.
(*ix*) Salemanship
(*x*) Advertising.
(*xi*) Pricing.
(*xii*) Insurance.

The functions of marketing may be classified into three categories as shown in the following table :

1. Marketing Research

It means the intelligence service of the organisation. Marketing research helps in analysing the buyer's habits, relative popularity of a product, effectiveness of advertisement media, etc. Its major task is to

Marketing Functions

Functions of Reserach
1. Marketing research
2. Product Planning and Development

Functions of Exchange
1. Buying and Assembling
2. Selling

Functions of Physical Treatment
1. Standardisation Grading and Branding
2. Packaging
3. Storage
4. Transportation

Functions which facilitate Exchange
1. Salesmanship
2. Advertising
3. Pricing
4. Insurance

provide the marketing manager with timely and accurate information so that better decisions can be made. The scope of marketing research is very wide. It may cover all the areas of business which have bearing on the marketing function. In the words of W.J. Stanton. "*Marketing research is the systematic search for an analysis of facts related to a marketing problem.* It is shifting from fact finding, information gathering activity to a problem solving and action recommending function."

2. Product Planning and Development

A product is something which is offered by a business firm to customers to satisfy their needs. It has great importance in all other areas of marketing management. For instance, marketing research is mainly directed towards knowing the needs of the customers and increasing the sale of the product ; and storage and transportation activities depend upon the nature of the product. Therefore, it is necessary to plan and develop products which meet the specifications of the customers. Products are the foundation of any marketing programme. The success of marketing department depends upon the nature of the product offered to the customers. The product must be so designed and developed that it meets the requirments of the customers.

Product planning and development involves a number of decisions, namely what to manufacture or buy, how to have its packaging, how to fix its price and how to sell it. The design, quality, colours, size and other features of the product can be determined by conducting marketing research. The production department will be guided by the requirements of the users.

3. Buying and Assembling

Procurement of raw materials, semi-finished or finished products has gained great importance for the modern industrial and commercial enterprises.

PRODUCT MIX

Product mix is the list of all products for sale by a company. It is defined as the composite of products offered for sale by a firm or a business. The product mix is three-dimensional : it has breadth, depth and consistency. Breadth is measured by the number or variety of products manufactured by a single manufacture. For example, Bajaj Electricals produce a variety of electrical appliances such as fans, mixers, lamps, etc. Depth refers to the assortment of sizes, colours, and models offered within each product line. For example, Bajaj Electricals manufacture different varieties or models of fans and lamps. Consistency refers to the close relationship of various product lines either or their end-use, or to production requirements or to distribution channels, or to other variables. Bajaj Electricals, for example, produce those goods which fall under the category 'Electrical Appliances'. So there is consistency in their products. In contrast to this, Godrej offers inconsistency in their product line, manufacturing process and even in their product mix, which offers a variety of products having no common relationship. For example, soaps and locks.

Factors Influencing Product Mix

The fundamental reason for changing product mix (adding or eliminating products) is due to the change in the market demand. Change in demand occurs due to the following factors :

(*a*) Population increase
(*b*) Changes in the level of the income of the buyers, and
(*c*) Changes in consumer behaviour

In India, there is an ever-increasing rate in the growth of population. This naturally adds to the number of buyers leading to a quantitative change in the volume production. The development programmes of the Government ensure increase in income enabling the consumers to spend more. This also adds to the stream of demand both qualitatively and quantitatively. In India 'rural markets' are involved mainly because of this reason. The change in consumer behaviour is a continuous source or a reason that invites changes in product planning. The other reasons could be stated as follows :

1. Marketing influences
2. Production influences and
3. Financial influences

All these arise out of the internal economies of a firm. As long as the profit motive is the criterion for the existence of a firm, changes in product mix and inevitable.

The product planning has assumed front-rank importance in the modern market-orientation business. In addition, product planning invites an intelligent, appropriate and scientific approach. The case history of the most successful companies has proved that product planning calls for the highest degree of top management ability and effort. It also makes it clear that under the changed marketing conditions one has to see things clearly before undertaking the production of any product. Hence, it is aptly said that "marketing activities precede production activities.

15. ORGANIZATIONAL BEHAVIORS

CONCEPT OF ORGANISATIONAL BEHAVIOUR

Organisational behavior is not a discipline in the usual sense of the term, but is rather an elective field of study involving the integration of the behavioural sciences (e.g., psychology, sociology, anthropology etc.) into the study of people's behavior within organisations. While those who conduct research in organisational behaviour often come from business schools, they may have their roots in diverse areas such as political sciences, sociology, psychology, or anthropology. It is the integration of relevant knowledge of these areas that has given us a new field of study - organisational behaviour. The organisational behaviour frequently abbreviated as OB.

Aldag and Brief have defined OB as follows :

"Organisational behaviour is a branch of the Social Sciences that seeks to build theories that can be applied to predicting, understanding and controlling behaviour in work organisation." Callahan et al have defined OB as a subset of management activities when they state that,

"Organisational behaviour is a subset of management activities concerned with understanding, predicting and influencing individual behaviour in organisational settings".

According to both these definitions, the basic ingredients of OB are the same, that is, understanding and controlling human behaviour though both treat OB as a field of study in different forms - a branch of the social science or a subset of management activities. We can define OB as follows:

Organisational behaviour is the study and application of knowledge about human behaviour related to other elements of the organisations such as structure, technology and social system.

Thus, OB is primarily concerned with that aspect of human behaviour which is relevant for organisational performance. It studies human behaviour at individual level, group level, and organisational level. It applies the knowledge gained about individuals, groups and the effect of organisation structure on behaviour towards the end of making organisations work more effectively.

Nature of Organisational Behaviour

Organisational behaviour is emerging as a separate field of study. Nature of OB is given as follows :

1. A Field of Study and not a Discipline: Organisational behaviour can be treated as a distinct field of study and not a discipline or even emerging discipline. A discipline is an accepted science with a theoretical foundation that serves as the basis for research and analysis. Organisational behaviour, because of its broad base, recent emergence and interdisciplinary orientation, is not accepted as science. We have just begun to synthesise principles, concepts and processes in this field of enquiry. Therefore, it is reasonable to call it a field of study rather than a discipline.

2. Interdisciplinary Approach: OB is basically an interdisciplinary approach. An inter disciplinary approach integrates the relevant knowledge drawn from different disciplines for same specific purpose. As OB draws from psychology, sociology and anthropology. Besides, it also takes relevant things from economies, political science, law and history. These disciplines exist separately, but OB integrates the relevant contents of these disciplines to make them applicable for organisational analysis. Thus OB is nothing apart from the integration of knowledge from different disciplines.

3. An Applied Science: The basic objective of OB is to make application of various researches to solve the organisational problems particularly related to human behaviour aspect. Unlike the pure science which concentrates on fundamental researches, OB concentrates on applied researches. Though many of the researches may be carried on in laboratory situations and controlled conditions, they are meant for general application in organisational analysis. Thus organisational behaviour is both science as well as art.

4. Normative And Value Centred: OB is a normative science. A normative Science, unlike the positive science which suggests only cause-effect relationships, prescribes how the various findings of the researches can be applied to get organisational results which are acceptable to the society. Thus, what is acceptable by the society or individuals engaged in an organisation is a matter of values to the people concerned. This aspect cannot be explained by positive science. The normative nature of OB is under scored by the proliferation of theories about management styles, ranging from 'how-to' prescriptions to polemics about change in basic practices.

5. **Humanistic And Optimistic:** OB focuses the attention on people from humanistic point of view. It is based on the belief that needs and motivation of people are of high concern. There is an acceptance of the value of the individual as a thinking, feeling organism, and without these considerations the organisations may not be fully operational as a social entity. Further, there is optimism about the innate potential of man to be independent, creative, productive, and capable of contributing positively to the objectives of the organisation. The man will actualise these potentials if given to him proper conditions and environments.

6. Oriented Towards Organisational Objectives: OB, being an applied Science and emphasising human aspect of the organisation, is oriented towards organisational objectives. Though an organisation may have several objectives and sometimes conflicting with individual objectives, it should not be understood that OB only emphasises the achievement of individual objectives at the cost of organisational objectives. In fact, OB tries to integrate both types of objectives so that these are achieved simultaneously.

7. A Total System Approach: OB is total systems approach wherein the living system of an organisation is viewed as an enlargement of a man. The systems approach is an integrative approach which takes into account all the variables affecting organisational functioning. In fact, the systems thinking in organisational analysis has been developed by behavioural scientists. Behavioural Science, while analysing organisational behaviour, does not take human being in isolation but as the product of Socio-psychological factors. Thus, his behaviour can be analysed keeping in view his psychological framework, interpersonal orientation, group influence, and social and cultural factors. Thus man's nature is quite complex, and OB by applying systems approach tries to find solution of this complexity.

ROLE OF ORGANISATIONAL BEHAVIOUR

OB offers several ideas to management as to how human factor should be properly emphasised to achieve organisational objectives. Human factor is not merely an instrument in the organisation but the very core of organisational existence. Barnard has observed that an organisation is a conscious interaction of two or more persons. This suggests that since organisation is the interaction of persons, they should be given adequate importance in managing the organisation. This becomes more important specially because of the changing dimensions of human behaviour, changing from money motivated behaviour to multimotivated behaviour. Mcgreger suggests that people are moving from Theory X assumptions to Theory 4 assumptions. The changing behavioural pattern suggests that organisational structure and process should be based on these characteristics. From this point of view, managers must understand the behavioural pattern of the people. Organisational behaviour provides this opportunity by analysing human behaviour for understanding and prescribing means for shaping human behaviour to a particular direction.

Understanding Human Behaviour

OB provides a way for understanding human behaviour in the organisation. For shaping human behaviour in definite direction for achieving certain predetermined objectives, managers must know how the people in the organisation behave. OB provides for understanding human behaviour in all the directions in which human beings interact. Thus, OB can be understood at the individual level, interpersonnel level, group level and intergroup level.

1. Individual Level: The behaviour of human beings as a social man is the first issue in behavioural science. It provides for analysing why and how an individual behaves in a particular way. As human behaviour is a complex phenomenon and is affected by a large numbers of factors—psychological, social, cultural, and others. OB integrates these factors to provide simplicity in understanding human behaviour.

2. Interpersonal Level: Human behaviour can be understood at the level of interpersonal interaction. Such interpersonal interaction is normally in paired relationship which represents man's most natural attempt at Sociolisation. When one focuses on the influence of one's peer and its effect in working relationship, or examines the superior-subordinate relationship, it is obvious that the two person relationship is inevitable in the organisation. OB provides means for understanding these interpersonal relation-ships in the organisation. Analysis of reciprocal relationship, role analysis, and traditional analysis are some of the common methods which provide such understanding.

3. Group Level: Though people interpret any thing at their individual level, they are often modified by group pressures which, thus, becomes a force in shaping human behaviour. Thus, individual should be studied in group also. Research in group dynamics has contributed vitally to OB and shows how a group behaves in its norms, cohesion, goals, procedures, communication pattern, leader-ship and membership. These research results are furthering managerial knowledge of understanding group behaviour which is very important for organisational morale and productivity.

4. Intergroup Level: The organisation is made up of many groups that develop a complex of relationships to build its process and substance. Understanding the effect of group relationships is important for managers in today's organisation. Intergroup relationship may be in the form of co-operation or competition. The co-operative relationships help the organisation in achieving its objectives. OB provides means to understand and achieve co-operative group relationships through interaction, rotation of members among groups, avoidance of win-lose situation, and focus on total group objectives.

Controlling and Directing Behaviour

After understanding the mechanism of human behaviour, managers are required to control and direct the behaviour so that it conforms to standards required for achieving organisational objectives. Thus, managers are required to control and direct the behaviour at all levels of individual interaction. For this purpose, OB helps managers in many areas: **Use of power and section, leadership, communication and building organisation climate conducive for better interaction.**

1. Use of Power and Sanction: Organisational behaviour can be controlled and directed by the use of power and sanction which are formally prescribed by the organisation. Power is referred to as capacity of an individual to take certain action and may be utilised in many ways. The use of power is related with sanction in the organisation. However, more use of power and sanction in the organisation is not enough for directing human behaviour. Moreover, these can be used in several ways and not all ways are equally effective. OB explains how various means of power and sanction can be utilised so that both organisational and individual objectives are achieved simultaneously.

2. Leadership: Another method of bringing human behaviour in tune with organisational requirement is leadership. Today, the difference between a successful and falling organisation lies in the quality of leadership of its managerial personnel. OB brings new insights and understanding to the theory and practice of leadership. It identifies various leadership styles available to a manager and analyses which style is more appropriate in a given situation. Thus managers can adopt styles keeping in view the various dimensions of organisations, individuals, and situations.

3. Communication: Communication is the building block of an organisation. It is communication through which people come in contact with others. People in the organisation, particularly, at higher level spend considerable time in communicating. To achieve organisational effectiveness, the communication must be effective. The communication process and how it works in interpersonal dynamics has been evaluated by organisational behaviour. The factors that affect communication have been analysed so as to make it more effective.

4. Organisational Climate: Organisational climate refers to the total organisational situations affecting human behaviour. Organisational climate takes a systems perspective and affects human behaviour. Organisational behaviour suggests that the approach to create organisational climate in totality rather than merely improving the physiological conditions or increasing employees satisfaction by changing isolated work process. Satisfactory working conditions, adequate compensation and the necessary equipments for the job are viewed as only small part of the requirements for sound motivational climate. Of greater importance is the creation of an atmosphere of effective supervision, the opportunity for the realisation of personal goods, congenial relations with others at the work place, and a sense of accomplishment. Thus OB has discovered a new approach of managing people in the organisation.

Organisational Adaptation

Organisations as dynamic entities are characterised by pervasive change. In this age of environmental variability, the real job of a manager is to provide continuity in organisations because the organisations have to adapt themselves to the environmental changes by making suitable internal arrangements. However, such organisational arrangements are mostly resisted by the internal people. Thus managers have to face dual problems, identifying need for change and then implementing the changes without adversely affecting the need for satisfaction of organisational people. It is also the essence of managing change. Management of change is seen as a self-perpetrating ever-evolving phenomenon.

PERSONALITY

Concept of Personality

Though the term personality is frequently used by people there does not seem to be any consensus about its meaning. It may mean different things to different people. To some, it means a general sum of traits or characteristics of the person; to others, it refers to a unitary mode of response to life situations. Thus, there prevails a great deal of controversy over the meaning of personality. We have categorised them into five areas as follows :

1. Omnibus: These definitions view personality as the sum total, aggregate or constellation of properties or qualities.
2. Integrative and configurational: Under this view of personality, the organisation of personal attributes is stressed.
3. Hierarchical: These definitions specify the various levels of integration or organisation of personality.
4. Adjustment: This view emphasises the adjustment (adaptation, survival and evolution) of the person to the environment.
5. Distinctiveness: The definitions for this category stress uniqueness of each personality.

Drawing from these approaches, We defined Personality as follows :

"Personality is the dynamic organisation within the individual of those psychological systems that determine his unique adjustment to his environment."

The term personality has been derived from Latin word 'persona' which means 'to speak through'. This Latin term denotes the masks which the actors used to wear in ancient Greece and Rome. Thus, personality is used in terms of influencing others through external appearance.

According to *Ruch*, personality should includes:

(*i*) external appearance and behaviour or social stimulus value;

(*ii*) inner awareness of self as a permanent organising force; and

(*iii*) the particular pattern or organisation of measurable traits, both inner and outer.

Maddi has defined personality as follows:

"Personality is a set of characteristics and tendencies that determine those commonalities and differences in the behaviour (thoughts, feelings and actions) of people that have continuity in time and that may not be easily understood as the soul results of the social and biological pressures of the movement.

Personality Theories

Many personality theorists, not only from the field of psychology but even from other field dealing with human behaviour also; have carried on researches to find answers to the questions; what is personality? What does personality constitute? How is behaviour governed by personality?

The most logical grouping of personality theories seems to be into psychoanalytic, socio-psychological, trait and self theories.

Psychoanalytic Theory

Psychoanalytic theory is based on the notion that man is motivated more by unseen forces that he is controlled by conscious and rational thought. Although Sigmund Freud is most closely related with this theory. The framework contains three aspects though interrelated but often conflicting. These are id, ego and super ego. They are so interrelated that they can only be artificially separated for individual study and analysis.

1. The Id: The id is the source of psychic energy and seeks immediately gratification for biological or instinctual needs. Freud believed that instinct could be classified under life instincts and death-instincts. Life-instincts are hunger, thirst, and sex; the energy involved in their activity is the libido. The id would proceed unchecked to satisfy motives, particularly the sexual relations and pleasures, were it not for the channeling activity into acceptable ways by the ego. As an individual matures, he learns to control the id. But even then, it remains a deriving force throughout life and an important source of thinking and behaving.

2. The Ego: The ego is the conscious and logical part of the human personality and is associated with the reality principle. While id represents the unconscious part, ego is conscious. Thus the ego keeps the id in check through the realities of the external environment through intellect and reason.

3. The Super Ego: The super ego represents social and personal norms and serves as an ethical constraint on behaviour. The super ego provides norms to ego to determine what is wrong or right. However, a person is not aware of the working of the super ego, and conscience is developed by absorption of cultural values and norms of society.

Socio-psychological Theory

Socio-psychological personality theory recognises the interdependence of the individual and society. The individual strives to meet the need of the society, while society helps the individual to attain his goal. Out of this interaction, the personality of an individual is determined. Thus, the theory is not exclusively sociological but rather a combination of two. The names associated with this theory are Adler, Horney, Forman, and Sullivan.

Social-psychological theory differs from psychoanalytic in two respects. First, social variables and not the biological instincts, are the important determinants in shaping personality. Second, behavioural motivation is conscious; man knows his needs and wants, and his behaviour is directed to meet these needs. The theorists accept that Socio-psychological factors determine personality.

Trait Theory

Trait factor theory represents a quantitative approach to the study of personality. This theory postulates that an individual's personality is composed of definite predispositional attributes called traits. A trait may be defined as any distinguishable, relatively enduring way in which one individual differs from another. Thus, traits can be considered as individual variables. There are basically three assumptions of this theory:

1. Traits are common to many individuals and vary in absolute amounts between individuals.
2. Traits are relatively stable and exert fairly universal effects on behaviour regardless of the environmental situation. Thus, a consistent functioning of personality variables is predictive of a wide variety of behaviours.
3. Trait can be inferred from the measurement of behavioural indicators.

Two most widely trait theories come from the work of Allport and Cattell. Allport bases his theory on the distinction between common traits and personal dispositions. Common traits are used to compare people. He has identified six categories of values: religious, social, economic, political, aesthetic and theoretical for comparative purpose. Besides the common traits, there are personal dispositions which are completely unique. These are cardinal, central or secondary. This uniqueness emphasises the psychology of the individual that Allport has developed.

Cattell has developed a similar set of traits through the construction of tests and the determination of factor or traits families which may emerge from these psychological measures. However, he has taken a different approach from Allport. He has identified two categories of traits— surface traits and source traits. He determined thirty-five surface traits by finding cluster of traits that are correlated. For example, wise-foolish, affectionate-cold, honest-dishonest and so on. Such traits lie on the surface of the personality and are largely determined by the underlying source traits. He identified twelve source traits. Examples of such traits are affectothymia (good nature and trustfulness) versus sizothymia (critical and suspicious); ego strength (maturity and realism) versus emotionality and neuroticism (immaturity and evasiveness); dominance versus submissiveness; surgency (cheerfulness and energy) versus desurgency (depressed and subdued feelings)

Trait theory gives recognition to the continuity of personality. This theory is based on personality research. In this research typical study attempts to find a relationship between set of personality variables and assorted behaviour. This contributes personality tests to the behavioural science. However, this theory is very descriptive rather than analytical, and is a long way from being comprehensive theory of personality.

Self Theory

The psychoanalytic, socio-psychological and traits theories of personality represent the more traditional approaches to explaining the complex human personality. Self theory, also termed as organic of field theory, emphasises on the totality and interrelatedness of all behaviour. This approach treats the organism as a whole to a greater degree than do any of the other theoretical formulation. Though there are many contributors, notably, Maslow, Herzberg, Lewin, etc.; the most important contribution comes from Carl Rogers. His self theory of personality is very relevant in organisational behaviour. He defines the self concept as organised consistent, conceptual, gestalt composed of perceptions of the "I" or "me" and the perceptions of the relationships of the "I" or "me" to others and to various aspects of lifes, together with the values attached to these perceptions. There are four factors in self concept.

1. Self-image: Self-image is the way one sees oneself. Every person has certain beliefs about who or what he is; taken together, these beliefs are a person's self-image or identity. Erikson has defined identity as 'a life-long development largely unconscious to the individual and his society. Its roots go back all the way to the first self-recognition; in the baby's earliest exchange of smiles, there is something of a self-realisation coupled with a mutual recognition.

2. Ideal-Self: The ideal-self denotes the way one would like to be. The ideal-self differs from self-image in the fact that the self-image indicates the reality of a person as perceived by him, while ideal-self indicates the ideal position as perceived by him. Thus, there may be a gap between these two characteristics. The ideal-self is important in stimulus selectively because a person will select those stimuli for processing which fit in with the characteristics of his ideal-self.

3. Looking Glass-self: The looking glass-self is the perception of a person about how others are perceiving his qualities and characteristics. This is the perception of other's perception, that is, the way one thinks people perceive about him and not the way people actually see him. Looking glass-self is pre-dominantly a social product which emerges from face-to-face interaction with others from the very beginning of the life. This interaction is directed towards cues about how others see him as an individual. Thus beliefs about self are in large measure a reflection of others' perception about the person.

4. Real-Self: The real-self is what one really is the first three aspects of self-concept are the functions of individual perception and they may be same, or different, as the real-self. An individuals self-image is confirmed when other persons' responses to him indicate their beliefs about who and what he corresponds with. In the face of feedback from the environment, the person re-evaluates himself and readjusts his self-image to be more consistent with the cues he was receiving. Thus, there is a mutual recognition of his real-self and the validity of his self-image is confirmed.

A person's self-concept gives him a sense of meaningfulness and consistency. Gellerman observes that 'the average individual is not particularly well acquainted with himself, so to speak, but he remains quite faithful to his not-so accurate image of himself and thereby acquires some consistency'. In analysing organisational behaviour, the self-concept plays a very significant role. A person perceives a situation depending upon his self-concept which has a direct influence on his behaviour. This implies that person with a different self-concept needs different types of managerial practices.

Personality Development

Human personality development is a continuous process. It starts since the child is in Fetal stage. After birth, the child develops and learns and this process continues throughout his life. Therefore, personality development can be seen through different stages of age of an individual. At each stage, a person develops different aspects of personality. These stages have been described differently by different personality theorists. These descriptions may be classified into:

1. Freudian stages.
2. Neo-Fraudian stages-Erikson's psychological stages.

Erikson's Psychological Stages

While formulating his stage theory of personality, Erikson has felt that relatively more attention should be given to the social rather than the sexual adaptations of the individuals. Based on this theme, he has identified eight psychological stages of personality development. Each stage covers a particular span of a person's life and in each stage, a particular type of crisis is experienced as shown in Table 1.

Erikson has asserted that a psychological crisis occurs within each of the stages and that in order to have a normal fulfilling personality, each crisis should be optimally resolved. However, these eight stages are not totally separable and the crisis at a particular stage is not fully resolved. A brief description of different stages of personality development is presented below:

1. Oral Sensory Stage: This is the stage of infancy and the child tries to resolve the crisis of trust versus mistrust. The infant who is cared well develops trust in people while the infant who is not well cared develop mistrust. This stage makes a serious impact on a child that influences his behaviour for the remaining life.

2. Muscular and Anal Stage: This is the early childhood stage of the life in which the child develops the sense of autonomy in his behaviour is approved by the parents and other people. If the child faces disapproval by the elders, he develops a sense of doubt and shame.

3. Locomotor Genital Stage: This is the play stage of the life and the child tries to resolve the

Table 1. Erikson's Psychological Stages

Stage of development	Age	Crisis
Oral sensory stage	0-1	Trust versus mistrust
Muscular and anal Stage	1-2	Autonomy versus doubt
Locomotor genital stage	3-5	Initiative versus guilt
Latency stage	6- puberty	Industry versus inferiority
Puberty and adolescence	12-19	Identity versus confusion
Early adulthood	Early 20s	Intimacy versus isolation
Young and middle adulthood	Late 20s	Generativity versus stagnation
Mature adulthood	30s	Integrity versus despair

crisis of initiative versus guilt. He tries to discover how much he can do. If the child is encouraged to experiment and to achieve reasonable goals, he develops the sense of initiative. If the child is blocked and made to feel incapable, he develops a sense of guilt and lack of self-confidence.

4. Latency Stage: This is the school-going stage of the life and the child tries to develop many new skills and social abilities. If the child experiences progress at a rate compatible with his abilities, he develops a sense of enterprise. In the reserve case, he develops a sense of inferiority.

5. Adolescence: This is the teenage stage of the life and the adolescent person tries to gain a sense of identity; a sense of feeling who he is and tries to establish himself as socially different from his parents. The autonomy, initiative and enterprise developed at the earlier stages of the life are very important in helping the teenager to resolve the crisis of identity versus confusion and to prepare himself for the adulthood.

6. Early Adulthood: This is the stage of clearly 20s of the life in which the person tries to resolve the crisis of intimacy versus isolation. The sense of identity developed during the teenage stage helps the early adult to develop deep and lasting relationships.

7. Young and Middle Adulthood: This the late 20s stage of the life in which the person tries to resolve the crisis of generativity versus stagnation or self-absorption. Generative persons attach more importance to the society as compared to themselves. Productivity at the work and societal advancement become more important for them. They try to become innovative and creative. Self-absorved persons do not develop an ability to look beyond themselves. They remain preoccupied with their own development and do not show concern for further generations.

8. Mature Adulthood: This is the 30s stage of the life in which the person faces the crisis of integrity versus desp r. At this stage the person gets maturity, wisdom and perspective that can guide the younger generation.

DETERMINANTS OF PERSONALITY

Personality represents of change and it relates to the psychological growth and development of individuals. While it may be possible to detect underlying personality characteristics, these characteristics may be useful only at that point of time and only for a limited number of situations. Therefore, it becomes important to know the factors that cause a given personality to change or develop. There are various determinants of personality and these have been categorised in different ways. Mc Clelland has categorised these factors into four fundamental theories— traits (acquired personality to respond), schema (beliefs, frame of reference, major orientations, ideas and values), motives (inner drives) and self-scheme (observation of one's own behaviour). Similarly, Scott and Mitchell have classified various determinants into heredity, groups and cultural factors, both physiological and psychological which play important role in human personality. These factors are interrelated and interdependent. However, for the purpose of analysis, these can be classified into four broad categories,

1. biological factors
2. family and social group factors
3. cultural factors, and
4. situational factors

The impact of these factors on the personality given in Fig. 1

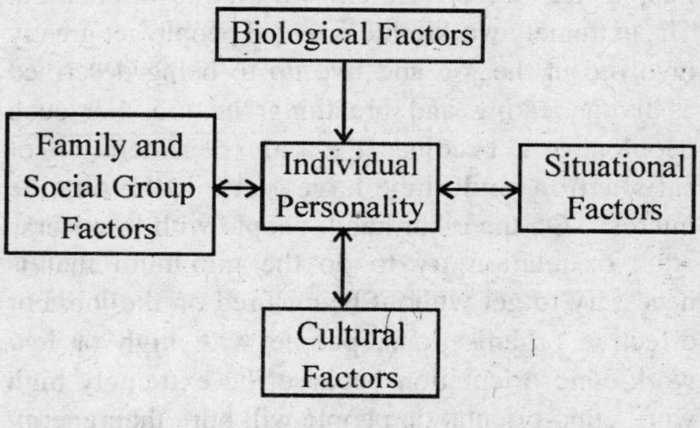

Fig. 1. *Determinants of personality*

PERSONALITY AND BEHAVIOUR

Personality has key influence on work performance. In jobs, particularly with high human relations content, where most of the working days is spent interacting with other people, personality is a major determinant of what will be done and how it will be done. Each man's personality reveals itself in the way he works with his superior, his subordinates, and other people. As a result, when the incumbent on a job changes, everyone has to adjust to a whole series of changes in the way work is accomplished. The result is that the organisation functions differently from the way the designers of the structure envisioned and what organisation really is reflects the personality of those who hold key jobs. This affects the individual performance and consequently organisational performance. Some of the important personality factors that determine what kind of performance will be achieved or what kind of behaviour is exhibited at work are self-concept and self-esteem, need patterns, machia vellianism, locus of control, tolerance for ambiguity, type A and B personalities, introversion-extroversion, and work-ethic orientation.

Self-concept and Self-esteem

Self-concept is the way individuals define themselves as to who they are and derive their sense of identity. Self-esteem denotes the extent to which they consistently regard themselves as capable, successful, important and worthy individuals. Self-esteem is an important personality that determines how managers perceive themselves and their role in the organisation. People with high self-esteem tend to take on more challenging assignments and contribute significantly to the organisational effectiveness if the organisation rewards them suitably for their contributions.

Need Patterns

According to the personality characteristics, there are four types of needs that people have at work. These are needs for achievement, affiliation, autonomy and dominance. Those who have high need for achievement engage themselves proactively in work behaviour in order to feel proud about their achievements and successes; those having high need for affiliation work co-operatively with others; those having need for autonomy like to work in an environment with less close supervision; and those with high need for dominance are very effective in an environment where they can actively enforce their legitimate authority.

Machiavellianism

Machiavellianism refers to manipulation of others as a primary way of achieving one's goals. Mach scale measures the extent to which an individual tends to be Machiavellian. People with high score on Mach scale, tend to be cool, logical in assessing the system around them, willing to twist and turn facts to influence others, and try to gain control of people, events and situations by manipulating the system to their advantage.

Locus of Control

Locus of control means whether people believe that they are in control of events or events control them. Those who have internal locus of control believe that they control and shape the course of events in their lives; those who have external locus of control tend to believe that events occur purely by chance or because of factors beyond their own control. Former category of people seek opportunities for advancement and rely more on their abilities and judgement at work; while latter category of people remain mostly inactive and allow the events occur on their own.

Tolerance for Ambiguity

Based on personality characteristics, some people can tolerate high level of ambiguity without experiencing undue stress and still function effectively while people who have a low tolerance for ambiguity may be effective in structured work setting but it is almost impossible to operate effectively when things are rapidly changing and much information about the future turn of events is not available. Generally managers have to work in an environment full of uncertainty because of rapid change; therefore, they have to develop high level of tolerance for ambiguity.

Type A and B Personalities

Personality has been grouped into two categories denoted by alphabets A and B. Type A people always feel a sense of time urgency are highly achievement-oriented, exhibit a competitive drive and are impatient when their work is slowed down for any reason. Such people are more prone to heart attack. On the other hand, type B people are easy-going, do not have urgency for time and do not experience the competitive drive.

Introversion and Extroversion

Introversion is the tendency in individuals which directs them to turn inward and experience and process feelings, thoughts and ideas within themselves. Extroversion refers to the tendency in individuals to turn outward of themselves searching for external stimuli with which they can interact. Introverts are quiet, reflective and intellectual people who prefer to interact with a small intimate circle of friends. They are more likely to be successful when they can work on highly abstract ideas such as research and development in a relatively quiet atmosphere. Extroverts, on the other hand, are sociable, lively, gregarious and seek outward interaction. They are likely to be more successful working in the sales activities, publicity departments, personal relations unit and so on where they can interact face to face with others.

Work-ethic Orientation

People may have different work-ethic orientation. The extremely work-ethic oriented people get greatly involved in the job and live up to being described as living, eating and breathing the job. For such people, work becomes the only consideration of satisfaction and they have very little outside interests. On the other hand, people with low work-ethic orientation try to do the minimum that is necessary to get without being fired on the job. For effective organisations, people with high or low work-ethic orientation because the extremely high work-ethic-orientation people will burn their energy too quickly creating lot of health problems, thus, affecting long-term organisational effectiveness adversely, while people with low work-ethic orientation will not be able to achieve anything meaningful for the organisation.

Based on the above discussion, some conclusion can be drawn about the desirable personality characteristics for effective managers. Apart from possessing the necessary managerial skills and abilities, managers need to have high level of self-concept, high level of tolerance for ambiguity, a type of personality, good mix of needs for achievement, affiliation and power, internal locus of control, relatively extroverts, and have high work-ethic orientation.

PERCEPTION

Concept of Perception

Perception is the cognitive process. In terms of S-O-B-C model, perception is the cognitive process which involves the O(organism) selecting organising and interpreting the S (stimulus). Thus, perception is the process of selecting, organising and interpreting or attaching meaning to the events happening in the environment. Robbins has defined perception as follows :

"Perception may be defined as a process by which individuals organise and interpret their sensory impressions in order to give meaning to their environment."

Based on the definition of perception, we may identify its following features :

1. Perception is the intellectual process through which a person selects the data from the environment, organises it and obtains meaning from it. The physical process of obtaining data from environment, known as sensation, is distinct from it.
2. Perception is the basic cognitive or psychological process. The manner in which a person perceives the environment affects his behaviour. Thus, people's actions, emotions, thoughts or feeling are triggered by the perception of their surroundings.
3. Perception, being an intellectual and psychological process, becomes a subjective process and different people may perceive the same environmental event differently based on what particular aspects of the situation they choose to absorb, how they organise this information and the manner in which they interpret it to obtain the grasp of situation. Thus, the subjectively perceived "reality" in any given setting may be different for different people.

Sensation and Perception

Sometimes confusion arises between sensation and perception as both are the cognitive processes and both are beads of the same string. Behavioural scientists generally acknowledge that all knowledge of the world depends on the senses and their stimulation, but the facts of raw sensory data are insufficient to produce or to explain the coherent picture of the world as experienced by the normal adult. In this context, it is important to understand the differences between sensation and perception.

Sensation may be described as the response of a physical sensory organ. The physical senses are vision, hearing, touch, smell, and taste. These senses are bombared by stimuli continuously, both external and internal to human body and reactions in particular sense organ take place because of these. Examples of sensation may be reaction of eye to colour, ear to sound, and so on. These examples show that sensation deals with very elementary behaviour that is, largely, determined by physiological functioning.

Perception is something more than sensation. It correlates, integrates and comprehends diverse sensations and information from many organs of the body by means of which person identifies things and objects, the sensations relate to. Perception classifies the stimuli based on past experience, feeling and motives. Thus perception is determined by both physiological and psychological characteristics of the organism. However, sensation only activates the organs of the body and is not affected by such psychological factors as learning and motives. Depey's statement further clarifies the difference between the two. 'By means of my eye, I see, but it is not my eye but I who see, and I tend to see an object in its totality, a thing or event with certain qualities, with a figure and form set against a background. Thus in seeing process, both sensation and perception are involved. Activation of eyes to see an object is sensation and the inference what is being seen is perception.

Boring has made distinction between sensation and perception. He says that "the distinction between sensation and perception is commonly made on the assumption that the sensation refers to the action by a receptor when it is stimulated and perception refers to the meaning given to the sensation."

Based on these observations, distinction between sensation and perception may be made as follows :

1. Sensation is a simple mental process whereas perception is comparatively a complex mental phenomenon. Perception is a complex process because it is affected by a number of variables.
2. By sensation, the person just becomes cautious of the quality of stimulus, he just becomes aware of the stimulus like colour, form, shape,

smell and meaning of the stimulus. By perception, he derives meaning of these.

3. The person is comparatively inactive in sensation whereas he becomes more active in perception because he tries to know the meaning of sensation in this process.
4. Sensation may be considered as a part of perception because the former is the first stage of the latter. The first experience of stimulation is sensation and the process related to the distinct knowledge of stimulus is perception. Only our organs and nerves are active in sensation but all our body becomes active in perception.

PERCEPTUAL PROCESS

Perception is a process consisting of several subprocesses. We can take an input-throughput-output approach to understand the dynamics of the perceptual process. This approach emphasises that there is input which is processed and gives output. The stimuli in the environment— subjects, events or people— can be considered as the perceptual inputs. The actual transformation of these inputs through the perceptual mechanisms of selection, organisation and interpretation can be treated as the throughputs and the resultant opinions, feelings, attitudes, etc., which ultimately influence our behaviour, can be viewed as the perceptual outputs.

This simplified process of perception is presented in Fig. 2.

The Fig. 2 is a simplified version of perception process. It does not present the whole factors which go in input-throughput-output process of perception. The Fig. 3 present a comprehensive view of process of perception.

The Fig. 3 presents three basic sub-processes or elements of perception. These are existence of stimuli, perception mechanism and perceptual outputs. Perceptual outputs alongwith other determinants of human behaviour affect and shape behaviour.

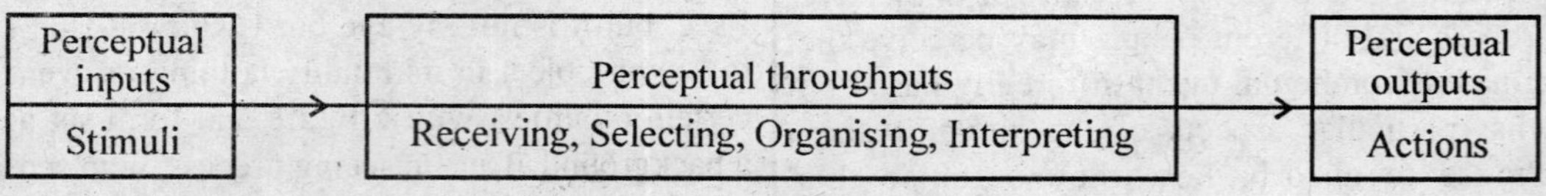

Fig. 2. *Simplified Process of Perception*

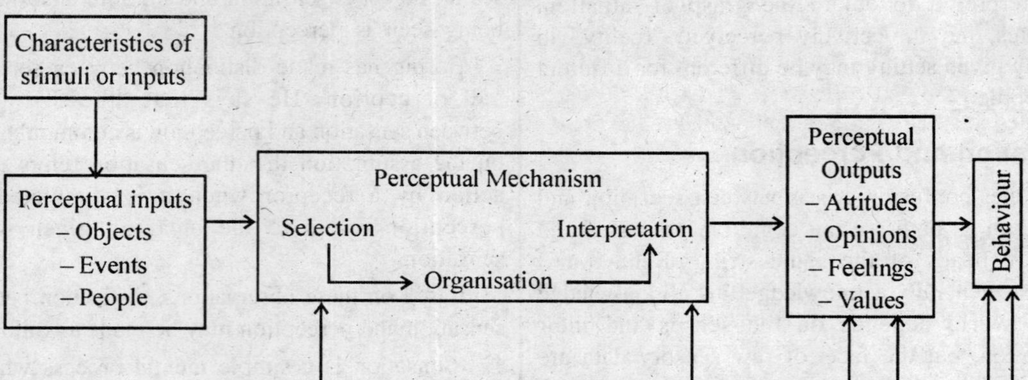

Fig. 3. *Complex Process of Perception*

Perceptual Inputs

Strictly speaking, perceptual inputs in the form of stimuli is not the part of actual perception process though these are necessary for the occurrence of perception. Stimuli may be in the form of objects, events or people. Thus, everything in the setting where events occur or which contribute to the occurrence of events, can be termed as perceptual inputs. Further, the characteristics of stimuli are important as these affect the extent to which the perceiver is attracted to these which affects the selection of stimuli for perception alongwith other variables affecting selection of stimuli like perceiver's characteristics and situational variables. When the perceiver interacts with a stimulus, sensation takes place which, we have seen earlier, starts perception process.

Perceptual Mechanism

Perceptual mechanism involves three elements—**selection of stimuli, organisation of stimuli** and **interpretation of stimuli**.

Selection of Stimuli

After receiving the stimuli from the environment, some are selected for further processing while others are screened out because it is not possible for a person to select all stimuli which he sees in the environment. There are two types of factors which affect selection of stimuli. These are external and related to stimuli and internal related to the perceiver. These external and internal factors are of several types.

Organisation of Stimuli

After the stimuli are received, these are organised in some form in order to make sense out of that. The various forms of organising stimuli are—ground, perceptual grouping, simplification and closure.

Interpretation of Stimuli

The perceptual inputs that have been organised will have to be interpreted by the perceiver so that he can sense and extract some meaning of what is going on in the situation. People interpret the meaning of what they have selectively perceived and organised in terms of their own assumptions of people, things and situations. They also become judgemental as well and tend to interpret the things as good/bad, beautiful/ugly, and so on which are quite relative terms. In such a process, there are chances of mis-interpretation. Interpretation of stimuli is affected by characteristics of stimuli, situations under which perception takes place, and characteristics of the perceiver. These factors also affect the total perception process. The characteristics of stimuli affect their selection for perception. At the same time, these may affect the interpretation also. Similarly, the physical, social and organisational settings in which an object is perceived, also affect the interpretation. In interpreting the stimuli, the perceiver may commit mistake in perceiving because of several reasons.

Perceptual Outputs

Based on perpetual mechanism which ends with interpretation of stimuli, perceptual outputs emerge. These outputs may be in the form of covert actions like development of attitudes, opinions, beliefs, impression about the stimuli under consideration. These outputs alongwith other factors affecting human behaviour may result in overt behaviour. For overt behaviour to occur, perception is not the sole decide though it is important. For example, when a person sees an advertisement of a product (stimulus), he may perceive that the product is good. This perception, however, may not be enough for the person to buy the product (over behaviour). The actual buying may depend on the availability of the product, perceiver's need for product, and his propensity and capacity to spend money for buying the product.

PERCEPTUAL SELECTIVITY

While discussing the perception process, we have mentioned that perception is a selective process and as the people can sense only limited amount of information in the environment, they are characteristically selective. By selection, certain aspects of stimuli are screened out and others are admitted. Those which are admitted remain in the awareness of the people and those which are screened out fall below the through hold. For example, when people read a newspaper, they do not read the entire newspaper but only those news which interest them. Similar things happen in other cases too. This is known as perceptual selectivity. This is caused by a variety of factors which may be grouped into two categories; external and internal.

ATTITUDES

The importance of attitudes in understanding psychological phenomenon was given formal recognition early in the history of social psychology. From the time of the concept's entry into the language of psychology until new, interest in attitudes has been strong and growing. However, over the years, attitudes have been studied with differing emphasis and methods. For example, between the 1920s and up to the World War II the attention of attitudes researchers was directed principally towards definitional issues and attitude measurement. In addition, there were studies concerned with relationship of attitudes to some social variables. World War II brought with it a growing concern about the place of the attitude concept in understanding prejudice, particularly antisemitism. This period also brought the measurement of attitudes and opinions concerning various facts of soldiering and war. After the war, the subject of attitudes was taken up by academicians, particularly in the context of attitude change. Till now, the researchers have developed a loosely structured theoretical framework formulating the psychological processes underlying attitude change and the direct application of the study to contemporary social problems.

CONCEPT OF ATTITUDES

It is necessary to be precise in defining attitudes—attitudes may be defined in two ways— conceptual and operational. According to **Allport**—"Attitude is a mental and neural state of readiness organised through experience, exerting and directive or dynamic influence upon the individuals response to all objects and situations with which it is related."

There is operational approach in defining the term attitude. **Reitz** has defined attitude as follows:

"Attitude is the persistent tendency to feel and behave in a favourable or unfavourable way towards some object, person or ideas."

Schermerhorm et al have defined attitude as follows :

"Attitude is a predisposition to respond in a positive or negative way to someone or something in one's environment."

Based on above definitions, an attitude has the following features:

1. Attitudes affect behaviour of an individual by putting him ready to respond favourably or unfavourably to things in his environment.
2. Attitudes are acquired through learning over the period of time. The process of learning attitudes starts right from childhood and continues throughout the life of a person.
3. Attitudes are invisible as they constitute a psychological phenomenon which can not be observe directly. They can be observed by observing the behaviour of an individual.
4. Attitudes are pervasive and every individual has some kind of attitudes towards the objects in his environment. In fact, attitudes are forced in the socialisation process and may relate to any thing in the environment.

Attitudes, Opinion and Belief

There are certain other terms, such as opinion and belief, which are used quite closely with attitudes. However, there is a basic difference in these terms. An opinion is generally the expression of one's judgement of a particular set of facts, an evaluation of the circumstances presented to him. Thurstone defines opinions as expression of attitudes. However, Kolasa observes that 'an opinion is response to a specifically limited stimulus, but the response is certainly influenced by the predisposition with which the individual is operating, that is, the attitude structure. Undoubtedly attitudes are basic to opinion as well as to many other aspects of behaviour. Although attitudes tend to be generalised predisposition to react in some way towards objects or concepts opinions tend to be focused on more specific aspects of the object or the concept. McCormick and Tiffin observe that 'the measurement of attitudes is generally based on the expressions of opinions. But we should distinguish between attitude scale which, like a thermometer or barometer, reflects the generalised level of individuals attitudes towards some object or concept and opinion surveys which typically are used to elicit the opinions of people toward specific aspect of, for example, their work situation.

A difference can also be made between attitude and belief. A belief is 'an enduring organisation of perceptions and cognitions about some aspects of individual's world. Thus, belief is a hypothesis concerning the nature of objects, more particularly, concerning one's judgement of the probability regarding their nature. In this sense, belief is the cognitive component of attitude which reflects the manner in which an object is perceived. Kolasa observes that 'beliefs are stronger than opinions, we hold them more firmly than we do the more changeable evaluations of minor or transitory events represented by opinions. Beliefs are less affected by the pro or con positions fundamental in attitudes than are opinions, but all three aspects may influence the others.'

The difference between attitudes, opinions and beliefs exist on conceptual basis. Most researchers believe that these three terms are so closely tied that it is difficult to separate them except on a limited conceptual basis. In the literature, often there is considerable amount of overlapping in these three terms. Most psychologists, however, believe that attitudes are more fundamental to human behaviour than are the related aspects. For this reason, more attempts have been made to analyse attitude as compared to others.

Attitudes And Behaviour

Individual's behaviour is not a simple and direct stimulus response relationship, rather it is affected by the individual concerned. The work situation is interpreted by the individual and attitudes play an important part in which the situation is interpreted. Only after individual's interpretation and comparison does the response occur. This means that response expected of a purely objective and rational consideration of the work situation and its characteristics may not be the actual response of the individual. His response depends completely on how he interprets the situation and on his own personal attitudes towards the situation. Obviously attitudes are an important consideration because of their central position in the process of transforming work requirements into efforts. The process of influence of attitudes on behaviour is presented in the following Fig. 4.

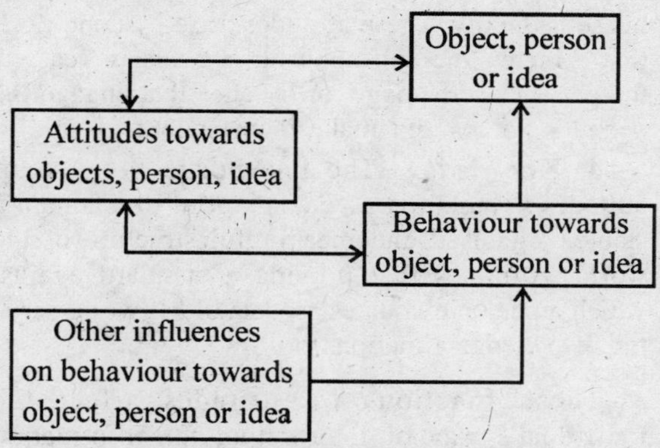

Fig. 4. *Attitudes and Behaviour*

Influence of Attitudes on Behaviour

Attitudes alone do not influence behaviour but these act with other factors in the individual influencing behaviour, such as personality, perception, motivation, etc. Further, attitudes are also affected by the individual dimensions as well as the objects, persons and ideas. Attitudes have been thought as serving four functions and thereby influencing the behaviour. These are utilitarian or instrumental, ego defensive, value orientation, and knowledge.

1. Instrumental: Attitudes serve as a means to reach a desired goal or to avoid an undesired one. Instrumental attitudes are aroused by the activation of a need or cues that are associated with the attitude object and arouse favourable or unfavourable feelings.

2. Ego-defensive: The ego-defensive function of attitude acknowledges the importance of psychological thought. Attitudes may be acquired and maintained to protect the person from facing threats in the external world or from becoming aware of his own unacceptable impulses. Ego-defensive attitudes may be aroused by internal or external threat, frustrating events, appeals or to the build-up or repressed impulses, and suggestions by authoritarian sources. The attitudes influence his behaviour by affecting his perception of the situation accordingly.

3. Value Orientation: The value-orientation function takes into account attitudes that are held because they express a person's values or enhance his self-identity. These attitudes arise by conditions that threaten the self-concept, appeals to reassert the person's self-image, or by cues that engage the person's values and make them salient to him.

4. Knowledge: The knowledge function of attitudes is based on a person's need to maintain a stable, organised and meaningful structure of the world. Attitudes that provide a standard against which a person evaluates aspects of his world serve the knowledge function too.

These functions of attitudes affect the individual's way of interpreting the information coming to him. Since attitudes intervene between work requirements and work responses, information about how people feel about their jobs can be quite useful in prediction about work response. Thus, these types of attitudes can portray areas of investigation for making the individual and the organisation more compatible.

THEORIES OF ATTITUDE FORMATION

These theories of attitude formation may broadly be classified into three categories, **cognitive-consistency theories, functional theories** and **social judgement theories.** However, there is frequent discontinuity between various groupings because related approaches have focused on different sets of phenomena. Nevertheless such classification is valid from practical point of view.

ATTITUDE MEASUREMENT

Attitudes are subjective attributes of people. They can be regarded as constructs in the sense that they are conceptualisations of human qualities that are formed on the basis of either rational consideration or statistical evidence. Thus, people may vary along a number of attitudinal dimensions. Keeping this measurement aspect into consideration, the attitudes might be defined operationally by describing the measurement systems that psychologists use to measure attitudes. Attitude measurement, developed largely by social psychologists, is concerned with efforts to tap these attitudes as they are characteristics of individual. There are many methods of attitude measurement. In pulling together numerous methods dealing with attitude measurement, Summers has used the following organisation which, in effect, is classification of methods of attitude measurement: (i) self-report (usually elicited with questionnaires dealing with beliefs, feelings and behaviours; (ii) indirect tests (such as projective techniques and disguised approaches; (iii) direct observation techniques; and (iv) psychological reaction techniques. However, attitude measurement of employees in organisations is most commonly carried out with self-respect questionnaires. Measurement of attitudes based on questionnaires uses several scaling methods. There are three types of attitude scaling which are commonly used in attitude measurement. Thurstone type of Scale, Likert Scale, and semantic differential.

The Thurstone type of scaling goes back to the early work of Thurstone and have, who collected a large number of statements relating to the area in which attitudes were to be measured. These statements may be relating to any object about which attitudes are to be measured. The statements are both favourable and unfavourable, and are placed in 11 piles, with most favourable statements being placed in pile 1 and the most unfavourable one being placed in pile 11. Other statements are placed in between their position depending on the degree of favourability or unfavourability. The scale is then presented to the respondents. Each respondent checks the statement with which he agrees. His attitude score is then based either on the average or the medium scale of the statements that he has checked.

Soon after Thurstone Scale, Likert experimented with certain other varieties of attitude scales Likert's attitude scale use five points. The statement relating to the measurement of attitudes is given to the person concerned and he is asked to check one of the five points given for every statement. These points show degree of agreement or disagreement with the given statements. The Likert Scale is considered better as compared to Thurstone because of several positive facts. For example, in this Scaling, there is not much problem in making numerous statements because for every aspect, only one statement is required which will show both positive and negative degrees. Seiler and Hough refer to Likert Scaling as equally or more reliable than the Thurstone, and faster, and equally or more valid.

The semantic differential, an attitude scaling technique that lends itself to various applications, was developed by Osgood, Suci, and Tannenbaum.

Semantic differential means a successive allocation of a concept to a point in the multidimensional space by selection from among a set of given scaled semantic alternatives. For any given purpose it consists of several or many pairs of opposite adjustive or phrases; with scale values in between. In using this scale, the respondent marks the position along each scale that reflects his attitude to the object. Scale values (often ranging from 1 to 7) are associated with the different responses and individual's attitude score usually is the sum of these.

Apart from these measures of attitudes, certain other scales have also been developed. These include the Guttman technique, the error-choice method, and the sentence completion method.

ATTITUDE CHANGE

There is often a paradox of attitudes in that people need them to provide stability to social world yet world is a changing one and people must change their attitudes appropriate to the situation. The attitude change appropriate to organisational requirement is more important because attitudes affect behaviour and only a certain behaviour is desirable from organisational point of view. Organisations adopt a number of techniques for changing attitudes of their members so that their behaviour corresponds to the organisational requirements. However, whatever the techniques for attitudes change are adopted, they can be effective only if basic characteristics of attitudes and their nature are kept in consideration. Though various theories of attitude formation and change have been presented earlier which help in understanding attitudes and the techniques through which they can be changed, the change techniques can be more effective, if three basic factors are considered adequately.

1. the characteristics of attitudes;
2. the personality of attitude holder; and
3. the group affiliation of the attitude holder,

These factors have been derived from two sources; theory of attitude formation and the factors affecting attitude formation.

METHOD OF ATTITUDE CHANGE

There are various methods through which a positive change in attitudes may be brought. In the social context, Cohen has suggested four methods for attitude change. These are :

1. communication of additional information
2. approval and disapproval of a particular attitude,
3. group influence, and
4. inducing engagement in discrepant behaviour

In some or the other, all these methods involve introducing discrepancies among the elements making up the individuals attitudes in the hope that the elements will be rebalanced through the effective component of the attitudes. Thus, in actual practice, the central variable in attitude change is the feeling component with the attitude object. From organisation's point of view, manager can take following actions in bringing change in attitudes of organisational members.

1. Group action
2. Persuation through leadership
3. Persuasion through communication, and
4. Influence of total situation.

VALUES AND ATTITUDES

Some researchers see values as consisting of large sets of related attitudes. For example, Fishbein and Ajzen have included three components in attitudes— informational (ideas, beliefs and values, and information), emotional (feelings of likes and dislikes or positive and negative), and behavioural (tendency to behave). Thus they have taken values as a part of attitudes. However, some differences exist between values and attitudes. Attitudes are specific and related to distinct objects, people, or ideas; values are more general and are not related to any object or situation. In addition to being more general than attitudes, values often contain statements of goodness or badness associated with the attitudes which people hold. Values are, then, beliefs about which attitudes we should have or how we should behave.

VALUES AND BEHAVIOUR

Behaviour of people is influenced by the values which they hold, particularly in terms of those stimuli which have some value orientations. In the organisational context, understanding the influence of individuals' value systems on their behaviour is important. Values influence the behaviour of individuals in the following manner:

1. Values influence an individual's perception about the problems he faces and consequently the decisions he makes to overcome those problems. For example, top management influences choice of organisational goals and strategies adopted to achieve those goals.
2. Values influence the way in which an individual looks at other individuals and groups of individuals, that is, interpersonal relationships. Values become the basis of such interpersonal interactions.
3. Individuals judge organisational success as well as its achievement on the basis of their value systems. Thus, for some individuals, organisational success may be in the form of high-profit earning irrespective of the means adopted whereas, this may be a mean thing for other individuals.
4. Individuals set limit for the determination of what is ethical or unethical behaviour for themselves as well as for others.
5. Values determine the context to which individuals accept organisational pressures and goals. If these do not match with the value held by them, they thwart the organisational pressure and goals and even leave the organisation.

LEARNING

Concept of Learning

According to the dictionary of psychology, learning means 'the process of acquiring the ability to respond adequately to a situation which may or may not have been previously encountered.

Sanford has defined learning as a relatively enduring change in behaviour brought about as a consequences of experience. In the context of organisational behaviour too, learning is defined in this way. Mitchell has defined learning as follows:

"Learning is the process by which new behaviours are acquired. It is generally agreed that learning involves changes in behaviour, practising new behaviours, and establishing permanency in the change."

We take learning as a relatively enduring change in behaviour due to experience.

Nature of Learning

Based on the definition of Learning, the nature of learning is as follows :

1. Learning involves a change in behaviour, though this change is not necessarily an improvement over previous behaviour. Learning generally has the connotation of improved behaviour, but bad habits, prejudices, stereotypes and work restrictions are also learned.
2. The behavioural change must be relatively permanent. Any temporary change in behaviour due to fatigue or any reason is not a part of learning.

3. The behavioural change must be based on same form of practice or experience.
4. The practice or experience must be reinforced in order for learning to occur.

Learning and Maturation

Any behavioural change because of physical maturation is not learning but this is natural outcome because of change in physical features. According to Boring, "maturity is a primary development which should exist before the learned action or behaviour. The development of physical abilities is called maturation". Nature of changes in behaviour due to maturation and learning is presented below:

1. Behavioural changes due to maturation are natural, while for learning, a person has to make efforts.
2. Changes in behaviour due to maturation are racial, but in the case of learning these changes are only in the person who learns.
3. Practice of behavioural change is necessary in learning but it is not necessary in the case of maturation.
4. Generally, maturation takes place upto the age of 25 years but a person can go on learning throughout the life.
5. Maturation takes place irrespective of the conditions, favourable or unfavourable, but learning is possible only in the favourable conditions.
6. Since maturity is a natural process, it does not require motivation to change behaviour but learning is cognitive process which is affected by motivation in some form.

Components of Learning Process

To understand the learning process, it is important to understand the role of various components of learning. These components are as follows :

- Drive
- Cue Stimuli
- Response
- Reinforcement, and
- Retention

Drive: Learning frequently occurs in the presence of drive— any strong stimulus that impels action. Without drive, learning does not take place because drive arouses an individual and keeps him readily to respond; thus, it is the basis for motivation. A motive differs from drive mainly in that it is purposeful, or directed towards the specific goal, whereas drive refers to an increased probability of activity without specifying the nature of the activity. Drives are basically of two types-primary or physiological drives and secondary or psychological drives. To predict behaviour, it is necessary to establish which drives are stimulating the most.

Cue Stimuli: Cue stimuli are any objects existing in the environment as perceived by the individual. It is common to speak of cue stimuli simply as stimuli or to use the term cue and stimuli interchangeably. The idea here is to discover the condition under which a stimulus will increase the probability of eliciting a specific response. There may be two types of stimuli so far as their results in terms of response are concerned; (1) generalisation and (2) discrimination.

1. Generalisation: Generalisation occurs when a response is elicited by a similar but new stimulus. If two stimuli are exactly alike, they will have the same probability of evoking a specified response, but the more dissimilar the stimuli become, the lower will be the probability of evoking the same response. The principal of generalisation has important implications for human learning. It makes possible stability in man's action across the time. Because of generalisation, a person does not have to completely relearn each of the new tasks or object which constantly confront him. It allows the organisational members to adapt to overall changing conditions and specific new or modified job assignment. The individual can borrow from past learning experience to adjust more smoothly to new learning situations. However, there are certain negative implications of generalisation for learning. A person may take false conclusion because of generalisation. For example, stereotyping or halo effect in perception occurs because of generalisation.

2. Discrimination: Discrimination is opposite of generalisation. This is process whereby an organism learns to emit a response to a stimulus but avoids making the same response to a similar but somewhat different stimulus. For example, a rat may learn to respond to the white colour but not to the black.

Discrimination has wide application in organisational behaviour. For example, a supervisor can discriminate between two equally high producing workers, one with low quality and other with high quality. The supervisor discriminates between the two workers and positively respond only to the quality conscious worker. As there is no positive response (reinforcement) the low quality producing worker may extinct his learning.

Responses: The stimulus results in responses. Responses may be in the physical form or may be in terms of attitudes, familiarity perception or other complex phenomena. Usually, learning psychologists attempt measurement of learning in behavioural terms, that is, responses must be operationally defined and preferable physically observable.

Reinforcement: Reinforcement is a fundamental condition of learning. Without reinforcement, no measurable modification of behaviour takes place. The term reinforcement is very closely related to the psychological process of motivation. Reinforcement may be defined as environmental events affecting the probability of occurrence of responses with which they are associated. The role of enforcement in learning is very important.

Retention: The stability of learned behaviour over time is defined as retention and the converse is forgetting. Some of the learning is retained over a period of time, while other may be forgotten. Extinction is a specific form of forgetting.

Extinction may be defined as a loss of memory. Extinction of a well learned response is usually difficult to achieve because once something is learned, it is never truly unlearned. Thus extinction merely means that the response in question has been repressed or it may be replaced by learning of incompatible response. Thus under repeated conditions of non-reinforcement, there is a tendency for the conditioned response to decrease or disappear.

The return of response strength after extinction, without intervening reinforcement, is called spontaneous recovery. Spontaneous recovery is not unusual among people when they are confused under stress or in other unusual states. In such situation, they sometimes will recover response tendencies that have been extinguished for many years. The original response strength of an extinguished behaviour can be recovered when a previously extinguished response is rewarded in an isolated instance.

Factors Affecting Learning

Since learning is an acquired process, it is quite natural that several factor may affect the process. Understanding of these factors is important for management because it can organise its learning programmes through training or otherwise for improving the behaviour of employees at the work place. The major factors affecting learning are as follows :

- Motivation
- Mental Set
- Nature of Learning Materials
- Practice
- Environment

Motivation: Learner's motivation is one of the major conditions for learning. Motivation is something that moves a person to action and continues him in the course of action already initiated. This course of action includes learning too. A positive behaviour developed through learning results into rewards while a negative behaviour results into punishment. Thus, the degree of the learner's motivation is positively associated with his learning.

Mental Set: Mental set refers to the preparation for an action, in this content learning. If a person is prepared to act, he can do the things quickly and in no time. Without mental set, learning cannot go smoothly and easily. It happens so because the person's mental set activates him to do the act, and due to his level of activation, he gets inclined to perform the act. Various research studies also support this view.

Nature of Learning Materials: Nature of learning materials affects learning by providing the clue for understanding. There are a number of features of the learning materials which affect learning. First, if the learning material is of easy nature, it is learned quickly whereas difficult material takes time to understand. Second, familiarity with learning materials affects learning. If the learner is familiar with the learning materials, he can learn more quickly as compared to when he is unfamiliar with these. Third, serial position, shape, and meaningfullness of learning materials also affect learning. If these features are positive, learning takes place at faster rate.

Practice: Practice is a very basic external condition of learning and affects all types of learning. The more a person practices, more he absorbs learning contents. Most of the motor skills (like typing, swimming, etc.) are learned based on this principle.

Environment: Environment in which learning process occurs, affects learning. Environment, here refers to the situational set up for learning. Environmental factors can be either strengthen or weaken the innate ability to achieve and learn. Environment with high pressure and high rate of change increases the likelihood of stress and has negative impact on learning. Environment with features of support, cohesion, and affiliation has positive impact on learning.

LEARNING THEORIES

Learning is the acquisition of new behaviour. People acquire new behaviour frequently. However, experts do not agree on what is the process through which new behaviour is acquired, and still there is disagreement on the theory behind it. This has resulted into the development of many theories of learning. Many of these theories are well-established while others are in the process of evolution. These theories can be grouped into three categories:

1. Conditioning theory
2. Cognitive Learning Theory
3. Social Learning Theory

MOTIVATION

Concept of Motivation

Today, virtually all people— lay people and scholars— have their own concept of motivation and they include various terms like motives, needs, wants, drives, desires, wishes, incentive, etc. in defining motivation. Technically, the term motivation can be traced to the Latin word mover, which means "to move". In order to understand the concept of motivation, we have to examine three terms: motive, motivating and motivation and their relationship Fig. 5.

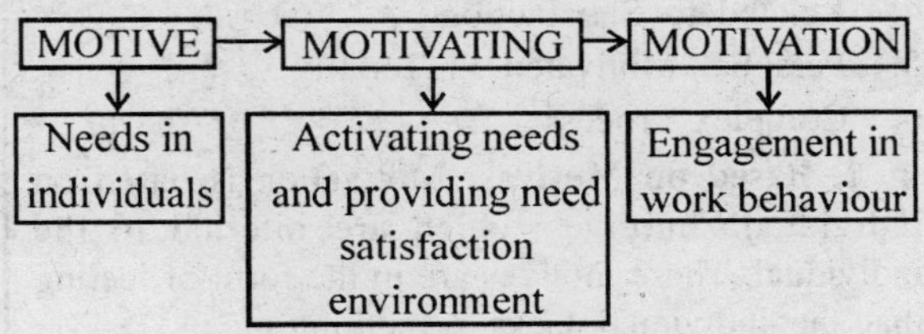

Fig. 5. *Relationship between Motive, Motivating and Motivation*

Motive: The word motive has been defined as follows :

"A motive is an inner state that energies, activates, or moves and that directs behaviour towards goals."

Motive has also been described as follows :

"A motive is restlessness, a lack, a yen, a force. Once in the grip of a motive, the organism does something to reduce the restlessness, to remedy the lack, to alleviate the yen, to mitigate the force."

Motivating: Motivating is a term which implies that one person, in the organisational context a manager, induces another, say employee, to engage in action by ensuring that a channel to satisfy the motive becomes available and accessible to the individual.

Motivation: Motivation depends on motives and motivating. Dubin has defined motivation as follows:

"Motivation is the complex forces starting and keeping a person at work in an organisation.

Motivation is something that moves the person to action, and continues him in the course of action already initiated.

According to McFarland: "Motivation refers to the way in which urges, drives, desires, aspirations, striving or needs direct, control or explain the behaviour of human beings."

Nature of Motivation

From the definition of motivation, we can derive the following characteristics of motivation:

1. Based on Motives
2. Affected by Motivating
3. Goal-directed Behaviour
4. Related to Satisfaction
5. Personal Motivated in Totality
6. Complex Process

1. Based on Motives: Motivation is based on individual's motives which are internal to the individual. These motives are in the form of feeling that the individual lacks something.

2. Affected by Motivating: Motivation is affected by way the individual is motivated. The act of motivating channelises the need of satisfaction.

3. Goal-Directed Behaviour: Motivation leads to goal-directed behaviour. A goal-directed behaviour is one which satisfies the causes for which behaviour takes place.

4. Related to Satisfaction: Motivation is related to satisfaction. Satisfaction refers to the contentment experiences of an individual which he derives out of need fulfillment.

5. Person Motivated in Totality: A person is motivated in totality and not in part. Each individual in the organisation is a self-contained unit and his needs are interrelated.

6. Complex Process: Motivation is a complex process; complexity emerges because of the nature of needs and the type of behaviour that is attempted to satisfy those needs. These generate complexity in motivation process in the following ways:

(*i*) Needs are internal feelings of individuals and sometimes, even they, themselves, may not be quite aware about their needs and the priority of these. Thus, understanding of human needs and providing means for their satisfaction becomes difficult.

(*ii*) Even if needs are identified the problems is not over here as a particular need may result into different behaviour from different individuals because of their differences.

(*iii*) A particular behaviour may emerge not only because of the specific need but it may be because of a variety of needs.

(*iv*) Goal-directed behaviour may not lead to goal attainment. There may be many constraints in the situation which may restrain the goal attainment of goal-directed behaviour. This may result frustration in an individual creating lot of problems.

Types of Needs: Needs may be grouped into following three categories:

1. Primary needs
2. Secondary needs
3. General needs

1. Primary Needs: Primary needs are also known as physiological, biological, basic, or unlearned needs. Primary needs are animal drives which are essential for survival. These needs are common to all human beings, though their intensity may differ. Some of the needs are food, sex, sleep, air to breathe, etc.

2. Secondary Needs: Secondary needs are not natural but are learned by the individual through his experience and interaction. Therefore, these are also called learned or derived needs. There may be different types of secondary needs like need for power, achievement, status, affiliation, etc.

3. General Needs: There are a number of needs which lie in the grey area between the primary and secondary classification. To be included in this category, a need must not be learned but at the same, it is not completely physiological. In fact, there are certain such needs like need for competence, curiosity, manipulation, affection, etc.

MOTIVATION AND BEHAVIOUR

Motivation causes goal-directed behaviour. Need is the base for motivation which is a kind of mental feeling in an individual that he needs something. This lack of something creates tension in the mind of the individual. Since, tension is not an ideal state of mind, the individual tries to overcome this by engaging himself in a behaviour through which he satisfies his needs. This is goal-directed behaviour and is presented in the Fig. 6.

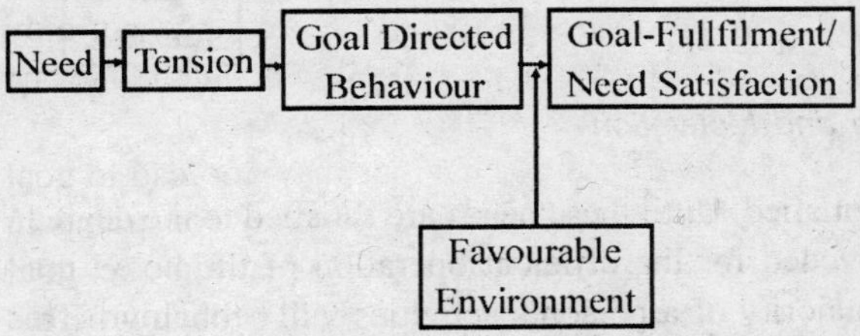

Fig. 6. *GDAL-Directed Behaviour*

Goal directed behaviour leads to goal-fulfillment and the individual succeeds in fulfilling his needs and thereby overcoming his tension in the favourable environment. The goal-directed behaviour is a continuous process.

However, if the need is not satisfied, the person may feel frustration which can be defined as the accumulation of tension due to non-fulfillment of needs. The type of behaviour may not be uniform but some common forms of behaviour are presented in the Fig. 7.

Defence Mechanism: Frustration may lead to any of the defence mechanism used by human organism, that is, any of the actions. Thus defence mechanism is the way of action for overcoming frustration because of non-fulfillment of needs so that the individual can protect his self-concept. There can be three types of mechanisms

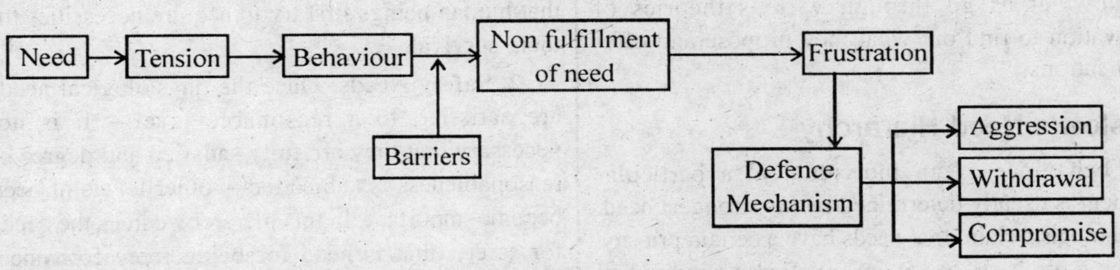

Fig. 7. *Need non-fulfillment and Defence Mechanism*

- aggression,
- withdrawal, and
- compromise

Motivation and Performance

Motivation is necessary for performance. If people do not feel inclined to engage themselves in work behaviour, they will not put in necessary effort to perform well. However, performance of an individual in the organisation depends on other factors too besides his level of motivation. How motivation works alongwith other factors to influence performance is present in the Fig. 8.

We can derive from figure that the performance of an individual in the organisation is affected by:

1. motivation of the individual
2. his sense of competence
3. his abilities
4. his role perception, and
5. organisational resources

THEORIES OF MOTIVATION

When human organisations were established, people had tried to find out the answer of 'what motivates people in the organisation most'. The starting was made by Fredric W. Taylor and his followers Frank Gilbreth, Lillian Gilbreath, and Henary Gnatt, in the form of scientific management and more particularly 'differential piece rate systems'. Maslow gave the theory of need hierarchy, Herzberg proposed two-factor theory; McClelland emphasised on power, affiliation, and achievement motives; and Alderfer proposed three groups of core needs: existence, relatedness, and growth (ERG model).

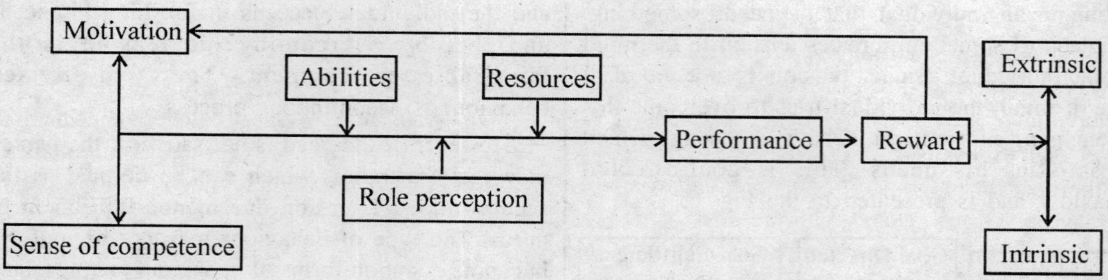

Fig. 8. *Performance and Motivation*

Some scholars tried to relate the nature of human beings with the work motivation. Though these propositions are not confined to work motivation, they offer some insights in understanding work motivation. Prominent theories in this group are Mcgregor's theories X and Y, and Ouchi's theory Z.

Now let us go through various theories of motivation to find out what they propose and offer implications.

Maslow's Need Hierarchy

The behaviour of an individual at a particular moment is usually determined by his strongest need. Psychologists claim that needs have a certain priority. As the more basic needs are satisfied, an individual seeks to satisfy the higher needs. If his basic needs are not met, efforts to satisfy the higher needs should be postponed. A. H. Maslow, a famous social scientist, has given a framework that helps to explain the strength of certain needs. According to him, hierarchy of human needs are arranged in the Fig. 9.

1. Physiological: The physiological needs are at the top of the hierarchy because they tend to have the highest strength until they are reasonably

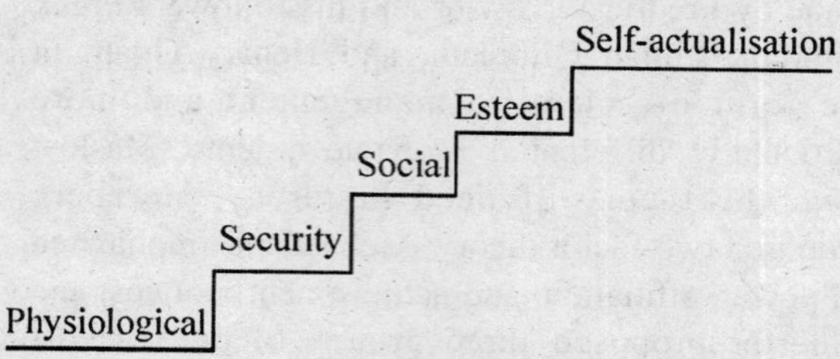

Fig. 9. *Maslow's Need Hierarchy*

satisfied. Until these needs are satisfied to the degree needed for the efficient operation of the body; the majority of a person's activities will probably be at this level, and the other levels will provide him with little motivation. A famous saying 'man can live on bread alone if there is no bread' suggests that human beings first try to acquire necessities for their survival.

2. Safety Needs: Once the physiological needs are satisfied to a reasonable level— it is not necessary that they are fully satisfied and degree of reasonableness is subjective— other levels of need become important. In this hierarchy comes the needs for safety, that is need for being free of physical danger or self-preservation. In the industrial society, safety needs may take considerable importance in the context of the dependent relationship of employees to employers. As pointed out by Mcgregor, the safety needs may serve as motivators in such circumstances as arbitrary management actions.

3. Social Needs: After the first two needs are satisfied, social needs become important in the need hierarchy. Since man is a social being, he has a need to belong and to be accepted by various groups. When social needs become dominant, a person will strive for meaningful relations with others.

4. Esteem Needs: The esteem needs are concerned with self-respect, self-confidence, a feeling of personal worth, feeling of being unique and recognition. Satisfaction of these needs produces feelings of self-confidence, power and control. The satisfaction of esteem needs is not always obtained through mature or adaptive behaviour.

5. Self-Actualisation Needs: Self-actualisation is the need to maximise one's potential, whatever it may be. This is related with the development of intrinsic capabilities which lead people to seek situations that can utilise their potential. This includes competence which implies control over environmental factors, both physical and social, and achievement. A man with high intensity of achievement needs will be restless unless he can find fulfillment in doing what he is fitted to do. As Maslow has put it, "this need might be phrased as the desire to become more and more what one is, to become everything that one is capable of becoming."

Maslow suggests that the various levels are interdependent and overlapping, each higher-level need emerging before the lower-level needs has been completely satisfied as shown in the Fig. 10. Since one's need does not disappear when another emerges, all needs tend to be partially satisfied in each area. When the peak of a need is passed, that need ceases to be the primary motivator. Even though a need is satisfied, it still influences behaviour because of interdependent and overlapping characteristic of needs.

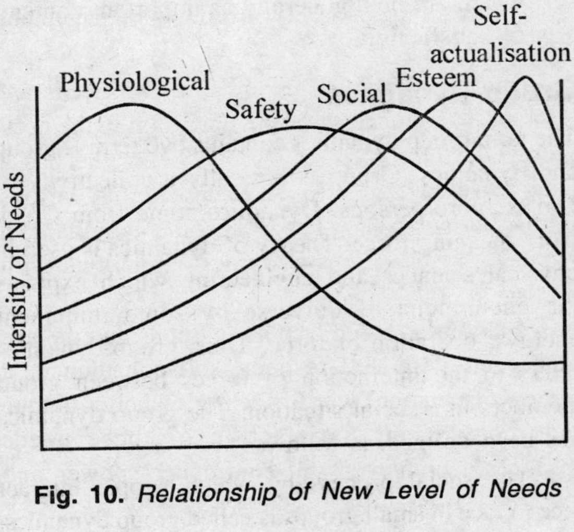

Fig. 10. *Relationship of New Level of Needs*

Critical Analysis of Maslow's Theory

Maslow's theory has reasonable support for the hypothesis that human needs have some hierarchy order. The theory is based on the assumption, it is true also that man is continuously wanting. His all needs are never fully satisfied.

1. There is a lack of hierarchy structure of needs as suggested by Maslow, though every individual has some ordering for his need satisfaction. This is based on the assumption that man has limited resources which he can use alternatively. Naturally, every person has to satisfy his needs in some order. However, this order may not follow Maslow's need hierarchy.
2. There is another problem, which is common with many other theories also that there is often a lack of direct cause-effect relationship between need and behaviour.
3. There is another problem in applying the theory into practice. A person tries for his higher-level need when his lower-order need is reasonably satisfied. What is this reasonable level is a question of subjective matter. Thus, the level of satisfaction for particular need may differ from person to person. Infact, needs and their satisfaction are mental feelings.

HERZBERG'S MOTIVATION-HYGIENE THEORY

It will be either directed towards achieving certain desirable positive goals or conversely towards avoiding other undesirable, negative consequences. Thus, a question may arises as to what variables are perceived to be desirable to achieve goals, and conversely, undesirable conditions to avoid. In this connection, a research study was conducted by Fredrick Herzberg of Case-Western Reserve University and associates. This study consisted of an intensive analysis of the experiences and feelings of 200 engineers and accountants in nine different companies in Pittsburgh area, USA. During the structured interview, they were asked to describe a few previous job experiences in which they felt 'exceptionally good' or 'exceptionally bad' about jobs. They were also asked to rate the degree to which their feeling were influenced— for better or worse— by each experience which they described.

In concluding the information from the interview, Herzberg concluded that there were two categories of needs essentially independent of each other affecting behaviour in different ways. His findings are that there are same job conditions which operate primarily to dissatisfy employees when the conditions are absent, their presence does not motivate them in a strong way. Another set of job conditions operate primarily to build strong motivation and high job satisfaction, but their absence rarely proves strongly dissatisfying. The first set of job conditions has been referred to as maintenance or hygiene factor and second set of job conditions as motivational factor.

Hygiene Factors; According to Herzberg, there are ten maintenance or hygiene factors. These are company policy and administration, technical supervision, interpersonal relationship with supervisors, interpersonal relationship with peers, interpersonal relationships with subordinates, salary, job security, personal life, working conditions and status. These are not intrinsic parts of a job, but they are related to conditions under which a job is performed.

Motivational Factors: These factors are capable of having positive effect on job satisfaction often resulting in an increase in one's total output. Herzberg includes six factors that motivate employees. These are achievement, recognition, advancement, work itself, possibility of growth, and responsibility. An increase in these factors will satisfy the employees; however, any decrease will not affect their level of satisfaction.

Sometimes, it is also influenced by the personality and characteristics of the individuals. From this point of view individuals may be classified into two parts — motivation seekers and maintenance seekers. The motivation seekers generally are individuals who are primarily motivated by the 'satisfiers' such as advancement, achievement and other factors associated with work itself. On the other hand, the maintenance seekers tend to be more concerned with factors surrounding the job such as supervision working conditions, pay, etc.

Critical Analysis of the Theory: Herzberg's model is based on the fact that most of the people are able to satisfy their lower order needs considerably. As such, they are not motivated by any further addition of satisfaction of these needs. Herzberg's model has been applied in the industry and has given several new insights. One of these insights is job enrichment. This job enrichment applies to improvement of jobs in such a way that they have more motivators than before.

However, Herzberg's model is not applied in all conditions. Besides, the research studies confronting the two factors-satisfiers and dissatisfiers many writers and thinkers on the subject have argued against the theory as follows :

1. In fact, job satisfaction and dissatisfaction are two opposite points on a single continuum. Individuals on the job are affected by any change either in the job environment or in the job content.
2. Herzberg's model is 'method bound', and a number of other methods used for similar study have shown different results not supporting his contentions. Thus, the theory has limitations in general acceptability.
3. This theory does not attach much importance to pay, status , or interpersonal relationships which are held generally as important contents of satisfaction.

Group Dynamics

The term group dynamics contains two terms : group and dynamics. Group is basically a collectivity of two or more persons. Dynamics come from Greek work meaning force. Theory of dynamics is used in physical sciences and engineering which explains the phenomena of universe by some immanent energy : operation of force. Thus, group dynamics refers to the interaction of forces between group members in a social situation. The group dynamics has been defined as follows:

"The social process by which people interact face to face in small groups is called group dynamics.

Features of Group

1. Two or More Persons: To form a group, there should be at least two persons because a single individual cannot interact. There is no specific limit on the maximum number of persons in a group.

2. Collective Identity: Members of the group must be aware about their membership of the group. Each member of the group must believe that he is a member of some specific group.

3. Interaction: Member of group interact among themselves. Interaction means that each member shares his ideas with others through communication and this communication can take place face to face, in writing, over the telephone, across a computer network, or in any other manner which allows communica-tion among group members.

4. Shared Goal Interest: Members of the group should subscribe to the attainment of some common objectives.

Types of Groups

An analytical classification of the group may be :

- Primary And Secondary Groups.
- Membership And Reference Groups.
- Command And Task Groups.
- In-Groups And Out-Groups.

1. Primary and Secondary Groups: A primary group is characterised by intimate, face-to-face association and co-operation. The membership of such a group is small and is based on intimate relationship. Examples of such groups may be family, friendship groups, or neighborhood groups. A secondary group is more formal, general and remote. The members of the secondary group may not have any interest in the problems and pleasures of others. The continuous interaction, intimacy, face-to-face interaction, co-operation and association of primary groups may not be found in secondary groups.

2. Membership And Reference Groups: A membership group is one to which an individual really belongs while a reference group is one with which the individual identifies or to which he would like to belong. In fact, an individual may be member of several groups at a time but he may not participate actively in all such groups but he would like to participate in that whose norms are more attractive and gratifying. The attractiveness of the reference group makes the norms of that group more attractive to the individual who aspires to it and its norms will, therefore, become more influential in determining behaviour. The reference groups have more relevance to organisational behaviour.

3. Command And Task Groups: A command group is composed of the subordinates who report directly to a common superior. This type of group is determined by organisational chart. Example of such a group may be a production manager and his subordinates in his department, a college principal and teachers, and so on. A task group is comprised of the employees who work together to complete a particular task or project. A task group is usually formed to solve a problem or perform an activity that involves a number of organisational units. Thus, membership of the task group may extend beyond the hierarchical command of a superior.

4. In-groups and Out-groups: The in-group represents a clustering of individuals holding prevailing values in a society or, at least, having a dominant place in social functioning. It can be a majority numerically, or it may represent the power structure with its pattern of behaviour considered desirable. The out-group is the conglomerate looked up as subordinate or marginal in the society, it is usually referred to as the minority group even though in certain instances, it may represent a numerical majority.

Formal And Informal Groups

In organisational setting, there may be two types of groups which are classified on the basis of structure. These are formal and informal.

Formal groups are created and maintained to fulfill specific needs or tasks which are related to the total organisational mission. Thus these are consciously and deliberately created. Such groups may be either permanent in the form of top management team such as board of directors or management committees, work units in the various departments of the organisation, staff groups providing specialised services to the organisation, and so on, or the formal groups may be constituted on temporary basis for fulfilling certain specified objectives. When such objectives are fulfilled they disappear. These may be in the form of temporary committee, task-force, etc.

On the other hands, informal groups are created in the organisation because of operation of social and psychological forces operating at the work place. Members create such groups for their own satisfaction and their working is not regulated by the general framework of organisational rules and regulations. Thus formal and informal organisations differ from each other, and understanding of difference between formal and informal organisation has important implications for managers.

Formal Groups

Almost in every large organisation, some formal groups are created to serve organisational purposes. These groups are required because of the following factors :

1. to accomplish tasks that cannot be done by employees individually;
2. to bring a number of skills and talents to bear on complex, difficult tasks;
3. to provide a vehicle for decision making that permits multiple and conflicting views to be aired and considered;
4. to provide an efficient means for control of employees' behaviour;
5. to provide changes in organisational policies or procedures;
6. to increase organisational stability by transmitting shared beliefs and values to new employees;
7. to aid individuals in gaining new skills and learning about the organisation and its environment; and
8. to satisfy important personal needs, specially needs for social acceptance and affiliations.

In an organisation, several groups may be created to serve specific needs. Such groups may be in the form of :

I. Committee
II. Task Force
III. Quality Circle

Informal Groups

Informal group, also called as informal organisation, is created because of the limitations of formal one. The actual organisational structure is the result of the formal and informal relationships. The first basic issue in analysing informal organisations is to identify the basic logic behind the formation of informal groups as these are not created by the management of the organisation but emerge on their own. Various theories have been formulated. These theories are :

1. Propinquity Theory
2. Homan's interaction Theory
3. Balance Theory, and
4. Exchange Theory

Characteristics of Formal Organisation

The formal organisation (mostly referred to structure) is deliberately designed to achieve some particular objectives. It refers to the structure of well-defined jobs, each bearing a definite authority, responsibility and accountability. According to classical theorists, the formal organisation is built on four pillars :

1. division of labour
2. scalar and functional processes
3. structure, and
4. span of control,

These are referred to as principles of organisation. From this point of view, characteristics of formal organisations are as follows :

1. Organisation structure is designed by the top management to fulfil certain requirements-performance of necessary activities thereby achieving organisational goals.
2. Organisation structure is based on the principles of division of labour and efficiency in operations.
3. Organisation concentrates more on the performance of jobs (conglomerate of

activities) and not on the individuals performing the jobs.

4. The authority and responsibility assigned to each job have to be adhere to by the job holders. Based on the concept of authority and responsibility, people are placed on hierarchy, and their status is determined accordingly.
5. Co-ordination among members and their control are well specified through processes, procedures, rules etc.

Characteristics of Informal Organisation

Informal organisation refers to the natural grouping of people on the basis of some similarity in an organisation. For example, Litterer has viewed that "the informal organisation refers to people in group associations at work, but these associations are not specified in the blueprint of the formal organisation. The informal organisation means natural groupings of people in the work situation. Whenever people work together, they evolve some sort of grouping or pattern of relationships among them which is not according to what is prescribed by the formal organisations. Such relationships may be more complex than the officially prescribed ones. For example, Davis observes that "beneath the clock of formal relationships in every institutions, there exists a more complex system of social relationships called the informal organisation". From this point of view, characteristics of informal organisation are as follows :

1. Informal organisation is a natural outcome at the work place. It is not designed and planned.
2. Informal organisation is created on the basis of some similarity among its members. The bases of similarity may be age, sex, place of origin, caste, religion, personality characteristics, linkings/dislikings, etc.
3. Membership in an informal organisation is voluntary. A person may become member of several informal organisations at the same time.
4. Behaviour of members of the informal organisation is co-ordinated and controlled by group norms and not by the norms of the formal organisation.

Formal and Informal Organisation: a Comparison

Basis of comparison	Formal organisation	Informal organisation
Formation	Planned and deliberate	Spontaneous
Purpose	Well-set goals	Social interaction
Structure	Well structured	Unstructured
Nature	Official	Unofficial
Focus	Positions	Persons
Leadership	Superior	Anyone
Source of power	Delegated	Given by group
Guidelines for behaviour	Rules and procedures	Group norms
Sources of control	Reward/punishment	Sanctions

COMMUNICATION

Concept of Communication

The word communica-tion has been derived from the Latin word communis which means common.

Newstrom and Davis have defined communication as follows :

"Communication is the transfer of information from one person to another person. It is a way of reaching others by transmitting ideas, facts, thoughts, feelings and values".

Communication Process

Communication has been defined as a process. The term process refers to identifiable flow of information through interrelated stages of analysis directed towards the achievement of an objective.

Elements of Communication Process: Communication, being a process must have some elements to complete the process. The elements of communication are given below (in Fig. 11) :

1. Sender
2. Message
3. Encoding
4. Channel
5. Receiver
6. Decoding
7. Feedback

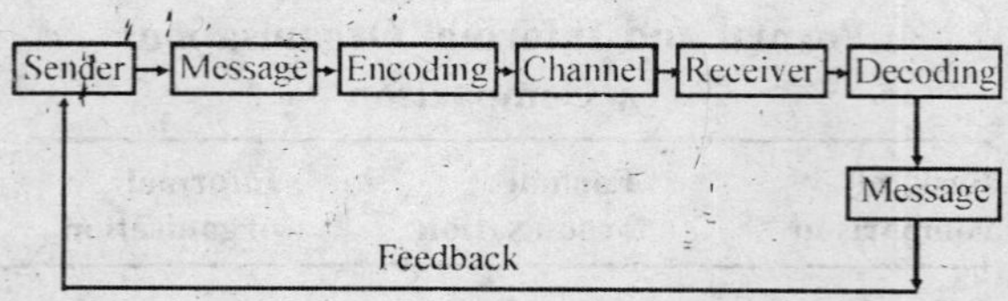

Fig. 11. *Communication Process With Feedback*

1. Sender: Sender of the message is the person who intends to make contact with the objective of passing the message to other persons. In organisational context, sender may be a superior, a subordinate, a peer, or any other person. The organisational position of the sender determines the direction of flow of the communication in an organisation.

2. Message: This is the subject matter of the communication which is intended to be passed to the receiver from the sender. The message may be in the form of ideas, opinions, feelings, views, suggestions, orders etc.

3. Encoding: Since the subject matter of communication is abstract and intangible, its transmission requires the use of certain symbols such as words, pictures, gestures, etc. The process of converting the message into communication symbols is known as encoding.

4. Channel: Message encoded into symbols is transmitted by the sender through a channel like written form, personal contact, phone call, etc. depending on the situation of two parties sender and receiver.

5. Receiver: Receiver is the person to whom the symbols are transmitted. Like sender, he may be a superior, subordinate, peer or any other person in the organisation.

6. Decoding: Decoding is the reverse of encoding. The receiver receives the subject matter of communication in the form of communication symbols in which the sender has encoded his message. The receiver decodes these symbols into message.

7. Feedback: Feedback is necessary to ensure that the receiver has received the message and understood it in the same sense as the sender intended. Further, it acts as an energising factor, thereby changing the course of action in the communication.

Functions of Communication

The various functions that are performed by communication are given as follows :

- Information Function
- Command and Instructive Function
- Influence and Persuasive Function
- Integrative Function

1. Information Function: Information is, vital for the functioning of any living system people or organisation. Living systems can achieve some viability in their environments only to the extent that they have some appropriate means of acquiring and processing information about themselves and their environments. This information is used as the basis for orientation to those environments and for determining their behaviour. The technology of communication has greatly enhanced man's information-generating capacities. It is our ability to affect each other communicatively which has so greatly increased the importance of the information giving and receiving aspect of our existence. As a consequence, we can create purposive organisations of people variously committed to some common endeavour. It is particularly the existence of such purposive organisations which gives rise to the importance of information-giving and receiving. No organisation can fulfil its purpose except to the extent that its communication process furthers its movement towards its specific goals in some way.

2. Command and Instructive Function: Communication performs command and instructive function. Those who are hierarchicaly superior—whether in family, business, civil, or millitary—often initiate communication not only for the purpose of informing their subordinates and often for the purpose of telling them what to do, directing them, or commanding their behaviour in some way. The command and instructive function of communication is more observable in formal organisations than it is in informal organisation. Individuals who are hierarchically superior within an organisation structure are both privileged and obligated to command and control certain task related behaviours of their subordinates. Those same subordinates have a similar obligation and privilege vis-a-vis their own subordinates, and so on from the top to the bottom of the organisational hierachy. Orders, directives, requests, procedures, even performance, appraisal all function as command messages.

3. Influence and Persuasive Function: Of all that has been written about communication over the years, perhaps more has been written about the persuasive function of communication than about any other aspect. There are those who take the position that all communication is persuasive in character. However, in management, influence and persuasion taken together represent one of the several functions as other functions are equally important. Managers can influence others either through coercively or communicatively. Since influence through coercion has its limitations in organisational setting, managers can do well to influence others through effective communication. In fact, leadership is more effective than exercise of authority in getting the maximum from the employees. Leadership, to a very great extent, depends upon how the manager communi-cates with his employees and others who may be related with the organisation in one way or the other.

4. Integrative Function: Communication performs the integrative function by relating various components of the organisation and maintaining equilibrium among them. In the broadest sense, the integration aspect includes all behavioural operations which (i) serve to keep the system in operation (ii) serve to regulate the interactional process, and (iii) relate the particular context to the larger context of which the particular interaction is but a special situation. The communication that occurs has the consequence of energising, organising and channelising the behaviour of living systems. However, if the messages we create in order to comprehend our environment are not cumulative and self-organising in some way, it would be impossible to gain or to maintain the necessary degree of equilibrium or stable state relations with various aspects of environment. For example, at the larger than face-to-face human groups, some formalisation takes place and integrative functions are provided in part by bureaucratisation, proceduralisation, institutionalisation etc. In fact, when a social system exceeds the integrative limits of face-to-face interactions, the necessary integrative mechanisms become embedded in the social system's literature, art folklore, mythology, beliefs, mores, institutional practices etc.

Communication Network

A network is a structured fabric of the organisation, made up of system of lines, or channels, which are interconnected. Communication networks, then, are those network channels or lines used to pass information serially from one persons to another. We can safely say that organisational communication is really the flow of information through the networks of interrelated human roles. Organizational

Table 2. Differences Between Formal Communication and Informal Communication

Formal Communication	Informal Communication
1. It is based on formal organisational relationships.	It emerges out of social interactions among the people.
2. The channels of communication are prescribed.	Channels of communication depend on individuals' relationships
3. It is rigid as deviations are not allowed.	It is quite flexible because nothing is prescribed
4. The speed of message travel is slow because of formalisation	Message travels faster
5. Chances of message distortion are low.	Message are often distorted
6. It is treated as authentic.	It is not authentic even if the message is correct.

communication network is made up of two types of channels which are formal and informal

A message coming through the formal channel is known as formal communication and that coming through informal channel is known as informal communication. Differences between the two are presented in Table 2.

Formal Channel: The formal channel as the very name implies, is the deliberately created. officially created path for flow of communication between the various positions in the organisation. It is a deliberate attempt to regulate the flow of organisational communication so as to make it orderly and thereby to ensure that information flows smoothly, accurately and timely to the points to which it is required. The officially prescribed communication network may be designed on the basis of a single channel or multiple channels as shows in Fig. 12.

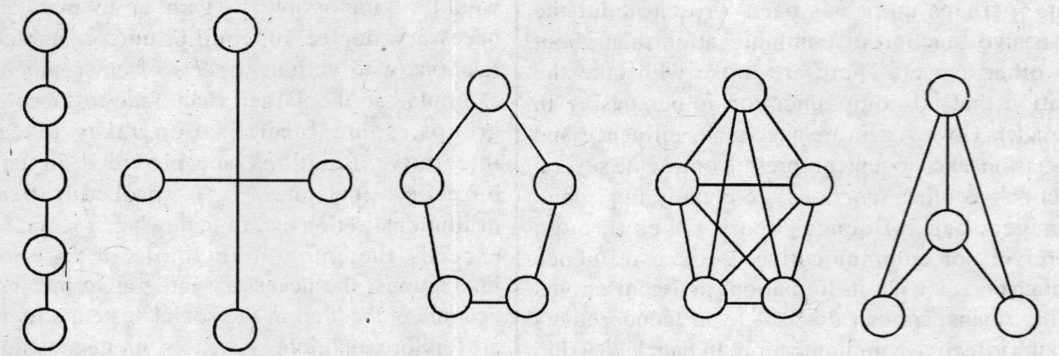

Chain Wheel Circular Free Flow Inverted

Fig. 12. *Communication Network*

Single Chain: Single chain communication network exists between a superior and his subordinate. Communication flows downward or upward through each successive level. Communication flow through the chain may be orderly and easy to control but it is very time consuming. We find such a communication network in bureaucratic organisations.

Wheel: In wheel network, all subordinates under one superior communicate through him only as he is the hub of the wheel. They are not allowed to communicate among themselves. Thus, there is no horizontal communication. In this network, problem of co-ordination is the main drawback.

Circular: In circular network, the communication moves in a circle. Each person can communicate with his adjoining two persons. In this network, communication flow is slow.

Free Flow: In this network, each person can communicate with others freely. In this network, communication flow is fast but problem of co-ordination exits. This is followed in free-form organisation or in task force.

Inverted V: In this network, an individual is allowed to communicate with his immediate superior as well as his superior's superior. In the later case, the subject matter of communication is prescribed. In such a network, communication travels faster.

Informal Channel or Grapevine: The informal channel of communication, also known as 'grapevine', is the result not of any official action, but of the operation of social forces at work place. The term grapevine arouse during the days of U.S. Civil War. At that time intelligence telephone lines were strung loosely from tree to tree in the manner of a grapevine, and the message thereon was often distorted, hence any rumour was said to be from the grapevine. Today, the term applies to all informal communication. Grapevine is more active when:

1. there is high organisational excitement such as policy changes like automation, computerisation etc., or personnel changes;

2. the information is new rather stale;
3. people are physically located close enough to communicate with one another; and
4. people cluster in cliques/groups along the grapevine, that is, they have trust among themselves.

Grapevine Network: Grapevine follows different types of network. Usually, there are four types of pattern through which grapevine travels. These are single strand, gossip, probability, and cluster. In each pattern, communication among different individuals is different as shown in the following Fig. 13.

In single strand network, the individual communicates with other individuals through intervening persons. In Gossip Network, the individual communicates non-selectively. In probability network, the individual communicates randomly with other individuals according to the law of probability. In Cluster Network, the individual communicates with only those individuals whom he trusts. Out of these informal networks, the cluster is the most popular.

Although grapevine informal tends to be orally, it may be in written form too. Sometimes, handwritten or typed notes are also used. In the modern electronic office, grapevine messages typically are flashed on computer screens, creating the new era of the electronic grapevine.

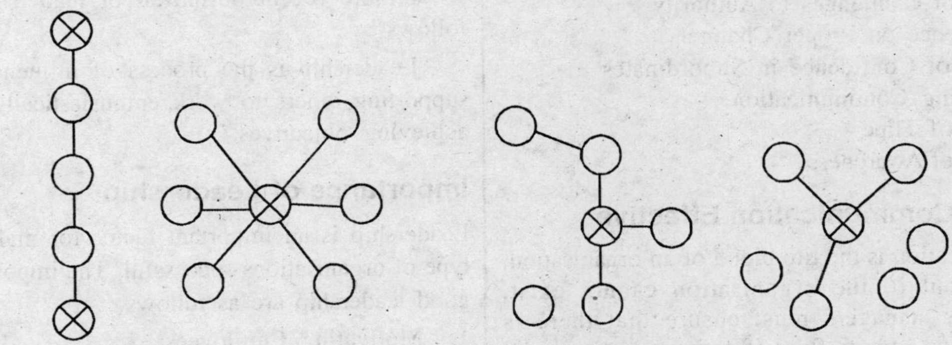

Fig. 13. *Informal communication Network*

Barriers In Communication

The problem of communication arises because there are various obstacles which may entirely prevent a communication, filter part of it out, or give it incorrect meaning. These obstacles are known as communication barriers.

Semantic Barriers: Semantics is the science of meaning, as contrasted with phonetics, the science of sounds. All communications are symbolic, that is, these use symbols (words, pictures, action, etc.) that suggest certain meanings. Semantic barriers arise from limitations in the symbols with which we communicate. Following types of semantic barriers are more prominent.

1. Symbols with Different Meanings
2. Badly Expressed Message
3. Faulty Translations
4. Unclarified Assumptions
5. Specialist's Language

Emotional or Psychological Barriers

Emotional or psychological factors are the prime barriers in interpersonal communication. Some emotional barriers are as follows:

1. Premature Evaluation
2. Inattention
3. Loss by Transmission and Poor Retention
4. Undue Reliance on the Written Word
5. Distrust of communicator
6. Failure to communicate

Organisational Barriers

An organisation being a deliberate creation for the attainment of certain specified objectives; day-to-day happenings within it require being regulated in such a manner that they contribute to attain these objectives in the most efficient manner. Major organisational barriers may be as follows :

1. Organisational Policy
2. Organisational Rules and Regulations
3. Status Relationships
4. Complexity in Organisational Structure
5. Organisational Facilities

Personal Barriers

1. Attitudes of Superiors
2. Fear of Challenges to Authority
3. Insistence on Proper Channel
4. Lack of Confidence in Subordinates
5. Ignoring Communication
6. Lack of Time
7. Lack of Awareness

Making Communication Effective

Communication is the life blood of an organisation, and without it, the organisation cannot exist. Therefore, managers must ensure that there is adequate and smooth flow of communication in all directions.

Steps for Making Communication Effective: Some general guidelines have been provided for effective communication:

1. Clarity in Idea
2. Purpose of Communication
3. Empathy in Communication
4. Two-way Communication
5. Appropriate Language
6. Supporting Words with Action
7. Credibility in Communication
8. Good Listening

LEADERSHIP

Concept of Leadership

Leadership is the process of influencing the behaviour of others to work willingly and enthusiastically for achieving predetermined goals. Tennenbaum *et al.* have defined leadership as follows:

"Leadership is interpersonal influence exercised in a situation and directed through communication process, towards the attainment of a specified goal or goals."

Terry has defined leadership in the context of enthusiastic contribution. He says that: "Leadership is essentially a continuous process of influencing behaviour. A leader breaths life into the group and motivates it towards goals. The lukewarm desires for achievement are transformed into a burning passion for accomplishment."

A more recent definition of leadership is as follows:

"Leadership is the process of influencing and supporting others to work enthusiastically toward achieving objectives."

Importance of Leadership

Leadership is an important factor for making any type of organisations successful. The importance of good leadership are as follows :

1. Motivating Employees
2. Creating Confidence
3. Building Morale

1. Motivating Employees: Motivation is necessary for work performance. Higher the motivation, better would be the performance. A good leader by exercising his leadership motivates the employees for high performance, good leadership in the organisation itself is a motivating factor for the individuals.

2. Creating Confidence: A good leader may create confidence in his followers by directing them, giving them advice and getting through them good results in the organisation. Once an individual with the help of a leader puts high efficiency, he tries to maintain it as he acquires certain level of confidence towards his capacity. Sometimes, individuals fail to recognise their qualities and capabilities to work in the absence of good direction.

3. Building Morale: Morale is expressed as attitudes of employees towards organisation, management and voluntary co-operation to offer their ability to the organisation. High morale leads to high productivity and organisational stability. Through providing good leadership in the organisation, employees' morale can be raised high ensuring high productivity and stability in the organisation.

Thus, good leadership is essentially in all aspects of managerial functions whether it be motivation, communication or direction. Good leadership ensures success in the organisation, and unsatisfactory human performance in any organisation can be primarily attributed to poor leadership.

LEADERSHIP THEORIES

Charismatic Leadership Theory

Charismatic leadership theory, also called **great man theory**. A leader has some Charisma which acts as influence. Charisma is a Greek word meaning gift. Thus, **Charisma** is a God-gifted attribute in a person which makes him a leader irrespective of the situations in which he works. **Charismatic leaders** are those who inspire followers and have a major impact on their organisations through thier organisations through their personal vision and energy.

The basic assumptions and implications of the theory are as follows :

1. Leaders in general, and great leaders in particular, have some exceptional inborn leadership qualities which are bestowed upon them by the divine power.
2. These inborn qualities are sufficient for a leader to be successful.
3. Since these qualities are inborn, these cannot be enhanced through education and training. Further, since these qualities are of personal nature, these cannot be shared by others.
4. These leadership qualities make a leader effective and situational factors do not have any influence.

Trait Theory

Trait is defined as relatively enduring quality of an individual. The trait approach seeks to determine 'what makes a successful leader' from the leader's own personal characteristic. From the very beginning, people have emphasised that a particular individual was successful leader because of his certain qualities or characteristics. A review of various research studies has been presented by Stogdill. According to him, various trait theories have suggested these traits in a successful leader :

(*i*) Physical and constitutional factors (heights, weight, physique, energy, health, appearance);
(*ii*) Intelligence
(*iii*) Self-confidence
(*iv*) Sociability
(*v*) Will (Initiative, persistence, ambition)
(*vi*) Dominance, and
(*vii*) Surgency (talkative, cheerfulness, geniality, enthusiasm, expressiveness, altertness, and originality).

The most important traits are a high level of personal drive, desire to lead, personal integrity, and self-confidence. Cognitive ability, business knowledge, charisma, creativity, flexibility, and personal warmths are also desired. The study highlighted 14 qualities. Accordingly, a chief executive thinks globally, anticipates cultural diversity, builds teamwork and partnership, embrace change, shows technological savvy, encourages constructive challenge, ensures customer satisfaction, achieves a competitive advantage, demonstrate personal mastery, shares leadership, and lives the values. The following are the major innate qualities in a successful leader:

1. Physical Features: Physical features of a man are determined by heredity factors. Heredity is the transmission of the qualities from ancestor to descendant through a mechanism lying primarily in the chromosomes of the germ cells. Physical characteristics and rate of maturation determine the personality formation which is an important factor in determining leadership success. To some extent, height, weight, physique, health and appearance are important for leadership.

2. Intelligence: For leadership, higher level of intelligence is required. Intelligence is generally expressed in terms of mental ability. Intelligence, to a very great extent, is a natural quality in the individuals because it is directly related to brain. The composition of brain is a natural factor, though many psychologists claim that the level of intelligence in an individual can be increased through various training methods.

Acquirable qualities of leadership are those which can be acquired and increased through various processes. In fact, when child is born, he learns many of the behavioural patterns through socialisation and identification processes. Following are the major qualities essential for leadership :

1. Emotional Stability
2. Human Relations
3. Empathy
4. Objectivity
5. Motivating Skills
6. Technical Skills
7. Communicative Skills
8. Social Skills

Implications of the Theory: This theory has two very important implications. **First** the theory emphasises that a leader requires some traits and qualities to be effective. **Second,** many of these qualities may be developed in individuals through training and development programmes. However, the theory suffers from two sets of limitations: generalisation of traits and applicability of traits.

Generalisation of Traits: There are problems in identification of traits which may be relevant for a leader to be effective in all situations. For example, Jennings has concluded that "fifty years of study has failed to produce a one-personality trait or set of qualities that can be used to discriminate leaders and non-leaders." A similar comment comes from House and Batez when they have concluded that the various studies on traits have failed to uncover any traits that clearly and consistently distinguish leaders and followers. Many other behavioural scientists hold similar views. From this point of view, the theory suffers from the following limitations :

1. There cannot be generalisation of traits for a successful leader.
2. No evidence has been given about the degree of the various traits.
3. There is a problem of measuring the traits.

Applicability of Traits: Another set of problems that hinders the full application of trait theory in practice, is that leadership as a process of influence reflects in leader's behaviour and not in his traits. There have been many persons with traits specified for a leader, but actually they could not become effective leaders. The reason for this phenomenon is that there is no direct cause-effect relationship between a trait of a person and his behaviour. The trait may be only one of the factors shaping behaviour; the other factors, sometimes even more important, are situational variables. These situational variables are not incorporated in trait theory.

Behavioural Theory

Behavioural theory of leadership emphasises that strong leadership is the result of effective role behaviour. Leadership is shown by a poison's act more than by his traits. Researchers exploring leadership role have come to the conclusion that to operate, effectively, groups need someone to perform two major functions: task-related functions and group maintenance functions. Task-related functions, or problem-solving functions, relate to providing solutions to the problems faced by the groups, in performing jobs and activities. Group maintenance functions, or social functions, relate to actions of mediating disputes and ensuring that individuals feel valued by the group. An individual who is able to perform both roles successfully would be an effective leader. These two roles may require two different sets of behaviour from the leader, known as leadership styles.

Leadership behaviour may be viewed in two ways: functional and dysfunctional. **Functional behaviour** influences followers positively and includes such functions as setting clear goals, motivating employees for achieving goals, raising the level of morale, building team spirit, effective two-way communication etc. **Dysfunctional** behaviour is unfavourable to the followers and denotes ineffective leadership. Such a behaviour may be inability to accept employees' ideas, display of emotional immaturity, poor human relations etc.

Situational Theory: Situational leadership approach was applied, for the first time, in 1920 in the armed forces of Germany with the objective to get good generals under different situations. In the business organisations much emphasis on the leadership researches was placed on the situations that surrounded the exercise of leadership since early 1950s.

The prime attention in situational theory of leadership (also known as contingency theory) is given to the situation in which leadership is exercised. Therefore, effectiveness of leadership will be affected by the factors associated with the leader and factors associated with the situation. These dimensions of leadership have been presented in the following Fig. 14.

Implications of the Theory

Situational theory has wide implications for managers in the sense that it offers clues why a manager who is successful in one situation, fails when there is change in the situation. Therefore, the managers may do better by adopting management practices including leadership which match with the situational variables. In fact, the systems and contingency approach have become the way of thinking in management and leadership is no exception.

This theory, however, should not be taken as the final word in leadership. The theory appears to be good on the surface but becomes quite complex in practice because of the presence of numerous contingent factors. However, managers can overcome this problem by diagnosing these factors suitably. This is not necessarily provided by the theory but experience has its role. One more important lacuna in this, the theory loses the insight of leadership and the leader is overwhelmed by the contingent factors.

LEADERSHIP STYLES

Leadership styles are the patterns of behaviour which a leader adopts in influencing the behaviour of his followers. These styles are either based on behavioural approach or situational approach of leadership. Some of the important theories/models prescribing leadership styles are given below:

Based on Behavioural Approach:

1. Power Orientation
2. Leaderships as a continuum
3. Employee-production orientation
4. Likert's management system
5. Managerial grid
6. Tri-dimensional grid

Based on Situational Approach

1. Fiedler's contingency model
2. Hursey and Blanchard's situational model
3. Path-goal model

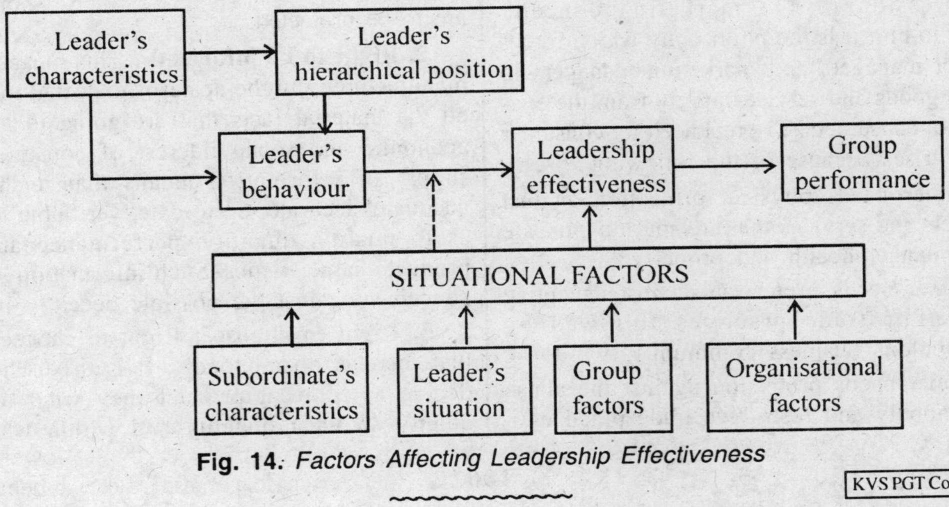

Fig. 14: *Factors Affecting Leadership Effectiveness*

16. CONSUMER PROTECTION

CONSUMER PROTECTION

In simple words consumer protection is a form of social action which is created to attain the well-being of consumers. Since an individual consumer is considered more vulnerable in the modern world, to exploilation and harassment by the manufacturers and distributors or sellers, it is necessary that the various groups of society such as government, judiciary, voluntary associations of consumers play their role to protect and promote the consumer interest—economic, social and environmental.

The Importance of Consumer Protection

The fundamental cause of consumer movement in any country has been the consumer disonance. Disonance means after-purchase doubts, disillusionment, disappointment and dissatisfaction. Dr. Peter Drucker rightly put 'consumerism' as 'the shame of modern marketing'. There will be no scope for consumerism in the case all marketers practise marketing concept in its real sense and entirety because, true marketing is 'consumer oriented'. Professor Philip Kotler, treated consumerism as the final expression of the marketing concept. According to him it is the philosophy which forces the product managers and marketing managers to look at the goods and services purely from the eyes and brains of consumers. The real need for consumer protection arises because of the following :

1. Consumer needs physical protection against products and services that are spurious, unsafe and endanger health and property.
2. Consumer needs protection against deceptive and unfair trade practices followed by unscrupulous business community.
3. Consumer needs protection against the abuse of monopoly and restrictive trade practices.
4. Consumer needs protection against sellers. In most of the cases the receipt as a documentary proof makes it clear that the goods once sold will not be taken back.
5. Consumer needs protection against pollution of all kinds.

Rights of Consumers

All consumers have some rights which no society or seller can ever deny. It was John F. Kennedy, the Ex. President of America who spelled out the consumer rights in 1962. These six rights have been outlined as under :

1. Right to protection of health and safety : There are good many products that are likely to cause physical danger to consumer health, lives and property, they contain potentially harmful substances that are dangerous from the consumer welfare point of view. The examples include food additives, colours, emulsifiers, preservatives. The health hazards that are likely to arise are to be eradicated or reduced considerably. The consumers who rely on the ads and buy the products and eventually find themselves cheated systematically are to be protected.

2. Right to be informed : This means that the manufacturer and the dealer is expected to disclose all the material facts that are going to affect the economic and social interest of consumers. The supply of information means that it should be adequate, accurate, up to date, verifiable and legal as to quality, quantity, performance and other product characteristics. Such information saves the consumer against the possible deceit.

3. Right to choose : Right to choose implies that there is no monopoly. It is they who are to decide as to what product they want to which quality, in what quantity and within what price range. It is not the producer to decide as to the quality, price and quantity. It means that consumers encourage competition among the producers and dealers so that there will be improvement in quality standards, reduction in costs and increase in quantity produced so that maximum number of consumers can be benefitted.

4. Right to be heard : Consumer has the right to express and register his dissatisfaction and get his complaint heard and weighed. The right is of vital importance because, all the earlier three rights are meaningless if this right is not granted. This gives scope for the government to intervene between the buyers and sellers and thus grant justice to the aggrieved party.

5. Right to be redressed : This right is one step ahead of the previous right. The complaints and protests are not just to be heard, the aggrieved party is to be granted compensation by bringing due adjustment in the transaction that has taken place. Further, the right to be heard means existence of an acceptable mechanism for asserting the rights.

6. Right to quality of life : Quality of life refers to the perceived well being of people, in groups and individually, and the well being of the environment in which these people live. Of late, consumerism has been defined as 'an improved quality of life'. It means that the environmental problems like air pollution, water pollution, food pollution, noise pollution and other related pollution, and the legacies of on-going industrialisation affect the very life of consumers. The social costs of these pollution is eating away the social benefits.

CONSUMER PROTECTION IN INDIA

Basically, consumer movement has its birth in 1960s though the rumblings of its formation has started as early as 1920s. It has been delayed and there is need for consumer protection in India at least for six solid reasons which are as under :

1. Consumer has no say : In India, at least, the consumers are not the kings. India presents a case of 'seller market' even today though we are daring to say that the things have changed.

2. Difficulty of get together : It is really very difficult to organise the consumers in India as India is a very vast country and the consumers are widely scattered speaking different languages, belonging to different religions, sects and sub-sects, cultures and sub-cultures, different political affiliations. Added to this, economic and social backwardness is acting as formidable barrier in coming together of consumers in the form of concrete organisation or organisations.

3. Ignorance and illiteracy : Ignorance, illiteracy, economic and social backwardness have given ample scope for the organised business community to exploit these consumers. The consumers need and should not depend on government registration alone.

4. To get latest goods and services : Today's science and technology is making available new ideas, products and services. The producers and dealers must made these available to the consumers. The latest products are comparatively lower in costs, better in quality and are available in sufficient quantities for right use.

5. False advertising : Consumer sovereignty is greatly influenced by advertising. Though advertisements are supposed to provide maximum possible information for consumer decision making, the consumers to take them at fairly high rate of discount. The truth is the ethics have reached the rock-bottom.

6. Environmental pollution : India is a rich nation so far as flora and fauna are concerned. However, if the things are left to themselves and unbridled, very soon the beauty of this country will be affected very badly by the pollution of water, air and noise, caused in the name of industrialisation. To raise voice against these factors that work against the quality of life, there is need for strong consumer organisations.

Method of Consumer Protection

In case, one thinks of ways and means of providing much warranted consumer protection, two alternatives are open :

I. Self-regulation
II. Government intervention

I. Self Regulation

When we discuss self-regulation, two types of associations come to the rescue of consumers and business community namely, consumer associations and business associations.

(i) Consumer associations : It is heartening to note that there are consumer associations coming up in a big way in every nook and corner of the country. At national level, four organisations are worth mentioning. These are Consumer Guidance Society of India of Mumbai, Consumer Education and Research Centre of Ahmedabad, Consumer Action Forum of Kolkata and Karnataka, Consumer Service Society of Bangalore. However, these regional organisations suffer from lack of persistent and motivated members, inadequate finance and are over-shadowed by the influence of politicians and big business shots. It means that such organisations succeed only when they are guranteed of timely and adequate finance, whole-hearted membership and effective leadership.

(ii) Business associations : Self-regulation by the business community through fair deal to resellers and consumers does wonders. Just as road accidents can be reduced by respecting traffic rules and regulations so also the item for confrontation can be eradicated if the business community behaves through the chambers of commerce and trade association. Oppositions, complaints, criticisms are to be accepted sportively and democratically as the part of the game for their own betterment and benefit.

II. Government Measures

When the efforts of self-regulation fails, that pave the way for government intervention as the last resort. It means that well organised business community has failed to regulate itself; the government as the custodian of the nation, takes the side of weaker side of the battle namely the consumers. This results in consumer legislation for protecting the legitimate interests of the consumers.

During post-war period, particularly after independence, Government of India has come with good piece of legislation containing the unethical practices and abuses in the arena of marketing. These enactments are Industries Development and Regulation Act of 1951, M.R.T.P. Act of 1969, Weights and Measures Act of 1956, The Prevention of Adulteration Act of 1954, The Drugs and Cosmetics Act of 1954, The Trade and Merchandise Act of 1958, The Essential Commodities Act of 1955 and Consumer Protection Act of 1986.

Of all these Acts, the last one is most specific and relevent to our discussion. There is now a greater recognition that consumers need to be protected not only from the effects of restrictive and unfair trade practices but also from defective goods or deficient services, over-charging of prices and unscrupulous exploitation. Further, ignorance of the consumer of his rights, lack of consumer movement and lack of due recognition to the consumer organisations have also been some important factors which led to the enactment of Consumer Protection Act 1986.

The Consumer Protection Act of 1986 has envisaged the setting up of the councils at the Centre and State levels called as Central Consumer Protection Council and the State Consumer Council. The Central Government is empowered to constitute the Central Consumer Protection Council which may consist of 150 members. Its term is three years. The council may meet as and when necessary but not less than three meetings of the council shall be held every year. The council is empowered to constitute among its members 'working groups'. Every working group so constituted shall perform such function as are assigned by the central council.

The objectives of the Central Council are to protect and promote the rights of consumers such as:

1. The right to be protected against marketing of goods which are hazardous to life and property.
2. The right to be informed about the quality, quantity, potency, purity, standard and prices of goods so as to protect the consumer against unfair trade practices.
3. The right to be assured, wherever possible access to a variety of goods at competitive prices.
4. The right to be heard and to be assured that consumer's interests will receive due consideration at appropriate forums.
5. The right to seek redressal against unfair trade

practices or unscrupulous exploitation of consumers; and

6. The right to consumer education. The State Governments are also empowered to establish State Consumer Protection Councils for their respective states. These councils shall consist of such members as may be notified by the State Government by notification from time to time. The objectives of State Council are to protect and promote the rights of consumers within the state as referred to in case of central council.

The Consumer Protection Act of 1986 provides for the establishment of three-tier quasi-judicial machinery for redressing the consumer grievances as under :

1. District forums
2. State Commissions and
3. National Commission

1. District Forums : A consumer dispute redressal forum to be known as "District Forum" is required to be established by the State Government with the prior approval of the Central Government. It consists of a president and two members appointed by the State Government. The president of the forum is required to be a person who is, or has been, or is qualified to be a District Judge. Of the two members one must be a person of eminence in the field of education, trade or commerce and another must be a lady social worker. The jurisdiction of the forum is to entertain complaints where the value of goods or services and the compensation claimed is less than rupees one lakh. The complaint may be lodged by affected consumer himself or the registered consumer association to which he belongs.

2. State Commission : A Consumer Disputes Redressal Commission to be known as "State Commission" is required to be established by the State Government with the prior approval of the Central Government in the State. It shall consist of a president and two other members to be appointed by the State Government. The president should be a person who is or has been a Judge of High Court, appointed by the State Government. The two other members should be persons of ability, integrity and standing and should have adequate knowledge or experience of or have shown capacity in dealing with problems relating to economics, law, commerce, accountancy, industry, public affairs or administration, one of whom should be a woman. The Jurisdiction of the State Commission is original as well as appellate. The original jurisdiction is vested in the commission in respect of complaint where the value of goods or services and the compensation so claimed exceed rupees one lakh but not more than rupees ten lakhs. The appellate jurisdication is confined to appeals from the orders of any District forum within the State. Further, the State Commission may call for the records and pass orders in any consumer dispute where it appears that a District forum has acted illegally or with material irregularity, or has exceeded its jurisdiction or has failed to exercise its jurisdiction.

3. National Commission : The highest authority to settle the consumer disputes under the Act is an independent statutory body called National Commission. This "National Commission" shall consist of a president and four other members to be appointment by the Central Government. The President should be a person who is or has been a judge of the Supreme Court. The persons to be appointed as members should be the persons of ability, integrity and standing with adequate knowledge or experience or capacity in dealing with the problems relating to economics, law, commerce, accountancy, industry, public affairs or administration. One of the members should be a woman. The jurisdiction of the National Commission is original as well as appellate. The original jurisdiction is limited to the complaints where the value of goods or services and compensation exceeds rupees ten lakhs. The appellate jurisdiction is confined to appeals against the orders of any State Commission. Thus, no appeal can lie to National Commission against the orders of the District Forum. It is the State Commission of each State which can entertain and appeal from the District Forums of the State. Further, the National Commission is empowered to call for records in any consumer dispute where it appears that the State Commission has acted illegally or with material irregularity or exceeded its jurisdiction or has failed to exercise its jurisdiction.

PART-II

FINANCIAL ACCOUNTING AND FINANCIAL STATEMENT ANALYSIS

1. ACCOUNTING

Definition of Accounting

Accounting is defined as "the art of recording, classifying, and summarising in terms of money transactions and events of a financial character and interpreting the results thereof".

Objectives of Accounting

The objectives of the term 'accounting' can be stated as follows:

(a) To maintain records of a business

(b) Calculation of profit or loss

(c) Depiction of financial position, and

(d) To make information available to various groups and users.

Functions of Accounting

Accounting embraces the following functions:

1. Keeping systematic records
2. Protecting properties of the business
3. Communicating the results
4. Meeting legal requirements

CONCEPTS OF ACCOUNTANCY

Accounting is the language of business. The financial transactions are recorded and reported by means of financial statements to a number of interested parties. In the absence of systematic approach, accountants may use their own language and whatever they will be writing, will not be understood necessarily in the same sense by others concerned. Thus, the uniformity in understanding of accounting records is possible only when some standard language is used. With a view to make the accounting language a standard language, certain accounting principles or concepts have been developed.

Accounting principles or rules or concepts are general guidelines for sound accounting practices. Their usefulness depend on general acceptability rather than individual acceptability. These are known as 'generally accepted accounting principles' having been formalised on the basis of usage, reason, and experience. As stated by the AICPA (American Institute of Certified Public Accountants) :

"Generally accepted accounting principles incorporate the consensus at any time as to which economic resources and obligations should be recorded as assets and liabilities, which changes in them should be recorded, when these changes should be recorded, how the recorded assets and liabilities and changes in them should be measured, what information should be disclosed and how should it be disclosed, and which financial statements should be prepared." Thus, generally accepted accounting principles (GAAP) comprises a set of rules, concepts and guidelines used in preparing financial accounting reports.

Following is a list of accounting concepts agreed to by accountants:

1. Business entity concept
2. Dual aspect concept
3. Going concern concept
4. Accounting period concept
5. Money measurement concept

6. Cost concept
7. Periodic matching of cost and revenue concept
8. Verifiable objective evidence concept
9. Realisation concept
10. Accrual concept
11. Disclosure concept
12. Materiality concept
13. Consistency concept
14. Conservatism concept

1. Business Entity Concept : According to this concept,'business is treated as a unit or entity apart from its owner, creditor, managers and others'. This concept is applicable to all forms of business organisations.

2. Dual Aspect Concept: According to this principle of accounting, every transaction has a dual aspect, i.e., two fold effect. Every receiver is also a giver and every giver is also a receiver.

Receiving and giving aspects are the two aspects of every business transaction. This principle is called double entry system of book-keeping. As per dual aspect, total assets and total liabilities must be equal. This equality is called 'Balance sheet equation or accounting equation. It can be stated as:

Liabilities = Assets

or

Capital + Liabilities (outside) = Assets

or

Capital = Assets – Liabilities.

3. Going Concern Concept: According to Kohler's Dictionary for Accountants, a going concern is defined as "any enterprise which is expected to continue operating indefinitely in the future".

This concept assumes that a business entity will continue to operate in definitely. Indefinitely existence means that the business enterprise will not be wound up within the foreseable future and therefore would be able to meet its contractual obligations and use its resources according to the plans and predetermined goals. This concept forms the basis for depreciation.

4. Accounting Period Concepts: Life of business is indefinitely, so, the measurement of income is not possible for a very, very long period. At frequent intervals properietor has to know "how things are going". Therefore, accountants choose some shorter and convenient time for the measurement of income. Normally, twelve month period is adopted for this purpose. The time interval is called "Accounting period."

5. Money Measurement Concept: The money measurement concept underlines the fact that is terms of money. A fact or a happening which cannot be expressed in terms of money is not recorded in the account book. As general health condition of the chairman of the company quality of products introduced by the enterprise etc. cannot be expressed in terms of money and thus are not recorded in the books.

As per this concept a transaction is recorded at its money value on the date of occurrence and the subsequent changes in the money value are ignored. Here, correct fact cannot be recorded in the book.

6. Cost Concept: The idea of cost assumption in that:

(i) asset is recorded at the price paid to acquire it-that is, at cost;

(ii) this cost is the basis for all subsequent accounting for the asset.

The cost concept implies that if nothing has been paid for acquiring something, it not be shown is the accounting books as an asset.

7. Periodic Matching of cost and Revenue concept: To compare profit or loss of an accounting period., it is necessary to match all expenses incurred in an accounting period with the revenue earned during that year.

Net income = Revenues – Expenses

8. Verifiable Objective Evidence Concept: This concept means that all accounting transactions should be evidenced and supported by business documents. These supporting documents (invoices, vouchers etc) provide the basis for making accounting entries and for later verification by auditors.

9. Realisation Concept: Kohler defines realisation concept as follows:

(i) A concept which gives accounting recognition to an exchange transaction, such as sale of goods or services only, when an inflow or outflow of cash equivalent results.

(ii) The realisation principle holds that revenue should be recognised with accompanying gains or losses at the point of sale in an arm's length transaction if the earning process is virtually complete.

10. Accrual Concept: Accrual means the recognition of events and conditions as they occur, rather than in the period of their incurrence, receipts or payments. Also the partial recognition of an item of revenue or expense and its related asset or liability: the result of the lack of coincidence of the accounting period and the contractual or benefit period.

11. Disclosure Concept: The disclosure principle implies that accounts must be prepared honestly, and all material information must be disclosed therein.

12. Materiality Concept: American Accounting Association (AAA) defines the term materiality as "An item should be regarded as material if there is reason to believe that knowledge if it would influence the decision of informed investor". It should be noted that an item material for one concern may be immaterial for another.

13. Consistency Concept: The principle of consistency plays its role when alternative accounting method is equally accepted.

14. Conservatism Concept: This is the policy of' Playing safe. It takes into consideration all prospective losses but leaves all prospective profit. Kohler defines 'Conservatism' as "a guidelines which chooses between acceptable accounting alternatives for recording events or transactions so that the least faveurable immediate effect on assets, income and owner's equity is reported." Following are the examples of this concept:

(a) Making the provision for doubtful debts and discount on debtors in anticipation of actual bad debts and discount.

(b) Valuing the stock-in-trade at market price or cost price whichever is less.

INCOME MEASUREMENT

The main purpose of accounting is to measure the income of a business because the business is started with the sole aim of organizing the various factors of production for the purpose of increasing its wealths.

Definition of Income : Income can be defined as the amount of change (favourable) in wealth which results from business activities.

The AAA Committee has defined the term 'Income' as "the realised net income of an enterprise measures its effectiveness as an operating unit and is the change in its net assets arising out of:

(a) the excess or deficiency of revenue compared with related expired cost, and

(b) Other gains or losses to the enterprise from sales, exchanges or other conventions of assets ..." The measurement of income is influenced by many concepts: Conservatism, consistancy, the entity business, the periodicity, the cost basis, and the realisation principles.

Conservatism

The approach of conservatism in the measurment of income, although shifts the income from one period to another, has been defended on the argument that the risk of understatement of income under the concept of conservatism cannot be equated with the danger of its over statement. The later approach to measurement of income may prove more disastrous for the business. The measurement of stock at cost or market price whichever is lower, the principle of amortization of intangible assets not recognizing the appreciation in the value of assets, are the examples of concepts of conservatism as applied to the measurement of income. But the concept of conservatism does not and must not lead towards bais for understatement of income by providing excessive depreciation, excessive reserves etc.

Consistency

To facilitate the comparison of performance of one year with that of another, it is essential that basis of measurement of income should remain the same from year to year. Therefore, the measurement of income in any particular year depends upon the basis followed in the previous year (s).

The Entity

The entity concept maintains that business should be regarded as an institution separate and distinct from its legal owners. Thus any measurement of income is to be done from the business point of view and not from the proprietor's point of view. The interest on the capital of partners, though income to individual partners, is considered as an expense of measuring income of a business.

The Accounting Period

It should be appreciated that income of an enterprise can precisely be determied only at the termination of entity's life. But inderterminable life-span of the entity makes the period so long and uncertain that no business can wait that long for finding out the fruit of hard work put in carrying the business. Moreover, if unfortunately, at that time it is found that results are unfavourable, it will be too late to correct the decision. It is thus essential for correct decision that interim progress of the business must be calculated. The satisfactory period for measuring income is either the calender year or a natural business year.

The Accrual Concept

With the choosing of calender year or natural business year as a period for reporting income, the continuous process of business does not come to standstill simply because the accounting period has ended. The flow of entity transactions does not confirm exactly to the prescribed time interval. Instead, there will be quantities unsold, goods-in-transit, accounts and bills to be collected, contract for services in the various stages of completion. This period convention has given rise to the accrual basis of accounting. This entails the necessity of recognising the revenue with the preiod in which it was realised and the application of costs to the period benefiting from services. For example, revenue from sales will be considered in the year in which shipment takes place regardless of when the payment is received. Rent, insurance, interest, salary etc., paid in advance will be prorated between successive years according to the specific period covered by the payments.

The Going Concern

Since the termination of business at the end of accounting period is a fiction and since life span of the business is indefinite, the determination of profits by means of assets appraisal is not considered proper. Any valuation of accounting income on the basis of appraisal of its assets on market value is much influenced by excessive emphasis on the liquidation rather than continuity.

EXPIRED COST AND INCOME MEASUREMENT

It has already been stated in the definition of income given by AAA that it is "... the excess or deficiency of revenue compared with related expired cost...". Thus any attempt to measure accounting income will be futile unless the correct measurement of the expired cost is available.

The costs which helps income determination may be direct cost or indirect cost, may be fixed cost or variable cost. The cost may be inclusive of purchase discount. Costs may be historical or standard. In order to have a more precise idea about the cost and its influence on the determination of income, it is studied under the following majorheads:

(a) Cost of property and its expiration: Property is constructed or acquired to provide a source of revenue and so long as it helps in providing revenue, each revenue increment derived from its usage should bear its proportionate share of the total actual cost of the property. As to what part of the cost of asset should go to determine income would much depend upon the determination of cost of asset itself.

The determination of the cost of asset, is a dificult process. The allocation of various overheads makes the cost of asset an intelligent expression of estimates if not an arbitrary one. Determination of life expectancy and scrap value of the asset pose a serious problem. The calculation of cost expiration for measuring income cannot be very accurate.

(b) Inventory Costs: Inventory costs include costs of those *(i)* which are held for resale, *(ii)* are in the process of production for sale, and *(iii)* are those which are currently consumed in the production of goods.

Determination of income depends much upon the determination of cost inventory as an expired cost. The calculation of inventory cost depends upon the direct cost, indirect cost efficiency on allocating costs between joint costs, by product costs, and so-on.

(c) Intangible Costs: The calculation of expiration costs of intangible assets like patent rights leasehold rights, goodwill, development expenses, advertisement, etc. is also in the way of determining correct income. But these intangible assets pose a serious problem because their useful life is absolutely unknown.

(d) Imputed Cost: In determining accounting income, besides taking same explicit or actual costs, some implicit or imputed costs like interest on capital, salary of a partner or proprietor, rent of the building owned by the proprietor are considered. The imputed costs are carved to facilitate comparison and management decision.

THE REALISATION PRINCIPLE AND INCOME MEASUREMENT

The definition of accounting concept of income by AAA lays emphasis on the realisation aspect of income. It aims at comparing the realised revenue with the corresponding expired cost. Thus in order to calculate proper amount of income it is essential and imperative to have a proper recognition of revenue.

The recognition of revenue leads to the problem of determination of precise point of time in income producing cycle when its realisation can be considered to be worthwhile and acceptable to standards. This leads to the consideration of following point :

(a) The sale as a basis of revenue recognition.

(b) The asset as a basis of revenue recognition, i.e., cash vs. mercantile system.

(c) Completed production as the basis of revenue recognition

(d) Recognition of revenue prior to productive completion, and

(e) Appreciation as the basis of revenue recognition.

(a) The sale as a basis of revenue recognition: The sale completes the transaction and receives the primary objective of manufacturing or purchasing goods, it provides a satisfactory measure of recognition of revenue. The sale also denotes the expiration of all proportionate costs and permits their comparison with revenue for measuring income. It eliminates all future speculation as to whether they will be selling or not and also to their prices at which they will be selling. From legal point of view also, sale point recognition is justified.

(b) Asset received as a basis of revenue recognition: The advocates of this principle want to postpone the recognition of revenue till its actual relisation in cash.

Cash vs. Accrual or Mercantile Basis of Accounting : According to cash basis, the actual receipts and payment in cash is the real basis of recording transaction in the accounting period. The revenue will be considered in a particular accounting period only when it is realised in cash. Similarly, an expense will be considered only when it is paid in actual cash in the accounting period.

(c) Completed production as the basis of revenue recognition: Where there are compelling reasons for the maintenance of large inventory for any purpose whatsoever, the revenue is recognised even before the sale takes place. The main purpose of holding the inventory in such business houses is to push up the sale price. The retention of goods in such industries serves the purpose of getting the revenues. The production basis of revenue recognition has its utility in agriculture, extractive industries (oil, gold, silver, other metals), etc.

(d) Recognition of Revenue prior to productive completion: In long-term contracts, the basis of recognition of revenue is discarded in as much as this will result in the postponement of income for a very long period. When all of a sudden heavy amount of revenue will be recognised. This type of procedure will bring frustration to shareholders during the period it is not recognised and also will attract high rate of income tax when it is recognised.

(e) Appreciation as the basis of revenue recognition: The value of an asset sometimes appreciates due to change in general price. Any increment in the value of asset due to above mentioned reasons, is treated as fictitious increment. It does not add to the source of revenue. It is more an expression of original cost into the currency as per the changed index number.

CONCLUSION

The calculation of income is an important affair in as much as its correct calculation determines the divident policy, acts as an important tool for measuring the effective use of money and managerial proficiency. It determines the future policy of the concern. But its determination is a difficult process as it is affected by:

(a) Various concepts and conventions

(b) Correct calculation of expired cost and

(c) Correct recognition of revenue

The concepts and conventions affecting the calculation of income are numerous, the calculation of expired cost is a difficult process and recognition of revenue is affected by various considerations. The job of measuring income is not an easy one.

Important Accounting Standards

Accounting standards may be defined as codified or written statements of uniform accounting rules and guidelines for preparing financial statements in a uniform and consistent manner and for their disclosures to the user of financial information. Accounting standards constitute a structural framework with the help of which credible financial statements can be prepared.

Accounting standards are prepared by the ICAI and are mandatory to be followed by the companies. So far, the ICAI has issued a number of standards. But, all of them are not equally important for the purpose of the examination. So, here we explain the important points of some standards which are important from the examination point of view and the rest are summarized in one. Also, for the reference, is given the list of all the standards so far issued. The list is as below :

AS1 Disclosure of Accounting Policies

AS2 Valuation of Inventories

AS3 Cash Flow Statements

AS4 Contingencies and Events Occurring after the Balance Sheet Date

AS5 Net Profit or Loss for the period, Prior Period and Extraordinary Items and Changes in Accounting Policies

AS6 Depreciation Accounting

AS7 Construction Contracts (revised 2003)

AS8 Accounting for Research and Development

AS9 Revenue Recognition

AS10 Accounting for Fixed Assets

AS11 Accounting for the Effects of Changes in Foreign Exchange Rates

AS12 Accounting for Government Grants

AS13 Accounting for Investments

AS14 Accounting for Amalgamations

AS15 Accounting for Retirement Benefits in the Financial Statement of Employers

AS16 Borrowing Costs

AS17 Segment Reporting

AS18 Related Party Disclosures

AS19 Leases

AS20 Earnings Per Share

AS21 Consolidated Financial Statements

AS22 Accounting for taxes on income.

AS23 Accounting for Investments in Associates in Consolidated Financial Statements

AS24 Discontinuing Operations

AS25 Interim Financial Reporting

AS26 Intangible Assets

AS27 Financial Reporting of Interests in Joint Ventures

AS28 Impairment of Assets

AS29 Provisions, Contingent Liabilities and Contingent Assets

APPLICABILITY OF STANDARDS

For the purpose of applicability of Accounting Standards, enterprises are classified into three categories, viz., Level I, Level II and Level III. Level II and Level III enterprises are considered as SMEs (Small and Medium Enterprises).

— Level I enterprises are required to comply fully with all the accounting standards.

— It has been decided that no relaxation should be given to Level II and Level III enterprises in respect of recognition and measurement principles. Relaxations are provided with regard to disclosure requirements. Accordingly, the applicability of various standards on them is as below :

Accounting Standards not applicable to Level II and Level III enterprises in their entirety:

I. AS3 Cash Flow Statements
II. AS17 Segment Reporting
III. AS18 Related Party Disclosures
IV. AS24 Discontinuing Operations.

(B) Accounting Standards not applicable to Level II and Level III enterprises since the relevant Regulators require compliance with them only by certain Level I enterprises:

(a) AS21 Consolidated Financial Statements
(b) AS23 Accounting for Investments in Associates in Consolidated Financial Statements
(c) AS 27, Financial Reporting of Interests in Joint Ventures (to the extent of requirements relating to consolidated financial statements)

(C) Accounting Standards in respect of which relaxations from certain disclosure requirements have been given to Level II and Level III enterprises:

(a) AS19 Leases
(b) AS20 Earnings Per Share
(c) AS29 Provisions, Contingent Liabilities and Contingent Assets

(D) Accounting Standard applicability of which is deferred for Level II and Level III enterprises:

AS 28, Impairment of Assets - For Level I Enterprises applicable from 1-4-2004

For Level II Enterprises applicable from 1-4-2006

For Level III Enterprises applicable from 1-4-2008

The important provisions of some of the standards are explained in points as under :

(A) AS1 Disclosure of Accounting Policies

1. All significant accounting policies adopted in the preparation and presentation of financial statements should be disclosed.
2. The disclosure of the significant accounting policies as such should form part of the financial statements and the significant accounting policies should normally be disclosed in one place.
3. Any change in the accounting policies which has a material effect in the current period or which is reasonably expected to have a material effect in later periods should be disclosed. In the case of a change in accounting policies which has a material effect in the current period, the amount by which any item in the financial statements is affected by such change should also be disclosed to the extent ascertainable. Where such amount is not ascertainable, wholly or in part, the fact should be indicated.
4. If the fundamental accounting assumptions, viz. Going Concern, Consistency and Accrual are followed in financial statements, specific disclosure is not required. If a fundamental accounting assumption is not followed, the fact should be disclosed.

(B) AS2 Valuation of Inventory

(a) Net realisable value is the estimated selling price in the ordinary course of business less the estimated costs of completion and the estimated costs necessary to make the sale.
(b) Inventories should be valued at the lower of cost and net realisable value.
(c) The cost of inventories should comprise all costs of purchase, costs of conversion and other costs incurred in bringing the inventories to their present location and condition.
(d) Interest and other borrowing costs are usually considered as not relating to bringing the

inventories to their present location and condition and are, therefore, usually not included in the cost of inventories.

(e) In determining the cost of inventories, it is appropriate to exclude certain costs and recognize them as expenses in the period in which they are incurred. Examples of such costs are: Abnormal amounts of wasted materials, labour, or other production costs; storage costs, unless those costs are necessary in the production process prior to a further production stage; administrative overheads that do not contribute to bringing the inventories to their present location and condition; and selling and distribution costs.

(f) The cost of inventories should be assigned by using the First-in First-out (FIFO), or weighted average cost formula.

(C) AS6 Depreciation Accounting

(1) This standard applies to all depreciable assets, except items to which special considerations apply like forests, plantations and similar regenerative natural resources; wasting assets including expenditure on the exploration for and extraction of minerals, oils, natural gas and similar non-regenerative resources; expenditure on research and development; goodwill; live stock.

(2) This standard also does not apply to land unless it has a limited useful life for the enterprise.

(3) Depreciation is a measure of the wearing out, consumption or other loss of value of a depreciable asset arising from use, effluxion of time or obsolescence through technology and market changes. Depreciation is allocated so as to charge a fair proportion of the depreciable amount in each accounting period during the expected useful life of the asset. Depreciation includes amortization of assets whose useful life is predetermined.

(4) Depreciable assets are assets which are expected to be used during more than one accounting period, have a limited useful life and are held by an enterprise for use in the production or supply of goods and services.

(5) Useful life is either (i) the period over which a depreciable asset is expected to be used by the enterprise; or (ii) the number of production or similar units expected to be obtained from the use of the asset by the enterprise.

(6) Depreciable amount of a depreciable asset is its historical cost, or other amount substituted for historical cost in the financial statements, less the estimated residual value.

(7) A change from one method of providing depreciation to another is made only if the adoption of the new method is required by statute or for compliance with an accounting standard or if it is considered that the change would result in a more appropriate preparation or presentation of the financial statements of the enterprise. When such a change in the method of depreciation is made, depreciation is recalculated in accordance with the new method from the date of the asset coming into use. The deficiency or surplus arising from retrospective re-computation of depreciation in accordance with the new method is adjusted in the accounts in the year in which the method of depreciation is changed. In case the change in the method results in deficiency in depreciation in respect of past years, the deficiency is charged in the statement of profit and loss. In case the change in the method results in surplus, the surplus is credited to the statement of profit and loss.

(D) AS7 Accounting for Construction Contracts

(a) The principal problem relating to accounting for construction contracts is the allocation of revenues and related costs to accounting periods over the duration of the contract.

(b) Construction contracts are formulated in two basic types: Fixed price contracts in which the contractor agrees to a fixed contract price, or rate, in some cases subject to cost escalation clauses; and Cost plus contracts where the contractor is reimbursed for allowable or otherwise defined costs, and is also allowed a percentage of these costs or a fixed fee.

(c) Two methods of accounting for contracts commonly followed by contractors are the Percentage of completion method and the Completed contract method.

(d) Under the percentage of completion method, revenue is recognized as the contract activity progresses based on the stage of completion reached. The costs incurred in reaching the stage of completion are matched with this revenue.

(e) Under the completed contract method, revenue is recognized only when the contract is completed or substantially completed. Costs and progress payments received are accumulated during the course of the contract but revenue is not recognized until the contract activity is substantially completed.

(f) Costs attributable to a contract include expected warranty costs. Warranty costs are provided for when such costs can be reasonably estimated.

(g) The selection of a method of accounting for a construction contract depends on various considerations. The contractor may use both methods simultaneously for different contracts depending upon circumstances.

(h) When current estimates of total contract costs and revenues indicate a loss, provision is made for the entire loss on the contract irrespective of the amount of work done and the method of accounting followed.

(i) Progress payments and advances received from customers in respect of construction contracts in relation to the work performed thereon are disclosed in financial statements either as a liability or shown as a deduction from the amount of contract-work-in-progress

(E) AS9 Revenue Recognition

(a) This standard deals with the issue as to when a business organization should recognize in the books of accounts that it has earned the revenue under various business conditions.

(b) Revenue can be recognized on the basis of one of the following methods i.e. Completed service contract method which recognizes revenue in the statement of profit and loss only when the rendering of services under a contract is completed or substantially completed and Proportionate completion method is a method of accounting which recognizes revenue in the statement of profit and loss proportionately with the degree of completion of services under a contract.

(c) Criterion for determining when to recognize revenue from a transaction involving the sale of goods is that the seller has transferred the property in the goods to the buyer for a consideration.

(d) Revenue from service transactions is usually recognized as the service is performed, either by the proportionate completion method or by the completed service contract method.

(e) Interest accrues, in most circumstances, on the time basis determined by the principal amount outstanding and the rate applicable.

(f) Royalties accrue in accordance with the terms of the relevant agreement and are usually recognized on that basis unless, having regard to the substance of the transactions, it is more appropriate to recognize revenue on some other systematic and rational basis.

(g) Dividends from investments in shares are not recognized in the statement of profit and loss until a right to receive payment is established.

(h) Where the ability to assess the ultimate collection with reasonable certainty is lacking at the time of raising any claim, e.g., for escalation of price, export incentives, interest etc., revenue recognition is postponed to the extent of uncertainty involved.

(i) When goods are sold on approval or return basis, revenue should not be recognized until the goods have been formally accepted by the buyer or the buyer has done an act adopting the transaction or the time period for rejection has elapsed or where no time has been fixed, a reasonable time has elapsed.

(j) When the consideration is receivable in instalments, revenue attributable to the sales price exclusive of interest should be recognized at the date of sale. The interest element should be recognized as revenue, proportionately to the unpaid balance due to the seller.

(k) In cases where installation fees are other than incidental to the sale of a product, they should be recognized as revenue only when the equipment is installed and accepted by the customer.

(l) If the membership fee permits only membership and all other services or products are paid for separately, or if there is a separate annual subscription, the fee should be recognized when received. If the membership fee entitles the member to services or publications to be provided during the year, it should be recognized on a systematic and rational basis having regard to the timing and nature of all services provided.

(F) AS10 Accounting for Fixed Assets

1. Fixed asset is an asset held with the intention of being used for the purpose of producing or providing goods or services and is not held for sale in the normal course of business.
2. The cost of an item of fixed asset comprises its purchase price, including import duties and other non-refundable taxes or levies and any directly attributable cost of bringing the asset to its working condition for its intended use; any trade discounts and rebates are deducted in arriving at the purchase price.
3. The expenditure incurred on start-up and commissioning of the project, including the expenditure incurred on test runs and experimental production, is usually capitalised as an indirect element of the construction cost.
4. Subsequent expenditures related to an item of fixed asset should be added to its book value only if they increase the future benefits from the existing asset beyond its previously assessed standard of performance.
5. When a fixed asset is acquired in exchange for another asset, its cost is usually determined by reference to the fair market value of the consideration given.
6. An increase in net book value arising on revaluation of fixed assets is normally credited directly to owner's interests (capital) under the heading of revaluation reserves and is regarded as not available for distribution of dividends.
7. Gains or losses arising on disposal are generally recognized in the profit and loss statement.
8. Goodwill, in general, is recorded in the books only when some consideration in money or money's worth has been paid for it.

(G) Other Accounting Standards

As regards other accounting standards, the following points are important :

(a) Cash flows arising from taxes on income should be separately disclosed and should be classified as cash flows from operating activities unless they can be specifically identified with financing and investing activities.

(b) The existence and amount of guarantees, obligations arising from discounted bills of exchange and similar obligations undertaken by an enterprise are generally disclosed in financial statements by way of note.

(c) The amount of a contingent loss should be provided for by a charge in the statement of profit and loss if it is probable that future events will confirm that, after taking into account any related probable recovery, an asset has been impaired or a liability has been incurred as at the balance sheet date, and a reasonable estimate of the amount of the resulting loss can be made.

(d) Contingent gains should not be recognized in the financial statements.

(e) Assets and liabilities should be adjusted for events occurring after the balance sheet date that provide additional evidence to assist the estimation of amounts relating to conditions existing at the balance sheet date or indicate that the fundamental accounting assumption of going concern (i.e., the continuance of existence or substratum of the enterprise) is not appropriate.

(f) Research and development costs are usually

charged to expense in the period in which they are incurred. If it can be demonstrated, however, that the product or process is technically and commercially feasible and that the enterprise has adequate resources to enable the product or process to be marketed, it may be appropriate to defer the costs of related research and development to future periods.

(g) Exchange differences arising on foreign currency transactions should be recognized as income or as expense in the period in which they arise.

(h) Exchange differences arising on repayment of liabilities incurred for the purpose of acquiring fixed assets, which are carried in terms of historical cost, should be adjusted in the carrying amount (book value) of the respective fixed assets.

(i) The cost of an investment should include acquisition charges such as brokerage, fees and duties.

(j) Extraordinary items should be disclosed in the statement of profit and loss as a part of net profit or loss for the period. The nature and the amount of each extraordinary item should be separately disclosed in the statement of profit and loss in a manner that its impact on current profit or loss can be perceived.

2. PROCESS OF ACCOUNTING

DOUBLE ENTRY SYSTEM

Rules of Debit and Credit : The transactions in the Journal are recorded on the basis of the rules of debit and credit. The rules are made according to the type of accounts as explained above. The rules are as under :

For Personal Accounts,

"DEBIT THE RECEIVER AND CREDIT THE GIVER"

For Real accounts,

"DEBIT WHAT COMES IN AND CREDIT WHAT GOES OUT"

For Nominal accounts,

"DEBIT ALL EXPENSES AND LOSSES AND CREDIT ALL INCOMES AND GAINS"

FUNDAMENTAL ACCOUNTING EQUATION

The fundamental accounting equation is based on the division of all types of accounts into only three categories:

(a) Assets

(b) Liabilities

(c) Equity

The equation is

Assets = Liabilities + Capital

This equation represents that what the company owes to outsides is equal to what the company has received from outsiders. Here, for the company, even the owners are outsiders and are a liability for the company which is shown separately as capital. Whenever, a firm enters into any transaction, this equation gets affected. But as per the double entry system, this equation will always hold true. This is explained with the help of following illustration:

Illustration 2 : Mr. Kothari starts a new business with a cash of Rs. 50,000.

Assets	=	Liabilities	+	Capital
(Cash – Rs. 50,000)		NIL		(Owner's capital - Rs. 50,000)

Now, he purchases building of Rs. 10,000 and stock worth Rs. 8,000 on credit.

Assets	=	Liabilities	+	Capital
(Cash - Rs. 40,000 Building - Rs. 10,000 Stock - Rs. 8,000)		(Creditors - Rs. 8,000)		(Capital - Rs. 50,000)

This accounting equation is fundamental in accounting as the double entry system is based on this equation. It is very necessary to understand this equation for proper learning of accounts. Like any other equation, this equation called also be presented in many ways like:

Assets – Liabilities = Capital

Assets – Capital = Liabilities

RECORDS AND TERMS IN ACCOUNTING

In an accounting system, various kinds of records are maintained and various terms are used. As a student of commerce, you must have learnt them. But, as a revision, these records and terms are explained hereunder:

1. Voucher : The basic record of any accounting system is 'Voucher'. A voucher is a documentary evidence in support of a transaction. For example, a cash memo showing cash sale, invoice showing credit sale etc.

2. Cash Book : It is meant to record all the cash transactions of the firm. Cash book can be single column, two column or three column. In one column cash book, only cash account is maintained. In two column cash book, the bank account is also maintained. Sometimes, cash is deposited in bank or withdrawn from the bank. In this case, entry is made on both the sides of the cash book. Such transactions are known as 'Contra' transactions or **'Contra Entry'**. Some firms also maintain a three-column cash book which apart from the above two accounts also maintains cash discount received and paid account. In case of cash and bank accounts, their closing balances are found out and carried forward but cash discount column is only totalled and not balanced.

3. Journal : It is the basic book of accounts which records all the transactions of a firm. In case the firm is maintaining the subsidiary books of accounts then the transactions which do not appear in those books, find their place in the journal.

4. Purchase and Sales Book : They constitute the bulk of the transactions of a trading firm. Since, most of the firms make sales and purchases on credit basis, they need to know the extent of it. For this purpose, these two subsidiary books are maintained. Only credit purchases and sales of goods in which the firm deals in are recorded in these books. The purchases are evidenced by credit bills received from the supplier whereas sales are supported by the invoice made out against the customer. With this, many firms also maintain separate books for goods returned to the suppliers and goods returned by the customers, which are known as 'Return Books'.

5. Debit and Credit Notes : A debit note is issued to a party for raising a debit against that party for various reasons like return of goods, availing some discounts etc. When the debit note is issued, the issuing firm debits the account of the person to whom it is issued and the person receiving it credits the sending firm. The reverse is for the credit note.

6. Ledger : The book which contains all accounts is known as the ledger. Since final information pertaining to the final accounts emerges only from accounts, the ledger is also called 'Principal book'. Other books like purchase or sales book, journal etc. merely facilitates the preparation of accounts or the ledger, they are known as subsidiary books or books of original entry. The cash book has unique position. It is a subsidiary book because cash entries are first entered here and then other accounts are prepared. But, it also contains the accounts of bank and cash itself and hence is a part of ledger. So, it is a book of original entry as well as the Principal book.

7. Operating Expenses : These are expenses of the business connected with the basic or day to day functioning of the enterprise. These include production, administration as well as selling expenses. Similarly, operating incomes are income from business activities.

8. Non-Operating Expenses : These are expenses not directly associated with the main activity of the enterprise like interest payment. Similarly, non-operating incomes are not associated with the principal activity of the business like dividend on investments.

9. Trade and Cash Discount : Trade discount is given by the seller at the time of sale of product which is deducted from price of product. The bill is raised by seller after deducting trade discount. Cash discount is provided to the buyer for making payment earlier than scheduled time. No journal entry for trade discount is made whereas cash discount is loss for seller and income for buyer.

10. Current Assets : These are assets of the enterprise which are expected to be converted into cash within the normal operating cycle of the business which is one year.

11. Current Liabilities : Such liabilities which will become due for payment within one year and are normally paid out of current assets.

12. Working Capital : It refers to the investment made by the enterprise in the business to keep the business going on smoothly. It is represented as the difference between the current assets and current liabilities. Sometimes, it is also referred as Net Working Capital. In such a case, Gross Working Capital is equal to the current assets.

Illustration 3 : From the following particulars, prepare a triple column cash book :

1. Opening Balance : Cash Rs. 500 and Bank Rs. 1,000
2. Received Rs. 490 from A in satisfaction of debt of Rs. 500 in cash
3. Paid Rs. 295 by cheque to B in satisfaction of claim of Rs. 300
4. Cash sales Rs. 2,000
5. Cash purchases by cheque Rs. 500
6. Rs. 500 withdrawn from bank
7. Rs. 600 salary paid
8. Rs. 1,500 deposited in bank

Particulars	L.F.	Disc. Allowed	Cash	Bank	Particulars	L.F.	Disc. Received	Cash	Bank
To Balance			500	1000	By B's A/c		5		295
To A's A/c		10	490		By Purchases				500
To Sales			2000		By Cash	C			500
To Bank	C		500		By Salary			600	
To Cash	C			1,500	By Bank	C		15,00	
					By Balance			1,390	
Total		10	1,490	2,500	Total		5	3,490	2,500

* 'C' represents Contra Entry

TRIAL BALANCE

Trial balance is a statement containing the ledger balances of all the accounts on a particular date. It has two sides viz., debit and credit to show the balance of a particular account. As under the double entry system, every transaction has two sides i.e. credit and debit which are equal. Therefore, when we take the balances of all the accounts, the total of accounts with debit balance should match with the total of accounts with credit balance. The following are the objectives of preparing the trial balance :

1. Checking the arithmetic accuracy of the accounting entries and their postings.
2. It gives a bird's eye view of the balances in various accounts.
3. It is a useful basis for the preparation of P&L account and Balance Sheet.
4. If the total of debit and credit side of Trial balance matches, it gives reasonable assurance of accuracy of accounts. But, still there can be some mistakes. This has been explained later.

GENERALLY ACCEPTED PRINCIPLES OF ACCOUNTING

The practice of accounting is influenced and guided by certain conventions, concepts and principles which from experience are proved acceptable and useful. The term 'Concept' is used to connote accounting assumptions or conditions upon which accounting is based. On the other hand, 'Convention' is used to signify customs or traditions as a guide to the preparation of accounting statements. While concepts have logical thinking and rationality at their base, the conventions are established by the practicability and use over a long period of time.

Conventions of Accounting

The following are treated as basic conventions of accounting :

(A) Consistency : The principle of consistency implies that the same accounting procedure and method should be continuously followed by a firm from year to year. They should not be changed frequently. This principle helps in making the statements comparable over a period of time. This principle applies more to items like depreciation, valuation of closing stock, deferred revenue expenditure etc. where a number of methods are available to accountant for valuation. According to this convention, whatever method suitable to the organization, once applied, should be applied every year.

If at all, any change in the accounting procedure or method is considered necessary, then such changes giving due explanation made and its effect should be clearly stated in the accounts.

(B) Conservatism : This is one of the most recognized and widely practiced accounting conventions. It recognizes the natural human behaviour of playing safe. According to this principle, all future losses and expenses are to be recognized whereas all future incomes and profits should be ignored. It is on this basis, the value of closing stock is taken at the cost or market price, whichever is lower. Some other examples of convention of conservatism are the provision for bad and doubtful debts and provision for fluctuation in the value of investment, showing joint life policy at surrender value, not providing for discount on creditors etc.

But, there are certain drawbacks of this convention. Excessive application of this concept leads to creation of secret reserves. It is contrary to the policy of full disclosure and consistency. Moreover, it conflicts with the concept of matching of revenues and costs. Therefore, it should be cautiously followed.

(C) Materiality : It implies that the accountant need not record events which are trivial considering the size of organisation and the work of recording them is not justified by the usefulness of the results. For example expenditure of Rs. 1,30,000.05 may be written as Rs. 1,30,000. Also, many small events can be clubbed under one accounting head instead of showing each of them separately. For example, many small expenses on different stationary items are clubbed under one head or certain petty expenses are clubbed as 'Sundry expenses'.

Materiality is a relative concept. What is material for one firm may be immaterial for another. Moreover, materiality is related not only to the monetary value but also with the importance of the item. An item is considered material if it is large enough to influence the judgement or decision based on accounting reports.

(D) Disclosure : The term disclosure suggests that all accounting statements should be honest and full disclosure of all significant information should be made. However, it does not mean that all information like sale price, details of customers should be disclosed but a sufficient disclosure of an information which is of material interest to proprietors, creditors and investors and affect their decision making should be made. This principle has more to do with the disclosures regarding the accounting policies and significant events of the firm. The accounting statements should conform to the generally accepted accounting principles. Moreover, where an important change has been made in presentation of information, as compared to preceding accounting periods, the nature of such change should be clearly indicated.

CONCEPTS OR ASSUMPTIONS OF ACCOUNTING

Of all the concepts and conventions, certain fundamental accounting assumptions underlie the preparation and presentation of financial statements. They are usually not specifically stated because their acceptance and use are assumed. Disclosure is necessary if they are not followed. The following have been generally accepted as fundamental accounting assumptions:-

(1) The Going Concern Concept : This concept is based on the assumption that the business will continue for the indefinite period or a sufficiently long period. Except the undertaking of a particular venture, it is assumed that business will last for a long time. It is due to this assumption that the fixed assets are usually stated in the balance sheet at the acquisition cost less provision for depreciation without any regard to the actual market value of the asset. The transactions are so recorded that the benefits likely to accrue in future of the money spent now are also taken into account.

For example, when a machine (expected to last for 10 years) is acquired, the total cost of the machine is not treated as an expense in the year in which it is acquired. Only a part of its cost is charged to profit and loss account every year in the name of depreciation. Similarly, the Contingent liabilities are shown at the footnote of the balance sheet with the assumption that the business is going to continue for a long time.

(2) Business Entity Concepts : According to this concept, business is considered as a distinct entity from its owners, managers and employees. In the accounting, the business has a separate personality and accountant must take note of the transactions between the business entity and its owners or employees just like the transactions with the third parties.

It should be remembered that companies and co-operative societies have legal existence or entity for all purposes but there is no separate legal entity for a sole proprietor or partnership. However, accounting will distinguish the business from the owners in all cases. So, even a sole proprietorship and partnership firm has a separate accounting entity though not separate legal entities.

Accordingly, all the transactions of the business are recorded in the books of the business from the viewpoint of the business entity and the owner is treated as a creditor to the extent of his capital. This is clear from the fact that capital is shown as a liability in the balance sheet. Any personal expense of the owner done from the money of the business is considered as reduction in capital (Drawings). If any expenditure does not involve the money of the business, it does not appear in the accounts.

(3) Money Measureent Concept : As per this concept, only such transactions and events which can be expressed in terms of money are recorded. In other words, the transactions and events on which money value cannot be put will not be recorded in the books of account even though the events may be extremely important. For example, if the chairman of the company dies in a plane crash, though the event may be a great loss to the company, it will not be recorded in the books of account, as it has no money value.

The main advantage of expressing events in monetary terms is that money provides a common denominator by means of which heterogeneous facts of the business can be expressed in one single object. It also avoids the subjective judgement about the importance of an event.

(4) Accounting Period Concept : Net income for the entire life of an organization is relatively easy to measure. It is the difference between the investments and returns. But, generally businesses run for several years. According to going concern concept, they are assumed to continue for indefinite period. Therefore, it is imperative for the management of the organization to know the results of their business at regular intervals. This leads to the Accounting period concept. It measures the activities of the organization for a period of time, called accounting period. Generally, it is one year since it is assumed that during this period, most of the kinds of business transactions does take place one or more times.

(5) Cost Concept : Under this concept, in accounting all transactions and events are recorded at their monetary cost of acquisition i.e. actual amount of money paid for the acquisition of the asset or for receiving the goods or services. Accounting should make a record of the transactions on the objective basis. The personal views of the people regarding the actual value of the asset are not considered.

Elaborating the concept, it means that if an asset does not cost anything, then such transaction would not be recorded in the books of account. Thus the knowledge and skill that is built up as business operates, the teamwork within the organization, managerial competence, a favourable location etc. in spite of being valuable assets do not appear in the books of account. However, if a tangible asset is acquired at free of cost, then the transaction is recorded at a nominal value of Re. 1 so that the record of the asset is available, according to convention of disclosure.

BASIC ACCOUNTING PRINCIPLES

Basic accounting principles are the general rules which are used as a guide in accounting and as a basis of practice. These principles are based upon logic and practical experience. These principles are flexible and are modified from time to time to meet the changing needs of business. These basic accounting principles are as follows:

(1) The Realisation Principle : According to this principle, revenue is deemed to be realised earned when the goods have been transferred or the services have been rendered to a customer. In the realisation of revenue, the receipt of cash is not significant. If a firm sells goods in April and receives cash in June, revenue will be considered as realised in April when the goods were sold.

Similarly, expenses are recognised not when the cash is paid but when the assets or services are used to produce revenue. For example, rent for January 1, 2001 to 31 March, 2001, though unpaid, will be recognised during the accounting year 2000-2001. Likewise, cost of goods lost by fire is immediately recognised in the year of loss.

(2) Maching Principle : According to Matching principle, the revenues or income and the expenses incurred to earn that income should be matched so that net income of the business operation is available in respect of a particular period. This principle has led to formation of rules regarding recognition of income as well as matching the expenses to that income.

This concept implies two principles. The first is that when revenue or sale is recognized to be earned, then all costs incurred to produce or sell must be considered. And secondly, that when the cost is incurred but sale or service is likely to be earned in the future, then such cost should not be considered during the current period. The result is that the figures shown in P&L Account are mutually interrelated and the resultant profit or loss is arrived at only after considering relevant revenue and relevant cost.

(a) When an item of revenue is included in the profit and loss account, all expenses incurred on it whether paid or not, should be included in the profit and loss account. Outstanding expenses are debited in the profit and loss account on this basis.

(b) If an amount is spent, but revenue from it will be earned in the next year, the amount should be carried down as an asset and should be shown as an expense next year. Prepaid expenses (e.g., prepaid insurance) are shown as assets in the balance sheet on this basis.

(c) Cost of goods remaining unsold at the end of the year together with expenses incurred on them must be carried forward to the next year. Therefore, closing stock is carried over to the next year as opening stock.

(d) Incomes received in advance must be treated as a liability, while income earned but not received should be recognised as revenue.

There is an exception to matching principle. In case of losses against which no revenue is earned or expected to earn, are debited to the P&L Account in the year in which they are incurred. For example, loss due to fire or theft.

(3) Accrual Principle : Accrual concept is very much related to the Matching principle. The mercantile system of accounting is based on accrual concept only. Under this, revenue is recognized when it accrues, whether received in cash or not. Accrual of income or expense arises when the right to receive income or the obligation to pay for the expenses is fixed.

According to this concept, as the income or expenses accrue, they are recorded in the books of account as outstanding income or expense, if cash is not received or paid at the same time. Whenever the cash is received or paid, the transaction is recorded again and the outstanding balance is cleared. Extending the concept, if any income is received or expense is paid in advance (i.e. not accrued), it is not taken into P&L Account, but is shown in the balance sheet as an asset or liability, as the case may be.

(4) The Dual Aspect Principle : The economic resources of an entity are called assets. The claims of various parties against these assets are called liabilities. Liabilities are of two types: Outside liabilities (or simply liabilities) and Capital (liability towards the owner). Since all types of assets of a business are claimed by someone and business does not have anything of its own, the total of these claims cannot exceed the amount of assets to be claimed, it follows that

ASSETS = LIABILITIES

As already explained, liabilities are of two types. So, the above equation can be rewritten as below:

ASSETS = OUTSIDE LIABILITIES + CAPITAL

This is the Fundamental Accounting Equation, which is the formal expression of the dual aspect concept. As per this concept, every transaction has a dual impact on the accounting records and this equation holds true all the time, as already explained earlier.

(5) The Principle of Full Disclosure : According to this principle, there should be complete and understandable reporting on the financial statements of all significant information relating to the economic affairs of the firm. To meet the requirements of this method of depreciation or method of valuation of stock, market value of investments and contingent liability are shown in foot notes. For example, change in the method of depreciation or method of valuation of stock, market value of investments and contingent liability are shown in footnotes. The Companies Act has prescribed the proforma and contents of Balance Sheet and Profit and Loss Account to ensure full disclosure of financial information.

(6) The Principle of Vertifiable Objective : This principle requires that all transactions recorded in the books of accounts must be evidenced and supported by business documents, such as cash memos invoices, vouchers, etc. These supporting documents provide the basis for making entries and for audit. Objectivity principle also requires that the accounting records must be free from the personal bias of the owners and managers.

ACCOUNTING CONVENTIONS OR MODIFYING PRINCIPLES

These principle are exceptions to the basic accounting principles stated above. These modifying principles are as under :

1. Principle of Materiality : This principle is an exception to the principle of full disclosure. According to this principle, items having an insignificant effect or irrelevant to the user need not be disclosed. American Accounting Association defines materiality as, "An item should be regarded as material if there is reason to believe that knowledge of it would influence decision of informed investor". Materiality of an item depends on its nature and amount. It should be noted that what is material for one firm may be immaterial for another. For example, the cost of small tools may be material for a small repair workshop but may be immaterial for TELCO. Therefore, the accountant should judge the importance of each transaction or event to determine its materiality.

2. Principle of Consistency : This principle states that accounting procedures and methods should remain consistent from one year to another. These should not be changed from year to year as otherwise the net profits of different years will not be comparable. For example, a firm can choose any one of the several methods of depreciation. But the method once chosen should be followed consistently year after year. However, change may be made to adopt improved techniques of accounting, to keep accounting flexible and to ensure better disclosure of financial information. In case a change becomes necessary, the change and its effect should be stated clearly.

3. Principle of Conservatism or Prudence : According to this principle record all anticipated losses but ignore all anticipated gains. Conservatism is thus, the policy of playing safe. Some examples of the application of this principle are :

(a) Closing stock is valued at cost price or market price whichever is less.

(b) Provision for doubtful debts is created in anticipation of actual bad debts.

(c) Joint life insurance policy is shown at surrender value as against the premiums paid.

The principle of conservatism should be applied carefully. Otherwise it may result in the creation of secret reserves which is against the principle of full disclosure.

4. Principle of Timeliness : Financial statements provide useful information on the basis of which users take important decisions. If the statements contain old and late information they are of little use. Therefore, this principle states that the financial statements should be prepared quickly at the end of the accounting period. They should be made available to the users at the earliest possible time. To ensure timely information, the Companies At requires companies to report quarterly results of their operations.

5. Principle of Industry Practice : Sometimes, the peculiar nature of an industry may required departure from the basic accounting principles. Three may be a long standing accounting practice in an industry. For example, a particular method of valuation of stock may be prevailing in an industry. While preparing its financial statements every firm in that industry must follow the prevailing accounting practice of that industry. Otherwise the results of the firm will not be comparable to those of other firms.

ERRORS IN ACCOUNTING

During the recording or summarizing the transactions, the accountant may make certain mistakes which leads to errors in the accounting The first major check to find out the errors is Trial Balance. If the trial balance does not tally, it means that there is some error in the accounting. But, even if the trial balance tallies, the accounts may have some errors. Before we understand that, errors are classified mainly into four types:

1. Errors of Omission - When the transaction is completely or partly omitted from the books of account
2. Errors of Commission - When transaction is recorded with wrong amount or in wrong account or error in casting totals.
3. Error of Principle - When the amount received or spent is not properly allocated between revenue and capital
4. Compensating errors - When two errors compensate each other in such a way that it does not affect the trial balance

Of the above, the error of complete omission, errors of principle and compensating errors do not affect the matching of trial balance and hence may be present even if the trial balance is matched.

Suspense Account : On knowing that there is some error in the accounts, the accountant should try to find it out and correct it. In case, he cannot find it and he is in hurry to close the books of account, he may transfer the difference between the credit and debit side of the trial balance to an account called 'Suspense account'. On location of the errors in the next year, the correct accounting entry is passed with the help of suspense account and the suspense account is closed.

Rectification of Errors : For rectification of errors, the following rules are observed.

(1) If the error is located at the trial balance stage, and it affects only one account, no Journal entry is passed. A correction is made in the ledger and explanation is given. If the error affects two or more accounts, those accounts are rectified by passing a journal entry.

(2) If the accountant fails to locate the errors at Trial Balance stage and it is important to prepare the Final accounts, the balance amount is transferred to Suspense Account. When the errors are located at subsequent stage, journal entry is passed by posting correct amount in the correct account and the second entry is made in suspense account.

(3) If the error comes to notice in the subsequent year, the Profit & Loss Adjustment A/c is opened and all the transactions where a revenue account is involved, instead to making entry in that account, P&L Adjustment account is used. The other entry is made in the concerned account and if no other account is involved, it is made to suspense account. The balance in P&L adjustment A/c is transferred to Capital account. This is done with an objective that due to the errors of previous year, the Profit & Loss A/c of current year should not be affected.

Illustration 4 : The following are certain illustrations regarding rectification of errors :

(1) Total of debit side of Salary account has been cast in excess by Rs. 100.

(2) One purchase of Rs. 25 has been posted from

day book to the ledger as Rs. 250.

(3) A cheque of Rs. 10,000 issued to Suresh for his past dues has been wrongly debited to the purchase account.

(4) Expenditure of Rs. 5000 incurred for trial run of the machine has been debited to the expenditure account.

(5) Expenditure of Rs. 250 was wrongly credited in the ledger as Rs. 520.

(6) Payment of Rs. 1100 received from Kamal was credited in the cash book.

(7) Purchase of Rs. 4500 from Rajan was entered in the Sales day book.

(8) Sale of Rs. 1500 to Surendra on credit was omitted from the day book.

(9) Sale of Furniture for Rs. 500 was entered in the Sales day book.

(10) Rent of office paid in advance Rs. 1200 was debited to the Rent account.

(11) Goods returned to Sunita valued Rs. 750 was debited to Anita's account.

(12) Rs. 1000 being purchase returns was posted to the Purchase day book.

(13) A sale of Rs. 1000 to Sanjay was entered in the Purchase day book from where the account of Sanjay was debited by Rs. 100.

No.	Particulars		Debit	Credit
1.	Suspense A/c	Dr.	100	
	To Salary A/c			100
2.	Creditor's A/c	Dr.	225	
	To Suspense A/c			225
3.	Suspense A/c	Dr.	10,000	
	To Purchase A/c			10,000
4.	Machine A/c	Dr.	5,000	
	To Expenditure A/c			5,000
5.	Expenditure A/c	Dr.	770	
	To Suspense A/c			770
6.	Cash A/c	Dr.	2,200	
	To Kamal A/c			2,200
7.	Purchase A/c	Dr.	4,500	
	Sales A/c	Dr.	4,500	
	To Rajan A/c			9,000
8	Surendra A/c	Dr.	1,500	
	To Sales A/c			1,500
9.	Sales A/c	Dr.	500	
	To Furniture A/c			500
10.	Advance Rent A/c	Dr.	1,200	
	To Rent A/c			1,200
11.	Sunita A/c	Dr.	750	
	To Anita A/c			750
12.	Creditor's A/c	Dr.	2,000	
	To Purchase Return A/c			1,000
	To Purchase A/c			1,000
13.	Suspense A/c	Dr.	1,100	
	Sanjay A/c	Dr.	900	
	To Purchase A/c			1,000
	To Sales A/c			1,000

3. ACCOUNTING FOR DEPRECIATION

DEPRECIATION

Depreciation means a permanent and continuing fall in the value of the asset. According to the Institute of Chartered Accountants of England, "Depreciation is that part of the cost of a fixed asset to its owner which is not recoverable when the asset is finally put out of use by him. Provision against this loss of capital is an integral cost of conducting the business during the effective commercial life of the asset and is not dependant upon the amount of profit earned." The term depreciation is used only in respect of fixed assets. Any diminution in the value of current assets is taken care of by valuing them for Balance sheet purpose 'at cost or market price whichever is less'. Depreciation is a charge against profit and hence is debited to P&L account but it is a non-cash expenditure as no cash is paid for it.

Causes of Depreciation

Depreciation may occur due to various reasons which are listed as below :

(a) Wear and tear (normal use of the asset)

(b) Exhaustion (in case of mineral mines, oil wells etc.)

(c) Obsolescence (due to change in the technology)

(d) Efflux of time (for patents, copyright, lease assets etc.)

(e) Accidents

Depletion and Amortization : These two terms are used interchangeably with depreciation but are different from depreciation. Depletion implies removal of an available but irreplaceable resource such as extracting coal from a coal mine or oil out of oil well.

Amortization is the process of writing off intangible assets. Intangible assets like patent, copyright, leasehold etc. have limited useful life after which they cease to be of any value to the owner. Therefore, the cost of acquiring them must be written off over the useful life of the concerned asset.

Methods for Providing Depreciation

The purpose of providing depreciation in the accounts is to show the true value of the assets of the firm, to ascertain the true profits of the firm earned during the year and make arrangement for the replacement of the asset after the end of its useful life. There are various methods of providing depreciation on assets. The important among them are as follows :

(1) **Straight Line Method :** Under this methods, depreciation remains same throughout the life of the asset. The total amount of depreciation is allocated to the useful life of the asset in equal proportion. This is most simple and widely used method of depreciation.

(2) **Reducing Balance Method :** Also, known as Written Down Value method, the depreciation is high in the initial years and less in the subsequent years. Since the maintenance expenditure is low in initial years and high in later years, this method leads to more or less uniform expenditure on depreciation and maintenance taken together, throughout the life of the asset. Though, the calculation of percentage of depreciation is complex, it is widely used and even for Income Tax purposes, only this method is used to calculate depreciation. In this method the value of the asset never becomes zero.

(3) **Annuity Method :** In this method, the depreciation is calculated based on the annuity

table, considering the amount to be required to replace the asset at the end of the useful life of the asset. Here also, the amount of depreciation remains same in all the years.

(4) **Depreciation Fund Method :** It is actually not a method of calculating depreciation but a method of providing depreciation in the books. In this method, the depreciation amount is calculated using the straight line or annuity method. The annual depreciation amount is set aside in an account called Depreciation Fund account and it is invested in safe and liquid securities. The annual depreciation amount is decided in such a way that the total amount accumulated from the depreciation and the income from the investments is nearly equal to the amount required to replace the assets at the end of the useful life. The journal entries are similar to the debenture redemption fund method, which is explained in the chapter of company accounts.

(5) **Depletion Method :** It is used for peculiar assets like mines, quarries etc. where an estimate of total quantity of output by the asset can be fairly known. The depreciation per unit of the asset is calculated based on the availability of total units. Each year depreciation is calculated according to the number of units extracted out of the asset.

(6) **Sum of Years Digit Method :** The amount of depreciation to be charged goes on decreasing every year. The following formula is used to calculate depreciation :

Remaining life of asset (including current year)

$$\text{Deprecation} = \frac{\text{Remaining life of asset (including current year)}}{\text{Sum of all digits of the life of asset in years}} \times \text{Original cost}$$

Sum of all digits of the life of asset in years

(7) **Machine Hour Rate Method :** This method is used when the life of the asset can be fairly known in terms of its usage in number of hours. In this method depreciation is calculated as below:

$$\text{Depreciation (Per machine hour)} = \frac{\text{Original cost of asset - Scrap value}}{\text{Life of asset in hours}}$$

(8) **Revaluation Method :** This method is used for items like loose tools, jigs etc. and cattle. At the end of the year, the market value of the assets on hand is calculated. Depreciation is taken as the difference between the value of assets at the beginning of the year and at the end of the year.

Apart from above, the following practices are followed in respect of various assets :

(a) No depreciation is charged on the Goodwill. It is generally written off over a number of years.

(b) In case of Freehold Land also, no depreciation is charged.

FINAL ACCOUNTS

Preparation of final accounts is the final step in the accounting cycle. Final accounts are prepared to achieve the objectives of accountancy. In order to know the profit or loss earned by a firm "Trading and Profit and Loss Account" i.e. income statement is prepared. Balance sheet of financial position statement will show the financial condition of the firm on a particular date. Under Section 210 of the Companies Act it has been made compulsory for companies to prepare their final accounts and present the same before the share holders for their approval, at every annual general meeting of the company.

TYPES OF FINAL ACCOUNTS

Every firm prepares final account to know the results of its operations as well as to know the current financial position of the firm. The following accounts are prepared for this purpose :

(1) Manufacturing account (only manufacturing firms)

(2) Trading account

(3) Profit & Loss account

(4) Balance sheet

(1) Manufacturing Account. It is prepared only by the manufacturing concerns. This account is prepared by the manufacturer to know the cost of production. So, all the expenses related to the manufacturing are debited to this account. The cost of production ascertained is then transferred to the Trading account.

(2) Trading Account. This account gives the overall result of trading i.e. purchase and sell, of goods. Trading account may be defined as an account which is prepared to ascertain the gross profit or gross loss of business concern for a given time period. It compares the cost of goods sold (which includes all the expenses on purchasing the goods) and sales price of goods. The difference between the two is called 'Gross Profit' or loss. Cost of goods sold can be defined as

Cost of goods sold = Opening stock + Net Purchases + Exp. on purchases – Closing Stock

Expenses on purchases include Wages, Customs and import duty, Freight, Carriage and cartage, Royalty, Gas, Electricity, Fuel etc., Packing materials and other similar items.

(3) Profit and Loss Account. Profit and Loss account is the account which is prepared to calculate the net profit or net loss of the business for a given accounting period. It may be defined as a financial statement that matches the gross profit and indirect revenues with the indirect expenses during an accounting period to show the net profit or net loss earned by a business firm. After knowing the gross profit, the owner is interested in finding out the net result of the operations of business. This is done with the help of P&L account. In this account, all the expenses other than those taken into trading account, are debited. These expenditures are related to the administration of the business as well as selling of the goods. Gross profit and other incomes of the business are credited. This also includes all incomes and expenses whether related to normal course of business or not. The net amount is 'Net Profit or Loss' of the business for the year.

(4) Balance Sheet. Balance sheet is a statement (not an account) of the assets and liabilities of the business concern. It shows the financial position of the business. Also, the trading and P&L accounts are prepared for a particular period (say a year) but balance sheet is prepared for a particular point of time (say a day) in business.

Form of Balance Sheet. Balance sheet means a financial statement which sets out the assets and liabilities of a trading or non-trading organisation as at a certain date.

There is no prescribed form of balance sheet for the sole proprietorship firm or partnership firm. The form of balance sheet for companies is contained in Schedule VI of Companies Act, 1956. but even for sole proprietorship and partnersihp firms the items of the balance sheet are shown in an orderly fashion. The order may be any of the following :

(a) Order of Permanence

(b) Order of Liquidity

These orders classify the assets in the order in which the expected time within which the asset can be converted into cash. Generally companies and manufacturing concerns use the order of permanence, which is mandated by the Schedule VI of Companies Act. In this order, the asset, which is most difficult

LIABILITIES	AMOUNT	ASSETS	AMOUNT
Capital		Goodwill	
Long Term Loans		Land	
		Building	
Sundry Creditors		Plant & Machinery	
Bills Payable		Furniture	
Outstanding		Closing Stock :	
Expenses		Raw material	
Bank Overdraft		Work in progress	
		Finished goods	
		Sundry Debtors	
		Bills Receivable	
		Prepaid Expenses	
		Cash at Bank	
		Cash in Hand	

to liquidate, is shown first and the asset, which is most liquid, is shown last. Hence, goodwill appears on the top (as goodwill is sold only after all other assets are sold) and cash on hand appears last. The reverse is the order when balance sheet is presented in the order of liquidity. The detailed explanation of order of permanence is given in the chapter relating to company accounts.

The following is the mode of a balance sheet prepared according to Permanency Order.

NOTE :

(a) Wages are debited to the Trading account whereas Salaries are debited to P&L account.

(b) Trading expenses are expenses related to trading but Trade expenses are petty or miscellaneous expenses which are debited to P&L account.

(c) Deferred revenue expenditure to the extent not written off appears on the asset side in the balance, but they are not represented by actual asset and hence are known as Fictitious Assets.

(d) Closing stock of raw material and work in progress appear in Manufacturing account, but stock of finished goods appears in trading account only.

(e) Freight, Carriage and Cartage are taken as direct expenses incurred on purchase of goods and hence they appear on the debit side of Trading account.

(f) Royalty is a direct expense, as it is paid on the production of goods. Hence it appears in the manufacturing account as a direct manufacturing expense. It royalty is paid on sales and not manufacturing, it is debited to Trading account.

(g) Treatment of packing material depends on the actual circumstances. Expenditure on packing to convert goods into saleable items are direct expenses and hence appear in the Trading account whereas packing expenses to make the goods look attractive for marketing is considered as marketing expense and hence should be debited to Profit & Loss account.

CLOSING ENTRIES

Final accounts i.e. Trading and P&L account and Balance Sheet are prepared by the accountant at the end of the year based on all the transaction of the year. At the end of the year, the accountant may know of certain adjustments to be made in the books of accounts to give a true picture of the performance of the business which is not taken into account till the stage of preparing Trial balance. These adjustments pertain to valuation of closing stock, annual interests on capital, provision for bad debts and discounts, depreciation, outstanding incomes and expenses, prepaid incomes and expenses, rectification of mistakes etc. Treatment of some important closing entries have been explained hereunder :

(1) Provision for Bad Debts. In business, generally a part of the credit sales do not materialize in cash and has to be foregone by the firm. This is known as bad debts. It is a loss of the business. Moreover, every year while preparing the final accounts, the businessman estimates the amount of bad debts that may occur in the subsequent year and considers it as a loss of this year because the debts belong to this year. For this purpose he debits the profit and loss account and creates a liability on the business by crediting Bad Debt Reserve account. This amount is shown as a deduction from the debtors in the balance sheet. The following is the format of showing bad debts and bad debt reserves in the P&L account and in the balance sheet.

PROFIT AND LOSS ACCOUNT

To Bad debts (old)	_____			
Add :				
Bad debts (new)	_____			
Bad debts Reserve(new)	_____			
Less :				
Bad debts Reserve (old)	_____	_______		

BALANCE SHEET

			Debtors	______	
			Less :		
			Bad debts(new)	______	
			Bad debts Reserve(new)	______	_____

Here, bad debts new refer to the bad debts given in the adjustment to be recognized while preparing the final accounts. Bad debts reserve (old) represents the balance in the account in the last year. Bad debts reserve(new) is the amount to be set aside out of the profits for the next year. It should be remembered that when bad debts reserve is to be created as a certain percentage of debtors it should always be calculated on the amount of debtors as reduced by the new bad debts. Next year when the actual bad debts happen, it is debited to the bad debt reserve account and not the profit and loss account. Similar treatment is given in case of discount and Discount Reserve on Debtors and Creditors. The only thing to remember is that new provision for discount on debtors is calculated on the net balance i.e. after deducting the Bad debt reserve, if any.

Illustration 1: In a trial balance, debtors are appearing at Rs. 1,08,000. a provision is to be made for doubtful debtors @5% on the debtors after considering following information:

1. An amount of Rs. 1,000 is included in debtors who is bankrupt and his estate is expected to realise 50 paise in a rupee.
2. Debtors include an amount of Rs. 5,000 for goods supplied to proprietor.
3. Bills receivable include a bill of Rs. 3,000, which is dishonoured.
4. Goods sold on 'Sale or return' basis amounting to Rs. 5,000 have been included in debtors.
5. Debtors include an amount of Rs. 1,000 from a customer whose financial position is doubtful.

The total provision to be made will be calculated as follows:

Debtors (Balance given)	1,08,000
Less : Debtor who is bankrupt [As the amount to be received and loss is certain]	(1,000)
Less : Goods supplied to proprietor [This amount needs to be debited to drawings]	(5,000)
Add : Dishonoured bill [After dishonour of bill, he is now again a debtor]	3,000
Less : Goods on 'Sale or return' basis [This amount cannot be considered as sale]	(5,000)
Amount on which provision is to be made1,00,000	
So, the provision to be made is	Rs. 5,000

(2) Closing Stock. As already explained, closing stock is valued at cost or market price, whichever is lower. Since closing stock is calculated on the last day of the year, it is taken as closing adjustment entry. Therefore, the value of closing stock appears at two places viz. credit side of Trading account and under Current assets in the Balance sheet. But, if the closing stock is given in the trial balance, it means that closing stock has been valued before preparation of trial balance and hence the accounting entry for closing stock has been made. The balance appearing in trial balance, therefore, is asset and will go to the asset side of balance sheet.

(3) Outstanding Expenses. Outstanding expenses mean those expenses, which are due to be paid by the firm, but they are still not paid in cash. Examples are outstanding salary, outstanding rent, Insurance premium etc. The following entry is made for outstanding expenses:

Expense A/c Dr.
To Outstanding Expense A/c

This will result in adding the outstanding amount to the amount appearing in the trial balance and showing the outstanding expense account as current liability in the balance sheet.

(4) Prepaid Expenses. Prepaid expenses are those which will become due for payment in the next year or the part of payment made belongs to the next year but the whole payment is made in the current year. Example are: Prepaid insurance, salary, commission etc. The following accounting entry is made for prepaid expenses:

Prepaid Expense A/c Dr.
To Expense A/c

This will result in reducing the account of the expense by the amount prepaid and showing the prepaid expense account as current asset in the balance sheet.

Illustration 2 : Trial balance as on 31-3-2005 shows Debit of Insurance premium account Rs. 6,000. But, Insurance premium paid Rs. 4,000 was for period from 1-1-2005 to 31-12-2005.

Here, Rs. 4000 were paid for the period from 1-1-2005 to 31-12-2005 out of which only 3 months i.e. 1-1-2005 to 31-3-2005 belongs to the current financial year. Rest 9 months' premium has been paid in advance.

So, the pre paid premium will be 4,000 * 9/12 = Rs. 3,000

The accounting entry to be passed is

Prepaid Insurance A/c Dr. 3,000
To Insurance A/c 3,000

(5) Outstanding Income. It refers to the incomes accrued to the firm but not received in cash. It may be commission, rent receivable etc. The accounting entry for outstanding income is:

Outstanding Income A/c Dr.
To Income A/c

Outstanding income will appear in the balance sheet as current asset.

(6) Income Received in Advance. Many a times, the firm may receive certain income in the current year which is due to it in the next financial year. Such receipt is known as income received in advance. The accounting entry will be:

Income A/c Dr.
To Income Received in Advance A/c

(7) Hidden Entries. Sometimes, some closing entries are hidden in the question which the reader is expected to notice. For example, the trial balance may give two figures : 6% Debentures : Rs, 50,000; Interest on debentures : Rs. 1,500. As one can notice that the total interest due for payment on these debentures was Rs. 3,000 for the year. But only Rs. 1,500 has entered the books. This means that the rest 1,500 is due but not paid and no accounting entry for this has been passed. Therefore, closing entry will be passed debiting the P&L account by Rs. 1,500 as Interest on debentures due but not paid and showing the same amount as current liability in the balance sheet.

(8) Commission Problem. A common type of question sometimes asked is about the calculation of commission of Manager, Director etc. In such questions, the wordings of the question are very important. For example, suppose, the net profit(before commission) of the firm is Rs. 11,000. The manager is entitled to get a commission of 10% on net profit. Now, since the net profit can be decided only after deducting the manager's commission, this profit involves the net profit as well as the manager's commission. So, if the net profit is say, 100 then after adding 10% commission, the profit before commission should be 110. So, in this case, the manager's commission will be (11000 * 10/110) = 1000 and net profit will be Rs. 10,000. In this way manager's commission is now 10% of the net profit.

But, there is catch. This procedure should be adopted only if the expenditure is to be deducted from the revenues for finding out the net profit. If any appropriation of profit is to be made, flat calculation should be made. For example, in the above case, if 10% of net profit is to be reserved for contingency, then the reserve amount will be (11000 * 10/100) = Rs. 1100. This is because reserve is created after calculating the net profit unlike the manager's commission which is calculated before finding net profit.

FINAL ACCOUNTS OF PARTNERSHIP

Final accounts of partnership firm are prepared in the same way i.e. Trading and Profit and loss accounts are prepared along with the balance sheet. Apart from these accounts, partnership firms also prepare an additional account i.e. Profit and Loss Appropriation account. This account is prepared to show the appropriation of the net profit and distributing the profit among the partners in their profit sharing ratio. Also, instead of preparing one capital account, separate capital account is prepared for each partner. The following is the format of profit and loss appropriation account:

Dr. **Profit and Loss Appropriation A/c** Cr.

Particulars	Amount	Particulars	Amount
To Transfer to general reserve		By Net profit for the year	
To Transfer to sinking fund			
To Transfer to capital accounts			
A's Capital account			
B's Capital account			
C's Capital account			

NATURE OF NON-PROFIT ORGANISATION

Charitable institutions like clubs, hospitals, schools etc. do not carry on trading and hence do not earn profit. They do not prepare a trading and profit and loss account. But they also want to know whether their incomes are sufficient to meet current expenses and what is their financial position at the end of the accounting period. Therefore, they prepare two types of accounts viz.,

1. Income and Expenditure A/c and
2. Receipt and Payment A/c

Apart from it, they also prepare Balance sheet like a trading firm.

Income and Expenditure Account. This account is very similar to the Profit and Loss Account. The difference between the revenues and expenses is not treated as profit or loss but considered as Surplus (excess of revenue over expenditure) or Deficit (excess of expenditure over revenue). This account contains all the incomes and revenues for the current year only whether received or paid in cash or accrued.

Receipts and Payment Account. Receipts and payments account is a summary of cash transactions appearing in the cash book. To keep a note of daily transactions of the organization, such organizations prepare receipts and payment account. It is like a cash or bank account. All the receipts and payments whether of the current year or any other year, whether capital or revenue gets recorded in this account. Accordingly, the closing balance of this account does not mean that income for the year has exceeded the expenditure by an amount equal to the balance in hand.

BALANCE SHEET

Balance sheet in case of a non-trading concern is prepared in the usual way and contains particulars of all assets and liabilities of the institution. The excess of assets over liabilities is termed as **'Capital Fund'**. The capital fund is made up of excess of income over expenditure and other incomes or surplus which might have been capitalized by the institution form time to time.

DISTINCTION BETWEEN R/P ACCOUNT AND I/E ACCOUNT

RECEIPTS AND PAYMENT A/C	INCOME AND EXPENDITURE A/C
It is a real account	It is a nominal account
It is like cash account of a business entity	It is like Profit and Loss account of a business entity
It has opening and closing balance of cash in hand and bank	It has no opening balance. The difference between credit and debit is transferred to balance sheet as excess of income over expenditure or vice-versa.
Receipts and payments relating to any accounting period are recorded in the year of receipt or payment	Income and expenditure of an accounting period gets recorded in the income and expenditure account of respective period only
It includes both capital and revenue receipts and payments	It includes only revenue incomes and expenditures
Balance sheet need not accompany this account	Balance sheet must accompany this account
Debit side of this account records receipts and the credit side records payments during the year.	Debit side of this account records expenses and the credit side records incomes for the year.

TREATMENT OF CERTAIN PECULIAR ITEMS

The treatment of certain peculiar receipts and payments in such organizations is as below:

(a) Any money received by such organizations for performing a specific activity in future like sports is called Endowment fund. It is capital receipt and figures only in the Receipt and Payment Account.

(b) General Donations received from time to time may be added to the Capital Fund or be treated as revenue receipts depending on the nature of the enterprise and the amount. But, in case of charitable institutions, they are treated as income.

(c) Specific Donations received for special purposes are to be used only for that activity. So, this amount is shown on the liability side of balance sheet and expenses done out of that fund are shown as deductions from the fund.

(d) Legacy is a sum received at the wish of a deceased person and should be treated as capital receipt.

(e) The Membership Fee or Entrance Fee should be treated as revenue receipt if it is received every year. If received once in the life time, it should be capitalized.

(f) Capitation Fee is collected by the educational institutions in a lump sum from the students seeking admission in a school or a college. This amount is quite heavy and is meant for development of the institution or incurring some capital expenditure. This amount is taken to balance sheet either as separate item or added to the Capital fund.

METHODOLOGY OF ANSWER

In the examination paper, generally the questions give figure appearing in one account i.e. either Income and Expenditure account or Receipt and payment account. With this certain additional information is also given. With the help of these, it is required to arrive at a figure which should appear in the other account. While solving such question, one should keep in mind the differences in the two accounts, the key among them are:

1. Receipts and payment account records receipts and payments relating to any year happening in the current year. But, income and expenditure account records income and expenditure relating to current year only

irrespective of the year in which it was received.

2. Receipts and payment account records revenue as well as capital receipts and payments whereas Income and expenditure account records only revenue incomes and expenditures.

Receipt and payment account to Income and expenditure account : If, in the question, the income appearing in the Receipts and payment account is given, the following steps should be followed to arrive at the income which should appear in the Income and expenditure account:

Step 1 : Take the income appearing in the Receipt and Payment account

Step 2 : Deduct the incomes which belongs to the year preceding and succeeding the current year but received in the current year.

Step 3 : Add the incomes received in the preceding or succeeding year but belonging to the current year.

This will give you the figure which should appear in the Income and Expenditure account. Same process should be followed for the expenditures. But, in case the figure given in the question belongs to Income and expenditure account, to arrive at the figure of Receipt and payment account the above steps should be reversed i.e. deduct will become add and add will be come deduct.

INCOME AND EXPENDITURE ACCOUNT OF PROFESSIONALS

Professionals like Doctors, lawyers etc. have a peculiar distinction from other organizations. Professionals prepare their accounts on the cash basis and therefore, they ignore outstanding incomes. They do take into account outstanding expenses but not income that has not yet been received. This is because they do not file suits for recovery of their dues. Hence they prepare **Receipt and Expenditure Account** which means that all incomes are considered on the receipt i.e. cash basis and all expenditures are considered on accrual basis. To reflect this, on one hand, they add the outstanding income to the corresponding income head, and on the other hand they debit the Receipt and Expenditure account with the outstanding income as reserve. This nullifies the effect of crediting the outstanding income.

PARTNERSHIP ACCOUNTS

INTRODUCTION

Partnership has been defined in the Indian Partnership Act, 1932. According to it, 'Partnership is the relation between two or more persons who have agreed to share profits of a business carried on by all or any of them acting for all'. It is voluntary for a partnership firm to register. But, the law provides certain benefits to the partnership firms which are registered. The partners may or may not have a written agreement. In absence of any agreement to the contrary, the following rules apply:

(a) Every partner is entitled to share the profits or losses equally.

(b) No partner is entitled to any interest on his capital nor interest is charged on drawings.

(c) A partner is not entitled to any salary from the firm for his work as a partner.

(d) A partner is entitled to interest @6% p.a. for any loans given by him to the firm.

PARTNERSHIP DEED

Partnership is created by an agreement but it is not necessary that the agreement should be in writing. But to avoid future disputes, it is always better to have it in writing. The document containing the important terms of partnership as agreed by the partners between themselves is called 'Partnership Deed'. It contains all the details regarding salary to be paid to any partner, interest on capital and drawings, duration of the firm, rules regarding operation of bank accounts, management of the firm etc. In the absence of any agreement in writing, the rights and duties of partners will be those as given in the Partnership Act, 1932.

RIGHTS OF PARTNERS

Every partner in a partnership firm has the following rights, according to the Indian Partnership Act:

1. Right to take part in the conduct and management of business.
2. Right to be consulted and heard in all matters affecting the business of the partnership.
3. Right of free access to all records, books and accounts of the business, and also to examine and copy them.
4. Right of share in profits equally, in absence of any agreement
5. Partner is entitled to be indemnified by the firm for all the acts done by him in the course of the partnership business, for all payments made by him in respect of partnership debts or liabilities and for expenses and disbursements made by him in an emergency for protecting the firm from the loss.
6. Every partner is a joint owner of the partnership property. He is entitled to have the partnership property used exclusively for the purposes of the partnership.
7. Every partner is entitled to prevent the introduction of a new partner into the firm without his consent.
8. Every partner has a right to retire according to the agreement or with the consent of the other partners. If the partnership is at will, he can retire merely by giving notice to other partners.
9. A retiring partner or the heirs of the deceased partner are entitled to share in the profits earned with the aid of the proportion of assets belonging to such outgoing partner until the accounts are finally settled.

DUTIES OF PARTNERS

(a) Every partner is bound to diligently carry on the business of the firm to the greatest common advantage.

(b) A partner is bound to keep and render true, proper and correct accounts of the partnership.

(c) A partner is bound to indemnify the firm for any loss caused by his willful neglect or fraud in the conduct of the business.

(d) A partner must not carry on a competing business, nor use the property of the firm for his private purposes.

(e) Every partner is bound to share the losses equally with the others.

(f) A partner is bound to act within the scope of his authority.

(g) No partner can assign or transfer his partnership interest to any other person so as to make him a partner in the business, without consent of other partners.

KINDS OF PARTNERS

Besides the usual partners who contribute to the capital of the firm and take part in its business who are known as Active Partners, the following types of partners may also exist :

(1) Sleeping Partner : A Sleeping partner does not take part in the day today activities of the business. He merely contributes capital and shares profit or losses. But, he is liable to outsiders for debts of the firm.

(2) Nominal Partner : A Nominal partner merely lends his name to the firm to be used as a partner but neither contributes capital not shares the profit/ losses. But, he is liable to those third parties who give credit to the firm on the strength of his being a partner.

(3) Partner in Profit Only : As the name implies, this kind of partner shares only profit and not the losses of business. But, in case of insolvency of firm, his liability to outsider for the payment of debts of the firm is similar to those of other partners.

(4) Partner by Estoppel and Holding Out : Partner by Estoppel is one who without really being a partner, so conducts himself as to lead others to believe him to be a partner. Similarly, if one is declared to be a partner in a firm and does not disclaim the partnership, he is treated as partner by Holding out. Such persons are also liable to third parties who give credit to the firm on the belief of his being a partner.

(5) Sub-Partner : A Sub-partner gets a share of profits of the firm from one of the partners. He has no rights against the firm and he is not liable to its debts also.

(6) Minor Partner : A minor can be admitted to the benefits of an existing partnership with the consent of all the partners. His position is peculiar in the firm. He is not personally liable for the debts of the firm like other partners, only his share in the partnership property and profits of the firm are liable. He can sue the firm for the accounts and his share when he wants to severe his connections with the firm but not otherwise. After attaining majority, within 6 months he has to decide whether he wants to become a regular partner in the firm or wants to withdraw from the firm.

CAPITAL ACCOUNT

Partners may maintain their capital accounts in either of two systems :

1. Fixed Capital System
2. Fluctuating Capital system

In Fixed Capital System a Capital A/c and Current A/c is opened for each partner. The initial capital brought by the partner is credited to the capital a/c. The adjustments regarding salary, interest, drawings, profit etc. are made in the current accounts of the partners. In the *Fluctuating Capital System,* only one Capital account is maintained and all the transactions related to the capital are recorded in this account.

To transfer the net profit of the firm between the partners, the firm prepares an account called "Profit and Loss Appropriation A/c" which contains all the appropriations out of the net profits including the reserves and distribution of profit to the partners.

JOINT LIFE POLICY

A partnership firm may decide to take a joint life insurance policy on the lives of all partners. The firm pays the premium and the amount of policy is payable to the firm in the event of death of any partner or on maturity of the policy. The objective is to minimize the financial hardship to the firm in the event of payment of a large sum to the legal representative of a deceased partner. The premium paid is treated as the revenue expenditure of the firm and debited to the P&L account. On maturity of the policy, the amount is received by the firm and is credited to all the partners' capital account in the profit sharing ratio.

Certain firms treat the insurance premium as capital expenditure. In that case a 'Joint Life Insurance Policy' account is opened and the premium paid is debited to this account. The surrender value of the policy is credited to this account as the balance to be carried forward to the next year. The difference between the premium paid and the surrender value is debited to P&L account as loss. Surrender Value remains to be shown on the asset side of the balance sheet till the maturity. On maturity of the policy the amount realized is credited to this account and final balance is distributed between all the partners in the profit sharing ratio.

ADMISSION OF A PARTNER

Sometimes, the firm may introduce a new partner to add to the capital of the business or associate with a renowned businessman or for any other purpose. But a new partner cannot be admitted without the consent of all the partners unless otherwise agreed upon. This admission of a new partner raises various issues.

(A) Legal Position. From admission of a new partner, the following legal consequences arise:

1. On admission of new partner, legally the old partnership is considered to be dissolved. However, the partnership firm is not dissolved. Profit sharing ratio of old partners is changed and partnership relation between all the partners (including the new one) comes into existence.
2. The new partner becomes liable for all future acts of the firm i.e., he becomes liable jointly and severally in respect of all liabilities created after his admission. However, he is not liable for liabilities created by the firm before he was admitted as a partner.
3. Old partners are liable for all the debts of the firm existing on the date of new partner's admission.

(B) Revaluation of Assets and Liabilities. To determine the share of the new partner as well as how much he should bring as capital and goodwill to be entitled to his share of profit, the true value of the firm as on the date of admission of the partner has to be calculated. For that purpose, all the assets and liabilities of the firm are revalued and the net value of the firm is found out.

This is done through an intermediary account called "Profit and Loss Adjustment Account" or "Revaluation Account". Any increase or decease in the asset or liability of the firm is shown in the revaluation account and the final balance of this account is transferred to the old partners in the old profit sharing ratio.

Sometimes, the partners decide that even though the assets and liabilities are revalued, the value in the books of account should not be changed. In such a situation, 'Memorandum Revaluation Account' is prepared. In this account the assets and liabilities are revalued and the resulting profit/loss is distributed between the old partners. Then again the assets and liabilities are brought to the original book values and the resultant profit and loss is shared by the new partners. In this process the net treatment in the old partners' capital account is in the Sacrifice ratio. An example of Memorandum revaluation account is shown as below :

MEMORANDUM REVALUATION ACCOUNT

To Furniture	500	By Land & Building	5,000
To Stock	1,000		
To Provision for bad debts	300		
To Machinery	2,000		
To Profit transferred to old Partners A 300 B 400 C 500	1,200		
	5,000		5,000
To Reverse entry for increase in value of L & B	5,000	By Reverse entry for decrease in value of assets	3,800
		By Loss transferred to new partners A 300 B 300 C 300 D 300	1,200
	5,000		5,000

The Journal Entries for revaluation of assets and liabilities are as follow :

(a) Increase in the market value of the asset

Asset A/c Dr.

To Revaluation A/c

(b) Decrease in the value of an asset

Revaluation A/c Dr.

To Asset A/c

(c) To reduce the debtors, new Bad Debts Reserve is created

Revaluation A/c Dr.

To Bad Debt Reserve A/c

(d) If any liability is to be brought to the books of account or increase in the liability

Revaluation A/c Dr.

To Liability A/c

(e) When a liability is cancelled or reduced by settlement

Liability A/c Dr.

To Revaluation A/c

(f) For recording income due but not received or prepaid expenses

Income Receivable A/c Dr.

Prepaid Expenses A/c Dr.

To Revaluation A/c

(g) To transfer the balance of the revaluation account to the partners' capital account (if Profit)

Revaluation A/c Dr.

To Old Partners' Capital A/c

If there is any Loss, reverse entry is passed.

(h) To transfer any balance in the Reserves account to the old partners

Reserve Fund A/c Dr.

To, Old Partners' Capital A/c

(C) New Profit Sharing Ratio of Partners after Admission. After the admission of new partner, the new profit sharing ratio of all the partners has to be determined for sharing future profits. For this purpose, the new partner may either get a fixed share in the firm's profits or he gets from the share of the old partners (purchase of share). In both the ways, the old partners have to sacrifice some part of their share in the profits in favour of the new partner. The proportion in which the old partners' contribute towards the share of the new partner is known as the **'Sacrifice Ratio'.**

(D) Capital of the New Partner. When the new partner is admitted to the firm, he generally brings capital to the firm. This capital may be brought in cash or in form of some asset. The amount of capital is determined by all the partners based on the value of the firm and the share of profit proposed to be given to the new partner. Sometimes, the new partner in his personal capacity may have given loan to the firm which is converted into his capital on being admitted as the partner. Moreover, it is not compulsory for the new partner to bring capital. For example, a manager of the firm may be made partner without bringing any capital to the firm.

(E) Distribution of Accumulated Profit. When a new partner is admitted, there may be existing accumulated profit in the firm. It may be in the name of Reserve Fund or credit balance of Profit and Loss Account. There may also be accumulated losses in the form of debit balance of Profit and Loss Account. This accumulated profit or loss belongs to the old partners and must be distributed among the old partners in the old profit sharing ratio before the new partner is admitted. The journal entry for this purpose is as below :

Reserve Fund A/c Dr.

Capital Reserve A/c Dr.

Profit & Loss A/c Dr.

To Old Partners' Capital A/cs

For accumulated losses, the entry will be reverse.

But, if there are specific reserves against assets in the books of the firm like Bad Debt Reserve, Depreciation Fund, Investment Fluctuation Fund etc., they are not free reserves and cannot be distributed among the partners.

(F) Treatment of Goodwill. On admission, the new partner has to pay some compensation, other than the capital, to acquire a share in the future profits of the firm, which is termed as goodwill. Goodwill is nothing but a possibility that the old customers will stick to the old firm.

The main base for calculation of goodwill is its profit earning capacity and hence past profits are taken into account for its calculation. There are many factors which determine the earning capacity of the business such as place of business, personal skills, control over raw material, latest technology, trade mark etc. In the following circumstances, the calculation of goodwill is necessary in the partnership firm :

(1) When a new partner is admitted into the firm
(2) When a partner retires or dies
(3) When firm is dissolved
(4) When Profit sharing ratio of partners is changed
(5) When method of computation of Profit is changed

VALUATION OF GOODWILL

There are various methods of calculation of goodwill. Some of them are explained here :

(1) Simple Average Profit Method. In this method, Goodwill is computed on the basis of 3 to 5 years' profit of the firm depending on the estimated period up to which the benefit of goodwill will be available. By taking average profit, the effect of fluctuation in the profits is eliminated. For example, if the average profit of the firm for last 5 years is Rs. 20,000 and goodwill is to be valued at 3 times the average profit of last 5 years, the value of goodwill will be Rs. 60,000.

(2) Weighted Average Profit Method. This method is similar to the earlier one. The difference is that in this method, higher weightage is given to the profits earned in the recent period based upon assumption that the recent trend is likely to continue in the future. So, weights are given to all the years whose average is taken. The formula for weighted average profit is :

$$\text{Weighted Average Profit} = \frac{\text{Total Weighted Profit}}{\text{Total Weights}}$$

For example,

Year	Profits	Weights	Weighted Profits
1999	12,000	1	12,000
2000	18,000	2	36,000
2001	26,000	3	78,000
2002	31,000	4	1,24,000
2003	40,000	5	2,00,000
Total		15	4,50,000

Weighted Average Profit = 4,50,000 / 15 = 30,000

Value of goodwill = 30,000 × 3 = Rs. 90,000

(3) Capitalisation Method. In this method, based on the current profits of the firm the capitalization is found out and it is compared with the present capitalization of the firm. The difference between the two is treated as goodwill. For example, the average profits of the firm for last 5 years are Rs. 16,000. The capitalization factor is 8%. So, the present capitalization of the firm is (16,000 *100 / 8) = 2,00,000. If the capital required to earn this much profit as per the market conditions is Rs. 2,50,000 then the goodwill of the firm is Rs. 50,000.

TREATMENT OF GOODWILL IN THE BOOKS ON ADMISSION OF PARTNER

Goodwill is an asset of the old firm and the old partners. So, when the new partner brings in goodwill, it is transferred to the old partners. The recording of goodwill in the books depends on how the partners wish to treat goodwill. In following different circumstances, the recording of goodwill in the books of account will be different:

(a) When the new partner pays the old partners goodwill in cash outside the firm :

In this case no record is made in the books of the firm. The amount is paid to partners outside the firm. So, the question of making any entry in the books of the firm does not arise.

(b) When goodwill is brought in cash and retained in the business :

In such a case, only two entries are made. The first is for bringing goodwill in cash i.e.

Cash A/c Dr.

To Goodwill A/c

Then this amount of goodwill is transferred to the old partners' capital account in the proportion of Sacrifice Ratio.

Goodwill A/c Dr.

To Old Partners' Capital A/c

(c) When goodwill is brought in cash and withdrawn by partners

Here, first, the above two entries will be passed. In addition, one more entry will be passed as below:

Old Partners' Capital A/c Dr.

To Cash A/c

Here also, the goodwill is credited to the old partners in the sacrifice ratio.

Note : It should be remembered that in all the above methods, the goodwill does not remain in the books. If the partners wish it to appear in the balance sheet, then the goodwill account is debited and the new partners' account is credited in the new profit sharing ratio. Moreover, if any old goodwill is already appearing in the books of the old firm, the same is to be written off to the old partners' capital account.

(d) Revaluation Method

In this case, the new partner does not bring goodwill in cash. Instead, the goodwill of the firm is valued and the old partners are given credit according to their sacrifice ratio. Here also, if the firm wishes the value of goodwill to appear in the books of account then only the following entry is passed :

Goodwill A/c Dr.

To, Old Partners' Capital A/c

(Old Profit sharing Ratio)

And if the firm does not want goodwill to appear in the books then after passing the above entry the following additional entry is passed :

All Partners' Capital A/c Dr.

(New Profit sharing ratio)

To Goodwill A/c

RETIREMENT/DEATH OF A PARTNER

When any partner retires from the partnership or if he dies, the following important points arise again:

(1) Treatment of Goodwill and New Profit Sharing Ratio. In this case, since the future profits will be shared only by the remaining partners, they stand to gain. So, they have to compensate the outgoing partner for this. This compensation is made by the remaining partners in the **'Gaining Ratio'.** The gaining ratio is decided based on what proportion of profit share of the outgoing partner is taken by which partner. So, it is again a difference between the old and new profit sharing ratios. On retirement, the treatment of goodwill may be done in any of the following ways :

(a) Goodwill may be raised in the books as an asset and credited to all the partners including the retiring partner in the old profit sharing ratio.

(b) After raising the goodwill as above, it is written off between the remaining partners in the new profit sharing ratio.

(c) Retiring partner's share of goodwill may be adjusted in the capital accounts of the continuing partners in the gaining ratio without opening the goodwill account.

The following is an example of treatment of goodwill in method (c) as above :

(2) Revaluation of Assets and Liabilities. On death or retirement of a partner, a Revaluation account or P&L adjustment account is prepared to find out the profit or loss on the revaluation of assets. As in the case of admission of partner, here also all the profits or losses on revaluation are taken into account in the P&L adjustment account. The net profit or loss on revaluation is transferred to all the old partners (including the retired or deceased partner) in their old profit sharing ratio.

(3) Distribution of Accumulated Profits and Reserves. As in the case of admission of partner, here also, all the existing accumulated profits and reserves of the firm are transferred to old partners' capital account (including the retiring or deceased partner) in the old profit sharing ratio. Many a times, firm may only transfer the share of the retiring or the deceased partner to his capital account. This can be used only when the profit sharing ratio of the remaining partners remains unchanged.

(4) Amount due to the Retiring Partner. The retiring partner's capital account is credited with his share of goodwill, profit on revaluation of assets, past profits and reserves etc. and is debited by drawings or accumulated losses etc. The balance in the capital account represents the amount due to him by the firm. This amount is transferred to the Partner's Loan account until it is paid off.

DISSOLUTION OF PARTNERSHIP

When a partnership ceases to exist, it is said to be dissolved. The dissolution may take place with the consent between the partners or by the decision of court in certain circumstances. The following issues arise on dissolution of the partnership.

(A) Realisation Account. A new account, called Realisation account is opened for arriving at the profit or loss made by the firm while dissolving the firm. All assets, other than cash and bank, are transferred to Realisation account at their book values. Similarly, all the liabilities other than capital and reserves are transferred to this account. The payments made for the liabilities are debited to the account and similarly the amounts realized from the assets are credited to this account. The expenses of dissolution are also debited to Realisation account.

The balance of Realisation account, profit or loss, is transferred to the capital accounts of the partners. Balances in the reserve account or P&L account are transferred to the partners' capital accounts in the profit sharing ratio. Partner's current accounts are also transferred to the Capital account. The balance in the capital account is their dues from the firm.

(B) Treatment of Goodwill. It is treated like any other asset in the balance sheet. Any balance appearing in the goodwill account is transferred to the Realisation account. Since, goodwill is not sold separately, generally no cash is realized against goodwill. It is reflected in the higher selling price of other assets.

(C) Insolvency of a Partner. When a partner is adjudicated as insolvent and he owes a sum of money to the firm, the uncollected portion of his dues is a loss to the firm. The question arises as to the distribution of this loss to the existing partners whether it should be divided into the capital accounts balance proportion or in the profit sharing ratio.

The decision in this regard was given by the court in the case of **Garner V/s Murray**. Court made a distinction between ordinary loss due to realization of assets and extraordinary loss due to insolvency of a partner. According to it, the following rules are observed for sharing the loss arising due to insolvency of a partner :

1. The solvent partners should bring in cash to make up their share of realization account loss.
2. The loss due to insolvency of a partner should be arrived at after transferring all the balances in the P&L A/c and reserves to all the partners in the profit sharing ratio.
3. The loss due to the insolvency of the partner is divided among the other partners in the fixed capital ratio, if the capital is fixed or in the ratio of capital balances after transferring any transferable balances appearing in the balance sheet but before adjusting profit or loss on the realisation, if the capital is fluctuating.
4. If any solvent partner has negative balance(debit) in the capital account, he will not share the loss arising due to insolvency of a partner. This will happen only in case of fluctuating capital account system. In fixed capital system, all the partners will have credit balance.

(D) When All Partners are Insolvent. When all partners are insolvent, the creditors of the firm will suffer as they cannot be repaid in full. In such a situation, the balance in the creditors' account should not be transferred to the Realisation account. A separate account should be opened for creditors. They should be paid whatever can be recovered from the private assets of the partners after paying the realisation expenses. The balance in the creditors' account should be transferred to the partners' capital account in the profit sharing ratio and the books of the firm are closed.

PIECEMEAL DISTRIBUTION OF ASSETS

In practice, when a firm is dissolved, all the assets are not sold on a single day. They are realized gradually and the liabilities are discharged as and when the cash is available. In this sequence, the liabilities to the third parties are first paid out, then the partners' loans, if any, and finally the partners' capital is returned. Here the question arises as to the basis of distribution of cash to the partners for their capital balances (when capital ratio is different from profit sharing ratio), after paying outside liabilities. For this purpose one of the following two methods may be adopted :

(1) Proportionate or Surplus Capital Method. In this method, the partners' capitals are arranged according to the profit sharing ratio by taking the least capital for one share as the base. If there is any surplus, the least surplus is eliminated and the extra surplus is determined. The extra surplus is first paid to the concerned partners in their due proportion. This results in equal ratio of capital and profit sharing. Now, the balance amount is distributed in this ratio.

(2) Maximum Loss Method. Under this method, it is assumed that every realization of assets is the final realization and according to that the loss is arrived at and divided among the partners in their profit sharing ratio. Any debit balance in the capital account will be transferred to other partners in the capital account ratio. Now, all the partners' balance will be equal to the available cash in hand and will be distributed to them according to their respective balances. This process will continue till the last asset is realized.

4. ACCOUNTING OF JOINT STOCK COMPANIES

Before going through this chapter, it is advisable to go through the salient features of the companies as well as the Companies Act (both explained in this book in detail) to get a full idea of the functioning of the companies and its salient features.

SHARE CAPITAL

A company is a legal entity separate from its owners. But as far as the accounting is concerned, the basic rules are same whether it is a company or a firm. Though there are some peculiarities in the company accounts which we shall discuss as we go along, the basic difference is that unlike in the partnership where there are few owners, in companies the owners may run into thousands. All of them hold share in the company. The various divisions of share capital are as follows :

Authorized or Nominal Capital : It is the capital mentioned in the Capital clause of the Memorandum of Association of the company with which the company is registered. The company cannot issue shares more than the authorized capital unless Capital clause is altered.

Issued Capital : It is that portion of authorized capital which is offered to the public for subscription. The remaining part of the Authorized capital is known as the 'Unissued Capital' which can be issued later on..

Subscribed Capital : Out of the issued capital, the portion for which public subscribe to the shares of the company is called subscribed capital.

Called up Capital : It is that portion of the subscribed capital which has been called up by the company from the shareholders. Capital is generally called on allotment as well as through various instalments known as 'Calls'.

Paid up Capital : It represents that portion of the Called up capital with regard to which the company has received call money from the shareholders.

Reserve Capital : According to Section 99 of the Companies Act a company may, by a special resolution determine that a portion of its uncalled capital should not be called up, except in the event of winding up of the company.

ISSUE OF SHARES

When the company issues shares to the public, the journal entries in respect of various transactions are explained as below :

TRANSACTION	ACCOUNTING ENTRY	
	DEBIT	**CREDIT**
(1) Receipt of application money	Bank A/c	Share Application A/c
(2) Application money in respect of shares allotted	Share Application A/c	Share Capital A/c
(3) Refund for rejected applications	Share Application A/c	Bank A/c
(4) Adjustment of excess application money towards allotment	Share Application A/c	Share allotment A/c
(5) Adjustment of excess application money towards calls-in-advance	Share Application A/c	Calls-in-advance A/c
(6) When allotment is made and money is due	Share Allotment A/c	Share Capital A/c
(7) Receipt of allotment money	Bank A/c	Share allotment A/c
(8) Where a call is made for the call money due	Share call A/c	Share Capital A/c
(9) Adjustment of money in calls-in-advance towards the call account	Calls-in-advance A/c	Share Call A/c
(10) Receipt of call money	Bank A/c	Share Call A/c

When the company receives applications for shares more than it wants to issue, it gives pro-rata allotment to the applicants. For example, if the company wants to allot 1000 shares and number of shares applied are 3000, the company will allot only 1/3rd of the shares applied by the applicants. The balance amount on application is either adjusted as calls in advance or is refunded to the applicants.

CALLS-IN-ADVANCE AND ARREARS

When the applicant sends more money than required, the excess money is called calls-in-advance. Such a calls-in-advance can be accepted only when the company is so authorized by its Articles of Association. If the company has adopted Table A, then it is required to pay 6% interest on such amount. The shareholder is not entitled to any dividend on the amount paid as calls-in-advance.

On the other hand, if shareholder makes default in sending call money according to conditions, then money not so sent is called calls-in-arrear. It is a liability of the shareholder and default to pay this may lead to forfeiture of shares.

ISSUE OF SHARES FOR CONSIDERATION OTHER THAN CASH

Shares are sometimes issued to certain persons for consideration other than cash. For example issue of shares to a vendor who sells some asset to the company or to the promoters for their services. In the first case, the treatment is simple. In place of making payment by cheque, the payment is made in the form of shares and hence the share capital account will be credited in place of bank account. But, when the shares are issued to the promoters, the following accounting entry is made :

Goodwill A/c Dr.

To Share Capital A/c

The amount is debited to Goodwill account because it is considered that without the work of the promoters, it would not have been possible to create the company.

ISSUE OF SHARES AT PREMIUM

When a share is issued at a price which is above its face value, then it is said that it has been issued at premium. Share premium is often charged by the company at the time of allotment of shares. As per the Companies Act, 1956, such premium whether received in cash of in kind must be credited to a separate account called "Share Premium Account". Under Section 78 of Companies Act, the amount to the credit of this account may be used wholly or in part for following purposes :

1. Paying up un-issued shares of the company to be issued to members of the company as fully paid bonus shares.
2. Writing off the preliminary expenses of the company.
3. Writing off the expenses of, or the commission paid or discount allowed on any shares or of any debentures of the company.
4. Providing for the premium payable on the redemption of any redeemable preference shares or of any debentures of the company.

ISSUE OF SHARES AT DISCOUNT

When a share is issued at a price which is less than its face value then it is said that it has been issued at discount. A Company can issue share at discount on fulfilling the conditions of Section 79 of the Companies Act.. Discount on issue of shares being a loss of capital nature, is shown on the asset side of the balance sheet and is amortised(written off) over a period of time decided by the company.

FORFEITURE OF SHARES

In case a member fails to pay any call on the day appointed for payment, the directors may, either by the adoption of Table A or by an express provision in its Articles, proceed to forfeit the shares held by such a defaulting shareholder. On forfeiture, the name of the shareholder is removed from the register of the company. But, before forfeiting shares, a proper notice requiring payment of the calls with interest should be served to the shareholder. It may be noted that share capital account, on forfeiture, is debited with the called up amount(excluding the share premium called and paid by the shareholder) and not with the face value of the share.

FORFEITURE OF SHARES ISSUED AT PREMIUM / DISCOUNT

When shares issued at premium are forfeited, the share premium which was due and not paid by the shareholder should be cancelled by giving a debit entry to the share premium account. But, the share premium which was due and paid by the shareholder should not be cancelled. This is according to Sec. 78 of Companies Act that share premium once collected cannot be cancelled even if the shares are forfeited.

On the other hand, discount on issue of shares is a loss and is debited at the time of issue of shares. When these shares are forfeited, the discount on issue of shares account is credited to cancel the effect of earlier debit entry.

RE-ISSUE OF FORFEITED SHARES

Shares forfeited on the non-payment of calls can be re-issued by the company as and when company finds it suitable and convenient. But, the amount collected on re-issue together with the amount already paid before the share were forfeited should not be less than the amount credited as paid up on re-issue of shares. When the shares forfeited are re-issued at a discount, such discount is to be debited to forfeited shares account. After setting off the amount earlier received on shares, if still there is some balance, it should be transferred to Capital Reserve Account. The accounting entries on re-issue of shares are similar to those at the time of issue of fresh shares.

VALUE OF RIGHT SHARE

In case a company makes a further issue of shares to its existing shareholders, it is known as a Right Issue. The existing shareholders may accept or reject the offer of shares. They can even sell these right shares in the market. In such a situation it is important to know the value of the share being offered by the company as right. The following method is employed.

ISSUE OF BONUS SHARES

Bonus shares are those shares which are allotted to the existing equity shareholders of the company without any consideration, either in cash or in kind. In other words, these are free shares issued by the company to the existing shareholders in some ratio of their existing shareholding. Bonus shares can be issued subject to the provisions of the Articles of Association and the Companies Act, 1956. Issue of bonus shares result into the capitalization of profits and reserves of the company. According to the SEBI guidelines, following conditions must be observed while making any bonus issue :

1. Bonus issue should be made out of free reserves built out of genuine profits or share premium collected in cash only.
2. Reserves created out of revaluation of fixed assets should not be capitalized.
3. The bonus issue cannot be made unless the partly paid shares, if any, are made fully paid up.
4. The company has not defaulted in payment of interest or principal in respect of fixed deposits or debentures.
5. Consequent to the issue of bonus shares, if the subscribed and paid up capital exceeds the authorized share capital, resolution shall be passed by the company at its general meeting for increasing the authorized capital.

BROKERAGE

Brokerage is merely the act of procuring subscriptions for shares or debentures without any responsibility. The company pays brokerage to the broker on the shares subscribed through him and he has no obligation to take up the shares that may remain unsold.

REDEMPTION OF PREFERENCE SHARES

According to Section 80, the following are the rules for redemption of preference shares :

(a) The shares to be redeemed should be fully paid up.

(b) They can be redeemed either out of the profits of the company which would otherwise be available for dividend or out of the proceeds of a fresh issue of shares (may be equity but not debentures) made for the purpose of redemption.

(c) The premium payable on redemption must be provided either out of accumulated profits of the company or the Share Premium account before the shares are redeemed.

(d) When the shares are redeemed out of the profits, an amount equal to the nominal value of the shares so redeemed should be transferred from the profits to a reserve account called **Capital Redemption Reserve** account which may be used in issuing the fully paid bonus shares by the company.

(e) Redemption of preference shares does not amount to reduction in the authorized capital of the company.

It is to be noted that in "Proceeds of fresh issue of shares" as mentioned above, only the nominal value of shares issued should be considered for determining the amount to be credited to Capital Redemption Reserve Account. It means that any premium received on issue of shares should be disregarded. But if the shares are issued at discount, the actual proceeds of the issue (Discounted price of shares) should be deducted from the face value of preference shares to be redeemed to arrive at the amount to be transferred to CRR A/c. The following journal entries are passed by the company on redemption of preference shares :

(a) If the company makes fresh issue of shares
Bank A/c Dr.
To Share Capital A/c
To Share Premium Account
(if issued on premium)

(b) When preference shares are redeemed at premium
Share premium A/c Dr.
Profit and Loss A/c Dr.
To Premium on Redemption A/c

(c) Transferring the amount to the CRR A/c
Profit & Loss A/c Dr.
General Reserve A/c Dr.
To CRR A/c
(Face value of shares to be redeemed - Face value of fresh issue of shares)

(d) Transferring the capital to the shareholders A/c
Preference shares A/c Dr.
Premium on Redemption A/c Dr.
To preference shareholders A/c

(e) When payment is made to the shareholders
Preference shareholders A/c Dr.
To Bank A/c

Illustration 1 : A company has to redeem 1,000 preference shares of Rs. 100 each at Rs. 103. For this purpose, it issues 500 equity shares of Rs. 100 each at a premium of 10%. The following figures will be important :

Total amount to be redeemed (105 * 1000)	1,03,000
Share premium on equity shares (10 * 500)	5,000
Amount to be transferred to CRR A/c (1,00,000-50,000)	50,000

The premium to be paid on redemption will be adjusted against the premium received from the new issue. The balance amount of premium by the new issue will not be considered for determining the amount to be transferred to the CRR A/c. If the fresh issue of shares is to be determined according to the divisible profit available with the company, the minimum possible number of shares to be issued has to be determined. This can be arrived at by applying the following equation:

Face value of preference shares + Premium on redemption = Share Premium account in the balance sheet + Divisible profit available (including reserves) + Fresh shares to be issued (say 'X') + Premium on issue of fresh shares.

Illustration 2 : Preference shares of Rs. 20,000 are to be redeemed at 10% premium and the Balance of Profit and Loss account and General Reserves is Rs. 4,000 and Rs. 6000 respectively. Share premium accounts balance is Rs. 1,000. Fresh issue of shares is to be made at 10% premium.

Applying the formula, the company needs to issue shares of Rs. 10,000.

ISSUE AND REDEMPTION OF DEBENTURES

The accounting entries for issue of debentures are same as that of equity shares. The only difference is that after the issue of debentures, the company has to make regular payment of interest to the debenture holders. It should be kept in mind that the amount of interest payable to the debenture holders is calculated at the rate of interest those debentures are carrying multiplying it with the face value of debentures irrespective of the fact that the debentures may have been issued at par, or at premium or at discount. Also first interest is payable from the date of issue of debentures to the date of payment of interest (quarterly, half yearly or yearly).

Illustration 3 : A company has issued 1000, 8% debentures of Rs. 100 each at Rs. 95 to be repayable at Rs. 105 each to be repayable after 5 years. The interest is payable half yearly. The interest to be paid at the end of each half year will be (1,000 * 100 * 8% / 2) = 4,000.

Another point is that if the debentures are issued at discount and to be redeemed at premium, the total loss on discount as well as the premium is booked at the time of issue itself by debiting the total amount to 'Loss on issue of debentures' A/c. This loss is considered as Deferred Revenue expenditure and is written off over the period of tenure of the debentures equally. If the debentures are repayable in installments, the amount is written off based on the proportion of the debentures outstanding at the end of each year.

Illustration 4 : In the above example, the total loss on issue of debentures is Rs. 10,000 (1,000 * 10). This loss will be written off over a period of 5 years i.e. Rs. 2,000 per year. If the debentures are to be redeemed in 5 installments starting from the end of the first year, the use of funds in 5 years will be Rs. 1,00,000, 80,000, 60,000, 40,000 and 20,000 respectively. So, the loss of Rs. 10,000 will be written off in the ratio of 5:4:3:2:1.

CUM-INTEREST AND EX-INTEREST PURCHASE OF DEBENTURES

Debentures may be purchased either on cum-interest basis or on ex-interest basis. If the debentures are purchased on cum-interest basis, it means that the price of the debenture includes the next installment of interest payable by the company. So, the purchaser of the debentures is entitled to the interest from the date of purchase. On the other hand, in ex-interest purchase, the next interest installment is received by the seller only and thereafter all the interests are received by the purchaser. So, ex-interest price of debentures is always lower than the cum-interest price.

MANNER OF REDEMPTION OF DEBENTURES

The debentures can be redeemed in any of the following ways :

(1) One time payment on maturity

(2) Payment in Instalments

(3) Purchase of debentures in open market

As regards, the first two manners, the accounting entries are simple. Complications arise in case debentures are redeemed by way of purchase in open market. Under this method also, the debentures may be purchased for two purposes :

(a) Purchase of debentures for redemption

(b) Purchase of debentures for investment

PURCHASE OF DEBENTURES FOR REDEMPTION

In this case, the company purchases debentures in the open market some time before the debentures are due for redemption. The purchased debentures are redeemed once the due date arrives and hence no payment need be made to the outsiders. In this case, the debentures may be purchased cum-interest or ex-interest.

Illustration 5: A company buys on 1-10-2004 own debentures of Rs. 10,000 of Rs. 100 each at Rs. 98 ex-interest for cancellation. Interest is payable @6% on 30th June and 31st December. The accounting entry will be

6% Debentures A/c	Dr.	10,000	
Interest on Debentures A/c	Dr.	150	
To Bank A/c			9950
To Profit on Redemption A/c			200

(Since the debentures were purchased ex-interest, original holder is entitled to the interest for the whole 6 months. On 31st December, since the debentures are held by the company, no interest will be paid. So, the interest will be paid to the original debenture holder for 3 months at the time of purchase and rest 3 months' interest is included in the purchase price. So interest will be debited only for 3 months instead of 6 months.)

In the same case, had the debentures been purchased on cum-interest, the company would have got the benefit of interest from October to December and hence the purchase price would have been only Rs. 98 and consequently, the profit would have been Rs. 350.

PURCHASE OF DEBENTURES AS INVESTMENT

Often, companies buy their own debentures as investment to save the interest which would otherwise have been payable. Such debentures are kept alive and can be disposed off again in the market. The accounting treatment is done like any other investment. When a company buys its own debentures as investment, an account called 'Own Debentures Account' will be debited with the amount actually paid, disregarding the nominal value of debentures purchased. When own debentures are bought and kept as investment, the interest on such debentures should be credited to the P&L account, the debit being given to the Interest on debentures account. In this manner, the interest on debentures account will show the full amount due on outstanding debentures. The credit to the P&L account shows the gain made by the purchase of own debentures.

The profit made by the company on redemption through open market purchase is a capital profit(which is considered when the debentures are cancelled). Any loss on issue of debentures may be written off against such profit. The balance of profit, if any should be transferred to Capital Reserve A/c.

Illustration 6 : A company issued 1000, 6% debentures of Rs. 1000 each. Interest is paid half yearly on 30th Sept. and 31st March. On February 1, 2004, the company purchased 20 of its own debentures as investment at Rs. 970. The journal entry will be as below:

Own Debentures A/c	Dr.	19,400	
Interest on Debentures A/c	Dr.	400	
To Bank A/c			19,800
(Debentures purchased ex-interest, interest for 4 months being payable extra)			
OR			
Own Debentures A/c	Dr.	19,000	
Interest on Debentures A/c	Dr.	400	
To Bank A/c			19,400
(Debentures purchased cum -interest, interest for 4 months included in the price)			
Interest on Debentures A/c	Dr.	200	
To Profit & Loss A/c			200
(Being the interest on debentures held by the company for 2 months)			
6% Debentures A/c	Dr.	20,000	
To Own Debentures A/c			19,400
To Profit on Redemption A/c			600
(Being the cancellation of the debentures purchased ex-interest. In case of cum-interest debentures, profit would be Rs. 1000)			

REDEMPTION AT PREMIUM OF DEBENTURES ISSUED AT DISCOUNT

Sometimes, to attract the investors, the company may issue the debentures on the discount and in addition promise to redeem the debentures at premium. In such a case, since both the losses are known at the time of issue of debentures, they are taken into the accounts and is written off over a period of time.

DEBENTURE REDEMPTION RESERVE/ SINKING FUND

When debentures are to be redeemed, the company has to arrange a large amount of cash for payment. This may affect the company's working capital. To avoid such a situation and to pay the debentures out of the profits, the company creates Debenture

Redemption Reserve. Every year, the company transfers some part of its profit to this account and this amount is invested by the company in some liquid assets. The transfer made every year and the income on such investments keeps on accumulating and when the debentures are to be redeemed, the company sells this investment and repays the debentures. The following journal entries are made in this respect :

(1) When amount is transferred to the reserve
P&L Appropriation A/c Dr.
To Debenture Redemption Reserve A/c

(2) When the amount is invested
DRR Investment A/c Dr.
To Bank A/c

(3) Interest on investment is received
Bank A/c Dr.
To DRR A/c

(4) When investing the total amount including the interest received
DRR Investment A/c Dr.
To Bank A/c

(5) On sale of investment
Bank A/c Dr.
To DRR Investment A/c

(6) Transferring the loss/profit on sale of investment
DRR Investment A/c (if Profit) Dr.
To DRR A/c

(7) Transfer of balance in DRR A/c
DRR A/c' Dr.
To General Reserve A/c

Note : The above entries are similar to those made for creation of sinking fund for replacement of a fixed asset.

FORM OF BALANCE SHEET

Every company has to follow the form of balance sheet as given in Schedule VI of Companies Act which has been reproduced as below :

Balance Sheet of XYZ Ltd. as at 31st March, 2008

PARTICULARS	AMT.	PARTICULARS	AMT.
SHARE CAPITAL Authorised shares of Rs------each Issued: (distinguishing between various classes of capital) ----- shares of Rs. ------ each Subscribed : ------- shares of Rs. ------ each Of the above shares, ----- shares are allotted as fully paid up pursuant to a contract without payment being received in cash. Of the above shares,-----shares are allotted as fully paid up by way of bonus shares. Less : Calls unpaid : a) My managing agent or secretaries b) By Directors c) By others. Add :Forfeited shares (amount originally paid up) (any capital profit on reissue of forfeited shares should be transferred to Capital Reserve)		**FIXED ASSETS** Distinguishing expenditure upon : a) Goodwill b) Land c) Buildings d) Leaseholds e) Plant and Machinery f) Furniture and fittings g) Patents, trademarks, and design h) Livestock i) Vehicles Under each of the assets, the original cost, additions and deductions during the year and total depreciation provided should be mentioned. If any amount is written off on reduction of capital, the balance sheet for the first 5 years after reduction shall also show the amount of reduction made.	

<table>
<tr><th>PARTICULARS</th><th>AMT.</th><th>PARTICULARS</th><th>AMT.</th></tr>
<tr><td>

RESERVES AND SURPLUS

1) Capital Reserves
2) Capital Redemption Reserve
3) Share Premium Account
4) Other Reserves specifying the nature of each reserve and the amount in respect thereof.
Less : Debit balance in profit and loss account (if any)
5) Surpluses i.e. balance in profit and loss account
6) Proposed additions to reserves
7) Sinking Funds.

(The word 'Fund' in relation to any reserve should be used only where such reserve is specifically represented by earmarked investments)

SECURED LOANS :

a) Debentures
b) Loans and advances from bank
c) Loans and advances from subsidiaries
d) Other loans and advances

(Loans from directors, secretaries, manager should be shown separately)(In case of debenture, terms of redemption or conversion is to be stated with the earliest date of redemption or conversion)

UNSECURED LOANS :

1) Fixed Deposits
2) Loans and advances from subsidiaries
3) Short term loans from :
a) Banks
b) Others

(Short term loans include those which are due for not more than 1 year as at the date of balance sheet)

Other loans and advances

CURRENT LIABILITIES AND PROVISIONS:

CURRENT LIABILITIES

a) Acceptances (Bills Payable)

</td><td></td><td>

INVESTMENTS

1) Investment in Govt. or trust securities
2) Investment in shares, debentures etc.
3) Immovable properties
4) Inv. In capital of partnership firm

Aggregate amount of the company's quoted investments and also the market value thereof shall be shown.

CURRENT ASSETS, LOANS AND ADVANCES

(A) Current Assets

a) Interest accrued on investment
b) Stores and spare parts
c) Loose tools
d) Stock in trade
e) Work in progress
f) Sundry debtors (less : provision)

Debts outstanding for more than 6 months should be stated separately.

g) Cash balance in hand
h) Bank balance

(B) Loans and Advances

1) Advances and loans to subsidiaries
2) Bills of exchange

MISCELLANEOUS EXPENDITURE AND LOSSES NOT WRITTEN OFF

a) Preliminary expenses
b) Expenses of commission or underwriting on issue of shares and debentures
c) Discount allowed on the issue of shares and debentures
d) Interest paid out of capital during construction
e) Development expenditure not adjusted
f) Debit balance of Profit and Loss account

</td><td></td></tr>
</table>

PARTICULARS	AMT.	PARTICULARS	AMT.
b) Sundry Creditors c) Subsidiary Companies d) Advance payments and unexpired discounts for the portion for which value has still to be given e) Unclaimed Dividends f) Other liabilities g) Interest accrued but not due on loans **PROVISIONS** 1) Provision for Taxation 2) Proposed dividends 3) For Contingencies 4) For Provident Fund scheme 5) For insurance, pension and other benefits 6) Other provisions. A foot note to the balance sheet may be added to show separately: a) Claims against the company not acknowledged as debts b) Uncalled liability on shares partly paid c) Arrears of fixed cumulative dividends d) Estimated amount of contracts remaining to be executed on capital account e) Other moneys for which the company is contingently liable			

Note : Now the companies have to disclose the names of all small scale industrial undertakings to whom the company owes any sum together with interest outstanding for more than 30 days in the balance sheet under the heading 'Current Liabilities and Provisions'.

5. FINANCIAL STATEMENT ANALYSIS

FINANCIAL STATEMENTS

Any business organization prepares various statements for different information and purposes. The income statement report what has actually happened to earnings during the given period. The balance sheet presents a summary of financial position of the company at a given point of time. Both of them are known as financial statements.

The analysis and interpretation of these statements is the job of a manager. This can be done in many ways. The important methods of analysis and interpretation of financial statements are as below :

(a) Comparative statement
(b) Common size statement
(c) Ratio analysis
(d) Funds flow analysis
(e) Cash flow analysis

COMPARATIVE STATEMENT

A financial statement gives a lot of information about the entity. But, the information is more useful and more clear to a lay man if it is given in a comparative form. The data of the current year is compared with that of last year or last few years. This can be done by showing the figures for more than one year for all items in the balance sheet or profit and loss account side by side. It can also be done by showing the actual figure for the current year and giving the difference from the previous year in rupees or in percentage. The following is an illustration of comparative profit and loss account and balance sheet.

Illustration 1 :

Comparative Balance Sheet

Particulars	For the period		Increase / Decrease	
	2007	2008	Absolute	Percentage
Share capital	1,00,000	1,00,000	Nil	----
Debentures	2,00,000	1,50,000	(-) 50,000	(-) 25%
Sundry creditors	60,000	72,000	12,000	20%
TOTAL LIABILITIES	3,60,000	3,22,000	(-) 38,000	(-) 10.5%
Plants and Machinery	1,00,000	1,50,000	50,000	50%
Investments	80,000	72,000	(-) 8,000	(-) 10%
Sundry debtors	80,000	70,000	(-) 10,000	(-) 12.33%
Cash at hand	1,00,000	30,000	(-) 70,000	(-) 70%
TOTAL ASSETS	3,60,000	3,22,000	(-) 38,000	(-) 10.5%

Comparative Income Statement

Particulars	For the period		Increase / Decrease	
	2007	2008	Absolute	Percentage
Sales	12,00,000	15,00,000	3,00,000	25%
Purchases	8,00,000	9,60,000	1,60,000	20%
Closing stock	30,000	25,000	(-) 5,000	(-) 16.67%
GROSS PROFIT	2, 45,000	3,50,000	1,05,000	43%
Operating expenses	1,00,000	1,50,000	50,000	50%
Non-operating expenses	80,000	72,000	(-) 8,000	(-) 10%
NET PROFIT	65,000	1,28,000	63,000	98%

BENEFITS OF COMPARATIVE STATEMENTS

Comparative statements are very useful for the financial statement analysis in the following ways:

(a) It reveals trend of the item concerned

(b) It helps the management to know the inefficiency in any part of the operations, if any

(c) It shows how the business has performed with respect to the last year

(d) It is also useful for comparing performance in the same year as compared to other firms placed similarly.

COMMON SIZE STATEMENTS

It is a method in which various items of a financial statement are compared to each other in terms of their weightage in the concerned financial statement. In this method, one figure of the statement is taken as base figure which is assumed as 100%. All other figures are then arrived at in percentage as a portion of the base figure. For example, in balance sheet the total of the statement is taken as 100 and all the assets and liabilities are expressed as a percentage with respect to total. Similarly, in profit and loss account, the base figure is taken as Sales. This is called 'Vertical analysis' and when the same type of statement is prepared for a number of years to show the trend, it is called 'Horizontal analysis'.

Illustration 2 : Taking the above figures, the common size statements may also be prepared :

Comparative Balance Sheet

Particulars	2007		2008	
	Amount	% of Total	Amount	% of Total
Share capital	1,00,000	27.8%	1,00,000	31.06%
Debentures	2,00,000	55.6%	1,50,000	46.58%
Sundry creditors	60,000	16.6%	72,000	22.36%
TOTAL LIABILITIES	3,60,000	100%	3,22,000	100%
Plants and Machinery	1,00,000	27.8%	1,50,000	46.58%
Investments	80,000	22.2%	72,000	22.36%
Sundry debtors	80,000	22.2%	70,000	21.74%
Cash at hand	1,00,000	27.8%	30,000	09.32%
TOTAL ASSETS	3,60,000	100%	3,22,000	100%

Comparative Balance Sheet

Particulars	2007		2008	
	Amount	% of Total	Amount	% of Total
Sales	12,00,000	100%	15,00,000	100%
Purchases	8,00,000	67%	9,60,000	64%
Closing stock	30,000	2.5%	25,000	01.67%
GROSS PROFIT	2, 45,000	20.42%	3,50,000	23.33%
Operating expenses	1,00,000	08.33%	1,50,000	10.0%
Non-operating expenses	80,000	06.7%	72,000	04.8%
NET PROFIT	65,000	05.42%	1,28,000	08.53%

Now, it is easy for a lay man also to analyse that the gross profit margin has increased due to reduction in the cost of purchases. Also, thought there is an increase in the operating expenses, due to reduction in non-operating expenses the net profit margin has increased.

While preparing the above statement, the figures are expressed in terms of percentage of the base figure like to find the percentage of cash for 2007 we took

1,00,000 / 3,60,000 × 100 = 27.8%

Similarly, to find the percentage for purchases in 2008

9,60,000 / 15,00,000 × 100 = 64%

RATIO ANALYSIS

Ratio analysis is a very powerful analytical tool for measuring performance of an organization. The ratio analysis concentrates on the inter-relationship among the figures appearing in the above mentioned and various other statements. It helps the management to analyze the past performance of the firm and to make further projections. Ratio analysis allows interested parties like shareholders, investors, creditors, government and analysts to make an evaluation of certain aspects of a firm's performance.

The calculation of ratios is a relatively easy and simple task but the proper analysis and interpretation of ratios can be made only by skilled analyst. While interpreting the financial information, the analyst has to be careful about limitations imposed by the accounting concepts and methods of valuation. Information of non-financial nature will also be taken into consideration before a meaningful analysis is made. Ratio analysis pinpoints the strengths and weaknesses of the business mainly in two ways. Firstly, by comparing current performance with that of past and secondly by comparing the performance of the business with that of the industry as whole or other firms in the industry.

INTERPRETATION OF RATIO

A ratio may be interpreted in many ways depending upon the purpose of the ratio.

1. It may be interpreted individually or as a stand alone ratio. For example, a ratio of 20% net profit on the sales shows a good margin in itself.
2. It may be interpreted by doing comparison between the ratio over a period of time. For example, if the same ratio is compared with the last year which was 30%, it means that margin have fallen this year.
3. It may also be interpreted by comparing with similar firms in the same industry. If the same ratio of a comparable firm is 16%, the margins of company under consideration is very good.
4. It may be interpreted by taking it together with other ratios. For example, in this case the margins are good but the return on capital employed is only 5%. It means the sales is very less but margins are high because of higher prices.

TYPES OF RATIOS

There are various ratios used in analysis. For the convenience of understanding, they can be divided into the following broad categories :

A. Long Term Solvency Ratios
B. Short Term Solvency Ratios
C. Turnover Ratios
D. Profitability Ratios
E. Operating Ratios
F. Market Test Ratios

We shall discuss various ratios under all the above categories.

A. Long Term Solvency Ratios

The long term financial stability of the firm may be considered as dependent upon its ability to meet all its liabilities, including those not currently payable. The following are important ratios measuring the long term solvency :

(1) Debt-Equity Ratio : Capital is derived from two sources : shares and loans. Every company has to raise equity capital. The effect of raising loan is to introduce an element of gearing or leverage into the capital structure of the company.

$$\text{Debt-Equity ratio} = \frac{\text{Long term debt}}{\text{Shareholders' Fund}}$$

Shareholders' fund is equal to the share capital plus reserves and surpluses less preliminary expenses, if any. This ratio indicates the relationship between loan funds and net worth of the company, which is known as gearing. A debt-equity ratio of 2:1 is accepted norm. Higher the ratio, higher is the gearing and higher is the risk of long term insolvency. As a general rule, gearing should be low in those industries where demand is volatile and profits are subject to fluctuations. Usually, in calculating the ratio, the preference share capital is excluded from debt, but if the ratio is to show effect of use of fixed interest sources on earnings available to the shareholders then it is to be included. On the other hand, if the ratio is to examine financial solvency, then preference shares shall form part of the capital.

The ratio may also be calculated as below :

$$\text{Debt-Equity ratio} = \frac{\text{Long term debt}}{\text{Shareholders' Fund} + \text{Long term Debt}}$$

(2) Capital Gearing Ratio : It is the proportion of fixed interest bearing funds to equity shareholders' funds.

$$\text{Capital Gearing Ratio} = \frac{\text{Fixed Interest Bearing Funds}}{\text{Equity Shareholders' Funds}}$$

The fixed interest bearing funds include debentures, long term loans, and preference share capital. This ratio indicates the degree of vulnerability of earnings available for equity shareholders.

(3) Fixed Assets To Long Term Funds Ratio

$$\text{F/A to L/T Funds Ratio} = \frac{\text{Fixed Assets}}{\text{Long Term Funds}}$$

Fixed assets represent the gross fixed assets minus depreciation till the date of calculation. The closeness of the ratio to 1 indicates that fixed assets are financed by long term funds. If the ratio is significantly less than 1, it means that long term funds are being used to finance current assets also. A very high ratio is dangerous for short term solvency as it implies that short term funds are also used to finance long term assets.

(4) Proprietary Ratio : It expresses the relationship between net worth and total assets.

$$\text{Proprietary Ratio} = \frac{\text{Net Worth}}{\text{Total Assets}}$$

Net worth = equity capital + Preference share capital + Reserves − Fictitious assets

Total assets = Fixed assets + Current assets

Reserves earmarked specifically for a particular purpose should not be included in calculation of net worth. A high proprietary ratio is indicative of strong financial position of the business.

(5) Dividend Cover

$$\text{Dividend Cover} = \frac{\text{Net Profit after Tax}}{\text{Dividend}}$$

This ratio indicates the number of times the

dividends are covered by net profit. This highlights the amount retained by a company for financing of future operations.

(6) Interest Cover

$$\text{Interest Cover} = \frac{\text{Profit before Interest, Depreciation and Tax (PBDIT)}}{\text{Interest}}$$

It shows how many times interest charges are covered by funds that are available for payment of interest. Here, PBDIT is used because interest is paid before payment of tax and depreciation is non-cash expense. In the dividend cover ratio as shown above, since the dividend is paid on PAT, PAT is in numerator. A high interest cover indicates that the firm is conservative in using debt and a very low ratio indicates excessive use of debt.

(7) Debt Service Coverage Ratio : It indicates whether the business is earning sufficient profits to pay not only the interest charges, but also the installments due to the 'principal' amount. This ratio is widely used by banks for analyzing the profitability of a project before financing it.

$$\text{DSCR} = \frac{\text{Profit before Interest and Tax}}{\text{Interest} + \text{Loan Installments}}$$

B. Short Term Solvency Ratios

These ratios measure the liquidity of the firm and its ability to meet its maturing short term obligations. Liquidity is defined as the ability to realise value in money, which is the most liquid of all assets. It refers to the ability to pay in cash, the obligations that are due. Excess liquidity, though a guarantor of solvency would reflect lower profitability. On the other hand, too little liquidity may lead to risk of insolvency. The important ratios to measure short term solvency are :

(1) Current Ratio

$$\text{Current ratio} = \frac{\text{Current Assets (including loans and advanced}}{\text{Current Liabilities (including Provision)}}$$

The ratio measures the solvency of the company in the short term. Current assets are those assets which can be converted into cash within a year. Current liabilities are those liabilities that are payable within a year. A current ratio of 1.33:1 is considered good. A very high ratio will have adverse impact on the profitability of the organization. To know the reason of high current ratio the next ratio is used.

(2) Quick Ratio/Liquid Ratio

This ratio shows whether high current ratio is due to piling up of inventory. If the difference between current ratio and quick ratio is significant, then the organization is carrying high inventory.

$$\text{Quick ratio} = \frac{\text{Quick Assets (Current Assets} - \text{Inventories} - \text{Prepaid Expenses)}}{\text{Quick Liabilities (Current Liabilities} - \text{Bank Overdraft)}}$$

It is also known as Acid-test ratio. It is used along with the current ratio.

(3) Absolute Liquidity Ratio

$$\text{Absolute Liquidity Ratio} = \frac{\text{Cash + Marketable Securities}}{\text{Current Liabilities}}$$

Absolute liquidity ratio is a subsequent innovation in ratio analysis. It eliminates uncertainty of receipts attached to the bills receivables. Therefore, this ratio excludes bills receivables also. The Absolute Liquidity Ratio only tests short-term liquidity in terms of cash and marketable securities.

C. Turnover Ratios

Turnover or activity ratios measure how effectively the firm employs its resources. These ratios involve comparison between the level of sales and investment in various assets - inventories, debtors, fixed assets etc. Activity ratios are used to measure the speed with which various accounts are converted into sales or cash. The following activity ratios are important:

(1) Inventory Turnover Ratio

$$\text{Inventory turnover ratio} = \frac{\text{Cost of goods sold}}{\text{Average Inventory}}$$

Average inventory is average of opening and closing stock. If the cost of goods sold is not available, sales figure is used. It shows how many times the company's inventory has been sold during the year. Higher the ratio, higher is the efficiency of the business.

(2) Debtor Turnover Ratio

$$\text{Debtor turnover ratio} = \frac{\text{Total Credit Sales}}{\text{Average Debtors}}$$

This ratio indicates the number of times of sales as compared to debtors. In other words, it shows the duration of credit given to debtors. The inverse of this ratio is Average collection period.

$$\text{ACP} = \frac{\text{Average Debtros}}{\text{Total Credit Sales}} \times 365$$

It shows in how many days the company receives payment for its credit sales. The actual collection period can be compared with the stated terms of the company. Higher this ratio(or lower the turnover ratio), lower is the efficiency in collection.

(3) Creditors Turnover Ratio : Similar to above ratios, the Creditor's turnover ratio or the Average payment period is :

$$\text{Creditors' Turnover ratio} = \frac{\text{Total Credit Purcases}}{\text{Average Creditors}}$$

$$\text{Average Payment Period} = \frac{\text{Average Creditors}}{\text{Credit Purchases}} \times 365$$

(4) Fixed Asset Turnover Ratio

$$\text{F/A turnover ratio} = \frac{\text{Sales}}{\text{Fixed Assets}}$$

This measures the company's ability to generate sales revenue in relation to the size of the investment. A high ratio indicates efficient utilization of fixed assets in generating sales and a low ratio indicates otherwise.

D. Profitability Ratios

The purpose of study and analysis of profitability ratios are to help assess the adequacy of profits earned by the company and also to discover whether profitability is increasing or declining. These ratios show the combined effects of liquidity, asset management and debt management. They are measured with reference to various items as below:

(1) Return On Capital Employed: ROCE or Return on Investment (ROI) is one of the fundamental ratios.

$$\text{ROI} = \frac{\text{Net Profit before interest and tax}}{\text{Capital Employed}} \times 100$$

Here, capital employed is equal to capital of the company (equity plus loan) less any fictitious assets and debit balance of Profit and Loss Account. This ratio encourages managers to obtain assets that will provide a satisfactory return on investment and to dispose of assets that are not providing an acceptable return.

(2) Earning Per Share (Eps) : It is one of the most widely used ratios to determine the market value of the firm.

$$\text{EPS} = \frac{\text{Profit after Tax - Preference dividend}}{\text{No. of equity shares}}$$

Higher EPS means better capital productivity. Growth in EPS is more relevant than the absolute value for pricing of share. It should be kept in mind that higher EPS does not necessarily lead to higher dividend payout.

(3) Gross Profit Margin:

$$\text{G/P Ratio} = \frac{\text{Gross profit (Sales-Cost of goods sold)}}{\text{Sales}} \times 100$$

Gross profit, as shown is calculated before taking into consideration the administrative and marketing expenses. It measures, the company's manufacturing or trading efficiency.

(4) Net Profit Margin: It is calculated as above after deducting the administrative and marketing expenses but before deducting interest and taxes.

$$\text{N/P Ratio} = \frac{\text{Net Profit after Tax (PAT)}}{\text{Sales}} \times 100$$

(5) Return On Net Worth:

$$\text{Return on Net worth} = \frac{\text{Net Profit after Tax}}{\text{Net worth}} \times 100$$

This ratio indicates the efficiency of utilization of assets in generating revenue.

E. Operating Ratios

The ratios of all operating expenses (material, labour, factory overheads, administration and selling expenses) to sales is the operating ratio. A comparison of the operating ratio would indicate whether the cost content is high or low in the figure of sales. If the annual comparison shows that the ratio has increased, the management would be naturally interested to know as to which element of the cost has gone up. It is not necessary that the management should be concerned only when the operating ratio goes up. If the operating ratio has fallen, though the unit selling price has remained the same, still the position needs analysis as it may be the sum total of efficiency in certain departments and inefficiency in others. An effective management is interested in making a complete analysis. It is therefore, necessary to break up the operating ratio into various cost ratios. They are :

$$\text{Material cost ratio} = \frac{\text{Material consumed}}{\text{Sales}} \times 100$$

$$\text{Labour cost ratio} = \frac{\text{Labour cost}}{\text{Sales}} \times 100$$

$$\text{Factory overheads ratio} = \frac{\text{Factory Expenses}}{\text{Sales}} \times 100$$

Administrative expenses ratio =

$$\frac{\text{Administrative Expenses}}{\text{Sales}} \times 100$$

Selling and Distribution Overhead ratio =

$$\frac{\text{Selling and Distribution Expenses}}{\text{Sales}} \times 100$$

$$\text{Operating ratio} = \frac{\text{Cost of Goods Sold}}{\text{Sales}} \times 100$$

F. Market Test Ratios

These ratios relate to the firm's stock price to its earnings and book value. They give management an indication of what investors think of the company's past performance and future prospectus. Market test ratios are as follows:

(1) Dividend Payout Ratio : Dividend payout ratio $= \frac{\text{Dividend per share}}{\text{Earnings per share (EPS)}}$

This ratio indicates the extent of the net profits distributed to the shareholders as dividend. A high payout signifies a liberal distribution policy and a low payout reflects conservative distribution policy.

(2) Dividend Yield : Dividend Yield = $\frac{\text{Dividend per share}}{\text{Market price of share}} \times 100$

This ratio reflects the percentage yield that an investor receives on his investment at the current market price of the share.

(3) Book Value : Book value = $\frac{\text{Net Worth}}{\text{No. of equity shares}}$

This ratio indicates the net worth per equity share. It is reflection of past earning and distribution policy of the company. A high book value indicates that the company has huge reserves and is a potential candidate for issue of bonus. Book value is considered as less relevant for market price as compared to EPS.

(4) Price Earning (P/E) Ratio : P/E ratio = $\frac{\text{Market Price of Share}}{\text{EPS}}$

This ratio indicates the number of times the earnings of the latest year at which the share price of a company is quoted. A low P/E ratio as compared to industry reflects under valuation of the price of the share. It is considered as barometer of market sentiment.

IMPORTANCE OF THE RATE OF RETURN ON INVESTMENT

Return on investment (R0I) is one of the most important ratios used by managers while making an investment. As already explained, ROI = $\frac{\text{Net Profit before Interst and Tax}}{\text{Capital Employed}} \times 100$

But, there is no unanimity over the use of capital employed or the profit taken. Managers may take net profit after tax, net profit before interest and tax, net profit after interest but before tax etc. For the purpose of simplicity, it is often taken as ROI = $\frac{\text{Net Profit}}{\text{Capital Employed}}$

American company DuPont has given a chart which shows how the Return on investment can be broken into various ratio and form this one ratio the whole analysis of the performance of the organization can be done. The chart is as below :

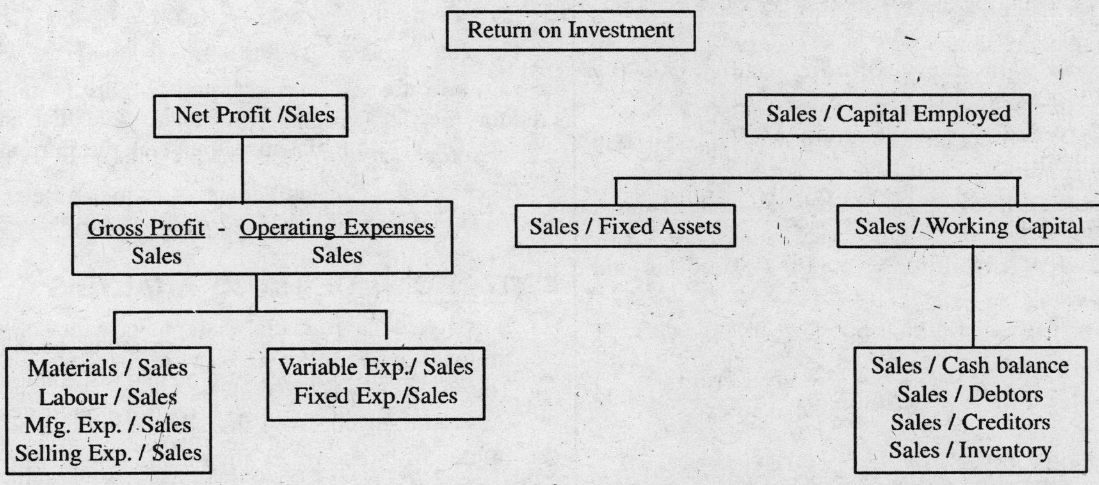

As the above chart shows that one single ratio may give a broad picture of the performance of the organization. Here, capital employed can be taken as Fixed assets and Net working capital, and operating expenses can be broken into various expenses. In the above chart, Sales/Capital employed is also known as 'Capital Turnover Ratio'.

Illustration 3 : From the following P&L A/c and Balance sheet calculate various ratios.

To opening Stock	10000	By Sales	100000
To Purchases	55000	By Closing Stock	15000
To Gross Profit	50000		
	115000		115000
To Administration expenses	15000	By Gross profit	50000
To Interest	3000		
To Selling expenses	12000		
To Net profit	20000		
	50000		50000

Balance Sheet

Capital	100000	Land and Building	50000
Profit and Loss A/c	20000	Plant and Machinery	30000
Creditors	25000	Stock	15000
Bills payable	15000	Debtors	15000
		Furniture	20000
		Bills receivable	12500
		Cash at bank	17500
	160000		160000

(1) Inventory Turnover Ratio = Cost of goods sold / Average Stock

Average Stock = Opening Stock + Closing stock / 2 = 10000 + 15000 / 2 = 12500

Cost of goods sold = Opening stock + Purchases – Closing stock = 10000 + 55000 – 15000 = 50000

Stock / Inventory Turnover ratio = 50000 / 12500 = 4 times

(2) Current Ratio = Current Assets / Current Liabilities

Current assets = 60000 (Stock, Debtors, Bills and Cash)

Current Liabilities = 40000 (Creditors and Bills)

So, Current Ratio = 60000 / 40000 = 1.5 : 1

(3) Net Profit Margin/Ratio = $\frac{\text{Net Profit}}{\text{Net Sales}} \times 100$;

$\frac{2000 \times 100}{100000} \times 100 = 20\%$

(4) Liquid Ratio = Liquid Assets / Current Liabilities

Liquid Assets = 45000 (Current assets - Stock)

Current Liabilities = 40000

Liquid Ratio = 45000 / 40000 = 1.125 : 1

(5) Proprietary Ratio = $\frac{\text{Shareholders' Funds}}{\text{Total Assets}} \times 100$;

$\frac{120000\,(\text{Capital} + \text{Profit})}{160000} \times 100 = 75\%$

Illustration 4 :

Current Ratio	2.5	Bank Overdraft	10000
Liquid Ratio	1.5	Working Capital	60000

From the above information, find out the value of inventory and creditors

If current ratio is 2.5, means Current assets and Current liabilities are in the ratio of 2.5 : 1

Working capital = Current assets – Current liabilities

So, 60000 = 2.5 Current Liabilities – Current Liabilities (since C/A = 2.5 C/L)

60000 = 1.5 Current Liabilities

Current Liabilities = 40000

Since, no information is given, it is considered that current liabilities comprise only Bank overdraft and creditors.

So, Creditors = 40000 – 10000 = 30000

Current Assets = 2.5 (40000) = 100000

Liquid Ratio is 1.5 and liquid liability is only creditors i.e. 30000

Therefore, Liquid Assets = 1.5 (30000) = 45000

Inventory = Current Assets – Liquid Assets

= 100000 – 45000 = 55000

LIMITATIONS OF RATIO ANALYSIS

(1) It is based on financial statements which are themselves subject to severe limitations. Therefore, any ratio analysis based on a mis-statement suffers from the similar limitations.

(2) In case of inter-firm comparison, no two firms are similar in age, size and product unit. Therefore, any comparison of ratios of two such firms must take these factors into account.

(3) Both, the inter-period and inter-firm comparisons are affected by price level changes. A change in the price level can affect the validity of ratios calculated for different time periods.

(4) The ambiguity in defining terms like gross profit, capital employed, operating profit, current assets etc. also leads to distortions in the ratio analysis and ratios based on different concepts can be misleading.

(5) Any decision cannot be taken based on a single ratio. The analyst has to use various ratios and other forms of accounting analysis before taking any decision.

(6) Conclusions from analysis of statements are not sure indicators of bad or good management.

(7) Ratio analysis is only a tool and is helpful to spot out the symptoms. The analyst has to carry out further investigations and exercise his judgement in arriving at a correct diagnosis.

6. FUND FLOW AND CASH FLOW STATEMENT

CONCEPT OF FLOW STATEMENT

A balance sheet is a snapshot view of the status of a firm's funds at one instance of time. But it does not give a picutre of from where the funds have come and how funds from various sources wree received and utilised during the year. A flow statement explains the changes that took place in a balance sheet account or group of accounts during the period between the dates of two balance sheets. Income statement is also a flow statement. Similarly two flow statements cash flow and fund flow are widely used. It contains all the details of the financial resources which have become available during an accounting period and the ways in which those resources have been used up.

The term fund has been defined differently be different authors. But, in general, it means 'working capital' which is excess of current assets over current liabilities.

PREPARATION OF FUNDS FLOW STATEMENT

The funds flow statement is not prepared alone. To take a holistic view, three statements are prepared:

(i) Funds flow statement

(ii) Statement of changes in working capital

(iii) Adjusted profit and loss account

(i) Funds Flow Statement. It is also known as Statement of Sources and Application of funds. This statement summarizes all the areas from which funds were received and the areas in which funds were used. The format of the statement is as below:

Sources	Amount	Application	Amount
Funds from Operations (Adjusted P&L A/c)		Funds lost in Operations	
Issue of share capitalIssue of Debentures		Redemption of preference shares/Debentures	
Raising Long term loans		Repayment of long term loans	
Receipt of calls on shares		Purchase of fixed assets/Investments	
Sale of Fixed assets or Investments		Non-trading payments like dividends/Tax	
Decrease in Working capital		Net increase in working capital	
Non-trading receipts like dividends			

This statement is like Cash account. All the receipts are considered as sources and all the payments are considered as application of funds.

(ii) Statement of Changes in Working Capital. The primary purpose of this statement is to determine the net changes in the working capital and that figure appears in the Funds flow statement as shown above. In this statement, all current assets and liabilities are individually listed. The acquisition of current assets and repayment of current liabilities will result into application of funds or increase in working capital. On the other hand, decrease in current assets and increase in current liabilities results in decrease in working capital and hence sources of funds.

(iii) Adjusted Profit and Loss Account. This is also called as Statement showing Funds generated from Operations. In this statement, we start with the profit/loss as shown in the profit and loss account. Then we exclude all the revenues and expenditures which do not pertain to the basic operations of the firm or are incidental losses and revenue. We add all the non-operational expenses and deduct all the non-operational revenues. The items are : Depreciation, Amortisation of fictitious assets, Appropriation of retained earnings, Loss/profit on sale of fixed assets, Payment or receipt of dividend, Taxation, Appreciation in value of fixed assets etc.

FUNDS FROM OPERATIONS

Funds from operations show the amount generated by the business activities. It is important to note that net profit as shown by the P&L account does not always mean the funds from operation. For this purpose only, adjusted P&L account is prepared as shown in the above example. The reasons for difference in net profit and funds from operations are many. One of them is there are certain expenses for which no payment is made like depreciation which does not affect the working capital. So, to arrive at the funds generated from operations, the following adjustments are made in the Profit and Loss Account.

ADD : Following items are added to the Net Profit as shown in P&L account :

(1) Depreciation on fixed assets

(2) Written off fictitious and intangible items like goodwill, preliminary expenses, discount on issue of shares etc.

(3) Loss on sale of fixed assets

(4) Appropriation of profits like transfer to general reserve or sinking funds.

(5) Dividend on shares

DEDUCT : Following items are deducted from net profit :

(a) Profit on sale of fixed assets

(b) Profit on revaluation of fixed assets

(c) Non-operating incomes like dividend, interest on investment, ret received etc.

In case there is net loss in the profit and loss account, the first set of items are deducted and the second set of items are added to the net loss to arrive at the figure of funds from operations.

Illustration 1 : Calculate funds from operations from the following P&L account :

To Expenses paid and outstanding	1,50,000	By Gross Profit	2,2,5000
To Depreciation	35,000	By gain on sale of land	30,000
To loss on sale of machine	2,000		
To Discount	100		
To Goodwill written off	10,000		
To Net Profit	57,900		
	2,55,000		2,55,000

Calculation of funds from operations :

Net Profit (as given)		57,900
Add : Non-operating items debited to P&L A/c		
Depreciation	35,000	
Loss on sale of machine	2,000	
Goodwill written off	10,000	47,000
		1,04,900
Less : Non-operating items credited to P&L A/c		
Gain on sale of land	30,000	30,000
FUNDS FROM OPERATIONS		74,900

TREATMENT OF SPECIFIC ITEMS

There are certain accounts which need specific treatment while calculating the funds flow.

(1) Provision For Taxation. While preparing funds flow statement, the provision for taxation may be treated either as appropriation of profit or as current liability. If it is treated as current liability, it is considered while preparing the statement of changes in working capital and showing it as current liability. If it is treated as appropriation of profit, no effect will be given on funds flow when the provision is made. But, the payment of tax is shown as application of funds. The amount of tax paid is calculated by opening Provision for Taxation account as follow :

To Bank A/c	By Opening balance
(Tax paid i.e. application of money)	By P&L Appropriation A/c
To Closing balance	(Provision made during the year)

(2) Proposed Dividend. This account can also be treated either as current liability or as appropriation of profit. When treated as current liability, like provision of taxation, it is also taken as current liability in the preparation of statement of changes in the working capital. In case it is treated as the appropriation of profit, the proposed dividend for the year is added back to the profit and proposed dividend for the last year is deducted form the profit while calculating the funds form operations.

(3) Interim Dividend. Interim dividend paid is shown as an application of fund in the funds flow statement. It is also added back in the net profit for calculating the funds from operations, if it has already been debited to P&L account.

Illustration 2 : From the following balance sheet, prepare funds flow statement :

Liabilities	2007	2008	Assets	2007	2008
Share Capital	30,000	40,000	Goodwill	11,500	9,000
Preference shares	15,000	10,000	Land & Building	20,000	7,000
General reserve	4,000	7,000	Plant	8,000	20,000
Profit and Loss A/c	3,000	4,800	Debtors	16,000	20,000
Proposed dividend	4,200	5,000	Stock	7,700	10,900
Creditors	5,500	8,300	Bills Receivable	2,000	3,000
Bills Payable	2,000	1,600	Cash in hand	1,500	1,000
Provision for Taxation	4,000	5,000	Cash at bank	1,000	800
	67,700	81,700		67,700	81,700

1. Depreciation of Rs. 2,000 on L&B and Rs. 1,000 on Plant has been charged in 2008.
2. Interim Dividend of Rs. 2,000 has been paid in 2008.
3. Income tax of Rs. 3,500 has been paid during the year 2008.

Statement of Changes in Working Capital

Particulars	2007	2008	Effect (+/-) on Working capital
CURRENT ASSETS			
Debtors	16,000	20,000	(+) 4,000
Stock	7,700	10,900	(+) 3,200
Bills receivable	2,000	3,000	(+) 1,000
Cash in hand	1,500	1,000	(-) 500
Cash at bank	1,000	800	(-) 200
TOTAL CURRENT ASSETS	28,200	35,700	
CURRENT LIABILITIES			
Creditors	5,500	8,300	(-) 2,800
Bills payable	2,000	1,600	(+) 400
Provision for taxation	4,000	5,000	(-) 1,000
Proposed dividend	4,200	5,000	(-) 800
TOTAL CURRENT LIABILITIES	15,700	19,900	
NET WORKING CAPITAL (Application of Funds)	12,500	15,800	(+) 3,300

Adjusted Profit and Loss Account

Particulars	Amount	Particulars	Amount
To Depreciation on		By Opening balance	3,000
Plant	1,000	By Funds from Operations	12,300
Building	2,000	(Balance figure)	
To Goodwill Written off	2,500		
To Transfer to G.R.	3,000		
To Interim dividend	2,000		
To Closing balance	4,800		
	15,300		15,300

Funds Flow Statement

Sources of Funds	Amount	Application of Funds	Amount
Issue of Equity shares	10,000	Redemption of Preference shares	5,000
Sale of building	1,000	Purchase of plant	13,000
Funds from operations	12,300	Dividend paid	2,000
		Net increase in working capital	3,300
	23,300		23,300

Note :

1. Sale of building figure has been calculated as (20,000 - 2,000 - 17,000 = 1,000)
2. Purchase of plant has been calculated as (1,000 + 20,000 - 8,000 = 13,000)

CASH FLOW ANALYSIS

It is very similar to Funds flow analysis. The major difference between the two is that cash flow statement analyses the receipts and application of cash only (which is a part of working capital) whereas funds flow statement analyses movement in the funds as a whole. According to SEBI guidelines, are listed companies have to present their cash flow statement in the Annual Report of the company. Cash flow statement during a period is classified into three categories

A. Operating activities

B. Investing activities

C. Financing activities

Operating activities are defined as all transactions that are not investing or financing activities. These transactions include the cash inflows associated with sales, interest and dividend revenues and outflows associated with purchases, operating expenses, interest, taxes etc. In nutshell, if we consider the format of the balance sheet, transactions occurring in current assets and current liabilities and transaction of profit and loss account fall under this category. While calculating cash from operations, all non-cash as well as non-operating incomes and expenditures are excluded.

Investing activities include acquiring or disposing off long term assets such as plants and equipments, securities, lending money etc. Increase or decrease in accounts receivables and inventory are not treated as investment activities; they are included in operating activities. In this category falls the transaction under the heads Fixed assets and Investments.

Financing activities include the borrowing of funds and issue of securities, their repayments etc. Transaction coming under the heads Capital and Reserves and surplus, Secured and Unsecured loans are financing activities.

BENEFITS OF CASH FLOW STATEMENT

A cash flow statement, when used in conjunction with the other financial statements, provides information that enables users to evaluate the changes in net assets of an enterprise, its financial structure, including solvency and liquidity, and its ability to affect the amount and timing of cash flows in order to adapt to changing circumstances and opportunities. Cash flow information is useful in assessing the ability of the enterprise to generate cash and cash equivalents and enable users to develop models to assess and compare the present value of the future cash flows of different enterprises. It also enhances the comparability of the reporting of operating performance by different enterprises because it eliminates the effects of using different accounting treatments for the same transactions and events.

CASH FROM OPERATIONS

Finding out cash from operations is similar to that finding out funds from operations with one change. In funds flow analysis, we prepare three statement viz., Adjusted P&L account, Statement of changes in working capital account and Funds flow account. But in cash flow analysis only two accounts are prepared i.e. Adjusted P&L account and Cash from operations.

So, while finding out the cash from operations, the adjustment regarding changes in the working capital is also made. Hence, to find out cash from operations, two steps are followed :

1. Find out the funds from operations as shown before
2. Add or deduct the net changes in working capital.

FUNDS FLOW ANALYSIS V/S CASH FLOW ANALYSIS

(a) Funds flow statement is based on accrual system while in preparing cash flow statement, only cash or cash equivalent items are considered.

(b) Funds flow analysis is more useful for long range financial planning. Cash flow analysis is more useful for identifying and correcting the current liquidity problem of the firm.

(c) Funds flow statement is a broader concept as cash itself is part of funds.

(d) Funds flow statement tallies the funds generated from various sources with various uses to which they are put. Cash flow statement starts with the opening balance of cash and reach to the closing balance of cash by proceeding through sources and uses.	(e) Cash flow statement is to be presented with the annual report of a company statutorily. Preparation of funds flow statement is not legally binding. (f) In cash flow statement, the changes in the working capital are incorporated in the cash flow from operating activities.

Illustration 3 : From the following information, calculate cash from operations.

Particulars	2008	2008
Debtors	50,000	47,000
Bills receivable	10,000	12,500
Creditors	20,000	25,000
Bills payable	8,000	6,000
Outstanding Expenses	1,000	1,200
Prepaid Expenses	800	700
Accrued Income	600	750
Income received in Advance	300	2,501
Profit made during the year		1,30,000

Cash from Operations :

Profit made during the year				1,30,000	
Add :	Decrease in Debtors			3,000	
	Increase in Creditors			5,000	
	Increase in outstanding expenses				200
	Decrease in Prepaid expenses			100	
				1,38,300	
Less :	Increase in Bills receivable	2,500			
	Increase in accrued Income	150			
	Decrease in Bills payable		2,000		
	Decrease in Income received in Advance		50		4,700
Cash from Operations				1,33,600	

Illustration 4 :

From following information prepare the cash flow statement for the year 2008. (Amounts in '000)

Net Profit	25,000	Interest Expenses	10,000
Dividend paid	8,535	Interest paid during the year	10,520
Provision for Income-tax	5,000	Increase in Working capital (except cash)	56,075
Income tax paid during the year	4,248	Purchase of Fixed asset	14,560
Loss on sale of asset	40	Investment in Joint Venture	3,850
Book value of asset sold	185	Expenditure on work-in-progress	34,740
Depreciation	20,000	Proceeds from calls in arrear	2
Amortisation of capital grant	6	Receipt of grant for capital project	12
Profit on sale of investment	100	Receipt from long term borrowings	25,980
Book value of investment sold	27,765	Receipt from short term borrowings	20,575
Interest income on investment	2,506	Opening cash balance	5,003
Closing cash balance	6,988		

Cash Flow Statement for the Year 2008

CASH FLOW FROM OPERATING ACTIVITIES		
Net profit before taxation (25000 + 5000)	30,000	
Adjustment for :		
Depreciation	20,000	
Loss on sale of asset	40	
Amortisation of capital grant	(6)	
Profit on sale of investment	(100)	
Interest income on investment	(2506)	
Interest expenses	10,000	
Operating profit before working capital changes	57,428	
Changes in working capital (Increase)	(56075)	
Cash generated from Operations	1,353	
Income tax paid	(4248)	
Net cash used in operating activities		(2,895)
CASH FLOW FROM INVESTING ACTIVITIES		
Sale of assets	145	
Sale of investments (27765 + 100)	27,865	
Interest income from investments	2,506	
Purchase of fixed assets	(14560)	
Investment in Joint Venture	(3850)	
Expenditure on work-in-progress	(34740)	
Net cash used in Investing activities		(22,634)
CASH FLOW FROM FINANCING ACTIVITIES		
Proceeds from calls in arrear	2	
Receipt of grant for capital project	12	
Receipt from long term borrowings	25,980	
Receipt from short term borrowings	20,575	
Interest paid	(10520)	
Dividend paid	(8535)	
Net cash from financing activities		27,514
Net increase in cash and cash equivalent	1,985	
Cash balance at the beginning of the period	5,003	
Cash balance at the end of the period	6,988	

7. COST ACCOUNTING

PROCEDURES INVOLVED IN COST ACCOUNTING

Cost accounting is an art because it involves costing techniques and methods, such as those of differential costing, marginal costing, standard costing etc. The application of these techniques helps the cost accountant in deciding how to control costs, whether to go for replacement of the existing plant by a new one or not etc.

The main objectives of cost accounting are :

(i) Determining selling price

(ii) Measuring and increasing efficiency

(iii) Facilitating preparation of financial and other statements

(iv) Providing basis for operating policy

In general 'cost' means "the amount of expenditure incurred on, or attribute to, a given thing."

ELEMENTS OF COST ACCOUNTING

- Materials
- Labour
- Expenses

There are two main methods used to determine costs :–

1. The job cost method
2. The process cost method.

It is possible to ascertain the costs under each of the above methods by two different systems:

1. *Historical costing*
2. *Standard costing*

1. Historical costing

Historical costing (conventional or orthodoc costing) is the determination of cost by actuals.

It may be in the nature of *(i)* Post costing or *(ii)* Continuous costing

(i) **Post costing :** It means ascertainment of cost after the production is completed. This is done by analysing the financial accounts at the end of the period in such a way as to disclose the cost of the units which have been produced. For instance, if the cost of product 'A' is to be calculated on this basis, one must wait till the materials are actually purchased and used labour actually paid, and overhead expenditure actually incurred. This system is useful only for ascertaining the costs but not useful for exercising my control over cost, as one comes to know of things after they had taken palce. It can serve as a guidance for future production only when conditions in future continue to be the same.

(ii) **Continuous costing:** In case of this system, cost is ascertain as soon as the job is completed or even when the job is in progress. This is done usually by charging the job or product with actual expenditure on materials and wages and estimated share of overheads. Hence, the figure of cost ascertained in this case is not exact. But it has an advantage of providing cost information to the management promptly there by enabling it to take the necessary corrective action in time. However, it neither provides any standard for judging current efficiency nor does it disclose what the cost of the job ought to have been.

2. Standard costing

Standard costing is a system under which the cost of the product is ascertained in advance on the basis of certain pre-determined standards. Taking the above example, the cost of product 'A' can be calculated in advance if one is in a position to estimate in advance the material, labour and overhead costs that should be incurred over the product. All this requires an efficient system of cost accounting. However, this system will not be useful if a vigorous system of controlling cost and keeping it upto standard cost is not in force.

Standard costing is becoming more and more popular now-a-days.

Marginal Costing

The Charted Institute of management Accountants, London defines the term marginal cost as "the amount at any given volume of output by which aggregate costs are changed if the volume of output is increased or decreased by one unit."

Marginal cost is, the total variable cost because within the capacity of the organisation, an increase of one unit in production will cause an increase invariable cost only. The variable cost consists of direct materials, direct labour, variable direct expenses and all variable overheads. The term "all variable overheads" include variable overheads plus the variable portion contained in semi-variable overheads.

The Accountant's concept of marginal cost differs from the Economist's concept of marginal cost. According to economists, the cost of producing one additional unit of output is the marginal cost of production.

Marginal cost = Direct material cost + Direct Labour cost + other variable costs

or

Total cost – Fixed cost

Marginal costing and Direct costing

Marginal costing and Direct costing are used by some accountants as synonymous terms since they take all "direct cost as variable cost".

Marginal costing and Differential costing : Marginal costing is sometimes confused with 'different costing'. Differential costing is the net increase or decrease in total cost resulting from a variation in production.

Marginal costing and Absorption costing : Marginal costing differs from absorption or traditional costing. Under absorption costing, full costs are charged to production. *i.e.,* all fixed and variable costs are recovered from production.

While, under marginal costing, only variables are charged to production. Fixed costs are ignored. There are two main differences between the absorption costing system and the marginal costing system :—

1. Valuation of stocks : Stocks of work-in-progress and finished goods are valued at works cost (including fixed works overheads) and total cost of production (including fixed works overheads and office overheads) respectively under absorption costing system. The two stocks are valued at marginal cost under marginal costing system.

2. Absorption of overheads : There can be under-recovery of overheads under marginal costing system as only variable overheads are absorbed to production. In marginal costing actual fixed overheads are wholly transferred to costing Profit and Loss Account, while in absorption costing, the over or under-recovery of overheads can be transferred to costing Profit and Loss Account.

On account of the above differences, the treatment of costs and profit differ under marginal costing and absorption costing systems. Since marginal costing system lays stress on *contribution i.e., sales minus variable cost,* any increase in contribution mean increase in profit, since fixed costs remain constant for all levels of production. Profit is arrived at after deducting fixed costs from the contribution fund. Under absorption costing, all the costs are first charged to products and then total costs are deducted from sales to arrive at the figure of profit. This would be clear from the following illustration.

Illustration: 1 from the following data prepare statements of cost according to both absorption costing and marginal costing systems :

	Product A *Rs.*	*Product B* *Rs.*	*Product C* *Rs.*
Sales	30,000	60,000	80,000
Direct Material	12,000	25,000	36,000
Direct Labour	8,000	10,000	14,000
Factors overheads :	6,000	8,000	6,000
Fixed variable	2,000	3,000	5,000
Administrative overheads	1,000	2,000	2,000
Fixed selling overheads	2,000	2,000	3,000
Fixed variable	1,000	3,000	3,000

Solution:

Statement of cost

(under absorption costing system)

Particulars	*Total Rs.*	*Product A Rs.*	*Product B Rs.*	*Product C Rs.*
Sales	1,70,000	30,000	60,000	80,000
Less: cost of sales:				
Direct Material	73,000	12,000	25,000	36,000
Direct Labour	32,000	8,000	10,000	14,000
Factory overheads	30,000	8,000	11,000	11,000
Administrative overheads	5,000	1,000	2,000	2,000
selling overheads	14,000	3,000	5,000	6,000
Total	1,54,000	32,000	53,000	69,000
Profit	16,000	(-)2000	7,000	11,000

Statement of cost

(under marginal costing system)

Particulars	*Total Rs.*	*Product A Rs.*	*Product B Rs.*	*Product C Rs.*
Sales	1,70,000	30,000	60,000	80,000
Less: Marginal costs of sales				
Direct Materials	73,000	12,000	25,000	36,000
Direct Labour	32,000	8,000	10,000	14,000
Variable factory overheads	10,000	2,000	3,000	5,000
Variable selling overheads	7,000	1,000	3,000	3,000
Total	1,22,000	23,000	41,000	58,000
Contribution Margin	48,000	7,000	19,000	22,000
Less: fixed costs (factory administration & selling)	32,000	9,000	12,000	11,000
Profit	16,000	(-)2,000	7,000	11,000

Contribution

The difference between selling price and variable cost (*i.e.,* the marginal cost) is known as 'contribution' or 'Gross Margin' or 'Contribution Margin'. In other words, fixed costs plus the amount of profit is equivalent to contribution. It can be expressed as

Contribution = Selling price – Variable cost

or = Fixed cost + Profit

We can derive from it that profit can not result unless contribution exceeds fixed costs. In other word, the point of 'no profit no loss' shall be arrived at where contribution is equal to fixed costs. We can see in the following example :

Variable cost = Rs. 50,000

Fixed cost = Rs. 20,000

Selling Price = Rs. 80,000

Contribution = Selling Price – Variable cost

= Rs. 80,000 – Rs. 50,000

= Rs. 30,000

Profit = Contribution – Fixed cost

= Rs. 30,000 – Rs. 20,000

= 10,000

Profit/Volume Ratio

This term is important for studying the profitability of operations of a business. Profit volume ratio establishes a relationship between the contribution and the sales value. The ratio can be shown in the form of percentage also. The formula can be expressed thus:–

$$\text{P/v Ratio} = \frac{\text{Contribution}}{\text{sales}}$$

$$= \frac{\text{Sales variable costs}}{\text{sales}}$$

This ratio can also be called as 'contribution/ sales' ratio. This ratio can also be known by comparing the change in contribution to change in sales or change in profit to change in sales. Any increase in contribution would mean increase in profit only because fixed costs are assumed to be constant at all levels of production. Thus,

$$\text{P/V Ratio} = \frac{\text{change in contribution}}{\text{change in sales}}$$

$$= \frac{\text{change in Profit}}{\text{change in sales}}$$

This ratio would remain constant at different levels of production since variable costs as a proportion to sales remain constant at various levels.

Example

	Rs.
Sales	2,00,000
variable costs	1,20,000
Fixed costs	40,000

$$P/V \text{ ratio} = \frac{\text{Rs. }2{,}00{,}000 - \text{Rs. }1{,}20{,}000}{\text{Rs. }2{,}00{,}000}$$

$$= 0.4 \text{ or } 40\%$$

The ratio is useful for the determination of the desired level of output or profit and for the calculation of variable costs for any volume of sales. The variable costs can be expressed as under :

V.C = s(1-P/V ratio)

Variable Cost = sales (1-P/V ratio)

In the above example

If we know the P/V ratio and sales before hand, the variable costs can be computed as follows:

Variable costs = 1-0.4 = 0.6 *i.e.,* 60% of sales

= Rs. 1,20,000 (60% of Rs. 2,00,000)

Alternatively by the formula:

$$P/V \text{ Ratio} = \frac{S-V}{S}, \therefore S - V = S \times P/V \text{ Ratio}$$

$$V = S - S \times P/V \text{ Ratio}$$

$$= S(1 - P/V \text{ Ratio})$$

Comparison of difference P/V Ratios is usually made by the management to find out which product is most profitable. Management tries to increase the value of the ratio by reducing the variable costs or by increasing the selling prices.

Key factor

"Key factor" is that factor which is the most important one for taking decisions about profitability of a product. the extent of its influence must be assessed first so as to maximize the profits.

Cost Volume Profit Analysis

Cost volume profit (CVP) analysis is an important tool of profit planning. It provides information about the followng matters :

1. The behaviour of cost in relation to volume
2. Volume of production or sales, where the business will break even.
3. Sensitivity of profits due to variation in output
4. Amount of profit for a projected sales volume.
5. Quantity of production and sales for a target profit level.

Cost volume profit analysis may therefore be defined as a managerial tool showing the relationship between various ingredients of profit planning, viz, cost (both fixed and variable), selling price and volume of activity, etc.

Such an analysis is useful to the Finance Manager in the following respects:

(i) It helps him in forecasting the profit fairly accurately

(ii) It helps in setting up flexible budgets, since on the basis of this relationship, he can ascertain the costs, sales and profits at different levels of activity.

(iii) It also assits him in performance evalution for purposes of management control.

(iv) It helps in formulating price policy by projecting the effect which different price structures will have on cost and profits.

(v) It helps in determining the amount of overhead cost to be charged at various levels of operation, since overhead rates are generally pre-determined on the basis of a selected volume of production.

Thus , cost-volume profit analysis is an important media through which the management can have insight into effects on profit on account of variation in costs (both fixed and variable) and sales (both volume and value) and take appropriate decisions.

BUDGETARY CONTROL

The budgetary control is an essential tool of the management for controlling costs and maximising profits.

Meaning of budget

A budget is a detailed plan of operations for some specific future period. It is an estimate prepared in advance of the period to which it applies. It acts as a business barometer as it is complete programme of activities of the business for the period covered. The chartered Institute of Management Accountants,

London, defines a budget as "a financial and/or quantitative statement, prepared prior to defined period of time, of the policy to be pursued during that period for the purpose of attaining a given objective". Thus, the essentials of a budget are :

(a) It is prepared in advance and is based on a future plane of actions

(b) It relates to a future period and is based on objective to be attained

(c) It is a statement expressed in monetary and/ or physical units prepared for the implementation of policy formulated by the management.

Meaning of Budgetary control: The chartered Institute of Management Accountants, London, defines budgetary control as "the establishment of budget relating to the responsibilities of executives to the requirements of a policy, and the continuous comparison of actual with budget results, either to secure by individual action the objective of that policy or to provide a basis for its revision." According to J.A. Scot "It is the system of management control and accounting in which all operations are forecasted and planned so far as possible ahead and the actual results compared with the forecasted and planned ones." Thus the budgetary control involves–

(a) establishment of budgets

(b) continuous comparison of actual with budgets for achievement of targets and placing the responsibility for failure to achieve the budget figures.

(c) revision of budgets in the light of changed circumstances.

The difference between budget, budgeting and budgetary control has been stated thus:

"Budgets are the individual objectives of a department, etc. whereas Budgeting may be said to be the act of building budgets. Budgetary control embraces all this and in addition includes the science of planning the budgets themselves and the utilisation of such budgets to effect an overall management tool for the business planning and control."

ADVANTAGES OF BUDGETARY CONTROL

It is a useful management tool for comparing the current items with pre-planned items with a view to attain equilibrium between ends and means, output and effort. It corrects the deviations from planned path through the media of observation, research, planning, control and decision making and thus helps in performance of future activities in an orderly way. It acts as a friends, philosopher and guide to the management. Its major advantages are given here below :–

1. It brings efficiency and economy in the working of the business enterprises. Even though a monetary reward is not offered, the budget becomes a game—a goal to achieve or a target to shoot at—and hence it is more likely to be achieved or hit than if there was no predetermined goal or target.
2. It establishes divisional and departmental responsibility. It thus prevents alibis and "buck-passing" when the budget figures are not met.
3. It co-ordinates the various divisions of a business, namely, the production, marketing, financial and administrative divisions. It "forces executives to think, and think as a group."
4. It guards against undue optimism leading to over-expansion because the targets are fixed by the executives after cool and careful thought.
5. It acts as a safety signal for the management. It shows when to proceed cautiously and when manufacturing or merchandising expansion can be safety undertaken. It serves as an automatic check on the judgement of the executives as losses are revealed in time which is a caution to the management to stop wastages.
6. Uniform policy without the disadvantages of a military type of business organisation can be pursued by all divisions of the business by means of centralisation of budgetary control.
7. Seasonal variation in production can be reduced by developing new "fill in" products. This results in decreasing the cost of production by increasing volume of output.
8. The use of budget figures as measures of

operating performance and financial position makes possible the adoption of the standard cost principle in divisions other than the production division.

9. It helps management in obtaining the most profitable combination of different factors of produc-tion. This results in a more economical use of capital.
10. Management which have developed a well-ordered budget plan and which operate accordingly, receive greater favour from credit Agencies.
11. It is the only means of predetermining when and to what extent financing will be necessary avoiding the possibility of both over and under-capitalisation.

LIMITATION TO BUDGETARY CONTROL

1. Opposition against the very spirit of budgeting : There will always be active and passive resistance to budgetary control as it points out at the efficiency or inefficeincy of individuals. The opposition is also due to human nature–the tendency to ressist change.

2. Budgeting and changing economy : The preparation of a 'budget which gives a realistic position of the firm' affairs under inflationary pressure and changing Government policies is really dificult. Thus, the accurate position of the business cannot be estimated.

3. Time factor : Accuracy in budgeting comes through experience. Management must not expect to much during the development period.

4. Not a substitute for management : Budget is only a management tool. It can not substitute management. Besides that no budgetary programme can be successful unless adequate arrangements are made for supervision and administration.

5. Co-operation required : The success of the budgetary control depends upon willing co-operation and teamwork. Budget officer must get co-operation from all departmental managers. These managers must feel the responsibility for achieving or bettering departmental goals laid down in the budgets.

Steps in Budgetary control

I. Organising Budgeting

II. Responsibility of Budgeting
1. Budget controller
2. Budget committee
3. Fixation of the budget period.

III. Budget procedure
1. Determination of key factor
2. Making of forecasts
3. Consideration of alternative combination of forecasts
4. Prepration of budgets

TYPES OF BUDGETS

I. Sales Budget

For the sales budget following factors should take into consideration:

(*a*) Past sales figures and trend
(*b*) Salesman's estimates
(*c*) Plant capacity
(*d*) General trade prospects
(*e*) Orders or hand
(*f*) Proposed expansion of discontinuance of products
(*g*) Seasonal fluctuations
(*h*) Potential market
(*i*) Availability of material and supply
(*j*) Financial aspect
(*k*) Other factors :–
  (*i*) The nature and degree of competition within the industry
  (*ii*) Cost of distributing goods
  (*iii*) Government control, rules and regulations related to the industry, and
  (*iv*) Political situation-national and international as it may have an influence upon the market.

II. Production Budget

This budget provides an estimate of the total volume of production productwise with the scheduling of operations by days, weeks and months a forecast of the closing finished product inventory. The responsibility of the total production budget lies with works manager and that of Departmental Production Budgets lies with Departmental Works Manager.

III. Performance Budgeting

Performance budgeting involves evaluation of the performance of an organisation in the context of both specific as well as over all objectives of the organisation. This requires the complete clarity about both the short-term and long-term organisational objectives.

The features of Performance Budgeting are given here below:–

1. The budget is prepared for each managerial level.
2. The jurisdiction of the authority and responsibility for different costs controllable by the executive concerned is fixed up.
3. The concerned executive is vested with the requisite authority required for the responsibility intrusted to him.

IV. Zero Base Budgeting

ZBB is a new technique designed to revitalise budgeting. A company should not only make decisions about the proposed new programmes but it should also from time to time review the appropriateness of the existing programmes.

Zero base budgeting as the term suggests, examines a programme or function be allowed. The manager proposing the activity has, therefore, to prove that the activity is essential and the various amounts asked for are really reasonable taking into account the volume of activity.

Standard costing

Standard costing is a specialised technique of costing under which standard costs are predetermined, actual costs are compared with such predetermined costs, the variations between the two are noted and analysed as to their causes so that corrective measures may be taken to control the factors leading to unfavourable variations. The system of standard costing, thus, involves various steps—from the setting up of stndards to finally exercising control over costs. It aims at assessing or prefixing the costs of a product, process or operation under standard operating conditions. It serves as an effective tool in the hands of the management for planning, co-ordination and control of various activities of the business. There is a continuous process of growth effected in business through the help of standard costing technique since the standard costs set in are realistic, capable of being attained and are revised from time to time according to needs and requirements of the business enterprise. This technique, if implemented in conjunction with the system of budgetary control, provides better and more successful functions of the business.

DEFINITION OF STANDARD COSTING

According to the Chartered Institute of Management Accountants. London Standard Costing is "the preparation and use of standards costs, their comparison with actual costs and the analysis of the variances to their causes and points of incidents". The definition given by W.W. Biggs makes concept of standard costing more clear. According to him, "Standard Costing discloses the costs of deviations from standard and classifies these as to their causes, so that management is immediately informed of the sphere of operations in which remedial action is necessary."

Thus, standard costing is a method of ascertaining costs where by statistics are prepared to show :

(a) the standard cost;
(b) the actual cost;
(c) the difference between these costs which is termed as variance.

Standard costs are determined for each element of cost—direct materials, direct labour, overheads (fixed and variable)—separately and then variations from actual costs are computed in respect of each element distinctly so as to detect which part of the costs needs control and to which department, process or operation, the responsibility may be placed. The standard costs are organised to uncover and report off-standard conditions. The management should strive for the attainment of standard costs because they are attainable ideal costs and are practical from the point of view of business.

Application of the Technique of Standard Costing

Standard costing is not a method of costing just as process or job or unit costing. It is a system or technique of cost accounting which can be used in conjuction with process, job or operating costing without any difficulty, whatsoever. Industries where standard costing is more suitable can be categorised as under :

1. Process industries where the method of production and nature of output are the same. The examples of such industries are chemical industries, distilleries, paper-making and metal processing etc.
2. Industries where the methods of manufacture are repetitive and products are more or less homogeneous, *e.g.*, agricultural and food products.
3. Service industries where operation costing is also applicable like transport, gas and water, electricity etc.
4. Engineering and textile industries where large range of products are manufactured.
5. Extraction industries such as coal, oil and timber.

Where the work is not repetitive, *e.g.*, construction work, contract work, ship-building and erection work etc., it is difficult to set standards and, therefore, standard costing would not be suitable. But in certain cases it can be applied partially though not fully, at least to some advantage of the concerns.

Advantages of Standard Costing

It is imperative for management to have prior knowledge of costs so that decision making can be effective. Management can control costs on information being provided to it immediately for comparison of results. The advantages of standard costing can thus be listed as follows :

1. Formulation of price and production policies: Standard costing acts as a valuable guide to management in the formulation of price and production policies. It assists management in the field of inventory pricing, product pricing, profit-planning and also further reporting to higher levels.

2. Comparison and analysis of data: Standard costing provides a stable and sound basis for comparison of actual costs with standard costs according to different elements separately. It brings out clearly the impact of external factors and internal causes on the cost and performance of the concern. Thus, it indicates places where remedial action in necessary and how far improvement is possible in the long run.

3. Cost consciousness: An atmosphere of cost consciousness is created among the staff, managerial as well as workmen, of the business. Standard costing also provides incentives to workers and middle and top executive personnel for efficient work.

4. Better capacity to anticipate: A tighter, more accurate and effective budget can be formulated for the coming years by once knowing the deviations of actual costs from standard costs. Data are available at an early stage and the capacity to anticipate about charging conditions is developed.

5. Delegation of authority and fixation of responsibility: The net profit is analysed and responsibility can be placed on the person incharge, for any variations from the standards. The sphere of operation of adverse variations is disclosed and particular production department or centre can be held accountable for it. Thus, delegation of authority and fixation of responsibility can be done by management to control the affairs in different departments.

6. Management by 'exception': The principle "management by exception" can be made applicable in the business. This helps the management in concentrating its attention on cases which are off-standard *i.e.,* below or above the standard set in. The trend of costs is portrayed and therefore, a pattern is provided for the elimination of undesirable factors causing damage to the business.

7. Better economy, efficiency and productivity: Managerial review of costs is more effective as the operations are scrutinised carefully and inefficiencies are disclosed. Men, machines and materials are more effectively utilised and thus economies can be effected in business together with increased productivity. Besides it, a lot of clerical labour is also saved and economy is attained in calculations and computations.

LIMITATIONS OF STANDARD COSTING

1. Fixation of standards may be costly and may require high order of skill and competency. Small concerns, therefore, feel difficulty in the operation of such system.
2. The industries which deal with non-standardised products and the jobs, which change according to customer's specifications, may find the system of standard costing unsuitable and costly.
3. Responsibility can be delegated upon a particular person, process or production only when the controllable and non-controllable factors are distinctly known—and this is a very hard nut to crack.

PRE-REQUISITES FOR INSTALLATION OF STANDARD COSTING SYSTEM

Installation of standard costing system for accomplishing the desired objectives require existence of certain pre-requisities. These pre-requisties can be put as follows:

1. Acceptance of the system: The standard costing system can have the desired effects only when the system is acceptable both to the management as well as to the workers. The management should take sufficient interest in the system to make it effective. Similarly the workers should also believe that in the long run, the system would be beneficial to all of them. This is possible by fixing the standards in a way that they are capable of being achieved by an average worker.

2. Judicious setting of standards: The standards should be fixed after a careful study of all technical processes and operations of the business. They should be fixed judiciously and should not be ideal but capable of being achieved. Setting of standards at too high a level will create resentment among the workers and depress their performance while setting of standards at too low a level will have adverse effects on personal initiative and costs. It will be appropriate to fix the responsibility of setting standards on a committee consisting of important persons such as Production Controller, Purchase Manager, Personal Manager Cost Accountant, etc.

3. Reasonable size: The system of standard costing can be introduced with advantage in concerns which are of a reasonable size. The system may not be suitable for small concerns since in their case careful scheduling of production may not be possible. For example, in a small concern a worker may be handling different machines and at times he may be called to handle different jobs and therefore, it may not be possible to correctly fix the standard time for different jobs or different operations handled by him. Moreover the system of standard, costing requires specialisation of jobs and processes which may not be possible in a small concern.

4. Competent staff: The successful operation of standard costing system requires existence of well qualified and trained staff for fixing the standards, measuring performance and reporting variances to different levels of management. The reports submitted help the management in applying the principle of "management by exception" which means that the management pays attention only to those cases where performance is below or above the standard.

5. Existence of budgetary control system: Existence of budgetary control system is a pre-requisite for the standard costing system. Budgets fix the targets which the executives have to achieve. They create a sense of discipline, financial or otherwise, among employees at different levels. Budgets are the projections for the future and therefore they are of great use to the effective functioning of the standard costing system.

6. Proper delegation of authority and responsibility: Standard costing system requires proper delegation of authority and responsibility at different levels. This is possible by drawing an organisation chart clearly laying down the authority and responsibility of different executives in the organisation.

7. Efficient accounting system: An efficient accounting system is also an essential requisite for successful operation of the standard costing system. The accounting information supplied should not only be accurate but also be complete and up to date. The system of coding may be used for speedy recording and analysing the accounting information. Appropriate cost centres should also be set up in the organisation.

MEANING OF STANDARD COSTS

Ideal costs

These are costs which should be there under ideal working conditions, ideal management and ideal plant capacity. Such an ideal is a myth, far from reality. Such a flight of imagination does not have any material significance in the eyes of practical manager who is aware of certain limitations which exist in spite of every possible check, control, care and caution. Perfection can never be achieved when one has to deal with men, materials and machines; and not simply figures. Perfection is not possible, even in biological and mathematical sciences, what to talk of management science which involves handling of man in particular whose behaviour is totally unpredictable at any given time. Sometimes, miraculous results are achieved due to certain abnormal conditions but we concern ourselves not with such abnormalities but with whatever is feasible if strived for. When the plant is working maximum capacity or even at more than its capacity level, perfection is a far cry and hence ideal costs cannot be regarded as standard costs for managerial control.

Normal costs

Such costs can be determined on the basis of the prevailing conditions of the business or industry. Thus, here it is assumed that plant is working at normal level of capacity and efficiency, workers are engaged in production activities performing their normal functions and the normal efficiency operations are being carried out. The cost shall thus be an average standard cost which is normally there in the business. Then, where would the management need control? How would the business progress and brighten its prospects, broaden and widen its field of activities and achieve prominence and success in the competitive market? Besides that, the meaning of 'normal' differs from one business to another. This suggests that normal levels of workmanship, efficiency, capacity and managerial operations are not significant and of worth for practical planning and control of costs.

Cost based on 'average of past performance'

If past is any guide for future action, as it popularly regarded the average of past performance should serve as the best ground for the ascertainment of standard costs. The costs which have been incurred during the past 3 or 5 years, for instance, as the case may be, are averaged out and same may be taken as standard costs for the following period. This, again, would not be a correct basis for the computation of standard cost because it is not logical and rational to assume that past trend will continue in future without any changes or reservation, whatsoever. No doubt, past results have a significant role to play in shaping the standards, yet they are not enough and self-sufficient to constitute standards. Several errors, wastes, ineconomies and inefficiencies of plant and business are comprised therein. The circumstances in the present set-up might have altogether changed; plant capacity might have increased or diminished, market conditions also might be adverse or more favourable. Besides that, different trends and tendencies might be foresighted. It is imperativge to take a record of all these factors and, therefore, historical costs cannot serve the purpose of standards costing.

Current costs

The costs which are currently or presently being incurred are also not a useful guide for standard costs since they are neither in rhythm with past trends nor are inclusive of factors and conditions to follow. Present is always required to be adjusted for past as well as future. Current costs have even a weaker ground for being regarded as a suitable basis for treatment as standards.

Current actual costs are, in one way, the costs which are more accurate to be assumed as standards if the conditions remain static and circumstances do not change. But this is seldom true in business and moreover we need cost control, the scope of which is absent if we adopt the current costs as standards.

Expected or anticipated costs

The costs which are expected to be incurred during a forthcoming period are costs which closely follow the pattern of present costs, though adjusted according to past behavioural pattern as well as future tendencies. But such costs would be an estimate of what the actual costs shall be in respect of the period for which the estimates have been prepared. As pointed out while distinguishing estimated costing from standard costing, such estimated costs do not provide any basis for comparison and control. Estimated cost is just a prediction of the actual costs; it is, in a way, better than what the cost is or what the cost shall be under normal conditions. A standard should be fixed assuming somewhat higher level of efficiency than what is reflected under simple estimation of actual costs.

Reasonably attainable costs

Costs which can be attained reasonably if the management tries for them, *i.e.,* it makes a sincere and concerned effort to achieve the targets set in, can be regarded as a satisfactory yardstick or benchmark for standards. Here, we assume a level of operation which is certainly above the normal level of efficiency. It neither means perfection (an ideal) not the current conditions nor even the normal conditions. The management by fixing costs at such a level can make wholehearted effort to bring down the actual costs to the level of standard and can achieve better efficiency in business operations. It is argued that reasonably attainable standards cannot be regarded as standards for our purpose because it is difficult to set a level in between actual costs and ideal costs. But, as a matter of fact, it is not at all difficult to set in such standards because we assume an efficiency level better than what is prevailing at present or even what shall prevail in the period for which standards are being fixed.

Standard Cost and Budgeted Cost

There is no conceptual difference between the terms "Standard cost" and "budgeted cost", expect that the term 'standard cost' is a unit concept while the term "budgeted cost" is a total concept. It other words, cost per unit, if carefully predetermined is termed as standard cost while total cost carefully predetermined is termed as budgeted costs.

PRELIMINARIES TO SETTING OF STANDARDS

Certain factors are to be borne in mind while fixing the standards :

Period of use

The first important criterion for establishment of standard costs is the length of the operation period for which standards are to be used. Long-term as well as short-term standards may be fixed ranging for different periods. For long-term planning and growth standards for a longer duration, say 3 to 5 years, may be justified while for planning and budgeting for the accounting period short term standards for a year or so are beneficial. For measuring the performance and exercising control over costs short-term standards are most suited. The standards according to length of time may be categorised as—

(a) **Basic standards:** These are not alerted over a long period of time; revisions are not frequent and there is a stability and stagnancy in standards fixed. These 'basic' or 'bogey' standards remain constants for a very long time and are applied in industries where only a *small range of products* are manufactured and *long-term planning* is required. But since the conditions do not remain static in this dynamic world. The standards become obsolete and require overhauling and, therefore, the long-term basic standards are not realistic.

(b) **Current standards:** Short-term standards are known as current standards. These are more suitable for business since they take into account the current conditions and are related to the budget period.

In business, it will be useful to set both—long term as well short term standards. This will help in finding out the variations in respect of both these standards in advance of actual production.

SETTING OF STANDARDS

The standard cost is determined for each and every element of cost distinctly. The elements can be divided under the following categories :

(i) Direct Material; *(ii)* Direct Labour; *(iii)* Overheads—*(a)* Fixed Overheads and *(b)* Variable Overheads.

Standards for direct material cost

The direct material cost is found out by multiplying the quantity of materials to be purchased with the rate or price at which they are available and hence the standards are to be set for both quantity and rate, separately, for the determination of standard cost of direct materials.

(i) **Quantity standards.** To know, 'how much materials is required' is a task which can be performed with the help of —

(a) records of past experience *i.e.*, historical data;

(b) mathematical or scientific computations and engineering specifications;

(c) test runs and experiments; or

(d) standard bills of materials.

(ii) **Price standards.** The material price standards can be set on the basis of either :

(a) prices paid in the past taking into account the anticipated trends of rise or fall of prices in the market during the period for which standards are to be determined; or

(b) average of the prices paid during the past period, *i.e.*, average or normal price; or

(c) 'basic' or 'bogey' prices which are static or fixed in nature. Market fluctuations are not incorporated while deciding such prices.

STANDARDS FOR DIRECT LABOUR COST

Just as for direct materials the standards are fixed separately for quantity and rate, similarly for direct labour also the standards are determined separately for quantum of labour to be employed in production and the rate of wages to be paid to them. The standard direct labour cost can be arrived at by multiplying the standard quantity with the standard rate. The quantity of labour can be fixed in terms of time required for performing the various operations involved in production. The standards regarding time and rate have been discussed below:

(i) **Standard time:** The time to be consumed by labourers can be measured by time, motion and fatigue studies. Works and methods analysis can be adopted and operation time for every activity noted down. The total time required is further adjusted for wastages.

(ii) **Standard rate:** The type of labour required for performing a specific job or activity would be the most important factor for deciding the rate of wage to be paid to the workers. Efficient and skilled workers having technical knowledge might have to be employed for certain types of technical jobs and therefore, the wages paid to such workers will be higher than those for unskilled and non-technical workers. Where the work requires some knowledge of art or science, specialisation in certain fields like product design or priduct specifications, engineerig etc. would be basically responsible for disparity in the rates of wages. Besides, production of certain commodities may requiere experienced workers-they also will have to be paid more. Then, if the management wants to provide some incentives to workers the rates of payment should be higher than what are expected by the workers. Again, the rates may be fixed according to look done, *i.e.*, piece rates or according to fixed hours of work, *i.e.*, time rates. The type of wage system to be followed is important in this respect.

The wages rates can be determined on the basis of one or more of the above considerations. Therefore, the standard may be set by computing the average of past figures and adjusting it further on the assumption that normal working conditions will continue. Estimates may be made on the grounds of judgement, intuition, guess or scientific calculations also.

STANDARDS FOR OVERHEADS

Overheads may be classified as manufacturing, administration, selling and distribution overheads. They may also be categories as fixed and variable. Before setting the standards in respects of overheads, the following points should be carefully gone through:

1. What level of activity has been taken as standard level? Does it represent current, or normal or reasonably attainable level?
2. The overheads would have to be classified into two broad categories— fixed and variable, because different standards are required to be fixed for them.
3. Quantum of expenses to be incurred on each item, according to each department for every process or operation will have to be determined. Flexible budgeting may be helpful in this connection.

Fixed overhead standards

Fixed overheads are not affected by the volume of production and therefore, fixation of standards for fixed overhead is relatively easy. The past figures shall be the best guide in this reference. In case the plant capacity is increased or business is carried on in more shifts, the fixed overheads might be more than what they were in the preceding period. A reasonable budgeted estimate of the same would be incorporated while determining fixed overhead standards. Normally, the fixed overhead rate per unit of output or per hour is determined so as to know the recovery of fixed overheads for the actual output or for actual time taken (as the case may be).

Variable overhead standard

The volume of production multiplied by the cost of overhead per unit of output would determine the total variable overhead cost for a period. The per unit variable cost is fixed and, therefore, it also depends to a large extent on the past data.

Manufacturing overhead standard

Indirect costs like indirect material cost, indirect labour cost and other manufacturing costs can be estimated with the help of the material and labour standards. The burden of overheads per hour can be determined. This standard overhead rate is to be applied for calculating standard cost for the total hours taken.

Office and administration overhead standard

The standards in respect of such overheads will depend upon the number of persons employed on the clerical and managerial staff, the hours of their work, the quantum of production, and the amount of control and vigilance exercised by the executives in this respect.

Selling and distribution overheads standard

The indirect selling expenses depend on the sale promotion efforts, channels of distribution, nature of the product, transportation and other difficulties for distribution of goods to different areas etc. A decision is to be taken in this regard and finally the total of such overheads is to be computed.

After fixing the standards for direct material cost, direct labour cost and overhead cost separately, the total standard cost of manufacturing a product or taking up a specific operation can be known by just aggregating the different costs.

STANDARD COST OF STANDARD OUTPUT

When the standard quantity which shall be manufactured during a particular period has been decided upon, the standard cost of standard production can be computed by a simple multiplication of the standard units to be produced by the standard per unit cost of production.

Standards of sales

Standards are to laid down both for the probable quantity of sales and the selling price, so as to know the standard value of sales. The budgeted estimate of the expected volume of sales and the selling price can be made by the management. The deviations of actual volume of sales and the price at which the goods are actually sold are also important for effecting managerial control over costs.

Standards for profit

The excess of standard sales over standard costs is the standard profit. Sometimes standards for profit are determined at a fixed percentage on cost or on selling price, keeping in view the minimum return expected on investment. This helps in determining standards for sales also.

Revision of standards

The standards set in are required to be revised from time to time according to change in circumstances. Any alterations effected in standards should represent the changed conditions of work, increased plant capacity, market contditions etc. If a new range of products is to be manufactured or some operations turn out to be unprofitable due consideration would have to be given to such factors in fixation of standards. Normally, there should not be frequent changes in standards, otherwise the very purpose of determination of standards shall be defeated. If variations from actuals occur in practice, they may be due to controllable or non-controllable causes.

8. COMPUTERS IN ACCOUNTING

USE OF COMPUTERS IN MANAGERIAL APPLICATIONS

What is a Computer

The word "Computer" comes from the word compute which means to calculate. So a computer is normally considered to be a calculating device that can perform arithmetic operation at an enormous speed. But more accurately, a computer may be defined as a device that operates upon data. Data can be anything, like bio-data of several applicants when the computer is used to assist us for recruiting personnel. Similarly, the data can be the details of passengers such as name, age, etc. when the computer is employed for making airline or railway reservations.

The two basic types of computers are the analog and the digital. The analog computer handles or process information which is of a physical nature, as for example, temperature, pressure, etc. The digital computer process information which is essentially in a binary or two-state form namely, zero and one. When talking about computers, we mostly refer to the **digital** type electronic machines.

Digital computers fall into ranges called microcomputers, minicomputers, mainframes, and supercomputers classified in ascending order of size—small, medium, large and very large.

Characteristics of Computers

Computer display the following characteristics depending on their type of use :

(*a*) The ability to perform calculations at a fast speed and to store that information for future retrieval or use.

(*b*) The ability to take in information and to store that information for future retrieval or use.

(*c*) The ability to take in and store a small variety of instructions for computers to obey.

(*d*) The ability to use simple logical rules to make decisions for their own internal control or for the control of some external activity.

(*e*) The ability to communicate with other computer systems.

(*f*) To carry out calculations accurately and speedily.

Applications of Computers

Computers may be used in the following fields/ institutions :

(*a*) Offices

(*b*) Book Publications

(*c*) Data Analysis

(*d*) Graphics

(*e*) CAM (Computer Aided Manufacture)

(*f*) Data Base Management

(*g*) Project Management

(*h*) Communications

(*i*) Education

(*j*) Medical Field

(*k*) Airways and Railways Ticket Reservations

(*l*) Industrial Control and Instruments

(*m*) Military

(*n*) Banks

(*o*) Designs and Research Work

(*p*) Other Applications

(*a*) **Office Uses:** The work done in offices is generally, the preparation of letters, reports, memoranda, copy of advertisement, publicity, minutes, contracts, forms, notes etc. All these tasks can be performed by computers more efficiently. Small offices, organizations and institutions can afford to have a personal computer because of its low price. A high end PC personal computer costs in the range of Rs. 35,000 to Rs. 50,000. This type of computer can help user in reports preparation, storing and retrieving and displaying of test. Word processing package like Microsoft Office 2000, Word Perfect, Word Pro etc. are available that help users to write, edit, manipulate, store, retrieving, display, and print the text. The paperless office needs much less office space and lesser number of workers to do the same job more smartly.

(*b*) **Publication of Books (Desk Top Publications):** Authors prepare manuscripts of books using Word processing programs. Tests is stored on a floppy disk and formatted by specialized personnel called type-setters. These are then printed using laser printers. Laser printers produce high quality print and the final copy is called the camera ready copy (CRC). These prints are sent to the offset press for printing purposes and then binding is done at the binding centres. The cover page of the books are made by artists or they are also designed using another graphic software such as corel DRAW. The cover is then sent for printing in another type of printing press which is specialized only in colour printing. Illustrations, pictures and tables are also created on specialized softwares such as Auto CAD. Such figures and diagrams are then imported and pasted in the text of the book using a word processor. These jobs are done very fast. Thus book publishing is revolutionized by computers.

(*c*) **Data Analysis:** Special software called spreadsheet program are used for data analysis. Data are entered in rows and columns in a spreadsheet. Using spreadsheet program one can tabulated results, and carry out interpolation of results such as the likely profits of the company based on the sales and expenses. These results are then compared by the actual results and corrections are accordingly applied from time to time. One can prepare product sales, profit, investment. Similarly, statistical packages are available for any kind of computation for data analysis. They have functions to calculate average, maximum and minimum, mean, mode and median values etc. They can accept data from other files and sort, merge and manipulate data as needed.

(*d*) **Graphics:** Computers are being used to make drawings, graphics and pictures. Corel DRAW, Harvard Graphics and Freelance Plus for Windows are some such software packages which help an artist in increasing his drawing capability. Preparation of drawings is a time consuming task if it is done by draftsman. But computers can draw sophisticated drawings in minutes. It can produce three-dimensional pictorial views. Graphics such as bar graphs, pie charts and line graphs are plotted from spreadsheet data and other tabulated form of stored data. Graphics packages are also used to recognize picture, process images, draw pictures etc.

(*e*) **Computer Aided Manufacture:** Computers are used to control production of engineering items, chemical processes etc. Designers use Computer Aided Design softwares to design machines and machine parts which are likely to be manufactured in large numbers. Computers are also used to control manufacturing machines such as lathes, drill or milling machines. Integrated approach of Computer Aided Design (CAD) and Computer Aided Manufacture (CAM) is used in automated factories. The designers design new machines using CAD. There are softwares packages to get design information from the CAD design database and convert them automatically into other programs which activate and control manufacturing machines such as lathes, drills, milling machines etc. A series of computer-controlled machines perform the whole task of production. Maruti Udyog in Gurgaon (Haryana) in India for the manufacturing and assembly Maruti Cars.

(*f*) **Database Management:** Computers are used to handle files which store a variety of information. The terms database is used to refer to one or more related files. Information can be seen on the computer screen. To handle files, database management packages are widely used. Let us suppose a computer stores information in a file regarding students, e.g. name of the students, roll number, marks subject wise, total percentage of marks subject wise, percentage of total, division awarded etc. If one asks computer to print the list of students who have secured total marks 75% and above, computer will be able to do so very easily. One can also ask it to print the names of the students who have secured the highest marks in different subjects. A database management system can provide information from more than one related files.

A user would like to have certain information which is not in a single file. The program will search all the required information from different files and supply it to user. Take an example of records maintained by an advocate. He maintains two files. One file contains the records of different clients. It may be named as client file. It records client number, client identification number, name of the client, address, phone number, amount due etc. He maintains another file which keeps the records of different cases. It may be named as the case file. It records case number, identification number of the client of different cases, attorney, court, judge, opening date, court date etc. Suppose the advocate wants information about which cases are to be taken up on a particular date, the details of the cases and details of clients to obtain information requires searching both the files—client files as well as case file. The software package will collect information from both the files. The case file gives the information about the cases that are due on a particular date. It also gives the identification numbers of the client corresponding to each case. For these identification numbers the details of clients are obtained from the client file. The information so retrieved is given to the user in a very short time.

(*g*) Project Management: A project work has a series of tasks which must be completed in scheduled time. Computers can be used to manage project work to plan, schedule and control man power, material and other resources needed to complete the project work in time at reasonable cost. What are the tasks to be performed, the sequence in which tasks are to be performed, time required to complete each task and the starting data—all this information should be supplied to the computer. The project management package shows the longest sequence of events in the project called critical path. It calculates total project time. In case a project lags behind the schedule, speed can be increased to reduce the time of completion of one or more tasks on the critical path to catch up the schedule. Project management package will show the impact of the delay. It will quickly show the modified schedule. It will also show the increased man power required for completing project in time.

(*h*) Communications: Computers are extensively used in sending and receiving information over long distances. For communication purposes one must have a computer, a data communication package and a modulator and demodular (modem). Telephone line is designate to transmit analog signals. On the other hand, a computer processes digital signals consisting of pulse or no pulse *i.e.*, presence or absence of an electrical voltage. Digital signals can not be transmitted over existing telephone lines which have been designed to transmit analog signals.

The Modulators/demodulators (Modem) are needed to convert or modulate digital signals to analog signals and vice versa to use existing telephone lines. The modem receives data from a computer or a terminal and converts (modulates) the digital signals into analog signals which can be transmitted over, telephone lines. The modem at the other end receives data from telephone lines and converts (or demodulates) the received analog signals into digital signals. These digital signals are processed by a computer at the receiving end. They are thereafter reproduced as the original information. Data can be transmitted in both directions. When data is being transmitted from one end, the modem placed at the other end performs demodulation. When data is received at the other end, the modem placed at this end performs demodulation. Computer communications are being used in electronic mail, video conference, banking, brokerage and to get information services etc.

(*i*) Education: In educational institutions computers are used as teaching aid, research tool and analysing system. When computer is used as a teaching aid it is referred to as computer—assisted instruction (CAI). The computer asks questions to test the students's ability to understand the subject. When a student gives an answer, the computer gives some comments to indicate that answer is right or wrong. If the answer is not correct, the computer gives some error signal. The CAI programs can be prepared in a variety of modes, such as tutorial, discovery, problem solving, modelling, and drill and practice. In tutorial mode the computer presents new ideas followed by text questions. In discovery mode the computer presents information and asks students to draw conclusions. In problem solving mode computer allows students to apply their concept in solving a problem. In modelling mode a process or a system is presented mathematically to make its analysis. Computers can also repeat the presentation of the material as many times as desired. This helps students make certain concepts clear if they are not clear in earlier attempts. Question bank may be prepared and stored in computer's memory. Test questions may be stored so that students can manage their examination to test their knowledge.

(*j*) **Medical Field:** Computers are widely used in hospitals to help doctors in diagnosis, get information on patients, diseases treatments, drugs etc. They are also used in administration of the hospital and in keeping patient records Doctors can discuss with colleagues about the diagnosis of a diseases using tele-conferencing. Doctors are taking help of expert system in the diagnosis and treatment of patients.

Presently expert systems are helping doctors but such systems are not the substitute for doctors. They are useful primarily in aiding doctors in diagnosis and treatment. Computers are also used in pathological laboratories also.

(*k*) **Airways and Railways Ticket Reservations:** The computer is capable of storing all necessary information in connection with ticket reservation, such as train number, stations in route, distance, number of seats available for each train in each class, fare etc. If seats are available, computer prints and issues ticket. Computer also prints reservation charts. It also gives information regarding train timings.

(*l*) **Industrial Control and Instrumentation:** Computers are extensively used in automatic control of temperature of a furnace, speed of a motor, generators voltage and power boiler's pressure, testing of products etc. Microprocessor based system have been developed for industrial control and instrumentation.

(*m*) **Military:** Computers are extensively used in defence. Modern tanks, torpedoes, missiles etc. employ computerized control systems. A guided missile uses internal computer for its own control. They can fly into dangerous zones without the risk of pilot's life. Communications. Radar systems employ computers for processing data and display images. Computerized control systems provide information about range, height, etc. of the target.

(*n*) **Banks:** Banks use computers to provide on line service to customers and to answer customer's enquiry regarding their bank balance, etc. To handle cash, banks use cash dispensing machines. With the use of a computer electronic transfer of funds from one account to another has become possible. A customer from his home, office or store can insert his identification number and type the transaction details on the terminal details on the terminal's keyboard. Immediately the amount he specifies will move out of his account and enter another's account.

(*o*) **Design and Research Work:** Design of bridges, towers, building, generators, motors, etc. need very complex calculations. In some cases, massive data are to be processed particularly in statistical analysis. Computers are suitable for both complex computations as well as processing of massive amount of data. Nowadays computers are a must for this type of work.

(*p*) **Other Applications:** Microprocessors which can control engine operations such as air fuel mixture, ignition timing etc. are available in the market for efficient operations. Computers also control door locks, air conditioning, braking, skidding and speed of the car. Smart watches are also in the market. Any smart product contains an embedded microprocessor. A microprocessor gives time, data, month etc. A number of smart products such as smart crane, smart material handler, smart camera, smart TV, smart thermostat, smart taxi meter etc. are available. The user can program a smart product to perform certain tasks as he desires.

Personal computers are also used in home for playing games, communicating with data base services, processing, computer aided education, home management, accounting etc. Computers are used in automatic electronic telephone exchange. An exchange can handle larger number of customers in faster and efficient manner. Many types of communications are controlled by computers. The computer-controlled telescope are able to detect and track satellites beyond radar range.

DATA PROCESSING

Manipulation of facts to the advantage of the users is called data processing. It may be done using manual or electronic methods. The main purpose of Electronic Data Processing (EDP) is to do complex job at incredible speed and accuracy.

Sometimes, a part of the data processing job may be done using manual methods. As an example, your class teacher may prepare the list of marks obtained by you in various tests and examinations manually. However, further processing into grades and merit may be done using electronic computers because electronic machines are faster and more accurate and calculations will not go wrong. Since electronic machines are faster in operation and reasonable affordable, one may prefer them over manual systems. Different cycle is which data processed electronically is given below :

I. Input Cycle
II. Processing Cycle
III. Output Cycle

I. Input Cycle: In this phase, data is prepared in some convenient form and on a medium most suitable for entry into a processing machine. For example, in a manual system, we may prefer to write data in a tabular form on a sheet of paper such as the marks sheet of students of a class. We do so, because it is very convenient to read the marks written in tabular form. In case of electronic data processing machines, we may record data on a magnetic tape or floppy disk.

II. Processing Cycle: In this cycle, we manipulate or combine the inputted data with other data as per the instructions. For example, in a manual processing cycle, a class teacher adds the marks secured by each student in different subjects. She divides this aggregate by the maximum marks and calculates the percentage of marks. She can also award a grade, based on the percentage of marks. In an electronic data processing system, these actions are performed automatically in accordance with a series of instructions called a program, which is stored in the computer. The computer will do exactly the same job as is told to it by the set of instructions or program.

III. Output Cycle: Once data are processed, the results need to be brought out in a form most suitable for the user. This is called the output cycle. For example, in the marks processing case, the marks of each student in each subject are transferred to printed report cards. Remarks like pass/fail are also recorded on this report along with the merit and the grades. This job is done by a class teacher in a manual data processing system and by a computer printer in an electronic data processing system. A block diagram of the three cycle is shown in the following Fig. 1.

Fig. 1. *Block Diagram of a Basic Data Processing Cycle*

INFORMATION SYSTEM

What is an Information System

An information system can be any organized combination of people, hardware, software, communications networks, and data resources that collects, transforms and disseminates information in an organization. People have relied on information system to communicate with each other using a variety of physical devices (hardware), information processing instructions and procedures (software), communications and channels (networks), and stored data (data resources) since the down of civilization. The following figure 2 represents the information systems :

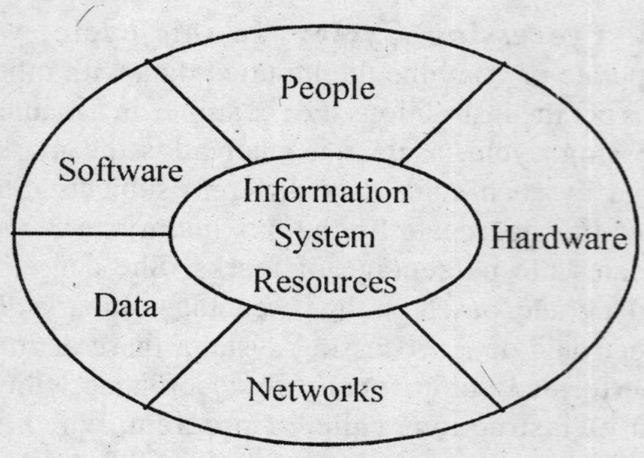

Fig. 2.

Components of Information System

An information system depends on :

→ The resources of people (end users and IS Specialists)

→ Hardware (machines and media)

→ Software (programs and procedures)

→ Data (data and knowledge bases), and

→ Networks (communications media and network support) to perform input, processing, output, storage, and control activities that convert data resources into information products.

The information system model highlights the relationship among the components and activities of information systems (see Fig. 3). It provides a framework that emphasizes four major concepts that can be applied to all types of information system :

- People, hardware, software, data, and networks are the five basic resources of information systems.
- People resources include end users and IS specialists hardware resources consist of machines and media, software resources include both programs and procedures, data resources can include data and knowledge bases, and network resources include communications media and networks.
- Data resources are transformed by information processing activities into a variety of information products for end users.
- Information processing consists of input, processing, output, storage, and control activities.

MIS AND DECISION MAKING

Management Information System (MIS) provide information in the form of reports and displays to managers and many business professionals. For example, sales managers may use their networked computers and Web browsers to get instantaneous displays about the sales results of their products and to access their corporate intranet for daily sales analysis reports that evaluate sales made by each salesperson.

MIS is one of the part of management support systems.

As MIS produces information products that support many of the day-to-day decision making needs of managers and business professionals. Reports, displays, and responses produced by such management support systems provide information that these decision makers have specified in advance as adequately meeting their information needs. Such predefined information products satisfy the information needs of decision makers at the operational and tactical levels of the organization who are faced with more structured typed of decision situations. For example, sales managers rely heavily on sales analysis reports to evaluate differences in performance among sales people who sell the same type of products to the same type of customers. They have a pretty good idea of the kinds of information about sales results they need to manage sales performance effectively.

Managers and other decision makers use an MIS to request information at their networked workstations that supports their decision making activities. This information takes the form of periodic, exception and demand reports and immediate responses to inquiries. Web browsers, application programs, and database management software provide access to information in the intranet and other operational databases of the organization. Remember, operational databases are maintained by transactions processing systems. Data about the business environment are obtained from Internet or extranet databases when necessary.

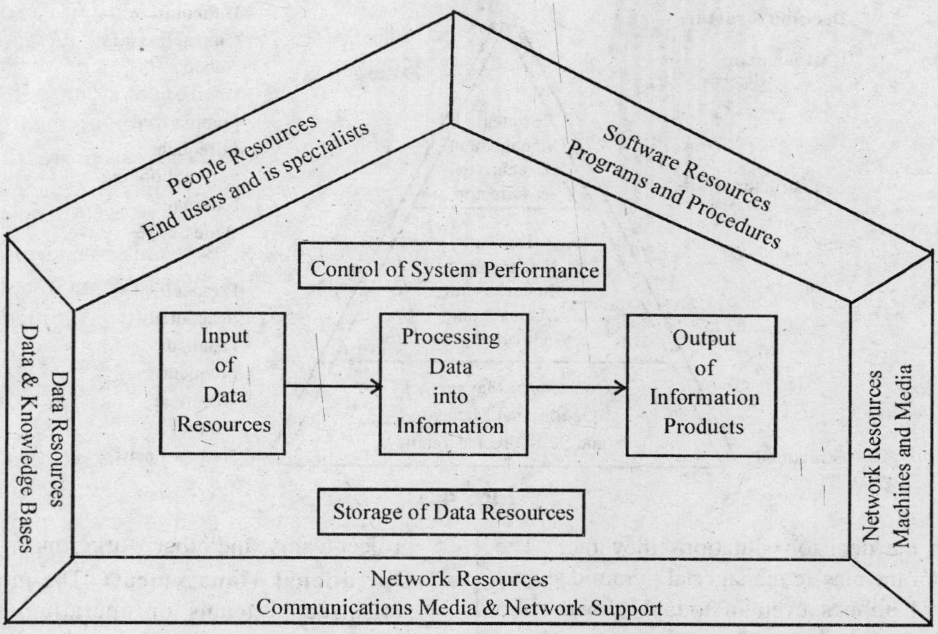

Fig. 3. *The Components of Information System*

Management Informaticn systems provide a variety of information products to managers. Four major reporting alternatives are provided by such systems:

1. Periodic Scheduled Reports: This traditional form of providing information to managers users a prespecified format designed to provide managers with informational on a regular basis. Typical examples of such periodic scheduled reports are daily or weekly sales analysis reports and monthly financial statement.

2. Exception Reports: In some cases, reports are produced only when exceptional conditions occur. In other cases, reports are produced periodically but contain information only about these exceptional conditions. For example, a credit manager can be provided with a report that contains only information on customers who exceed their credit limits. Exception reporting reduces information overload, instead of overwhelming decision makers with periodic detailed reports of business activity.

3. Demand Reports and Responses: Information is available whenever a manager demands it. For example, Web browsers and DBMS query languages and report generators enable managers at PC workstations to get immediate responses or find and obtain customized reports as a result of their requests for the information they need. Thus, manager do not have to wait for periodic reports to arrive as scheduled.

4. Push Reporting: Information is pushed to a manager's networked workstation. Many companies are using webcasting software to selectively broadcast reports and other information to the networked PCs of managers and specialists over their corporate intranets.

Decision Making Process

A process of intelligence, design, and choice activities that result in the selection of a particular course of action.

Information requirements of decision makers are depicted in the following Fig. 4.

The type of information required by decision makers in a company is directly related to the level of management decision making and the amount of

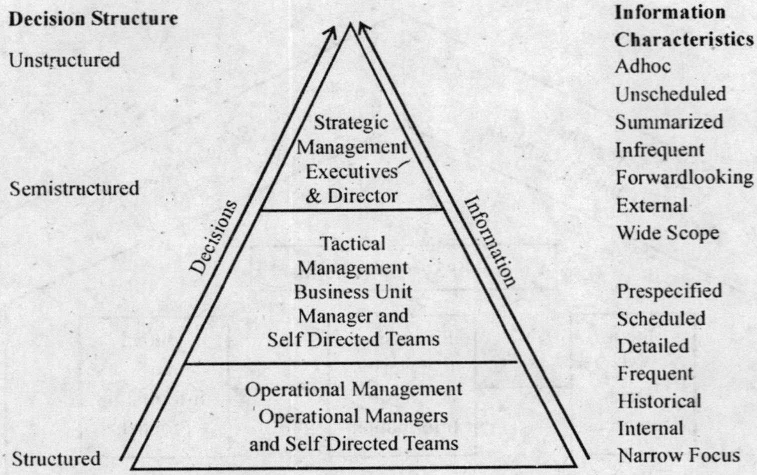

Fig. 4

structure in the decision situations they face. The framework of the classic managerial pyramid shown in the Fig. 4 applies even in today's down sized organizations and flattened or non hierarchical organizational structures. Levels of management decision making still exist, but their size, shape and participants continue to change as today's fluid organizational structures evolve. Thus, the levels of managerial decision making that must be supported by information technology in a successful organization are :

- **Strategic Management:** Typically, a board of directors of an executive committee of the CEO and top executives develop overall organizational goals, strategies, policies and objectives as part of a strategic planning process. They also monitor the strategic performance of the organization and its overall direction in the political, economic and competitive business environment.
- **Tactical Management:** Increasingly, business professionals in self-directed teams as well as business unit managers develop short-and medium-range plans, schedules, and budgets and specify the policies, procedures and business objectives for their subunits of the company. They also allocate resources and monitor the performance of their organiza-tional subunits, including departments, divisions, process teams, project teams, and other workgroups.
- **Operational Management:** The members of self-directed teams or operating managers develop short-range plans such as weekly production schedules. They direct the use of resources and the performance of tasks according to procedures and within budgets and schedules they establish for the teams and other workgroups of the organization.

Decisions made at the operational management level tend to be more structured, those at the tactical level more semistructured, and those at the strategic management level more unstructured. Structured decisions involve situations where the procedures to follow when a decision is needed can be specified in advance. The inventory reorder decisions faced by most businesses are a typical example. Unstructured decisions involve decision situations where it is not possible to specify in advance most of the decision procedures to follow. At most, many decision situations are semistructured. That is, some decision procedures can be prespecified, but not enough to lead to a definite recommended decision. For example, decisions involved in starting a new line of E-commerce services or making major changes to employee benefits would probably range from unstructured to semistructured. Table 1 provides a variety of examples of business decisions by type of decision structure and level of management.

Table 1

Decision	Operational	Tactical	Strategic
Structure	Management	Management	Management
Unstructured	Cash Management	Business process reengineering Work Group performance analysis	New E-commerce initiatives Company reorganization
Semistructured	Credit Management	Employee performance appraisal	Product Planning
	Production Scheduling	Capital budgeting	Mergers and acquisitions
	Daily work assignment	Program budgeting	Site location
Structured	Inventory Control	Program Control	

Therefore, information systems must be designed to produce a variety of information products to meet the changing needs of decision makers throughout an organization. For example, decisions makers at the strategic management level require more summarized, ad hoc, unscheduled reports, forecasts, and external intelligence to support their more unstructured planning and policy making responsibilities. Decision makers at the operational management level, on the other hand, may require more prespecified internal reports emphasizing detailed current and historical data comparisons that support their more structure responsibilities in day-to-day operations.

SYSTEMS ANALYSIS AND DESIGNS

Systems

The term system is derived from the Greek word systema, which means an organized relationship among functioning units or components. A system exists because it is designed to achieve one or more objectives. We come into daily contact with the transportation system, the telephone system, the accounting system, the production system, computer system etc.

A system is an orderly grouping of interdependent components linked together according to a plan to achieve a specific objectives.

System analysis and design are the application of the systems approach to problem solving generally using computers. To reconstruct a system the analyst must consider its elements—outputs and inputs, processors, control, feedback and environment.

Systems fall into three classifications :

(*a*) Physical (tangible entitles) or abstract, such as models or formulas.

(*b*) Open (allowing inputs and providing outputs) or closed, which isolates it from the environment.

(*c*) Man made such as information systems.

A system may be schematic (two dimensional), a flow system to abstract the real world (e.g., PERT Chart), a static (exhibiting one relationship such as Gnatt Chart) or a dynamic system model that approximates the business organization.

An information system is an open system that allows inputs and facilitates interaction with the user. The main characteristics of an open system are input from outside, processing, output, operating in cycles through feedback, differentiation, and equifinality.

There are three levels of information in organizations that require a special type of information system :

(*a*) Strategic information relates to long range planning policies and upper management. It is achieved with the aid of decision support systems.

(*b*) Managerial information helps middle management and department heads in policy implementation and control. It is maintained with the aid of management information systems.

(*c*) Operational information is daily information needed to operate the business. It is established by data processing systems.

The nature of information and managerial levels is related to whether decision making is structured or unstructured. A relatively closed stable, and mechanistic business tends to develop a more structured information process for planning and control. Open, dynamic organizations are associated with uncertain environments where more unstructured rather than structured decisions are made to cope with uncertainty.

The informal communications network of employees in the organization is a useful source for examining systems, since computers cannot provide all the information user staff support is important.

Managerial levels determine the kind of information needed to solve a problem. Lower-level management needs detailed information to make day-to-day structured decisions. Higher-level management requires summarized information to attain goals. MIS is combination of information for various managerial levels.

The key element of MIS is the data base-ideally, a nonredundant collection of interrelated data items that are processed through application programs. The data base offers several advantageous to end users and is the wave of the future.

The historical nature of MIS reports and the need to deal with unstructured problem situations prompted the introduction of Decision Support System (DSS). The concept is future oriented, emphasizing decision making in problem situations, not information processing; it requires a computer aided environment and accentuates a combined "mean", machine, and decision environment.

System analysis and design are keyed to the life cycle. The stages are :

(*a*) Recognition of the need for change

(*b*) Feasibility study

(*c*) Analysis of the present system

(*d*) Design of a candidate system

(*e*) Testing and implementation of the system

(*f*) Post implementation

The idea for change originates in the environment (government, consumers, union, etc.) or from within the firm (user, analyst, etc.). Once the problem is verified, an initial investigation is conducted to determine whether change is feasible. If the answer is yes, a feasibility study is authorized.

Analysis is a detailed study of the various operations performed by a system. This involves gathering information and using structured tools for analysis.

System design refers to the technical specifications that will be applied in implementing the candidate system. This involves input/output, file, and processing design.

Implementation is concerned with detail—the physical creation of the candidate system. The key point is actual operation and user acceptance testing before the system is released to the user.

After implementation, maintenance begins. This includes enhancement, modifications, or any change from the original specifications. This phase terminates the system development life cycle.

In deciding on the project to design, a number of factors are considered: technical (availability of qualified specialists), operational (user's experience with similar projects), and economic (cost effectiveness of the proposed system). Political considerations also play a role in the final selection.

To ensure the success of the system, careful and often extensive planning is required. This work falls under project management, where a project is organized into work unit levels involving tasks (lowest level), activities, phases and milestones. The overall management process is crucial to the successful completion of systems.

A system analyst is a person who conducts a study, identifies activities and objectives and determines a procedure to achieve the objectives. Systems analysis is that a history dating back to Taylor. Early analysts worked in factories, specializing in improving work methods and setting time standards for production. With the advent of the computer, the analyst assumed the role of a problem solver and a specialist in developing computer applications.

Success in systems analysis requires interpersonal and technical skills. Interpersonal skills emphasize communication and interface with the user, whereas technical skills include creativity, problem solving, and managing the overall project. During analysis, there is greater need for interpersonal skills, but during design there is greater emphasis on technical skills. During implementation, both skills are needed.

A career in system analysis requires academic preparation, experience, and good interpersonal relations. The person must be familiar with the inner-workings of business and competent in system tools and methodologies. The personal qualities include creativity and communications skills and being systematic and sensitive.

Analyst perform a multitude of sales—as change agent, investigator, architect, psychologist, salesperson, and motivator. They also need to understand politics.

An important aspect of system development is the viability of the relationship between the analyst and the user. Research indicates that the probability of system failure increases without a good interface.

Three behavioural issues are related to system success :

1. establishing user motivation,
2. narrowing analyst/user differences, and
3. neutralizing political factors.

Related to system success also is the extent of the commitment to avoid future conflict. Therefore, coordination of people's ideas for system design is important for system development.

The analyst is the key member of the MIS organization. An MIS facility consists of four major areas :

(*a*) Administration, which handles user liaison, long-range planning, budget planning and control, and personnel.

(*b*) Systems analysis and design, which is organized as project oriented, pool oriented or functional.

(*c*) Programming, which is structured around applications, software, and maintenance. It is organized on a pool or a team basis.

(*d*) Operations, which deals with job scheduling, supplies inventory and the data library.

Of all the managerial and administration positions in the MIS area the position of the analyst is perhaps the most crucial. The job carries considerable responsibility, high status, and attractive pay.

The tasks that make up system development are changing. To perform them well, assistance is becoming available from paraprofessionals. Although less experienced than the systems analyst, they perform general support tasks and specific system development tasks such as drafting data flow diagrams and maintaining data dictionaries. Care must be taken to determine what tasks should be assigned to the paraprofessional.

Another new position in systems work is the technical writer, who is brought to when the candidate system is near completion. The main contribution is quality documentation.

Under the System Development Life Cycle following stages have been followed :

1. Recognition of need
2. Feasibility study
3. Analysis
4. Design
5. Implementation
6. Post-implementation and maintenance

INFORMATION TECHNOLOGIES

Under the topic Information Technologies generally we studied about Major Concepts, developments, and management issues in information technology—that is, hardware, software, networks, data resource management, and many Internet-based technologies.

Business professionals rely on many types of information system. Some information systems use simple manual (paper-and-pencil) hardware devices and informal (word-of-mouth) communication channels. However, in this text, we will concentrate on computer based information systems that use computer hardware and software, the Internet and other telecommunications networks, computer based data resource management techniques, and many other information technologies to transform data resources into an endless variety of information products for consumers and business professionals.

Basic Strategies in the Business Use of Information Technology are:

Lower Costs

- Use IT to substantially reduce the cost of business processes.
- Use IT to lower the costs of customers of suppliers.

Differentiate

- Develop new IT features to differentiate products and services.
- Use IT features to reduce the differentiation advantages of competitors.
- Use IT features to reduce the differentiation advantage of competitors
- Use IT features to focus products and services at selected market niches.

Innovate

- Create new products and services that include IT components.
- Develop unique new markets or market niches with the help of IT.
- Make radical changes to business processes with IT that dramatically cut costs, improve quality, efficiency, or customer service, or shorten time to market.

Promote Growth

- Use IT to manage regional and global business expansion.
- Use IT to diversify and integrate into other products and services.

Develop Growth

- Use IT to create organisations of business partners.
- Develop interenterprise information systems linked by the Internet and extranets that support strategic business relationships with customers, suppliers, subcontractors, and others.

With the help of information technology the business enterprises cut their costs and maximize the benefits.

Information technology plays a major role in reengineering most business process. The speed, information processing capabilities, and connectivity of computers and Internet technologies can substantially increase the efficiency of business processes, as well as communications and collaboration among the people responsible for their operation and management. For example, the order management process illustrated in the following Fig. 5 is vital to the success of most companies. Many of them are reengineering this process with enterprise resource planning software and Web-enabled electronic business and Commerce systems.

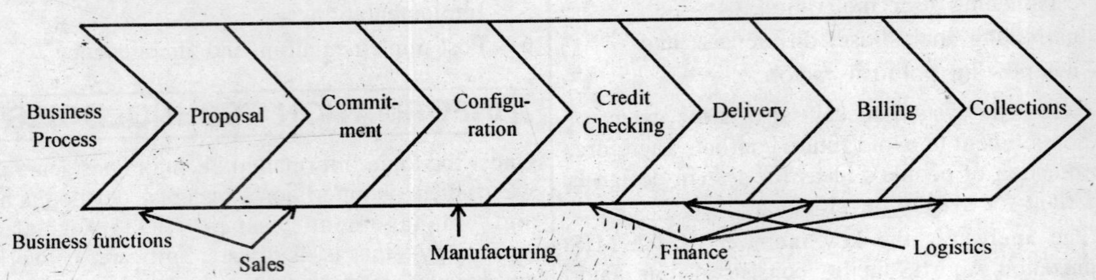

Fig. 5

The order management process consists of several business processes and crosses the boundaries of traditional business functions.

Examples of information technologies that support re-engineering the sales and order management processess:-

- Customer relationship management systems using corporate intranets and the internet.
- Supplier managed inventory systems using the internet and extranet.
- Cross functional EROP software for integrating manufacturing, distribution, finance, and human resource processes.
- Customer-accessible E-Commerce websites for order entry, status checking, payment, and service.
- Customer, product, and order status databases accessed via intranets and extranets by employees and suppliers.

INTERNET

The Internet is a worldwide network of networks. It is a conglomeration of smaller networks and other connected machines spanning the entire globe. Around the world, each country has at least one backbone network that operates at a very high speed and carries the bulk of the traffic. Other smaller networks are connects to that backbone.

The word internetted was used as early as 1849, meaning interconnected or interwoven. The word Internet was used in 1945 by the United States War Department in a radio operator's manual, and in 1974 as the shorthand form of Internetwork. Today, the term Internet most commonly refers to the global system of interconnected computer networks, though it may also refer to any group of smaller networks.

The Internet has no central authority—networks on the Internet simply agree to cooperate with each other. Individual computers on these networks can share files and transmit information. Various networks connected to Internet format messages with Internet Protocol (IP). IP is often used in conjunction with TCP (Transmission Control Protocol). The Combination of TCP/IP has made the Internet robust and flexible.

Purpose of Internet

The Internet has revolutionized the communication methods around the world. Sitting at a workstation or PC, one can get any kind of information one wants. The latest technological advances have enabled it to be used as a business tool as well, with the result that companies are today spending considerable amount of money on Internet research. The amalgamation of computer and communication technologies has resulted in the integration of data, sound and video on the Internet, which in turn has made it a powerful tool for re-engineering business process the world over.

One can use the Internet for the following purpose :

(*a*) To exchange electronic mail with friends all over the globe for a small price.

(*b*) To participate in group discussions on topics of interest, through public news groups.

(*c*) To find educational tools. Universities around the world, book stores, and libraries are sharing on line-information.

(*d*) To shop-commercial electronic store fronts are growing in number in the USA and Europe. One can order different products over the Internet.

(*e*) In the case of business one can get technical support for products one is using. One can publish information such as technical or marketing literature.

(*f*) Because the Internet is electronic, one can make changes to reflect late breaking news that would be impossible for printed publications. Change becomes easier, updates are simpler and information is instant.

(*g*) The Internet has become the first global venue for publishing information. This network has enough users now and it is benefitting from the positive feedback loop: the more users it gets, the more content it gets; and the more content it gets, the more users it gets.

(*h*) Internet's main asset is freedom. An alternative to controlling its freedom is to train and educate the user.

Typical applications of Internet are as follows :

1. Internet connectivity
2. Electronic mail server
3. Corporate communications
4. Database services
5. Remote job applications
6. Travel reservations
7. Electronic fund transfer
8. Credit and verifications

The most popular internet applications are E-mail, browsing the sites on the World Wide Web, and participating in newsgroups and chat rooms. Internet E-mail messages usually arrive in seconds or a few minutes anywhere in the world, and can take the form of data, text, fax and video files. Internet browser software like Netscape Navigator and Microsoft Explorer enables millions of users to surf the World Wide Web by clicking their way to the multimedia information resources stored on the hyperlinked pages of business, government, and other websites. Websites offer information and entertainment, and are the launch sites for electronic commerce transactions between businesses and their suppliers and customers.

The Internet provides electronic discussion forums and bulletin board systems formed and managed by thousands of special interest newsgroups. You can participate in discussions or post messages on thousands of topics for other users with the same interests to read and respond to. Other popular applications include downloading software and information files and accessing databases provided by thousands of business, government, and other organizations. You can make online searches for information at websites in a variety of ways, using search sites and search engines such as Yahoo!, Google and Fast Search. Logging on to other computers on the Internet and holding realtime conversations with other Internet users in Chat rooms are so popular uses of the Internet.

Surf: Point and click your way to thousands of hyperlinked websites and resources for multimedia information, entertainment, or electronic commerce.

E-mail: Exchange electronic mail with millions of Internet users.

Discuss: Participate in discussion forums or post message on bulletin board systems formed by thousands of special-interest newsgroups.

Chat: Hold realtime text conversations in website chat rooms with Internet users around the world.

Buy and Sell: You can buy and sell practically anything via E-Commerce retailers, wholesalers, service providers, and online auctions.

Download: Transfer data files, software, reports, articles, pictures, music, videos, and other types of files to your computer system.

Compute: Log on to and use thousands of Internet computer systems around the world.

Other Uses: Make long-distance phone calls, hold desktop video conferences, listen to radio programs, watch television, play video games, explore virtual worlds, etc.

9. HUMAN RESOURCE ACCOUNTING

SOCIETAL ACCOUNTING

Since society is one of the stakeholders and user of accounting information, the business or accounting should provide for societal accounting. In other words, the accounting should provide for the benefits it has provided to the society and the costs it has inflicted upon the society. For this purpose the organization can prepare a society account like any other personal account. All the benefits given to the society can be credited and all the costs inflicted upon the society will be debited. Some examples of debit items are as below:

(a) Pollution of air and water in excess of permissible limits
(b) Harm caused by unsafe products
(c) Stress caused to employees because of unethical practices
(d) Injuries to the workers
(e) Subsidy burden borne by the society for infrastructural facilities like water, transport etc.
(f) Services provided by the society free of cost like education, medical facilities etc.

Similarly some of the credit items may be as below:

(1) Development and training of workers
(2) Development of entrepreneurial activities
(3) Employment generated in the society
(4) Development of new products useful to the society
(5) Excess rates paid for some services to provide subsidy to the society like fuel cost
(6) Expenditure done on community development
(7) Expenditure done on protection of the environment

As it is very difficult to put money value to all these costs and benefits, the organization may provide narrative and quantitative figures for each of the item which will help to known how much the business is contributing to the society and how much costs are incurred by the society.

VALUE ADDED STATEMENT

Another method to show the contribution of the business towards society is to use value added statement. This statement shows the value addition made by the business and utilization of such value addition. The total value addition done by the business can be arrived at by deducting the cost of material from the total value of the goods produced. This value addition is then bifurcated into its utilization in terms of payments made to employees, payment made to outsiders for operating expenses, taxes paid, payment of interest on loans, payment of dividend, retention of profits etc. This statement gives a much clear picture as to the functioning of organization from the point of view of society rather than conventional P&L account. Public sector undertakings like BHEL have started preparing such value added statements.

HUMAN RESOURCE ACCOUNTING

Another aspect which is growing acceptance in corporate world is human resource accounting. With the growth of IT industry which is driven solely by the performance of human resources, need has been felt that an organization should value its human resources. For this prupose, various methods have been suggested by different researchers. Some of the popular methods are:

(a) Historical cost method
(b) Replacement cost method
(c) Opportunity cost method (by Heikimain and Jones)
(d) Adjusted present value method (by Hermanson)
(e) Economic value method (by Lev and Schwartz)

MULTIPLE CHOICE QUESTIONS

1. Profits can be fraudulently inflated by:
A. Suppression of sales returns
B. Treating capital expenditure as revenue
C. Overestimation of liabilities
D. Omission of prepaid expenses

2. A credit sale of goods to Shivendra should be debited to:
A. Sales Account
B. Goods Account
C. Shivendra Account
D. Purchase Account

3. Which of the following assets does not depreciate?
A. Machinery and equipment
B. Patents
C. Land
D. Furniture

4. Valuing the stock in trade at market price or cost price which is less is an example of the convention of:
A. consistency
B. disclosure
C. knowing the value
D. None of these

5. Double entry principle means:
A. Having debit for every credit and similarly credit for each debit.
B. Writing all the entries twice in the book.
C. Maintaining the double account for all business transactions.
D. Writing two times the same entry.

6. A sale of goods to Vaibhav Deep for cash should be debited to:
A. Vaibhav's A/c B. Cash A/c
C. Sale of goods A/c D. None of these

7. A withdrawal of cash from business by the proprietor of the firm should be credited to:
A. Capital Account
B. Cash Account
C. Drawing Account
D. Proprietor's Account

8. The preparation of a trial balance helps in:
A. Locating errors of principle
B. Locating errors of omission
C. Locating clerical errors
D. Locating compensatory errors

9. A cheque received and deposited in the bank on the same day is recorded in the:
A. Cash column of the cash book
B. Bank column of the cash book
C. Credited in the cash book
D. Debited in the cash book

10. Petty cash may be used to pay:
A. the expenses relating to postages and conveyance
B. salaries and wages to the final staff
C. for the purchase of furniture and fittings
D. None of these

11. A reserve is charge against:
A. Trading account
B. Profit and loss account
C. Profit and loss appropriation account
D. None of these

12. The payment side of cash book is under cost by ₹ 200 when overdraft as per pass book is the starting point:
A. ₹ 200 will be deducted
B. ₹ 200 will be added
C. No effect will be in the pass book
D. None of these

13. An amount of ₹ 300 is debited twice in the pass book when overdraft as per the cash book is the starting point:
A. ₹ 600 will be added
B. ₹ 500 will be deducted
C. No effect will be in the cash book
D. None of these

14. Expenditure incurred by a publisher for acquiring copy rights is a:
A. Capital expenditure
B. Revenue expenditure
C. Deferred revenue expenditure
D. None of these

15. Immediately after purchasing a new truck ₹ 1,000 is paid to have the name of the company and other advertising material painted on the truck. This ₹ 1,000 is a:
A. Capital expenditure
B. Deferred revenue expenditure
C. Revenue expenditure
D. None of these

16. A return Inwards book is kept to record:
A. return of goods sold
B. returns of anything purchased
C. returns of goods purchased
D. returns of anything sold

17. Bill Receivable Book is a part of the:
A. Ledger
B. Balance sheet
C. Journal
D. Profit and Loss Account

18. A sales of ₹ 2000 wrongly entered in the purchase book:
A. decreases the gross profit by ₹ 2000
B. increases the gross profit by ₹ 2000
C. increases the gross profit by ₹ 4000
D. None of these

19. Which of the following are current assets?
A. Bank loan for three years
B. Account receivable
C. Long-term investments
D. Debentures sinking fund investments

20. Insurance unexpires accounts is a:
A. Real account B. Personal account
C. Nominal account D. None of these

21. Goodwill account is a:
A. Nominal Account B. Real Account
C. Personal Account D. None of these

22. Bank overdraft account is a:
A. Personal Account B. Real Account
C. Nominal Account D. All of these

23. Contingent liability is shown due to:
A. Convention of full disclosure
B. Convention of conservatism
C. Convention of materiality
D. Dual aspect concept

24. Which item is shown on the debit side of a trial balance?
A. Rent outstanding
B. Prepaid Expenses
C. Purchases
D. Excess of income over expenses by the firm

25. Purchase for office furniture on account is recorded in:
A. General Journal B. Cash book
C. Purchase book D. Sales book

26. Sales on account is recorded in:
A. Cash book B. Journal
C. Sales book D. General Journal

27. The credit balance in the bank account is:
A. Capital B. a liability
C. an asset D. an expense

28. Cash sales are recorded in:
A. Sales book B. Cash book
C. Journal D. Purchase book

29. Error of commission do not permit:
A. The trial balance to agree
B. Correct the total of balance sheet
C. Correct totalling of trial balance
D. None of these

30. An item of ₹ 72 has been debited to a personal account as ₹ 27, is an error of:
A. Commission B. Omission
C. Principle D. None of these

31. Sales to Shyam of ₹ 500 not recorded in the books would affect:
A. Shyam's account B. Cash account
C. Sales account D. None of these

32. Which of the following accounts is increased by credit entries?
A. Bank Overdraft
B. Purchases Account
C. Goodwill Account
D. Sales Return Account

33. Profit and loss account of business shows the:
A. Net profit earned
B. Gross profit earned
C. Balance of all accounts
D. Capital employed in business

34. If a receipt of ₹ 200 from Rajesh out debtor has not been recorded in the books the profit would show:
A. an increase of ₹ 200
B. a decrease of ₹ 200
C. neither an increase nor a decrease
D. None of these

35. Closing stock is valued at:
A. Market price
B. Cost price
C. Cost price or market price whichever is lower
D. Cost price or market price whichever is higher

36. Unearned income account is:
A. an liability B. a liability
C. an expernse D. an income

37. Depreciation is provided on:
A. Current Assets B. Liquid Assets
C. Fictitious Assets D. Fixed Assets

38. A bill of exchange is drawn by a:
A. Creditor B. Debtor
C. Shareholder D. Debenture holder

39. Bills receivable account is:
A. a revenue Account
B. an expense Account
C. a liability Account
D. None of these

40. When goods are purchased for the joint venture out of joint bank A/c the amount is debited to:
A. Joint bank A/c
B. Joint venture A/c
C. Purchases account
D. None of these

41. Bills receivable endorsed are debited to:
A. Debtor's Account
B. Creditor's Account
C. Bills payable Account
D. Bills receivable Account

42. Subscription received during the year were ₹ 800 for the current year. ₹ 100 for the previous year and ₹ 100 for the next year. In the receipts and payments account the receipts from subscriptions would appear at:
A. ₹ 700 B. ₹ 800
C. ₹ 900 D. ₹ 1000

43. Any donation received for a specific purpose is a:
A. Liability
B. Assets
C. Revenue receipts
D. Capital receipts

44. The convention of conservatism will have the effect of:
A. Over statement of assets
B. Under statement of assets
C. Under statement of liabilities
D. Under statement of provision for bad and doubtful debts

45. Expenditure incurred by a publisher for acquiring copyright is a:
A. Capital expenditure
B. Revenue expenditure
C. Deferred revenue expenditure
D. None of these

46. Expenses incurred on resarch and development is an example of:
A. Capital expenditure
B. Revenue expenditure
C. Deferred revenue expenditure
D. None of these

47. Amount spent on increasing the seating capacity in a cinema hall is:
A. Capital expenditure
B. Revenue expenditure
C. Deferred revenue expenditure
D. None of these

48. Which of the following is not capital expenditure?
A. Cost of issuing shares and debentures
B. Wages paid for construction of building
C. Repairs on a second-hand machinery newly purchased
D. Purchase of new spark plug at a cost of ₹ 8.50 for a two-year old car

49. Window dressing is prohibited due to:
A. Convention of conservatism
B. Convention of disclosure
C. Convention of materiality
D. Accrual concept

50. Quantitative transactions are not recorded in accounts due to:
A. dual concept
B. accrual concept
C. money measurement concept
D. None of these

51. Concept of Realisation implies:
A. When cash is received from debtors
B. When goods are delivered to customer
C. When order is received
D. None of these

52. Which of the following are not current liabilities?
A. Bank overdraft
B. Redeemable debentures
C. Provision for doubtful debts
D. Accounts payable

53. Provision for doubtful debts account is a:
A. Personal account B. Real account
C. Nominal account D. None of these

54. LIFO inventory method was used in year I, FIFO in year II and weighted average in year III. Which accounting principle is violated?
A. Cost principle
B. Consistency
C. Materiality
D. No principle of accounting is violated

55. Land was reported at its selling price which is substantially higher than its cost. The increase in value was included in the income statement, which accounting principle is violated?
A. Cost principle
B. Going concern concept
C. Entity concept
D. Conservatism

56. The cost of three small files (of ₹ 4 each) was charged to expenses when purchased even though they had a useful life of several years. This was done according to the:
A. Cost principle
B. Conservatism principle
C. Full disclosure
D. Materiality

57. The amount spent on unsuccessful patent rights is a:
A. Capital expenditure
B. Deferred revenue expenditure (if the amount is large)
C. Revenue expenditure (even though the amount is large)
D. None of these

58. Double entry system of book keeping refers to a system where:
A. the number of accounts with a debit balance must agree with the number of accounts with the credit balance
B. each transaction is recorded twice, once in journal and then in ledger
C. equal debit and credit entries are made for each transaction
D. each transaction is recorded in two set of account books

59. An entry of ₹ 500 was wrongly posted to wages account instead of machinery account, as wages are to be capitalised. It is an error of:
A. Commission B. Omission
C. Principle D. Clerical error

60. Which of the following statements best explains the relationship between journal and ledger?
   A. First recording in journal and then posting to ledger completes the double entry of the transaction.
   B. The journal is the book of original entry where as the ledger is the book of second entry.
   C. The journal is the book for analytical record and ledger is the book for chronological record.
   D. The process of recording, in the journal is called journalising, the process of recording in the ledger is called posting.

61. In order to determine the amount of sales, to which of the following records one should refer?
   A. Sales book
   B. Sales account
   C. Journal
   D. Total debtors account

62. Which of the following errors is revealed by trial balance?
   A. Wrong amount entered in the book of original entry
   B. Wrong amount entered in a ledger account
   C. Complete ommission of an entry from the book of original entry
   D. All of these

63. Which of the following errors are revealed by trial balance?
   A. Omission of an amount from the trial balance
   B. Posting of the wrong amount
   C. Wrong totalling of the book of original entry
   D. None of these

64. Which of the following errors will cause the trial balance to be out of balance?
   A. The total of the purchase book is ₹ 1000 short
   B. Good received back from Mahesh, ₹ 250 have not been entered in the Returns inward book
   C. Office furniture purchased from Ravi and Co. ₹ 950 has been entered in the purchase book
   D. A purchase of ₹ 251 from Gopal and Co. has been entered in the purchase book as ₹ 215.

65. Which of the following errors will not cause the trial balance to be out of order?
   A. ₹ 590 received from P. Das has been debited to ₹ 10 Das
   B. A purchase of ₹ 258 from Lekhi has been debited to his account as ₹ 285
   C. The total of the discount column of the cash book (cr.) is ₹ 20 short
   D. An invoice for ₹ 460 is entered in the sales book as ₹ 640

66. Which of the following errors will not cause the trial balance to be out of balance?
   A. ₹ 310 for goods sold, was posted to the credit of charges
   B. Purchases returns book for December 1978 was overcast by ₹ 220
   C. Sales book carried forward ₹ 2400 instead of ₹ 2004
   D. All of these

67. An invoice of ₹ 560 is entered in the sales book as ₹ 650. The total of the debit side of the trial balance is ₹ 21,440. Assuming no other error what is the total of the credit side of the trial balance?
   A. ₹ 21,240 B. ₹ 21,350
   C. ₹ 21,330 D. None of these

68. Which of the following books should be used to record purchase of a typewriter on account?
   A. Cash books B. Purchase book
   C. Sales book D. Journal

69. Which of the following books should be used to record purchase of merchandise an account?
   A. Cash book B. Purchase book
   C. Sales book D. Journal

70. Agreement of the trial balance may not indicate that:
   A. no error remains undetected
   B. double entry has been completed

C. arithmetic accuracy is reasonably proved
D. all ledger accounts have been correctly posted

71. Networking capital of a firm is the:
A. Effective capital of the company when the business is in full swing.
B. Capital borrowed from banks.
C. Difference between the current assets and current liabilities.
D. Capital provided by shares holders only.

72. If sales are ₹ 60,000; gross profit 1/3 on cost. Purchases are ₹ 49,000 and the closing stock is ₹ 9,000. The opening stock will be:
A. Nil B. ₹ 5,000
C. ₹ 20,000 D. ₹ 49,000

73. A company has inadvertently overstated its ending inventory. This will:
A. Increase the income of the succeeding year.
B. Decrease the income of the current year.
C. Have no effect on the income of the succeeding year.
D. Decrease the income of the succeeding year.

74. Modern Leasing Co. Ltd. has debt equity ratio 8 : 1. It has decided to issue bonus shares in the ratio of 1 : 1. The debt-equity ratio after the issue would be:
A. 8 : 1 B. 4 : 1
C. 1 : 8 D. 1 : 4

75. Which one of the following ratio is the indicator of the long term solvency of the firm?
A. Acid test ratio
B. Debt-equity ratio
C. Time interest earned ratio
D. None of these

76. To test the liquidity of a concern which of the following ratios are useful?
A. Acid test ratio
B. Capital turnover ratio
C. Bad debts to sales ratio
D. Inventory turnover ratio

77. A low inventory turnover ratio may be the result of:
I. Obsolescence of some of the stock
II. Slow moving inventory
III. Frequent stock-outs
IV. Fast moving inventory
Of these statements:
A. I and II are correctB. II alone is correct
C. IV alone is correctD. II and III are correct

78. If earning per share of X limited is ₹ 15 and the price-earnings ratio of other similar companies is ₹ 10, then the market value of the share of ₹ X Ltd. will be:
A. ₹ 300 B. ₹ 150
C. ₹ 75 D. ₹ 25

79. Which one of the following is least suited for measuring return on investment?
A. Income invested capital
B. Net operating income before interest and taxes average total assets
C. Operating income ratio total assets turnover
D. Net income after interest but before taxes average total share holder equity

80. Given in the following table is data for various companies in the same industry:

	A	B	C	D
Current Assets	150	140	100	120
A/c Receivable	60	50	50	70
Turnover Ratio	6.5	5.0	5.5	5.0
Current Liabilities	100	120	80	130

The two firms which appear to be having better liquidity position are:
A. A and B B. B and C
C. A and C D. B and D

81. While calculating the Net Present Value under discounted cash flow method of return on Investment analysis the operations involved are:
I. Cash out flow
II. Discounted net cash flow
III. Cash inflow
IV. Net present value

The correct sequence of these operations is:
A. I, II, III, IV B. I, III, II, IV
C. IV, I, III, II D. III, I, IV, II

82. Rate of return on investment is meaningful to:
I. Shareholder
II. Creditors
III. Management
Of the statements given above:
A. I alone is true B. I and III are true
C. II and III are true D. I, II and III are true

83. Purchase of machinery and equipment for cash by firm:
A. Increase the total assets
B. Keeps total assets unchanged
C. Decreases the total assets
D. Increases the liability of the firm

84. Which of the following is an operating expense?
A. Depreciation of plant
B. Expired insurance
C. None of the above
D. All of these

85. Which of the following are current assets?
A. Bank loan for three years
B. Account Receivable
C. Long-term investments
D. Debentures sinking fund investments

86. Purchase of office equipment results in:
A. Decrease in liability
B. Decrease in capital
C. Increase in capital
D. Increase in fixed Assets

87. Payment of a liability results in:
A. Increase in total Assets
B. Decrease in total Assets
C. No change in total Assets
D. None of these

88. Which one of the following is correct about 'margin of safety' ratio?
A. Capital employ/net worth
B. Contribution/sales volume
C. Operating profit/contribution
D. Contribution/sales of BEP

89. If the profit is 25% of the cost price, then it is:
A. 20% of the sale price
B. 25% of the sale price
C. 30% of the sale price
D. 33% of the sale price

90. Repayment of loan results into:
A. Source of fund B. Application of fund
C. No flow of fund D. All of these

91. Sale of building results into:
A. Source of fund
B. No flow of fund
C. Application of fund
D. None of these

92. The term 'funds' as used in funds flow statement means:
A. Cash
B. Current assets
C. Current liabilities
D. Current Assets minus current liabilities

93. Payment of interim dividend is a:
A. Source of fund B. Application of fund
C. No flow of fund D. All of these

94. If the rate of gross profit is 25% on cost of goods sold and the sales are ₹ 200000 the amount of profit will be:
A. ₹ 50000 B. ₹ 40000
C. ₹ 45000 D. None of these

95. Quick ratio is a good indicator of the liquid position of a concern. The ideal quick ratio is:
A. 2 : 1 B. 1 : 1
C. 3 : 1 D. 4 : 1

96. When current ratio is 4 : 1 and the amount of current liabilities ₹ 12,000. What is the amount assets?
A. ₹ 12,000 B. ₹ 4,000
C. ₹ 48,000 D. ₹ 60,000

97. Which of the following is a non–operating income?
A. Profit on the sale of used plant in manufacturing company.
B. Revenue from sales in a trading concern.
C. Dividends received by an investment company.
D. Premiums received by an insurance company.

98. Which of the following is correct?
- A. Cost of goods sold + closing stock – opening stock = Purchases
- B. Cost of goods sold – closing stock + opening stock = Purchases
- C. Opening stock + closing stock – cost of goods sold = Purchases
- D. Closing stock – cost of goods sold + opening stock = Purchases
- E. None of these

99. Which of the following is not correct?
- A. Purchases + Opening stock – Cost of goods sold = Closing stock
- B. Opening stock + Purchases – Closing stock = Cost of goods sold
- C. Closing stock + Cost of goods sold – Purchase = Opening stock
- D. Cost of goods sold – Closing stock – Purchases = Opening stock

00. The equation for the Debt Equity Ratio is:
- A. Long-term debt/Equity capital
- B. Liquid Assets/current liability
- C. Current Assets/current liabilities
- D. Net profits/net sales

1. Opening stock – ₹ 15,000, Purchases – ₹ 40,000; cost of goods sold – ₹ 52,000; Sales – ₹ 57,000 what is the amount of gross profit or loss?
- A. ₹ 12,000
- B. ₹ 5,000
- C. ₹ 5,000 (Loss)
- D. ₹ 7,000

2. Sales return – 2,500; Sales – ₹ 12,800; Purchases – ₹ 8,400; Gross profit ₹ 2,100 What is the amount of cost of goods sold?
- A. ₹ 10,700
- B. ₹ 10,500
- C. ₹ 8,200
- D. ₹ 6,300

3. For the purpose of final accounts, stock is valued according to:
- A. Cost or market value whichever is less
- B. First–in first–out basis
- C. Last–in first–out basis
- D. Any of these

4. The works manager gets commission of 10% on the profits after charging such commission. If the profit is ₹ 2,200 what is the amount of his commission:
- A. ₹ 220
- B. ₹ 200
- C. ₹ 240
- D. ₹ 244.44

105. If profits are 25% of selling price, what is the percentage of profit to cost?
- A. 20%
- B. 25%
- C. 30%
- D. 33%

106. In which of the following methods, inventory is valued at the latest prices prevailing in the market?
- A. Last-in first-out (LIFO)
- B. First-in first-out (FIFO)
- C. Replacement price method
- D. Weighted average method

107. In ABC Analysis, which category represents those items which are used in largest quantity but their value is not high?
- A. 'A' items
- B. 'B' items
- C. 'C' items
- D. None of these

108. FIFO is advisable in case of:
- A. Rising prices
- B. Falling prices
- C. Constant prices
- D. All of these

109. Which of the following methods results in lower valuation of inventory and lower income when prices are rising?
- A. FIFO
- B. LIFO
- C. Simple average
- D. Weighted average

110. When current ratio is 2 : 1, an equal increase in current assets and current liabilities would:
- A. Increase the current ratio
- B. Decrease the current ratio
- C. Not change the current ratio
- D. Will affect some other ratio

111. When the current ratio is 2 : 5, and the amount of current liabilities is ₹ 25,000 what is the amount of current assets?
- A. ₹ 62,500
- B. ₹ 12,500
- C. ₹ 10,000
- D. None of these

112. When quick ratio is 1.5 : 1 and the amount of quick assets ₹ 30,000 what is the amount of quick liabilities?
- A. ₹ 20,000
- B. ₹ 50,000
- C. ₹ 45,000
- D. ₹ 30,000

113. Which of the following items is not taken into account while computing current ratio?
A. Sundry creditors B. Sundry debtors
C. Furniture D. Bank over draft

114. Which of the following items is not an operating expense?
A. Advertising
B. Depreciation of office equipment
C. General management salaries
D. Power consumed

115. When net sales for the year are ₹ 2,50,000 and debtors ₹ 50,000, the average collection period is (assuming year of 360 days):
A. 60 days B. 45 days
C. 42 days D. 72 days

116. Given-fixed long term liabilities ₹ 5,50,000, fixed assets ₹ 12,00,000, capital ₹ 8,50,000, current liabilities ₹ 2,50,000, current assets ₹ 4,00,000, solvency ratio is:
A. 5 : 12 B. 8 : 16
C. 15 : 17 D. 10 : 15

117. If the cost of goods sold is ₹ 1 lakh, the value of opening and closing stock is ₹ 20,000 and ₹ 30,000 respectively, the stock turnover ratio will be:
A. 3.3 times B. 4 times
C. 5 times D. 6 times

118. Dividing net sales by average debtors would yield:
A. Acid test ratio
B. Return on sales ratio
C. Debtors turnover ratio
D. None of these

119. Which of the following transactions change the current ratio?
A. Purchase of goods for cash
B. Plant acquired on account
C. Sold goods on credit
D. Debentures converted into equity capital

120. When the operating ratio is 91.5, the ratio of operating profit to sales:
A. Will be 91.5%
B. Will be 8.5%
C. Cannot be known from the given information
D. None of these

121. In calculating the Earning per Shares (EPS) the net profit is dividend by:
A. Number of equity shares
B. Number of preference shares
C. Number of equity plus preference shares
D. Total liabilities

122. Given net profit ₹ 1,50,000, preference dividend ₹ 25,000, taxes ₹ 10,000. What is the Earning per Shares (EPS), If there are 1 la shares?
A. ₹ 1.50 B. ₹ 1.25
C. ₹ 1.15 D. None of these

123. Accounting information given by a company

Total assets turnover	3times
Net profit margin	10%
Total assets	₹ 1,00,000

The net profit is:
A. ₹ 10,000 B. ₹ 15,000
C. ₹ 25,000 D. ₹ 30,000

124. Given that

Assets	₹ 20,00,000
Tax	₹ 25,000
Profit before tax	₹ 2,25,000
Net worth	₹ 10,00,000

What is the Return on Investment (ROI)?
A. 10% B. 12.5%
C. 20% D. 25%

125. The immediate solvency ratio is:
A. Quick ratio
B. Current ratio
C. Stocks turn ratio
D. Debtors turnover ratio

126. Pay out ratio means:
A. Ratio of debtors to creditors
B. Ratio of earning that are distribut through dividends
C. Ratio of profit distributed to profit retain
D. Ratio of profit to capital

127. Current ratio is increased by:
I. Cash received from debtors
II. Issue of redeemable debentures

III. Selling the old machine for cash
IV. Converting debentures into equity capital
A. I, II and III B. II and III
C. I and III D. III and IV

128. ROI takes into account:
A. Share holders investment
B. Interest on working capital
C. Interest on fixed assets
D. All of these

129. Match the following:

I.	Test of liquidity	(*a*)	ROI
II.	Test of profitability	(*b*)	Debtors turnover
III.	Test of solvency	(*c*)	Acid test ratio
IV.	Test of activity	(*d*)	Debt equity ratio

Codes:

	I	II	III	IV
A.	(*a*)	(*d*)	(*b*)	(*c*)
B.	(*d*)	(*a*)	(*c*)	(*b*)
C.	(*b*)	(*c*)	(*a*)	(*d*)
D.	(*c*)	(*a*)	(*d*)	(*b*)

130. A person interested in investing for growth in the market price of shares should invest in a company with:
A. High net profit ratio
B. High gross profit ratio
C. High payout ratio
D. Low payout ratio

131. Given Current ratio = 2.5 : 1
Net working capital = ₹ 30,000

What is the amount of current liabilities?
A. ₹ 20,000 B. ₹ 30,000
C. ₹ 50,000 D. ₹ 60,000

132. In Computing Debt/Equity ratio, debt means:
A. Debentures only
B. Short-term creditors
C. Short-term as well as long-term creditors
D. All of these

133. Which of the following liabilities are taken into account for acid test ratio?
I. Trade creditors
II. Bank overdraft
III. Bills payable
IV. Outstanding expenses
V. Redeemable debentures

Codes:
A. I, II, III, IV and V B. I, III and IV
C. I, II, III, and IV D. I, III, IV and V

134. Which of the following results in the flow of funds?
A. Creditors issued bills payable
B. Loss on the sale of machinery
C. Transfer to general reserve
D. Building sold on credit

135. A transaction results in the flow of fund when:
A. Non-current asset is purchased out of a current asset
B. Debentures are redeemed
C. Preference share capital is issued
D. All of these

136. Which of the following is not a source of fund?
A. Purchase of machinery
B. Profit earned during the year
C. Issue of share capital
D. Long term loan raised

137. If net profit is ₹ 25,000 after writing off preliminary expenses of ₹ 5,000 then the funds from operation will be:
A. ₹ 25,000 B. ₹ 30,000
C. ₹ 20,000 D. ₹ 22,000

138. Which of the following items is not added to net profit for computing the amount of funds from operations?
A. Depreciation on machinery
B. Profit on sale of machinery
C. Goodwill written off
D. Loss on sale of furniture

139. When net profit is ₹ 23,000 and profit on the sale of a fixed asset is ₹ 2,000, what is the fund from operations?
A. ₹ 23,000 B. ₹ 21,000
C. ₹ 25,000 D. ₹ 24,000

140. Plant and machinery on 1st January 1982 is ₹ 50,000 and on 31st December 1982 it is ₹ 80,000. Depreciation of ₹ 10,000 was provided during the year. This has resulted in:

A. Source of funds of ₹ 30,000
B. Application of funds of ₹ 30,000
C. Application of funds of ₹ 40,000
D. Source of funds of ₹ 40,000

141. While preparing 'Annual financial statements' 'Credit Balance' shown by the Bank pass Book should be treated as:
A. A liability
B. An income
C. An excess of payments over receipts
D. An asset

142. The joint life policy a account received on the death of a partner is credited to the:
A. Joint life policy reserve account
B. Capital accounts of all the partners in their profit sharing ratio
C. General ratio
D. Profit and loss account

143. Consider the following activities connected with the accounting information system:
I. Preparation of the table of accounting.
II. Communication of accounting information
III. Preparation of accounting information report.
IV. Collection of accounting data.

The correct sequence of these activities is:
A. IV, I, III, II B. I, IV, III, II
C. IV, III, I, II D. I, II, IV, III

144. A cooperative store having a turnover of ₹ 10 lakh and profit of ₹ 50, 000 purchased locks costing ₹ 300 for use in the shop. The accountant charged it in the P & L A/c of current year, but the auditor raised an objection saying that it should be capitalised. On which one of the following conventions could the accountant be defended?
A. Disclosure B. Materiality
C. Conservatism D. Consistency

145. Consider the following statements:

Notes forming part of accounts of companies invariably display significant Accounting Policies
I. as per the requirement of SEBI guidelines for disclosure and investor protection.
II. because it is a mandatory requirement under the Companies Act, 1956.
III. as required by As-I-disclosure of accounting policies, which is mandatory.
IV. as it is required under the listing agreement with the stock exchanges.

Which of the above statements are correct?
A. I, II, and III B. II, and III
C. II, III and IV D. I and IV

146. Match List-I with List-II and select the correct answer using the codes given below the Lists:

List-I	List-II
I. Showing joint life policy at surrender value	(*a*) Concept of consistency
II. Team spirit and dedication of cost employees are not recorded in the books of accounts	(*b*) Concept of cost
III. Methods of depreciation and inventory valuation should not be changed frequently	(*c*) Concept of conserva-tism
IV. Fixed assets are recorded at 'cost less depreciation'	(*d*) Concept of money measure-ment

Codes:

	I	II	III	IV
A.	(*c*)	(*d*)	(*a*)	(*b*)
B.	(*c*)	(*d*)	(*b*)	(*a*)
C.	(*d*)	(*c*)	(*a*)	(*b*)
D.	(*d*)	(*c*)	(*b*)	(*a*)

147. If depreciation is calculated on the basis of the formula, $\frac{n(n+1)}{2}$, then which one of the following methods is adopted?
A. Diminishing value method
B. Annuity method
C. Sum of years Digits Method
D. Sinking Fund Method

148. Consider the following methods of inventory valuation:
I. Simple Average II. First-in-first-out
III. Last-in-first-out IV. Weighted Average

Which of these methods do not match current cost with current revenues?

A. I and III B. I, II and III
C. I, II, and IV D. II, III and IV

149. Consider the following fundamental assumptions:

I. Prudence II. Going concern
III. Accrual IV. Consistency

As per Accounting standard-1, which of these assumptions are taken into consideration while preparing financial statements?

A. I and IV B. II and III
C. I, II, III and IV D. II, III, and IV

150. Which one of the following statements is correct?

A. Preliminary expenses are revenue expenses
B. Cost of issuing shares and debentures and rising loans, such as legal expenses and under writing commission are capital expenditure
C. Interest on loan is a capital expenditure
D. Cost of machinery purchased is a revenue expenditure

151. The ending balance of owner's equity is ₹ 21,000. During the years the owner contributed ₹ 6,000 and withdrew ₹ 4,000. If the firm had ₹ 8,000 net income for the year, what was the owner's equity at the beginning?

A. ₹ 23,000 B. ₹ 21,000
C. ₹ 19,000 D. ₹ 11,000

152. The ending balance of the accounts receivable amount was ₹ 12,000. Services billed to customers for the period were ₹ 21,500 and collection on account from customers was ₹ 23,600. The beginning balance of account receivable was:

A. ₹ 33,500 B. ₹ 14,100
C. ₹ 9,800 D. ₹ 33,300

153. Which one of the following is a capital expenditure?

A. Compensation paid for breach of a contract of supply of goods
B. Interest on borrowings during the period of construction of works
C. Loss of stock by fire
D. Loss due to embezzlement by the Manager

154. A company issued 14% debentures of ₹ 10,00,000 at a discount of 10%. The discount allowed will be treated in the account books as:

A. Capital expenditure
B. Revenue expenditure
C. Deferred revenue expenditure
D. Capital loss

155. A building standing in the books at ₹ 30,000 was sold for ₹ 45,000. The gain on the sale of building was transferred to profit and loss account thus taking the net profit to ₹ 1,70,000. The fund from operation will be:

A. ₹ 2,15,000 B. ₹ 1,17,000
C. ₹ 1,55,000 D. ₹ 2,00,000

156. Match List-I with List-II and select the correct answer using the codes given below the Lists:

List-I	**List-II**
I. Lease hold property	(*a*) Depreciation Fund Method
II. Mines, quarries, etc.	(*b*) Annuity Method
III. The interest lost on the acquisition of an asset	(*c*) Fixed Instalment Method
IV. To provide for replacement of asset at the end of its useful life	(*d*) Depletion Method

Codes:

	I	II	III	IV
A.	(*b*)	(*a*)	(*d*)	(*c*)
B.	(*c*)	(*d*)	(*a*)	(*b*)
C.	(*c*)	(*d*)	(*b*)	(*a*)
D.	(*d*)	(*c*)	(*a*)	(*b*)

157. Following are the extracts from the Trial Balance of a firm:

Particulars	**₹ Dr.**	**₹ Cr.**
Sundry debtors	50,000	–
Provision for doubtful debts	–	5,000
Bad debts	3,000	–

Additional Information:

I. Additional bad debts ₹ 3,000.

II. Keep the provision for bad debts @ 10% on debtors.

The net amount of bad debts that will appear in the Profit and Loss Account will be:

A. ₹ 8,000
B. ₹ 7,500
C. ₹ 5,700
D. ₹ 4,500

158. A and B sharing profits in the ratio of 3 : 2 and having capitals of ₹ 30,000 and ₹ 15,000 respectively decided to dissolve the firm. After paying off all liabilities, they realised from various assets is ₹ 15,000. This amount will be distributed between A and B as:

A. ₹ 9,000 and ₹ 6,000 respectively
B. ₹ 10,000 and ₹ 5,000 respectively
C. ₹ 7,500 and ₹ 7,500 respectively
D. ₹ 12,000 and ₹ 3,000 respectively

159. A, B and C are partners sharing profits in the ratio of 6 : 3 : 1. They dicided to dissolve the firm when their capitals were ₹ 8,000, ₹ 3,000 and ₹ (–1) 1,000 respectively other liabilities and assets were-Bank over draft ₹ 3,500; A's advance to the firm ₹ 500; sundry creditors ₹ 2,500; plant and machinery ₹ 7,500; stock-in trade ₹ 2,500; Sundry debtors ₹ 6,000 and Cash ₹ 500. Plant and machinery realised at 20% less, stock-in trade at 25% less and sundry debtors at 30% less than their respective book value. Expenses of dissolution amounted to ₹ 250. C become insolvent and his private estate yielded ₹ 100 only. What is the loss on realisation?

A. ₹ 4,125 B. ₹ 4,150
C. ₹ 4,175 D. ₹ 4,225

160. A, B and C are the partners in a business firm sharing their profits in the ratio of 4 : 3 : 2. A new partner D enters the firm. The new profit sharing ratio for A, B, C and D is 5 : 4 : 2 : 1. D contributes a goodwill of ₹ 36,000. This good-will is to be allocated among A, B and C. Which one of the following will be the correct allocation?

	A ₹	B ₹	C ₹
A.	16,000	12,000	8,000
B.	12,000	8,000	16,000
C.	12,000	Nil	24,000
D.	24,000	Nil	12,000

161. A, B and C are equal partners in a firm with capital of ₹ 16,800, ₹ 12,600 and ₹ 6,000 respectively with bills payable ₹ 3,300; creditors ₹ 6,000; cash ₹ 600; debtors ₹ 10,800; stocks ₹ 11,400; furniture ₹ 2,400 and building ₹ 19,500. E is admitted to the firm and brings ₹ 9,000 as goodwill and ₹ 15,000 as capital. Half the goodwill is withdrawn by old partners, and stock and furniture is depreciated by 10%. A provision of 5% on debtors is created and value of building is taken at ₹ 27,000. The profit on revaluation will be:

A. ₹ 5,500 B. ₹ 5,580
C. ₹ 5,400 D. ₹ 5,680

162. A and B are partners in a firm sharing profits in the ratio of 3 : 2. They admit C as a new partner for 1/3 share in the profits of the firm. The new profit-sharing ratio of A, B and C is:

A. 3 : 2 : 1 B. 3 : 2 : 2
C. 3 : 2 : 3 D. 6 : 4 : 5

163. Under the net worth method, the basis of ascertaining profit is the:

A. Difference between the liabilities on two dates.
B. Difference between the gross assets on two dates.
C. Difference between the capital on two dates.
D. Increase in net worth before adjusting for drawings and additions to capital.

164. A non-performing asset with a financial institution denotes an asset on which:

A. Regular dividend is not being received
B. Interest is on default for two quarters or more
C. Repayment of capital appears difficult
D. There is no earning of profit

165. A company forfeited 100 shares of ₹ 10 each owing to the default in the payment of share call money of ₹ 5 each. These shares were issued at ₹ 9 each, payable at ₹ 2 on application, ₹ 2 on allotment and the balance of ₹ 5 on call. The shares were then reissued to another share holder at a price of ₹ 6 per share.

The amount to be debited to forfeited shares account on account of discount on reissue of shares would be:

A. ₹ 100 B. ₹ 300
C. ₹ 400 D. ₹ 500

166. The issue of bonus shares must be in accordance with the guidelines issued by the:

A. Company Law Board
B. Controller of Capital Issues
C. Securities and Exchange Board of India
D. Registrar of Companies

167. Consider the following statements:

I. Obsolescence of some of the stock
II. Slow-moving inventory
III. Frequent stock-outs
IV. Fast-moving inventory

Which of the above statement (s) is/are correct?

A. I and II B. IV alone
C. II alone D. II and III

168. Consider the following ratios:

I. Acid test ratio
II. Capital turnover ratio
III. Bad debts to sales ratio
IV. Inventory turnover ratio

Which of these ratios are more appropriate for testing the liquidity of a concern?

A. I and III B. I and IV
C. II and IV D. II and III

169. Consider the given data:

I. Proprietary ratio = 0.75
II. Current ratio = 2 : 1
III. Proprietary fund = ₹ 60,000
IV. Fixed assets = ₹ 50.000

The working capital will be computed as:

A. ₹ 10,000 B. ₹ 15,000
C. ₹ 20,000 D. ₹ 25,000

170. Consider the following Balance sheet of ABC Company Limited as on March 31, 2008:

Liabilities	₹	Assets	₹	₹
Equity Shares Capital	20,00,000	Fixed assets	60,00,000	
Preference Share Capital	10,00,000	Less depreciation	20,00,000	40,00,000
General reserve	5,00,000			
10% Debentures	11,00,000	Debtors		10,00,000
Creditors	7,00,000	Stock		6,00,000
Outstanding expenses	3,00,000	Cash		1,00,000
Profit & Loss A/c	1,05,000	Formation Expenses		5,000
	57,05,000			**57,05,000**

The current ratio of ABC Company is:

A. 2.00 B. 1.90
C. 1.85 D. 1.70

171. Match List-I with List-II and select the correct answer using the codes given below the Lists:

List-I	List-II
I. Current assets ÷ Current liabilities	(*a*) Performance of equity capital
II. Fixed assets ÷ Long-term funds	(*b*) Short-term solvency
III. Debt Equity	(*c*) Capital structure
IV. Earnings after interest and taxes ÷ Number of shares issued	(*d*) Over all performance

Codes:

	I	II	III	IV
A.	(*b*)	(*e*)	(*c*)	(*d*)
B.	(*a*)	(*b*)	(*c*)	(*d*)
C.	(*b*)	(*e*)	(*d*)	(*c*)
D.	(*a*)	(*b*)	(*d*)	(*c*)

Directions (Qs. No. 172 & 173): *These questions are based on the following Balance-sheet of Messrs A Limited as on 31st Dec., 2008:*

Liabilities	₹ (in lakhs)	Assets	₹ (in lakhs)
Owned funds	25.00	Fixed assets	27.00
Long term debt	1.50	Current assets	6.10
Current liabilities	5.00	Other assets	0.40
Unclaimed dividends	0.20		
Provisions	1.80		
	33.50		**33.50**

Study the Balance sheet carefully and attempt the following questions:

172. 'Owned funds' would be:
A. ₹ 25 lakh
B. ₹ 8.50 lakh
C. ₹ 25.20 lakh
D. ₹ 27 lakh

173. The 'margin of safety'. *i.e.*, the cushion of protection for creditors is:
A. 4.06 : 1
B. ₹ 4.60 lakh
C. 0.20 : 1
D. ₹ 22 lakh

174. If the management of A Limited want to evaluate the general efficiency, which one of the following additional information is required?
A. Sales and earnings after income-tax and interest.
B. Break-up of owned funds into share capital, reserves and surpluses, etc.
C. Earnings before income-tax and interest.
D. Operating expenses and sales.

175. Financial indicators of four companies are as follows:

Company	Current ratio	Debt equity ratio	Rate of return on investment	Fixed assets turnover
A	2.0 : 1	2.5 : 1	10%	5
B	2.5 : 1	3.0 : 1	25%	4
C	1.5 : 1	4.0 : 1	20%	3
D	1.0 : 1	3.5 : 1	15%	2

In general, which of the above companies would fall in the highest risk class?
A. A and B B. B and C
C. C and D D. A and D

176. Consider the particulars given below:
Sales = ₹ 60,000
Variable cost = ₹ 25,000
Fixed cost = ₹ 30,000

Based on these data, the operating leverage shall be:
A. 5 B. 7
C. 8 D. 9

177. Consider the following statements:

Redeemable preference shares of a company can be redeemed out of
I. Profits of the company which would otherwise be available for dividend.
II. Company's share premium account.
III. Fresh issue of shares made for the purpose of redemption.

Which of the above statements are correct?
A. I and II B. I and III
C. II and III D. I, II and III

178. The main purpose of depreciation accounting is to:
A. Charge the cost of asset.
B. Allocate the cost of the asset over its estimated useful life.
C. Provide replacement of the asset on the expiry of its useful life.
D. Value the assets on the closing date of the year.

179. Which one of the following pairs is not correctly matched?
A. Increase in working capital – Application of fund
B. Increase in current liability – Source of fund
C. Issue of shares – Source of fund
D. Issue of bonus shares – Source of fund

180. Consider the following statements:
I. Operational loss is a source of funds.
II. Decrease in working capital is a source of funds.
III. Additions to fixed assets are an application of funds.
IV. Fresh introduction of capital is an application of funds.

Which of the above statements are applicable while preparing the funds flow statements?
A. I and II B. I and III
C. II and III D. I, III and IV

181. A company's reported current profit is ₹ 70,000 after incorporating the following: Loss on sale of investments ₹ 10,000; Premium on redemption of debentures ₹ 1,500; Depreciation on machinery and plant ₹ 20,000; Goodwill and preliminary expenses written off ₹ 30,000; Gain from sale of non current assets ₹ 40,000. The net inflow of funds from the operation would be:

A. ₹ 91,500 B. ₹ 80,000
C. ₹ 70,000 D. ₹ 59,500

182. For the purpose of analysing changes in financial position, enterprises prepare:

A. Balance sheet and Profit and Loss A/c.
B. Cash flow statement and funds flow statement.
C. Statement of cash from Operations and Balance sheet.
D. Statement of changes in working capital and statement of cash from operations.

183. Materiality in accounting is decided:

A. By the size of an item.
B. By the knowledge as to whether an individual item is having a significant influence on financial statement.
C. Solely by the discretion of the accountant.
D. By the physical volume of the transaction.

184. Match List-I (Event) with List-II (Result) and select the correct answer using the codes given below the Lists:

List-I	List-II
I. Collusion between two or more persons	(*a*) Payments of dividends otherwise not possible
II. Falsification of accounts to increase apparent profits	(*b*) Error of principle committed
III. Operation of an effective system of internal check	(*c*) Trial balance may agree
IV. Purchase of raw materials is debited to Loose tools and concealed	(*d*) Frauds perpetrated and account
	(*e*) Possiblility of errors and frauds is considerably reduced

Codes:

	I	II	III	IV
A.	(*c*)	(*d*)	(*e*)	(*b*)
B.	(*d*)	(*a*)	(*e*)	(*b*)
C.	(*d*)	(*a*)	(*b*)	(*e*)
D.	(*b*)	(*d*)	(*a*)	(*c*)

185. Accounting is the process of matching:

A. Benefits and costs
B. Revenues and costs
C. Cash inflows and outflows.
D. Potential and real performance.

186. A had started business with ₹ 20,000 in the beginning of the year. During the year he borrowed ₹ 10,000 from B. He further Introduced ₹ 20,000 in the business. He also gave ₹ 5,000 as loan to his son. Goods given away as charity by him was ₹ 2,000. Profits earned by him was ₹ 25,000. He also withdrew ₹ 3,000 from the business. His capital at the end of the year would be:

A. ₹ 50,000 B. ₹ 40,000
C. ₹ 62,000 D. ₹ 48,000

187. Match List-I with List-II and select the correct answer using the codes given below the list:

List-I	List-II
I. A long term debt instrument on which interest is accumulated and paid on maturity	(*a*) Mutual fund
II. A debt instrument on which rebate is available under the Income Tax Act	(*b*) Deep Discount Bond
III. Pooling together the money of different investors and investing it in diversified securities	(*c*) Infrastructure Bond
IV. Buying the right but not the obligation to sell a security for a specific price	(*d*) Put option

Codes:

	I	II	III	IV
A.	(*d*)	(*a*)	(*b*)	(*c*)
B.	(*b*)	(*c*)	(*a*)	(*d*)
C.	(*c*)	(*a*)	(*b*)	(*d*)
D.	(*c*)	(*a*)	(*d*)	(*b*)

188. To guard against the dangers of excess payment arising out of double insurance or over-insurance made by the insured, insurance companies provide in their agreement:
A. Average clause B. Subrogation clause
C. Risk clause D. Indemnity clause

189. A person insured his property worth ₹ 10,000 against fire for ₹ 8,000. His actual loss by fire is ₹ 5,000 and there is an average clause in the policy. His claim will be:
A. ₹ 10,000 B. ₹ 8,000
C. ₹ 5,000 D. ₹ 4,000

190. In the Balance sheet, under the sub-heading 'current liabilities and provisions', disclosure of the name (s) of small-scale industries/ undertakings is required if the company owes a sum:
A. Exceeding ₹ 1 lakh as outstanding for more than 6 months.
B. Not exceeding ₹ 1 lakh as outstanding for more than 6 months.
C. Exceeding ₹ 1 lakh as outstanding for more than 30 days.
D. Exceeding ₹ 50,000 as outstanding for more than 2 months.

Directions (Qs. No. 191-205): *These questions consist of two statements, one labelled the Assertion (A) and the other labelled the Reason (R). You are to examine these two statements carefully and decide if the Assertion (A) and the Reason (R) are individually true and if so, whether the Reason is a correct explanation of the Assertion. Select your answers to these items using the codes.*

191. Assertion (A) : Management accounting provides management with information for decision making.
Reason (R) : Management accounting is a branch of cost accounting.

Codes:
A. Both (A) and (R) are true, and (R) is the correct explanation of (A).
B. Both (A) and (R) are true, but (R) is not a correct explanation of (A).
C. (A) is true, but (R) is false.
D. (A) is false, but (R) is true.

192. Assertion (A) : Under diminishing balance method of depreciation, the charge for depre-ciation keeps on diminishing year after year in all subsequent years.
Reason (R) : Under diminishing balance method, the rate per cent at which depreciation is written off goes on diminishing from year to year.

Codes:
A. Both (A) and (R) are true, and (R) is the correct explanation of (A).
B. Both (A) and (R) are, true, but (R) is not a correct explanation of (A).
C. (A) is ture, but (R) is false.
D. (A) is false, but (R) is true.

193. Assertion (A) : No item of capital expenditure finds its place in the Trading and Profit & Loss Account or some other form of revenue accounts.
Reason (R) : Capital expenditure consists of expenditure, the benefit of which is not fully consumed in one accounting period but is spread over several periods.

Codes:
A. Both (A) and (R) are true, and (R) is the correct explanation of (A).
B. Both (A) and (R) are true, but (R) is not a correct explanation of (A).
C. (A) is true, but (R) is false.
D. (A) is false, but (R) is true.

194. Assertion (A) : Now-a-days many companies prepare their Balance sheet in a vertical form rather than in the traditional horizontal form.
Reason (R) : Part IV of schedule IV to the Companies Act, 1956 permits both the forms.

Codes:
A. Both (A) and (R) are true and (R) is the correct explanation of (A).
B. Both (A) and (R) are true, but (R) is not a correct explanation of (A).
C. (A) is true, but (R) is false.
D. (A) is false, but (R) is true.

195. Assertion (A) : When pro-rata allotment of shares is made, the surplus application money is transferred to share allotment A/c.

Reason (R) : The company is not required to pay any interest on such surplus application money.

Codes:
A. Both (A) and (R) are true, and (R) is the correct explanation of (A).
B. Both (A) and (R) are true, but (R) is not a correct explanation of (A).
C. (A) is true, but (R) is false.
D. (A) is false, but (R) is true.

196. Assertion (A) : One single primary ratio, that measures the financial outcome of all recorded business activities, is ROI.

Reason (R) : In practice, however, variations are also found in the ratio because capital and return are subject to different interpretations by firms.

Codes:
A. Both (A) and (R) are true, and (R) is the correct explanation of (A).
B. Both (A) and (R) are true, (R) is not a correct explanation of (A).
C. (A) is true, but (R) is false.
D. (A) is false, but (R) is true.

197. Assertion (A) : ROI is the index to study management efficiency.

Reason (R) : Earning power in relation to total investment is measured by ROI.

Codes:
A. Both (A) and (R) are true, and (R) is the correct explanation of (A).
B. Both (A) and (R) are true, but (R) is not a correct explanation of (A).
C. (A) is true, but (R) is false.
D. (A) is false, but (R) is true.

198. Assertion (A) : For a company, every debt is not a loan, but every loan is a debt.

Reason (R) : In the case of deposit of money with the company, it is the depositor who is the prime mover, where as in the case of loan it is the company who is the prime mover.

Codes:
A. Both (A) and (R) are true, and (R) is the correct explanation of (A).
B. Both (A) and (R) are true, but (R) is not a correct explanation of (A).
C. (A) is true, but (R) is false.
D. (A) is false, but (R) is true.

199. Assertion (A) : A company is accountable to the society since it makes use of community owned assets and other infrastructural facilities and concessions provided by the state from the tax payers' money.

Reason (R) : The best way of social responsibility reporting is to prepare a Value-Added Statement (VAS) which shows the income earned by share holders.

Codes:
A. Both (A) and (R) are true, and (R) is the correct explanation of (A).
B. Both (A) and (R) are true, but (R) is not a correct explanation of (A).
C. (A) is true, but (R) is false.
D. (A) is false, but (R) is true.

200. Assertion (A) : The matching concept requires that costs be recognised as expenses in the period in which revenue is realised.

Reason (R) : There may not be a match between expenditure and expenses over a short period.

Codes:
A. Both (A) and (R) are true, and (R) is the correct explanation of (A).
B. Both (A) and (R) are true, but (R) is not a correct explanation of (A).
C. (A) is true, but (R) is false.
D. (A) is false, but (R) is true.

201. Assertion (A) : According to International Accounting Standards Committee, fixed pro-duction expenses should be included in inventory valuation on the basis of normal capacity. According to the Institute of Chartered Accountants of India, it is for the management to decide the Question.

Reason (R) : The Question to be decided is whether the fixed production expenses be excluded from inventory valuation and charged wholly to the revenue of that year or whether these expenses be included on the basis of normal level of production. The former method, is called 'marginal costing' and the latter 'absorption costing?

Codes:
A. Both (A) and (R) are true, and (R) is the correct explanation of (A).
B. Both (A) and (R) are true, but (R) is not a correct explanation of (A).
C. (A) is true, but (R) is false.
D. (A) is false, but (R) is true.

202. Assertion (A) : The fixed assets in the balance sheet of a limited company are required to be shown at cost less depreciation.

Reason (R) : The balance sheet and profit and loss account are to disclose a true and fair view.

Codes:
A. Both (A) and (R) are true, and (R) is the correct explanation of (A).
B. Both (A) and (R) are true, but (R) is not a correct explanation of (A).
C. (A) is true, but (R) is false.
D. (A) is false, but (R) is true.

203. Assertion (A) : Share premium amount can be refunded in cash to equity share holders.

Reason (R) : Share premium is usually collected when the market price of the shares is higher than the face value of the share.

Codes:
A. Both (A) and (R) are true, and (R) is the correct explanation of (A).
B. Both (A) and (R) are true, but (R) is not a correct explanation of (A).
C. (A) is true, but (R) is false.
D. (A) is false, but (R) is true.

204. Assertion (A) : Conventionally, a newly-started company should adopt a low geared capital structure where the share of equity capital and reserves is higher than the share of fixed interest bearing securities.

Reason (R) : During initial years, the profit is low and the company tries to strengthen its financial position.

Codes:
A. Both (A) and (R) are true, and (R) is the correct explanation of (A).
B. Both (A) and (R) are true, but (R) is not a correct explanation of A.
C. (A) is true, but (R) is false.
D. (A) is false, but (R) is true.

205. Assertion (A) : A new firm can be profitable and yet not be able to pay its debts as they become due.

Reason (R) : New firms often have the problem of having increased investments in inventory and fixed assets at an amount which exceeds cash generated from operations.

Codes:

A. Both (A) and (R) are true, and (R) is the correct explanation of (A).
B. Both (A) and (R) are true, but (R) is not a correct explanation of (A).
C. (A) is true, but (R) is false.
D. (A) is false, but (R) is true.

206. Which one of the following routines best describes the chronology of steps taken in the selling process?
A. Receipt of order, invoicing, processing order, shipment of goods.
B. Invoicing, processing order, shipment of goods, accounting for sale.
C. Receipt of order, processing order, accounting for sale, shipment of goods
D. Processing order, invoicing, shipment of goods, accounting for sale.

207. When prices show a rising trend, which one of the following methods of inventory valuation will result in lower income and lower valuation of inventory?
A. FIFO
B. LIFO
C. Simple average method
D. Weighted average method

208. Under which one of the following methods of depreciation is the amount of the assets never reduced to zero?
A. Straight line method
B. Diminishing balance method
C. Sum of years digit method
D. Annuity method

209. Consider the following statements:
Secret reserves serve the purpose of
I. enabling the directors to tide over unfavourable items
II. meeting exceptional losses
III. increasing the working capital
Of these statement:
A. I and II are correct
B. II and III are correct
C. I and III are correct
D. I, II and III are correct

210. ABC analysis is a:
A. System of profit and loss appropriation
B. technique of financial planning
C. technique of inventory control
D. technique of profit determination

211. A sum of ₹ 50,000 was spent by a factory in over – hauling its existing plant and machinery and it enhanced its working life by five years.
The aforesaid expenditure is:
A. Capital expenditure
B. Partly capital and partly revenue expenditure
C. Revenue loss
D. Deferred revenue expenditure

212. Match List-I (Items of Expenditure and Receipt) with List-II (Nature of Expenditure and Receipt) and select the correct answer using the codes given below the lists:

List-I	List-II
I. Replacement cost of an old a sset	(*a*) Revenue expenditure
II. Special repairing charges of an asset	(*b*) Capital receipt
III. Huge advertisement expenses	(*c*) Deferred revenue expenditure
IV. Sale value of an old motorcar	(*d*) Capital expenditure

Codes:

	I	II	III	IV
A.	(*d*)	(*a*)	(*c*)	(*b*)
B.	(*d*)	(*a*)	(*b*)	(*c*)
C.	(*a*)	(*d*)	(*c*)	(*b*)
D.	(*a*)	(*d*)	(*b*)	(*c*)

213. Which one of the following is not a capital expenditure?
A. Legal expenses incurred in raising a debenture loan
B. Compensation paid to a dismissed employee
C. Brokerage paid to the broker at the time of purchase of land
D. Expenses for pulling down an old structure

214. Out standing wages is an item of:
A. Current asset
B. Current liability
C. Non-current asset
D. Non-current liability

215. A and B partners sharing profits and losses in the ratio of 3 : 1. They have agreed to admit C into the partnership firm. C is given 1/4 th share of future profits which he acquires in the ratio 2 : 1 from A and B. The new profit sharing ratio would be:

A. 4 : 3 : 1 B. 7 : 2 : 3
C. 3 : 1 : 7 D. 7 : 3 : 2

216. A, B, C were partners sharing profits in the proportion of 1/2, 1/3 and 1/6 respectively. On 31st March, 1997 their capital stood as follows:

A = ₹ 4,00,000
B = ₹ 3,00.000
C = ₹ 2,50,000

A sum of ₹ 1,20,000 also appeared as reserve fund in their balance sheet on this date. B retires on this date when the goodwill of the firm was valued at ₹ 1,80,000.

Profit and loss adjustment account prepared on that date without taking goodwill and reserve fund into consideration showed a net profit of ₹ 28500. The net amount payable to B will be:

A. ₹ 3,82,500 B. ₹ 4,09,500
C. ₹ 3,63,800 D. ₹ 4,04,000

217. X and Y are partners sharing profits in the ratio of 1 : 1. They admit Z for 1/5 th share who contributed ₹ 25,000 for his share of goodwill. The total value of the goodwill of the firm will be:

A. ₹ 25,000 B. ₹ 50,000
C. ₹ 1,00,000 D. ₹ 1,25,000

218. On the death of a partner, the amount of joint life policy should be credited to the capital accounts of:

A. all partners including the deceased partner in their profit-sharing ratio.
B. remaining partners in the new profit sharing ratio.
C. remaining partners equally.
D. all partners including the deceased partners in their capital ratio.

219. In the absence of any contract to the contrary, capital profit or arising on dissolution of a partnership firm is credited to the partners' capital account in:

A. Equal proportion
B. Capital ratio
C. Profit-sharing ratio
D. Proportion to assets realised

220. Writing off the expired cost of an intangible asset is called:

A. Amortisation B. Capitalisation
C. Depletion D. Depreciation

221. The debt : equity ratio of a company is 8 : 1. It was decided to issue bonus shares in the ratio of 1 : 2. The debt : equity ratio after the issue of bonus shares would be:

A. 8 : 1 B. 4 : 1
C. 1 : 8 D. 1 : 4

222. Profit prior to incorporation is an example of:

A. Revenue reserve B. Secret reserve
C. Capital reserve D. General reserve

223. Interest on calls in arrears is charged according to Table A of schedule I to the Companies Act, 1956 at the rate of:

A. 5% p.a. B. 6% p.a.
C. 12% p.a. D. 10% p.a.

224. The ratios which measure the relative contribution of financing by owners and financing provided by outsiders are called:

A. Liquidity ratios B. Leverage ratios
C. Activity ratios D. Profitability ratios

225. Right's shares are the shares that are offered to the:

A. Directors of the company
B. Debenture holders
C. Existing share holders
D. Creditors of the company

226. Unpaid calls are shown in the balance sheet of a company:

A. By adding it to the share capital
B. By deducting it from the called-up share capital
C. Under the head 'current assets'
D. Under the head 'current liabilities'

227. Pro-rata allotment of shares means allotment of shares:

A. Equally amongst the applicants
B. At the discretion of the directors
C. To all the applicants in proportion to the shares applied for
D. To only a few selected applicants

228. Match List-I with List-II and select the correct answer using the codes given below the Lists:

List-I	List-II
I. Acid test ratio	(*a*) Liquidity ratio
II. Gearing ratio	(*b*) Profitability ratio
III. Working capital turnover ratio	(*c*) Leverage ratio
IV. Return on capital employed	(*d*) Long-term solvency ratio
	(*e*) Activity ratio

Codes:

	I	II	III	IV
A.	(*a*)	(*c*)	(*e*)	(*b*)
B.	(*b*)	(*e*)	(*a*)	(*c*)
C.	(*a*)	(*e*)	(*d*)	(*b*)
D.	(*e*)	(*c*)	(*d*)	(*a*)

229. Which of the following transaction(s) will improve the Current Ratio?

I. Bills receivable dishonored.
II. Cash collected from customers.
III. Issue of new shares.
IV. Payment of preliminary expenses by way of equity shares.

Select the correct answer using the codes given below:

Codes:

A. I, II and III   B. IV alone
C. III alone   D. II and IV

230. In the case of a particular depreciation method, the periodic depreciation is smaller than the asset's actual annual depreciation cost. The annual net incidence on profit and loss account remains constant due to incorporation of only fixed depreciation. The periodic depreciation is not recorded through the asset account. The depreciation method used in this case is:

A. Sinking fund method
B. Diminishing balance method
C. Annuity method
D. Sum-of-years digits method

231. X Ltd. forfeited 30 shares of ₹ 10 each fully called up for non-payment of allotment money of ₹ 3 per share and call money of ₹ 4 per share. These shares are reissued for ₹ 8 per share fully paid. What is the amount to be transferred to capital Reserve Account?

A. ₹ 300   B. ₹ 60
C. ₹ 30   D. ₹ 90

232. Credit sales of a company during the year are ₹ 1,20,000, Debtors ₹ 20,000 and Bills Receivable ₹ 10,000. The average collection period is:

A. 3 Months   B. 4 Months
C. 5 Months   D. 6 Months

233. Collection of sundry debtors would:

A. Increase current ratio
B. Decrease current ratio
C. Have no effect on current ratio
D. Increase debtors' turnover

234. Which one of the following statements is not correct? A high gross profit margin ratio is the result of:

A. higher sales price, cost of goods sold remaining constant
B. lower cost of goods sold, sales price remaining constant
C. an increase in the proportionate volume of higher margin items
D. increase in the sales return, cost of goods sold remaining the same

235. A company with a paid-up capital of 5000 equity shares of ₹ 10 each has a turnover of four times with a margin of 8% on sales. The ROI of the company will be:

A. 28%   B. 32%
C. 35%   D. 42%

236. The best definition of 'Capital employed' in calculating the rate of return on investment is:

A. Current assets + gross fixed assets
B. Current assets + net fixed assets
C. Working capital + gross fixed assets
D. Working capital + net fixed assets

237. While calculating the net present value under discounted cash flow method of return on investment analysis, the calculations involved are:

I. Cash outflow
II. Discounted net cash flow
III. Cash inflow
IV. Net present value

The correct sequence of these calculations is:

A. IV, I, III, II B. I, III, II, IV
C. I, II, III, IV D. III, I, IV, II

238. Patents and copyrights fall under the category of:

A. Current assets B. Liquid assets
C. Intangible assets D. Nominal assets

239. Match List-I (Balance sheet items) with the List-II (Classification) and select the correct answer using the codes given below the Lists:

List-I	List-II
I. Discount on debenture	(*a*) Current liability
II. Forfeited shares	(*b*) Non-current asset account
III. Income tax payable	(*c*) Current asset
IV. Debtors' acceptance	(*d*) Non-current liability

Codes:

	I	II	III	IV
A.	(*b*)	(*d*)	(*a*)	(*c*)
B.	(*d*)	(*b*)	(*c*)	(*a*)
C.	(*b*)	(*d*)	(*c*)	(*a*)
D.	(*d*)	(*b*)	(*a*)	(*c*)

240. Ajoy Ltd. makes a net profit of ₹ 1,00,000, after providing for depreciation on assets amounting to ₹ 20.000 and writing off preliminary expenses amounting to ₹ 10,000 and gain of ₹ 5,000 on sale of a piece of machinery. Funds from operation of Ajoy Ltd. would be:

A. ₹ 1,00,000 B. ₹ 1,20,000
C. ₹ 1,25,000 D. ₹ 1,35,000

241. According to the Principle of Subrogation:

A. The insured must take all nècessary steps to minimise the loss
B. The actual amount of loss, not exceeding the amount of the policy, shall be paid
C. The actual amount of loss should be distributed among the different insurers of the same risk
D. On making good the loss, the insured to succeed to all the rights of the insured regarding the subject matter of insurance

242. The persons who agree to insure cargo, hull or freight are called:

A. undertakers B. caretakers
C. underwriters D. bookkeepers

Directions (Q. 243-245): *In the given context of the statement, mark the answer according to the following codes.*

Codes:

A. Both (A) and (R) are true, and (R) is the correct explanation of (A)
B. Both (A) and (R) are true, but (R) is not a correct explanation of (A)
C. (A) is true, but (R) is false.
D. (A) is false, but (R) is true.

243. Assertion (A) : The liability of shareholders in a private limited company is limited to the amount unpaid on shares.

Reason (R) : The number of shareholders of a private limited company is limited to fifty.

244. Assertion (A) : High capital gearing leads to greater speculation.

Reason (R) : Proportion of equity the share capital in relation to the total capital comprising the other securities is small leading to capitalisation being highly geared.

245. Assertion (A) : Special rules and procedures are follo-wed in the import and export trade.

Reason (R) : The need for import and export trade is explained by the principles of comparative Cost Theory.

246. Partnership is a form of business organisation in which business debts can be recovered:
A. the managing partners
B. all the managers and partners
C. the firm and the managers
D. the firm and all the partners

247. Of the following organisations the easiest to wind up is the:
A. Public Limited Company
B. Multinational Corporation
C. Private Limited Company
D. Partnership Firm

248. Match List-I with List-II and select the correct answer using the codes given below the lists:

List-I	List-II
I. Partners and Firms	(*a*) agent and principal relationship
II. Sole Proprietorship	(*b*) prospectus
III. Public Limited company	(*c*) personal supervision
IV. Nominal partnership	(*d*) firm image

Codes:

	I	II	III	IV
A.	(*a*)	(*b*)	(*c*)	(*d*)
B.	(*b*)	(*c*)	(*a*)	(*d*)
C.	(*a*)	(*c*)	(*b*)	(*d*)
D.	(*d*)	(*b*)	(*a*)	(*c*)

249. The main object of stock exchange is to:
A. Provide facilities for speculation
B. Safeguard the interest of investors
C. Help in the capital formation the country
D. Provide a ready market for securities

250. Fishing has been classified as:
A. Extractive Industry
B. Genetic Industry
C. Manufacturing Industry
D. None of these

251. 'Fishing Culture' is classified in:
A. Extractive Industry
B. Genetic Industry
C. Construction Industry
D. None of these

252. If a partnership firm is not registered with the Registrar of firms:
A. it has to pay penalty for non-registration
B. the members can file suits against the third party
C. the members can enforce their rights among themselves
D. None of these

253. Which of the following is not an economic activity?
A. A doctor practising
B. A lawyer practising law
C. A professional cricketer playing cricket
D. A student playing cricket

254. In order an activity may be called business which of the following condition need not be satisfied?
A. There should be exchange or transfer of goods or services
B. There should be continuity of dealings
C. Dealings may be either in goods or services
D. There should be certainty of profit

255. Fish culture, should be classified as:
A. extractive industry
B. genetic industry
C. manufacturing industry
D. construction industry

256. In a private business enterprise profit should be regarded as:
A. the legitimate reward for honest end labour
B. the supreme objective of business
C. the sole objective of business
D. subsidiary to service motive

257. Which of the following should be regarded as the most important factor for deciding the form of business organisation?
A. Types of business, trading manufacturing, etc
B. Expected volume of business
C. Financial requirements
D. Area of operations

258. An establishment insured its property worth ₹ 50 lacs for ₹ 30 lacs against fire. The actual loss due to fire was ₹ 40 lacs. The firm can get:
A. ₹ 50 lacs B. ₹ 40 lacs
C. ₹ 30 lacs D. None of these

259. The liability of a sole proprietor is:
A. limited to the extent of his capital invested in the business
B. limited to the extent of the value of business assets
C. limited to the extent of the value of business assets and his all private assets
D. None of these

260. The maximum number of partners in a firm for a general business is:
A. 7 B. 10
C. 50 D. 20

261. The agreement of partnership:
A. must be in oral
B. must be in writing
C. can be either oral or in writing
D. must be in writing on a stamp paper

262. Liability of partners in respect of the firm's debts is:
A. limited up to the amount of his capital in the business
B. unlimited
C. limited up to the amount of guarantee given by the partner
D. limited up to the amount of his capital and loan to the firm if any

263. Partnership may come into existence:
A. by the operation of law
B. by an express agreement only
C. by an express or implied agreement only
D. by inheritance of property

264. A partner has an implied authority to:
A. acquire immovable property on behalf of the firm
B. enter into a partnership on behalf of the firm
C. to borrow money on behalf of the firm
D. to compromise or relinquish any claim or portion of a claim by the firm

265. If a firm is not registered with the registrar of firms:
A. it has to pay penalty for non-registration
B. it introduces certain disabilities which make registration necessary at one time or the other
C. the members of the unregistered firm can enforce their rights between themselves
D. the members of the unregistered firm can file suit against third parties

266. Dissolution of firm takes place:
A. by the death or insolvency of any one partner
B. the retirement of any one partner
C. by the expiry of the term
D. by the insolvency of all but one partner

267. Registration of Joint Stock Company is:
A. compulsory
B. optional
C. compulsory for public companies and optional for private company
D. compulsory for companies with liabilities limited by shares and optional for companies with liabilities limited by guarantee

268. The minimum number of member require for registration of a co-operative society is:
A. two B. seven
C. ten D. twenty

269. Co-operative and public companies are similar in respect of:
A. the liability of members
B. the minimum number of members required for registration
C. the maximum number of members
D. None of these

270. Profits earned by a co-operative society are distributed:
A. to members in the ratio of capital held by them
B. to member in the ratio of purchases made by them
C. by providing a nominal rate of interest on capital contribution by members and remaining in the ratio of purchases made by members
D. by declaring divided at a specific rate and remaining transferring to general reserves

271. Management of a co-operative organisation is in the hands of:
A. persons nominated by the Registrar of co-operative societies

B. an elected body by the members
C. some persons nominated by Registrar of cooperative societies and other selected by the member
D. the promoters of the co-operative organisation

272. Which of the following is an example of a company incorporated by a special act of parliament?
A. Delhi Cloth Mills Ltd.
B. Tata Iron and Steel Co. Ltd.
C. Industrial Finance Corporation.
D. Swadeshi Cotton Mills Ltd.

273. Which of the following documents need not be prepared and Registered with the Registrar of companies in Public limited companies?
A. Memorandum of Association
B. Articles of Association
C. Statutory Declaration
D. Directors of undertaking to take up and pay for qualification shares

274. The term, 'capitalisation' is used in relation to:
A. sole-proprietorship
B. partnership
C. joint stock companies
D. co-operative societies

275. Which of the following methods provide a better basis of capitalisation for an established concern?
A. Add up the cost of fixed assets and working capital required
B. Add up the cost of fixed assets, working capital and cost of promotion etc.
C. Capitalise the profits to be earned
D. Estimate on the basis of financial position of other similar companies

276. Watered capital means:
A. over-capitalistation
B. under capitalistation
C. excessive capital
D. part of the capital not represented by assets

277. Over capitalisation may be remedied by:
A. increasing the number of equity shares
B. increasing the per value of shares
C. issuing additional preference shares
D. redemption of debentures

278. Under Capitalisation can be remedied by:
A. issue of bonus shares
B. redemption of preference shares
C. redemption of debentures
D. reduction of interest of debentures

279. Capital gearing means:
A. proper capitalisation
B. watered capital
C. fixation of a proper ratio between two or more types of securities
D. trading on equity

280. A company is said to be low geared when the proportion of:
A. equity capital to the total capital is small
B. preference capital to the total capital is small
C. debentures capital to the total capital is small
D. both preference and debentures capital to the total is small

281. Working capital can be used for the purchase of:
A. machinery
B. goodwill
C. land and building
D. raw material

282. Which of the following sources is not used for medium term financing?
A. Issue of equity shares
B. Issue of preference shares
C. Issue of debentures
D. Terms loan from banks

283. Working capital is represented by:
A. current liabilities
B. current assets minus current liabilities
C. total assets minus current liabilities
D. cash-in-hand plus stock-in-trade

284. Participating preference shares are those which participate:
A. in the voting
B. in the general meeting of the company
C. in the management of the company
D. in the profits over and above their fixed dividend

285. In which of the following, rate of interest/ dividends is not fixed?
A. equity capital B. debentures
C. preference capital D. public deposits

286. To which of the following types of companies, debentures suit as a source of finance?
A. companies with fluctuating earnings
B. campanies which stable earnings
C. companies which cannot earn a rate of profit higher than the rate of interest, payable on debentures.
D. All of these

287. First debentures are those:
A. which are issued before share capital
B. which are repayable before other debentures
C. which are secured by a floating charges
D. which are secured by a fixed charges

288. Underwriters are persons who:
A. purchase the shares and debentures of a company
B. work as agents of the company for the sale of shares and debentures
C. manage the issue of shares and debentures
D. undertake to buy those shares and debentures not subscribed for by the public

289. Which of the following institutions undertake underwriting of shares and debentures of companies?
A. Unit Trust of India
B. Industrial Development Bank of India
C. State Finance Corporations
D. All of these

290. Which of the following sources of finance do not pose a burden on the company?
A. Public deposits
B. Debentures
C. Loans from financial institutions
D. Retained earnings

291. Which of the following is not a component of the new issue market?
A. Stock Exchange
B. Unit Trust of India
C. Financial Institution of India like IFC, IDBI
D. LIC

292. When an existing company offers its shares for sale to the existing shareholders, it is known as:
A. private placing B. bonus issue
C. rights issue D. offer for sale

293. The first stock exchange was set up in India in:
A. Kolkata B. Mumbai
C. Delhi D. Chennai

294. The first stock exchange was set up in India in:
A. 1887 B. 1905
C. 1908 D. 1923

295. Which of the speculators expects the price of securities to rise in the near future?
A. bull B. bear
C. stag D. lame duck

296. Which of the following speculative activities is based on disparity in quote prices in different markets?
A. Option dealings B. Arbitrage
C. Margin trading D. Blank transfers

297. Contango charge is paid by a:
A. bull speculator to bear speculator
B. bear speculator to bull speculator
C. lame duck to bull speculator
D. bull to lame duck speculator

298. Listing of securities in a stock exchange for the purpose of trading indicates that:
A. at the time of listing, the company is financially sound
B. at the time of listing, the company is legally organised
C. the stock exchange guarantees about the financial soundness of the company
D. All of these

299. An existing company raising additional capital:
A. must offer the new shares to the existing shareholders
B. need not offer the new shares to the existing shareholders
C. issues share to debenture holders
D. issue shares to preference share holders

300. Stock exchange deals with the:
A. second hand securities
B. issues of equity shares
C. issue of preference shares
D. issue of debentures

301. One of the impelling causes of business combination is:
A. desire for bigness
B. wasteful competition
C. influence of tariffs
D. rationalisation

302. When a cement mill, a steel mill and a chemical company combine, it is a case of?
A. horizontal combination
B. vertical combination
C. diagonal combination
D. circular combination

303. Which of the following is an example of vertical integration?
A. One small steel mill combines with a big steel mill
B. Two steel mills of the same combine
C. Iron ore firm combines with iron melting firm
D. Paper mill combines with a publishing company

304. Combination of plants at the same stage of production or in the same trade or commerce is called a:
A. horizontal combination
B. vertical combination
C. diagonal combination
D. allied combination

305. One of the main advantages of vertical combination is that.
A. it helps in avoiding competition
B. it helps in controlling the market
C. it helps in controlling the quality of raw material and finished output
D. it brings about coordination between activities of combining units

306. Pools are a type:
A. horizontal combinations
B. vertical combinations
C. allied combinations
D. None of these

307. Cartel is a type of:
A. horizontal combination
B. vertical combination
C. allied combination
D. mixed combination

308. FICCI was formed in the year:
A. 1920 B. 1925
C. 1926 D. 1951

309. Business combinations are formed to derive the advantages of:
A. enabling the units to join hands and establish a monopoly
B. avoiding wasteful competition
C. enabling business units to withstand the rigors of a depression
D. All of these

310. Match the following:

List-I	List-II
I. Trust	(*a*) Company A holds more than 51% share capital of the company B
II. Merger	(*b*) Existing companies A and B are merged into company C
III. Holding Company	(*c*) Business of number of firms is entrusted to the care of Board of Trustees
IV. Amalgamation	(*d*) Company A takes over Company B

Select the correct answer from the code given below:

Codes:

	I	II	III	IV
A.	(*b*)	(*c*)	(*a*)	(*d*)
B.	(*a*)	(*b*)	(*c*)	(*d*)
C.	(*c*)	(*d*)	(*a*)	(*b*)
D.	(*b*)	(*a*)	(*d*)	(*c*)

311. MRTP Act came into force in:
A. 1969 B. 1970
C. 1971 D. 1980

312. Resale price maintenance is a:
A. Restrictive trade practice
B. Monopolistic trade practice
C. None of these
D. Both of these

313. When custom duty is levied according to the value of the goods, it is known as:
A. revenue duty B. excise duty
C. specific duty D. ad-valorem duty

314. When custom duty is levied according to the weight of good, it is known as:
A. revenue duty B. excise duty
C. specific duty D. ad-valorem duty

315. Import procedure begins with:
A. mate's receipt B. marine insurance
C. indent D. shipping bill

316. Shipping order is issued by the owner of the ship when:
A. whole of the ship is hired
B. major part of the ship is hired
C. freight is reserved for the exporter
D. ship starts its journey

317. A shipping bill is prepared when:
A. goods are damaged in the ship.
B. goods reach their destination in satisfactory condition.
C. goods are not cleared by the custom authorities.
D. None of these

318. Entrepot trade means:
A. import trade
B. export trade
C. foreign trade
D. goods imported for re-export

319. A letter of credit means:
A. a letter sent by importer to exporter sanctioning credit deal.
B. a letter sent by exporter to importer sanction credit deal.
C. a letter containing conditions of credit purchase or sale.
D. a bank agreeing to accept and pay on due date.

320. A bill of loading transferable to another person by:
A. mere delivery
B. endorsement and delivery
C. any of the above
D. this one is not transferable

321. Charter party means:
A. an agreement by which the ship owner agrees to place the entire or part of the ship at the disposal of the merchant.
B. the party who works as a middle man between shipper and shipping company.
C. the party who performs loading or unloading operations on the ship.
D. the party working as a middleman between importer and exporter.

322. State Trading Corporation of India was established:
A. by a special Act of Parliament
B. under the companies Act, 1956 as a private limited company.
C. under the companies Act, 1956 as a public limited company.
D. as departmental undertaking.

323. Which of the following is not a subsidiary of the State Trading Corporation of India?
A. Indian Motion Picture Export Corporation of India
B. Handicraft and a Handlooms Export Corporation of India Ltd.
C. Project and Equipment Corporation of India Ltd.
D. All of these

324. Mate's receipt is issued by:
A. the exporter
B. the importer
C. the captain of the ship or his assistant
D. the bank

325. Under which of the following principles of insurance, parties to the contract must disclose and material facts known to them?
A. Indemnity B. Utmost good faith
C. Subrogation D. Insurable interest

326. A person can insure:
A. any body's property
B. only his own property
C. only that property in which he is interested
D. only that property in which he has financial interest

327. In the case of fire insurance, the insured must have insurable interest in the thing insured at the time:
A. when policy is taken
B. when loss is incurred
C. through out the period of contract of insurance
D. both when policy is taken and when loss is incurred

328. In marine insurance, the insured must have insurable interest at the time:
A. when policy is taken.
B. when the event happens.
C. when policy is taken as well as event happens.
D. when throughout the period of contract of insurance.

329. A person had insured his goods worth ₹ 10,000 for ₹ 8,000 against fire and his loss by fire was ₹ 9,000. His claims is:
A. ₹ 8,000 B. ₹ 9,000
C. ₹ 10,000 D. None of these

330. A person insured his property worth ₹ 10,000 against fire for ₹ 8,000 only. His actual loss by fire is ₹ 5,000 and there is average clause in the policy. His is claim is:
A. ₹ 10,000 B. ₹ 8,000
C. ₹ 5,000 D. ₹ 4,000

331. According to the principle of cause proximate the insured can recover the loss from the insurer:
A. if it is proximity caused by any of the perils insured against
B. if it is caused by any of the remote cause
C. if it is caused by any reason, what so ever
D. All of these

332. The principle of subrogation applies to:
A. all types of insurance
B. fire insurance only
C. marine insurance only
D. fire and marine insurance

333. The principle of contribution applies when:
A. there is two or more insurance on one risk
B. the insured does not take necessary steps to mitigate the loss
C. the insured insures the same risk partly with other insurers
D. the premium is not paid by the insured

334. Surrender value of a life policy is the amount payable by Life Insurance Corporation when:
A. the life policy matures by death.
B. the life policy matures after the expiry of the policy period.
C. the life policy is withdrawn before its maturity.
D. the payment of premiums is discontinued and the amount is payable at the maturity of the policy.

335. Principle of subrogation states that:
A. the actual amount of loss should be distributed among the differenced insurers of the same risk.
B. on making good the loss, the insurers is entitled to succeed to all the rights of the insured regarding the subject matter of insurance.
C. the insured must take all necessary steps to minimise the loss.
D. the actual amount of loss, exceeding the amount of the policy, shall be paid.

336. Average clause in a fire policy is inserted in order to check mainly:
A. under-insurance
B. over-insurance
C. both other-insurance and under-insurance
D. All of these

337. X mortgages certain property with Y who has insurable interest in property:
A. only X B. only Y
C. both X and Y D. None of these

338. Principle of insurable interest applies to:
A. life insurance only
B. fire insurance only
C. fire and marine insurance only
D. all types of insurance

339. In which of the following kinds of insurance, insurable interest should be present only at the time of loss subject-matter:
A. life insurance B. fire insurance
C. marine insurance D. All of these

340. Unless the marine policy otherwise provides, insurer is liable:
A. if the loss is caused by ordinary wear and tear.
B. if the loss is caused by peril insured against.
C. if the loss is caused by ordinary leakage and breakage.
D. if the loss is caused by inherent nature of the subject-matter.

341. Which one of the following defines co-ordination?
A. Actuating force which inspires a person to put his best for the fulfillment of a task
B. Orderly arranged of group effort to provide unity of action in the pursuit of a common purpose.
C. Process of transmitting information from one person to another or from one unit to another.
D. Process of determining what is to be accomplished and what has been accomplished and if necessary applying corrective measures.

342. Consider the following basic steps involved in the process of control:
I. Identifying the strategic control points
II. Establish the standards
III. Measuring performance against standards
IV. Correcting deviations from the standards

The correct sequence of the above steps in the process of control is:
A. I, IV, III, II B. IV, III, II, I
C. II, I, IV , III D. II, III, I, IV

343. Match List-I with List-II and select the correct answer using the codes given below the lists:

List-I (Management thinkers)	List-II (Contribution/work)
I. Elton Mayo	(*a*) Importance of integrating the company's and employee's goal
II. Frederic W. Taylor	(*b*) Social problems of Industrial Civilisation
III. Henri Fayol	(*c*) General and Industrial Management.
IV. Mary Parker Follet	(*d*) Principles of Scientific Management

Codes:

	I	II	III	IV
A.	(*a*)	(*d*)	(*c*)	(*b*)
B.	(*d*)	(*c*)	(*b*)	(*a*)
C.	(*b*)	(*d*)	(*c*)	(*a*)
D.	(*c*)	(*d*)	(*a*)	(*b*)

344. An organisation structure is effective if it enables individuals to contribute to the objectives of the enterprise. This is known as:
A. Scalar Principle
B. Principle of functional definition
C. Principle of unity of objectives
D. None of these

345. Which one of the following orders indicates the correct logical order of managerial functions?
A. Organising, planning, directing, staffing, coordination and control.
B. Planning, organising, staffing, directing, coordination and control.
C. Planning, directing, organising, staffing, control and coordination.
D. Organising, planning, staffing, directing, control and coordination.

346. Effective direction does NOT depend on the:
A. Communication process
B. Forces at the subordinate level
C. Ability of the manager
D. Deployment of human resources

347. Planning refers to:
A. Looking backward
B. Looking forward

C. Looking forward and backward
D. Looking and actual performance to decide action to be taken

348. Which one of the following formulae is used calculate "Cross relationship" under span of control?

A. n (n–1) B. $n(2^n/_2 -1)$
C. $n(2^n/_2 + n-1)$ D. None of these

349. V.A. Graicunas has identified three sets of superior subordinate relationships, which are: Direct single relationship, Direct group relationship and cross relationship. Now if there are two, three, four and five subordinates respectively under one superior then in this context which one of the following Pairs is correctly matched?

	Number of the subordinates	Total number of relationships
A.	2	8
B.	3	18
C.	4	48
D.	5	98

350. Leadership is a function of all the following factors except:

A. Workgroup B. Product or service
C. Leader D. Situation

351. The main difference between delegation and decentralisation is that:

A. delegation refers primarily to transfer of authority from one individual to another while decentralisation refers to systematic delegation of authority to all units in an organisation.
B. delegation of authority can take place without decentralisation where as there cannot be decentralisation without delegation of authority.
C. delegation represents sharing of excessive burden of key managerial personnel while decentralisation refers to division of top managerial operations.
D. delegation may take place due to administrative, technical and routine reasons while decentralisation involves deliberate action for the smooth functioning of the organisation.

352. Management by exception introduces:

A. selective, responsibility oriented reporting
B. reporting of significant variances
C. requirement of full reports on performance
D. computation of actual in different spheres of performance

353. Consider the following office equipments used in various offices:

I. Fax
II. Typewriter
III. Dictaphone
IV. Letter opener

The correct order in which they are used is:

A. I, II, III, IV B. IV, III, II, I
C. II, IV, III, I D. III, II, IV, I

354. Control refers to:

I. Establishment of standards
II. Measurement of actual performance against the set standards
III. Correction for deviation from standards

Of these statements:

A. I alone is correct
B. III alone is correct
C. I and II are correct
B. I, II, and III are correct

355. Which one of the following is not related to the trait theory of leadership?

A. Physical factors such as height
B. Intelligence and extroversion
C. Self confidence and ambition
D. Training and experience of employees

356. Match List-I with List-II and select the correct answer from the codes given below the lists:

List-I	List-II
I. Planning	(*a*) Training
II. Staffing	(*b*) Forecasting
III. Directing	(*c*) Evaluating
IV. Controlling	(*d*) Motivating
	(*e*) Grouping

Codes:

	I	II	III	IV
A.	(*c*)	(*a*)	(*d*)	(*e*)
B.	(*c*)	(*e*)	(*a*)	(*b*)
C.	(*b*)	(*a*)	(*d*)	(*c*)
D.	(*b*)	(*e*)	(*a*)	(*c*)

357. Decentralisation of an organization is commended on account of which of the following advantages?

I. Reduced burden on top executives
II. Executive development
III. Improvement of morale
IV. Solves problems of coordination

Select the correct answer from the codes given below and mark your answer sheet accordingly:

Codes:

A. II and III B. I, II and IV
C. I, II and III D. III and IV

358. In a functional organisation:

A. There are no advisers, the executives alone having the authority and competence
B. There are specialist advisers having no authority
C. The entire organisation is divided into functions with specific role for specialists
D. The organisation is divided into functions with specialists having authority

359. The process of grouping activities into units for the purpose of administration may be referred to as:

A. Departmentalisation
B. Decentralisation
C. Co-ordination
D. Specialisation.

360. Span of control means that:

A. an organisation consists of various departments
B. each person's authority is clearly defined
C. every subordinate has one superior
D. a manager can supervise only a limited number of subordinates

361. If a general manager asks the sales manager to recruit some sales men on his behalf, it is an instance of:

A. division of authority
B. decentralisation of authority
C. delegation of authority
D. delegation of responsibility

362. Which one of the following principles states that recurring decisions should be handled in a routine manner by lower level managers whereas problems involving unusual matters only should be referred to higher levels?

A. Principle of unity of command
B. Scalar principle
C. Principle of exception
D. Principle of commitment

363. MBO is a technique which requires that the objectives of the enterprise:

A. be written and defined in broad terms
B. lay down the time period for achieving the results
C. include a plan of action for achieving the desired results
D. be defined in terms of measurable results

Directions (Qs. No. 364 and 365): *In the given context of the statement, mark the answer using the given codes:*

Codes:

A. Both (A) and (R) are true, and (R) is the correct explanation of (A).
B. Both (A) and (R) are true, but (R) is not a correct explanation of (A).
C. (A) is true, but (R) is false.
D. (A) is false, but (R) is true.

364. Assertion (A) : Management is a continuous operation or process involving the interaction of all functions.

Reason (R) : Managers first plan, then organize and finally perform the function of controlling.

365. Assertion (A) : When the span of control is wide, coordination and control becomes difficult.

Reason (R) : In a narrow span levels of authority decrease.

366. In the field of management some of the important techniques, relate to budgeting, cost accounting, planning and control are through:

A. Operational research
B. PERT & CPM
C. Budgetary control
D. Financial Administration

367. Which of the following management functions are closely related?
A. Planning and organising
B. Staffing and control
C. Planning and control
D. Planning and staffing

368. "Human Relations Approach" to management was originated by:
A. Henery Fayol B. Winslow Taylor
C. Elton Mayo D. Peter F. Drucker

369. The famous book "The Philosophy of Management" was written by:
A. Henery Fayol B. Oliver Sheldon
C. F.W. Taylor D. Urwick

370. Policy making is an important part of the process of:
A. Planning B. Co-ordinating
C. Organising D. Motivating

371. A firm has these characteristics : It is involved in the manufacture of custom built machinery, its products have shorter life span, the products are processed through different specialists and the products have a rigid time schedule to be met. In such a circumstance, which one of the following would be the form of organisation best suited to achieve the objectives?
A. Functional organisation
B. Line and staff organisation
C. Project (Matrix) organisation
D. Line organisation

372. The managerial function of organising is:
A. to review and adjust plan in the light of changing conditions
B. to establish a programme for the accomplishment of objections
C. to create a structure of functions and duties to be performed by a group of people
D. to get things done through and with the help of people

373. Span of management means:
A. A good organisation should consist of departments
B. Authority of each person must be clearly defined
C. Each subordinate should have one superior
D. A manager can supervise a limited number of executives

374. Which of the following is the oldest type of organisation?
A. Functional organisation
B. Line organisation
C. Line and staff organisation
D. Committee organisation

375. 'Unity of command' principle of effective direction means:
A. Subordinates should be responsible to one superior
B. Boosting the morale of the subordinates
C. decreasing the productivity of subordinates
D. All of these

376. In line organisation:
A. the organisation is divided according to the skill required to perform a work.
B. the organisation is divided according to the type of work involve.
C. the authority flows from the man at the top to the lowest man vertically.
D. each worker serves a number of supervisors.

377. The function of 'staff' in 'line and staff' organisation is to:
A. take advice from the line
B. advice the line
C. hold authority and responsibility
D. fix responsibility for performance of tasks in a definite manner upon certain individuals

378. Control function of management implies:
A. to bring harmony in various activities
B. to keep the work force constant
C. taking corrective course of action
D. to provide sufficient finance

379. The main advantage of line and staff organisation is:
A. Simplicity
B. Specialisation
C. Availability of expert advice
D. Speedy decision making

380. The terms speed boss, route clerk etc. are used in relation to:
A. Line organisation
B. Line and staff organisation
C. Functional organisation
D. None of these

381. General manager has delegated authority to production Manager for achieving budgeted production. Who is responsible for low production to Board of Directors?
A. Production Supervisors
B. Production Manager
C. General Manager
D. None of these

382. Delegation can be:
A. upward B. downward
C. side ward D. All of these

383. Unity of command is violated under:
A. Line organisation
B. Line and staff organisation
C. Functional organisation
D. None of these

384. 'Theory Y' states that:
A. Workers prefer to be directed
B. Workers exercise self-direction and self control
C. Workers have inherent disliking for work and will avoid it if they can
D. None of these

385. 'Theory X' and 'Theory Y' is given by:
A. Maslow B. Herzberg
C. Mc Gregor D. Norman

386. The Need – Hierarchy Theory of Motivation is given by:
A. Maslow B. Herzberg
C. Vroom D. Mc Gregor

387. Under the Need – Hierarchy Theory, when UDC designation is changed into 'Assistant', it is an example of:
A. Social needs
B. Esteem needs
C. Self-actualisation needs
D. All of these

388. Maslow's Need – Hierarchy Theory of Motivation has classified the human needs into five categories as follows:
I. Safety needs II. Esteem needs
III. Social needs IV. Physiological needs
V. Self-actualisation needs

What is the sequence of domination of these needs?
A. I, IV, III, II, V B. IV, I, III, II, V
C. V, III, II, IV, I D. IV, I, III, II, V

389. Under Expectancy Theory of Motivation, increase in motivation results when:
A. Valence increases
B. Valence decreases
C. No effect on valence
D. None of these

390. Which one of the following is a motivating factor as per Herzberg's Theory?
A. Salary and allowances
B. Job design
C. Working conditions
D. None of these

391. Match List I with List-II and select the correct answer using the codes given below the lists:

List-I (Company Issue)	List-II (Company Documents)
I. Affirmation of compliance Certificate with the registration formalities	(*a*) Incorporation
II. Classes of shares in which share capital is divided	(*b*) Statutory declaration
III. Rules for forfeiture of shares	(*c*) Memorandum of association
IV. Name and address of the company auditor	(*d*) Articles of association
	(*e*) Prospectus

Codes:

	I	II	III	IV
A.	(*a*)	(*d*)	(*c*)	(*e*)
B.	(*e*)	(*d*)	(*c*)	(*a*)
C.	(*b*)	(*c*)	(*d*)	(*e*)
D.	(*d*)	(*a*)	(*e*)	(*b*)

392. A special resolution for the alteration of the objects clause of the memorandum of association of a company having been passed, the aeration is to be confirmed by the:
A. Court concerned
B. Central government
C. Company law board
D. Creditors of the company

393. Which one of the following statements is NOT connected with the conversion of share into stock and reconversion into shares?
A. Only shares that are fully paid up can be converted into stock
B. Articles of association shall permit such conversion through a special resolution
C. Conversion can take place by passing an ordinary resolution as provided in the articles
D. Memorandum of association shall permit such conversion

394. Under the Indian companies Act 1956, a person can be a director in:
A. 7 companies B. 10 companies
C. 20 companies D. 25 companies

395. When a person transacts with a company on a matter which is beyond the power of the company, the person will be governed by the doctrine of:
A. Indoor management
B. Self assessment
C. Constructive notice
D. Management by exception

396. Which one of the following statements illustrates the doctrine of indoor management?
A. Persons dealing with the company are bound to inquire into the regularity of the internal proceedings
B. Persons dealing with the company are bound to inquire as to whether the general meeting of the shares holders was convened on proper notice
C. Persons dealing with the company are entitled to assume that what has been done has been regularly done by the company and therefore they can hold the company liable even if the internal formalities are found not to have been completed
D. Persons dealing with the company can easily assume that all acts done are introverts the company

397. According to Section 2 (45) of the Companies Act (as amended in 1974), a company secretary must possess the qualifications prescribed from time to time by the:
A. Company Law Board
B. Central Government
C. Registrar of Companies
D. Parliament

398. The company secretary files copies of resolution passed in an extraordinary general meeting with the Registrar of Companies under section:
A. 173 B. 192
C. 193 D. 208

399. The first annual general meeting of a company must be held within:
A. One month from the date of its incorporation
B. Six months from the date of its incorporation
C. 12 months from the date of its incorporation
D. 18 months from the date of its incorporation

400. Which one of the following statements relating to a company secretary is not correct?
A. He is not likely to perform duties towards shareholders
B. He is the mouth piece of the Board of Directors
C. He may be considered to be the head of the administrative section of a company
D. He is to arrange for Board meetings

401. The last page of the record of proceeding of each meeting in minutes book shall be dated and signed by the chairman of the same meetings within a period of 30 days of the conclusion of the meeting or in the event of death or inability of the chairman within that period by:

A. The managing director
B. A director
C. A director duly authorised by the Board for that purpose
D. The secretary

402. Which of the following statements are correct?

I. Minutes are not required to be read at a subsequent general meeting
II. Confirmation of minutes is not an item of agenda in general meetings
III. The chairman may disallow any matter within his opinion is detrimental to the interests of the company from being included in the minutes
IV. Members cannot obtain copies of minutes though they can inspect them during business hours

Select the correct answer using the codes given below:

Codes:

A. I and II   B. I, II and III
C. I, III and IV   D. II, III and IV

403. The agenda of the first Board meeting of a limited company generally consists of the following items:

I. Election of chairman
II. Approval of draft prospectus
III. Appointment of officers, *viz.*, the secretary, the manager and the accountant
IV. Incorporation of the company and the legal adviser to report on the same

The correct order in which the above items of the agenda usually appear is:

Codes:

A. I, II, III, IV   B. IV, III, II, I
C. III, IV, I, II   D. IV, I, III, II

404. Keeping the company's register of charges and making it available for inspection is a:

A. Contractual duty of the secretary
B. Duty of the secretary general
C. Statutory duty of the secretary
D. Duty delegated to the secretary by the Board

405. The maximum period for which the register of members can be closed at a time after giving 7 days pre-notice is:

A. 7 days   B. 15 days
C. 30 days   D. 45 days

406. The company secretary may be held liable for not holding the statutory meeting:

A. On the resolution of the general body
B. On the resolution of the Board of Director
C. Under section 165 of the companies Act
D. On the petition of the creditors

407. The minutes book containing the proceedings of general body meeting shall, at the registered office of company:

A. Be kept for inspection for 10 days
B. Be kept for inspection for one day
C. Be kept for inspection for two hours per day
D. Not be kept for inspection

408. Perpetuity and separate legal entity are the two most important distinctive features of:

A. Sole proprietorship form of business
B. Partnership
C. Company
D. Joint Hindu Family Firm

409. Partnership is a form of business organisation in which business debts can be recovered from:

A. The managing partners
B. All the managers and partners
C. The firm and the managers
D. The firm and all the partners

410. Of the following organisation, the easiest to wind up is the:

A. Public Limited Company
B. Multinational Corporation
C. Private Limited Company
D. Partnership Firm

411. Match List-I with List-II. Select the answer from the codes given below the lists:

List-I	List-II
I. Partners and firm	(*a*) Agent and principal relationship
II. Sole proprietorship	(*b*) Prospectus

III. Public limited company (*c*) Personal supervision
IV. Nominal partnership (*d*) Firm image

Codes:

	I	II	III	IV
A.	(*a*)	(*c*)	(*b*)	(*d*)
B.	(*b*)	(*c*)	(*a*)	(*d*)
C.	(*d*)	(*b*)	(*c*)	(*a*)
D.	(*a*)	(*b*)	(*d*)	(*c*)

412. Qualification share is a requirement prescribed for:
A. The officers of the company
B. Creditors of the company
C. Directors of the company
D. Auditors of the company

413. Most of the public sector enterprises in India are joint stock companies because this enable the:
A. Company to earn high profits
B. Government to enter any business
C. Government to exercise greater control
D. Management to work with high operational autonomy

414. The contracts signed by the promoters of a company:
A. Are legally binding upon the company after it is formed
B. Can be ratified by the company after its incorporation
C. Cease to be the personal liability of the promoters after the company is formed
D. Continue to be personal liability of the promoters

415. Doctrine of indoor management is reflected in:
A. Royal British Bank vs Turquands case
B. Solomon vs Solomon Ltd.
C. Daimler Ltd. vs Continental Tyre and Rubber Co. Ltd.
D. Kindston Cotton Mills case

416. The liability of share holders of a public company is limited to the extent of:
A. Paid up value of the share
B. The face value of the share
C. Called up value of the share
D. All of these

417. A company is called an artificial person because:
A. It does not have the shape of a normal man
B. It cannot be sued in the sort of law
C. It is invisible and intangible
D. It exists only in contemplation of law

418. Which of the following is the top administrative organ of the company?
A. Shareholders B. Managing Director
C. General Manager D. Board of Directors

419. The Board of Directors has to call the general body meeting giving a constructive notice of M days to all members entitled to attend the meeting. Here M stands for:
A. 7 B. 11
C. 14 D. 21

420. The doctrine by which an outsider is presumed to have a prior knowledge of the contents of memorandum and articles of association of a company is technically known as:
A. Doctrine of constructive notice
B. Doctrine of indoor management
C. Doctrine of retrospective notice
D. *Ignorantia legis haud excus at*

421. Converting Public Company into a Private Ltd. Company requires:
A. Special resolution
B. Central governmentt approval
C. Special resolution and central government approval
D. Special resolution and Company Law Board approval

422. The first directors of a public company are appointed by the:
A. Public B. Shareholders
C. Promoters D. Government

423. Rules concerning meetings and report of a joint stock company are contained in its:
A. Prospectus
B. Memorandum of Association
C. Articles of Association
D. Bye-Laws

424. Consider the following statements:
I. A letter of credit eliminates the risk of payment in foreign trade
II. Revolving letter of credit and circular letter of credit are two different entities
III. Revocable letter of credit is a confirmatory letter of credit
A. I only B. II and III
C. I and III D. I, II and III

425. Consider the following statements:
I. A public limited company can commence business only after getting the certificate of commencement of business
II. In a public limited company, directors can not borrow from the company without the approval of the Central Government
A. I only B. III only
C. Both I and II D. Neither I nor II

426. Consider the following statements:
I. Sole-proprietorship type of business unit is not governed by the Contract Act.
II. A private limited company is governed by the partnership act where as a public limited company is governed by the Companies Act.
A. I only B. II only
C. Both I and II D. Neither I nor II

427. A change in the exchange rate will change the amount of local currency receivable on a bill denominated in a foreign currency. The risk involved is called:
A. Foreign exchange risk
B. Import risk
C. Transaction risk
D. Monetary risk

428. The marine policy which insures incidental in land risks along with the marine perils is called:
A. Block policy
B. Currency policy
C. Blanket policy
D. Voyage policy

429. Which of the following does not meant the Qualified Institutional Buyer (QIB) under the SEBI (Disclosure & Investor Protection) guidelines as amended by the recent DIP circular?
A. Mutual funds
B. Pension fund with a corpus below ₹ 20 crore
C. Pension funds with minimum corpus of ₹ 25 crore
D. Provident funds with minimum corpus of ₹ 25 crore

430. When can an Annual general meeting be called after giving shorter notice than that specified?
A. If consent is accorded to by all the memebers entitled to vote
B. If consent is accorded to by 30 % of the members entitled to vote
C. If Board of Directors takes a majority decision in this regard
D. If the company secretary so wishes

ANSWERS

1	2	3	4	5	6	7	8	9	10
A	C	C	D	A	B	B	C	B	A
11	**12**	**13**	**14**	**15**	**16**	**17**	**18**	**19**	**20**
C	B	B	A	C	A	C	D	B	B
21	**22**	**23**	**24**	**25**	**26**	**27**	**28**	**29**	**30**
B	B	A	B	A	C	C	B	A	A
31	**32**	**33**	**34**	**35**	**36**	**37**	**38**	**39**	**40**
C	A	A	C	C	B	D	A	B	B
41	**42**	**43**	**44**	**45**	**46**	**47**	**48**	**49**	**50**
B	D	D	B	A	C	A	D	A	C

51	**52**	**53**	**54**	**55**	**56**	**57**	**58**	**59**	**60**
B	B	B	B	B	D	C	C	C	D
61	**62**	**63**	**64**	**65**	**66**	**67**	**68**	**69**	**70**
C	B	C	A	D	D	B	D	B	D
71	**72**	**73**	**74**	**75**	**76**	**77**	**78**	**79**	**80**
C	B	D	B	B	A	A	B	C	C
81	**82**	**83**	**84**	**85**	**86**	**87**	**88**	**89**	**90**
B	B	B	B	B	D	B	D	A	B
91	**92**	**93**	**94**	**95**	**96**	**97**	**98**	**99**	**100**
A	D	B	B	B	C	A	A	D	A
101	**102**	**103**	**104**	**105**	**106**	**107**	**108**	**109**	**110**
B	C	D	B	A	C	C	A	B	B
111	**112**	**113**	**114**	**115**	**116**	**117**	**118**	**119**	**120**
C	A	C	B	D	B	B	C	B	B
121	**122**	**123**	**124**	**125**	**126**	**127**	**128**	**129**	**130**
A	C	D	C	A	C	B	A	D	A
131	**132**	**133**	**134**	**135**	**136**	**137**	**138**	**139**	**140**
A	A	C	D	D	A	B	B	B	C
141	**142**	**143**	**144**	**145**	**146**	**147**	**148**	**149**	**140**
D	B	A	B	B	A	C	C	D	B
151	**152**	**153**	**154**	**155**	**156**	**157**	**158**	**159**	**160**
D	B	B	C	C	C	C	D	C	C
161	**162**	**163**	**164**	**165**	**166**	**167**	**168**	**169**	**170**
B	D	D	D	B	C	C	A	B	D
171	**172**	**173**	**174**	**175**	**176**	**177**	**178**	**179**	**180**
A	A	D	D	C	B	B	B	D	C
181	**182**	**183**	**184**	**185**	**186**	**187**	**188**	**189**	**190**
A	B	B	B	B	C	B	D	D	C
191	**192**	**193**	**194**	**195**	**196**	**197**	**198**	**199**	**200**
C	C	A	A	C	B	A	A	C	C
201	**202**	**203**	**204**	**205**	**206**	**207**	**208**	**209**	**210**
C	A	C	A	A	D	B	B	A	C
211	**212**	**213**	**214**	**215**	**216**	**217**	**218**	**219**	**220**
A	A	D	B	B	B	D	A	A	A
221	**222**	**223**	**224**	**225**	**226**	**227**	**228**	**229**	**230**
A	C	A	B	C	B	C	A	C	A
231	**232**	**233**	**234**	**235**	**236**	**237**	**238**	**239**	**240**
C	A	C	D	B	D	B	C	A	C
241	**242**	**243**	**244**	**245**	**246**	**247**	**248**	**249**	**250**
D	A	B	D	B	D	D	C	B	A

251	252	253	254	255	256	257	258	259	260
B	D	D	D	B	D	D	D	C	D
261	262	263	264	265	266	267	268	269	270
C	B	C	C	B	D	A	C	A	D
271	272	273	274	275	276	277	278	279	280
B	C	B	C	C	D	D	A	D	D
281	282	283	284	285	286	287	288	289	290
D	A	B	D	A	B	B	D	D	D
291	292	293	294	295	296	297	298	299	300
A	C	B	A	A	B	A	B	A	A
301	302	303	304	305	306	307	308	309	310
B	D	C	A	C	A	A	C	D	C
311	312	313	314	315	316	317	318	319	320
D	A	D	C	C	C	D	D	A	C
321	322	323	324	325	326	327	328	329	330
A	B	D	C	B	D	D	B	A	D
331	332	333	334	335	336	337	338	339	340
A	D	A	C	B	A	C	D	C	B
341	342	343	344	345	346	347	348	349	350
B	B	D	C	B	C	D	A	B	B
351	352	353	354	355	356	357	358	359	360
A	B	B	D	D	C	C	D	A	D
361	362	363	364	365	366	367	368	369	370
C	C	D	A	C	B	C	C	B	A
371	372	373	374	375	376	377	378	379	380
C	C	D	B	A	C	B	A	C	D
381	382	383	384	385	386	387	388	389	390
C	B	C	A	B	A	B	D	A	C
391	392	393	394	395	396	397	398	399	400
C	C	D	C	C	C	B	C	D	A
401	402	403	404	405	406	407	408	409	410
C	C	D	C	C	C	C	C	D	A
411	412	413	414	415	416	417	418	419	420
A	C	D	D	A	B	D	D	A	A
421	422	423	424	425	426	427	428	429	430
C	C	C	A	C	D	D	C	B	A

●●●

2402